ISBN 978-1-331-02773-7
PIBN 10135309

FB &c Ltd, Dalton House, 60 Windsor Avenue, London, SW19 2RR.
Company number 08720141. Registered in England and Wales.

For support please visit www.forgottenbooks.com

1 MONTH OF
FREE
READING

at

www.ForgottenBooks.com

By purchasing this book you are eligible for one month membership to ForgottenBooks.com, giving you unlimited access to our entire collection of over 700,000 titles via our web site and mobile apps.

To claim your free month visit:
www.forgottenbooks.com/free135309

Similar Books Are Available from
www.forgottenbooks.com

Legal Maxims, Vol. 1
With Observations and Cases, by George Frederick Wharton

Readings on the History and System of the Common Law
by Roscoe Pound

A Handbook of Bankruptcy Law
Embodying the Full Text of the Act of Congress, by Henry Campbell Black

The Principles of Pleading and Practice in Civil Actions in the High Court of Justice
by W. Blake Odgers

Real Estate Principles and Practices
by Philip A. Benson

The New Law-Dictionary
by Giles Jacob

On Foreign Jurisdiction and the Extradition of Criminals
by George Cornewall Lewis

Principles of the Law of Contract
by William Reynell Anson

A Treatise of the Law Relative to Merchant Ships and Seamen, Vol. 1 of 4
by Charles Abbott

A Manual of Constitutional History, Founded on the Works of Hallam, Creasy, May and Broom
by Forrest Fulton

Patent and Trade Mark Laws of the World
by B. Singer

Thomas Aquinas
Treatise on Law (Summa Theologica, Questions 90-97), by Thomas Aquinas

A Treatise on the Conflict of Laws, and the Limits of Their Operation in Respect of Place and Time
by Friedrich Carl von Savigny

A Summary of the Law of Lien
by Basil Montagu

Introduction to Roman Law
In Twelve Academical Lectures, by James Hadley

The Science of Law
by Sheldon Amos

The Oldest Laws in the World
Being an Account of the Hammurabi Code and the Sinaitic Legislation, by Chilperic Edwards

The Law of Torts
by Francis M. Burdick

Cases on Criminal Law
by Jerome C. Knowlton

Constitution and Laws of the Cherokee Nation
by Cherokee Nation

THE

PRACTICE IN CRIMINAL CASES

IN

CERTIORARI, HABEAS CORPUS, APPEALS,

AND PROCEEDINGS BEFORE

MAGISTRATES AND JUSTICES OF THE PEACE.

WITH FORMS.

AND

AN ALPHABETICAL SYNOPSIS OF OFFENCES,

WITH FORMS OF CHARGES, ETC.

SECOND EDITION.

BY

CHARLES SEAGER

OF OSGOODE HALL

BARRISTER-AT-LAW, CROWN ATTORNEY COUNTY OF HURON.

TORONTO:

CANADA LAW BOOK COMPANY, LIMITED

LAW BOOK PUBLISHERS,

32, 34 TORONTO STREET.

CANADA LAW BOOK COMPANY, LIMITED, LAW PRINTERS, TORONTO.

TABLE OF CONTENTS.

CHAPTER X.

CHAPTER XI.

CHAPTER XII.

CHAPTER XIII.

CHAPTER XIV.

CHAPTER XV.

TABLE OF CASES

NOTE.—Errors in citation in the text have been corrected in this Table.

C.—MAG. MAN.

PRACTICE

IN

MAGISTRATES'

CRIMINAL CASES.

CHAPTER I.

CERTIORARI, AND MOTIONS TO QUASH CONVICTIONS.

Certiorari is a writ issued from a superior court to an inferior tribunal exercising summary judicial jurisdiction, by which the latter is required to certify and return its judicial proceedings into the superior court, in order that such court may by virtue of its prerogative authority, examine upon their legality and determine accordingly.

So, if any proceeding by a magistrate or justice appears to be in excess of his jurisdiction, or is for any reason irregular or invalid, the superior courts of criminal jurisdiction of the different provinces will, in the exercise of their inherent authority, order the cause in which such proceeding has been taken to be brought up by certiorari for the purpose of its being quashed, or such order being made in regard to it as may be right. This supervising authority is inherent in the superior courts and requires no special law or statute: R. v. The Manchester & Leeds Ry. Co., 8 A. & E. 413; R. v. Cushing, 26 A.R.P. 248.

By what Court.

The expression "superior courts of criminal jurisdiction" is defined, and the courts in the different provinces which have the authority to exercise this jurisdiction in criminal matters, are indicated by sec. 2 (35) of the Criminal Code, viz

In Ontario, the High Court of Justice.

In Quebec, the Court of King's Bench; and the Superior Court of Quebec: R. v. Mercier, 6 Can. Cr. Cas. 44.

1—MAG. MAN.

In Nova Scotia, New Brunswick and British Columbia, the Supreme Court.

In Prince Edward Island, the Supreme Court of Judicature.

In Manitoba, the Court of Appeal, or the Court of King's Bench (Crown side).

In Saskatchewan and Alberta, the Supreme Court of the North-West Territories, until the same is abolished, and thereafter such court as is by the legislatures of these provinces substituted therefor: (now the Supreme Court of these provinces).

In the Yukon Territory, the Territorial Court.

What may be Removed by Certiorari.

Not only a conviction, but any judicial proceeding may be brought up by certiorari and quashed; *e.g.*, a search warrant: R. v. Kavanagh, 2 Can. Cr. Cas. 271; R. v. Morgan, 5 Can. Cr. Cas. 272; R. v. Townsend (No. 2), 11 Can. Cr. Cas. 129; R. v. Kehr, 11 Can. Cr. Cas. 52, and cases cited in notes to that case; or a preliminary or interlocutory order: Ex p. Kavanagh, 2 Can. Cr. Cas. 267; R. v. J. J. Sutherland, (1901), 2 K.B. 357; a minute of adjudication without a formal conviction: R. v. Mancion, 8 O.L.R. 24, 8 Can. Cr. Cas. 218. But a warrant of commitment for non-payment of a fine is a ministerial act and not a judicial one, and is not the subject of certiorari and motion to quash, even if improperly issued; habeas corpus being the appropriate remedy where by any improper warrant, a person is deprived of his liberty: Ex. p. Bertin, 10 Can. Cr. Cas. 65. Two writs of certiorari will not be allowed in the same matter, one for an interlocutory proceeding and another for the conviction. It is the whole cause which is removed by certiorari.

Who may Apply for Certiorari.

The writ may be granted either at the instance of the prosecutor or defendant. To the former it is granted as a matter of right and of course, as he represents the Crown: Re Ruggles, 5 Can. Cr. Cas. 163; but to the defendant it may be granted or refused as a matter of discretion; *ibid*.

Certiorari lies to inferior tribunals, when exercising judicial acts only, and not merely ministerial functions: R. v. Sharman (1898), 1 Q.B. 578; R. v. Manchester (Jus.), (1899), 1 Q.B. 571: R. v. New Glasgow, 30 N.S.R. 107; R. v. Cotham

(1898), 1 Q.B. 802; R. v. Waterman's Co. (1897), 1 Q.B. 659;
R. v. Kehr, 11 Can. Cr. Cas. at p. 56, and cases there cited as
to what proceedings are the subject of certiorari, also, R. v.
Aberdare Canal Co., 14 Q.B. 854.

Rules of Court.

By Code 576 the superior courts of criminal jurisdiction in
the provinces are authorized to make rules regulating the practice and procedure in criminal matters, including certiorari,
mandamus, habeas corpus, prohibition, and also including cases
stated under Code 761-769: In Ontario the court authorized to
make such rules is the Supreme Court of Judicature: Code 576
(3) ; see R. v. Creelman, 25 N.S.R. 404; Re Barrett, 7 Can. Cr.
Cas. 1; 52 Vict. ch. 40 (Can.).

No such rules have been passed in Ontario. The rules of
court made under statutes of the provincial legislatures do not
apply to criminal proceedings for offences against Dominion Statutes; and the provincial legislatures have, since Confederation,
no authority to deal with procedure in criminal cases under Dominion laws: Re Boucher, 4 A.R. at p. 193; R. v. McAuley, 14
O.R. at p. 657; R. v. Beemer, 15 O.R. 266, 270; R. v. Beale, 11
Man. R. 448; R. v. Crothers, 11 Man. R. 567; R. v. Toland, 22
O.R. 505; R. v. Levinger, 22 O.R. 690; R. v. Wason, 17 A.R. 221.
So the Ontario Judicature Act and the Consolidated Rules under
it, do not apply to any proceeding for an offence against Do-
minion laws: R. v. McAulay, 14 O.R. 643; R. v. Eli, 13 A.R. 526;
Con. Rule 3 (Ont.) ; R.S.O. c. 51, s. 191.

There are consequently no rules of court in Ontario relating
to the practice in certiorari and proceedings to quash convictions, in criminal cases, for offences against Dominion laws, except the Crown Rule of 17th November, 1886, which relates only
to the recognizance or deposit required, as will be presently mentioned.

In British Columbia Crown Rules, 1896, prescribe the practice in certiorari. These are quoted in full in 8 Can. Cr. Cas. p.
162; and provide that a summons to shew cause against the issuing of a writ of certiorari, upon the application of any person
other than the Attorney-General on behalf of the Crown, is to
issue unless the court is of opinion that the writ should issue
forthwith, or that the order for the writ should be made ex parte
or otherwise.

These rules also provide, for the six days' notice which will
be presently mentioned; and that the application must be made
within six months after the conviction or order in question has
been made; that a recognizance in the sum of $100 shall be
entered into and filed with the registrar with affidavits of justification and execution; unless the application is made by the
Attorney-General acting for the Crown, in which case no recognizance is necessary; that a copy of the conviction or proceeding
in question, verified by affidavit, shall be produced and filed in
court before the application is made; and that in case cause is
shewn on the application for the writ against the order nisi for
certiorari, an order absolute that the conviction or proceeding be
·quashed may be granted, in which case no recognizance is required; and that no objection on account of any mistake or
omission by the justice shall be allowed unless it has been specified in the order for certiorari.

In Nova Scotia Crown Rules have been made providing for
a four days' notice to the magistrate or justice and the opposite
party; and for a recognizance in $200; and that the application
must be made within six months after the conviction; that a
copy of the conviction, verified by affidavit, must be produced;
and that any mistake or omission upon which the application is
made must be stated in the notice of motion: see 5 Can. Cr. Cas.
p. 284.

In the North-West Territories the practice is governed by
Crown Rules, 1900.

The rules made under the Judicature Act in Ontario, and
the provincial rules and laws regulating civil procedure, do not
apply to criminal proceedings; and so not to certiorari, in a case
under a Dominion law, which is itself a matter of criminal
law: O'Shaunessy v. Montreal, 9 Can. Cr. Cas. 45, and note at
p. 46: R. v. Cushing, 26 A.R. 248.

Otherwise than as provided in the provinces where Crown
Rules have been passed, the practice on applications for certiorari provided by the Imp. Statute, now referred to, will prevail.

Notice to Justice.

By 13 Geo. II. ch. 18 (Imp.), sec. 5, six days' notice of
application for certiorari must be given to the justice, or to
two of the justices if more than one sat on the case. This section
of the Act is in force in Ontario: R. v. Peterman, 23 U.C.R. 516;
R. v. Munro, 24 U.C.R. 44; R. v. McAllan, 45 U.C.R. 402.

The above Imp. Act sec. 5, provides as follows:

5. And for the better preventing vexatious delays and ex-·
pense, occasioned by the suing forth writs of certiorari, for the
removal of convictions, judgments, orders and other proceedings
before justices of the peace, be it further enacted by the authority aforesaid that from and after the twenty-fourth day of June,
which shall be in the year of our Lord, one thousand seven hundred and forty, no writ of certiorari shall be granted, issued forth
or allowed, to remove any conviction, judgment order or other
proceedings had or made by or before any justice or justices of
the peace of any county, city, borough, town-corporate, or liberty,
or the respective general or quarter-sessions thereof, unless such
certiorari be moved or applied for within *six calendar months*
next after such conviction, judgment, order or other proceedings
shall be so had or made, and unless it be duly proved upon oath
that the said party or parties suing for the same hath or have
given *six days' notice* thereof in writing to the justice or justices.
or to two of them (if so many there be) by and before whom
such conviction, judgment, order, or other proceeding shall be
so had or made, to the end that such justice or justices or the
parties therein concerned, may shew cause, if he or they shall so
think fit, against the issuing or granting such certiorari.

Notice a Condition Precedent.

The effect of the Statute 13 Geo. II. ch. 18, sec. 5, is to imperatively require that six days' notice shall be given, and to make
the giving of it a *condition precedent* to the issuing of the writ,
and the convicting justices are not driven to make an independent application to quash the certiorari for the want of such
notice, but can set up the defect in answer to the rule nisi obtained by the defendant to quash the conviction. R. v. McAllan,
1880, 45 U.C.R. 402, 406.

This notice should specify the objections to the conviction:
see, R.S.B.C. ch. 42, sec. 2. But it would seem the notice is
good without stating the objections: Re Taylor v. Davey, 1 P.R.
346; R. v. McGregor, 10 Can. Cr. Cas. 313.

FORM OF SIX DAYS' NOTICE TO MAGISTRATE.
In the High Court of Justice.
The King against A.B.
To C.D., Esquire,
Police magistrate (*or* one of His Majesty's justices of the peace) for
the of

Whereas you did on the   day of   , A.D. 19   , at the
of   , in the County of   , convict A.B. of the   of
, in the County of   , for that he did on the   day of   ; A.D.
19   , at the   of   , in the said County of   unlawfully
(*here set out the charge as in the conviction*).

And whereas the said conviction is invalid in that it does not shew
that the said alleged offence was committed within the territorial jurisdiction of you, the said C.D., as such police magistrate (*or justice*), *or*
that the penalty imposed is illegal and in excess of your jurisdiction, *or*
of the penalty authorized by law for the said offence; (*or as the case may
be, inserting the various grounds of objection*), as well as on other grounds.

Wherefore the said A.B., being resolved to seek a remedy for the injury
he has received and sustained by reason of the said conviction, I do hereby
on behalf of the said A.B. give you notice that a motion will be made on behalf
of the said A.B. before the presiding judge of the High Court of Justice in
Chambers at Osgoode Hall, Toronto, after the expiration of six clear days from
the time of your being served with this notice, namely on the   day of
, A.D. 19   , at ten o'clock in the forenoon, or as soon thereafter as
the motion can be heard, for an order for a writ of certiorari to issue out
of the High Court of Justice to be directed to you and to the clerk of the
peace for the County of   , for the removal of such conviction into the
said court for the purpose of having the same quashed and the said A.B.
discharged upon the grounds hereinbefore stated.

Dated at   this   day of   , A.D. 19

                                      A.B.

by E.F., of No.   Street, in the   of   , his Solicitor.

If the notice is given by more than one person it must be
signed by or on behalf of all of them: R. v. Cambridge, J.J , 3.
B. & Ad. 887; R. v. Kent, J.J , 40 L.J.M.C. 76.

A notice that the writ of certiorari is to be directed to the
justice alone if he has sent the proceedings to some other officer,
is not sufficient: R. v. Starkey, 6 Man. R. 588; 7 Man. R. 489.
In such event the notice must also state that the writ is to be also
directed to the officer in whose custody the proceedings to be
moved against, are now on file, *e.g.*, the clerk of the peace.

The notice must be served on the justice or magistrate to
whom it is directed six clear days before the application for
certiorari: 13 Geo. II. ch. 18, sec. 1.

The notice need not be served on the prosecutor, unless provided for by Crown Rules above indicated. He will afterwards
be served with the rule nisi to quash: Re Lake, 42 U.C.R. 206;
R. v. Murray, 27 U.C.R. 134.

FORM OF AFFIDAVIT OF SERVICE.

In the High Court of Justice.

The King v. A.B.

I,   of the   of   , in the County of   (*fill in
occupation*), make oath and say:

1. That I did on the   day of   A.D. 19   , personally serve
C.D., the police magistrate (*or.* justice of the peace) named in the
notice now shewn to me marked Exhibit A, with a true copy of the said

notice, by delivering to and leaving with him, the said C.D., personally, at the   of   in the County of   , on the said day a true copy of the said notice.

2. That I was present at the trial and conviction of the said A.B. for the offence mentioned in the said notice, and I personally know the person so served by me as aforesaid to be the said C.D., police magistrate (*or*, justice) by whom the said conviction was made (*or as the case may be, shewing the means of identification of the magistrate or justice*).

Sworn, *etc.*

The affidavit will be insufficient unless it identifies the justice or justices served as the convicting justice or justices: Re Lake, 42 U.C.R. 206; R. v. J. J. Shrewsbury, 11 A. & E. 159; R. v. J. J. Lancashire, 11 A. & E. 144.

The service of the notice is the first step to be taken; and it is unnecessary that the affidavits to be used on the application should be sworn or filed before giving it: R. v. Starkey, 6 Man. R. 588, 7 Man. R. 489. If the conviction in question has been affirmed on appeal to the Sessions, the justices of the Sessions must also be served: R. v. Ellis, 25 U.C.R. 324; R. v. Peterman, 23 U.C.R. 516; see R. v. McAnn, 4 B.C.R. 587, 3 Can. Cr. Cas. 110. The notice is a condition precedent to the application, and the court has no jurisdiction to grant certiorari unless it has been given: R. v. McAllan, 45 U.C.R. 402; and service on the justice of a rule nisi for certiorari returnable six clear days or more after service is not a good substitute for the notice: Re Plunkett, 3 B.C.R. 484; 1 Can. Cr. Cas. 365; R. v. McAllan, *supra*.

A notice given of a previous unsuccessful application, does not enure to the benefit of the defendant on a second application, but a fresh notice must be given: R. v. McAllan, *supra.*

No notice is required of an application by the Crown or by the prosecutor: Paley on Convictions, 8th ed. 451.

Application for Certiorari.

By 13 Geo. II. ch. 18, sec. 5, the certiorari must be applied for within six calendar months after the conviction except in those provinces where some other period is prescribed by Crown Rule as above stated.

Great delay has been held, in New Brunswick and Nova Scotia (where the Imperial Statute is not in force), to be a ground for refusal of the application: Ex p. Kyle, 32 N.B.R. 212; unless the delay is accounted for: Ex p. Long, 27 N.B.R. 495: see also R. v. Nichols, 24 N.S.R. 151. Under a similar provision in England it was held that the six months was to be computed from the date of the conviction if there had been no appeal, but if an appeal was taken the time counted from the hearing of the appeal: Paley on Convictions, 8th ed. 457(*b*). And when the applicant had filed the affidavits and had done all he could to make the application on the last day of the time limited, but there was no judge in Chambers until the next day, the application was granted on that day: R. v. Allen, 4 B. & S. 915.

Affidavits for Certiorari.

The application for certiorari must be supported by affidavits shewing the grounds of it: see 1 Can. Cr. Cas. 156. But if it is applied for by the Attorney-General on behalf of the Crown or by the prosecutor, certiorari is granted as a matter of right and of course, and no affidavit is required: Re Ruggles, 5 Can. Cr. Cas. 163, and see Crown Rules mentioned above pp. 3, 4. R. v. Boultbee, 4 A. & E. 498. Neither are the restrictions as to time of applying, nor notice, nor recognizance applicable in such case: Paley on Convictions, 8th ed. 451.

The affidavits must be entitled in the court: Ex parte Nohro, 1 B. & C. 267; R. v. Plympton, 37 W.R. 334; and need not be otherwise entitled; but are unobjectionable if headed "In the matter of," etc.: Breeden v. Copp, 9 Jour. 271.

A copy of the proceedings must be produced and verified by affidavit; or the affidavit must shew positively that a copy could not be obtained, and must disclose what the proceedings were; otherwise the application will be refused: Ex parte Emerson (N.B.), 1 Can. Cr. Cas. 156, and notes thereto; 33 N.B.R. 425; see R. v. Wells, 28 N.S.R. 547. The affidavits for certiorari or habeas corpus cannot be sworn before the prosecutor or his solicitor: R. v. Marsh, 25 N.B.R. 370. The statutory requirements must be strictly complied with, and where a local statute required that on the application for certiorari to remove a conviction under a provincial law an affidavit of the defendant should be filed, the want of such affidavit was held fatal to the application, when the matter was within the justice's jurisdiction: R. v. Stevens, 31 N.S.R. 125; R. v. Bigelow, 31 N.S.R. 436 and cases cited.

AFFIDAVIT FOR CERTIORARI.
Verifying proceedings.

In the High Court of Justice.
The King v. A.B.
I   , of the   of   in the County of
(*occupation*), make oath and say:

1. That the hereto anneXed several paper writings, marked respectively exhibits A., B. and C., being the information, evidence taken before the justice, the justice's minute of adjudication, the formal record of conviction and other papers connected therewith, to this my affidavit, were copied by me from the originals of which the same purport to be copies now in the hands of   Esquire, police magistrate (or justice of the peace, etc., or now on file in the office of the clerk of the peace for the County of   ) and the said anneXed paper writings are true copies of the said originals respectively.

2. That I have eXamined the warrant of commitment now in the hands of the keeper of the common gaol for the County of   (or as the case may be), upon which the said A.B. is now held in custody in the said gaol (or as the case may be).

3. That the paper writing hereto anneXed, marked exhibit D., to this my affidavit, is a true copy of the said warrant of commitment now in the hands of the said keeper of the said gaol (or as the case may be), upon which the said A.B. therein named is held for trial (or is committed under the said conviction).

4. I have carefully compared the said copy of the said warrant of commitment, marked exhibit D., with the said original thereof in the hands of the said keeper, and the said copy is a true copy of the said original warrant of commitment.

Sworn, etc.

If copies of the proceedings before the justice cannot be procured, it should be stated in clear and positive terms what efforts have been made to procure them and the reason why they cannot be obtained, setting out what the proceedings were as fully as possible.

AFFIDAVIT BY DEFENDANT.

Same heading as above.

I, A.B., of, etc.

1. I am the above named defendant, A.B., and the person on behalf of whom the notice now shewn to me marked exhibit A., of this application for a writ of certiorari in this case was given (*R.* v. *J. J. Kent*, 3 *B. & Ald.* 250).

2. (*State the facts shewing why the conviction or commitment and warrant are bad and forming the grounds for the application to quash*).

Application—To Whom Made.

The application for certiorari (which may issue on an ex parte application: Symonds v. Dimsdale, 2 Exch. 533), is made in Ontario, to a judge of the High Court in Chambers; in Manitoba it must be made to the full court and by rule nisi: R. v. Beale, 11 Man. R. 448; in British Columbia to a judge of the Supreme Court, for summons to shew cause, unless otherwise ordered: Crown Rules, 1896, *ante,* p. 3; R. v. Tanghe, 8 Can. Cr. Cas. 160.

ORDER FOR CERTIORARI.

In the High Court of Justice.
The Honourable The Chief Justice
or The Honourable Mr. Justice
In Chambers.
The King against A.B.

Tuesday, the
day of   , A.D. 19

1. Upon the application of the said A.B. upon reading the six days' notice served herein, and the affidavit of service thereof, upon   , Esquire, the police magistrate (or justice of the peace) therein named, and upon reading the affidavit of   filed, and the exhibits therein referred to, and the other papers filed on behalf of the said A.B. upon this motion, and upon hearing what was alleged by the solicitor (or counsel) for the said A.B. and for the prosecutor E.F., and also for the convicting or committing magistrate (as the case may be).

2. It is ordered that a writ of certiorari do issue out of this Court directed to C.D., Esq., police magistrate (or one of His Majesty's justices) for the County of   , and also to   , Esquire, the clerk of the peace for the County of   (as the case may be), to remove and return into this Court all and singular the information, process, depositions, evidence, minute of adjudication, conviction and all other proceedings, and all things touching the same, had and taken against the said A.B. before the said magistrate (or justice of the peace), upon the information of   for that the said A.B., at the   of   , in the County of   , on the   of   , A.D. 19   , did unlawfully (here set out the charge).

Clerk in Chambers.

Recognizance.

By Code s. 1126 the court having jurisdiction to quash convictions, etc., is authorized to make a rule requiring the defendant to enter into a recognizance or to deposit money as security, as a condition precedent to a motion to quash a conviction or any proceeding brought up on certiorari. No such rule has been made in Ontario, since the Criminal Code was passed; but under the Dominion Statute, 49 Vict. ch. 49 sec. 6, which on the passing of the Criminal Code was re-enacted as sec. 892, (now 1126), the High Court passed a general order on 17th November, 1886, as follows:—

"No motion shall be entertained by this Court or by any Division of the same, or by any judge of a Division sitting for the court, or in Chambers, to quash a conviction, order or other proceeding, which has been made by or before a justice of the peace (as defined by the said Act), and brought before the court by a certiorari, unless the defendant is shewn to have entered into a recognizance with one or more sureties in the sum of $100 before a justice or justices of the county or place within which such conviction or order has been made, or before a judge of the county court of the said county, or before the judge of the Superior Court, and which recognizance with an affidavit of the due execution thereof shall be filed with the registrar of the court in which such motion is made, or is pending, or unless the defendant is shewn to have made a deposit of the like sum of $100 with the registrar of the court in which such motion is made, with or upon the condition that he will prosecute such certiorari at his own cost and charges, and without any wilful or affected delay, and that he will pay the person in whose favour the conviction, order or other proceeding is affirmed, his full costs and charges to be taxed according to the course of the court, in case the conviction, order or proceeding is affirmed.''

This rule remains in force under the Criminal Code without being repassed: R.S.C. c. 1, sec. 20 (a); R. v. Robinet, 16 P.R. 49, 2 Can. Cr. Cas. 382; and a similar rule was adopted by the Supreme Court of British Columbia, 27th April, 1889, the amount to be $100: see R. v. Ah Gin, 2 B.C.R. 207; and so in Nova Scotia, the amount to be $200: see McIsaac v. McNeil, 28 N.S.R. 442. And there is a similar rule in the N.W.T., dated 8th June, 1889, requiring a recognizance in $300, or $200 deposit.

The above rule is also expressly made applicable to certiorari proceedings in respect to offences against Ontario laws, by 1 Edward VII. (Ont.), ch. 13, secs. 3, 4.

FORM OF RECOGNIZANCE.

In the High Court of Justice.

The King v. A.B.

Be it remembered that on the   day of   A.D. 19 , in the   year of the reign of our Sovereign Lord, Edward VII., of the United Kingdom of Great Britain and Ireland, and His Majesty's other Dominions beyond the seas, King, Defender of the Faith, Emperor of India, personally came before me, E.F., one of His Majesty's justices of the peace in and for the County of   (or police magistrate in and for the

of   , in said County of   ), A.B. (*defendant*), of the
of   , in the County of   , (*occupation*), G.H., of the   of
          , in the County of   , (*occupation*), K.L., of the   of
          , in the County of   , (*occupation*), and acknowledged themselves to owe to our Sovereign the King the sum of $100 of lawful money of Canada to be levied upon their goods, chattels, lands and tenements to His Majesty's use, upon condition that if the aforesaid A.B. (*defendant*) shall prosecute with effect without any wilful or affected delay at his own proper costs and charges, a writ of certiorari issued out of the High Court of Justice for Ontario to remove into the said court all and singular the records of conviction and of whatsoever trespasses and contempts against the form of the statute known as the Criminal Code of Canada, sec. (*or insert whatever the Statute may be, under which the defendant was convicted*), and particularly the offence whereof the said A.B. was convicted before C.D., Esquire, police magistrate (*or one of His Majesty's justices of the peace*) in and for the   of   , as aforesaid (*set out the charge*), and shall pay as and when the same may be ordered by the Court to the person or persons in whose favour the said conviction may be

affirmed, all his or their full costs and charges to be taxed according to the course of the said Court in case the said conviction is affirmed.

Then this recognizance to be void; otherwise to remain in full force and virtue.

Taken and acknowledged the day and year ⎤ A.B. (seal).
first above mentioned at the   ⎬ E.F. (seal).
of   aforesaid, before me.   ⎬ G.H. (seal).
           R.S.   (seal). ⎦

A justice of the peace in and for the
County of
Witness to the execution by the
parties and justice above named.
       M.N.

This recognizance must be taken before a justice of the peace or magistrate, or before a judge for the County or place within which the conviction has been made, pursuant to the rule above mentioned, or before a judge of the Superior Court. If it is taken before a justice in another County the application to quash cannot be entertained: R. v. Johnston, 8 Can. Cr. Cas. 123; R. v. Robinet, 16 P.R. 49.

One surety is sufficient if he can qualify in the amount mentioned.

This recognizance may be estreated and enforced in the manner prescribed by Code 1096.

In analogy to the general practice in the High Court, the sureties must, in Ontario cases, justify in $100 over and above what they are otherwise sureties for (or the affidavit must negative the fact that they are sureties in any other matter, *if such be the case*), and also over and above their other liabilities: R. v. Robinet, 16 P.R. 49, 2 Can. Cr. Cas. 382; but see R. v. Ashcroft (N.W.T.), 2 Can.Cr.Cas. 385, in which it was held that in the N.W.T. it is not necessary to negative the sureties being securety in any other matter.

A cash deposit may be made with the registrar of the court in which the motion is made according to the requirements of the above Ontario rule, or any rule in the other provinces, in the place of a recognizance. The deposit need not be accompanied by any writing stating the conditions on which it is made: R. v. Davidson, 6 Can. Cr. Cas. 117.

The security or deposit must be filed or deposited in the court in which the motion to quash is made and before making it, and cannot be put in pending such motion; but it is not required before certiorari is applied for. If it be delivered to the justice and filed in court with his return to certiorari, that was held sufficient: R. v. Cluff, 46 U.C.R. 565, in which case the practice and procedure are fully stated: see, also, R. v. Robinet, 16 P.R. 49; R. v. Ashcroft, 2 Can. Cr. Cas. 385.

An affidavit of justification by the surety or sureties is necessary: R. v. Richardson, 17 O.R. 729; R. v. Petrie, N.W.T.R. vol. 1, pt. 2, p. 3. The rule nisi to quash the conviction was quashed in these cases for want of a sufficient recognizance or deposit; but fresh security having been put in pending the proceedings, leave was given to issue another rule nisi. In R. v. Abergele, 5 A. & E. 795, an adjournment was made to perfect the security; see also R. v. McAllan, 45 U.C.R. 402.

In McIsaac v. McNeil, 28 N.S.R. 442, however, it was held that the requirements of the rule as to filing affidavits of justification are imperative, and where they are not complied with the judge is bound to give effect to the objection and dismiss the application; and that leave to file the affidavit pending the motion to quash cannot be granted.

FORM OF AFFIDAVIT OF JUSTIFICATION BY SURETY.
In the High Court of Justice.
The King v. A.B.
I, E.F., of the   of   in the County of
(occupation) make oath and say:
1. That I am the surety (or one of the sureties, as the case may be) proposed and named for the above named A.B. in the recognizance in this matter hereunto annexed.
2. That I am a freeholder (or householder residing at No.   St.   in   of   in the said County of   .
3. That I own and am worth property to the amount of one hundred dollars over and above what will pay all my debts and liabilities and every other sum for which I am now liable, or for which I am bail, or surety in any other matter.
4. That I am not bail or surety for any person except in this matter and except (stating in what matter and for how much, if any).
5. That my said property to the amount of the said sum of one hundred dollars consists of household furniture (or farm stock, implements, money deposited in bank or bank stock or land, (describing it, or whatever it consists of), to the value of about   dollars.
Sworn before me at the   .
          of   in the   E.F.
County of   on the
          day of   A.D. 19 .
          Signed: O.P.,
          A Commissioner, etc.

The affidavit need not shew residence of surety for any specific time: R. v. Burke, 7 Can. Cr. Cas. 538.

If there are two sureties, a second affidavit similar to the foregoing will be made, and in that case each may justify in $50, so as to make up the $100 required.

As to the sufficiency of the affidavit of justification: see R. v. Burke, 7 Can. Cr. Cas. 538.

It has not been decided whether there must be a description or statement of the property on which the surety qualifies, but it is submitted that it is not required: see Tidd's Prac. 242, 267; Short and Melton, 662. The Crown may question the sufficiency of the sureties by affidavits in answer, though there is no right to cross-examine the surety on this point.

FORM OF AFFIDAVIT OF EXECUTION.

In the High Court of Justice.
The King v. A.B.
I, M.N., of the   of   in the County of   ,
(*occupation*) make oath and say:

1. That I was personally present and did see the hereunto annexed recognizance duly signed, sealed and executed by A.B., and E.F. and G.H., the parties thereto, and by R.S., the justice of the peace for the said County of   , before whom the same was taken and acknowledged.

2. That the said recognizance was so executed, taken and acknowledged at the   of   in the said County of   .

3. That I know the said parties and the said justice.

4. That I am a subscribing witness to the said recognizance.

Sworn before me at the   ⎫
        of   in the County ⎬   M.N.
of   , this   day of ⎭
        A.D. 19
            T.U.,
            A Commissioner, etc.

Under the Nova Scotia Crown Rules an affidavit in any form verifying the recognizance suffices: R. v. Burke, 7 Can. Cr. Cas. 538.

The Ontario Crown Rule (see *ante*, page 10) requires "an affidavit of the execution" of the recognizance," and the Court will not entertain an application to quash a conviction without such affidavit: R. v. Ah Gin, 2 B.C.R. 207.

No recognizance is required on an application made by the Crown or the prosecutor, see *ante*. p. 8.

It is to be observed that by Code 1126, and the Ontario Crown Rule above mentioned the recognizance or deposit is only required in the case of a conviction or proceeding "brought before the court by certiorari;" and it has been held that if the conviction is already regularly on the files of the court, as for instance, if it has been filed on a motion for habeas corpus under a certiorari in aid of the latter writ, or if it has been returned by the justice to the clerk of the court under the provisions of a statute requiring such return to be made, then there is no necessity for a writ of certiorari to bring up the case for the purpose of its being reviewed and the conviction being quashed: R. v. Wehlau,

45 U.C.R. 396; R. v. Nunn, 10 P.R. 395; R. v. Allen, 45 U.C.R. 402. In the North-West Territories, where the conviction had been returned by the justice under Code 757 or 793 to the registrar of the Supreme Court, it was held that a motion to quash might be properly made without certiorari; and that the notice under the 13 Geo. II., and the recognizance or deposit provided for by the Crown Rule before mentioned, were not requisite: R. v. Rondeau, 9 Can. Cr. Cas. 523.

There is a conflict of opinion in the cases in different provinces on this point. The cases, in addition to those above mentioned, are: R. v. Frawley, 45 U.C.R. 227; R. v. Levecque, 30 U.C.R. 509; R. v. Ashcroft, 2 Can. Cr. Cas. 385; R. v. Monaghan, 2 Can. Cr. Cas. 488; R. v. Hostyn, 9 Can. Cr. Cas. 138; R. v. Ames, 10 Can. Cr. Cas. 52; R. v. Gehrke, 11 Can. Cr. Cas. 106; R. v. McDonald, 5 Can. Cr. Cas. 279.

The notice of the intended application for certiorari which is provided by the statute, 13 Geo. II., and required by the court before a conviction can be quashed, seems clearly to be necessary in every case, inasmuch as the justice would otherwise have no notice of the intended proceedings by which he will be exposed to an action if the conviction is quashed: R. v. Peterman, 23 U.C.R. 516. It is also argued that the effect of allowing an application to be made to quash a conviction which happens to be filed in the office of the person who is the registrar of the court, without requiring the notice or recognizance above mentioned, would open the way to abuse of the procedure of the court, and an avoidance and nullification of what was clearly intended by the statute and rule; viz., that no application to quash a conviction should be made without the previous notice under the 13 Geo. II., or Crown Rule, and without fitting security for the costs; the former depriving the justice of his right to rectify a technical error in a proper case; and the latter depriving the prosecutor and justice of the security for their expenses which is provided by law.

It may also be noticed that it is questionable whether a conviction on file in the office of the person who is also the registrar of the court can be said to be thereby before the court, or even on the files of the court, for the purposes of a motion to quash it. And further that certiorari in aid of habeas corpus merely brings up certain proceedings (and not necessarily the whole record) for the information of the court: R. v. Nunn, 10 P.R. 395;

whereas the scope and consequence of the proceedings by certiorari for the purpose of reviewing the justice's proceedings and determining upon the same and quashing, amending or confirming them, is the removal of the whole record and of the cause itself, out of the jurisdiction of the justice and into the Superior Court to be determined there upon the return of the certificate of the same and all the proceedings therein and all things touching the same: R. v. Hampshire, J. J., 33 L.J.M.C. 104; R. v. Foster, 7 Can. Cr. Cas. 46; and it would seem that the justice is the only functionary who can accurately, and as a matter of fact, certify to the court a complete record of them: R. v. Gehrke, 11 Can. Cr. Cas. at p. 113.

The case of R. v. McDonald (No. 2) in the Supreme Court of Nova Scotia, 5 Can. Cr. Cas. 279, would point to the conclusion that until the cause itself and all matters connected with it, have been brought into the Superior Court by a regularly certified return by the justice, the court will not entertain proceedings to quash the same: R. v. Gehrke, 11 Can. Cr. Cas. 109. A writ of certiorari will not be allowed to bring up intermediate proceedings alone, in a case where there has been final judgment; but the judgment and all proceedings must be brought up for review, otherwise two or more writs of certiorari might be required in order to get the whole record before the court; and there cannot be two writs of certiorari in one case: R. v. Townsend (No. 2), 11 Can. Cr. Cas. 115.

If a cash deposit is made instead of giving a recognizance, it is in court for the purposes of security only, and on the terms mentioned in the rule of court, and not for any collateral or other purpose; and if the conviction is sustained no portion of the deposit can be applied towards the fine and costs imposed by the conviction; but any surplus after paying any costs of the application for certiorari must be repaid to the defendant: Wing v. Sicotte, 10 Can. Cr. Cas. 171.

Writ of Certiorari.

If the conviction has been returned to the clerk of the peace, under Code 757 or 793, the writ of certiorari must also be directed to the latter; it is properly addressed to the officer having the custody of the papers: R. v. Frawley, 45 U.C.R. at p.

231; and where there has been an appeal to the county judge, and the papers are in his hands, it seems that the writ should be directed to him also.

If the justice having the possession of the papers dies before a return is made to the writ, it may be directed to his executors who must make the return, with the documents: 2 Hawkins P.C. ch. 27, sec. 41, Paley, 8th ed. 105.

The writ is issued on *præcipe* by the registrar of the High Court on production of the order therefor.

The original writ is served on the party to whom it is addressed. It is not necessary to serve the prosecutor, who will be served with the proceedings to quash, subsequently.

The writ supersedes the justice's authority from the time of its delivery to him, and all subsequent proceedings by him on the conviction are void: Paley, 8th ed. 464; even if nothing further be done upon the writ. *Ibid.* But the justice may fix the amount of the fine (if not already done) in order to return the complete judgment: Paley, 8th ed. 464. The writ has no effect upon the execution of warrants previously in the constable's hands, and in course of execution by him, and he may proceed to sell under distress warrant goods he already has levied on: R. v. Nash, 2 Lord Raymond 990.

The question of the validity of the conviction or commitment is sometimes argued on the application for certiorari, and if the proceedings are held to be valid certiorari will be refused: R. v. Cunerty, 2 Can. Cr. Cas. 325.

Return to Writ.

On being served with the writ of certiorari the justice or officer to whom it is addressed endorses on the back of the writ the following:—

"RETURN TO WRIT OF CERTIORARI."
"The answer of C.D., the justice of the peace within mentioned."
The execution of this writ appears in the schedule hereunto annexed.
C.D.,
Justice of the peace.
SCHEDULE (*to be attached to the writ*).
I, C.D., of the   of   in the County of   , one of the justices of the peace of our Sovereign Lord, the King, assigned to keep the peace within the said County of   , and to hear and determine divers offences committed in the said county, by virtue of this writ of certiorari to me delivered, do hereby certify unto His Majesty in His High Court of Justice for the Province of Ontario, the record of conviction with the in-

formation, summons (or warrant to apprehend) and the depositions and evidence and minute of adjudication and all proceedings taken before me, of which mention is made in the said writ, together with all matters touching the same.

    In witness whereof I the said C.D. have to these presents set my seal.

    Given at the   of   the   day of   .A.D. 19 .

                                     C.D.

                                     J.P. [Seal].

The return must be under seal: 2 Hawkins P.C. ch. 27, sec. 70; Paley, 8th ed. 315.

The originals and not copies of the conviction and other papers, are to be annexed, with the above schedule, to the writ of certiorari and returned along with it and the recognizance or deposit above mentioned: Askew v. Hayton, 1 Dowl. 510; and in Ontario are to be transmitted to the registrar of the High Court of Justice, Osgoode Hall, Toronto.

If the conviction has been returned by the justice to the clerk of the peace, the above return will be made by the latter.

Upon being served with the writ of certiorari the justice of the peace or magistrate must make a return to the writ, even if the papers have been filed with the clerk of the peace, in which case the following form of return may be used:—

The answer of C.D., the justice of the peace (or police magistrate) within mentioned.

The execution of this writ appears in the schedule hereunto annexed.·

                               C.D.,

                        Justice of the peace

                        (or police magistrate).

                   SCHEDULE.

I, C.D., justice of the peace (or police magistrate), to Our Sovereign The King, do certify that before the coming of the writ of Our said Lord the King, to me directed and to this schedule annexed, to wit, on the day of   , A.D. 19 , an information was laid on oath by against A.B. charging him with (state the charge), and the said charge was laid before me as such justice (or police magistrate), and the matter of the complaint was enquired into by me, and the depositions of witnesses were taken.

The Crown was represented by   , Esquire (County Crown Attorney, or as the case may be), and the prisoner by his counsel, Esquire (or as the case may be).

At the close of the examination, and upon hearing counsel for the Crown and counsel for the prisoner (or as the case may be), I did duly convict the said A.B. and prepare and sign a record of conviction of the said A.B. (or I did by warrant in due form of law) commit the said A.B. to the common gaol of the County of   , there to be kept until he should be thence delivered by due course of law (or as the case may be, describing the proceedings taken). The said warrant was sent to the gaoler with the said prisoner (if such be the fact), and the information and depositions were afterwards and before the receipt of the said writ by me sent and delivered to the clerk of the peace of the said County of , according to law, and at the time of the receipt of the said writ by me, I had not, nor have I now, any of the said information, depositions, evidence, commitment or proceedings aforesaid remaining in my custody, control or keeping whatsoever.

And this is my return to the said writ this day of , A.D. 19

[Seal].
Justice of the peace.
(*or* police magistrate).

Motion to Quash Conviction.

The motion to quash a conviction or commitment brought up under certiorari must be made to the full court in Ontario: R. v. McAulay, 14 O.R. p. 656; R. v. Beemer, 15 O.R. 266; and in Manitoba: R. v. Beale, 11 Man. R. 448; and so in the North-West Territories. The case of R. v. Ames, 10 Can. Cr. Cas. 52 (N.W. T.), was decided under the Dominion statute 54-5 Vict. ch. 22, sec. 7, but that statute was subsequently repealed: see schedule A, R.S.C. 1906, p. 2946. The motion for rule nisi should be set down with the registrar of the high court the day before the application is to be made, and the following motion paper is to be filed:

MOTION PAPER ON APPLICATION FOR RULE NISI.

In the High Court of Justice.

Before the Court } Monday the day of
A.D. 19

The King v. A.B.

Motion on behalf of the above named A.B. upon reading the writ of certiorari granted herein on the day of A.D. 19 , and the papers filed in Chambers on the application therefor, the return to the said writ and the papers thereto attached, and the recognizance also filed for an order calling upon C.D., Esquire, justice of the peace (*or* police magistrate), for the of and E.F. (*the informant*), upon notice to them of such order to be given to them respectively, to shew cause why the conviction of the said A.B., upon the information of the said E.F. for that he did (*set out the charge as in the conviction*), should not be quashed with costs upon the following, among other grounds: (*State the grounds.*)

Of counsel for the said A.B.

RULE NISI TO QUASH CONVICTION.

In the High Court of Justice.
The Divisional Court.

day, the day
The Honourable Chief of A.D. 19 .
Justice. Upon the application of the said A.B.
The Honourable Mr. upon reading the writ of certiorari issued on
Justice. the day of A.D. 19 , and
The Honourable Mr. the affidavits of the said C.D. and A.B. and
Justice. other papers filed in Chambers on the ap-
The King v. A.B. plication therefor, the return of C.D.,

Esquire, justice of the peace (or police magistrate, for the   of
     , or the clerk of the peace for the County of   as the case
may be), to the said writ and the papers thereto attached, and also the
rcognizance entered into by the said A.B., with a surety (or sureties),
with affidavits of justification and execution also filed, and upon hearing
counsel for the said A.B.

     It is ordered that C.D., Esquire, justice of the peace (or police magis-
trate), for the   of   and E.F., the prosecutor, upon notice
to them of this order, to be given to them respectively, shall, on
the   day of   A.D. 19 , at   o'clock, in the forenoon, or so soon thereafter as counsel can be heard before this court at
Osgoode Hall, Toronto, shew cause why a certain conviction made by the
said C.D., justice of the peace (or police magistrate), on the information
of the said E.F., whereby the said A.B. was convicted for that (set out
the charge as in the conviction), and which said conviction has been removed into this court under certiorari should not be quashed with costs,
on the following grounds, amongst others: (Set out the grounds.)

     On motion of Mr.   , of counsel for the said A.B.

                  By the court.

                         Registrar.

The grounds of objection to the conviction or proceeding need
not be stated in the rule nisi: R. v. McGregor, 10 Can. Cr. Cas.
313. But it is usual and proper to so state them.

Proceedings to Quash Certiorari.

The objection to the want of the six days' notice mentioned
at p. 5, ante, or other objection to the proceedings to quash a
conviction should be raised by the prosecutor or magistrate by a
substantive application to supersede the certiorari; but that
course is not essential in some instances; and the objection may
be allowed to be raised on the return of the motion to quash the
conviction. Objection for the ground of defects of form or of a
trifling or technical nature in the proceedings to quash will not be
allowed to be brought up on the motion to quash a conviction; and
a substantive motion will be necessary, so as to give an opportunity
for ordering an amendment, if proper, and upon proper terms;
and that is generally the proper and necessary course to take: R.
v. Davidson, 6 Can. Cr. Cas. 119; R. v. Fordham, 11 A. & E. 73.

But if the defect is a fundamental one, it is not too late to
bring it up on the motion for rule absolute to quash the conviction: R. v. McAllan, 45 U.C.R. 402, distinguishing R. v. Levee-
que, 30 U.C.R. 509; R. v. Davidson, 6 Can. Cr. Cas. 117; R. v.
Hoggard, 30 U.C.R. 152.

So objection to the certiorari on the ground that the security
required is defective or has not been properly given, should be
raised by a substantive motion to supersede the writ of certiorari:

R. v. Cluff, 46 U.C.R. 565; and see Re Bishop Dyke, 20 N.S.R. 263; R. v. Porter, *ib.* 352.

Care must be taken, not to do anything which would be held to be a waiver of an objection (for instance, of the objection of absence after six days' notice required by the Crown Rule), and either a substantive motion should be made to supersede the certiorari, or the justice or prosecutor should cause notice to be served that he will take the objection of want of six days' previons notice or other objection on the return of the motion to quash the conviction. Should he not do this he may, by acquiescence in the motion or by delay, (such as allowing an adjournment to be ordered without raising the objection), be held to have waived it: R. v. Whittaker, 24 O.R. 437; following R. v. Basingstoke, 19 L.J.M.C. 28; and distinguishing on this point R. v. McAllan, 45 U.C.R. 402. In the case of R. v. McAllan, it was stated that the six days' notice to the justice was a condition precedent and its want "a most substantial defect;" and that if the objection were only to the recognizance required by the High Court rule, it might be got over, as was done in R. v. Abergele, 5 A. & E. 795, by allowing a new recognizance to be given, and enlarging the application for that purpose; but the want of the notice could in no way be cured or waived.

But in the more recent case of R. v. Whittaker, 24 O.R. 437, it was distinctly held, that it might be waived. Great delay in taking objections to the certiorari proceedings will be considered as waiving them: R. v. Davidson, 6 Can. Cr. Cas. 117, and notes at p. 122.

Quære whether the truth or falsity of a return to certiorari can be enquired into by a motion to quash it: R. v. Nichols, 24 N.S.R. 151.

FORM OF NOTICE THAT ON THE MOTION TO QUASH, AN OBJECTION WILL BE TAKEN TO THE CERTIORARI.

In the High Court of Justice.
The King v. A.B.
Take notice that upon the motion to quash the conviction of you, the above named A.B., objection will be taken on behalf of C.D., the prosecutor (or of   , the convicting magistrate *or* justice), that the writ of certiorari herein and the return thereto are invalid on the ground that six clear days' previous notice was not given to the said convicting magistrate (*or* justice, *or* two of the convicting justices, *as the case may be*), of the application for the said certiorari, or that the recognizance filed is insufficient, for the following reasons: (stating the objections or stat-

ing any other grounds on which it is contended that the certiorari is invalid).

Dated, etc.

To the said A.B.

E.F.,

Solicitor for the said C.D., prosecutor,

(or G.H., the magistrate or justice above named).

If a substantive motion to supersede the certiorari is made, then instead of the next preceding notice the following forms may be used:

AFFIDAVIT IN SUPPORT OF MOTION TO SUPERSEDE CERTIORARI.

In the High Court of Justice.

The King v. A.B.

I   , of the   of   , in the County of
, make oath and say:

1. That I am the prosecutor (or the magistrate or justice as the case may be) named in the writ of certiorari issued herein, a true copy of which is now shewn to me marked exhibit A.

2. [If the objection is that the notice was served on the magistrate less than six clear days, state the facts clearly, and shew when it was served, and negativing service for six clear days as required by the 13 Geo. II. If no notice was served at all on the magistrate, state the fact. If the copy of notice served is claimed to be insufficient in form, the copy of notice should be verified and marked as an exhibit. If the objection is to the sufficiency of the recognizance, or of the affidavit of execution, or justification, or in form or substance or manner of execution, state any facts necessary to shew this. If the objection is to the sufficiency of the sureties shew this, and state fully the means of knowledge of the deponents, and what the sureties' property, if any, is worth. If the application is made on the ground of delay in prosecuting the writ of certiorari and in moving to quash, then set out the proceedings taken and the facts shewing that there has been laches and undue delay.]

NOTICE OF MOTION TO SUPERSEDE CERTIORARI.

In the High Court of Justice.

The King v. A.B.

Take notice that a motion will be made on behalf of E.F., the convicting justice (or magistrate), or on behalf of C.D., the prosecutor herein. before the presiding judge of this court in Chambers, at Osgoode Hall, in the City of Toronto, on the   day of   , A.D. 19 , at ten o'clock in the forenoon, or so soon thereafter as the motion can be made for an order superseding or quashing the writ of certiorari issued herein, and succeeding the order therefor, and for the return of the conviction and other proceedings and papers to the said convicting justice (or magistrate), or to the clerk of the peace for the County of   ,
on the ground that no notice was given to the said magistrate six clear days before the application for the said writ, as required by the statute in that behalf; or that the notice was insufficient in this that
(setting out its defect); or that no recognizance was filed as required by the rule of court; or that the recognizance is insufficient, or was not duly entered into and executed, in this that   (setting out defects);
or that the sureties named in the said recognizance were not possessed of sufficient property to justify as such, and were not worth $100 over and above what they are otherwise sureties for, and over and above their other liabilities, (see Re Robinet, 16 P.R. 49); or for want of prosecution and delay in prosecuting the certiorari on the part of the said A.B., within

the time limited by the statute in that behalf, and for an order that the said defendant do pay to the said prosecutor (or convicting magistrate *or* justice) his costs of, and incidental to the application for certiorari and this application; or for such further or other order as may seem meet.

And take notice that upon such application will be read the affidavit of   the exhibits therein referred to and the orders, proceedings and papers herein.

Dated this   day of   A.D. 19 .

G.H., Solicitor for the said prosecutor
(or convicting magistrate *or* justice).

To the said C.D. and
E.F., his solicitor.

After the quashing of a writ of certiorari and the return of the conviction to the justice a second writ of certiorari will not be granted: R. v. Nichols, 21 N.S.R. 288, noted in 7 Can. Cr. Cas. p. 51; even if the prior certiorari was dismissed on a technicality, *e.g.*, for omission to file the recognizance: R. v. Geiser, 7 Can. Cr. Cas. 173. This decision is based on the judgment in R. v. Bodmin, (1892), 2 Q.B. 21, in which the court refused to entertain a second application for this high prerogative writ, which is an extraordinary remedy and cannot be repeatedly applied for.

Service of Rule Nisi, to Quash Conviction.

The rule nisi to quash the conviction must be served four days before the day on which the application for the rule absolute is to be made.

Motion for Rule, Absolute.

The case must be set down with the registrar of the High Court for argument, at the latest the day before the time fixed for the argument, in analogy to C. R. 364, and the motion paper signed by counsel should be filed with the registrar. (The motion paper will be similar in form to that filed on application for the rule nisi, *ante*, p. 19).

The court will not hear a motion to quash a return to certiorari pending an appeal from the order granting certiorari: R. v. Hurlburt, 26 N.S.R. 123, 2 Can. Cr. Cas. 331.

RULE ABSOLUTE QUASHING CONVICTION.
In the High Court of Justice.

The Honourable the
Chief Justice of the
The Honourable   Monday, the
Mr. Justice   day of
The Honourable   A.D., 19
Mr. Justice

The King against A.B.

1. Upon the application of A.B. upon reading the rule nisi issued on the   day   , A.D. 19   , and the affidavit of service thereof, the writ of certiorari, dated the   day of   , A.D. 19   , the return of the said writ and the papers thereto attached, and the recognizance filed, and upon hearing counsel for the prosecutor, E.F., and for the appellant, A.B., and for C.D., Esquire, justice of the peace (*or* police magistrate), (*or* no one appearing for the said E.F. or C.D., although duly notified).

2. It is ordered that the conviction of the said A.B. by C.D., Esquire, justice of the peace (*or* police magistrate) for the   of   on information of the said E.F. for that (*set out the charge*) be and the same is hereby quashed (*and if costs are ordered*) with costs to be paid by the said   to the said A.B.

3. And it is further ordered that the said A.B. be and he is hereby discharged from custody under the warrant of commitment issued upon the said conviction.

4. And it is further ordered that no such action as is provided for by section 1131 of the Criminal Code of Canada, and by the Revised Statutes of Ontario, chapter 88, section 11, shall be brought against the said C.D. and E.F., or either of them, or any person whomsoever.

On motion of Mr.   of counsel for said A.B.

By the court,

_____

Registrar.

The court on quashing a conviction has the right to impose the condition that no action shall be brought against the justice or officer, Code **1131**, Ont. St., 1 Edw. VII. ch. 13, sec. 1, but the applicant may accept or reject this condition; and if rejected, the court, may, if it sees fit, for special reasons and in the substantial interest of justice, dismiss the application with costs, although it finds the justice exceeded his jurisdiction: R. v. Morningstar, 11 Can. Cr. Cas. 15, but *quære,* whether the court being seized of the whole matter and having the right conferred by the above statutes, could not impose the condition *ipso facto* on the applicant; and whether any objection by him was of any force: see notes in 11 Can. Cr. Cas. 18.

Costs.

The court has no authority under its general powers or otherwise to award costs to the successful party in cases under Dominion laws; except as against an unsuccessful applicant for the writ, and that is by force of the recognizance he has given: see 5 Can. Cr. Cas. p. 460: R. v. Banks, 1 Can. Cr. Cas. 370; R. v. Bennett, 5 Can. Cr. Cas. 456; R. v. Bowers, 6 Can. Cr. Cas. 100; R. v. Rondeau, 9 Can. Cr. Cas. p. 528; R. v. Mancion, 8 Can. Cr. Cas. p. 218; London County

Council v. West Ham. (1892), 2 Q.B. 176. Code 751 does not apply to certiorari or habeas corpus proceedings which do not constitute an appeal on which costs may be awarded under that section: R. v. Graham, 1 Can. Cr. Cas 405.

But the successful applicant may recover his costs by a civil action, unless such action is barred by order of the court: R. v. Somers, 24 O.R. 244.

In prosecutions for breaches of Ontario laws, however, costs' may be awarded, R. v. Mancion, 8 Can. Cr. Cas. 218. By the Ontario Judicature Rule, 1238, passed 7th June, 1902, the costs of and incidental to proceedings in the Court of Appeal and High Court of Justice in relation to the quashing of convictions or orders are in the discretion of the court which has authority to direct by whom, to whom and to what extent they shall be paid, whether the conviction is affirmed or quashed in whole or in part.

This rule is only operative under the Ontario Judicature Act, and not being a rule promulgated under Code 576, can only operate in prosecutions for offences under Ontario statutes and not in proceedings to quash convictions under any Dominion statute: R. v. Eli, 13 A.R. 526; R. v. Wason, 17 A.R. 221; R. v. McAuley, 14 O.R. 657; R. v. Bennet, 5 Can. Cr. Cas. 456; R. v. Mancion, 8 Can. Cr. Cas. 218, and other cases noted above.

If the conviction is affirmed without amendment the prosecutor is entitled to his costs of opposing the motion: Paley, 8th ed. 476.

But when the proceeding to quash was justified when launched, but the conviction was amended and affirmed, or an amended conviction was returned under the certiorari, costs are not given against the defendant: R. v. Whiffin, 4 Can. Cr. Cas. 141; R. v. Highan, 7 E. & B. 557; Re Plunkett, 3 B.C.R. 484; 1 Can. Cr. Cas. 365; R. v. Little, 6 B.C.R. 321; R. v. McAnn, 3 Can. Cr. Cas. p. 120. The principle upon which the question of costs is dealt with is discussed in the case of R. v. Crandall, 27 O.R. 63; and see Re Rice, 20 N.S.R. 437; R. v. Roche, 32 O.R. 20; R. v. Banks, 1 Can. Cr. Cas. 372; R. v. McLeod, 1 Can. Cr. Cas. 10; R. v. Graham, 1 Can. Cr. Cas. 405.

An application by way of certiorari to set aside a conviction is not an appeal within the meaning of Code 751 and 754; and the proceedings, therein provided, for the recovery of the costs,

do not apply. Any costs should be ordered to be paid to the
opposite party, and not to the clerk of the peace; and can only
be recovered by estreating the recognizance under Code 892, or
by process of the High Court: R. v. Graham, 1 Can. Cr. Cas. 405.

Notice of Application for Costs.

It was suggested in R. v. Westgate, 21 O.R. 621, that if, with
the notice of application for certiorari, a notice was served stating that unless the prosecution was forthwith abandoned, the
costs of further necessary proceedings to obtain relief would be
asked, such notice would be a ground for asking costs, when the
conviction is manifestly bad, and when it appears clearly unjust
or unfair to put the defendant to such further costs.

FORM OF SUCH NOTICE.

To   (*the informant*).
     of the   of   in the County of
Take notice that hereto anneXed and served on you herewith is a true
copy of a notice served on C.D., Esquire, police magistrate (*or* one of His
Majesty's justices of the peace) for the   of   of a
motion for certiorari to issue out of the High Court of Justice, directed
to the said magistrate (*or* justice), and to the clerk of the peace for the
County of   , for the removal into the said High Court of Justice
of the record and conviction of A.B. upon the information of you, the
said   , for that he did on the   day of   A.D. 19 ,
at the   of   in the County of   unlawfully (*set out the
charge*).
     And take notice that unless the said conviction, and the prosecution
thereunder, be forthwith abandoned by you, and notice given by you to the
said A.B., or to me as his solicitor, to that effect with your consent to
the quashing of the proceedings, the said A.B. will apply to the court on
the quashing of the said conviction for an order that you pay the costs of
the further proceedings necessary in the premises.
     Dated this   day of   A.D. 19 .

_____

Solicitor for said A.B.

This proceeding can only apply to proceedings under Ontario
laws and not to those under Dominion laws; as there is no authority to order payment of costs by the prosecutor in the latter:
ante, p. 24.

Proceedings on Refusal to Quash.

An order being made refusing to quash the conviction the
registrar of the court is forthwith to return the conviction with
the order, to the justice, who may then proceed to enforce the
conviction; and it is not necessary to issue a writ of procedendo:
Code 1127 dispensing with the necessity for that writ:
R. v. Zickrick, 5 Can. Cr. Cas. 380. If however the

conviction is quashed, even on the ground that the justice's summons was not duly served, the justice is *functus officio,* and cannot issue, and cause a fresh summons to be served upon the same information; and the papers should remain on file in the High Court. As the justice can only proceed when procedendo would have been ordered, prohibition will be ordered restraining him from any attempted proceeding: R. v. Zickrick, 5 Can. Cr. Cas. 380; and any such proceeding if taken will be quashed: R. v. Foster, 7 Can. Cr. Cas. p. 51.

Death of Prosecutor.

The death of the prosecutor (who is also the informant) after conviction and before service of proceedings, does not prevent the High Court from dealing with the matter: R. v. Fitzgerald, 29 O.R. 203, 1 Can. Cr. Cas. 140.

The Remedy by Certiorari.

The prerogative of the Sovereign to review and keep within their jurisdiction the proceedings of inferior legal tribunals, and which prerogative is vested in and delegated to the High Court is not dependent upon statutory provisions. The authority to issue certiorari applies, therefore, to all convictions and proceedings by justices and magistrates acting under the authority of a Royal Commission, and whether executing the laws of the Dominion or of a province: R. v. Cushing, 26 A.R. p. 248.

By the provisions of Code 798 none of the clauses in part XIII and XV of the Criminal Code (ss. 705-769) apply in any way to convictions or orders made by magistrates under part XVI (ss. 771, etc.); but by Code 1130, such convictions are not to be quashed for want of form; and a warrant of commitment by a magistrate is not to be held void for any defect whatever, if it is alleged theren that the defendant was convicted, and it appears that there is a· valid conviction to sustain it. In such cases, if the conviction itself is also bad, a defective commitment is not cured by the statute: R. v. Gibson, 29 O.R. 660, and cannot be amended by the court, the section as to amendment (Code 1124) not applying to summary trials before magistrates: R. v. Randolph, 32 O.R. 212.

The Remedy by Certiorari for Offences Against Ontario Laws.

In Ontario by Stat. 1 Edw. VII. ch. 13, secs. 889 to 896 (now secs. 1124 to 1129) of the Criminal Code are made applic-

able to proceedings in connection with offences against Ontario
laws. Sec. 1126 of the Criminal Code, deals with the conditions
upon which a motion to quash will be heard; and by sec. 3 of
the above Ontario statute, similar authority is conferred upon
the High Court of Justice with regard to the recognizance or
deposit of $100, to those mentioned, *ante*, p. 10.

By Ontario Stat. 2 Edw. VII. ch. 12, sec. 14, it is further provided that certiorari is not to be allowed except in cases where
an appeal would not afford an adequate remedy; and by sec. 15
powers of amendment or modification given by Code 883 and 889
(now 1124 and 754) to the court on applications to quash, are also
made applicable. By R.S.O. vol. 3, ch. 324, the application for
certiorari must be made within six calendar months, and the six
days' notice before referred to(*ante*, p. 5) must also be given
to the justice or justices.

The Ont. Stat. 2 Edw. VII. ch.12, sec. 15, authorizing amendment of an irregular conviction only applies to convictions under
summary proceedings before a justice of the peace, and not to
proceedings under the Liquor Act: R. v. Foster, 7 Can. Cr. Cas.
46.

Certiorari in Police Magistrates' Convictions.

Certiorari lies against convictions by police magistrates when
acting under the Justices Summary Convictions Clauses of the
Criminal Code, or when, acting in cases for violation of an Ontario statute. And on a conviction by a magistrate under his
jurisdiction under Part XVI. of the Criminal Code, for an indictable offence, it was held by the Court of Appeal in Ontario in
R. v. St. Clair, 3 Can. Cr. Cas. 551, that although Code 791 says
that such conviction shall *have the same effect* as a conviction
upon an indictment, nevertheless *it is not the same thing*, and is
different from a judgment of a court of record, and can be enquired into by certiorari and motion to quash, or upon habeas
corpus: see also O'Reilly v. Allen, 11 U.C.R. 526.

But it was held otherwise in Quebec: R. v. Racine, 3 Can.
Cr. Cas. 446; R. v. Marquis, 8 Can. Cr. Cas. p. 350.

In Ontario the question is settled by the St. Clair case.

In cases of convictions by magistrates or two justices under
Code 773(*a*) or (*f*) an appeal is allowed by Code 797, whether
the conviction is by justices or magistrate. The present Code
797 differs from the amendment of the old sec. 782 made in 1895,

the latter only providing for an appeal if the conviction was by two justices; but the present sec. 797 allows an appeal from a conviction under sec. 773(a) or (f) by magistrates as well as by justices.

In cases of convictions by magistrates or justices under the sub-sections last mentioned certiorari lies.

Jurisdiction and Powers of the Court.

Upon certiorari and motion to quash a conviction, the court cannot sit in appeal from the justice's or magistrate's decision, on the merits, and, therefore, cannot quash an adjudication, otherwise valid, upon an objection that the justice erroneously found a matter either of fact or of law which he was competent to try: Colonial Bank v. Willan, L.R. 5 P.C. p. 443; R. v. Grainger, 46 U.C.R. 382; R. v. Green, 12 P.R. 373; R. v. Walsh, 29 N.S.R. 521; reversing R. v. McDonald, 19 N.S.R. 336; R. v. Stevens, 31 N.S.R. 125; R. v. Beagan, 6 Can. Cr. Cas. 54; R. v. Can. Pac. Ry. Co., 9 Can. Cr. Cas. 328; R. v. Urquhart, 4 Can. Cr. Cas. 256.

The court has no power to review the decision of the justice upon the evidence, in a matter within his jurisdiction, as that is a matter of appeal, and this is so even if an affirmative finding was essential to jurisdiction: R. v. Cunerty, 26 O.R. 51, 2 Can. Cr. Cas. 325; Ex p. Nugent, 1 Can. Cr. Cas. 126.

And the court refused to interfere by certiorari, when the magistrate was alleged to have made a conviction on the evidence of a witness precluded by statute, the proper remedy being by appeal: R. v. Walsh, 29 N.S.R. 521; followed in R. v. Stevens, 31 N.S.R. 125; or to review an erroneous ruling as to the admission of evidence: R. v. Geo. McDonald, 29 N.S.R. 33, citing R. v. Dunning, 14 O.R. 58; R. v. Brown, 16 O.R. 45; Ex p. Armstrong, 31 N.B.R. 411; Ex p. Hopwood, 15 Q.B. 121; Colonial Bank v. Willan, L.R. 5 P.C. p. 443.

But the refusal of the magistrate to allow the defendant to give evidence, is to deny the defendant his full right of defence to which he is entitled, and so is a matter going to the jurisdiction: Ex p. Legere, 27 N.B.R. 292.

The court will not interfere in a case in which the magistrate has jurisdiction over the subject matter; even if it would have come to a different conclusion upon the evidence: Ex p. Levesque, 32 N.B.R. 174; Ex p. McKeen, 32 N.B.R. 85.

In R. v. Bolton, 1 Q.B. p. 72, Denman, C.J., said that if the conviction is valid the court cannot go into the evidence at all to consider whether or not the justice's decision was supported by it; that is for the justice, or the appellate court; and this is so, even if the evidence leads to the irresistible conclusion that the offence was not committed, and so, in one sense, was not within the justice's jurisdiction.

In Ex p. Partington, 6 Q.B. 656, the same judge said: "We are not authorized to review his (the justice's) decision. It may be that there may be no court competent to review it . . . . It is clear only that we have not that power." See also the review of the numerous decisions to the same effect and the opinion of the Supreme Court on the same point, in Re Trepanier, 12 S.C.R. at p. 111.

In R. v. Wallace, 4 O.R. 127, a conviction, which was valid on its face, had been made upon evidence which manifestly did not prove any offence, and in that case, Wilson, C.J., said that the provision for referring to the evidence made by the Imperial statute 41 Vict. ch. 16, sec. 117, (the same as Code 1124,) "would seem to warrant an examination of the merits; but it is probably only so when a conviction is substantially defective on its face, to allow it to be supported by the evidence proving the offence." In the same case, Hagarty, C.J., said: "If the justice refused to hear any evidence or decided without hearing evidence, or if there was a clear dereliction of duty or improper conduct on his part, the court would probably have authority to interfere, but not if there has been any *decision* of the justice arrived at by him, on the merits, however erroneous; and the court has to see that the justice 'acted within his authority, duly heard the case, and gave his decision upon the evidence as laid before him'." But Cameron, C.J., in the same case said, that when the evidence is taken, but it does not shew any offence, the justice has no jurisdiction, and the court may issue certiorari to quash the conviction.

The above were not appealable cases; and so there was no remedy except by certiorari.

In R. v. Coulson (No. 1), 24 O.R. 246, 1 Can. Cr. Cas. 114, it was held by the judges of the Queen's Bench Division, following the above case of R. v. Wallace, 4 O.R. 127, that, if the conviction is valid on its face, the court cannot, on a motion to quash, look at the evidence to see whether an offence was established or not, as that was a matter for the justice and the appellate court, if any. But this was not followed in the subsequent case of R. v. Coulson (No. 2), 27 O.R. 59, before the judges of the Common Pleas Division, in which it was held that, even in an appealable case, and even if the conviction is apparently a valid one, the depositions should be looked at for the purpose of ascertaining whether there was any evidence which would have been sufficient to go to a jury; and if not, the conviction should be quashed, as being made without jurisdiction.

In R. v. St. Clair, 27 A.R. 308, (which was the case of a conviction by a magistrate under part XVI of the Criminal Code and so there was no appeal upon the merits), Osler, J., said: "If there was evidence upon which the magistrate might have convicted, he was the judge of the *weight* to be attached to it, and it is not for us to re-hear the case or sit in appeal from it." And in R. v. Hughes, 29 O.R. 179, Boyd, C.J., said: "It may be that when a conviction is good on its face, and there is an appeal to the Sessions, the court, on certiorari, will not go into the facts; but it is a serious thing, and a doubtful thing, to say that the court will not do so, even although the conviction is good on its face, when there is no such appeal."

The result of the cases is that where there is no appeal, even if the conviction is valid on its face, the court will, without weighing the evidence, see that there is some evidence, such as would justify a case going to a jury, and upon which the conclusion of guilt may fairly be drawn; and in any case, a conviction not based upon any proper proof of guilt whatever, is void as against natural right, and in excess of jurisdiction, and will be quashed even if it is valid on its face. See White v. Feast, L.R. 7 Q.B. 353; R. v. Davey (Ont. App.), 4 Can. Cr. Cas. p. 33; Ex p. Dalley, 27 N.B.R. 129; Ex p. Coulson, 33 N.B.R. 341, 1 Can. Cr. Cas. 31.

The granting of certiorari is discretionary in any case; and if it appears that the grounds of objection are more properly the subject of appeal, and an appeal lies, the court will refuse certiorari unless special grounds are shewn: R. v. Whitbread, 2 Doug. 553; Ex p. Ross, 1 Can. Cr. Cas. 153; Ex p. Young, 32 N.B.R. 181. And after a conviction has been affirmed on appeal, certiorari will not be granted: Code 1121; except for excess of jurisdiction: R. v. Lynch, 12 O.R. 372; R. v. Herrell (No. 2), 3 Can. Cr. Cas. 15; and in appealable cases certiorari will be re-

fused, unless special circumstances are shewn therefor: Ex p.
Ross (S.C.N.B.), 1 Can. Cr. Cas. 153. But when a gross perversion of justice had occurred through the justice's misconduct
the court in the exercise of its discretion granted certiorari although the statute provided another mode of reviewing the conviction: Ex p. Cowan, 9 Can. Cr. Cas. 454. And certiorari will
be granted even after an appeal, if it was abortive in consequence
of the justice's default in not returning the deposit on appeal ·
R. v. Alford, 10 Can. Cr. Cas. 61; or in returning the conviction:
Ex p. Cowan, *supra,* or even in an appealable case if in the exercise of a sound judicial discretion and under exceptional circum
stances it is in the interests of justice: Re Traves, 10 Can. Cr.
Cas. 63.

The court, in its discretion, refused certiorari when defendant
pleaded guilty, and there was an appeal: Ex p. Barbarie, 31.
N.B.R. 368.

Certiorari does not lie to bring up a warrant of commitment
on grounds not affecting the conviction, or if the conviction is
valid; the proper procedure for reviewing upon grounds not
affecting the conviction but only the validity of the commitment
being by way of habeas corpus: R. v. Garland, 8 Can. Cr. Cas.
385; Ex p. Bertin, 10 Can. Cr. Cas. 65.

But in non-appealable cases the court will go into both facts
and law: R. v. Hughes, 29 O.R. 179, 2 Can. Cr. Cas. 5.

Conviction not Quashed, if Depositions Disclose an Offence.

If it appears from the evidence that the defendant was guilty
and properly convicted, the court will not quash the conviction,
however invalid it may be on its face: R. v. Menary, 19 O.R. 691.

But the court must be satisfied from the depositions that, if
trying the defendant in the first instance, it would have convicted
him upon the same evidence: R. v. Herrell, 1 Can. Cr. Cas. 510;
R. v. Law Bow, 7 Can. Cr. Cas. 468.

If the conviction is irregular, informal or defective on its face,
it is the duty of the court to examine the evidence; and if satisfied upon perusal of the depositions that an offence of the nature
described has been committed, over which the justice had jurisdiction, and that the punishment is not in excess of the justice's
jurisdiction, the conviction or warrant is not to be held invalid
for any defect or insufficiency: Code 1124. So a conviction which
omitted to allege scienter of defendant which was essential

to the offence, is valid if the.evidence shewed it: R. v. Crandall, 27 O.R. 63; or which omitted to shew time and place of offence, but they appeared in the evidence: R. v. Lewis, 6 Can. Cr. Cas. 499. But an inherent defect in the proceedings by which the defendant was deprived of a fair trial is not cured by this section: R. v. Sing Kee, 5 Can. Cr. Cas. 86; and a conviction which improperly included two persons cannot be amended by separating them: R. v. Sutton, 14 C.L.J. 17. So, also, if the offender has not been dealt with by the justice according to law or there has been a mistrial, these defects go to the jurisdiction and are fatal: R. v. Nurse, 8 Can. Cr. Cas. 173; and when neither the evidence nor the conviction shews territorial jurisdiction in the justice, the conviction is bad and cannot be amended: R. v. Gow, 11 Can. Cr. Cas. 81, 84. A warrant signed by the justice with the letters J.P., and containing a reference to himself or some other justice of the peace for (naming the county) sufficiently shewed jurisdiction: Ex p. Hilchie, 11 Can. Cr. Cas. 85.

Amendment of Conviction by the Court.

And by the same section, 1124, even if the punishment is in excess of what may lawfully be awarded, the court shall have the like powers of amendment, and to deal with the case as seems just, as are by Code 754 conferred in Ontario upon the General Sessions, and in the other provinces upon the courts named on an appeal under Code 749.

By these sections, the court is given express power, on an application to quash a defective conviction, to refer to the evidence, and to modify or amend the conviction, or to make such other conviction as the court thinks just, and to deal with the case as the justice ought to have done: Code 1124.

And this applies whether the punishment is in excess of the justice's jurisdiction or not: Code 1124; R. v. Crandall, 27 O.R. 63; Ex p. Conway, 31 N.B.R. 405.

The powers conferred by Code 1124 were acted upon by the court and approved on appeal by the Ontario Court of Appeal in the case of R. v. Murdock, 4 Can. Cr. Cas. 82; and it was held in the same case that this might also be done on application for *habeas corpus*. There is a further provision made by Code 1120, authorizing the court, on application for certiorari and habeas corpus, in cases of indictable offences, to make an order detaining

3—MAG. MAN.

the accused and directing the judge or justice, under whose warrant he is in custody, or any other judge or justice, to take further evidence, or such further proceedings as the court deems will best further the ends of justice. But this will only be done in exceptional cases: R. v. Randolph, 32 O.R. 212, 4 Can. Cr. Cas. 165.

Sections 754 and 1124 (Cr. Code) only apply to summary convictions, under Part XV, and in cases under Part XVI, relating to summary trials by magistrates, the court cannot amend: R. v. Randolph, *supra*; R. v. Gibson, 29 O.R. 660.

But where excessive imprisonment had been awarded in a conviction, in a case which the magistrate was competent to try, either as a magistrate, or as an *ex officio* justice, and there was nothing to preclude the court from assuming that he was trying it in the latter capacity, the court so assumed; and in view of the fact that the defendant had pleaded guilty, and that the ends of justice would be better served by amending the conviction, under Code 1124, the court amended it, so as to impose the proper punishment: R. v. Spooner, 4 Can. Cr. Cas. 209. In this case the court ordered the defendant to be brought up on habeas corpus to receive the new sentence.

In Ex p. Nugent (S.C.N.B.), 1 Can. Cr. Cas. 126, the difficulty in amending a conviction, in which the quantum of punishment is in the justice's discretion, is discussed; and it was argued that the court would by such amendment make the justice appear to have exercised a discretion which he had not exercised, and would inflict a punishment which had not been inflicted by the justice; see also R. v. Lake, 7 P.R., p. 230.

Code 1124 gives very wide powers, and confers upon the court, on examining the evidence, the like powers to deal with the case as are conferred by Code 754 upon the General Sessions on an appeal. The court may hear and determine the charge upon the merits as disclosed in the depositions and vary, reverse or modify the justice's decision and adjudicate *de novo*: R. v. Whiffin, 4 Can. Cr. Cas. 141.

In R. v. Murdock, 4 Can. Cr. Cas. 82, the Ontario Court of Appeal changed the statement of the offence to a different one, but "of the same nature as that described in the conviction," and reduced the punishment which the justice had put at the maximum and added provision for levying by distress before imprisonment. In R. v. Mickleham, 10 Can. Cr. Cas., p. 382, the court amended the conviction from "unlawfully allowing liquor to be sold" to "unlawfully selling liquor without a license," the evidence warranting such change. See also R. v. Myers, 7 Can. Cr. Cas. 303.

In the case of Ex p. Nugent, it was decided that when the penalty is a fixed sum, specified in the particular statute, and the justice has, in error, awarded an additional punishment, the court may amend on the assumption that it was manifest that the justice added the unauthorized punishment by inadvertence or through ignorance. And in that case the Supreme Court of New Brunswick ordered that the conviction, on being returned under the certiorari, should be amended by striking out the unauthorized clause. But where under a similar statute the justice imposed less than that fixed by the statute the court refused to amend: R. v. Hostyn, 9 Can. Cr. Cas. 138.

Where the conviction did not shew that the offence was committed within the justice's jurisdiction, it was held to be invalid: R. v. Chandler, 14 East 267.

But the court may amend in such case if the evidence shews that the case was in fact within the justice's jurisdiction: R. v. Elliot, 12 O.R. 524; R. v. Perrin, 16 O.R. 446.

But when neither the conviction nor the evidence shewed that the place mentioned was within the justice's jurisdiction the conviction was quashed: R. v. Young, 5 O.R., 184a.

When the conviction did not shew territorial jurisdiction the evidence was looked at; and it appearing from the caption that the charge, as laid, was read to the defendant, the court referred to the charge stated in warrant to apprehend, which was returned with the certiorari; and the warrant shewing that the offence was one which arose within the justice's jurisdiction, the conviction was amended, the court being thereby satisfied, in accordance with Code 1124, that an offence of the nature described in the conviction, and over which the justice had jurisdiction, had been committed: R. v. McGregor (Ont.), 2 Can. Cr. Cas. 410, 26 O.R. 115.

A conviction which is invalid as not negativing an exception in the statute, will be amended if the evidence negatives the exception: R. v. Smith, 31 O.R. 224.

In R. v. Hays, 5 O.L.R. 1898, 6 Can. Cr. Cas. 357, the omission of the word "knowingly" which was essential to the offence was held not to be an "irregularity, informality or insufficiency,'' which was cured or could be amended under this section; but in that case the evidence did not supply the omission.

So the omission of the essential word "wilfully" cannot be supplied by amendment: R. v. Tupper, 11 Can. Cr. Cas. 199; Ex p. O'Shaunessy, 8 Can. Cr. Cas. 136. These omissions do not come within this section of the Criminal Code; but a new conviction and commitment even after proceedings to quash are taken, may be substituted even where such omissions had been made if there is evidence to sustain such conviction: Re Plunkett, 1 Can. Cr. Cas. 365; R. v. Barre, 11 Can. Cr. Cas. 3.

The provisions of Code 1124 and Code 1125, are that none of the defects therein enumerated shall invalidate a conviction or other proceeding.

There are many other defects within the saving provision of Code 1124, 1125. For instance, if the adjudication and conviction omit to fix the amount of costs payable; or a provision for distress before imprisonment: R. v. Flynn, 20 O.R. 638: R. v. Clarke, 20 O.R. 642; or omission to reswear an information after amendment when the particular statute required a sworn information: R. v. Lewis, 6 Can. Cr. Cas. 499, and such amendment will not invalidate a conviction if defendant did not object at the trial: same case.

A manifestly clerical error will be amended: Ex p. Kavanagh (S.C.N.B.), 2 Can. Cr. Cas. 267.

And, generally, a proceeding to quash a conviction or to discharge the defendant must be based upon some substantial defect in the justice or legality of the proceeding, and not a mere informality: R. v. Barker, 1 East 186.

The provisions of the Criminal Code above cited apply also to warrants of commitment, and all other warrants to enforce convictions: Re Plunkett, 3 B.C.R. 384.

When Affidavits of Extrinsic Facts are Receivable.

When the application for certiorari rests on the ground of defective jurisdiction, matters on which the defect depends may be apparent on the face of the proceedings, i.e., the conviction and evidence and other documents returned by the justice; but if not so appearing they may be brought before the court by affidavits.

Such grounds must, however, be extrinsic of the adjudication impeached, to warrant affidavits being received as to them: Paley on Convictions, 8th ed. 450.

Such objections on which affidavits may be received may be founded either on a defect in the constitution and authority of the justice or magistrate, or upon the absence of some preliminary proceeding which was essential to jurisdiction: Colonial Bank v. Willan, L.R. 5 P.C. 417.

Affidavits will be received to shew that the justice had no authority to enter upon the enquiry: R. v. Bolton, 1 Q.B. 66; Thompson v. Ingham, L.R. 14 Q.B. 710, 718.

The court is to consider the evidence before the justice, but is not bound to confine itself to that evidence, but may receive affidavit evidence to arrive at a determination of the question of jurisdiction:.R. v. Evans (Ex p. Rice Jones), 19 L.J.M.C. 151; R. v. Farmer (1892), 1 Q.B. 637.

When Certiorari Taken Away.

By Code 1129, if the defendant appeared before the justice, and the case was tried on its merits, and the defendant has not appealed in an appealable case, or if he appealed and the conviction was sustained, it is not afterwards to be vacated for defect of form, but the construction is to be such a fair and liberal one as is agreeable to justice.

Code 1121 provides that no conviction or order, affirmed on appeal, shall be quashed for want of form, or removed by certiorari; and no warrant of commitment shall be held void by reason of any defect, provided it is therein alleged that the defendant was convicted, and there is a good and valid conviction to sustain it. And by Code 1122 no certiorari is to be allowed to remove a conviction or order if the defendant appealed; nor is the order or conviction made on appeal to be so removed. This is also applicable to convictions under Ontario laws: 2 Edw. VII. ch. 12, secs. 14, 15, but not under the Liquor Act, 1902: R. v. Foster, 5 O. L.R. 624; and by Code 725, no information or conviction to be held defective for stating the offence to have been committed in different modes; or in respect of several articles, either disjunctively or conjunctively.

So a charge of stealing "in or from" a building is good: R. v. White, 4 Can. Cr. Cas. 430; or of unlawfully distilling spirits and making or fermenting beer: R. v. McDonald, 6 Can. Cr. Cas. 1.

Giving notice of appeal is "appealing" within sec. 749 of the Code: R. v. Howard, 6 C.L.T. 526; R. v. Lynch, 12 O.R. p. 378.

But the giving of notice, and filing a recognizance for an appeal, does not take away the right to certiorari on the ground of excessive jurisdiction: R. v. Ashcroft, 2 Can. Cr. Cas. 385.

See also, R. v. Wallace, 1 East, P.C. 127; R. v. Johnston, 30 U.C.R. 423; R. v. Levecque, 30 U.C.R. 509; R. v. Scott, 10 P.R. 517; R. v Starkey, 7 Man. R. 489.

The right to certiorari is also declared to be taken away by many statutes in particular cases. It will, however, be held not to be taken away by implication, nor otherwise than by express words, and not by a statute authorizing an appeal to the Sessions which was empowered to "hear and *finally* determine" the matter: R. v. Jukes, 8 T.R. 542.

Nor by a statute which provides that no other court than the one appealed to shall intermeddle, but that it shall be *finally* determined by the Sessions only: R. v. Morley, 2 Burr. 1041.

Unless the word "certiorari" is used and barred, such statutes will be construed as only referring to matters of fact tried by the justice: R. v. Plowright, 3 Mod. 95; 2 Hawkins, P.C. 6th ed., ch. 27, sec. 23; and see notes 1 Can. Cr. Cas. p. 155; and even though an act of parliament take away certiorari in express words, the Crown is an exception and is not construed to be within the general restriction, unless there be words in the statute which shew a clear intention in the legislature to take it away: R. v. Eaton, 2 T.R. 90. And the same rule applies to the prosecutor who represents the Crown: R. v. Cumberland, 6 T.R. 194; R. v. Davies, 5 T.R. 626; R. v. Allen, 15 East, 333, 337, 341.

In pursuance of Code 1122, the court will not order a conviction to be returned by certiorari for the purpose of review, on any ground, other than excess of jurisdiction, after an appeal under Code 749, *et seg.*, or after any appeal authorized by law: R. v. Lynch, 12 O.R. 372; citing R. v. Wallace, 4 O.R. 127.

But whenever the right to certiorari is expressly taken away, whether by the clauses of the Cr. Code (such as clause 1121), or by the particular statute relating to the offence, a party has, nevertheless, always the right to certiorari on the ground of want of jurisdiction of the justice to do what is complained of.

Certiorari is a prerogative right: R. v. Lynch, 12 O.R. p. 372; and it cannot be taken away by any legislation in any case in which the justice has acted without or in excess of jurisdiction; and the evidence may be looked at upon that question: Ex p. Bradlaugh, 3 Q.B.D. 511; R. v. Dowling, 17 O.R. 698; see also Tupper v. Murphy, 3 R. & G. (Nova Scotia) 173; R. v. McKenzie, 23 N.S.R. 620; R. v. Major, 29 N.S.R. 373; R. v. Bigelow, 31 N.S.R. 436, and cases therein cited.

And the statute purporting to take away the right to certiorari will be construed as only doing so in so far as relates to the High Court reviewing the proceedings as to their regularity or validity, otherwise than upon the question of jurisdiction; and the authority of the High Court in the latter respect, cannot be taken away by statute: Hespeller v. Shaw, 16 U.C.R. 104; Re Holland, 37 U.C.R. 214; R. v. Horning, 8 Can. Cr. Cas. 268.

"It is settled even in cases where no restraint is placed by the legislature upon review by certiorari that an adjudication by a tribunal having jurisdiction over the subject matter is, if no defects appear on the face of it, to be taken as conclusive of the facts therein stated; and the court will not on certiorari quash an adjudication upon the ground that the fact, however essential, has been erroneously found. But when the right (of certiorari) is taken away by statute, it is to be deemed as still existing in cases of want or excess of jurisdiction or fraud:" per King, J., The Queen v. "The Troop," 29 S.C.R. p. 673. Referring to Colonial Bank v. Willan, L.R. 5 P.C. 417 he adds: "There is a distinction between the merits of the case, and points collateral to the merits upon which the limit of jurisdiction depends. In the former, whenever by statute the adjudication is final, no mere error of the tribunal, whether as to law or fact involved, can make the adjudication open to review on certiorari."

As decided in Re Holland, 37 U.C.R. 214, the adjudication may, notwithstanding, be removed to the High Court, not for review as to its regularity or validity, or the sufficiency of the evidence, if there is any evidence at all to support it, but on the sole question of jurisdiction. But the conviction in such case will not be quashed except upon the ground of clear excess or want of jurisdiction, or upon the ground of fraud: Colonial Bank v. Willan, L.R. 5 P.C. 417.

An appeal is no obstacle to certiorari based upon an excess of jurisdiction: R. v. McAnn, 4 B.C.R. 587, 3 Can. Cr. Cas. 110; R. v. Starkey, 6 Man. R. 588, 7 Man. R. 489; R. v. McKenzie, 23 N.S.R. 20; Re Ruggles, 5 Can. Cr. Cas. 163.

But under a conviction for an offence under an Ontario statute, a certiorari can only be granted (after an appeal) upon the ground of want of jurisdiction: R. v. Horning, 8 Can. Cr. Cas. 268; R.S.O. ch. 90, sec. 7; and the fact that the justice convicted the defendant without taking down the evidence *in writing*, as required by Code 682 (3), is a defect in the proceeding which goes to jurisdiction, and in such circumstances the conviction was quashed in the case of Denault v. Robida, 8 Can. Cr. Cas. 501, the taking of a writ of certiorari being held to waive the defendant's right to appeal.

Nothing, not even the defendant's consent, will confer jurisdiction, and he may object to the jurisdiction of the tribunal he has himself selected: R. v. Smith, 3 Can. Cr. Cas. 467. As to what matters the accused person may admit or consent to: see R. v. Rogers, 6 Can. Cr. Cas. 419, and notes at p. 421.

The question of the powers of the court on application for certiorari, in cases where it has been taken away, is reviewed in R. v. Chantrell, L.R. 10 Q.B. p. 589.

When a question as to the validity of a conviction has been decided by the court, on a case stated, the matter is *res judicata*, and certiorari will not be granted on the same ground: R. v. Monaghan (N.W.T.), 2 Can. Cr. Cas. 488.

A conviction for breach of a by-law was quashed when proof of the by-law required by the Ontario Evidence Act, as amended, had not been properly given, the omission leaving no evidence on which a conviction could legally be founded, and the justice had no jurisdiction to convict: R. v. Dowslay, 19 O.R. 622. So a justice or magistrate, holding a preliminary enquiry is without authority, even after hearing all the evidence and even if the defendant does not object, to convict for a lesser offence included in the offence charged; Ex p. Duffy, 8 Can. Cr. Cas. 277; R. v. Dungay, 5 Can. Cr. Cas. 38.

Returning Amended Conviction.

If a certiorari is obtained upon a defective memorandum of adjudication, and before any formal conviction is made out, the justice is not precluded from making out and returning a formal conviction remedying the defect in the adjudication: R. v. Smith, 46 U.C.R. 442; R. v. Mcnary, 19 O.R. 691; Jones v. Williams, 36 L.T. 559; Paley, 8th ed. 320.

So also in his return to certiorari, the justice may make out and return an amended conviction, in substitution for the first one made out, and on which the certiorari was obtained, if the latter was defective: R. v. Hartley, 20 O.R. 481; followed by R. v. Mc-Ann, 4 B.C.R. 587; R. v. Whitesides, 8 O.L.R. 622.

But if this is done the return must state that the justice intended to amend the first conviction by the second one which is in substitution of the other; if not, the return will be bad: R. v. Venôt, 6 Can. Cr. Cas. 212.

An amended conviction may be made out and returned to the court under certiorari, even after a previous formal conviction has been returned to the clerk of the peace; provided such new conviction is according to the truth, and is supported by the facts of the case, as proved before the justice: R. v. Barker, 1 East, 186; Selwood v. Mount, 9 C. & P. 75; Wilson v. Graybiel, 5 U.C.R. 227; but see R. v. McKenzie, 23 N. S.R. 20; R. v. Learmont, ib. 24. And he may do so even after a writ of certiorari has been served: R. v. McKenzie, 6 O.R., 165; and even after the first formal conviction has been returned to the court under it: and, in fact, at any time before the conviction has been actually quashed, or the defendant released: R. v. Lawrence, 43 U.C.R. p. 168; R. v. Lake, 7 P.R. p. 235; R. v. Hartley, 20 O.R. 481; R. v. Bennett, 3 O.R. 45; Chaney v. Payne, 1 Q.B. 712; Charter v. Graeme, 13 Q.B. 216; R. v. House, 2 Man. R. 58; R. v. Smith, 46 U.C.R. 442; R. v. Richardson, 20 O.R. 514; Jones v. Williams, 36 L.T. 559; R. v. McDonald, 26 N.S.R. 402; R. v. Bigelow, 31 N.S.R. 436. So with regard to an invalid warrant of commitment; if a good warrant be returned, the court will not enquire into the validity of a previous document under which the defendant was committed; Paley, 8th ed. 319, 322; Re Plunket, 1 Can. Cr. Cas. 365, 3 B.C.R. 484. "The right to substitute a good for a bad conviction or commitment after a motion for habeas corpus has long been recognized." R. v. Barre, 11 Can. Cr. Cas. at p. 3.

Even after argument of an appeal from an order refusing a writ of habeas corpus a further return may be made by the justice with a new and corrected commitment, curing defects in the one against which the proceedings were directed: R. v. LeConte, 11 Can. Cr. Cas. p. 45.

If there is a good conviction returned with a bad commitment, the court may adjourn the case to enable an amended commitment to be filed in conformity with the conviction: R. v. Lavin, 12 P.R. 642.

But the justice cannot make out and return a conviction, or amended conviction, substantially differing from his memorandum of adjudication, giving effect to a change of intention, as regards the adjudication of guilt or punishment: R. v. McAnn, 3 Can. Cr. Cas. 110. A justice cannot convict a man of one offence, and on certiorari, inform the court that he convicted him of another: Re Houghton, 1 B.C.R. p. 89. Nor can he award punishment of one sort, and return a conviction awarding another. But a conviction awarding one month's imprisonment, upon a minute of adjudication by which thirty days' imprisonment is awarded, is not such a variance as the court will take notice of: Ex p. Rogers, 7 Can. Cr. Cas. 314; and where hard labour was illegally awarded by the minute and conviction, the justice was allowed to return an amended conviction leaving out hard labour notwithstanding the amended conviction differed from the minute of adjudication: R. v. Whiffen, 4 Can. Cr. Cas. 141.

But it is otherwise as regards the consequences which follow the default of payment of the fine; and any error or excess in that respect may be remedied by making out a new conviction without amending the minute of adjudication: R. v. Mcnary, 19 O.R. p. 696; R. v. Hartley, 20 O.R. 481; R. v. McAnn, *supra;* R. v. Doherty, 32 N.S.R. 235, 3 Can. Cr. Cas. 508. But see R. v. Perley, 25 N.B.R. 43.

When the justice has exercised his judgment in the case, and has nominated the fine and fixed the term of imprisonment, the formal conviction must be in accordance with the fact; and the fact is shewn by the minute of adjudication; and in order to change the latter there would have to be a new judgment, which could only be done in presence of the defendant, as suggested by Wilson, C.J., in R. v. Brady, 12 O.R. p. 363. But where the excess was in awarding measures in default of payment, (as. where defendant was illegally ordered to be committed to the stocks, Barton v. Breckwell, 13 Q.B. 393; or where distress was illegally ordered, R. v. Mcnary, 19 O.R. 691; and R. v. Hartley, 20 O.R. 481, followed on this point in R. v. Southwick, 21 O.R. p. 674; see also R. v. Walsh, 2 O.R. 206), the conviction may be amended by making out a new one, omitting the excess, even after the formal conviction containing the defect has been returned and attacked upon certiorari: R. v. McAnn, 3 Can. Cr. Cas. 110, 4 B.C.R. 587.

The leading case of R. v. Hartley, 20 O.R. 481, was followed on the above point by R. v. Richardson, 20 O.R. 514, and overruled the decisions to the contrary on this point in R. v. Brady, 12 O.R. 358, and R. v. Higgins, 18 O.R. 148.

An alteration which would be more onerous to the defendant cannot be made in his absence, and can only be made by amending the adjudication in his presence: R. v. Brandon, 3 L.T. 559; and see Jones v. Williams, 36 L.T. 559.

A conviction which imposes less than the minimum punishment provided for the offence is not invalid: Code 1125 (b), but see R. v. Verdon, 8 Can. Cr. Cas. 352; nor one which omits to negative circumstances, the existence of which would make the act lawful whether stated in the section under which the offence is laid or under another section: Code 1125 (c).

If the original adjudication imposing measures for enforcing the penalty has been acted upon (as where hard labour was added improperly to imprisonment in default of payment and the defendant has been imprisoned at hard labour under it) the defect cannot be corrected by an amended conviction omitting the improper provision; R. v. McAnn, 4 B.C.R. 587; 3 Can. Cr. Cas. p. 121; Barton v. Bricknell, 13 Q.B. 393.

A commitment imposing unauthorized conditions of discharge (such as a provision that the defendant be imprisoned until the costs of conveying him to gaol are paid, in cases where that is not provided for) and which has been acted on, is bad in whole and must be quashed: Ex p. Lon Kai Long, 1 Can. Cr. Cas. 120.

That part of an adjudication improperly awarding imprisonment, in default of a payment of a fine, may be quashed, without quashing the rest of the conviction: R. v. Dunning, 14 O.R. 52. A conviction may be severable; as where imprisonment and a fine are both properly awarded, and the imprisonment is being undergone; the defendant is not, while undergoing such imprisonment, entitled to be discharged, nor to have the conviction quashed, because the imprisonment also ordered in case of default of payment of the fine is illegally imposed: R. v. Carlisle, 7 Can. Cr. Cas. 470.

There is a distinction between making out a conviction containing more than the adjudication (and thus creating a variance between them), and one which omits something which was improperly included in the adjudication. The above-mentioned case of R. v. Hartley, decides that the conviction is good in the latter state of facts, while in the former it is not.

If the adjudication is erroneous, or the punishment awarded is not in accordance with law, the justice is not *functus officio,* even after he has made out and returned a formal conviction; but he may still bring the parties before him and amend the minute of adjudication in their hearing, and return a new conviction, even after certiorari has been issued: R. v. Hartley, *supra;* R. v. McAnn, 3 Can. Cr. Cas. p. 121, 4 B.C.R. 587; R. v. Dunning, 14 O.R. p. 52; R. v. Brady, 12 O.R. 363, per Wilson, C.J.

An unsealed conviction is bad and cannot be amended by the court; but an amended conviction with seals may be made out and filed before the first one is quashed: Bond v. Conmee, 16 A.R. 398; R. v. Phipps, 11 W.R. 730. It was held that a warrant of commitment for non-payment of a fine is invalid if it does not shew on its face a return to a distress warrant, or that the justice ordered distress to be omitted under Code 744 upon an adjudication on that point, and such defect cannot be in any way cured: R. v. Skinner, 9 Can. Cr. Cas. 558; but *quaere* whether the powers of amendment are not sufficient to cover this defect: see *ante,* p. 33.

Where costs not properly chargeable were included in a lump sum allowed for costs in the conviction the court refused to amend, as it was unable to distinguish the costs improperly included or to say how much of the same allowed was in respect of the improper costs: R. v. Townsend, 11 Can. Cr. Cas. 153.

A conviction against a person by wrong name is not defective if objection was not taken before the justice, when he could have amended the proceedings: Ex p. Corrigan, 2 Can. Cr. Cas. 591.

If the conviction is under a particular statute, which does not provide how the penalty is to be enforced, the adjudication and conviction are not defective for not providing for it; and Code 739 supplies the measures to be taken: R. v. McKenzie, 6 O.R. p. 168.

If other costs than those in the tariff are ordered, as where a conviction contained an order to pay costs, including $1 which had been paid for the use of the hall where the trial was held, it is in excess of the justice's jurisdiction and the conviction is bad. The court held that it had no power to amend by omitting that item, on the ground that it would create a variance between the adjudication and the conviction, coming within R. v. Walsh,

2 O.R. 206; and that the court had no power to interfere with an adjudication; R. v. Elliott, 12 O.R. 524; but in R. v. Murdock, 4 Can. Cr. Cas. 82, the Ontario Court of Appeal held that there was power to amend such a defect: see *ante*, p, 33.

A *judgment* of the General Sessions cannot be removed by certiorari, it being a Court of Record, and the judgment being by a court of competent jurisdiction the matter is *res adjudicata*. But an order of General Sessions issued in excess of authority may, as a judicial act of an inferior tribunal, be so removed; for instance, an order directing the sheriff, under a judgment of the General Sessions, to abate a nuisance, was removed by certiorari and quashed, the Sessions having no authority to substitute such order for the writ *de nocumento amovendo* which ought to have been issued: R. v. Grover, 23 O.R. 92.

As to removal by certiorari of proceedings on indictable offences, where there is reason to apprehend that the accused may not be fairly tried: see R. v. Hart, 45 U.C.R. 1; R. v. Adams, 8 P.R. 462.

On a conviction being quashed the justice may, in the province of Quebec, be compelled by coercive imprisonment to refund any money received by him under the conviction: R. v. Plamondon, 6 Can. Cr. Cas. 223.

Appeals.

An appeal lies to the High Court from an order for certiorari granted by a judge, or for an order refusing certiorari, but not from a judge in Chambers to another judge in court: R. v. Graham, 1 Can. Cr. Cas. 405.

There is no appeal to the Court of Appeal from the High Court on an application for certiorari; nor from an order made on an application to quash a conviction under a Dominion law; nor is there any such appeal in cases under Ontario statutes, except upon a certificate of the Attorney-General for Ontario, that the decision involves a question of the construction of the B.N.A. Act: See R.S.O. ch. 91, sec. 3; and in a case where such certificate had been obtained, but it plainly appeared to the Court of Appeal that the decision did not in fact involve any such question, and that the certificate had been granted inadvertently, the court quashed the appeal: R. v. Reid, 26 A.R. 181.

An appeal was allowed by R.S.O. ch. 245, sec. 121, to the Court of Appeal, under the Ontario Liquor License Act: R. v. Hodge, 7 A.R. 246; but unless there is a special provision in the statute relating to the particular offence, for an appeal from the High Court to the Court of Appeal, no such appeal lies; either in cases under Dominion laws: R. v. Eli, 13 A.R. 526; R. v. McAuley, 14 O.R. 643; or under Ontario statutes, the Judicature Act and the rules under it, not applying in either case: R. v. Cushing, 26 A.R. 248; and there being no general provision for appeals to the Court of Appeal in penal matters. There is no appeal in any case except it is specially provided by statute: R. v. London (Jus.), 25 Q.B.D. p. 360; Ellis v. The Queen, 22 S. C.R. p. 11.

CHAPTER II.

HABEAS CORPUS.

The writ of habeas corpus is defined as "a writ directed to the person detaining another, commanding him to produce the body of the prisoner before the court or judge at a certain time or place, with the day and cause of his caption and detention, to do, submit to and receive whatsoever the court or judge awarding the writ shall consider in that behalf:" Bour. L. Dic.; Crowley's Case, 2 Swans. 68; R. v. Cowle, 2 Burr. 855.

Origin of Habeas Corpus.

The writ is a high prerogative one, and the right to it is not created by statute, but is a common law right of very ancient origin: Re Bessett, 6 Q.B. 481; but it has been confirmed and regulated by various statutes: See Crabb's Hist. Eng. Law, 525.

The Imperial Act,

1679, 31 Car. II., ch. 2, sec. 2 (which is the original Habeas Corpus Act, and the text of which may be seen in Vol. III. R.S.O., 1897), provides for the issuing of the writ in all cases where a person is committed or detained for any cause (except for felony or treason plainly expressed in the warrant) upon the application of the person detained or any one in his behalf. This statute applies only to cases of detention or imprisonment for "criminal or supposed criminal offences."

It is in force in Canada, except as varied by Canadian legislation: R. v. Cameron, 1 Can. Cr. Cas. 169.

Canadian Legislation Regarding Habeas Corpus.

The statute of the late Province of Canada (comprising the present Provinces of Ontario and Quebec), 29 & 30 Vict. ch. 45, extended the remedy by habeas corpus to include other than criminal matters; and varied the practice under the Imperial statute.

It remains still in force in Ontario and Quebec, having been passed before Confederation, regarding matters of criminal law over which the Dominion Parliament now has jurisdiction: R. v.

Marquis, 8 Can. Cr. Cas. 346; without regard to the fact that it has been included in the subsequent revisions of the provincial statutes, and without regard to any changes made by the latter statutes; and except only as amended or varied or impliedly repealed by the Criminal Code of Canada or some Dominion legislation: 1 Can. Cr. Cas. 213; R. v. Bougie, 3 Can. Cr. Cas. 487.

The effect of the statute 29 & 30 Vict. is not only to extend the writ to other than criminal matters, and also to vary the practice on applications for the writ from that under the Imperial statute; but by section 7 it also extends to all writs awarded under the Imperial statute all the benefits of the provisions of the Canadian statute.

The statute 29 & 30 Vict. was embodied from time to time in Ontario, in the revised statutes of that province, and is now contained in R.S.O. 1897, ch. 83; and in Quebec in the R.S.L.C. 1861, ch. 95.

The revised statutes mentioned into which the 29 & 30 Vict. has been transferred, with the Imperial statute of Charles, and the provisions of the Criminal Code, and any rule passed thereunder, contain the provisions governing the right to, and the practice upon, applications for habeas corpus in Ontario and Quebec respectively; except that anything contained in the above mentioned revised statutes of those provinces, and which was not comprised in the original anti-confederation statute from which they were taken, will have no operation as regards criminal matters, which are exclusively within the jurisdiction of the Dominion Parliament: R. v. Cameron, 1 Can. Cr. Cas. p. 170; but the provincial statutes mentioned including as well the provisions taken from the 29 & 30 Vict. as others which were added by the Provincial Legislatures afterwards, will apply to cases of offences against provincial laws: See 2 Can. Cr. Cas., at p. 306.

The rules under the Ontario Judicature Act, and that Act itself, will also apply to the latter class of cases.

Section 576 of the Criminal Code empowers Superior Courts of Criminal Jurisdiction to pass rules relating to the procedure by writ of habeas corpus. In some of the provinces rules have been passed and duly promulgated under that section; and such rules, together with the Imperial statute mentioned, will control the right to and the practice in habeas corpus, in cases for offences under Dominion statutes, in those provinces.

No such rules have been passed in Ontario; the rules under the Ontario Judicature Act having neither been passed nor promulgated under Code 576, and therefore only apply to cases of offences under Ontario laws.

In the several provinces where there has been provincial legislation on the subject of habeas corpus since they entered into the Canadian Confederation: See R.S.N.S. 117; R.S.N.B. 41; R. v. Cameron, 1 Can. Cr. Cas. 169; such legislation is only operative as to habeas corpus proceedings for offences under provincial laws.

Restraint of Liberty.

Habeas corpus may be applied for whenever the person has been in any manner restrained of his liberty to any degree whatever. It is not necessary that he should be actually incarcerated, but he may apply whenever he is deprived of the privilege of going when and where he pleases; so he may apply immediately upon being arrested, and while in the custody of a constable: 2 Just. 589; Re Cloutier, 2 Can. Cr. Cas. 43.

But a merely moral restraint is not sufficient: R. v. Davis, 1 Burr. 638(n); Hurd. 201.

As to what constitutes an arrest, see *post* "Execution of Warrant."

Every restraint upon a man's liberty is, in the eye of the law, an imprisonment, whatever may be the place, or the manner in which the restraint is effected: 1 Kent. 631; 2 Just. 482, 589; Hurd. 201.

A person discharged on bail will not be considered as restrained of his liberty, so as to be entitled to a writ of habeas corpus directed to his bail: Hurd. 201; but there is actual restraint if he be taken by the bail and delivered into custody, though not if he voluntarily surrenders himself: 15 Am. & Eng. Enc. 159. But under the R.S.L.C. ch. 95, which contains special provisions authorizing it, the accused who was on bail was discharged and the recognizance vacated, after he had twice appeared at the court to which he was bailed, and no indictment had been preferred: R. v. Cameron, 1 Can. Cr. Cas. 169. "Bail is custody, and he is constructively in gaol; and has the same rights . . . as he would have to be released from an imprisonment:" *Ibid.*

Exceptions to the Operation of the Statute.

The statute 31 Car. II. ch. 2, sec. 2, excepts from the benefit of habeas corpus persons committed for felony or treason, plainly expressed in the warrant; as well as persons convicted or in execution by legal process. And the statute of Ontario excepts persons imprisoned for debt or by process issued in any action or by the judgment, conviction or order of a Court of Record, Oyer and Terminer or General Gaol Delivery or General Sessions. Such persons are, therefore, not entitled to the writ: R.S.O. ch. 83, sec. 1.

A County Judge's Criminal Court is a Court of Record, and its process within the above exception: R. v. St. Denis, 8 P.R. 16; R. v. Burke (N.S.), 1 Can. Cr. Cas. 539; R. v. Murray (Ont.), 1 Can. Cr. Cas. 452; Re Sproule, 12 S.C.R. 140; R. v. Goodman, 2 O.R. 468; Re Ferguson, 24 N.S.R. 106; R. v. Kavanagh, 5 Can. Cr. Cas. 507; and so also is a decision of the General Sessions on an appeal from a summary conviction: R. v. Beamish, 5 Can. Cr. Cas. 388.

But if any court whatever should entertain a criminal prosecution beyond its jurisdiction, the proceeding would be void; and the accused will be released on habeas corpus, as not being in custody under any valid legal proceeding: Re Sproule, 12 S.C.R. p. 205; and see notes 1 Can. Cr. Cas. 546.

Where the party is in custody *in execution*, after conviction on indictment by a court having general jurisdiction of the case, for a criminal offence, the exception in the statute applies, and habeas corpus cannot be obtained: Ex. p. Lees, El. Bl. & El. 828: Re Newton, 16 C.B. 97; Ex. p. Dunn, 5 D. & L. 345; R. v. Crabbe, 11 U.C.R. 447; Re Sproule, 12 S.C.R. 140; R. v. Burke, 1 Can. Cr. Cas. p. 544; Fleming v. Clarke, 12 Allen (N.B.) 191; Brenan's Case, 10 Q.B. 502.

An order to commit, in a civil suit in the County Court, is a "process of a Court of Record" within the exception in section 1 of the statute: Re Anderson v. Vanstone, 16 P.R. 243.

The remedy of habeas corpus, and certiorari in aid of the same (as to the latter see *post* 70), applies not only to the case of a conviction and warrant of commitment by a justice of the peace, but also by a police magistrate under sections 773, 774 of the Criminal Code. Although section 791 provides that a conviction in the latter case shall have the *same effect* as a conviction upon an indictment by a Court of Record, yet it is not the *same thing;* and the magistrates' court is *not* a Court of Record, against the judgment of which habeas corpus does not lie: R. v. Gibson, 29 O.R. 660; R. v. St. Clair, 27 A.R. 308, and cases there cited: see also O'Reilly v. Allén, 11 U.C.R. 526; see, however, the remarks and cases cited *ante,* p. 28, and R. v. Marquis, 8 Can. Cr. Cas. (Que), 346; R. v. Racine, 3 Can. Cr. Cas. 448; and notes in 8 Can. Cr. Cas. p. 350.

Application for Writ, to What Court.

The Superior Courts of Criminal Jurisdiction, having authority in habeas corpus are: In Ontario, the High Court of Justice; in Quebec, the Court of King's Bench and the Supreme Court; in Nova Scotia, New Brunswick and British Columbia, the Supreme Court; in Prince Edward Island, the Supreme Court of Judicature; in Manitoba, the Court of King's Bench, Crown side; in Saskatchewan and Alberta, the Supreme Courts of those provinces respectively, and in the Yukon, the Territorial Court.

As to the jurisdiction of the Supreme Court of Canada in habeas corpus see *post.*

By Whom Application to be Made.

The application may be made by the prisoner himself or by an agent or friend on his behalf, *e.g.,* by the prisoner's husband · Cobbett v. Hudson, 15 Q.B. 988; Re Daley, 2 F. & F. 258; or the prisoner's father: Re Thompson, 30 L.J.M.C. 19; Hurd. 203; Anne Gregory's Case, 4 Burr. 1991; R. v. Clarke, 1 Burr. 606.

A young child may petition for certiorari, though too young to bring action in respect of civil rights: Re A. B., 9 Can. Cr. Cas. 390.

It is not necessary that any legal relationship should exist between the applicant and the prisoner: The Hottentot Venus Case, 3 East. 195; but it cannot be made by a mere stranger, who shews no authority whatever on behalf of the person detained, and no right to represent him: Ex. p. Child, 15 C.B. 238. But express authority from the prisoner is not necessary; it is sufficient if it appears that the prisoner is suffering involuntary and wrongful restraint: Hurd. 204; see Re Carmichael, 1 C.L.J. 243. It has been held that the writ may be applied for by an officer holding a warrant for the prisoner's arrest in another proceeding: Re Mineau, 45 Fed. Rep. 188.

The writ will be granted to aliens as well as to British subjects: Hottentot Venus Case, 3 East. 195; R. v. Bessett, 6 Q.B. 481; but not to an alien prisoner of war: R. v. Schiever, 2 Burr. 765.

The fact that, at the time of the application, the person against whom the writ is asked, has not in his custody or power the person said to be detained, is no ground for refusing the writ, if it appears that the person has illegally parted with such custody: R. v. Barnardo, 24 Q.B.D. 283; Barnardo v. Ford (1892), A.C. 326; Barnardo v. McHugh, 61 L.J.Q.B. 721, disapproving, R. v. Barnardo, 23 Q.B.D. 305.

"When the detention has ceased the writ is inapplicable, but when a counterfeited release has taken place and a pretended ignorance of the place of custody, or of the identity of the present custodian, is insisted on, the court ought to examine into the facts;" and if a doubt is entertained by the court as to the proper disposition of the person detained, it is entitled to use the pressure of the writ to test the truth of the allegations and to require a return to be made to it: Barnardo v. Ford (1892), A.C. 326.

A person confined or restrained of his liberty is entitled to one writ only, to be granted by any judge of the High Court, returnable before himself or another judge in Chambers, or before the court: R.S.O. ch. 83, sec. 1; Taylor v. Scott, 30 O.R. 475.

The application may be made at any time: R.S.O. ch. 83, sec. 1; Re Paton, 4 Gr. 147; Re Hawkins, 3 P.R. 239; and may be made either to a judge in Chambers or to the full court: R. v. Barre, 11 Can. Cr. Cas. p. 3. It is usually made to a judge in Chambers.

An order of suspension of part of the punishment (*e.g.*, whipping) may precede the order for the writ: R. v. Goldsberry, 11 Can. Cr. Cas. 159.

Security, etc., not Required.

On habeas corpus the court can only deal with the question of the custody and restraint of the person, and has no power to quash the conviction or warrant. The rules passed under the statute of Geo. II., or under Code 892 (now 576), requiring security, and notice to magistrate or justice to be given, do not, therefore, apply to these proceedings, and no such security or notice is necessary; even when certiorari in aid is asked: R. v. Nunn, 10 P.R. 395; see *post* p. 70.

Affidavit in Support of Application.

An affidavit by the person imprisoned, disclosing grounds upon which the court can exercise its discretion, must be made; unless it is shewn that he is so coerced as to be unable to make an affidavit: R. v. Hobhouse, 3 B. & Ald. 420; Re Parker, 5 'M. & W. 32; Re Ross, 3 P.R. 301; see R.S.O. ch. 83, sec. 1; 31 Car. II. ch. 2, sec. 2. This is imperative under Ontario decisions: R. v. Black, 8 Can. Cr. Cas. 465; but in R. v. McIvan, 7 Can. Cr. Cas. 184, it was held by Townshend, J. (S.C.N.S.). that the affidavit may be made "on behalf of" the prisoner by his solicitor, that being the wording of the provincial statute and the offence being one against a provincial statute.

A copy of the warrant under which the person is detained must be produced, or the affidavit must shew that a copy has been denied: 31 Car. II. ch. 2, sec. 3; in which case it must also be shewn that there was a written demand for a copy, signed by the person in custody or someone on his behalf: Re Carmichael, 1 C.L.J. 243; Ex p. Pollock, Ramsay's Case (Que.), 187 This demand must be served on the gaoler himself, if he is there, and not on the turnkey: Huntley v. Luscombe, 2 B. & P. 530.

The affidavit must be entitled in the court applied to: Re Ross, 3 P.R. 301; and must set forth the facts on which the defendant considers himself entitled to be discharged, unless the commitment shews invalidity on its face: Hands Prac. 73. See as to other points of practice: 6 Can. Cr. Cas. p. 212.

When a warrant of arrest was issued in Quebec and endorsed in Ontario, where the defendant was arrested, and the proceedings were not *ultra vires,* it was held that the High Court had no jurisdiction, on application for habeas corpus, to try on affidavits under section 4 of R.S.O. ch. 83, the question as to where the alleged offence was committed (Ex. p. Smith, 3 H. & N. 227), nor to make an order under section 5, these sections not applying when no preliminary enquiry has taken place: and that an enquiry could not be made, in the manner provided for in Code 752 (now 1120), as to the question of the legality of the arrest, as that section only applies when the habeas corpus is issued in the same province where the warrant of arrest was issued, the court in Ontario having no authority over a magistrate in Quebec: R. v. Defries, 25 O.R. 645. A court or judge in Ontario has no authority over a justice in Quebec to compel him to take any proceedings or hear evidence in a prosecution under Can. Cr. Code: R. v. Tamblyn, 25 O.R. 645.

The affidavit must not be sworn before the prosecutor or his solicitors: R. v. Marsh, 25 N.B.R. 370.

Form of Affidavit.

The form of affidavit for certiorari at page 9 *ante*, may be adapted adding the following clause:

"That the paper writing now shewn to me marked exhibit A. to this my affidavit is a true copy of the warrant of commitment (*or* to apprehend) under which I am now confined in close custody of the keeper in the county gaol of the County of   under the said warrant" (*or as the case may be*) and I am not in such custody as a prisoner in said gaol under any other warrant, or other authority, or for any other cause or matter.

If the warrant is defective on its face and does not disclose any ground for the detention of the prisoner, an affidavit in the following form will be sufficient:—

In the High Court of Justice.
The King against A. B.
I, A. B. of the   of   in the County of (*occupation*) make oath and say:—
1. I am the above named defendant.
2. That the paper writing shewn to me marked exhibit "A." to this my affidavit is a true copy of the warrant of commitment produced to me by the gaoler of the common gaol of the County of   (*or by the warden of the Central Prison in the city of Toronto, or as the case may be*) as that under which I am now held in close custody in said goal (*or* Central Prison) namely, on the   day of   A.D. 19 .
3. That I am not guilty of the offence therein mentioned.
Sworn, etc.

The affidavit must be entitled as in the case of an affidavit for certiorari: See *ante*, p. 8.

If the affidavits satisfy the court that the commitment was clearly without jurisdiction, the prisoner may be at once discharged on the application for the writ: Re Authers, 22 Q.B.D. 345; see 15 L.J.Q.B. 235.

Notice of Application.

In criminal cases, notice of application for habeas corpus must be given to the Attorney-General: R. v. Taylor, 7 D. & R. 622; Hurd. 227. The application is by notice of motion to a judge in Chambers, and not by rule *nisi*, and such rule if made

NOT

will be discharged: R. v. Smith, 24 U.C.R. 480. In Quebec, when there is a judge of the Court of King's Bench then within the limits of the judicial district to which he belongs, and in which the applicant is imprisoned, a judge of that court sitting in another district has no jurisdiction to entertain an application; the prisoner must apply to a judge who is in the district in which he is confined: Ex p. Tremblay, 6 Can. Cr. Cas. 147. And in the absence from the Montreal district of the judges of the Court of King's Bench during the sittings at Quebec, applications in respect to prisoners in the Montreal district cannot be heard at Quebec and must be made to the Superior Court: Re Gaynor & Green, 9 Can. Cr. Cas. 255. See further, Ex p. Goldsberry, 10 Can. Cr. Cas. 392, as to the jurisdiction of the courts in the Province of Quebec.

The following form of notice may be used:—

NOTICE OF MOTION FOR WRIT OF HABEAS CORPUS.

In the High Court of Justice.
The King on the information of E.F. against A.B.
Take notice that a motion will be made on behalf of the above-named A.B. before the presiding judge in Chambers at Osgoode Hall Toronto, on the day of A.D. 19 , at ten o'clock in the forenoon. or so soon thereafter as the motion can be heard, whereon you are to shew cause why a writ of habeas corpus should not issue to the keeper of the common gaol of the County of (or as the case may be) directing him to have before a judge of the High Court of Justice for Ontario the body of the said A.B.. a prisoner detained in his custody, that the court may cause to be done thereupon what of right and according to law the court shall see fit to be done, and for a writ of certiorari in aid thereof, for the following among other reasons:
1—(State the reasons and grounds of application) And take notice that in support of such application will be read the affidavits of , filed, and the exhibits therein referred to.
Dated this day of · A.D. 19
To the Attorney-General for the
Province of Ontario and to E.F..
the prosecutor, and to C.D., the   Solicitors for the
convicting magistrate (or Justice).   said A.B.

Requisites of Writ.

The writ must be marked in the margin *"Per statutum tricesimo primo Carli Secundi Regis,"* and must be signed (usually in the margin) by the judge himself who grants it; and if not so signed no one is bound to obey it (see 1 and 2 Phil. & M. ch. 13, sec. 7) : 31 Car. II., ch. 2, sec. 3; R. v. Roddam, Cowp. 672; R. v. St. Clair, 27 A.R. 308; see also R. v. Arscott, 9 O.R. 541; Arscott v. Lilly, 11 O.R. 153; Re Hallock, *per* Meredith, C.J., 15

C.L.T. 9; and it must be sealed with the seal of the court: R.S.O. ch. 83, sec. 2.

The writ is good without being marked *"per statutum,"* etc. if it can be supported at common law, which was held not to be abrogated by the statute: Wilson's Case, 7 A. & E. N.S. 984; but, *quære*, whether the 29 & 30 Vict. now embodied in the Ontario statute above mentioned has not so limited the issuance of the writ that it cannot now be issued at common law: Re Sproule, 12 S.C.R. 140. The omission of the above words or of the judge's signature, is not a ground of objection to the writ, after a return has been made to it: United States v. Browne; 11 Can. Cr. Cas. 171.

The person to be produced may be designated by his name, if known, or if it is unknown or uncertain, by any description, so as to make known who is intended.

Order for Habeas Corpus.

In the High Court of Justice.

Before the Honourable ⎱ Tuesday, the
Mr. Justice ⎰ day of
In Chambers A.D. 19 .

The King against A.B.

Upon the application of the above named A.B., upon reading the affidavit of the said A.B. filed, and a copy of the warrant of commitment marked "A." thereto and upon hearing counsel for the defendant.

1. It is ordered that a writ of habeas corpus do issue out of the High Court of Justice directed to the keeper of the common gaol for the County of   (*or the warden of the Central Prison for the Province of Ontario, in the City of Toronto, or as the case may be, mentioning the head official of the place where the defendant is detained or the constable in whose custody he is*), directing him to have before a Judge of the High Court of Justice for Ontario presiding in Chambers at Osgoode Hall, Toronto, forthwith on the receipt of the said writ the body of A.B. a prisoner detained in the custody of the said keeper of the said common gaol (*or warden or as the case may be*), that there may be caused to be done thereupon what of right and according to law it shall be seen fit to be done.

Clerk in Chambers.

To Whom Writ Directed.

The writ must be directed to the person in whose custody or power the party confined or restrained is: R.S.O. ch. 83, sec. 1. In criminal matters to the constable having the prisoner in charge; or the gaoler, and not to the sheriff, when the prisoner is in gaol: Bac. Abr. tit. Hab. Cor. sec. 6; it should not be directed in the disjunctive, *e.g.*, to the sheriff *or* the gaoler: *ib.*: R. v. Fowler, 1 Salk. 293, 350; Ld. Raym. 586.

Habeas Corpus cannot be issued against a person who is at the time out of the jurisdiction: R. v. Pinckney, (1904), 2 K.B. 84; but it is no objection that the person in custody is not in the jurisdiction (1892), A.C. 326.

Issue of Writ.

The writ is issued from the office of the registrar of the High Court on præcipe, which may be endorsed on the order as follows:—

Required a writ of habeas corpus pursuant to the within order. Dated, etc.

Solicitor for the within named A.B.

Service of Writ.

The original writ must be served: R. v. Rowe, 71 L.T. 578; by delivering it to the person having the custody of the prisoner and to whom it is directed, or by leaving it with a servant or agent of such person at the place where the prisoner is in custody, who is to include it in his return: R.S.O. ch. 83, sec. 2. If directed to more than one person the original is to be left with the principal person and copies with the others.

Application to Quash Writ of Habeas Corpus.

If it is considered that the writ has, for any reason, been improperly obtained or objection is taken to it, a motion may be made to quash it, in the same manner as a motion to quash certiorari, as described *ante*, p. 20; and such application may be entertained in the absence of the prisoner: Re Sproule, 12 Can. S.C.R. 140.

Return to Writ.

The officer or person to whom the writ is directed must, when service has been made on him, make a return: R.S.O. ch. 83; and the body of the prisoner must be produced with the return, "upon payment or tender of the charges of bringing the prisoner, to be ascertained by the judge, and endorsed on the writ, not exceeding 12 pence per mile," and upon security being given by the prisoner in his own bond, for payment of the charges of conveying him back to gaol, if he shall be remanded, and that he will not make any escape by the way: 31 Car. II. ch. 2, sec. 1. A return stating that the prisoner is not produced for want of means is not a good return: R. v. Reno, 4 P.R. 281; see Ex p. Martins, 9 Dowl. P.C. 194.

The court will, however, on consent of the prisoner, dispense with his attendance on the argument of a writ of error: Richards v. The Queen (1897), 1 Q.B. 574; and the court usually dispenses with his attendance on habeas corpus, on the consent of his solicitor, endorsed on the writ, as follows:—

"I hereby dispense with production of the body of the within named A.B., in pursuance of the within writ.
Dated, etc.

E.F.,
Solicitor for the said A.B."

By R.S.N.S. 1900, ch. 181, sec. 3, if it is not convenient to bring up the body of the prisoner, the court, instead of ordering a writ of habeas corpus to issue, may make an order in the nature of habeas corpus, directing the gaoler to make a return of the cause of imprisonment: Re Ferguson, 24 N.S.R. 111. There is no such provision in the R.S.O. ch. 83; but the prisoner's production is always dispensed with on the above consent.

FORM OF RECOGNIZANCE TO GAOLER.

To be Given if the Production of the Prisoner is not Dispensed with.

Know all men by these presents that I A.B., of the   of
             in the County of   (*occupation*) am held and
firmly bound unto   , keeper of
the common gaol of the County of   , in the sum
of   for which sum
to be well and truly paid I bind myself, my heirs, executors and administrators, by these presents.
Sealed with my seal and dated this   day of
             A.D. 19 .
Whereas I am now confined as a prisoner in the common gaol of the County of   and a writ of habeas corpus has been issued by the High Court of Justice for Ontario to inquire into the cause of my detention directed to the said gaoler.
Now the condition of this obligation is such that if I shall well and truly pay or cause to be paid to the said gaoler upon demand, the charges of carrying me back to said goal, if I shall be remanded on the said habeas corpus and if I shall not escape by the way either in going to or returning from the place where I am to be produced under the said habeas corpus then this obligation shall be void, otherwise the same is to remain in full force and virtue.
(Sd.)   [Seal.]

The return to a writ of habeas corpus must be in writing, signed by the party to whom the writ is directed, stating the time and cause of the caption and detention of the prisoner: R. v. St. Clair, 27 A.R. 308; and his production before the court, or, if the prisoner be not produced, then the reasons for not pro--

ducing him: Hurd. 235, see Barnardo v. Ford (1892), A.C. 326; Barnardo v. McHugh, 61 L.J.Q.B. 721; 15 Am. & Eng. Enc. of Law 195; unless his production has been dispensed with.

The original warrant under which the prisoner is detained should be attached to the return; a copy is not sufficient: Re Carmichael, 10 C.L.J. 325; Re Ross, 3 P.R. 301, ·not followed.

The law requires certainty in the statement of the facts: Watson's Case, 9 A. & E. 731; see Douden's Case, *ib.* 294; Nash's Case, *ib.* 295; Re Parker, 5 M. & W. 32. A return which on its face is ambiguous is bad: R. v. Roberts, 2 F. & F. 272. As to the form of return, see R. v. McDearmid, 19 C.L.T. 329.

If the person confined is too weak, or too much deranged to be brought into court, it is a good return: R. v. Wright, 2 Burr. 1099; R. v. Turlington, 8 Burr. 1115; or if dangerously sick: Hurd. 249. In such cases an order may be made giving access to the prisoner detained; but only to persons who have some pretentions to demand it: R. v. Clarke, 3 Burr. 1362.

Affidavits by physicians or other satisfactory proofs should be produced to satisfy the court of the correctness of a return that the prisoner is too sick to be produced: Hurd. 249.

The consequences of an evasive return are fully exemplified in the leading case of Buller v. Winton, 5 T.R. 89; see also R. v. Suddis, 1 East 306; Ex p. Krans, 1 B. & C. 258; Re Parker, 5 M. & W. 32: Watson's Case. 9 A. & E. 731: R. v. Richards. 5 Q.B. 926: Ex p. Bessett, 6 Q.B. 481; R. v. Roberts, 2 F. & F 272; Re Mathews, 12 Ir. R.C.L. 241; R. v Jackson (1891), 1 Q.B. 671.

FORM OF RETURN TO HABEAS CORPUS.

By virtue of the within Order, I, G.H., keeper of the common gaol at   in and for the County of   do hereby return to the Honourable Mr. Justice   (or, to the High Court of Justice for Ontario; *or as the writ directs*) that A:B. is a prisoner in the County Gaol at   aforesaid under and by virtue of a Warrant of Commitment which is hereto annexed, and that the said A.B. was committed to the said common gaol under and by virtue of the said warrant on the   day of   A.D. 19 , and the said A.B. is now detained in the said common gaol by virtue of the said warrant and for no other cause or reason whatsoever (*or as the case may be, setting out any other warrants of detention*).

Dated at   this   day of   A.D. 19 .

(Signed)   G.... H....,

Keeper of the said common gaol.

A form of return to habeas corpus by a constable having a prisoner in his custody and to whom a writ of habeas corpus is directed, is given in R. v. Defries, 1 Can. Cr. Cas. 207.

Note.—When the production of the body of the prisoner has not been dispensed with by an endorsement on the writ to that effect by the solicitor for the prisoner, a clause is to be added to the above form stating that the body of the prisoner is produced; or if, for any sufficient reason, the prisoner cannot or should not be produced, state that fact, and give fully and particularly the reasons for the same, as, for instance, that the prisoner's case comes within the exception in clause 1 of R.S.O. ch. 83. A return must be made even if the person has been released from custody by the person detaining him: R. v. Gavin, 15 Jur. 329; and the impossibilty of producing the party in obedience to the writ is, except under special circumstances noted elsewhere, a sufficient return, the writ being remedial and not punative: see Barnardo v. Ford (1892), A.C. 326, overruling R. v. Barnardo, 23 Q.B.D. 305.

But the return in such case must state distinctly and un-equivocally why it is not obeyed with the facts shewing the reason therefor: R. v. Winton, 5 T.R. 89.

The return need not be verified by affidavit: Watson's Case, 9 A. & E. 731; but may be so fortified if defective, or the facts are insufficiently stated: R. v. Roberts, 2 F. & F. 272.

When Return to be Made.

The return must be made immediately: R.S.O. ch. 83, sec. 1 By 31 Car. II. ch. 2, sec. 2, the time making the return was limited according to the distance, not exceeding twenty days.

Delay may be allowed if for good cause shewn: R. v. Clarke, 3 Burr. 1362.

It is not indispensable that the person making the return should himself attend with the prisoner: Re Hakewell, 22 Eng. L. and Eq. 395; 12 C.B. 223.

To Whom Made.

As to whom the return is to be made, see R.S.O. ch. 83, sec. 1.

Amending Return.

Before the return is filed, any defect may be amended by the officer making it: Anon. 1 Mod. 102; but after the return is filed, it becomes a record of the court, and cannot be amended without leave of the court: Re Clarke. 2 A. & E. N. S. 619; 2 Q.B. 619; R. v. Batcheldor, 1 P. & D. 516; Watson's Case, 9 A.

& E. 731; R. v. Wixon, 8 L.J.Q.B. 129. In R. v. Defries, 1 Can. Cr. Cas. 211, a clerical error in the return was allowed to be amended.

Return—How Enforced.

Any person who wilfully neglects or refuses to make a return or pay obedience to the writ is deemed guilty of contempt of court, and the court or judge, upon proof by affidavit of the service of the writ and of wilful disobedience, may order a warrant to be issued for apprehending and bringing before the court or judge, the person so disobeying, to the end that he may be bound over in two sureties to appear in court at a day mentioned to answer the contempt: R.S.O. ch. 83, sec. 2; Cyrus Wilson's Case, 7 Q.B. 984.

If he refuses or neglects to become bound, he may be committed to gaol until he becomes bound or is discharged: R.S.O. ch. 83, sec. 3.

If a person wilfully puts it out of his power to obey the writ, e.g., by transferring the custody of the prisoner to some other person; or if he otherwise disposes of the prisoner, he is liable to attachment for contempt and to pay the costs: R. v. Barnardo, 23 Q.B.D. 305.

Proceedings for Contempt.

An application to commit will not be entertained except on notice to the party, informing him of the consequences of failure to obey: R. v. Hallock, 15 C.L.T. 9.

On motion to commit, an affidavit of service of the writ is required, and of search in the proper office, and that no return has been filed; or if an insufficient return has been made, an affidavit shewing that fact and verifying a copy of the return: Ex p. Harrison, 2 Sm. 408; R. v. Winton, 5 T.R. 89; R. v. Gavin, 15 Jur. 329; R. v. Barnardo, 23 Q.B.D. 305; 24 Q.B.D. 283.

Contradicting the Return.

Although the return is good and sufficient in law, the court or a judge, before whom the writ is returnable, may examine into the truth of the facts set forth by affidavit or other evidence: R.S.O. ch. 83, sec. 4. And a judge in Chambers has power to refer the matter to the court: R. v. Reader, 1 Stra. 531: Re Taurner, 15 L. & M. ch. 140. Matters wholly and exclusively within the province of the justice or magistrate will not be enquired into on application for habeas corpus, nor on motion to quash a conviction, such matters being proper subjects for appeal. But in matters extrinsic and collateral and going to jurisdiction, the return may be contradicted: see further at p. 66 and *ante*, p. 36 upon this subject.

Notice of Application for Discharge.

Upon serving the writ of habeas corpus a notice of application for the discharge of the prisoner must be served on the Attorney-General in criminal matters.

NOTICE OF MOTION FOR DISCHARGE.

In the High Court of Justice.
The King against A.B.
Take notice that (*if short notice of motion is to be given, add,* by special leave of the Honourable Mr. Justice   this day given), an application will be made before the presiding judge in Chambers at Osgoode Hall, Toronto, on   day, the   day of   A.D. 19   , or so soon thereafter as the motion can be made, for the discharge of the said A.B. from the common gaol of the County of   (*or as the case may be*) upon the return of the writ of habeas corpus this day issued in pursuance of the order of Mr. Justice   , directing the keeper of the common gaol (*or as the case may be*) of the County of   to have before one of the judges of the High Court of Justice for Ontario the body of the said A.B. now in custody under the Warrant of Commitment issued in pursuance of a conviction made by C.D., Esquire, police magistrate (*or*, a justice of the peace) for the   of   , for that the said A.B. at the   of   in the County of   on the   day of   A.D. 19   , did unlawfully (*insert the charge as in the conviction or warrant*). And take notice that in support of such application will be read the affidavits of   and   and the exhibits therein referred to and the return to the said writ of habeas corpus and to the writ of certiorari issued in aid thereof.
Dated at   this   day of   A.D. 19
To
　　The Attorney-General for　　　　　　　　　　Solicitor for the
　　　the Province of Ontario.　　　　　　　　　　said A.B.
And to E.F.
　　　　　The Prosecutor.

The Hearing.

On the return to habeas corpus the prisoner's counsel moves that it be filed, and that the prisoner be brought into court, and then proceeds with the application for discharge. The court, although the return is good in law, may proceed to examine the truth of the facts set forth in it by affidavit or other evidence, and may order and determine touching the discharging, bailing, or remanding the prisoner: R.S.O. ch. 83, sec. 4.

Habeas corpus does not apply to mere irregularities or errors. It is the proper remedy, only, when the proceeding is void, and not merely voidable; and in the latter case, the remedy is by certiorari and motion to quash the proceeding: see Ex p. Bertin, 10 Can. Cr. Cas. 65.

The court will examine the proceedings including the evidence to see if they authorize the detention, and if insufficient, will discharge the prisoner: Ex p. Beebe, 15 L.T. 235; and see 17 C.L.T. 18. The court will discharge the prisoner if the evidence taken on a preliminary enquiry, and brought up on certiorari, does not shew any grounds to warrant his commitment for trial: R. v. Mosier, 4 P.R. 64, in which case the subject of jurisdiction on habeas corpus was fully discussed; or if the evidence on which the party was convicted did not disclose any offence known to the law: R. v. Collette, 10 Can. Cr. Cas. 286; or if a fact found by the justice be one essential to jurisdiction, it may be shewn that there was no evidence whatever to warrant such finding; but if it was a finding on the merits of the case or part of it, it is not reviewable by certiorari or habeas corpus, the remedy being by appeal: Paley, 8th ed., 442 (o). If there is any evidence upon which the magistrate may convict, he is the judge of its weight, and the court will not rehear the case, or sit in appeal from his decision: R. v. St. Clair, 27 A.R. p. 310; R. v. Gillespie (Que.), 1 Can. Cr. Cas. p. 561; R. v. Bougie, 3 Can. Cr. Cas. 487; R. v. Trepannier, 12 Can. S.C.R. 113; R. v. St. Clair, 3 Can. Cr. Cas. 551. See also the cases cited ante, p. 29, "Certiorari."

The court will not question the justice's decision on the weight of the evidence, nor sustain objections to the justice's conduct of the case: R. v. Munro, 24 U.C.R. 44.

Amendment by the Court.

By the provisions of the curative clauses of the Criminal Code, many defects which formerly invalidated convictions and warrants of magistrates and justices will not now do so; and certain powers of amendment are given: see Code 1121 to 1125, 1128 to 1132. These sections and the powers to return amended convictions and warrants, and the powers of the courts as to amendments are fully discussed in the previous pages on the subject of certiorari and motions to quash proceedings, ante, p. 33 et seq., and what is there stated applies in these respects to proceedings on habeas corpus. The court may on certiorari amend a conviction under the powers given by Code 754 and 1124 (formerly sections 883 and 889), whether the certiorari is one preliminary to an application to quash a conviction, or is in aid of habeas corpus: R. v. Murdoch, 4 Can. Cr. Cas. 82: see also R. v. Phipps, 11 W.R. 730; Ex p. Dauncey, 8 Jur. 829; Ex p. Welsh, 4 Rev. de Jur. 437; R. v. Reno, 4 P.R. 281; Ex p. Cross, 2 H. & N. 354; R. v. Skinner 9 Can. Cr. Cas. 558.

The prisoner will not be discharged in the case of a defective warrant of commitment, if a conviction is recited, the court assuming it to be a valid one: R. v. Roper, 1 D. & R. 156; R. v. Taylor, 7 D. & R. 622; but the warrant must refer to a conviction, so as to give notice of it to those concerned; then both will be read together, and if the conviction justifies the warrant, it is sufficient: Daniel v. Phillips, 5 Tyr. 293; but if both are defective the prisoner will be discharged.

If the commitment is bad the prosecutor is the party to produce the conviction: 9 Q.B. 92, note; and this he can do by applying in time to bring it into court when the prisoner is brought up: see *post*, p. 70. It is for those who allege the conviction to be different from the recital of it, in the commitment, to bring it into court. *Primâ facie* it is as so recited: Ex p. Reynolds, 8 Jur. 192; Arscot v. Lilly, 11 O.R. 153, 14 A.R. 297; Re Timson, L.R. 5 Exch. 257.

The commitment must state a conviction over which the magistrate had jurisdiction, and it will not be presumed: see Arscott v. Lilly, 11 O.R. 153; R. v. Kent, 8 Jur. 271; R. v. Kennedy, 11 Man. R. 338.

If there has been an appeal from the conviction, the court cannot review the justice's proceedings again under habeas corpus, for all questions could be raised on the appeal and so the confirmation of the conviction by the court appealed to is conclusive of such questions; and besides, the defendant having elected his remedy by appeal, is bound by its result: R. v. Beamish, 5 Can. Cr. Cas. 388.

Order for Detention under Code 1120.

The court, on habeas corpus proceedings, may make an order in any case for the further detention of the accused, and direct the justice to take any proceedings, hear such evidence and do such further act, as in the opinion of the court, may best further the ends of justice: Code 1120.

Under this section the accused may be sent back for further evidence to be taken before the justice, or to be dealt with by a fresh warrant of commitment or otherwise.

Where there was a valid conviction but defendant was imprisoned thereunder without a formal commitment having been issued, the court refused habeas corpus and allowed a formal commitment to be put in, directing the detention of the prisoner under Code 1120 until that could be done: R. v. Morgan, 5 Can. Cr. Cas. 63, 272. See also the several examples of the application of Code 1120 in 5 Can. Cr. Cas. p. 66. But where the magistrate exceeds his jurisdiction the court will not order the detention of the prisoner under Code 1120 to have the proper thing done: R. v. Randolph, 4 Can. Cr. Cas. p. 165. Nor where his proceeding is altogether without authority, *e.g.*, where he made a conviction for an indictable offence, the court refused to order prisoner's detention and direct the proper preliminary enquiry to be taken: R. v. Blucher, 7 Can. Cr. Cas. 278.

When unauthorized punishment was awarded and partly undergone, the court refused to act under section 752 (now 1120), and discharged the prisoner, although he had pleaded guilty to the charge: R. v. Hayward, 6 Can. Cr. Cas. 399. A mistake of the justice as to his authority to compel a witness to attend without being prepaid his witness fees whereby the defendant was deprived of the witness's evidence, is not a matter reviewable on habeas corpus, but is the subject of appeal: R. v. Clements, 4 Can. Cr. Cas. 553.

If the conviction and commitment omit some statement essential to the offence; *e.g.*, if the word "wilful" was omitted in a case in which it was an essential ingredient of the offence, there is no offence stated over which the justice has jurisdiction, and the defect cannot be cured: Ex p. O'Shaunessy, 8 Can. Cr. Cas. 136. So when the conviction and commitment failed to shew that the offence was committed within the time limited for prosecution, the objection goes to the jurisdiction and is fatal: R. v. Adams, 24 N.S.R. 559; R. v. Boutelier, 8 Can. Cr. Cas. 82; or when the conviction and commitment failed to shew that the information had been laid before two justices when that was required by the statute relating to the offence: R. v. Ettinger, 3 Can. Cr. Cas. 387.

5—MAG. MAN.

Affidavits Showing Grounds Avoiding Return.

The court will not receive affidavits to contradict the matters found by the justice and appearing on the face of the proceedings returned: Re Clarke, 2 Q.B. 619; Dimes' Case, 14 Q.B. 554, but will receive affidavits to establish collateral and extrinsic facts going to the jurisdiction of the justice: Re Defries, 1 Can. Cr. Cas. 207; R. v. Munro, 24 U.C.R. 44; Paley, 8th Ed. 440. So affidavits are receivable to shew that the trial or judicial proceeding took place on Sunday and was therefore void: Re Cooper, 5 P.R. 256; R. v. Cavalier, 1 Can. Cr. Cas. 134; Ex p. Garland, 8 Can. Cr. Cas. 385; or that the justice or one of the justices who signed the warrant was not a duly qualified justice of the peace: R. v. Boyle, 4 P.R. 256; or that the warrant of commitment had been issued after part of the fine had been paid and had not been refunded or tendered back to the defendant: Ex p. Bertin, 10 Can. Cr. Cas. 65; or that the justice convicted the defendant in his absence without due ·service of the summons for his appearance: R. v. Lyons, 10 Can. Cr. Cas. 131; or that the justice had amended the information in the absence of the defendant and had convicted him in such absence, of a different offence to that stated in the summons served on the defendant (*e.g.*, by changing the charge from one for illegally selling liquor to that of illegally keeping liquor for sale): R. v. Lyons, *supra.*

So if the constable made an untrue return of no goods to a distress warrant, it was held by the S.C. New Brunswick that the facts may be proved by affidavit and the prisoner will be discharged, as the warrant is void if issued on a false return: Ex p. Kirkpatrick, 5 Can. Cr. Cas. 191; but otherwise in Ontario: R v. Sanderson, 12 O.R. 178; and extrinsic evidence may be given to shew that there has been an appeal: R. v. Beamish, 5 Can. Cr. Cas. 388; or that the justice conducted the case in a wholly unauthorized and illegal manner so as to exclude his jurisdiction over it: R. v. Randolph, 4 Can. Cr. Cas. 165; R. v. Blucher, 7 Can. Cr. Cas. 278; or that there was no evidence of any offence having been committed: Re Bailey & Collier, 3 E. & B. 607; or that the defendant had been previously convicted of the same offence: Ex p. Baker, 2 H. & N. 219.

Affidavits will not be received to contradict the statement in a conviction and commitment returned to the court, that the offence was committed within the territorial jurisdiction of the justice: Ex p. Newton, 16 C.B. 97.

See also on this subject: Ex p. Beeching, 4 B. & C. 136; Re Crawford, 13 Q.B. 613; R. v. Douglass, 12 L.J.Q.B. 49; Ex p. Mainville, 1 Can. Cr. Cas. 528; R. v. Whiteside, 8 Can. Cr. Cas. 480.

Habeas Corpus with Motion to Quash Conviction.

On certiorari and motion to quash a conviction, if it appears clearly that the accused is in custody illegally the court may order habeas corpus to issue, and hear, together, the motion to quash and a motion for the prisoner's discharge: R. v. Spooner, 4 Can. Cr. Cas. 209.

Returning Amended Commitment, etc.

If the return to habeas corpus shews a valid commitment, the court will not inquire when it was lodged with the gaoler, or whether there was a previous invalid commitment. So a valid commitment may be lodged with the gaoler, in place of an invalid one, even after habeas corpus has been served, and thus defeat the writ: Charter v. Graeme, 13 Q.B. 216; Chaney v. Payne, 1 Q.B. 712; Re Plunkett, 1 Can. Cr. Cas. 365; R. v. House, 2 Man. R. 58; see also Ex p. Cross, 2 H. & N. 354, 20 L.J.M.C. 201; Re Fell, 15 L.J.M.C. 25; Re Marks, 3 East 57; Re Anderson, 20 U.C.R 162; p. Pap, 1 B. & Ald. 568; R. v. Gordon, 1 B. & Ald. 572; Ex p. Smith, 27 L.J.M.C. 186; Hammond's Case, 9 Q.B. 90. A supplementary return may be made of a second warrant intended to remedy a defect in the first one returned; Re Murphy, 2 Can. Cr. Cas. 578.

In R. v. Richards, 5 Q.B. 926, Denman, C.J., said: "It is impossible not to see that there is a good warrant under which the party may lawfully be detained." See also R. v. Walton, 10 Can. Cr. Cas. 269. But the return must shew in express terms that the second commitment is in substitution or amendment of the first one: R. v. Venot, 6 Can. Cr. Cas. 209; Re Emy v. Sawyer, 1 A. & E. 843.

In R. v. Wright, 10 Can. Cr. Cas. 461 leave was given on the motion for habeas corpus to return an amended sentence, correcting the date and inserting the date when imprisonment was to commence.

And in Re Lavin, 12 P.R. 642, similar leave was given to return an amended warrant changing the date of the conviction by substituting the year 1887 for 1888, the conviction returned on certiorari shewing the correct date.

If the commitment is bad on its face in not alleging that there was a conviction, a formal conviction cannot be received to remedy the defect, Code 1121, 1123, 1130, only applying when the warrant alleges a conviction and there is in fact a valid conviction: R. v. Lalonde, 9 Can. Cr. Cas. 501.

After service of habeas corpus the prisoner cannot be arrested under an amended warrant unless he has been first liberated from arrest under the first warrant, or except by permission of the court: Ex p. Cohen, 8 Can. Cr. Cas. 312.

ORDER DISCHARGING PRISONER ON HABEAS CORPUS.

In the High Court of Justice.
The Honourable
    Mr. Justice
                In Chambers.
       or (if the application is to the court)
The Honourable
    The Chief Justice
The Honourable   day, the   day
    Mr. Justice   of   , A.D. 19 .
The Honourable
    Mr. Justice
                The King v. A.B.

1. Upon the application of the above-named A.B., upon reading the writ of habeas corpus issued herein on the   day of A.D. 19 , and the return made thereto by   , keeper of the common gaol for the County of   (or, as the case may be,) the writ of certiorari, issued on the said last-mentioned day, in aid of the said writ of habeas corpus. Upon reading the information, conviction and proceedings returned by   , Esquire, police magistrate (or justice of the peace) for the   of   , in compliance with the said writ of certiorari upon reading the affidavits of   and the exhibits therein referred to, and upon hearing counsel for the Crown (and for the private prosecutor) and for the said A.B.

2. It is ordered that the said A.B. be, and he is hereby discharged, out of the custody of the said   , the keeper of the said common gaol, (or, as the case may be,) as to his commitment made by the said   , Esquire, police magistrate (or justice of the peace), aforesaid, on the information of   for that (set out the charge, as in the commitment,) in so far as the said A.B. is held under the said warrant, and that this order be sufficient authority to the said keeper of the said common gaol for the discharge of the said A.B.

{ Seal of
  Court. }

                        Clerk in Chambers,
                              or
                          Registrar.

Effect of Discharge.

By section 6 of 31 Car. II., no person discharged on habeas corpus shall be again imprisoned or committed for the same offence, other than by legal process or order of the court wherein he is bound by recognizance to appear, or other court, having jurisdiction of the cause. This section has no application to a case in which the person was confined under a warrant in execution: Hunter v. Gilkinson, 7 O.R. 735; nor to the case of a person discharged from a commitment for trial, for defects in the proceedings; but only to prevent a prisoner, who has been committed for trial, and bailed under habeas corpus, from being re-arrested for the same offence, except by process or order of the court wherein he was bound under such bail to appear: Attorney-General v. Kwok-a-Sing, L.R. 5 P.C. 179.

In Arscott v. Lilly, 11 O.R. 153, Wilson, C.J., decided that when a prisoner had served a portion of the imprisonment under conviction, and had been released on bail pending appeal, and was afterwards discharged on habeas corpus for invalidity of the warrant; and a second warrant having been issued for the full period originally awarded, without deducting the time previously served in gaol, the second warrant was valid, as the time so served might be endorsed upon the warrant or otherwise provided for.

Conditions on Discharge.

The court may impose terms on discharging a prisoner that he undertake that no action shall be brought against any person: Code 1131; R. v. Hoton, 3 Can. Cr. Cas. 84 (N.S.); R. v. Quirke, 32 C.L.J. 779. But see R. v. Keeping, 4 Can. Cr. Cas. 494 (N.S.) 32 C.L.J. 779. But see R. v. Keeping, 4 Can. Cr. Cas. 494 (N.S). in which it was held that only the gaoler can be protected.

Costs.

Costs may be ordered on an application for habeas corpus, but the power to award costs, should only be exercised in extreme cases, if at all: Re Murphy, 28 N.S.R. 196; London County Council v. Westham Overseers (1892), 2 Q.B. 173; R. v. London (Jus.), (1894), 1 Q.B. 453; R. v. Jones (1894), 2 Q.B. 382; Freeman v. General, etc., Co. (1894), 2 Q.B. 380; Re Fisher (1894), 1 Ch. 453; see section 190 Cr. R. N. S.; Ord. 63, r. 1, N.S. Jud. R. The Crown Rules, Nova Scotia, were made under

the power conferred on the Superior Courts of criminal jurisdiction in the various provinces, by the Dom. Statute, 1889, ch.
40.

Certiorari in Aid of Habeas Corpus.

Where the legality, or otherwise, of the restraint does not
depend upon the validity or invalidity of the warrant, but upon
that of the conviction or the sufficiency or insufficiency of the
evidence, it will be necessary for the party on whom the burden
of proof lies, to bring up those proceedings; and a writ of certiorari may be obtained by either party for that purpose, as
provided by R.S.O. ch. 83, sec. 5; Ex p. Reynolds, 8 Jur. 192;
Arscott v. Lilly, 11 O.R. 153, 165, 14 A.R. 297. Certiorari in aid
of the writ of habeas corpus may be applied for at the same time
as the latter writ; or it may be issued at any time, and the case is
then heard upon the habeas corpus and the proceedings brought
up on certiorari: 1 Chitty's Cr. Law 127, 129; 2 Strange 911,
note 1; R. v. Marks, 3 East 157. If the habeas corpus proceedings are based upon a bad warrant of commitment, it will be
necessary for the prosecution to take steps, by certiorari, in sufficient time to have the evidence and conviction brought into court,
when the prisoner is brought up on the writ of habeas corpus
for the court may not adjourn the application for the prisoner's
discharge and detain him in gaol, on the suggestion that there is
a good conviction. Ex p. Timson, L.R. 5 Ex. 257.

But a judge of the Canadian Supreme Court on application
to him for habeas corpus cannot grant certiorari in aid of the
writ: Re Trepannier, 12 Can. S.C.R. 111, 129, see *post* under
"Appeals."

FORM OF ORDER FOR CERTIORARI IN AID OF HABEAS CORPUS.
In the High Court of Justice.
The King on the information of C.D. against A.B.
1. Upon the application of C.D., the prosecutor above named (*or of A.
B.* above named, a prisoner now confined in close custody in the common
goal of the County of   ) upon reading the affidavit of the said
     , and the exhibits therein referred to, this day filed, and a writ
of habeas corpus having been issued to bring the body of the said A.B.
before a judge of this court.
2. It is ordered that a writ of certiorari in aid of the said writ of
habeas corpus, do issue out of the court (*proceed as in Form ante p. 10*).

If the certiorari is applied for at the same time as the writ
of habeas corpus, both may be inserted in one order, and writ.

No notice under the statute of Geo. II., nor any recognizance
or deposit is required on issuing certiorari in aid of habeas
corpus: R. v. Nunn, 10 P.R. 395.

Custody Pending Argument.

The writ of habeas corpus supersedes all other processes under which the party may be detained; consequently, on the return of the writ, and production of the body of the person detained, he is in the custody of and subject to the order of the court to which the return is made, and he may be bailed *de die in diem,* or remanded to any gaol under the control of the court. He may be brought before the court, from time to time, by its order until the matter is finally disposed of as provided by Code 1120: R. v. Bethel, 5 Mod. 19.

Appeal.

In Ontario and Quebec a person who has been brought before the court or a judge on habeas corpus and remanded to custody, upon the original warrant of commitment or by virtue of any warrant, order or rule of such court or judge, may appeal from the judgment to the Court of Appeal in Ontario, or to the Court of King's Bench in Quebec: see Ex p. Tremblay, 6 Can. Cr. Cas. 147. The writ, the return thereto, the affidavits, depositions, evidence, conviction, and other proceedings, are then certified by the proper officer (the Registrar or Clerk in Chambers), under the seal of the court, to the Court of Appeal, which is required to hear and determine the matter without formal pleadings: 29 & 30 Vict. ch. 45 (R.S.O. ch. 83), sec. 6.

If the Court of Appeal determines that the restraint is illegal, the fact must be certified by such court under seal to the person having the custody or charge of the person confined or restrained, and order his immediate discharge, and he shall be discharged accordingly: *ib.*

The right of appeal must be exercised in the manner provided by section 6 of the statute 29 & 30 Vict.; and therefore an appeal from a judge in Chambers, as well as from the full court if the original application was to the latter, must be made direct to the Court of Appeal: Re Harper, 23 O.R. 63; Taylor v. Scott, 30 O.R. 475.

The statute 29 & 30 Vict. ch. 45, substituted the right of appeal in habeas corpus cases, for successive applications from court to court, and such applications will not now be entertained in Ontario or Quebec unless new facts are stated: Ex p. Tremblay, 6 Can. Cr. Cas. at p. 148. But in the other provinces successive applications may be made to the different judges of the court,

although previously refused: R. v. Carter (S.C.N.B.), 5 Can.
Cr. Cas. 401; Re Bowack (S.C.B.C), 2 B.C.R. 222; Re James
Black, Nova Scotia Dig. 614; R. v. Heckman (S.C.N.S.), 5 Can.
Cr. Cas. 242; Re Piaget (N.S.), 21 C.L.T. 536; Re Bryan (N.B.),
22 N.B.R. 436. In extradition cases the application must be
made to the full court: N.S. Crown Rules 150. In other provinces than Ontario and Quebec there is no law providing for
appeals and no appeal lies in habeas corpus cases, but applications may be made successively to the judges for the writ: R. v.
Barre, 11 Can. Cr. Cas. 1; Ex p. Woodhall, 20 Q.B.D. 823; Bell
Cox v. Hakes, 15 App. Cas. 514; Re Hall, 8 A.R. 135.

The Supreme Court of Canada.

There is no appeal in any criminal case unless it is provided
by some special Act; and appeals from any of the provincial
courts to the Supreme Court are not only unprovided for, but
they are expressly prohibited by R.S.C. 1906, ch. 139, sec. 36 (a)
in habeas corpus, certiorari or prohibition proceedings arising out
of a criminal charge; and there is no appeal in any criminal case
in regard to any other matter except as provided in the Criminal
Code: Attorney-General v. Scully, 6 Can. Cr. Cas. p. 384. The
Supreme Court has therefore no appellate jurisdiction in habeas
corpus cases over the provincial courts: R. v. Patrick White, 4
Can. Cr. Cas. 430.

But each judge of the Supreme Court of Canada has concurrent jurisdiction with the provincial courts to grant writs of
habeas corpus, except in extradition cases, and if a judge of that
court refuses the writ or remands the prisoner, an appeal lies
from him to the full court; R.S.C. 1906, ch. 139, s. 62; Re
Boucher, Cassel's Dig. 182; Re Trepannier, 12 S.C.R. 111; Re
Lazier, 29 S.C.R. 630; R. v. The Troop, 29 S.C.R. 662; Ex p.
Macdonald, 27 S.C.R. 683; Re Sproule, 12 S.C.R. 140; Rice v.
The King, 5 Can. Cr. Cas. 529; R. v. Vancini (No. 2), 8 Can.
Cr. Cas. 228, 34 S.C.R. 621.

But such jurisdiction is limited to cases under Dominion
statutes and no application can be made to a judge of the Supreme Court of Canada for habeas corpus if the party is in
custody on a charge under a provincial statute: Re Sproule, 12
S.C.R. 140. The jurisdiction is also limited merely to an enquiry into the cause of commitment as disclosed in the warrant
of commitment: Ex p. Macdonald, 27 S.C.R. 683; for the Su-

preme Court of Canada or a judge has no authority to issue certiorari in aid of habeas corpus, s. 66 of the Supreme Court Act not applying to habeas corpus: Re Trepannier, 12 S.C.R. 111.

The Supreme Court has no power to quash a conviction, but if the conviction shews a want of jurisdiction, or if it is shewn, in any way, that the magistrate had no jurisdiction, the conviction with commitment thereon is a nullity; and the court will discharge the prisoner on habeas corpus, because he is not held by process of any legal tribunal. But a valid conviction standing against the prisoner, and the warrant being regularly issued, the court cannot discharge him or undertake the duty of sitting in appeal from magistrates' decisions, either by way of certiorari or habeas corpus: Re Trepannier, 12 S.C.R. 111.

The Supreme Court has authority to quash a writ of habeas corpus improvidently issued by a judge of that court; and section 36 of the Supreme Court Act does not deprive the court of that authority: Re Sproule, 12 S.C.R. 140. The only means of enforcing obedience to a writ of habeas corpus issued by a judge is by an application to the full court for an attachment: *Ibid.*

The Supreme Court or a judge will not grant habeas corpus after it has been refused on application to a provincial court; this being on the ground that it would be practically entertaining an appeal from the provincial court: Re Patrick White, 31 S.C.R. 383.

Appeals to Privy Council.

Code 1025 prohibits any appeal in any criminal proceeding from any court in Canada to the Privy Council.

It was said in Falkland Is. Co. v. The Queen, 1 Moo. P.C. N.S. 312, that "it may be assumed that the Queen has authority by virtue of her prerogative, to review the decisions of all colonial courts, whether the proceedings be of a civil or criminal character, unless Her Majesty has parted with such authority.'

In the same case it was further stated, that "the incon venience of entertaining such appeals, in cases of a strictly criminal nature, is so great, the obstruction which it would offer to the administration of justice is so obvious, that it is very rarely that applications to this Board have been attended by success."

The Privy Council will not in any case grant leave to appeal in criminal cases, unless it is shewn that by a disregard of the forms of legal process, or by some violation of the principles

of natural justice, or otherwise, some substantial and grave injustice has been done: see Ex p. Dillet, L.R. 12 A.C. 459, in
which leave to appeal was allowed; re-affirmed in Ex p. Carew
(1897), A.C. 719, in which it was refused. See also Riel v.
Regina, L.R. 10 A.C. 675.

Rules of Court.

The High Court is authorized to make rules: R.S.O.
ch. 83, sec. 8; Code 576. No. rules have been made in Ontario under these provisions. The rules made under the
Ontario Judicature Act do not affect procedure in criminal matters: Con. R. 4; see also section 191 of the
Act, R.S.O. ch. 51; R. v. Eli, 13 A.R. 526; R. v. Cushing, 26 A.R. 248. As to what are "criminal matters," the test
under the section of the English Act, which is almost identical
with the above section 191, was held to be whether it is a matter
in the result of which the party may be fined or imprisoned: Seaman v Burley (1896), 2 Q.B. 344; R. v. Fletcher, 2 Q.B.D. at p.
47. In the latter case the term "criminal proceeding" was held
to include proceedings in the High Court in respect of matters
before justices and magistrates: see also R. v. Central Cr. Court,
18 Q.B.D. 314; Ex p. Schofield (1891), 2 Q.B. 428; Ex p. Bowman, 22 L.R. Ir. 334.

And an application by a party to a civil suit against a person
who is not a party for contempt is a "criminal matter": O'Shea
v. O'Shea, 15 P.D. 59; Ellis v. The Queen, 22 S.C.R. 7, distinguishing R. v. Barnardo, 23 Q.B.D. 305, the distinction being
that in the Barnardo case the proceedings were to enforce obedience to an order made against the party to a civil suit; while in
the case of Ellis v. The Queen, the original proceeding was for
a "punitive" purpose. A proceeding to recover a penalty for
the infraction of a statute is a criminal matter: Southport v.
Berkdale, 76 L.T. 318.

As to other cases on the same point, see Re Hardwick, 12
Q.B.D. 148; Ex p. Eede, 25 Q.B.D. 228; Cox v. Hakes, L.R. 15
App. Cas. 506.

CHAPTER III.

PROHIBITION.

Prohibition will be granted by the High Court, as a matter of prerogative, at any time and in any case, to restrain an inferior judicial officer from assuming to exercise a jurisdiction which he does not possess: Re Chapman and London, 19 O.R. 33; and that the proper remedy: Mayor of London v. Cox, L.R. 2 H.L. 239.

Only Granted for Excess of Jurisdiction.

It is however, an extreme measure, and is only granted in a very plain case of excess of jurisdiction: Re Birch, 15 C.B. 743; Re Grass v. Allan, 26 U.C.R. 123; Re Cummings and County of Carleton, 25 O.R. 607, 26 O.R. 1; Beaudry v. Lafontaine, 17 Que. S.C.R. 396; and if no other equally convenient and adequate remedy exists: Tessier v. Desnoyers, 17 Que. S.C.R. 35.

Prohibition will not be granted on the ground of objection to the due appointment of a *de facto* official, the adequate and appropriate remedy being by *quo warranto*: Re Garner and Green, 9 Can. Cr. Cas. 240; nor in case there is a complete relief by some more ordinary remedy, *e.g.*, by appeal: R. v. Amyot, 11 Can. Cr. Cas. 232.

It will be granted where the justice's judicial proceedings are a denial or perversion of right, which is always an excess of jurisdiction: For instance, a defendant having been served with summons almost immediately before the trial, and the justice having refused to adjourn, the proceeding was held to be in denial of right and contrary to natural justice, and so, in excess of jurisdiction: R. v. Eli, 10 O.R. 727; R. v. Mabee, 17 O.R. 194; R. v. Smith, L.R. 10 Q.B. 604. And so when an adjournment of a case was made for more than eight days at one time, without the consent of the defendant, the justice is *functus officio*, and will be prohibited from proceeding with the case afterwards: Paré v.

Recorder of Montreal, 10 Can. Cr. Cas. 295; or when the ad‑ journment was made by the justice's clerk in the absence of the justice: *ibid.*

Prohibition will not be granted as a means of review or appeal; but only to keep the inferior court within the limits of its jurisdiction, from which it has departed, or is about to depart: Hudson's Bay Company, etc. v. Joanette, 23 S.C.R. 415; nor to correct an illegal or wrong judgment, not going to juris- diction: Elliott v. Biette, 21 O.R. 596; R. v. Murdock, 27 A.R. 443; R. v. Amyot, 11 Can. Cr. Cas. 232.

It will not be granted to remedy an illegality in procedure merely, unless it amounts to an excess of jurisdiction: R. v. Mayor of London, 69 L.T. 721; or violates some fundamental principle of justice, per Lush, J., in Martin v. Mackonachie, 3 Q.B.D. p. 739.

It will not be granted for refusal to hear a witness, an adequate remedy existing by appeal, or certiorari and motion to quash proceedings improperly taken; and if there is no such appeal, then there is no remedy: Mayor of London v. Cox, *supra;* Breton v. Landry, Q.R. 13 S.C. 31.

It will not be granted to rectify a decision upon a matter of fact, within the jurisdiction of the justice, however erroneous: Bar of Montreal v. Honan, Q.R. 8 Q.B. 26; Re Field v. Rice, 20 O.R. 309; R. v. Cunerty, 26 O.R. 51; Beaupre v. Desnoyers, Q.R. 11 S.C. 541; R. v. McIntosh, 17 C.L.T. 407; nor the mis- construction of a statute, if the justice does not thereby wrongly give himself jurisdiction: Elston v. Rose, L.R. 4 Q.B. 4; R. v. Judge of Lincolnshire, 20 Q.B.D. 167; Re Long Point Co. v. Anderson, 18 A.R. 401; Re Dyer v. Evans, 30 O.R. 637; nor for the erroneous determination of a question of law or fact with- in the officer's jurisdiction: Re Chisholm and Oakville, 12 A.R. 225.

If the officer has jurisdiction over the subject matter, pro- hibition does not lie upon the ground that he may have made a mistake in the manner of exercising it: R. v. J. J. Kent, 24 Q.B.D. 181; *e.g.,* on the ground that the justice has appointed an inconvenient place for the hearing: R. v. Chipman, 1 Can. Cr. Cas. 81.

But a justice's decision, not only on a matter of law, but on a matter of fact also, is reviewable on application for prohibi- tion, if such decision is on a matter essential to jurisdiction; but only upon clear grounds: Liverpool v. Everton, L.R. 6 C.P. 414. When neither the information nor the evidence shews that the proceedings were commenced within the time prescribed, the justice's jurisdiction not appearing on the face of the proceedings, he is without jurisdiction in the case; and he will be prohibited from proceeding further, on an application made during an adjournment to consider his finding: R. v. Breen, 8 Can. Cr. Cas. 146; R. v. Boutelier, 8 Can. Cr. Cas. 82; and see R. v. Adams, 24 N.S.R. 559; Ex p. Hopper, 27 N.B.R. 496; R. v. Ettinger, 3 Can. Cr. Cas. 387; R. v. Brine, 33 N.S.R. 43.

Prohibition was granted *ex parte* in the above case of R. v. Breen, as the justice's proceeding was manifestly without jurisdiction.

After a conviction has been quashed on the ground that the summons was not properly served, a justice has no jurisdiction to issue another summons on the same information, and he will be prohibited from doing so: R. v. Zickrick, 11 Man. R. 452, 5 Can. Cr. Cas. 380.

Prohibition will be granted against the unlawful exercise of judicial functions; but not against merely ministerial acts, such as improperly issuing a distress warrant, if the conviction is valid on its face, and within the justice's jurisdiction: R. v. Coursey, 27 O.R. 181; reversing S.C. in 26 O.R. 685.

It will be granted against any officer attempting to exercise judicial (but not ministerial) functions over a person who is not properly before him: Re Hickson and Wilson, 17 C.L.T. 303.

Prohibition lies to a coroner: R. v. Hertford, 3 E. & B. 115; Re Haney v. Mead, 34 C.L.J. 330.

Who May Apply For.

Prohibition may be granted even upon the application of a stranger to the proceedings when a justice is clearly exceeding his jurisdiction, as such is a contempt of the Crown: Worthington v. Jaffries, L.R. 10 C.P. 379; Chambers v. Green, L.R. 20 Eq. 552; De Haber v. Portugal, 17 Q.B. p. 171; Wallace v. Allan, L.R. 10 C. P. 607.

Against Whom Prohibition Lies.

Prohibition may be granted against a justice of the peace to prohibit him from assuming to exercise powers which he does not possess: Re Chapman and London, 19 O.R. 33; *e.g.*, in the case of a justice of the peace proceeding to try summarily an indictable offence: R. v. T. Eaton Co., 29 O.R. 591.

It will be granted against police magistrates: R. v. London, 32 O.R. 326; and against the Court of General Sessions to prohibit an appeal over which it has no authority; Re Brown and Wallace, 6 P.R. 1; *e.g.*, an appeal from a police magistrate: Re Murphy and Cornish, 8 P.R. 420. But there is no authority to interfere where the General Sessions or County Court, on an appeal, over which it has jurisdiction, has given a decision on the legal merits; nor to say whether such decision is right or wrong: R. v. Middlesex, J.J., 2 Q.B.D. 516; Strang v. Gillatly, 8 Can. Cr. Cas. 17.

Prohibition will be granted against a special sessions of the peace in Quebec: Molson v. Lamb, 15 Que. S.C.R. 253.

When prohibition had been granted against the General Sessions of the Peace, the court afterwards refused mandamus to the clerk of the peace requiring him to tax the costs of opposing the appeal in the case: Re Coleman, 23 U.C.R. 615.

Prohibition must be granted as a matter of right, if the total want of jurisdiction appears on the face of the proceedings; and in that case no consent or waiver will deprive the applicant of it: Farquharson v. Morgan (1894), 1 Q.B. 552. But if the want of jurisdiction is not apparent on the proceedings, it is discretionary with the court to grant or refuse prohibition; and it may then be refused if the grounds of want of jurisdiction were not brought by the applicant before the attention of the justice: Farquharson v. Morgan, *supra;* Broad v. Perkins, 21 Q.B.D. 533. If, however, the grounds of want of jurisdiction were brought to the justice's notice, it is the same as if the defect was apparent on the proceedings: Sherwood v. Cline, 17 O.R. 30.

Waiver.

Taking a step in the proceedings is a waiver: Re Jones v. James, 19 L.J. Q.B. 257. But it is not necessary that the applicant should have made personal objection, and had it over-ruled: De Haber v. Portugal, 17 Q.B. 171; see Chapter on "Waiver" *post.*

If any justice who is interested in the subject matter sits on the case, prohibition will be issued against the proceeding; see *post* "Disqualifying Interest." Daigneault v. Emerson, 5 Can. Cr. Cas. 534.

When Application to be Made.

The application for prohibition may be made at the outset of the proceedings, or at the latest stage if the want of jurisdiction is apparent and there remains anything to prohibit: Re Brazill v. Johns, 24 O.R. 209.

An appeal is no bar to prohibition: Harrington v. Ramsay, 8 Exch. 879; Re Rochon, 31 O.R. 122; but pending an appeal, prohibition will not be allowed: Wiltsey v. Ward, 9 P.R. 216.

Costs.

Costs will be allowed to the successful party. The proceeding for prohibition is not one belonging exclusively to the Crown side of the court; but being in the nature of a civil remedy, the Court may exercise its inherent discretion to allow costs: McLeod v. Emigh (2), 12 P.R. 503; Wallace v. Allan, L.R. 10 C.P. 607; R. v. J. J. London (1894), 1 Q.B. 453; R. v. Purley, 6 T.L.R. 37; 5 Can. Cr. Cas. p. 459. Costs should be given unless there has been impropriety on the part of the applicant: Re McLeod v. Emigh 12 P.R. 503; Re London J.J., (1894), 1 Q.B. 453. Costs were refused when the objection was not taken in the court below: Re Murphy and Cornish, 8 P.R. 420; Nerlich v. Clifford, 6 P.R. 212.

To Whom Application to be Made.

The application is made to a judge of the High Court in Chambers (in Ontario); or it may be made to a single judge in court: Con. Rule 1100.

Appeal.

An appeal may be made from a judge to the Divisional Court and to the Court of Appeal; but there is no appeal from the latter to the Supreme Court of Canada: Re Kemp and Owen, 10 M.C.L.J. 269; R. v. Scolly, 6. Can. Cr. Cas. at p. 384; Re Gaynor and Green, 10 Can. Cr. Cas. 21; Code 1025.

The superior courts of criminal jurisdiction have authority to pass rules regulating the practice and procedure in prohibition in criminal cases: Code 576.

No rules under this section have been passed in Ontario; but the application for prohibition is not a proceeding in a criminal matter in any case, and the Ontario Judicature Act and Rules of court in civil matters apply: R. v. Meehan, 5 Can. Cr. Cas. 307.

FORM OF NOTICE OF MOTION FOR PROHIBITION.

In the High Court of Justice.

In the matter of an information (*or* complaint) laid before E.F., justice of the peace in and for the County of   , by A.B. against C.D., for (*set out the charge*).

Take notice that a motion will be made on behalf of the above named C.D. before the presiding Judge in Chambers at Osgoode Hall, in the City of Toronto, on   , the   day of   , 19   (*a judge sits on Mondays and Fridays*), at the hour of   o'clock in the forenoon, or so soon thereafter as the motion can be made, for an order that E.F., Esquire,   , a justice of the peace in and for the County of   , be prohibited from taking any further proceedings in the said matter, and particularly from convicting the said C.D. on the said charge (*or as the case may be*), on the grounds that the said E.F. has no jurisdiction over the same (*or as the case may be, stating the grounds*), and upon grounds disclosed in the affidavit of the said C.D. (and   ), filed herein, or for such other order as may be proper. And take notice that upon such motion will be read the affidavit of the said C.D., this day filed herein (*and any other affidavits*), and the exhibits therein referred to.

Dated this   day of   , A.D. 19   .

(Signed)   G.H.,

Solicitor for the said C.D.

To the said A.B., and to
E.F., Esquire, the said justice.

FORM OF AFFIDAVIT FOR PROHIBITION.

In the High Court of Justice.

In the matter of an information (or complaint) laid before E.B., Esquire, a justice of the peace in and for the County of   , by A.B. against C.D. for (*set out the charge*).

I,   , of the   of   , in the County of (*merchant*), make oath and say:—

1. That I am the above named C.D.

2. That on or about the   day of   , A.D. 19   , an information was laid by the above named A.B., a true copy of which is now shewn to me marked Exhibit A.

3. On the   day of   , A.D. 19   , I was served with the copy of summons thereon, which is now shewn to me marked Exhibit B.

4. That the said matter came on for trial before E.F., of the   or   , in the County of   , a justice of the peace in and for the said county, and I thereupon, through G.H., my counsel or agent (*as 'the case may be*), objected to the jurisdiction of the said justice of the peace to entertain the said information and proceedings, or to hear the said matter, inasmuch as I claimed to justify the said alleged trespass by right and title to the land upon which the said trespass was alleged to have been committed.

5. That I did there and then offer to prove before the said justice that I did *bonâ fide* claim the right and title to the said land, and that the same was my land and freehold (*or whatever other fact or facts were relied on before the said justice as shewing the want of jurisdiction*), and that I had reasonable grounds for my said claim.

6. That the said land upon which the said alleged trespass was supposed to be committed is (*describe the property*).

7. That I did at the time when the said supposed trespass was committed *bonâ fide* claim, and from thence continually hereto have *bonâ fide* claimed and still claim the soil or freehold of the said land (*or as the case may be*) by virtue of a conveyance (*or as the case may be*) thereof heretofore made to me by one G.H., dated the   day of   , A.D. 19   (*or in such other way as the party claims title*).

8. That the said land so alleged to have been trespassed upon is a part of the land so conveyed (*or as the case may be*) as aforesaid; and that the said A.B. in the said proceeding claims the said land adversely to me, and contends, as I believe, that it belongs to him, which, I say, is not the case.

9. That the said justice (*or magistrate*), notwithstanding my first objection, and notwithstanding my said offer to prove my said claim of title, and that I had reasonable ground therefor, did proceed, and is proceeding, to hear and determine the said matter.

Sworn, etc.

The above affidavit may be so framed, and set forth such facts, as are necessary to meet the particular case.

The affidavits are usually intitled in the court merely, and not in any cause: R. v. Plymouth, 37 W.R. 334; Re Miron v. McCabe, 4 P.R. 171; Re Siddall v. Gibson, 17 U.C.R. 98; but it is no objection that they are intitled in the names of the parties, as in the above form: Breeden v. Capp, 9 Jur. 781; Re Burrows, 18 U.C.C.P. 493.

FORM OF ORDER FOR PROHIBITION.

In the High Court of Justice.	Monday, the
The Honourable Mr. Justice	day of
In Chambers.	A.D. 19 .

In the matter of an information laid before E.F., Esquire, a justice of the peace (*or police magistrate*), for the   of   by A.B. against C.D. for (*set out the charge*).

Upon the application of the above named C.D. and upon reading his affidavit filed, and upon hearing the solicitors (*or counsel*) for said A.B. and C.D. and E.F. respectively (*as the case may be*) and it appearing that the said E.F., Esquire, as such justice of the peace (*or magistrate*) has no jurisdiction to hear and determine the said matter, by reason that (*state facts shewing want of jurisdiction*), it is ordered that the said E. F., Esquire, as such justice (*or magistrate*), be and he is hereby prohibited from further proceeding in the matter of the said information; and it is further ordered, that the costs of this application be paid by the said A.B. to the said C.D. forthwith after taxation thereof.

The writ of prohibition is abolished; and an order has the same effect: Con. Rules (Ont.) 1100.

CHAPTER IV

MANDAMUS.

The superior courts of justice are invested with the inherent, prerogative right to compel by mandamus inferferior tribunals and public officials,—such as justices and magistrates—to exercise the jurisdiction which they possess, and to perform any specific act which it is their legal duty to perform. This remedy is intended for those extraordinary cases in which a party would be left without effectual means to compel the performance of some duty in which the applicant is interested; and to the performance of which he has a specific legal right: R. v. Lewisham (1897), 1 Q.B. 498. This is called the Prerogative Mandamus; and is not dependent upon or affected by any enactments.

A legislative right to mandamus has been enacted in Ontario, by R.S.O. 1897, ch. 88, sec. 6, which is as follows:

In all cases where a justice of the peace refuses to do any act relating to the duties of his office as such justice, the party requiring the act to be done may, upon an affidavit of the facts, apply to the High Court, or to the judge of the County Court of the county or united counties in which the justice resides, for an order nisi calling upon the justice, and also the party to be affected by the act, to shew cause why the act should not be done; and if, after due service of the order, good cause is not shewn against it, the court or judge may make the same absolute, with or without, or upon payment of costs, as may seem meet; and the justice upon being served with the order absolute, shall obey the same, and shall do the act required; and no action or proceeding shall be commenced or prosecuted against the justice for having obeyed the order, and done the act required as aforesaid.

This statute is a transcript of the Imperial Act, 11 & 12 Vict. ch. 44, sec. 5.

In other provinces similar legislation exists; and the mandamus so authorized is called a statutory mandamus.

Neither the provincial statutes referred to, nor any other enactments, in any way interfere with the inherent right of the court to issue prerogative mandamus; and either the latter, or the statutory mandamus may be applied for. There is practically no difference; but prerogative mandamus is the usual and appropriate remedy to compel the performance of legal duty by a justice or magistrate.

The authority of the court under the statutes referred to is not extended by such statutes, and is limited to cases in which, before the statutes, mandamus could be issued: R. v. Bristol, J.J., 3 E. & B. 479 (B.); Ex p. McLeod, 25 J.J. 84; and see Glossop v. Heston, 12 Ch. D. 122.

Section 576 of the Criminal Code authorizes the Superior Courts of criminal jurisdiction to pass rules relating to mandamus. No rules have been passed in Ontario expressly under this section; but mandamus is a civil and not a criminal proceeding in any case; and the practice is governed by provincial legislation and rules of court regulating civil procedure: R. v. Meehan, 5 Can. Cr. Cas. 307. So the Ontario Judicature Act, sec. 58 (9), and Con. Rules thereunder, 1080, 1084 to 1093, govern the practice, in all applications for mandamus in Ontario: R. v. Meehan, *supra.*

By Whom It May be Applied For.

The applicant must be a person who has the legal right to the performance of the act required to be done: Ex p. Napier, 18 Q.B. p. 692; R. v. Hertford, 3 Q.B.D. p. 701; R. v. Littledale, L.R. 12 Ir. p. 101; R. v. Lewisham, (1897), 1 Q.B. 498; Peebles v. Oswaldtwistle, (1897), 1 Q.B. 625; R. v. Peterborough, 44 L.J.Q.B. 85.

It will not be granted to a person who has no interest in the performance of the act required; nor to a person who is not applying *bona fide*: R. v. Liverpool Ry. Co., 21 L.J.Q.B. 284 A person who is not a party to the proceedings below has no *locus standi*: R. v. Case (No. 2), 7 Can. Cr. Cas. 212; and the court will exercise its discretionary power to refuse mandamus on behalf of a person who is himself in fault: R. v. Wigan, L. R. 1 App. Cas. 622; R. v. G. W. Ry. Co., 62 L.J.Q.B. 572, 69 L.T. 572.

At What Time It May be Applied For.

There is no statute of limitations applicable to a claim for mandamus: Ward v. Lowndes, 1 E. & E. 940; but it must be

applied for promptly: R. v. West Riding, J.J., 2 Q.B. 505; R.
v. Case (No. 1.), 7 Can. Cr. Cas. p. 211—twelve months being held
too late: Cook v. Jones, 4 L.T. 306. It may be granted at any
stage of the proceedings before the justice, if the latter illegally
refuses to proceed: R. v. Brown, 7 E. & B. 757.

Against Whom Granted.

It will be granted to all inferior tribunals or public officers
upon whom any statutory or legal duty devolves, and is refused;
against justices and magistrates; the clerk of the peace, the
Court of General Sessions: R. v. Kesteven, J J., 3 Q.B. 810; R.
v. Flintshire, J.J., 11 Jur. 185; or a county judge, e.g., in regard
to an appeal from a justice; R. v. Middlesex, JJ., 2 Q.B.D. 516:
Strang v. Gellatly, 8 Can. Cr. Cas. 17. It will not be granted
against the Crown: McQueen v. McQueen, 16 S.C.R. 1; Queen
v. The Lord Commissioners of the Treasury, L.R. 7 Q.B. 387
But it will be granted against an officer of the Crown to compel
the performance of a public duty by him: Re Massey Man. Co.,
11 O.R. 444. So it will be granted to compel the clerk of the
peace to deliver certified copies of records in his office: R. v.
Scully, 5 Can. Cr. Cas. 1.

In What Cases.

Mandamus is not a matter of strict right; but is one as to
which the court is to exercise a judicial discretion; and it will
be granted or refused as the particular circumstances of each
case are deemed to require: R. v. Garland, L.R. 5 Q.B. 269; Re
Wigan, L.R. 1 App. Cas. 622.

If there is some other specific remedy, equally convenient
and adequate, such as an appeal from the justice, the remedy
by mandamus will not be adopted: R. v. Askew, 4 Burr. p. 2188;
R. v. Halls, 3 A. & E. 491; Pasmore v. Oswaldtwistle, (1899), A.
C. 387; R. v. Wigan, L.R. 1 App. Cas. 622; R. v. Joint Stock
Co.'s Registrar, 21 Q.B.D. 131; Re Marter and Gravenhurst,
18 O.R. 243; R. v. Charities Commissioners, (1897), 1 Q.B. 407;
R. v. Mayor of Hastings (1897), 1 Q.B. p. 49, e.g., when an appeal by special case for the opinion of the court is more convenient: Luton Local Board v. Davis, 24 J.P. 677. Mandamus will
not be entertained merely to put in motion the justice when he
has not decided upon his course of action; he must first decide
upon the matter one way or other, and then the court above will

say what the final decision should be: R. v. Kesteven, J.J., 3 Q.B. 810; Ex p. Lewis, 21 Q.B.D. 191. But when the justice declines to act (*e.g.*, upon a claim of right being raised by the defendant) it was held a proper case for an application for mandamus: R. v. Phillimore, 14 Q.B.D. 474; R. v. Biron, 14 Q.B.D. 474. In applications under the statute the right is not confined to those in which the justice needs protection in the discharge of his duties, *ibid*: R. v. Paynter, 7 E. & B. 328.

Mandamus cannot be made the occasion or mere means of obtaining the opinion of the court on some doubtful question of law: R. v. Case, 7 Can. Cr. Cas. p. 206. It is only granted to compel the performance of a duty and not to undo what has been done: Ex p. Nash, 15 Q.B. p. 92.

But even if there is another remedy, mandamus will be granted, if the former is not equally advantageous: R. v. Stewart (1896), 1 Q.B. 303; R. v. Leicester (1899), 2 Q.B. 632; or if the alternate remedy is doubtful, or if the adoption of such remedy might work an injustice: R. v. Garland, L.R. 5 Q.B. 269.

And the court will be vigilant to apply the remedy by mandamus where it is reasonably applicable: Mayor of Rochester v. The Queen, 27 L.J.Q.B. 434.

The application must be for the performance of an act which it is the legal duty of the officer to perform: Ex p. Nash, 15 Q.B. p. 92; R. v. G.W.R. Co., 62 L.J.Q.B. 572; R. v. Bexley, (1898), A.C. 210.

And the officer's jurisdiction must be clear: Pearson v. Glazebrook, L.R. 3 Ex. 27; Trainor v. Holcombe, 7 U.C.R. 548; Re Jackson v. Clarke, 36 C.L.J. 68.

If the justice is interested in the subject matter (see *post*. "Disqualifying Interest") he is right in refusing to take the case, and the court will not compel him to act: Re Co. Judge of Elgin, 20 U.C.R. 588.

The obligation to perform the act must be imperative; and a mandamus will not be ordered to enforce a mere discretionary power, not amounting to an absolute duty: R. v. Mayor of Westlove, 5 Dowl. & Ry. 414; R. v. Bishop of Oxford, 4 Q.B.D. 553.

The word "may" in statutes is construed as permissive or optional, and the word "shall" as imperative: R.S.O. ch. 1, sec. 8 (2) ; R.S.C. ch. 1, sec. 34 (24).

Such is the natural meaning of these words; and the general principle of statutory construction is that the words "may," or "it shall be lawful," or "if he deems it advisable," are in themselves merely permissive, and do not import a duty. But notwithstanding the above general rule of interpretation, if the subject matter shews that it must have been intended that the exercise of the power should be imperative, it will be so: per Crompton, J., Re Newport, 29 L.J.M.C. 53; Julius v. Oxford, L.R. 5 A.C. 214; Paley, 8th ed. p. 41; R. v. Bailiffs, 1 B. & C. 86; Girdlestone v. Allen, 1 B. & C. 61; Re Goodspeed, 7 Can. Cr. Cas. 240.

"May" was held compulsory in McDougall v. Paterson, 11 C.B. 755; and directory in R. v. Bishop, 29 L.J.Q.B. 23.

So when the statute by any of the above mentioned words confers authority upon a judicial officer to do an act, whether judicial or ministerial a duty is imposed to perform the act when the occasion for it arises, and it is applied for by a person entitled to have it done; and it is imperative: Cameron v. Wait, 3 A.R. p. 193.

The word "may" in such cases imports a judicial discretion, and not a power to arbitrarily refuse; but confers authority to consider and decide, which the officer is bound to exercise. As, for instance, a mandamus will be ordered to compel a justice to issue a search warrant under Code 629, the word "may," conferring a power and involving a duty, which must be done upon the arising of the contingency calling for its exercise: see Maxwell on Statutes, 4th ed. 360; Cameron v. Wait, *supra;* McDougall v. Paterson, 11 C.B. 755; Crake v. Powell, 3 E. & B. 210; Aitcheson v. Mann, 9 P.R. 473; Barnardin v. Dufferin, 19 S.C.R. 581; Dwyer v. Port Arthur, 21 O.R. 175; Matton v. The Queen, 5 Ex. C.R. 401.

A power given for the furtherance of justice, or when the thing to be done is for the public benefit, or in advancement of public interest, is given to be exercised, and is a command: R. v. Bishop of Oxford, 4 Q.B.D. p. 553; Julius v. Bishop of Oxford, L.R. 5 A.C. 214; and see cases in Short on Informations 274; Douglas Summary Procedure, 8th ed. 76.

Mandamus will be ordered to compel the performance of judicial as well as ministerial powers; and where the duty is merely ministerial, its performance will be compelled as a matter of course: R. v. Mayor of Fowell, 2 B. & C. 596; R. v. Payne, 6 A. & E. 309.

As a general rule the court in the exercise of its discretion, will refuse to compel a justice by mandamus to issue a warrant of distress or commitment: Ex p. Thomas, 11 J.P. 295; Re Delaney v. McNab, 21 C.P. 563; Ex p. Lewis, 21 Q.B.D. 191; Ex p. Gilbert, 10 Can. Cr. Cas. 38.

If the duty is of a judicial character, its performance will be enforced only where it has been refused, and not where it has been improperly performed. The court will not dictate what judgment another tribunal shall give: R. v. Middlesex (Jus.), 9 A. & E. p. 546; R. v. Case, 7 Can. Cr. Cas. p. 206.

Where a discretion is vested in a subordinate tribunal the court cannot compel a particular course to be adopted: R. v. Carden, 5 Q.B.D. 1; the *bona fide* exercise of the discretion by the tribunal, is a complete justification: Re White v. Galbraith, 12 P.R. 513; Re Jackson v. Clark, 36 C.L.J. 68; Ex p. Cook, 3 Can. Cr. Cas. 72. But where the justice is required by the law to exercise his judicial discretion, he is not at liberty to arbitrarily refuse to perform the act in question, or to refuse to consider the matter; and if he does so, or if he by wrongly deciding a preliminary point of law, or upon extraneous considerations or otherwise, (upon a mistaken view of the law,) improperly refuses to hear a case, or to do what the law provides that it is his duty to do, the court will order a mandamus. But if he really and *bona fide* considers the matter and exercises his discretion, his decision however erroneous, will not be interfered with by mandamus; but it is a ground of appeal from his judgment: R. v. Richards, 20 L.J.Q.B. 352; R. v. J. J. North Riding, 2 B. & C. 291; R. v. Worcester (Jus.), 3 E. & B. 477; R. v. West Rid. (Jus.), 11 Q.B. D. 417; Churchward v. Coleman, L.R. 2 Q.B. 18; R. v. J. J. Middlesex, 2 Q.B.D. 516; R. v. De Rutzen, 1 Q.B.D. 55; R. v. King 20 Q.B.D. 430; R. v. Conolly, 22 O.R. 220; R. v. Bowman (1898), 1 Q.B. 663; R. v. Sharman (1898), 1 Q.B. 578; Re E. J. Parke, 3 Can. Cr. Cas. 122.

The justice's discretion must be exercised *bona fide* and not arbitrarily: R. v. Cumberland (Jus.), 4 A. & E. 695; R. v. Fawcett, 19 L.T. 396; R. v. Adamson, 1 Q.B.D. 201.

Mandamus will be ordered to compel a justice to receive an information, which is a ministerial duty: Code 654, 708; R. v. Kent (Jus.), 14 East, 317; R. v. Richards, 20 L.J.Q.B. 352; Re Monmouth, L.R. 5 Q.B. 251.

On receiving an information a justice is required by Code
655 to hear and consider (personally, so that he may properly
form his judgment: Dixon v. Wells, 25 Q.B.D. 249), the allegations of the complainant, and determine whether further proceedings are warranted or not. This is a judicial act: R. v. Ettinger,
3 Can. Cr. Cas. 387; Hope v. Evered, 17 Q.B.D. 338; Ex p.
Lewis, 21 Q.B.D. 191; Lea v. Charrington, 23 Q.B.D. 45, 272;
and the justice cannot in mere caprice refuse to issue a process.
He must hear the matter and adjudicate, either that a *prima
facie* case is stated, or that even assuming the prosecutor's statement to be true, it is clear that no offence within the justice's
cognizance is shewn; or that it is of too frivolous a character to
justify legal proceedings: Selwood v. Mount, 9 C. & P. 75; R.
v. Bather, 42 L.T. 532; R. v. Huggins, 60 L.J.M.C. 139; R. v.
Ingham, 14 Q.B. 396; R. v. Meehan, 5 Can. Cr. Cas. 312. So, if
the justice holds, contrary to law, that an offence is not indictable, and so he has no jurisdiction to hold a preliminary enquiry,
mandamus will lie to compel him to do so: R. v. Meehan, *supra.*
But the fact that the justice did not appreciate the evidence submitted to him on an application for a warrant of arrest for an
offence, is not a ground for mandamus to compel him to issue a
warrant against his opinion formed in good faith: Thompson v.
Desnoyers, 3 Can. Cr. Cas. 68.

If the justice should act from mere caprice, or opinion as
to what the law ought to be, instead of administering the law as
it is; or if he refuses to proceed upon an erroneous ruling in
regard to a point of law, the court will compel him to hear and
determine the matter, free from such erroneous view: R. v.
Botelier, 4 B. & S. 959; R. v. Durham (Jus.), 19 L.T. 596; R.
v. Gooderich, 19 L.J.Q.B. 413; Fournier v. De Montigny, Q.R.
10 S.C. 292. The test whether the justice has exercised or de-
clined jurisdiction is this: if the objection be such that, whatever
the merits of the case, the justice holds contrary to law that he
can not decide on the merits owing to an objection, (such as that
a claim of right or title to land arises in the case), such holding
is a declining of jurisdiction and not an adjudication: R. v.
Brown, 26 L.J.M.C. 183.

But if he really adjudicates and decides, in the exercise of his
judgment, that the facts do not constitute any offence over which
he has authority, his decision is not open to question on an application for mandamus, but is a subject of appeal: R. v. Paynter,

7 E. & B. 327; R. v. Dayman, 7 E. & B. 672; Ex p. McMahon, 48 J.P. 70; Ex p. Reid, 49 J.P. 600; R. v. Cotham, (1898), 1 Q.B. 802; Re Parke, 30 O.R. 498, 3 Can. Cr. Cas. 122; R. v. Carden, 5 Q.B.D. 1; Re Holland, 37 U.C.R. 214; R. v. Connolly, 22 O.R. 220.

The justice is not bound to announce the reasons for his decision, but it will be assumed that he did his duty properly, unless the circumstances shew the contrary: Thompson v. Desnoyers, 3 Can. Cr. Cas. 68.

But where the facts so clearly established a *prima facie* case that the court saw that the justice's refusal to proceed was really a declining of jurisdiction improperly, a mandamus was issued: R. v. Adamson, 1 Q.B.D. 201.

A mandamus will not be ordered upon improper rejection or reception of evidence: R. v. Yorkshire (Jus.), 53 L.T. 728; R. v. Sanderson, 15 O.R. 106; R. v. Connolly, 22 O.R. 220; nor if the decision is wrong, in law or in fact, as to whether an offence is made out; if the justice has really and *bona fide* exercised his judgment and discretion: R. v. Byrde, 60 L.J.M.C. p. 19; R. v. Blanchard, 18 L.J.M.C. 110. But if he refuses to receive any evidence offered on a material or essential point mandamus will be allowed: R. v. Marsham, 56 J.P. 164.

If, by misconstruing a statute, he decides improperly, that he has no jurisdiction, mandamus will be granted: R. v. Cloete, 64 L.T. 90; or if he refuses to act on any ground from a mistaken view of his jurisdiction amounting to a declining of it: R. v. Fawcett, 11 Cox C.C. 305; R. v. Mead, 77 L.T. 462; (1898) 1 Q.B. 110; or upon considerations outside the provisions of the law: R. v. London (Jus.) (1895), 1 Q.B. 214, 616; R. v. Cotham (1898), 1 Q.B. 802.

If a justice refuses to grant process, the prosecutor is not entitled to require the justice to bind him to prosecute, under Code 688, as that section is only applicable when the defendant has been before the justice and the case is dismissed: Ex p. Reid, 49 J.P. 600; but see Ex p. Wason, L.R. 4 Q.B. 573. And after a summary trial by a police magistrate, on defendant's consent, on a charge of an indictable offence, on which the magistrate dismisses the case, the prosecutor is not entitled to require the magistrate to bind him over to prosecute by indictment, under Code 688: R. v. Burns, 1 O.L.R. 341.

If a justice refuses to hear any evidence for the defence on the ground that it is not so provided by statute, he will be compelled by mandamus to do so, for it is a clear miscarriage of justice, and the refusal to hear one side is the same as if the case had not been heard at all: Re Holland, 37 U.C.R. 214; R. v. Washington, 46 U.C.R. 221; R. v. Sproule, 14 O.R. 375, 384.

But a justice's adjudication as to the reception or rejection of evidence is not open to review on a motion for mandamus: R. v. Yorkshire (Jus.), 53 L.T. 728; R. v. Connolly, 22 O.R. 220; nor upon a question of fact upon which he has adjudicated: R. v. Shiel, 49 J.P. 68; see Re Brighton Sewers Act, 9 Q.B.D. 723.

The court will not compel a justice to proceed with a criminal case arising out of a pending civil proceeding, except so far as is necessary to hold the party to bail; or unless the judge in the civil proceeding so orders: R. v. Ashburn, 8 C. & P. 50; R. v. Ingham, 14 Q.B. 396.

To What Court Application to be Made.

The High Court in Ontario has jurisdiction in mandamus: Re Stratford and Huron Ry. and County of Perth, 38 U.C.R. 156; Toronto Pub. Lib. Board v. Toronto, 19 P.R. 329; and see Re Paris Skating Rink Co., 6 Ch. D. 731.

The Practice.

Ontario Con. Rule 1090 provides for the issuing of a peremptory mandamus in the first instance; and Rule 1091 that the application is to be made upon affidavit to a judge of the High Court in Chambers, upon notice of motion to be served on persons who may be interested in the order (e.g., the defendant and the justice, as the case may be). Rule 1092 provides for an order absolute in the first instance if the judge sees fit; and Rule 1093, that the notice of motion may be served personally or substitutionally, as the judge directs. The mode of procedure mentioned is that generally adopted: see R. v. Scully, 5 Can. Cr. Cas. 1; Toronto Pub. Lib. Board v. Toronto, 19 P.R. 329; Holmsted and Langton's Jud. Act and Rules, 1296. An order nisi may be made upon application to the court if so desired; and if mandamus is applied for under the R.S.O. ch. 88, sec. 6, it is so provided, and that course is the one to be taken. R. v. Scully, 5 Can. Cr. Cas. 1; R. v. Meehan, 5 Can. Cr. Cas. 307.

FORM OF NOTICE OF MOTION FOR MANDAMUS.

In the High Court of Justice.
In the matter of an information (*or* complaint) laid before E.F., Esquire, a justice of the peace in and for the County of
by   A.B. against C.D.
for (*set out the charge*).

Take notice that a motion will be made in behalf of the above named A.B. before the presiding judge in Chambers at Osgoode Hall in the City of Toronto, on   day, the   day of   , A.D. 19   , at the hour of   o'clock in the forenoon, or so soon thereafter as the motion can be made, for a mandamus requiring the said E.F., Esquire, as such justice, (*state the proceeding required, for example*, "to take the recognizance of the said A.B. to prefer and prosecute an indictment against the said C.D. before the court by which the said C.D. would be tried if the said E.F. had committed him for trial on the charge above mentioned.") or for such other order as may be proper.

And take notice that upon such motion will be read the affidavit of   , filed herein, and the exhibits therein referred to.

Dated this   day of   , A.D. 19   .
To the said C.D.

                    (Signed)   G.H., Solicitor for the said A.B.
and to the said E.F.

AFFIDAVIT FOR MANDAMUS.

In the High Court of Justice.
In the matter of, etc. (*as in the above notice of motion*).
I, A.B. of the   of   in the County of
          (*occupation*) make oath and say:—

1. I am the above named prosecutor in the matter above mentioned.

2. That on the   day of   A.D. 19   , at the   of   in the County of   I duly laid an information on oath before E.F., Esquire, a justice of the peace in and for the said County of   , a true copy of which information is now shewn to me, marked exhibit "A." to this my affidavit.

3. That on the   day of   A.D. 19   , the said matter came on to be heard at the said   of   before the said justice in the presence and hearing of the said C.D., and of myself, and all witnesses called by both parties having been duly examined in the presence and hearing of the said C.D. and myself, and the said matter having been duly heard, the said E.F. as such justice dismissed the charge and discharged the said C.D.

4. That immediately thereupon, and at the said time and place, I, as the prosecutor, verbally informed the said justice that I desired to prefer an indictment respecting the said charge, and I then and there verbally required the said justice to bind me over to prefer and prosecute such an indictment before the Court at which the said C.D. would have been tried if the said justice had committed him for trial, and I then and there offered to enter into the recognizance required by section 688 of the Criminal Code of Canada.

5. The said justice answered my said request by saying that he would not bind me over or take any further step in the said matter (*or otherwise setting out what the justice said, in answer to the request*) and the said justice then and there refused and still refuses to accede to or comply with my said request, and to bind me over to prefer and prosecute an indictment as hereinbefore stated.

Sworn, *etc.*

The affidavit must shew a demand and a refusal; and must state distinctly what was demanded, how the demand was made, and how answered: Re Bruce, 11 C.P. 575; Re Peck & Peterborough, 34 U.C.R. 129; Young v. Erie and Huron Ry. Co., 27 O.R. 530; Re Irving v. Askew, 28 L.T. 84; R. v. Pontypool, 71 L.T. 17; Re Guillot and The Sandwich & Windsor G. R. Co., 26 U.C.R. 246. But when the officer's affidavit in answer to the motion shed that he had refused to act, and it appeared the demand if made would have been refused, this removed all objection to the want of proof of demand: Re Davidson & Miller, 24 U.C.R. 66.

ORDER FOR MANDAMUS.

In the High Court of Justice.
The Honourable Mr. Justice.
                    In Chambers.
        the   day of
        19 .
In the matter of, etc. (*as in the above form of notice of motion.*)
Upon the application of the above named A.B. (*or as the case may be*), upon reading the notice of motion served herein that an order of mandamus do issue, directed to E.F., requiring him to (*here state the duty to be performed, or the thing to be done, as claimed or ordered*), and the affidavit of service thereof upon reading the affidavits of A.B. and G.H., and upon hearing the counsel or solicitor for the said A.B., C.D., and E.F., (*as the case may be*) and it appearing that (*here insert the necessary inducements and averments*).
It is ordered peremptorily that the said E.F. be and he is hereby commanded that he do forthwith after the service hereof (*here insert the duty to be performed, or the thing to be done as ordered*).
And it is hereby further ordered that the costs of this application be paid by the said C.D., to the said A.B., forthwith after taxation thereof.
                                        Clerk in Chambers.

The notice of motion takes the place of the order nisi, and the order when granted is usually an absolute and peremptory order in the first instance: see Re Board of Education v. Napanee, 29 Grant 395, Holmsted and Langton, 1297, 1302.

The writ of mandamus is abolished by Con. Rule 1080; and the order has the same effect.

If an absolute and peremptory mandamus is not issued the order nisi will provide for the act being done unless cause to the contrary is shewn by a return to be made. In that case the justice may make a return shewing reasons why he has not done what is required.

Return to Mandamus.

A return must be made to the mandamus; shewing why the act required was not done; or that the mandamus has been complied with; and the return should be very minute: Con. Rule (Ont.) 1085; R. v. Southampton, 1 B. & S. 5. As to the sufficiency of the return: see R. v. Mainwaring, El. B. & E. 474; R v. King, 20 Q.B.D. 430.

The return may state according to the fact that the justice has obeyed the order and done what was required; giving particulars to shew that there has been a real compliance; or in case of an order nisi the return may justify the non-performance of the matter in question; and in that event the facts must be fully and explicitly stated and the grounds fully given, shewing such justification; so that the court may be able to judge of the legality or otherwise of the reasons offered for not doing the act in question; e.g., by stating facts shewing that the justice heard the statements of the prosecutor and any witnesses he produced and duly considered the information and evidence and came to the conclusion that no criminal offence was disclosed; or that the alleged offence arose wholly in another county and the defendant was not present or residing in the justice's county and so the latter had no jurisdiction; or such other sufficient facts and grounds according to the circumstances of the case; see notes in Holmsted and Langton's Jud. Act and Rules p. 1298.

FORM OF RETURN.

Indorse on the back of the order the fallowing:

The answer and return of E.F., one of His Majesty's justices of the peace (or police magistrate) for the   of   to this order appear in the schedule hereunto annexed.

E.F.
J.P.

SCHEDULE.

I. E.F., one of His Majesty's justices of the peace (or police magistrate) for the   of   do most humbly certify and return, in accordance with the annexed order, as follows:

1. That I have (*if the return is in obedience to the mandatory part of the order, the words in that part of the order should be inserted here in the past, instead of the future, tense*) as by the said order I am commanded.

E.F. (Seal).
J.P. (or P.M.).

The return with the order is to be filed in the proper office.

No return is admissible to an order absolute, except explicit obedience thereto.

Attachment for Default.

If a return is not made to an order nisi, a peremptory order will be issued; and if a return is not made to a peremptory order, it is a contempt of court: Con. Rule (Ont.) 1085; and it may be enforced by process of attachment: Con. Rule 1093; Demorest v. Midland Ry. Co., 10 P.R. 82.

The application for attachment is made, on notice of motion, to a judge of the High Court in Chambers, on an affidavit of the service of the order, and an affidavit of search, and of no return being filed in the proper office.

Amendment of Return.

Clerical errors may be allowed to be amended.

Objections to Return.

If the return is evasive, or frivolous; hypothetical or uncertain, a motion may be made to quash it: Con. Rule (Ont.) 1089; or a motion for attachment or to commit for contempt may be made: Con. Rule 1085, 1093. See also Rule 882: Holmsted and Langton 1299.

Amendment.

The court cannot, on application for mandamus, amend the conviction in question; and the provisions of the Criminal Code as to amendment of an invalid conviction do not apply: R. v. Case, 7 Can. Cr. Cas. 204.

Costs.

The costs of the application are in the discretion of the judge, and are usually, though not necessarily granted to the successful party: R. v. Surrey, J.J., 14 Q.B. 684; R. v. Harding, 6 T.L.R. 53, 157; R. v. London, J.J., (1894), 1 Q.B. 453; R. v. Meehan, 5 Can. Cr. Cas. 312. Costs will generally be refused if the question was a fairly arguable one: Coswell v. Cook, 11 C.B. (N.S.) 242; and see Re Brookfield v. Township of Brooke, 12 P.R. 485.

Appeal.

An appeal lies from a judge to the Divisional Court: R. v. Meehan, 5 Can. Cr. Cas. at p. 310; Atty.-Gen. v. Scully, 5 Can. Cr. Cas. 1; and to the Court of Appeal, Atty.-Gen. v. Scully, 6 Can. Cr. Cas. 167.

There is no appeal to the Supreme Court of Canada: Atty. Gen. v. Scully, 6 Can. Cr. Cas. at p. 384.

Statutory mandamus under R.S.O. ch. 88 sec. 6, may be granted by a judge of the County Court; and an appeal from his decision is given by sec. 52 of ch. 55 of the County Courts Act: see R. v. Meehan, 5 Can. Cr. Cas. at p. 310.

If an application for mandamus is dismissed, a second application will not be entertained; unless perhaps if the first application was dismissed on a technicality: R. v. Mayor of Bodmin, (1892), 2 Q.B. 21.

CHAPTER V.

APPEAL AND CASE STATED.

The Right of Appeal,

In any form, exists only when it is given by statute, either expressly or by necessary implication; and the procedure to be employed therein must be distinctly laid down by statute: R. v. London, JJ., 25 Q.B.D. 360; Superior v. Montreal, 3 Can. Cr. Cas. 379.

A provision by statute for an appeal, without the same or some other statute providing any procedure by which it is to be exercised, would be wholly ineffectual and illusory; and so, the procedure, when provided, must be strictly and implicitly followed.

Provisions of the Criminal Code.

An appeal and the procedure to be adopted, are provided by sections 749-761 of the Criminal Code, from the decision of a justice of the peace, in any case in which he acts, under his summary jurisdiction under Part XV. (sections 705-770), of the Criminal Code, and either convicts (or makes an order), or dismisses the information.

Case Stated.

Sections 761-769 also provide for an appeal, and procedure thereon, by way of *case stated* upon the ground that the justice's decision is erroneous in point of law, or is in excess of his jurisdiction and authority. The first named appeal is upon the merits of the case; including the legal merits: R. v. Gilmour, 7 Can. Cr. Cas. at p. 217; R. v. Bombadier, 11 Can. Cr. Cas. 216; and the only means by which the justice's finding on the facts and merits of the case can be reviewed, is by appeal under sections 749-760; R. v. Urquhart, 4 Can. Cr. Cas. 256.

Case stated under Code 761-769 is an appeal only upon a point of law or jurisdiction. Upon a pure question of jurisdiction, however, the appropriate remedy is by certiorari, rather than by case stated: Re Ruggles, 5 Can. Cr. Cas. 163.

In What Cases Appeal Lies.

These provisions as to appeal and case stated, under the above sections of the Criminal Code, only have reference to a case in which the charge is for an offence against the Criminal Code or some law having force throughout Canada; and not to a case for an alleged offence under a provincial law. The latter is dealt with by provincial statutes regarding appeals; and will be presently mentioned with reference to appeals under Ontario Statutes.

Cases before Police Magistrates.

The above mentioned provisions of the Criminal Code for appeal and case stated, are also limited to cases of summary convictions or orders, by justices of the peace when acting under Part XV. of the Cr. Code (the summary convictions clauses); and do not apply to cases of convictions by police magistrates on summary trials of indictable offences, Code 798: R. v. Egan, 1 Can. Cr. Cas. 112; R. v. Racine, 3 Can. Cr. Cas. 446; R. v. Bougie, 3 Can. Cr. Cas. 492; R. v. Portugais, 5 Can. Cr. Cas. 100. Sections 749-769 are comprised in Part XV. (the summary convictions clauses) of the Cr. Code; and Code 706 provides that the provisions of Part XV. shall apply only to matters under Canadian Statutes punishable on summary conviction or order.

So also the provisions in Code 749-769 do not apply to convictions or orders by police magistrates, even in summary convictions cases, tried by them as such, but which are also within the summary jurisdiction of a justice of the peace under Part XV. and appealable if tried by the latter. There is no appeal from a police magistrate in any case tried by him as such magistrate, except as specially provided by Code 797 (which will be presently mentioned), and by Code 1013 and 1014 which only apply to summary trials under Code 777 for the indictable offences there mentioned.

But the same right of appeal lies from a police magistrate as from a justice of the peace, when he is merely acting as an *ex officio* justice; *e.g.*, in a case summarily tried by a police magistrate for a town, for an offence committed in the same county, but not within the town.

Appeal is expressly provided by Code 797 from a conviction by a police magistrate or any of the functionaries mentioned in

7—MAG. MAN.

Code 771 (except a judge of a Superior Court in Saskatchewan or Alberta); upon a conviction for an offence under Code 773 (a), for theft, false pretences or receiving stolen property, not exceeding $10 in value; or under Code 773 (f) for keeping or being an inmate of a disorderly house. Such appeal lies, notwithstanding Code 776 declares the jurisdiction of certain magistrates to be absolute: R. v. Wirth, 5 B.C.R. 114. The provisions of Code 749-760 and the procedure there laid down apply to these appeals. It will be observed that the appeal last mentioned is confined to a case of *conviction,* and not of *dismissal* of the charge. This appeal lies *in all the provinces,* including the N.W. Territories; the reasons for holding that the appeal would not lie in the N.W.T., given in R. v. McLennan, 10 Can. Cr. Cas. 14, not being now applicable, under Code 797. As above mentioned an appeal, by reservd case on a question of law only, is provided by Code 1013-1014, from any conviction by a magistrate proceeding under Code 777, on the trial of one of the offences there referred to. This appeal will be referred to separaately, under "Reserved Case" *post.*

Sections 749-769 do not apply to this appeal, which is governed by sections 1013-1014 only.

Where Appeal Provided for by a Particular Statute.

In some cases the particular statute relating to the offence prohibits any appeal from a conviction under it, and such prohibition will prevail: while, in other cases, special provisions and procedure regarding appeals are made by the particular statute. In such last mentioned cases Code 749-769, or such portions of them, as may be inconsistent with such special Act, are excluded by their terms, which make them applicable "unless it is otherwise provided by any special Act." But such portions of these clauses as are not inconsistent with the provisions of the special Act, are to be read into the latter provisions: R. v. McIntosh, 2 Can. Cr. Cas. 114. And the special appeal provided by the Fisheries Act, R.S.C. ch. 45, sec. 103, to the Minister of Marine and Fisheries, does not take away the general right of appeal under the Criminal Code, but is additional thereto: R. v. Townsend, 5 Can. Cr. Cas. 143.

1. APPEALS FROM SUMMARY CONVICTIONS UNDER PART XV. OF THE CRIMINAL CODE—CODE 749-760.

To what Court Appeal to be made.

Unless it is otherwise provided in any special statute, under which a conviction takes place, or an order is made by a justice for the payment of money, or dismissing an information or complaint, any person who thinks himself aggrieved by any such conviction or order or dismissal, may appeal: Code 749

In Ontario:—If the conviction adjudges *imprisonment only,* the appeal is to be to the Court of General Sessions of the Peace; and in *all other cases* to the Division Court of the division of the county in which the cause of complaint arose: Code 749(*a*).

In Quebec:—The appeal in all cases is to the Court of Kings Bench, Crown side: Code 749(*b*). An appeal under the Seamen's Act of Canada, for an offence committed in Quebec, must be taken under this section to the Crown side of the Court of King's Bench, and not under Code 1013 (formerly 742), to the appeal side: R. v. O'Dea, 3 Can. Cr. Cas. 402.

In Nova Scotia, New Brunswick and Manitoba:—The appeal is to the County Court of the district or county where the cause of complaint arose: Code 749 (*c*).

In British Columbia:—To the County Court, at the sittings thereof held nearest to the place where the cause of complaint arose: Code 749(*d*).

In Prince Edward Island:—To the Supreme Court: Code 749(*e*).

In Saskatchewan and Alberta:—To a judge of the Supreme Court of the N.W.T. pending the abolition of that court; and thereafter, to a judge of such court as may be substituted for the Supreme Court of the N.W.T.: Code 749 (*f*). A court called the Supreme Court of the Province of Saskatchewan, has been recently established there; and a similarly named Court in Alberta. These now take the place of the former Territorial Court named.

In the North-West Territories:—To a stipendiary magistrate: Code 749(*g*).

In the Yukon:—To a judge of the Territorial Court: Code 749(*h*).

In Nipissing (*Ont.*) :—To the general sessions of the peace
for Renfrew County, when the conviction adjudges *imprisonment only;* and in *all other cases* to the Division Court of Renfrew County, held nearest to the place where the cause of complaint arose; or at the nearest place thereto where a court is appointed to be held: Code 749(2).

Who May Appeal.

The appeal may be taken by the prosecutor or complainant,
as well as by the defendant: Code 749.

The defendant may appeal although he pleaded guilty before
the justice. That plea only concludes him as to the matter
stated in the information or charge upon which he was
tried; and he may shew that the conviction is bad in law,
or upon an objection to the information or summons taken
before the justice and over-ruled by him. A person may
plead guilty and be convicted, and yet the conviction be
bad in law and liable to be quashed on appeal: R. v. Brook, 7
Can. Cr. Cas. 216. But the case of a defendant who has pleaded
guilty before the justice, should not be re-opened, and witnesses
called on the merits, in order to revise the punishment, if the
justice has not acted oppressively: R. v. Bowman, 2 Can. Cr.
Cas. 89.

A party who has been convicted and paid his fine, may nevertheless appeal, if he paid under compulsion and protest: Ex p.
Mason, 13 U.C.C.P 159; or with any intimation of an intention
of appealing; but not if he paid the fine voluntarily: R. v.
Neuberger, 6 Can. Cr. Cas. 142. In *Ex p. Mason, supra,* the defendant said he would pay his fine, and paid it; but stated also
that he would see further about it; and the court held that
there was no waiver of the right to appeal; which should not
be taken away on any doubtful ground. In R. v. Tucker, 10.
Can. Cr. Cas. 217, the payment of the fine accompanied by enquiries for information as to time allowed for appeal, was held
not to be a waiver. Code 749 gives an appeal to either party
who "thinks himself aggrieved," by the conviction or order.
But that does not mean a person who groundlessly fancies he is
aggrieved; but one who has some legal ground for it: Harrup v.
Bailey, 6 E. & B. 218. So a person who has pleaded guilty, is
not a party aggrieved, so far as the facts relating to his guilt

or innocence are concerned, as to which he is estopped by his plea: R. v. Gilmore, 7 Can. Cr. Cas. p. 218.

Where an information was laid by an individual describing himself as an agent for a society named, the society is not a party aggrieved, and has no *locus standi* to appeal; Canadian Society v. Lauzon, 4 Can. Cr. Cas. 354, and see Robinson v. Curry, 7 Q.B.D. 465.

Code 749 does not authorize an appeal under it on a conviction for an offence under a provincial statute; and has no application to such a conviction, any appeal from which is the subject for provincial legislation only: Lecourse v. Hurtubise, 2 Can. Cr. Cas. 521. In Ontario the practice and procedure in appeal and case stated has been assimilated to that provided by the sections of the Cr. Code now under consideration: R. S.O. 1897, ch. 90, s. 8, amended by 1 Edw. VII. ch. 13, s 2.

When Certiorari Barred by Appeal.

Code 1122 provides that certiorari shall not be allowed to remove any conviction or order if the defendant has appealed; nor any order or conviction made on such appeal. But this does not take away the right to certiorari if the appellate court has acted without jurisdiction, or in excess if it: see ante, "Certiorari": Ex. p. Bradlaugh, 3 Q.B.D. 509; Colonial Bank v. Willan, L.R. 5 P.C. 443; *e.g.*, when the appellate court refused to hear evidence other than that given before the justice: R. v. Washington, 46 U.C.R. 221.

Notice of Appeal.

The appellant must give notice of appeal in writing, by filing in the office of the clerk of the court appealed to, and serving the respondent with a copy thereof, a notice in writing setting forth, with reasonable certainty, the conviction appealed against, and the court appealed to, within ten days after the conviction or order complained of was made: Code 750(*b*).

NOTICE OF APPEAL AGAINST A CONVICTION OR ORDER.

To C.D., of   , (*the name and addition of the* prosecutor).

Take notice, that I, the undersigned A.B. of   intend to enter and prosecute on appeal at the next general sessions of the peace in and for the County of   (or of the Division Court of the County of   , *as the case may be*) to be holden at   , in the County of   , against a certain conviction (or order) bearing date on or about the day of   , instant, and made by J.S., Esquire, a justice of the

peace in and for the said County of   whereby I, the said A.B., was
convicted of having (*or* was ordered to pay   , *here state the offence
as in the conviction;* or *the amount* ordered *to be paid, etc., as correctly as
possible*).

Dated at   this   day of   , one thousand nine
hundred and

                                                            A.B.

The above notice may of course be changed to suit the case of
an appeal by the prosecutor.

The notice need not state that the appellant is a "party
aggrieved" by the conviction or order appealed from: R. v. Jordan, 5 Can. Cr. Cas. 438.

Requisites of the Notice.

The notice must state with reasonable certainty the conviction or order appealed against; and a notice of appeal purporting to be from a conviction for "looking on" while persons were playing in a common gambling house, (Code 229)
is not a good notice of appeal from a conviction for "playing in" a common gambling house, (Code 229): R. v. Ah Yin,
(Cy. Ct. Vancouver), 6 Can. Cr. Cas. 63. A notice stating
merely to what judge and place the appeal was to be made, but
not stating "to the next sittings" of the Court, nor when that
would be, is insufficient: R. v. Brimacombe, 10 Can. Cr. Cas.
169. The wording of the section in the Cr. Code 1906, is the
same as that of 1892 under which this decision was given.

Notice to be Addressed to the Opposite Party.

A notice not addressed to the respondent and not served
personally upon him is invalid; but if it is served personally on
the respondent, although not addressed to him, it would
seem to answer the rquirements of Code 750 (*b*) in
the Act of 1906. It was so held under the similar
clause in the English statute in R. v. Essex, JJ., (1892),
1 Q.B. 490; Doe v. Wrightman, 5 Esp. 5, and in some Canadian
cases, but contrary in several other cases under the Criminal
Code of 1892: see Cragg v. Lamarsh, 4 Can. Cr. Cas. 246.
The latter were decided on the ground that the form
of notice N.N.N. in the Criminal Code of 1892 was addressed to the respondent, and the Act required this form, or
one to the same effect, to be used; and so the English decisions
did not apply, as the English Act did not furnish any form of
notice of appeal; see R. v. Jordan, 5 Can. Cr. Cas. 438, and the

cases cited there and in 5 Can. Cr. Cas. at p. 161. But the Criminal Code, of 1906, has omitted the form of notice of appeal; and the reasons on which the Canadian decisions (requiring the notice to be addressed to the respondent), were founded seem to be removed; and section 750(b) of the Criminal Code being similar to that in the English Act, the decisions there would seem to apply: See also R. v. Davitt, 7 Can. Cr. Cas. 514 and notes.

Notice to be Signed.

Code 750 (b) does not expressly require the notice to be signed by any person; and the same reasons for holding a notice not addressed to any person to be sufficient, would be applicable to the omission of a signature to it if the name of the party giving the notice is mentioned in it. The reasons, given in R. v. Bryson, 10 Can. Cr. Cas. 398, and in the cases cited in that decision for so holding, are even more cogent now that the form of notice is omitted from the statute, than they were when that decision was given. A notice signed on the appellant's behalf, by his solicitor, is undoubtedly a sufficient compliance with the statute: R. v. Nichol, 40 U.C.R. 76; R. v. Kent, J.J., L.R. 8 Q.B. 305. The proper practice of course, is to address the notice to the respondent, and to have it signed by the appellant or his solicitor.

Service of the Notice.

Personal service is not required in express terms, by the Act; and where not so required, is not imperatively demanded in any case, unless the purpose of a notice is to charge the party with contempt of court for not performing some act, required by the document served: Ward v. Vance, 9 C.L. J. 214; 3 P.R. 130. Service by leaving the copy of the notice at the place of residence of the respondent, with some grown-up person residing there is sufficient: R. v. N.R. of Yorkshire, J.J., 7 Q.B. 154; and cases cited in Bicknell and Seager D.C. Act 198. Personal service is expedient and should be made when possible.

Service of the notice on Sunday is void: Paley, 8th ed. 380: see "Sundays and Holidays" *post*.

When Notice to be Served.

The ten days within which it must be served and filed under Code 750(b), are computed from the day on which the justice announced his decision and made the minute of adjudication required by Code 727; and not from the time of making out the formal record of conviction, if the latter is done afterwards, as it may be, (see the same section); and which may be transmitted to the court appealed to at any time before the appeal is to be heard: Code 757: See R. v. Derbyshire (Jus.), 7 Q.B. 193; Ex p. Johnson, 3 B. & S. 947. The time for appealing from a judgment begins to run when the decree or order for judgment is put into intelligible shape, so that the parties may clearly understand what they have to appeal from, (such as the minute of adjudication must be, see *post,* "Summary Convictions,"), and not from the entry of formal judgment: Koksilah Quarry Co. v. The Queen, 5 B.C.R. 600.

The day next following that on which the decision was announced will be the first day counted; and the day of serving the notice will be excluded: Radcliffe v. Bartholomew (1892), 1 Q.B. 161. If the last day for service falls on a holiday the notice may be served on the next following day which is not a holiday: R.S.C. ch. 1, sec. 31 (*h*); R.S.O. ch. 1, s. 8, 17: see "Sundays and Holidays" *post.*

Filing Notice of Appeal.

The notice must be both filed and served within the ten days: Code 750(*b*).

To What Sitting.

If the conviction or order is made more than fourteen days before the sitting of the court to which the appeal is given, the appeal is to be to the then next sitting of that court: but if less than fourteen days, then to the second sitting after such conviction or order: Code 750.

The "sittings of the court" refers to the sittings fixed by law; and not to sittings which had begun within the fourteen days, but were adjourned, the adjourned sittings taking place after the fourteen days: R. v. Bombadier, 11 Can. Cr. Cas. 217.

Fourteen *clear* days is meant, so that an appeal from a conviction made on or before, say, 28th May, would have to be to the sitting beginning on, say, 12th June; but if the conviction was after the 28th May, and the next sitting began on 12th June, the appeal must be to the second sitting, *e.g.,* in Ontario to the December general sessions.

The general sessions in Ontario are held on the second Tuesday in June and December, R.S.O. ch. 56, sec. 4: except in the County of York, where they are held on the first Tuesday in March and December, and the second Tuesday in May and September: sec. 4(2).

The Second Notice.

By Code 750(b) a second notice is now required to be given to the respondent or his solicitor, *at least* five days before the hearing of the appeal, setting forth the grounds of the appeal. This notice must be given five *clear* days before the first day of the sitting of the court appealed to, excluding both the day on which the notice is given and the first day of the sitting of the court appealed to: R. v. Middlesex, J.J., 14 L.J.M.C. 139; R. v. Sallop, J.J., 8 A. & E. p. 173; R. v. Thornton, 11 Can. Cr. Cas. 71; R. v. Dolliver, 10 Can. Cr. Cas. 405. This notice and the previous one may possibly be combined in one notice; but, if so, would have to be filed and served within the ten days provided by Code 750(b).

FORM OF THE FIVE DAYS' NOTICE GIVING GROUNDS OF APPEAL.

In the Court of General Sessions of the Peace (or in the Division Court) for the County of

In the matter of the appeal, from the conviction of the appellant, by E. F. Esquire, justice of the peace for the said county, dated the day of A.D. 19 , for (*state the charge as in the conviction*).

Between
A.B.
Appellant.
and
C.D.
Respondent.

Take notice that the following are the grounds of the appeal herein:

1. That the said A.B. is not guilty of the offence stated in the said conviction.

2. That the said justice had no jurisdiction to convict the said A.B., the alleged offence not having arisen within the territorial limits of the said justice (*or stating any other grounds on which is contended the justice had no jurisdiction over the case*).

3. That the evidence taken before the said justice did not disclose any criminal offence, for which the said A.B. could be convicted.

4. (*And proceed to state any other grounds*).

5. And upon such other grounds as appear upon the proceedings and conviction.

Dated, etc.

To C.D.,
The Respondent and to G.H., Esq., his solicitor.

A.B.,
Appellant.

The giving of both of the above notices is a condition precedent to the due lodgment of the appeal; and if not implicitly complied with, the appeal is not duly lodged, the court appealed to has no jurisdiction to hear the appeal, and the objection cannot be waived or cured: R. v. Middlesex, J.J., 12 L.J.M.C. 59; R. v. Oxfordshire, J.J., I M. & S. 446; Alderson v. Pallister, 70 L.J.K.B. 935; R. v. Dolliver, 10 Can. Cr. Cas. 405. The court appealed to can only hear the appeal on the grounds stated in the notice; and cannot quash the conviction, even if invalid, on grounds not so expressly stated: R. v. Boultbee, 4 A. & E. 498.

Other Requirements of Appeal.

The N.W. Terr. ordinance requiring an affidavit to be filed by the appellant denying his guilt, is not *ultra vires,* not being inconsistent with the provisions of the Criminal Code: and the omission to file such affidavit within the time limited, goes to jurisdiction, and cannot be waived or cured: Cavanagh v. McIlmoyle, 6 Can. Cr. Cas. 88.

Waiver of Right to Appeal.

The taking of certiorari proceedings is a waiver of the right to appeal: Denault v. Robida, 8 Can. Cr. Cas. 501.

And by Code 769 any person who appeals by way of case stated under Code 761, shall be taken to have abandoned his right to appeal under Code 749, finally and conclusively and to all intents and purposes.

Recognizance on Appeal.

If the appeal is from a conviction adjudging imprisonment, the appellant must either "remain in custody until the holding of the court to which the appeal is given," or enter into a recognizance, Form 51 to the Cr. Code, before a county judge, clerk of the peace or any justice of the peace for the county in which the conviction was made with two sufficient sureties conditioned personally to appear at the court and try the appeal, and abide by the judgment on appeal, and pay such costs as may be awarded by the court: Code 750 (c).

The recognizance is good, and the proceedings are regular, even if the defendant was not "in custody" when the recognizance was given: R. v. Jordan, 5 Can. Cr. Cas. 438.

The recognizance must be taken before a justice for the county in which the conviction was made; and if taken before a justice for another county it is invalid, the appeal is not properly launched, and the court appealed to has no jurisdiction to hear the appeal: R. v. Johnston, 8 Can. Cr. Cas. 123; R. v. Robinet, 16 P.R. 49.

Upon giving the recognizance, the appellant, if in custody, is to be liberated by the justice: Code 750(c).

If the appeal is from a conviction awarding only a penalty or sum of money to be paid, without directing imprisonment on default of payment, the appellant need not give any recognizance on appeal.

Time within which Recognizance to be Given.

The recognizance need not be entered into within the ten days required for giving the notice of appeal: but it must be given and filed in the appellate Court, before the sittings of the court appealed to, begin: Kent v. Olds, 7 U.C.L.J. 21. It is too late if this is not done before the opening of the court: Bestwick v. Bell, 1 Terr. L.R. 193; McShadden v. Lachance, 5 Can. Cr. Cas. 43.

The giving of the recognizance is a stay of proceedings on the conviction, by the justice; but until the recognizance is entered into he may proceed to enforce the conviction, notwithstanding the notice of appeal: Simington v. Colbourne, 4 Can. Cr. Cas. 367.

FORM OF RECOGNIZANCE ON APPEAL: FORM 51 CR. CODE.

Canada.   ⎫
Province of   ⎬
County of   ⎭ .

Be it remembered that on the   day of   A.D. 19 , A.B. of the   of   , in the County of   (occupation), and C.D. of the   of   , in the County of (occupation), and E.F. of the   of   in the County of (occupation), personally came before the undersigned, G.H., a justice of the peace in and for the said County of   , and severally acknowledged themselves to owe to our Sovereign the King the several sums following, that is to say, the said A.B. the sum of   the said C.D. the sum of   , and the said E.F. the sum of   . each (*the amount filled in should be double the amount of any money penalty, and the costs awarded by the conviction and the probable costs of the appeal*), of good and lawful money of Canada to be levied on their several goods and chattels, lands and tenements respectively, to the use of our said Sovereign the King, his heirs and successors, if the said A.B. fails in the condition hereunder written.

Taken and acknowledged the day and year first above mentioned at the   of   , in the County of   , before me.

(Signed)   G.H.

J.P., County of

The condition of the above written recognizance is such that if the said A.B. personally appears at the (next) general sessions of the peace; (*or name the court to which the appeal is made according to Code* 749) to be holden at the   of   , in the County of   , on the   day of   , A.D. 19 , in and for the said County of   , and tries an appeal against a certain conviction bearing date the   day of   A.D. 19 , and made by me the said justice of the peace for the County of   , whereby he, the said A.B., was convicted for that he the said A.B. did at   in the said County of   on the   day of   A.D. , (*set out the offence as stated in the conviction*) and also abides by the judgment of the court upon such appeal and pays such costs as are by the court awarded, then the said recognizance to be void, otherwise to remain in full force and virtue.

(Signed)   G.H.

J.P.

Notice of Recognizance.

Notice of recognizance—Form at the end of Form 51 to the Cr. Code—should be given by the justice to the parties bound by it. The omission to do so, however, will in no way effect the appeal; the notice, being merely a matter of proceedure by the justice, is directory to him, and does not affect the proceedings.

FORM OF NOTICE OF RECOGNIZANCE TO BE GIVEN TO THE APPELLANT AND HIS SURETIES.

Take notice that you, A.B., are bound in the sum of   , and you, L.M. and N.O., in the sum of   , each, that you the said A.B. will personally appear at the next general sessions of the peace (*or as the case may be, naming the court appealed to*) to be holden at   , in and for the said County of   , and try an appeal against a conviction (or order) dated the   day of   , (*instant*), whereby you A.B. were convicted of (or ordered, etc.), (*stating offence or the subject of the order shortly*), and abide by the judgment of the court upon such appeal and pay such costs as are by the court awarded, and unless you the said A.B. personally appear and try such appeal and abide by such judgment and pay such costs accordingly, the recognizance entered into by you will forthwith be levied on you, and each of you.

Dated at   , this   day of   , one thousand nine hundred and   .

(Signed)   G.H.

J.P.

Several Appellants.

Where there are several appellants there must be two sureties besides the appellants, (who must also be joined in the recognizance) : R. v. Joseph, 6 Can. Cr. Cas. 144.

Defects in Recognizance,

If the word "personally" is omitted from the condition in the recognizance, for the appellant's appearance at the court, the recognizance is void, the appeal has not been properly lodged and the appeal cannot be heard. Ex p. Sprague, 8 Can. Cr. Cas. 109. The object of that condition in the recognizance is to secure personal appearance so as to give the court control over the appellant's person: *ibid.* But the omission of the words "try such appeal" was held to be immaterial, if the appellant actually appeared to prosecute: R. v. Tucker, 10 Can. Cr. Cas. 217.

The sureties must be *sufficient;* (Code 750(c); and they may be required by the justice before whom the recognizance is entered into, to justify, either by affidavit, or by being sworn and examined before the justice as to their property, etc.; and if the sureties and recognizance are sufficient the justice has no authority to refuse to act upon it on the ground of the insufficiency of the notice of appeal, as that is a matter for the Appellate Court only: R. v. Carter, 24 L.J.M.C. 72.

Sufficiency of Sureties is for the Justice.

The sufficiency of the sureties and recognizance is, however, a matter for the justice alone, before whom it is entered into; and it will not be enquired into by the court appealed to; and so the absence of an affidavit of justification is no objection to the appeal: Cragg v. Lamarsh, 4 Can. Cr. Cas. 246.

It is not for the justice to assume the determining whether the appeal is in time; that is for the court appealed to: R. v. Slavin, 38 U.C.R. 557.

The justice must see however that he has proof of the sureties' sufficiency: Cragg v. Lamarsh, 4 Can. Cr. Cas. 246. The sureties need not be freeholders; it suffices if they have property enough of any kind. A person who is not a resident of the county should not be accepted as a surety: R. v. Lyon, 9 C.L.T. 6.

In case of an appeal by a corporation, it was said in the case of Sourthern Cos. Bank v. Boaler, 11 T.L.R. 568, that it is the practice to accept the recognizance of some member of the corporation—usually a director—with the usual sureties: and see R. v. Manchester, J.J., 7 E. & B. 453.

Money Deposit Instead of Recognizance, Abolished.

It will be noticed that the alternative of depositing money as security on appeal, (which was provided for in the Criminal Code of 1892), instead of recognizance, has been omitted from the statute of 1906: and a recognizance must now be entered into in every case.

Transmission of Conviction, etc., to Court.

The justice is required to transmit the conviction or order appealed from, to the court to which an appeal is given, *before* the time the appeal is to be heard; there to be kept among the records of the court: Code 757.

In Ontario the papers must be sent to the clerk of the peace, if the appeal is to the general sessions; or to the clerk of the Division Court, if the appeal is to the latter court.

It is for the appellant to see that this is done, and that the papers with recognizance are on file before the opening of the court, and that all of the conditions upon which an appeal is allowed by the statute have been strictly complied with, otherwise the appeal is not duly lodged and cannot be heard: R. v. Gray, 5 Can. Cr. Cas. 24; McShadden v. Lachance, 5 Can. Cr. Cas. 43; Ex p. Cowan, 9 Can. Cr. Cas. 454; R. v. Joseph, 6 Can. Cr. Cas. 144; R. v. Neuberger, 6 Can. Cr. Cas. 142. And any defect therein cannot be cured, as it goes to jurisdiction: R. v. Dolliver Mining Co., 10 Can. Cr. Cas. 405; Re Meyers and Wonnacott, 23 U.C.R. 611.

Entering the Appeal.

The provisions of provincial Acts or rules of court requiring an entry of the appeal to be filed with the registrar or clerk of the court: see Gibson v. Adams, 10 Can. Cr. Cas. 32; do not apply to appeals under the Criminal Code; the only conditions essential to the hearing of the appeal are those comprised in the sections of the Criminal Code; and these do not require the appeal to be formally entered with the clerk of the court. It is usual, however, to so enter the appeal.

Proceedings on the Hearing of Appeal.

At the opening of the court appealed to it is for the appellant to call the person who served the notices before mentioned, and prove the due service of them. The conviction or order is presumed not to have been appealed against until the contrary is shewn: Code 757(2).

It is then for the respondent to begin; and to produce evidence to sustain the charge against the accused; and unless he does so the court may quash the conviction: Whiffin v. Bligh, (1892) 1 Q.B. 362.

Adjournments of Hearing.

The court (if the proof of service of the notice has been made at the opening of the count), may adjourn the hearing of the appeal from time to time, and from one sitting to another or others of the court, if in the interests of justice; but such adjournments must be "by order, endorsed on the conviction": Code 751(3). This last provision as to endorsing the order on the conviction is probably directory merely and the failure to endorse the written order of the court on the back of the conviction, will not invalidate the order.

No Jury.

On the trial of an appeal under the Criminal Code there was at no time any right to a jury: R. v. Washington, 46 U.C.R. 221; R. v. Bradshaw, 38 U.C.R. 564; nor is there now any authority for the court to allow a jury: Code 881: R. v. Malloy, 4 Can. Cr. Cas. 116. The sections of the Criminal Code, which are the authority for the appeal and the procedure thereon, do not provide for a jury; and any provincial statute providing for a jury on an appeal under provincial laws, will not apply to an appeal under Dominion law. Although it is expressly provided by Code 749 (3), that appeals under the Code in Saskatchewan, Alberta, the N.W.T. and the Yukon are to be tried without a jury, this provision does not furnish affirmative legislation by implication that a jury can be allowed elsewhere, in the absence of express authority for so doing.

Procuring Attendance of Witnesses.

Witnesses anywhere in the province may be required to attend, by subpœnas issued out of the court appealed to: Code 971 providing that every witness duly subpœnaed to attend and give evidence at any criminal trial shall be bound to attend. Code 972, 973, contain provisions for enforcing this.

A witness in Canada but not in the province may also be compelled to attend on a subpœna in like manner as if he was a resident in the province: Code 974. Code 975, 976 provide the means of compelling obedience to the subpœna.

In R. v. Gillespie, 16 P.R. 155, Chancellor Boyd, held that an order for a subpœna to a witness in Canada, but out of the province to attend at the hearing of an appeal to the general sessions in Ontario, might be made by a judge of the High Court or County Court under Code 584 (now 676); as Code 843 (now 711), which incorporates Code 584 (now 676), declares that the provisions of the latter, as to procuring attendance of witnesses, shall apply to "any hearing" under the summary convictions clauses of the Criminal Code; and these words are large enough to cover, not only the hearing before the justice, but also the hearing of an appeal from the action of the justice.

But it would seem that a subpœna for any witness anywhere in Canada is authorized by Code 974, without an order.

Hearing the Appeal.

When the appeal has been lodged in due form in compliance with the requirements of the statute, the court appealed to is to hear and determine the matter of the appeal, and make such order therein, with or without costs to either party, including costs of the court below, as seems meet to the court; and in case of a dismissal of an appeal by the defendant, and the affirmance of the conviction or order, the court shall order and adjudge the appellant to be punished according to the conviction, or to pay the amount adjudged by the order, and to pay such costs as are awarded; and shall if necessary issue process for enforcing the judgment of the court: Code 751. And the court is to try, and shall be the absolute judge as well of the facts as of the law, in respect to such conviction or order: Code 752.

The court is empowered to consider the law as it affects the whole conviction. See further as to the powers and duty of the court: R. v. Tebo, 1 Terr. L.R. 196; McLellan v. McKinnon, 1 O.R. 238; R. v. Lizotte, 10 Can. Cr. Cas. 316.

Any of the parties may call witnesses and adduce evidence, either as to credibility of witnesses or any other material fact, whether such witnesses were called or evidence was adduced at the hearing before the justice or not: Code 752(2); see R. v.

Washington, 46 U.C.R. 221; and any evidence taken before the justice at the hearing, certified by the justice, may be read on the appeal and shall have the same effect as if the witness was there examined, if the court is satisfied by affidavit or otherwise that the personal attendance of the witness cannot be obtained by any reasonable efforts: Code 752(3)

Depositions as Evidence.

Code 881, in the statute of 1892, (now 752), required that the deposition before the justice, in order to be receivable as evidence must have been "signed by the witness" as well as being certified by the justice. The requirement as to signature of the witness is omitted in sec. 752, the Criminal Code of 1906; as it is not essential that depositions before a justice on a summary trial should be signed by the witness.

FORM OF AFFIDAVIT TO LET IN DEPOSITIONS AS EVIDENCE ON APPEAL, UNDER CODE 752(3).

In the Court of General Sessions of the Peace for the County of   ,
(or in the   Division Court of the County of   , as the case may be).

In the matter of an appeal.
Between

      A.B.

                        Appellant.

             and

      C.D.

                        Respondent.

I,   , of the   of   , in the County of   (occupation, e.g., constable, or as the case may be), make oath and say:

1. That on the   day of   A.D. 19 , I was directed on behalf of (the appellant or respondent, as the case may be) to serve a subpoena or summons then delivered to me for that purpose upon one,   , of the   of   in the County of   (occupation), who was one of the witnesses, and who gave evidence at the hearing of the said charge before   , Esquire, the convicting justice, in order to obtain the personal attendance of the said   as a witness at the present sitting of this court on the hearing of the appeal herein now pending in said court.

2. That on the   day of   , A.D. 19 , I accordingly, called at the place of residence of the said   , at the said   for the purpose of serving him with the said subpoena and enquiring there for the said   , I was informed by the wife of the said (or as the case may be, shewing the person to be a grown up resident of the place mentioned), that the said   was not then at home. I then stated to the said wife of the said   (or other person spoken to) the nature of my business, and told her (or him) that I would call again for the purpose of serving the said subpoena at   (naming the day and hour at which the call was to be made), and that I accordingly

8—MAG. MAN.

*(here state whatever calls were made and other attempts to effect service,
and if the witness has a place of business, shew what efforts were made to
serve him there; also, state what the persons seen at the witness' residence
and place of business said in reply to the questions asked as to the where-
abouts of the witness, giving the questions and answers. If the witness has
gone abroad, shew if possible where he is alleged to have gone to, and state
such facts and circumstances as would satisfy the court that all reasonable
efforts have been made to obtain the personal attendance of the witness to
give evidence. What the officer said; and the answers to his questions
should be distinctly stated: Dubois v. Lowther, 4 C.B. 228; Fisher v. Good-
win, 2 C. & J. 94; Tomlinson v. Goatley, L.R. 1 C.P. 230).*

3. That I have made all resonable efforts and used all due means in
my power to serve the said   with the said subpœna, and to procure
his personal attendance at the hearing of the said appeal, and I have not
been able to do so.

Sworn, etc.

What will be deemed reasonable efforts, depends upon the
circumstances of each particular case; as to that: see R. v. Nelson, 1 O.R. 500; Tomlinson v. Goatley, L.R. 1 C.P. 236; Stroud's
Dic. 1670; Re Hibbert and Schilbroth, 18 O.R. 399; Cannington
v. Willoughby, 23 Sol. J. 230; Re Turner (1897), 1 Ch. 536; Re
Kay (1897), 2 Ch. at p. 519; Perkins v. Bellamy (1899), 1 Ch.
800. These cases furnish various illustrations of the subject.

If the personal attendance of the witness cannot be obtained
in consequence of his illness or death, this must be proved by a
witness who knows the fact otherwise than by hearsay: Robinson v. Maskes, 2 M. & Rob. 375. Sickness must be such as to
preclude the hope of the witness attending the trial within a
reasonable time: Beaufort v. Crawshay, L.R. 1 C.P. 699; Davis
v. Lowndes, 7 Dowl. 101.

A similar form of affidavit to the above may be used on an
appeal from a conviction under an Ontario law, the proof required being that witness is ''dead, or so ill as not to be able to
attend and give evidence, or is absent from Ontario,'' or after
diligent enquiry cannot be found to be subpœned: R.S.O. ch. 90,
sec. 10.

Objections to Convictions.

No objection is to be allowed to any information, complaint,
summons or warrant to apprehend, for any defect therein in
substance or in form, or for any variance between the information or process and the evidence adduced at the hearing before
the justice, unless it is proved before the court hearing the appeal that such objection was made before the justice, and that,
notwithstanding it was shewn to the justice that by such vari-

ance the defendant was deceived or misled, the justice refused to adjourn the case to some further day: Code 753.

It was held under the Summary Convictions Act of British Columbia, which contains similar provisions to Code 753, that the objection that a by-law under which the defendant was convicted was *ultra vires*, could not be taken on appeal, if the defendant pleaded guilty and did not raise the objection before the justice; even if he was not then aware of the invalidity of the by-law: R. v. Bowman, 2 Can. Cr. Cas. 89; see Rogers v. Cavanagh, 27 C.P. 537; and see R. v. Poirier, 19 C.L.T. 378. And on an appeal from a conviction upon a plea of guilty, the case will not be re-opened to revise the punishment imposed, if the justice has not acted oppressively: R. v. Bowman, *supra;* and see *ante,* p. 100.

Powers of the Court.

If the appeal is by the defendant, and it is dismissed and the conviction affirmed, the court must order and adjudge the appellant to be ·punished according to the justice's conviction, or to pay the amount adjudged by the justice's order, and to pay such costs as the court may award: Code 751.

It was held in R. v. Surrey (Jus.), (1892) 2 Q.B. 721, that the court has no jurisdiction to modify the punishment awarded by a valid conviction by the justice. This was under similar provisions to sections 751, 754 of the Cr. Code. The provisions in the latter, which would seem to empower the court to ''modify the decision of the justice'' or ''make such other conviction or order in the matter as the court thinks just,'' and ''exercise any power which the justice might have exercised,'' apply only when the justice's conviction is invalid or the punishment imposed, or the order made, was in excess of the justice's jurisdiction. Otherwise the measure of punishment is for the justice and not for the court appealed to; and Code 751 so provides.

If the conviction is quashed, an order is to be endorsed on the conviction accordingly: Code 751 (4); and a copy of the conviction and order certified by the clerk of the court is evidence: Code 751(5).

Enforcement of Order on Appeal.

In either result of the appeal the court may, if necessary, issue its own process for enforcing its judgment against either party according to the result: Code 751, 754(3); or if the appeal against a conviction or order is decided in favour of the respondent, the justice who made the conviction or order, or any other justice for the same "territoral division," may issue the warrant of distress or commitment as if no appeal had been brought: Code 756; and for that purpose the clerk of the court appealed to is to remit the conviction and all papers, except the notice of appeal and recognizance, to the justice: Code 757(4).

By Code 754 the court, notwithstanding any defect in the conviction or order, or that the punishment or order was in excess of the justice's jurisdiction is, on the appeal, to hear and determine the charge or complaint upon the merits, and may confirm, reverse or modify the justice's decision, or make such other conviction or order as the court thinks just; and may by its order exercise any power which the justice might have exercised, and any such conviction or order shall have the same effect, and be enforced in the same manner, as if it had been made by the justice; and any conviction or order made by the court on appeal, may also be enforced by process of the court itself: Code 754.

Abandonment of Appeal before Hearing.

The appellant may at any time abandon the appeal, by giving to the opposite party six *clear* days' notice in writing before the sitting of the court appealed to: Code 760. The six days are to be reckoned exclusively of both the day of serving the notice and the first day of the sittings of the court: R. v. Aberdare, 14 Q.B. 854; Re Sams and Toronto, 9 U.C.R. 181.

FORM OF NOTICE OF ABANDONMENT OF APPEAL.

In the Court of General Sessions of the Peace for the County of
(or in the   Division Court of the County of
In the matter of an information (*or* complaint) laid before   ,
Esquire, a justice of the peace in and for the County of   , by
A.B. against C.D. for that (*set out the charge*).

Take notice that I do hereby abandon my appeal to this court against the conviction of me, the said C.D., for the alleged offence above mentioned.

Dated this   day of   , A.D. 19
                                        C.D.,
                                        by E.F., his Solicitor.

Costs.

On hearing and determining the appeal the court may award costs against either party; including the costs of the proceedings in the justice's court: Code 751, 754.

On dismissing the defendant's appeal and confirming the conviction, the court may order the appellant to pay such costs as the court may award: Code 751.

The provisions of Code 754 are wide enough to include the costs of a successful appeal by the prosecutor; and his costs may be added to the amount awarded on conviction of the defendant by the court appealed to; and payment may be enforced by distress and imprisonment on default: R. v. Hawbolt, 4 Can. Cr. Cas. 229.

On the appellant giving notice of abandonment of his appeal, as above mentioned, no order of the court for costs or otherwise, is necessary: Code 760 providing that in that event the justice is to add the costs of the appeal, so far incurred, to the amount already adjudged against the appellant, if any; and proceed on the conviction as if there had been no appeal; viz., by distress, and commitment on default; inserting a clause in the warrants, adding the costs of appeal: Code 760.

Costs when Appellant Neither Serves Notice of Abandonment, nor Appears at the Hearing.

In that event, the court may, upon proof of the respondent having been served with the notice of appeal, make an order, at the sittings for which the notice was given, for the payment by the appellant of the respondent's costs; although the notice of appeal was invalid; and such costs may be recovered in the same way as costs on the hearing of an appeal are recoverable: Code 755(2); that is, either by estreating the recognizance, or by the means provided by Code 759.

Costs when both Parties Appear, but the Appeal is Dismissed upon a Preliminary Objection to the Appeal Proceedings.

In R. v. Ah Yin No. 2, 6 Can. Cr. Cas. 66, it was held that there is nothing comprised in the provisions of the Criminal Code which would include authority to award costs in the case of an appeal which is prosecuted, but dismissed on the ground of some objection to the appeal proceedings; there being no authority to award costs not specifically provided for by statute; and so no costs could be awarded in such case. But in Ex p. Sprague, 8 Can. Cr. Cas. 109, the Supreme Court of New Brunswick held that there is authority to award costs in such circumstances. See also the decision to the same effect in R. v. Dolliver,

10 Can. Cr. Cas. 405; and the authorities cited in the judgments in these cases, and in 8 Can. Cr. Cas. at pp. 119-122. These latter authorities appear to correctly state the law that there is authority to award costs.

Costs must be applied for and awarded, if at all, at the sittings for which notice of appeal was given, or one to which the hearing of the appeal was adjourned as above mentioned; there is no jurisdiction in any subsequent general sessions, or sittings of the Appellate Court, to deal with the question of costs: McShadden v. Lachance, 5 Can. Cr. Cas. 43; Bothwell v. Burnside, 4 Can. Cr. Cas. 450.

But after the court has given judgment and fixed the costs, and nothing remains to be done but to issue the order, that may be done by the clerk of the court after the close of the session, and the order dated as of the first day of the session; and no subsequent session can interfere by amendment or otherwise with an order ·made on appeal: Re Rush and Bobcaygeon, 44 U.C.R. 199.

The amount of the costs must also be fixed at the sittings at which the appeal is heard; and cannot be referred to the clerk of the court, as he has no authority; but the judge, before issuing the order, may direct the costs to be taxed by the clerk of the court, for the judge's guidance in fixing the amount to be inserted in the order: R. v. McIntosh, 28 O.R. 603.

On quashing the conviction appealed from, the costs must be fixed and included in the formal order; and an order referring the costs to the clerk of the peace for taxation was quashed :⁹ Re Bothwell and Burnside, 4 Can. Cr. Cas. 450; Re Rush and Bobcaygeon, 44 U.C.R. 199.

The costs of appeal include solicitors' costs and counsel fees, if any, if the appeal is from a conviction for an offence against the Criminal Code or any other Dominion statute, although there may be no express provision by such statute for the payment of such costs: R. v. McIntosh, 28 O.R. 603.

Quantum of Costs.

There is no provision as to the scale of costs, and no tariff of same; but by Code 751, 754, they are entirely in the disposal of the judge, who may make any reasonable allowance in his discretion; R. v. McIntosh, *supra*.

To Whom the Costs are to be Ordered to be paid.

The order must direct the costs to be paid to the clerk or other proper officer, of the court appealed to: to be paid over by him to the person entitled to the same; and the order must state within what time the costs are to be paid: Code 758.

Enforcement of Order for Payment.

If the costs are not paid as directed by the order, and the party ordered to pay them has not been bound by recognizance to pay the costs, the clerk of the peace is to so certify:—Form 52 to the Cr. Code;—on application of the person entitled to the costs and on payment of the officer's fee; and on production of the certificate to any justice of the county, he may enforce payment of such costs by warrant of distress: Form 53 to the Cr. Code; and in default of distress, by warrant of commitment: Form 54 to the Cr. Code; for not more than one month, unless the same and the costs of distress and commitment and of conveying the party to prison, (if the convicting justice so orders), are sooner paid: Code 759. The amount of these costs is to be stated in the commitment.

FORM OF CERTIFICATE UNDER CODE 759.
Form 52.

Office of the clerk of the peace for the County of   (or of the Division Court of the County of   ).

I hereby certify that at a court of general sessions of the peace (or, *the name of the court to which the* appeal *was made, as the case may be*), holden at   , in and for the said county, on   last past; an appeal by A.B. against a conviction (or order) of J.S., Esquire, a justice of the peace in and for the said county, came on to be tried, and was there heard and determined, and the said court of general sessions (*or other court, as the case may* be) thereupon ordered that the said conviction (or order) should be confirmed (*or* quashed), and that the said (*appellant*) should pay to the said (*respondent*) the sum of   for his costs incurred by him in the said appeal, and which sum was thereby ordered to be paid to the clerk of the peace for the said county, on or before the   day of   (*instant*), to be by him handed over to the said (*respondent*), and I further certify that the said sum for costs has not, nor has any part thereof, been paid in obedience to the said order.

Dated at   , this   day of   , one thousand nine hundred and

(Seal of Court).

G.H.,
Clerk of the Peace.

(*or* Clerk of the   Division Court, County of   ).

WARRANT OF DISTRESS FOR COSTS OF AN APPEAL AGAINST A CONVICTION OR ORDER. FORM 53.

Canada,
Province of $\left. \begin{array}{c} \\ \bullet \\ \\ \end{array} \right\}$
County of

To all or any of the constables and other peace officers in the said county of   .

Whereas A.B. of the   of   in the County of (*occupation*) was on the   day of   A.D. 19 , duly convicted before   , a justice of the peace in and for the County of   , for that (*set out the offence as stated in the conviction*) [*or* if the appeal was from an order for the payment of money the following will be substituted for the above recital—see Form 40 to the Cr. Code:— "Whereas on the   day of   , A.D. 19 , a complaint was made before   , a justice of the peace in and for the said county, for that (*set out the matter complained of as in the order*), and thereupon the matter of the said complaint having been considered, the said A.B. was adjudged to pay the said C.D. the sum of   , on or before the   day of   , A.D. 19 , and also to pay to the said C.D. the sum of   for his costs in that behalf]. And whereas the said A.B. appealed to the court of general sessions of the peace (*or other court, as the case may be*), for the said county, against the said conviction or order, in which appeal the said A.B. was the appellant, and the said C.D. was the respondent, and which said appeal came on to be tried and was heard and determined at the last general sessions of the peace (*or other court, as the case may be*) for the said county, holden at   , on   ; and the said court thereupon ordered that the said conviction (*or* order) should be confirmed (*or* quashed) and that the said (*appellant*) should pay to the said (*respondent*) the sum of   , for his costs incurred by him in the said appeal, which said sum was to be paid to the clerk of the peace for the said county (*or* to the clerk of the said Division Court) on or before the   day of   , one thousand nine hundred and   , to be by him handed over to the said C.D.; and whereas the clerk of the peace of the said county (*or* to the clerk of the said Division Court) has, on the   day of (*instant*), duly certified that the said sum for costs had not been paid: *These are, therefore, to command you, in His Majesty's name, forthwith to make distress of the goods and chattels of the said A.B., and if, within the term of   days next after the making of such distress, the said last mentioned sum, together with the reasonable charges of taking and keeping the said distress, are not paid, then to sell the said goods and chattels so by you distrained, and to pay the money arising from such sale to the clerk of the peace for the said County of   , (*or* to the clerk of said Division Court) that he may pay and apply the same as by law directed; and if no such distress can be found, then to certify the same unto me or any other justice of the peace for the same county, that such proceedings may be had therein as to law appertain.

Given under my hand and seal this   day of   in the year   , at   , in the county aforesaid.

                                        O.K.,   [*seal.*]
                                        J.P., (*County of*   ).

CONSTABLE'S RETURN TO A WARRANT OF DISTRESS.

I, J.K., Constable, of the   of   , in and for the County of   , hereby certify to   . Esquire, a justice of the peace for the County of   , that by virtue of this warrant I have made diligent search for the goods and chattels of the within named A.B. and that I can find no sufficient goods or chattels of the said A.B. whereon to levy the sums mentioned in the within warrant.

Witness my hand, this   day of   , A.D. 19
                    (Signed)
                                        J.K.,
                                                Constable.

WARRANT OF COMMITMENT FOR WANT OF DISTRESS IN THE LAST CASE.

FORM 54.

Canada,
Province of   ,
County of   .
To all or any of the constables and other peace officers in the said County of   .

Whereas (etc., as in form 53 to the asterisk* and then thus): And whereas, afterwards, on the   day of   , in the year aforesaid, I, the undersigned, issued a warrant to all or any of the peace officers in the said County of   , commanding them, or any of them, to levy the said sum of   , for costs, by distress and sale of the goods and chattels of the said A.B.; And whereas it appears to me, as well by the return to the said warrant of distress of the peace officer who was charged with the execution of the same, as otherwise, that the said peace officer has made diligent search for the goods and chattels of the said A.B., but that no sufficient distress whereupon to levy the said sum above mentioned could be found: These are, therefore, to command you, the said peace officers, or any one of you, to take the said A.B., and him safely to convey to the common gaol of the said County of   , at   aforesaid, and there deliver him to the said keeper thereof, together with this precept: And I do hereby command you, the said keeper of the said common gaol, to receive the said A.B. into your custody in the said common gaol, there to imprison him (and keep him at hard labour) for the term of   , unless the said sum and all costs and charges of the said distress (and for the commitment and conveying of the said A.B. to the said common gaol amounting to the further sum of   , are sooner paid unto you the said keeper; and for so doing this shall be your sufficient warrant.

Given under my hand and seal this   day of   , A.D. 19 , at the   of   in the County aforesaid.

(Signed)
   O.K.,   [seal]
   J.P., County of

Appeal from Order for Restoration of Mined Metals.

The provisions of Part XV. of the Criminal Code (secs. 749-769) relating to appeals from summary convictions by justices, are, by Code 750(d), made applicable to an order made by a justice under Code 637 for the restoration of mined metals.

On such an appeal the appellant is to give security by recognizance to the value of the property, to prosecute his appeal at the "next" sittings of the court, and to pay such costs as are awarded against him: Code 750(d).

The notices and procedure is, in other respects, the same as in other appeals under Code 749-760.

Appeal Does Not Abate by Death of Parties.

The appeal does not abate by the death of the informant: R. v. Fitzgerald, 1 Can. Cr. Cas. 420.

Case Reserved for Court of Appeal.

The court or judge who hears an appeal from a summary conviction may state a case at the request of either party, upon any queston of law, for the opinion of the Court of Appeal: Code 1013, 1014; and if the judges of the Court of Appeal are unanimous in their decision, it is final; otherwise there is an appeal to the Supreme Court of Canada: Code 1013 (2), (3), 1024.

If the court or judge refuses to reserve a case for the opinion of the Court of Appeal, an application may be made to the latter, for leave to appeal; and if leave is granted, a case is to be stated as if the question of law had been reserved by the judge: Code 1015-1016. For fuller provisions see sections 1017-1018.

Certiorari and Motion to Quash Order on Appeal.

Certiorari will be granted by the superior courts of criminal jurisdiction, to bring up the proceedings taken before the justice, and the order and proceedings on appeal, for the purpose of a motion to quash an order on appeal; but only on the ground of absence or excess of jurisdiction of the Appellate Court: *e.g.* on the grounds of defects in the notice of appeal or recognizance; or that the conviction was by a police magistrate, and so there was no right of appeal, or that the defendant had paid his fine voluntarily, and so had waived his right to appeal; or on any ground on which the Appellate Court acted without or in excess of jurisdiction: R. v. Tucker 10 Can. Cr. Cas. 217.

2. CASE STATED BY A JUSTICE, ON THE SUMMARY TRIAL OF AN
· OFFENCE AGAINST A DOMINION LAW, UNDER PART
XV. OF THE CRIMINAL CODE.

Any person aggrieved, the prosecutor or complainant, as well as the defendant, who desires to question a conviction, order, determination, or other proceeding of a justice under Part XV. (the summary convictions clauses), of the Cr. Code, *on the ground that it is erroneous in point of law, or is in excess of jurisdiction,* may apply to such justice to state and sign a case, setting forth the facts of the case as found by the justice, and the legal grounds on which the proceeding is questioned; and if the justice declines to state the case, the party may apply to "the court" for an order requiring a case to be stated: Code 761. This mode of appeal is only for the purpose of the review of questions of law; and if it is desired to review both facts and law, the appeal must be taken under Code 749: see *ante* p. 112; when the whole case as to facts and law may be tried, *de nova*: R. v. McNutt, 33 N.S.R. 14, 4 Can. Cr. Cas. 392.

Nor does it apply to cases of offences tried by *magistrates,* under Part XVI. of the Cr. Code: R. v. Egan, 1 Can. Cr. Cas. 112; R. v. Racine, 3 Can. Cr. Cas. 446. But it applies to a conviction by two justices, in a case tried by them under Part XVI. Code 773 (*a*) or (*f*); as the right of appeal is specially provided in such case, by Code 797; and "case stated" is a mode of appeal: R. v. Robert Simpson Co., 2 Can. Cr. Cas 272; R. v. Oland, 8 Can. Cr. Cas. 206.

To What Court.

The term "the court" to which this appeal lies under Code 761 means any superior court of criminal jurisdiction for the province in which the proceedings referred to are carried on; and the Superior Courts of Criminal jurisdiction, are stated by Code 2, sec. 35, to be in Ontario, the High Court of Justice for Ontario; in Quebec, the Court of King's Bench; in Nova Scotia, New Brunswick, British Columbia and the North West Territories, the Supreme Court; in Prince Edward Island, the Supreme Court; and in Manitoba the Court of Appeal or the Court of King's Bench (Crown side); in the provinces of Saskatchewan and Alberta, the Supreme Court of the North West Territories, until the same is abolished, which has now been done; the Supreme Court of these provinces respectively being substituted; in the Yukon, the Territorial Court.

The right of appeal, under Code 749, is barred by taking a proceeding by way of case stated: Code 769.

When the right of appeal is taken away by any special Act, there can be no appeal by case stated: Code 769 (2).

When, and how, Application to be Made.

Application to the justice to state a case, must be made within such time and in such manner as is from time to time directed by rules or orders to be made under Code 576: Code 761 (2). In Ontario, no Rules or orders have been passed under this provision, and there is no other provision limiting the time within which the application must be made; and the application for the case need not be made in writing; R. v. Bridge, 54 J.P. 629. In other provinces where such Rules have been passed, the provisions as to form, manner and time of the application to the justice, must be strictly complied with; as defects therein go to the jurisdiction of the court to hear the case, and they cannot be waived or cured; and the objection on the grounds of such defects may be raised even when the case comes on for argument before the court: R. v. Early No. 1, (N.W.T) 10 Can. Cr. Cas. 280; Cooksley v. Nakasheba, 5 Can. Cr. Cas. 111; and if such Rules so require the request to the justice must be in writing; R. v. Early No. 2, 10 Can. Cr. Cas. 337.

These cases relate to the requisites of the application and its form, as laid down in the Terr. Sup. Ct. Rules 1900, (given in full at page 337, 10 Can. Cr. Cas.), which provide the practice, requiring the application to be in writing, and to be made within four days of the "making of the conviction," i.e. the decision in the case by the justice and not the making out of the formal conviction; see ante p. 104. The provisions of the Criminal Code, secs. 761, 762 as to procedure on the application to the justice, also go to jurisdiction and must be strictly followed, otherwise the court will have no authority to hear and determine a case which has otherwise been duly stated: see the above cases: also South Staffordshire v. Stone, L.R. 19 Q.B.D. 168; Lockhart v. St. Albans, 21 Q.B.D. 188. If two or more justices sit on the case, application must be made to all of them: Westmore v. Payne (1891), 1 Q.B. 482; and the minority of such justices have no power to state a case. Ib.

FORM OF APPLICATION TO JUSTICE TO STATE A CASE: CODE 761.

To E.F., Esquire, a justice of the peace for the County of (*or to E.F. and G.H., Esquires, justices, etc., as the case may be*).

Pursuant to sec. 761 of the Criminal Code, I the undersigned, C.D., the person named in the conviction hereinafter mentioned, desire to question the said conviction of me, the said C.D. made by you on the **day of** A.D. 19 , for that (*state the charge*) on the ground that the said conviction is erroneous in point of law (*or is in excess of jurisdiction*) for the reasons herein stated: And I do hereby apply to you to state and sign a case setting forth the facts of the case and the grounds on which the same is questioned by me as aforesaid, to wit:

1. (*State the points of law desired to be raised; or the grounds on which excess of jurisdiction is claimed.*)

Dated   day of   A.D. 190

C.D.

by J.K.

his Solicitor.

Refusal of Justice to State a Case.

If the justice is of opinion that the application is merely frivolous, but not otherwise, he may refuse to state a case, and shall, on the request of the applicant, sign and deliver to him a certificate of such refusal; Code 763. But the justice cannot refuse to state a case where the application is made to him by or on behalf of the Attorney-General of Canada, or of any province: Code 763.

FORM OF CERTIFICATE OF REFUSAL TO STATE A CASE UNDER CODE 763.

I, , a justice of the peace in and for the County of do certify at the request of C.D., who was on the day of A.D. 19 , summarily convicted before me on the information of A.B. for (*state the charge*) that after the said conviction was made, namely, on the day of A.D. 19 , the said C.D. desiring to question the said conviction on the ground that it is erroneous in point of law in that (*state the ground of objection*), or that the same is in excess of my jurisdiction as such justice (*or as the case may be*), applied to me as such justice to state and sign a case setting forth the facts of the case and the grounds on which the said conviction is questioned. And I further certify that the said application being in my opinion merely frivolous (*or if the question proposed to be raised is one of fact and not upon a point of law or jurisdiction and so not the proper subject of a case stated, so state*). I did thereupon refuse to state a case thereon; and this certificate thereof is signed and delivered by me to the said C.D. at his request pursuant to section 763 of the Criminal Code of Canada.

Given under my hand at the of in the County of this day of A.D. 19 .

_____ _____

The justice of the peace above named.

For form of certificate of refusal on other grounds than that it was frivolous, *e.g.*, that it was not on a point of law or jurisdiction, etc., see 52 J.P. 235; R. v. Bridge, 24 Q.B.D. 609.

Upon What Points a Case May be Stated.

It was held under the construction put upon the language
of R.S.C. 1886, ch. 174, sec. 259, which provided for the reservation of questions of law "arising on the trial" that only
questions so arising could be made the subject of a case stated:
R. v. Gibson, 16 O.R. 704; R. v. Barnett, 17 O.R. 649;
and not those, arising before or after the trial; R. v. Murray,
1 Can. Cr. Cas. at p. 456; Moran v. The Queen, 18 S.
C.R. 407; R. v. Faderman, 1 Den. C.C. 565; Brisbois v. The
Queen, 15 S.C.R. 421. But Code 761 is differently worded;
and it was held by Judge Wetmore, in the Sup. Ct. N.W.T.,
that it is in the discretion of the court to hear an objection not
taken before the justice: Simpson v. Lock, 7 Can. Cr. Cas. 294;
and such seems to be the law, see the cases cited in Paley 8th
ed. 426. Judge Wetmore, in the subsequent case of R. v.
Nugent, 9 Can. Cr. Cas. 1, distinguished that case from Simpson
v. Lock, and held that only questions raised before the justice,
and stated in the "case" could be dealt with by the Appellate
Court. A case cannot be stated, if it is in the opinion of the
justice merely frivolous: Code 763; R. v. Bridge, 54 J.P. 629;
Ex p. Hawke, 10 T.L.R. 677; nor, upon a question of fact; but
only upon a question of law, or whether the justice's decision
is in excess of jurisdiction; Code 761; R. v. Letang, 2 Can.
Cr. Cas. 505; R. v. Shiel, 50 L.T. 590; Hobbs v. Dance, L.R. 9
C.P. 30; R. v. Yeomans, 24 J.P. 149; R. v. Pollard, 14 L.T.
599; Sweatman v. Guest, L.R. 3 Q.B. 262.

A question depending purely on the weight of evidence
such as the question, whether the failure of a husband to
provide necessaries for his wife would be likely to permanently
injure her health, cannot be made the subject of a case stated:
R. v. McIntyre, 31 N.S.R. 422, 3 Can. Cr. Cas. 413; see R. v.
Bowman, (N.S.) 3 Can. Cr. Cas. 410; R. v. Robinson (Ont.), 1
Can. Cr. Cas. 28.

Questions of Law.

A case should not be granted unless some doubtful point
of law has been raised, fit to be submitted to the court. The
question, whether there is sufficient evidence to support a criminal charge, is a question of fact, but a question, whether there
is any evidence, is one of law: R. v. Lloyd, 19 O.R. 352; Greene
v. Pensance, 22 J.P. 727. A case may be stated upon the ques-

tion, whether the facts stated constitute any evidence to warrant the finding: R. v. Pilkington, 13 L.J.M.C. 64; R. v. Cohon, 6 Can. Cr. Cas. p. 393. A question may be stated as to the meaning of a statute: R. v. Bridge, 24 Q.B.D. 609. And a case may be stated even if the particular statute relating to the offence contains a clause declaring that the justice's decision should be final: Leicester v. Hewitt, 57 J.P. 344; Sweatman v. Guest, L.R. 3 Q.B. 262. As to what are questions of law upon which a case may be stated, see R. v. Garrow, 5 B.C.R. 61; R. v. Fortier, 7 Can. Cr. Cas. 417, in which the court decided that the question, whether a slot machine was or was not a game of chance, was a question of fact and not of law.

It is improper to send up the whole body of the evidence, and ask the court to say whether it justifies a conviction. The essential facts as found by the justice, and the effect of the evidence given, or extracts from it, which the justice has found to be true, should be given: R. v. Cohon, 6 Can. Cr. Cas. 386; so the forwarding of the whole of the depositions, and asking the court whether there is any legal evidence to sustain a conviction, is not the proper course: the justice must certify his finding of fact, and then specify the points of law in question: R. v. Giles, 3 C.L.J. 33; R. v. Letang, 2 Can. Cr. Cas. 505.

The Appellate Court has to take the facts to have been proved as the justice has found and stated them to be, and decide the points of law in the light of those facts and those only: R. v. Cohon, *supra*.

The proper course is to submit a point or points of law and not to seek the opinion of the court upon the evidence generally as to its sufficiency to support the conviction: R. v. Brennan, 6 Cox C.C. 381.

The question what threats are such a menace as constitutes a crime under Code 452, is a question of law: R. v. Gibbons, 12 Man. R. 154, 1 Can. Cr. Cas. 340.

A case should not be granted when the magistrate has no doubt whatever on the question of law raised; but the party may then apply to the court for leave: R. v. Letang, 2 Can. Cr. Cas. 505.

Question of Jurisdiction of Justice.

The question whether the justice acted in a case in which he had no jurisdiction may be submitted: R. v. Paquin, Q.R. 7 Q.B. 319.

The question, whether the justice had authority, when hearing several charges against the same defendant at one time, to postpone the adjudication of the first until he has heard the others, is a question of jurisdiction, and it was held that he must adjudicate upon each case at its conclusion, or if necessary to take time to consider the first one, he must adjourn the others and adjudicate on the first one tried before proceeding with the others: R. v. McBerny, 29 N.S.R. 327.

The general rule is that a case is not to be stated upon the point which was not raised on the trial before the justice: Perkins v. Huckstable, 23 J.P. 197.

But on an obvious point going to the root of the whole matter, and of which the justice should himself have taken cognizance, a case may be stated, even if it has not been raised on the trial: Ex. p. Markham, 21 L.T. 748; and see *ante* p. 126, after an appeal to the County Court on which a conviction is affirmed, another mode of appeal by case stated, cannot be taken, as the matter is then *res adjudicata*: R. v. Townsend No. 2, 6 Can. Cr. Cas. 519: so also after an appeal by case stated no appeal can be taken: Cooksley v. Toomaten, 5 Can. Cr. Cas. 26. Nor can the same question be reviewed by certiorari: R. v. Monaghan, 2 Can. Cr. Cas. 488. Even if the former appeal was abortive on the ground of non-compliance with some condition precedent to the right of appeal, it is a bar: Cooksley v. Toomaten, 5 Can. Cr. Cas. 26. But see R. v. Caswell, 33 U.C.R. 303.

Recognizance.

At the time of making the application, and before a case is stated and delivered to him by the justice, the appellant must, in every instance, enter into a recognizance before such justice or any other justice exercising the same jurisdiction, with or without surety or sureties, and in such sum as to the justice seems meet, conditioned to prosecute his appeal by case stated without delay, and to submit to the judgment of the court, and pay such costs as are awarded by the same; and must, at the same time, pay to the justice such fees as he is entitled to; and the appellant, if in custody, is to be then liberated, upon the recognizance being further conditioned for his appearance before the same or such other justice as is then sitting, within ten days after the judgment of the court has been given, to abide by such judgment, unless the justice's decision appealed against is reversed: Code 762.

FORM OF RECOGNIZANCE ON CASE STATED UNDER CODE 762.

Canada,
Province of Ontario,
County of .

Be it remembered that on the   day of
, A.D. 19 , C.D. of the
of   in the County of   (*occupation*), G.H. of the same
place (*occupation*) and J.K. of the same place (*occupation*) personally
came before me, the undersigned, one of His Majesty's justices of
the peace, in and for the said County of   and severally acknowledged themselves to owe to our Sovereign Lord the King the several
sums following, that is to say: The said C.D. the sum of
dollars, and the said G.H. and J.K. the sum of   dollars each of
lawful money of Canada to be made and levied of their goods and chattels, lands and tenements respectively, to the use of our said Lord the
King, his heirs and successors, if he, the said C.D., fails in the condition
hereunder written.

Taken and acknowledged the day and year first above mentioned at
the   of   in the County of   before me,
[Seal.]
M.L., a justice of the peace, in and for the
County of

Whereas the above bounden C.D. was on the   day of   A.D.
19 , convicted before   , a justice of the peace in and for the said
County of   for that the said C.D. (*state the charge*) and afterwards
on the   day of   A.D. 19 , the said C.D. desiring to question the said conviction on the ground that it is erroneous in point of
law (*or is in excess of jurisdiction*) applied to the said   as such
justice to state and sign a case for the opinion of (*name the court, e.g.,
the High Court of Justice for Ontario*).

The condition of the above written bond or obligation is such that if
the said C.D. shall prosecute his appeal without delay and submit to the
judgment of the said High Court of Justice (*as the case may be*) and pay
such costs as shall be awarded by the same. (*If the appellant is not in
custody the condition as above is sufficient; but if he is in custody, it
will be necessary, before he can be liberated, to add the following clause
to the condition of the above recognizance*: Code 762(2)), and further if
the said C.D. shall appear before the said   the same justice by
whom he was convicted as aforesaid or such other justice as is then sitting, within ten days after the judgment of the said court has been given,
to abide such judgment, unless the judgment appealed against is reversed,
then the recognizance to be void, otherwise to stand in full force and
virtue.

Note.—The appellant must also pay the justice's fees before he is entitled to have the case delivered to him: Code 762: they are 25 cents for
taking the recognizance, item 7 of tariff in Code 770: and 5 cents for folio
for any necessary copy of evidence.

The recognizance need not be entered into at the time
the application is first made to the justice, but must be entered
into before the case is made up and delivered to the applicant:
Chapman v. Robinson, 1 E. & E. 25; Stanhope v. Thorsby, L.R.
1 C.P. 423.

9—MAG. MAN.

A cash deposit cannot be substituted for the recognizance, which is a condition precedent to the jurisdiction of the court to hear the appeal: R. v. Geiser, 5 Can. Cr. Cas. 154.

The recognizance may be estreated as provided by Code 1097-1100.

Application to Court for Order for Case Stated.

Where the justice refuses to state a case the appellant may apply to the court, upon an affidavit of the facts, for a rule calling upon the justice, and also upon the respondent, to shew cause why such case should not be stated; and the court may make a rule absolute or discharge the application, with or without payment of costs, as to the court seems meet; and the justice, upon being served with such rule absolute, shall state a case accordingly, upon the appellant entering into the recognizance, above mentioned as provided by Code 762: Code 764.

Where the objection raised was that the justices had improperly received evidence, a rule ordering them to state a case was refused; it must appear that the decision was wrong in point of law: R. v. Maclesfield, 2 L.T. 352; see Christie v. St. Luke, Chelsea, 8 E. & B. 992. All the requirements of the statute must be complied with before the justice will be deemed to have refused to state a case.

A case may be reserved at any time, however remote from the judgment, if it is possible that some material benefit may accrue to the defendant therefrom, unless by statute a time is specially limited: R. v. Paquin, Que. R. 7 Q.B. 19.

FORM OF AFFIDAVIT (CODE 764).

In the High Court of Justice.
In the matter of the King on the information of A.B. against C.D.
I, C.D., of the   of   in the County of   , (*occupation*) make oath and say:—

1. That I am the above-named defendant C.D.

2. That on the   day of   A.D. 19   , I was served with a summons (*or arrested upon a warrant*) herein, a true copy of which is now shewn to me marked Exhibit "A," and issued upon an information, a true copy of which is now shewn to me marked Exhibit "B."

3. On the   day of   A.D. 19   , I appeared before E.F., Esquire, the justice of the peace named in the said proceedings, to answer to the charge therein mentioned, and the said justice thereupon proceeded to hear and determine the said charge in presence of the said informant, A.B., and of myself, and upon hearing the evidence the said justice convicted me of the said charge.

4. That the paper writing now shewn to me marked Exhibit "C" is a true copy of the evidence upon the said hearing as taken down by the said justice.

5. That upon the said hearing I took the objection before the said justice that the said conviction was erroneous in point of law (*or*, was in excess of his jurisdiction) upon the grounds following (*here state the questions of law or jurisdiction raised*).

6. That I thereupon applied to the said justice to state a case for the opinion of this court upon the said questions so raised, but he refused to do so on the ground that the same were merely frivolous; and a certificate of such refusal was then granted by the said justice, which certificate is now shewn to me marked Exhibit "D."

7. (*State any facts which may be necessary to shew that the questions raised are substantial.*)

RULE NISI TO COMPEL A JUSTICE TO STATE A CASE UNDER CODE 764.

In the High Court of Justice.

The Honourable Chief Justice	
The Honourable Mr. Justice	} day the day of
The Honourable Mr. Justice	A.D. 19 .

In the matter of the King upon the information of A.B. against C.D.

Upon the application of the said (C.D.), upon reading the certificate of E.F., one of His Majesty's justices of the peace in and for the County of   , of his refusal to state a case for the opinion of this court, at the request of the said C.D., touching the question of the validity of a certain conviction made on the   day of
                    A.D. 19 , by the said justice for that (*set out the charge*) upon the ground that the same is erroneous in point of law (*or* in excess of the said justice's jurisdiction), upon reading the affidavit of the said C.D. and upon hearing counsel for the said C.D.:

It is ordered that the said E.F. and the said A.B., upon notice to them of this order to be given to them respectively, shall on the
          day of   A.D.   , at   o'clock in the forenoon or so soon thereafter as counsel can be heard before this court, at Osgoode Hall, Toronto, shew cause why the said E.F., as such justice, should not be ordered to state and sign a case for the opinion of this court upon the following questions:

1. (*Set out the points of law on which the conviction is claimed to be erroneous, or the question as to the justice's jurisdiction.*)

On motion of Mr.   of counsel for the said C.D.

By the court,
                    Registrar.

RULE ABSOLUTE TO STATE A CASE UNDER CODE 764.

In the High Court of Justice.

The honourable Chief Justice	
The Honourable Mr. Justice	} day the day of
The Honourable Mr. Justice	A.D. 19 .

In the matter of, etc., (*as in the above form of rule nisi*).

Upon the application of the above named C.D. upon reading the rule *nisi* issued on the   day of   A.D. 19 , the therein mentioned certificate of E.F., a justice of the peace for the County of   of his refusal to state a case (*as in the above form of rule nisi*) upon reading the affidavits of   and   filed, and upon hearing counsel for the said A.B., C.D. and E.F. the convicting justice, respectively (*or* no one appearing for the said   although duly notified).

1. It is ordered that the said E.F. do forthwith state and sign and transmit to this court, a case for the opinion of this court upon the following questions:

(1) (*Set out the questions to be submitted*).

2. And it is further ordered that the costs of and incidental to this application be paid by the said A.B. to the said C.D. forthwith after taxation thereof.

On motion of Mr.   of counsel for the said C.D.

By the court,

Registrar.

Statement of Case.

In drawing up the case stated care should be taken that it contains every question to be submitted for the opinion of the court, as the court will not decide upon any question not raised by the justice for its opinion: St. James, Westminister v. St. Mary, Battersea, 29 L.J.M.C. 26; see Hills v. Hunt, 15 C.B. 1, where the court refused an amendment of a case stated.

The duty of the court on a case stated is simply to answer a question of law put to them by the justice: Buckmaster v. Reynolds, 13 C.B.N.S. 62.

Form of Case.

The case should be stated in a complete form, and it should be signed by the justice.

FORM OF CASE STATED.

(Code 761.)

In the High Court of Justice.

In the matter of the King upon the information of A.B. (*Respondent*) and C.D. (*Appellant*).

Case stated by E.F. one of His Majesty's justices of the peace in and for the County of   under the provisions of section 761 of the Criminal Code of Canada.

1. On the   day of   A.D. 19 , an information was laid, under oath, before me by the above named A.B. for that the said C.D. on   at   (*state the offence*).

2. On the   day of   A.D. 19 , the said charge was duly heard before me in the presence of both parties, and, after hearing the evidence adduced and the statements of the said A.B. and C.D. and their solicitors (*or* counsel) I found the said C.D. guilty of the said offence and convicted him thereof, but at the request of the solicitor (*or* counsel) for the said C.D. I state the following case for the opinion of this Honourable Court:—

It was shewn before me that (*here set out the findings of fact under which the point of law arises*).

The solicitor (*or* counsel) for the said C.D. desires to question the validity of the said conviction on the ground that it is erroneous in point of law (*or* is in excess of jurisdiction) the questions submitted for the judgment of this Honourable Court being: (*here state the questions submitted, as for instance*).

1. Whether the Municipal Act, R.S.O. ch. 223, sec. 569(4), is constitutionally valid and binding upon the appellant, or is he, by reason of the above mentioned facts, not bound by the provisions thereof (*or as the case may be*).

2. (*State other points of law in question for the opinion of the court, if any.*)

Settling the Case.

The usual course is for one of the parties to the proceedings to draw up a special case, and serve notice of a time and place for settling the same, with a copy of the case, having first obtained an appointment for the purpose.

FORM OF NOTICE.

In the High Court of Justice.

The King on the information of A.B. against C.D.

Take notice that E.F., Esquire, a justice of the peace for the County of   , has appointed   the   day of   , A.D. 19   , at the hour of   o'clock in the   noon, at   , in the   of   , for settling the case to be submitted by him herein, a copy of which is served herewith.

Dated this   day of   , A.D. 19   .

To   ⎱ Solicitor for the above named A.B.
Solicitor for the said C.D. (*or* A.B. ⎰(*or* C.D.
                    Respondent. ⎰   Appellant.

Notice of Hearing.

Notice of hearing should be served on the respondent with a copy of the case.

NOTICE OF HEARING CASE STATED.

(*Heading and style of cause as in above.*)

Take notice that an application will be made before a judge of this court in Chambers at Osgoode Hall, Toronto, on   , the   day of   , A.D. 19   , at   o'clock in the forenoon, or as soon thereafter as the application can be made, for the hearing and determining by the court of the questions of law arising on the case stated by E.F., Esquire, a justice of the peace for the County of   , in this matter.

Dated this   day of   , A.D. 19

                                                     G.H.

To the above-named A.B., and to E.F., the justice of the peace above named. }   Solicitor for the said C.D.

The Hearing.

The court to which the case is transmitted shall hear and determine the questions of law arising thereon, and affirm, reverse or modify the conviction, order or determination, or remit the matter to the justice with the opinion of the court, and may make such other order in relation to the matter, and as to costs, as the court sees fit; such orders are final and conclusive upon all parties: Code 765.

The court has no authority on a case stated to reduce the penalty awarded by the justice: Evens v. Hemingway, 52 J.P. 134.

The court will not affirm a conviction when material evidence was improperly received, even if there was sufficient good evidence to support the conviction: R. v. Dixon, 29 N.S. R. 462; and see R. v. Woods, 5 B.C.R. 585, distinguishing Mackie v. Attorney-General (1894), A.C. 57. If the point has been previously decided it is *res judicata,* and will not be again entertained on case stated: R. v. St. John, 2 Jur. 46; Hastings v. St. James, L.R. 1 Q.B. 43.

If the particular statute relating to the offence, provides that there is to be no appeal, then no stated case can be substituted that being a mode of appeal: R. v. Robert Simpson Co., 2 Can. Cr. Cas. 272. See as to case stated under Nova Scotia Liquor License Act: R. v. Oland, 8 Can. Cr. Cas. 206-208, and notes at p. 207.

Amendment.

If the court thinks fit, it may order the case to be sent back to the justice for amendment, and the case may be amended accordingly, and judgment shall be given after amendment: Code 766.

The application to amend may be made before the day of argument: Yorkshire Tire Co. v. Rotherham L.B., 4 C.B.N.S. 362; but there must be some substantial insufficiency: Townsend v. Read, 4 L.T. 447; Pedgrift v. Chevalier, 8 C.B.N.S. 246; Hodgson v. Little, 16 C.B.N.S. 202.

So the court may remit the case to the justice for re-hearing: R. v. Strauss, 1 Can. Cr. Cas. 107.

Who May Hear.

The authority and jurisdiction vested in the court by Code 765-766, for the opinion of which a case is stated, may, subject to any rules and orders of court in relation thereto, be exercised by a judge of such court sitting in chambers: Code 766 (2).

Quære, whether Code 766 (2), applies to an application to compel justice to state a case: per Channell, B., Ex. p. Smith, 27, L.J.M.C. 186. In England the application to compel a justice to state a case, is made to a Divisional Court of the Queen's Bench Division, under Rule 80, C.O.R. (1886). It is submitted that in Ontario the application for the "Rule to shew cause," and "Rule absolute," should be made to the court. and not to a judge in chambers: see Code 764.

FORM OF ORDER.

In the High Court of Justice.

(Date).

Before the Hon.
Mr. Justice
In Chambers.

The King, upon the Information of A.B., Appellant.
C.D., Respondent.

Upon the application of the above named C.D., upon reading the case stated by E.F., Esquire, a justice of the peace for the County of
in this matter touching the question of the validity of a certain conviction of the said C.D. made by the said justice of the peace on the
day of   A.D. 19 , for that (*set out the charge*) upon the grounds that the same is erroneous in point of law (*or in excess of jurisdiction or as the case may be*) and submitting the following questions for the opinion of this court thereon, namely:

1. (*Set out the questions submitted.*)
Upon hearing counsel for the said C.D. and for the said A.B. and E.F. respectively (*or no one appearing for the said
although duly notified*).
It is ordered that the said conviction be and the same is hereby affirmed (*or quashed, as the case may be,* see Code 765).

2. And it is further ordered that the costs of and incidental to this application be paid by the said   to the said
forthwith after taxation thereof.

Clerk in Chambers.

Costs.

The court has power to award costs, but any justice who states and delivers a case in pursuance of the Code, shall not be liable to any costs in respect to or by reason of such appeal: Code 765.

But when the justice improperly refused to state a case, the court, on ordering a case stated, may award costs against him: R. v. Bradford (Jus.), 48 J.P. 149.

Costs should be applied for on the disposal of the case by the court, and may not be entertained afterwards: Budenburg v. Roberts, L.R. 2 C.P. 292; Carswell v. Cook, 12 C.B.N.S. 242; Cook v. Montague, L.R. 7 Q.B. 418.

The applicant is generally entitled to his costs on a decision in his favour; even if the respondent does not appear to support the justice's decision: Shepherd v. Folland, 49 J.P. 165; Wednesbury v. Stephenson, 9 L.T. 731.

On quashing a conviction, costs are given against the prosecutor: Venables v. Hardnan, 1 E. & E. 79, and may be allowed against an officer of the crown who is prosecutor: Moore v. Smith, 23 J.P. 133; Walsh v. The Queen, 16 Cox C.C. 435.

On abandonment, or where the appeal by case stated was dropped, costs were ordered against appellant: Crowther v. Boult, 13 Q.B.D. 680, and so, even if no notice of the hearing of the appeal is given; and, so under the English practice the appeal could not be heard, costs were given against appellant: South Dublin v. Jones, 12 L.R. Ir. 358.

Where the decision of the justice was reversed on a point not raised before him costs were refused: Stinson v. Browning L.R. 1 C.P. 321. For other examples, see Paley 8th ed. 427-428.

The justice is not entitled to the costs of obtaining legal assistance in preparing a case stated: Luton, L.B. v. Davis, 2 El. & El. 678.

But the costs of the successful party may include charges for preparing and amending the case stated: Glover v. Booth, 31 L.J.M.C. 270.

Death of Respondent.

The death of the respondent does not prevent the court from dealing with the matter: Gainsbury v. Ryne, 34 J.P. 810; R. v. Fitzgerald, 29 O.R. 203.

After Decision Justice may Issue Warrant.

After the decision of the court, in relation to the case stated, the same or any other justice exercising the same jurisdiction, shall have the same authority to enforce any conviction, order or determination affirmed, amended or made by the court, as the justice who originally decided the case would have had, if it had not been appealed against: Code 767.

If the justice refuses to act in accordance with the judgment of the court upon a case stated, he may be compelled by mandamus to do so R. v. Haden Corser, 8 T.L.R. 563.

Court May Enforce its Own Order.

If it deems it necessary or expedient, the court may enforce any order by its own process: Code 767 (2).

Certiorari not Necessary.

No certiorari or other writ is required in aid of this proceeding: Code 768.

3. RESERVED CASE BY A MAGISTRATE, ACTING UNDER PART XVI. CRIMINAL CODE.

In What Cases.

The only appeal from a conviction, or other decision, by a police magistrate (or any of the other functionaries mentioned in Code 771; except that provided by Code 797, which is mentioned below), is that given by Code 1013, *et seq.;* viz., by way of a case reserved for the opinion of the "Court of Appeal," upon a question of law only; and that applies only to cases tried under Code 777. There is no other appeal from a police, stipendiary or district magistrate, when acting as such under Code 771 *et seq.,* with the exception above referred to: R. v. Racine, 3 Can. Cr. Cas. p. 446; R. v. Bougie, 3 Can. Cr. Cas. p. 487; R. v. Nixon, 5 Can. Cr. Cas. 32; Rice v. The King, 5 Can. Cr. Cas. 529; R. v. Smith, 10 Can. Cr. Cas. 362; nor from the recorder of Montreal holding a "Summary Trial": R. v. Portugais, 5 Can. Cr. Cas. 100.

Cases Under Code 773, (a) or (f).

As above mentioned an appeal is given by Code 797, from a *conviction* only, for an offence under Code 773, sub-section (a) for theft under $10, or under sub-section (f) for keeping or being an inmate or habitual frequenter of a disorderly house; which appeal is to be taken in the same way as an appeal from a decision of a justice in a summary conviction case, under Code 749, or Code 761, as described *ante* p. 99. This sec. 797 applies to convictions by police magistrates, as well as to those by two justices, for the offences named. It was contained in the amendment of 1895 to the Criminal Code 1892, sec. 782, as sub-section (v); which gave authority to two justices, as well as magistrates, to try these offences, and provided for the appeal from a decision, by such justices only; but the present sec. 797, in the Criminal Code 1906, does not restrict the appeal to a case tried by justices; and there is an appeal from a conviction under Code 773 (a) or (f), whether it be by two justices or a magistrate. This appeal only applies, however, to convictions for these particular offences, under the sub-sec. of Code 773 (a) or (f); and not to other offences tried under other sections of Part XVI.

Police Magistrate, Acting in his Capacity as Such.

The appeal provided by Code 749-769, in summary convictions cases, tried by justices under Part XV. of the Criminal Code 1906, does not apply to a conviction by a magistrate acting in a "Summary Trial" under Part XVI. Code 798, expressly excluding the same: R. v. Egan, 1 Can. Cr. Cas. 112; R. v. Bougie, 3 Can. Cr. Cas. p. 492; nor to a conviction by a police magistrate, even on the trial of a case, of a breach of a Dominion law, which is within the summary jurisdiction of a justice under Part XV., if the magistrate is acting therein by virtue of his office of police magistrate, e.g., if the offence arose within the place for which he is police magistrate.

Police Magistrate Acting as Ex Officio Justice.

But in cases, in which he acts as an *ex officio* justice, e.g., for offences arising in other parts of the same county, (for which he is, by R.S.O. ch. 87, secs. 27 and 30, an *ex officio* justice), an appeal lies under Code 749 or 761 from his decision.

There is, however, no appeal from his decision in any case in which he acts under Part XVI., (except as above mentioned, under Code 797), other than by reserved case, as provided by Code 1013. This is so, although the case may be one which he may summarily try under that Part. XVI., without the defendant's consent: R. v. Nixon, 5 Can. Cr. Cas. 32. The decision *contra* in R. v. Hawes, 4 Can. Cr. Cas. 529, is clearly not good law; as Code 798 expressly excludes the provisions of Part XV., (formerly XVIII.), and therefore also the provisions for appeal contained therein, from applying to any magistrates cases under Part XVI; and there is no other provision for appeal, except as above stated; see notes in 4 Can. Cr. Cas. 532. The Egan and Racine cases above cited expressly so decide. The proceeding of case reserved under Code 761 is a form of appeal: R. v. Robert Simpson Co., 2 Can. Cr. Cas. 272.

As to appeal and case stated by magistrates or justices on the trial of an offence against a provincial law, see *post* p. 146.

Appeal by Reserved Case.

A police or other "magistrate," *i.e.*, any of the functionaries mentioned in Code 777, when acting under Code 777 may reserve and state a case upon a point of law only for the opinion of the "Court of Appeal": Code 1013.

To What Court.

"The Courts of Appeal," referred to, in the different provinces, are defined by Code 2 (7) ; viz. :

In Ontario, the Court of Appeal for Ontario; in Quebec, the Court of King's Bench, appeal side; in Nova Scotia, New Brunswick, and British Columbia, the Supreme Court *in banc;* in Prince Edward Island, the Supreme Court; in Manitoba, the Court of Appeal; in Saskatchewan and Alberta, the Supreme Court of the North West Territories, *in banc,* until the same is abolished; and thereafter such court as is by the respective legislatures of those provinces, substituted therefor; in each of these provinces the court called the Supreme Court of the province has now been established, and is the court to which the above appeal is to be taken; in the Yukon, the Supreme Court of Canada. Secs. 1014-1025 of the Criminal Code apply to this proceeding, by implication, and evidently apply, by the wording of Code 1013, to the mode of appeal provided by that section: see R. v. Burns, 1 O.L.R. at p. 337.

The magistrate before which any accused person is tried may, either during or after the trial, reserve any question of law arising either on the trial or on any of the proceedings preliminary, subsequent or incidental thereto, for the opinion of the "Court of Appeal," in manner provided by Code 1014. (2).

Who May Appeal by Reserved Case.

Either the prosecutor or the accused may, during the trial, apply, orally or in writing, to the magistrate to reserve any such question, and the magistrate, if he refuses so to reserve it, must, nevertheless, take a note of the objection: Code 1014 (3).

A case is to be stated by the magistrate for the opinion of the court appealed to: Code 1014 (6).

After a question is reserved the trial may proceed as in other cases: Code 1014 (4).

If the result is a conviction the magistrate may postpone sentence or respite execution until the question has been decided, and may commit the person convicted to prison or admit him to bail, with one or two sufficient sureties, in such sums as the magistrate thinks fit, to surrender at such a time as the magistrate directs: Code 1014 (5).

If Reserved Case Refused.

If the magistrate refuses to reserve a case, the party may, on notice of motion to the opposite party, apply to the "Court of Appeal," for leave to appeal: Code 1015.

Formerly, the consent of the Attorney-General had to be obtained for leave to apply to the Court of Appeal, for leave to appeal by case reserved; but by the amendment of 1900, now Code 1015, the application may be made direct to the "Court of Appeal." If leave is given by the "Court of Appeal," a case is to be stated for the opinion of the court, as if the question had been reserved: Code 1016.

The Court of Appeal (Ont.), refused to direct a reserved case when the magistrate had jurisdiction, and the question was whether the evidence in a perjury trial was sufficiently corroborated; which was a question of fact for the magistrate to determine, as he had done: R. v. Burns, 1 O.L.R. 336.

A case may be reserved, under Code 1014, at any time, however remote from the judgment, if it is possible that some material benefit may accrue to the defendant thereon: R. v. Paquin, Que. R. 7 Q.B. 319, 2 Can. Cr. Cas. 134.

It is a question whether the case, when stated by order of the court, is to be settled by the "Court of Appeal," or by the magistrate. In R. v. Coleman, 30 O.R. 93, the Court of Appeal made an order for leave, which included in detail the form of the case to be stated, and a direction to state the case so set forth: See note, 2 Can. Cr. Cas. 539.

Notice of appeal must be served on the accused, if accquitted, and not on his solicitor: R. v. Williams, 3 Can. Cr. Cas. 9.

Evidence for "Court of Appeal."

If on appeal the trial magistrate thinks it necessary, or if the "Court of Appeal," so desires, the former shall send to the court a copy of the evidence or such part as may be material: Code 1017.

The Court of Appeal, may also send back any case to the magistrate by whom it was stated, to be amended or re-stated: Code 1017 (3).

Wide powers are conferred upon the "Court of Appeal," in dealing with cases reserved by magistrates by Code 1018: and by Code 1019 no conviction is to be set aside, even if some evidence was improperly rejected or admitted or something not according to law was done at the trial; unless it appears that some substantial wrong or miscarriage was thereby occasioned. When two persons are jointly convicted, the court may, on deciding the objection raised by case stated by one of them only, also quash the conviction of the one who has not appealed: R. v. Saunders (1899), 1 Q.B. 490.

The proceedings consequent upon the decision of the appeal, are provided by Code 1018 and 1020 (2).

Appeal to the Supreme Court.

An appeal lies from the decision of the "Court of Appeal," to the Supreme Court of Canada, on the case stated by a magistrate under Code 1013; but only in the event of some of the judges of the "Court of Appeal," dissenting: Code 1013 (2), (3); and only in the case of the conviction being affirmed: Code 1024; R. v. Cunningham, Cassell's Dig., 2nd ed. 107. And an appeal also lies to the Supreme Court from a decision of the "Court of Appeal," refusing a motion for a reserved case, under Code 1015 (3), if any of the judges of the latter court dissent; or when the appeal is based on two grounds and any of the judges have dissented upon one of them; but only as to the ground upon which there was such dissent: McIntosh v. The Queen, 23 S.C.R. 180. But not when a new trial was ordered, by the Court of Appeal: Viau v. The Queen, 29 S.C.R. 90. No appeal is allowed to the Supreme Court, if the Court of Appeal is unanimous: Code 1013 (2): 1024.

The proceedings on appeal to the Supreme Court are regulated by Code 1024; the proceedings being commenced by notice, which must be given within 15 days.

Code 1025 prohibits any appeal in a criminal case to the Privy Council; see *ante* p. 73 and Riel v. Regina, L.R. 10 A.C. 675.

A reserved case can only be stated by a magistrate under Code 1013 (formerly 742), in cases under Code 777 (formerly 785), and not in cases under Code 773 (formerly 783).

4. APPEAL AND CASE STATED BY JUSTICES AND MAGISTRATES IN CASES UNDER PROVINCIAL STATUTES.

The provisions of the Criminal Code, relating to appeal and case stated, being by Dominion legislation, do not in themselves have any application to appeals from convictions for offences against provincial laws; and can have no such application, unless it is so expressly provided by some provincial enactment: R. v. R. Simpson Co., 28 O.R. 231; Lecours v. Hurtubise, 2 Can. Cr. Cas. 521; Scottstown v. Beauchesne, Que. R. 5 Q.B. 554; Superior v. Montreal, 3 Can. Cr. Cas. 379.

But in some of the provinces, provincial statutes relating to such appeals, have made the provisions of the Criminal Code apply to such appeals. These and the provincial laws regarding appeals, so far as they relate to the Province of Ontario, will now be more fully mentioned.

(A) *Appeal to General Sessions, or Division Court, in Cases of Offences Against Provincial Laws.*

Sometimes the particular Ontario statute relating to the offence, or to a class of offences, provides for an appeal from the decision on a summary trial of such offence. For instance, in Ontario, the Liquor License Act, the Public Health Act, and certain other statutes provide for the appeal, and also lay down the practice and procedure on the same; in such cases the provisions of the particular statute will apply to the appeal referred to; and the general provisions for appeals and case stated, will only apply in so far as they are not inconsistent with what is provided by the particular statute.

The mode of appeal provided by the Ontario Health Act, R.S.O. ch. 248, only applies to convictions for offences against the Act itself and not to offences against the general by-law at the end of that statute, to which the provisions for appeal in the body of the Act have no application: R. v. Coursey, 26 O.R. 685; 27 O.R. 181.

The Appeal.

In Ontario, R.S.O. ch. 90, secs. 7 to 11, provides for an appeal in all cases, when the particular statute does not stipulate to the contrary, or give some other mode of appeal. Such appeal lies even if no appeal is expressly allowed by the statute relating to the offence:—

Until the Act of the recent session of the legislature, 7 Edw. VII. ch. 23, was passed, the R.S.O. ch. 90, sec. 7, only allow-

ed an appeal to the general sessions; but by the statute of
1907 the Dominion Statute of 1905, ch. 10, was made applicable also to appeals for offences against Ontario laws; and
since the 20th April, 1907, the appeal, as well under Ontario
laws as under Dominion laws, is to be as follows: to the
general sessions, when the conviction adjudges imprisonment
only, (no fine); and in *all other cases*, to the Division Court of
the division of the county in which the cause of information and
complaint arose. The justice must transmit at once the depositions conviction, and all papers, either to the clerk of the
peace, if the appeal is to the general sessions, or to the clerk
of the Division Court, if the appeal is to the latter court.

The practice and procedure on the appeal and preliminary
thereto, and otherwise in respect thereof, is the same as the
practice and procedure under the statutes of the Dominion,
except when otherwise expressed: R.S.O. ch. 90, sec. 8.

So the appeal from a conviction by a justice or magistrate,
for an offence under an Ontario statute, is to the same court,
and the notice and practice and all proceedings are precisely the
same as those described, *ante* p. 99, *et seq.*: and the forms and
steps there mentioned will be followed.

Formerly in the above provisions of the Ontario law, there
was no provision for an appeal when the justice or magistrate
dismissed the case; but only in the event of a *conviction;* but
there is now an appeal also by the prosecutor, provided by Ont.
stat. 1903, ch. 7, sec. 20.

Code 750 (2) provides that the notice of appeal must be
served and filed "within ten days after" the conviction or
order: while in R.S.O. ch. 7, sec. 21, it is to be "within ten days
at the latest." There is no difference in the effect; the day
on which the conviction took place, is excluded and, the day
on which the notice is served is included in the ten days: see
ante p. 104.

It is to be remembered that a second notice giving reasons
for appeal is required: see *ante* p. 105.

The recognizance must also be given; the provisions for a
cash deposit instead of a recognizance being abolished: see
ante pp. 106, 110.

Either party may call witnesses and adduce evidence in addition to the witnesses and evidence adduced before the justice:
R.S.O.. ch. 90, sec. 8: Code 752 (2).

On an appeal under the Ontario revised statute, the rule as to reading the depositions of a witness taken upon the hearing before the justice is different from that in an appeal under the Code 749. In the latter, the depositions may be read on the appeal and are to have the same force as if the witness was then and there examined, if the court appealed to is satisfied by affidavit or other evidence that the personal attendance of the witness cannot be obtained by any reasonable efforts: Code 752 (3); but under sec. 10 of R.S.O. ch. 90, the depositions can only be read when it is proved that the witness is dead, too ill to attend, or is absent from Ontario, or that after diligent inquiries he cannot be found to be served with a subpœna.

To let in the depositions under the Ontario statute, it must also be proved that the depositions were taken in the presence of the accused, and that he or his counsel or solicitor had full opportunity to cross-examine; and the depositions must purport to be signed by the justice, by or before whom they purport to have been taken: sec. 10.

Upon the appeal to the general sessions, the whole case is up for trial *de novo* before the court appealed to: R.S.O. ch. 90, sec. 8.

Abandonment of Appeal.

The appellant may abandon his appeal by giving six days' notice, sec. 11; for form, etc., see p. 116 and thereupon the justice or magistrate may tax any additional costs of the respondent, adding the same to the original costs, and proceed on the original conviction or order, as if there had been no appeal.

Jury.

Ontario stat. 1903, ch. 7, sec. 21 (3), allows a jury if the court so directs; but there is no authority for a jury on an appeal under Code 749.

A special sessions of the peace may be held at any time, to hear these appeals, if there is no jury; Ont. stat. 1903, ch. 7, sec. 21 (4).

The provisions of the Cr. Code as to amendment on appeal, also apply to appeal cases under Ontario laws; Ont. stat. 1902, ch. 12 sec. 15. And all the saving clauses of the Cr. Code (formerly secs. 889 to 896, now) 1124 to 1129, also, similarly apply: Ont. stat. 1901, ch. 13, sec. 1.

10—MAG. MAN.

Appeal from the Sessions Thereon.

Such appeal lies to the Court of Appeal, only in case the Attorney-General certifies that a question of law is involved, of sufficient importance to justify the case being appealed: Ont. Stat. 1901, ch. 12, sec. 11: and see *ante* p. 122.

(B) *Appeal to County Judge in Ontario.*

An appeal may be made to the county judge in Ontario from a conviction or order of a justice of the peace, for an offence against an Ontario statute: but this can only be done in a case in which by some Ontario statute this mode of appeal is especially allowed: R.S.O. 1897, ch. 92, sec. 2; otherwise the appeal, if any, is to the general sessions or division court as already mentioned.

There is no appeal from a magistrate when acting in that capacity; but if he is acting as an *ex officio* justice of the peace there is such appeal: R. v. Smith, 10 Can. Cr. Cas. 362.

The appeal under consideration may now be made by either party, prosecutor as well as defendant, Ont. stat. 1903, ch. 7, sec. 20.

If the party has previously appealed in some other form, *e. g.*, by case stated, he cannot appeal again. And this appears to be so, even if the first appeal was not perfected, or gone on with: Cooksley v. Toomaten, 5 Can. Cr. Cas. 26.

The following are the proceedings on an appeal to the county judge, under R.S.O. 1897, ch. 92.

If the appeal is against a conviction whereby only a money penalty is imposed, the person convicted and desiring to appeal, may deposit with the justice the amount of the penalty and costs, and also $10; or, instead of so doing, he may enter into a recognizance before any justice in double the amount of the penalty and costs: R.S.O. 1897, ch. 92, sec. 3 (*a*). The form of recognizance is given in the above statute at page 999.

If, however, the appeal is against a conviction awarding imprisonment as a punishment for the offence, the person convicted must enter into a recognizance (Form 2 in the statute, p. 1000) in not less than $100, or more than $200, as the convicting justice directs, and also in double the amount of the penalty and costs awarded: sec. 3 (*b*).

If, in either of the above cases, the person convicted is in custody and does not make the deposit or enter into the above recognizance, he must remain in custody pending the appeal:

sec. 5; and must also deposit with the convicting justice $10: sec. 3 (c).

If sec. 3 (a) and (b) has been complied with, proceedings on a conviction are to be stayed, and the justice is to issue his warrant (Form 3 to the statute) to liberate the appellant: sec. 4.

Entering into the recognizance or making the $10. deposit is merely for the appellant to have his liberty, and to stay execution; and is no condition of the appeal: R. v. Davitt, 7 Can. Cr. Cas. p. 517.

The payment of his fine by the defendant does not debar him from appealing, if he did so under circumstances that shewed an intention to appeal: R. v. Tucker, 10 Can. Cr. Cas. 217, and see *ante* p. 100.

The appellant may within ten days after the justice has pronounced his adjudication (unless the delay is caused by the fault of the convicting justice, and then within one calendar month at latest) apply to the county judge for a summons to quash the conviction: sec. 6.

Upon the return of the summons, the judge, either with or without hearing further evidence, as he sees fit, may affirm, amend or quash the conviction, and fix the costs, if any, allowed upon the appeal: sec. 7.

The judge has the same authority as to costs as the general sessions have under secs. 751, 754 of the Cr. Code, and may allow solicitor's costs and counsel fees. And there is no appeal to the High Court from the discretion of the judge as to such costs: R. v. McIntosh, 28 O.R. 603.

FORM OF SUMMONS.

In the County Court of the County of
His Honour , Judge of the County ⎫ day the day of
Court of the County of in Chambers. ⎭ A.D. 19

In the matter of the appeal between A.B., appellant, and C.D., respondent.

Upon reading the conviction made herein on the day of A.D. 19 , the depositions of witnesses taken before the convicting justice (*or* justices) the notice of appeal and affidavit of service thereof and other papers filed with the clerk of this court and upon hearing what was alleged; let the above named respondent C.D. (*the complainant*) and the County Crown Attorney for the County of attend before me at my chambers in the court house in the of in the County of on day the day of A.D. 19 , at o'clock in the forenoon and shew cause why the conviction of the above named appellant made upon the complaint of the respondent dated the day of A.D. 19 , and now on file with the clerk of this

court and made by   , a justice of the peace in and for the County
of   (*or as the case may be*) whereby the said appellant A.B. was
convicted for that (*set out the charge*) the said C.D. being the informant,
and the said justice (*or justices*) adjudged the said A.B. for his said
offence (*set out the adjudication*) should not be set aside and quashed
with costs on the grounds:

    1. (*Here state the grounds of objection to the conviction.*)
and upon grounds disclosed in said affidavits and papers filed.

Judge.

ORDER ON APPEAL TO COUNTY JUDGE.

    In the County Court of the County of
His Honour
The Judge of the County Court of the   }   day the   day of
    County of   in Chambers.   A.D. 19

    In the matter of, etc. (*as in above summons*).
    Upon reading the summons granted herein on the   day of
    A.D. 19 , the information, depositions of witnesses, the con-
viction herein and all others the papers filed, and upon hearing counsel
for the appellant and respondent (*or as the case may be*) *or* the said
        not appearing although duly notified in that behalf as required
by law as by affidavit of service appears.

    I,   , judge of the County Court of the County of   , do
order and adjudge that the conviction of the appellant made upon the
complaint of the respondent dated the   day of   A.D. 19 ,
and now on file with the clerk of this court, and made by   , a
justice of the peace in and for the county of   (*or as the case
may be*) whereby the said appellant A.B. was convicted for that (*here
set out the charge as in the conviction*) the said C.D. being the informant,
and whereby it was adjudged that the said A.B. (*set out adjudication*) be
and the same is hereby quashed, rescinded and set aside without costs (*or
with costs to be paid by the said C.D. to the said A.B. forthwith with taxation* (*as the case may be*).

Judge.

If the conviction is amended and affirmed, and even a reduced punishment inflicted by the judge, the defendant if in
custody must be brought before the judge to receive the fresh
punishment. The defendant cannot be punished in his absence,
unless such absence is by his own default: R. v. Johnston, 11
Can. Cr. Cas. 10.

Upon the judge's order affirming the conviction being produced before the justice, the latter is to issue a warrant of distress, and if there is no sufficient distress, he is to issue a warrant of commitment, for the recovery of such further costs as
the sum deposited is insufficient to pay; but if a recognizance
has been given, no warrant is to be issued and the recognizance
is to be estreated in the manner described by sec. 8.

If the conviction is quashed by the judge, he is to order the
money deposited to be returned to the accused, and he may also

allow and fix the costs to be paid by the complainant, and, if necessary, may issue a distress warrant to levy the same. If the conviction adjudged imprisonment for the offence, and it is affirmed, or amended and affirmed by the judge, or if the person convicted fails to prosecute the appeal within the time limited by sec. 6, the judge is to issue a warrant (Form 4, p. 1001 of the statute) committing the defendant to prison; and if the defendant does not surrender himself into custody of the constable entrusted with the warrant within one week after the date of the order, the recognizance given shall be deemed broken, and upon an affidavit of the constable or other proof of such non-surrender, the judge may certify (Form 5 to the statute) the default on the back of the recognizance, and transmit the same to the clerk of the peace: sec. 9; and the recognizance may be estreated at the next sitting of the general sessions: sec. 9 (2).

The above mentioned proceedings upon the recognizance do not relieve the defendant from undergoing the punishment awarded by the justice; and he may be arrested under the warrant of the judge in any part of Ontario, and imprisoned accordingly: sec. 9 (2). If it appears that the person convicted has served a portion of the time of imprisonment, the warrant of commitment is to be only for the residue of the term: sec. 11. The warrant is to be executed in the same manner as warrants of commitment upon summary convictions under the Cr. Code: sec. 12.

So that if the accused is not in the judge's county, the warrant would have to be "backed" as described *infra*, before being executed elsewhere.

If the justice's conviction against the defendant was for a money penalty only, no warrant of commitment can be issued; but upon an affidavit of default of payment, the judge is to certify upon the recognizance the fact of such default, and the recognizance is to be sent to the clerk of the peace to be estreated at the next general sessions.

The justice is to retain the money deposited with him on the appeal for six calendar months unless judgment is sooner given by the judge; and upon such judgment or on the expiration of six months from the date of the conviction, the money is to be paid over to the person entitled to it according to the judgment, but if no judgment is given within six months the conviction is to stand, and any justice for the county may issue the warrant of commitment for the unserved portion of the imprisonment awarded by the conviction, and the appeal falls to the ground: sec. 14.

(C) Case Stated under Ontario Laws.

An appeal by way of "case stated," in prosecutions under Ontario laws is provided by R.S.O. 1897, ch. 91, sec. 5. The provisions of the Cr. Code apply to such proceeding. The case is to be stated to the Court of Appeal, and it is only to be allowed upon a question of the constitutionality of the statute under which the conviction or order is made: R. v. Wason, 17 A.R. 221; R. v. Edwards, 19 A.R. 706; R.S.O. ch. 91, sec. 5.

It is restricted solely to that question, and does not extend to a case in which the decision depends upon the question whether the statute is applicable to the defendants: R. v. Toronto Ry. Co., 26 A.R. 491; nor whether it is applicable to a given state of circumstances: Monkhouse v. G.T.R., 8 A.R. 637; nor does it extend to a question of the validity of some other statute such as a statute regulating procedure or evidence, and which arises in the case: R. v. Edwards, 19 A.R. 706. The following are the proceedings provided by R.S.O. ch. 91:

A "case" is to be stated to the Court of Appeal; and either party may apply to a justice after he has announced his decision to state a case for the opinion of that court. A recognizance is to be entered into by the applicant before the justice who heard the case, with or without sureties as the justice may see fit: R.S.O. ch. 91, secs. 5, 6.

See *ante* page 128, for form of recognizance.

If the appellant is in custody and desirous to be liberated, the recognizance is to be further conditioned that the accused will appear before the same justice, or, if that is impracticable, before some other justice, within ten days after the judgment of the Court of Appeal shall be given, to abide such judgment unless the determination appealed from is reversed: sec. 6 (3). See *ante* p. 129 for form.

The appellant is also to pay to the justice the fees mentioned in schedule A to the statute, and any other fees to which the justice is entitled by law: sec. 6 (2).

The fees are given in the schedule at the end of the statute: R.S.O p. 994. And the justice is also entitled, under the Ontario Tariff R.S.O. ch. 95, schedule 1, item 12, to 10 cents per folio of one hundred words, for copies of any papers required to be attached.

Upon entering into the above recognizance conditioned as provided by sec. 6 (1) (3), the appellant, if in custody, is to be liberated: sec. 6 (3). If the recognizance is not conditioned as required by sec. 6 (3), but only under sec. 6 (1), the appellant, if in custody, is to so remain, pending the hearing of the case stated by the Court of Appeal: sec. 6 (3).

No security is required if the appeal is brought by or under the directions of the Attorney-General for Ontario: sec. 6 (4); nor·is the justice to refuse to state a case if required by the Attorney-General or under his direction: sec. 6 (5).

In other cases the justice may refuse to state a case if of opinion that the application is merely frivolous; and in that event he is to grant a certificate of such refusal upon the applicant's request: sec. 6 (6).

Form of certificate is given *ante* p. 125.

The applicant may apply upon such certificate to a judge of the Court of Appeal in Chambers, or to the court upon notice and an affidavit of the facts: see p. 130 for forms; and, if ordered, the justice must state a case accordingly upon the above recognizance being entered into: sec. 6 (7).

The Court of Appeal may reverse, affirm, or amend the justice's decision, or may remit the matter back to him with its opinion, and make any order as to the same and as to costs; but no costs are to be awarded against the justice: sec. 7.

Upon an order of the Court of Appeal being presented to him, the justice who heard the case, or any other justice having the same jurisdiction, is given the same authority to enforce the conviction or order affirmed, amended or made by the Court of Appeal, as the justice who originally heard the case would have had, if his decision had not been appealed from: sec. 9. No writ of certiorari is necessary in aid of the proceedings before the Court of Appeal: sec. 10. If the conviction is affirmed, and the recognizance entered into is not complied with, it is to be transmitted by the justice to the clerk of the peace to be estreated, with a certificate endorsed by the justice stating in what respects it has not been complied with: sec. 12.

Form of certificate *ante* p. 119, may be adapted.

After the above proceedings by way of case stated, no appeal lies to the county judge or general sessions from the justice's decision: sec. 13.

For form of application to the justice to state a case, see *ante* p. 124.

CHAPTER VI.

EVIDENCE.

The ordinary rules of evidence which apply to criminal trials, as acted upon in courts of justice, are also applicable to proceedings before justices, and these rules are generally the same in criminal as in civil cases; except when varied by statutes applicable to civil proceedings only: Roscoe's Cr. Ev., 10th ed. 1; Paley, 6th ed. 124; R. v. Burdett, 3 B. & Ald. 717; and see R. v. White, 4 F. & F. 384.

The Canada Evidence Act, R.S.C. 1906, ch. 145; and also the clauses of the Cr. Code relating to evidence on trials before the High Court, will govern the taking of evidence in summary trials and preliminary inquiries before justices and magistrates under Dominion laws. But they do not apply to trials under Ontario laws; provision being made for the latter by the Ontario Evidence Act, R.S.O. ch. 73.

Competence of Witnesses.

No witness in any criminal case is now incompetent through crime or interest: Can. Ev. Act, sec. 3; Ont. Ev. Act, R.S.O. ch. 73, sec. 2.

The character or condition of a witness, or his interest in the subject matter, only affects the weight to be attached to his evidence; and everyone is now a competent witness; except idiots and lunatics, the former (idiots) being totally incapable of giving evidence, while a lunatic may give evidence during any lucid interval: 3 Russell, 6th ed. 654.

Deaf-mutes.

A deaf-mute may give evidence if it clearly appears he has a proper sense of the obligation he is undertaking, and is able to communicate his testimony! *Ib.* A person who is mute may give his evidence in any way he can make it intelligible: Can. Ev. Act. sec. 6.

Husband and Wife.

By sec. 4 of the Can. Ev. Act, the accused, or the wife or husband of the accused, is a competent and compellable witness for the prosecution, without the consent of the person charged, on a trial against him for any of the offences there enumerated: sec. 4 (2) ; or for the defence in any case, sec. 4 (1) ; but the husband or wife is not compellable to disclose any communication made during marriage: sec. 4 (3).

So in any proceeding, whether it is a summary trial or a preliminary examination under any Dominion law, the wife, or husband of the accused may give evidence on behalf of the latter in any case; or may be called and compelled to give evidence for the prosecution in any of the cases mentioned: Gosselin v. The King, 7 Can. Cr. Cas. 139; subject to the prohibition in regard to communications during marriage.

A communication sent to a wife by the accused, by direction of counsel, sent by the accused to give the communication, is not within this exception: Gosselin v. The King, 7 Can. Cr. Cas. 139; see note in 7 Can. Cr. Cas. at p. 91.

Incriminating Questions.

No witness is excused from answering a question upon the ground that the answer may tend to incriminate him, or establish his liability to an action: Can. Ev. Act, sec. 5.

If however he objects on that ground, he must answer; but his answer will not be receivable as evidence in any criminal proceeding against him afterwards, other than a prosecution for perjury, in the giving of the evidence: sec. 5 (2): R. v. Clark, 5 Can. Cr. Cas. 235; R. v. Van Meter, 11 Can. Cr. Cas. 207; but if he does not object the evidence he has given may be used in a prosecution against him on a charge for any offence which it may tend to prove: R. v. Van Meter, 11 Can Cr. Cas. 207.

The accused when called on his own behalf, may be cross-examined as to any previous convictions or as to any relevant matters; the only exception to his competency and liability to testify being in respect to communications between husband and wife: R. v. D'Aoust, 3 O.L.R. 653.

In trials for infractions of Ontario laws, however, the law is somewhat different.

The Ontario Legislature, by Ont. Ev. Act, R.S.O. 1897, ch. 73, sec. 9, has enacted that (although a *witness* cannot be compelled to answer incriminating questions, sec. 5), the *accused* (or the *wife*, or *husband*, of the accused), is not only a competent witness, but may be called and compelled to give evidence for the prosecution, before any justice of the peace, mayor or police magistrate on the trial of any proceeding, matter or question, cognizable by him, under any Ont. Act: R. v. Nurse, 2 Can. Cr. Cas. 57; R. v. Fee, 13 O.R. 590; R. v. Askwith, 31 O.R. 150; 3 Can. Cr. Cas. 78.

Section 9 of the Ontario statute, which makes the defendant a compellable witness, applies, whether or not the charge is of the class of infractions of Ontario laws, which may be designated as "crimes." The words "not being a crime" contained in R.S.O. 1887, ch. 61, sec. 9, are omitted, (as no longer necessary), from sec. 9 of the Revised Statutes of 1897; it having been held that the Ontario Legislature has jurisdiction to regulate the proceedings and evidence in cases under its own laws, whether the offence may be considered "a crime" or not: R. v. Bittle, 21 O.R. 605; Maritime Bank v. Receiver Gen. (1892), A.C. 437; R. v. Davitt, 7 Can. Cr. Cas. p. 517; and that it may impose punishments for infractions of laws which it has power to enact. B.N.A. Act, sec. 92 (15); Attorney-General of Canada v. Attorney-General of Ontario, 23 S.C.R. 458: see also R. v. Douglass, 1 Can. Cr. Cas. 221; 11 Man. R. 401.

Under the Canada Evidence Act, a witness who is not a party to the particular case which is being tried, is liable to be called as witness and cannot be excused from answering, on the ground that he is himself also a defendant in a separate prosecution, in connection with the same transaction, and that his answers would tend to incriminate himself; though if he makes objection, his evidence cannot afterwards be used against himself: R. v. McLinehy (Que.), 2 Can. Cr. Cas. 416; R. v. Clark, 5 Can. Cr. Cas. 235; R. v. Viau, Que. R. 7 Q.B. 362; see also R. v. Jackson, 6 Cox C.C. 525; R. v. Gallagher, 13 Cox. C.C. 61. But a defendant cannot be compelled to give evidence against his co-defendant, in the same case; though he may testify if he chooses: R. v. Connors, 5 Can. Cr. Cas. 70; and a voluntary confession or statement made by one defendant may be given in evidence against him, even if it tends also to inculpate his co-defendant: R. v. Martin, 9 Can. Cr. Cas. 371; R. v. Connors, 5 Can. Cr. Cas. 70.

The exception under the Can. Ev. Act, that the evidence given by a witness cannot be made use of in any *proceeding thereafter instituted* against him, does not include the *then pending* proceeding: R. v. Skelton, 4 Can. Cr. Cas. 467.

The privilege allowed, in Ontario cases, under the Ontario Evidence Act, of refusing to answer incriminating questions, can only be claimed by the witness himself; and he may answer if he chooses, notwithstanding any of the parties object to it.

It seems to be a question for the justice or magistrate, and not for the witness, to determine from the nature of the question and the circumstances, as to whether the privilege claimed is well founded or not; that is, whether the answer would really have the tendency to incriminate the witness; and a witness must pledge his oath to it. It must appear that the danger to be apprehended by the witness is real and appreciable, and not of an unsubstantial character, having reference to some improbable and remote contingency, or such as any reasonable man should not be affected by, and which ought not to obstruct the administration of justice: R. v. Boyes, 1 B. & S. 311; *ex parte* Reynolds, 20 Ch. D. 294; Osborn v. London Dock Co., 10 Ex. 698. The question cannot be argued by counsel: R. v. Adey, 1 M. & Rob. 94.

If it is not clear, however, that the answer would not tend to incriminate the witness, the privilege of not answering should be allowed: Russell, pp. 644, 645. If the witness cannot be prosecuted by reason of the matter being barred by lapse of time, the evidence could not tend to render him liable to prosecution; and it is not privileged and must be given if it is relevant to the issue: Russell, 615; and so where the party had previously been pardoned for the offence: R. v. Boyes, 1 B. & S. 311. If the question in any substantial degree has a tendency to incriminate a witness, even though it does not do so directly, the witness is privileged from answering: Power v. Ellis, 6 S.C.R. 1; Lamb v. Munster, 10 Q.B.D. 110; Weiser v Heintzman, 15 P.R. 258; D'Ivry v. The World, 17 P.R. 387.

Upon this subject see further matters stated *post* under "Admissions in Depositions."

Questions Affecting Character.

The privilege and protection given as above to a witness in regard to incriminating questions, does not extend to questions affecting the witness's character. The witness is bound to answer all questions bearing upon the subject matter of the trial, even if the evidence may effect his character and reputation. But the justice should exercise his discretion, by refusing to allow questions concerning stale matters, not bearing upon the issue; and especially if they are such as are not calculated to affect the question of the witness's veracity, and the witness is not bound to answer questions as to matters not pertinent to the issue, and which relate to matters of an odious and infamous character. But questions bearing on the witness's present moral character, and upon his veracity, or shewing him to be profligate, must be allowed.

A defendant in a criminal trial may offer the evidence of witnesses as to his character for the purpose of shewing that he is not a person who is likely to have committed the alleged offence. Such evidence must be confined to statements as to the general reputation of the defendant, and not as to the witness's own personal opinion of the defendant's character: Archibald's Cr. Pl. & Ev. 288. If such evidence is given on behalf of the prisoner or accused; or if the accused questions the witnesses for the prosecution, upon that point: R. v. Long, 5 Can. Cr. Cas. 493; the prosecution may offer evidence of bad character; but not otherwise: Archibald, 288. And if the defendant claims the right to give evidence, he comes under the ordinary rules as to cross-examination in criminal cases, and must answer all pertinent questions even if they may implicate him or go to shew bad character: R. v. Connors, 5 Can. Cr. Cas. 70; R. v. D'Aoust, 5 Can. Cr. Cas. 407; and see on this subject generally, Phipson on Evidence, 2 ed. 164, 478. It is obvious that such evidence can only be of any value at all in doubtful cases, where the evidence of guilt is not strong: Archibald, 288.

As a general rule it is not admissible for the prosecution to prove facts not directly connected with the particular offence charged against the defendant, which are of a nature to impair his general reputation; but there are necessary exceptions to this rule. One exception is that when any act done by any person is relevant to the issue, any fact which supplies a motive for that act, is relevant even if proof of it tends to damage such person's good character: Stephen's Digest of the Law of Evidence, article 7; R. v. Barsalon, 4 Can. Cr. Cas. 347; R. v. Hutchinson, 8 Can. Cr. Cas. 486.

Evidence of other similar acts being committed by the accused, is not admissible in corroboration of the fact that he committed the offence charged; but upon proof of the act charged, such evidence is admissible to prove criminal intent:

R. v. Komenski, 7 Can. Cr. Cas. 27; R. v. Collyns, 4 Can. Cr. Cas. 572; Maken v. Atty-Gen. (1894), A.C. p. 65; R. v. Geering, 18 L.J.M.C. 215; R. v. Dossett, 2 C. & K. 306; R. v. Gray, 4 F. & F. 1102; R. v. Oddy, 2 Den. C.C. 264; in which cases the subject is fully discussed.

Previous Written Statements.

A witness may be cross-examined as to previous statements made by him in writing or reduced to writing, without the writing being shewn to him; but if it is intended to contradict the witness by the writing, his attention must, before such contradictory proof can be given, be called to such parts of the writing as are to be so used; and the judge may at any time during the trial, require the writing to be produced for his inspection, and may make such use of it at the trial as he thinks fit; Can. Ev. Act, sec 10: Ont. Ev. Act, sec. 17.

And a witness may be cross-examined as to any inconsistent statements he may have made, relative to the subject matter; and if he does not distinctly admit making them, proof may be given; but the circumstances of the supposed statements, sufficient to designate the particular occasion, must be mentioned to the witness, he must first be asked whether or not he made them: Can. Ev. Act, sec. 11; Ont. Ev. Act, sec. 18.

Questions as to Previous Convictions.

A witness may also be asked whether he has been convicted of any offence; and if he denies or refuses to say, the fact may be proved by a certificate from the clerk of the court having the records, and by proof of the identity of the witness: Can. Ev. Act, sec. 12; Ont. Ev. Act, sec. 19.

Except as above provided the answer of a witness in cross-examination upon questions irrelevant to the issue must be accepted as final, and cannot be rebutted: 2 Taylor on Ev., 9th ed. 947; R. v. Lapierre, 1 Can. Cr. Cas. 413.

Adverse Witness.

A party cannot impeach the credit of his own witness, by general evidence of bad character, but if the witness proves adverse, the party may be allowed to call evidence to contradict him, or to shew that such witness previously made inconsistent statements, but the witness must first be asked if he made such statements; and circumstances sufficient to designate the particular occasion when such statements are alleged to have been made, must be stated to the witness: Can. Ev. Act, sec. 9; Ont. Ev. Act, sec. 20. In proceedings under the Summary Convictions Clauses of the Cr. Code, the prosecution is not entitled to give evidence in reply, if the defendant has adduced no evidence, except as to general character: Code 721 (4).

Depositions in Previous Cases.

By consent of the defendant, or his counsel, the evidence taken in another case against either the same, or another defendant may be read as evidence in the case: R. v. St. Clair, 27 A.R. 308.

Sufficiency of Evidence.

As to the sufficiency of the evidence, see Paley on Convictions, 8th ed. 138.

The general rule is that the evidence must support the charge in every material fact, with specific date and place. But a variance as to time between the evidence and the information, summons or warrant, on the summary trial, is not material if the information was, in fact, laid within the time limited by law: Code 724 (2); nor as to the place, if the offence was in fact committed within the justice's jurisdiction: Code 724 (3); nor any other variance: Code 724 (4).

But if the defendant appears to have been misled, the justice must adjourn the case to give the defendant time to meet the new facts, if he so desires: Code 724 (4).

These provisions also apply to summary prosecutions under Ontario laws: R.S.O. ch. 90, sec. 2.

Privileged Official Communications.

Communications and reports of officers, and other official information of Government are privileged, if it is declared to be against the public interest to disclose them, and they cannot be disclosed without the consent of the Government: Horne v. Bentinck, 2 B. & B. 130, 162; Atty.-Gen. v. Briant, 15 M. & W. 169; R. v. O'Connor, 4 St. Tr. N.S. 935; Hennessy v. Wright, 57 L.J.Q.B. 594; R. v. O'Brien, 7 St. Tr. N.S. 1; Hardy's case, 24 St. Tr. 199, 753; and generally a police or other public officer cannot be required to give the names of persons on whose information he has acted, unless it is directly and necessarily in the interests of the prisoner: R. v. Richardson, 3 F. & F. 693; Marks v. Beyfus, 25 Q.B.D. 494; Humphrey v. Archibald, 21 O.R. 553.

This is on the ground of injury to the public service, and the question of allowing such evidence to be given is for the Government, or head of the department concerned, and not for the judge or magistrate.

And also upon grounds of public policy, it is the rule that, in all cases in which the Government is directly concerned (as in offences against the Revenue laws), an informer cannot be asked any questions tending to the discovery of the source of his information, or to shew the channels by which the disclosure of an offence was made to the officers of justice: 3 Russell, 592.

But in other cases such questions may be put, if, for any reason, the ends of justice require it: *ib.;* but not otherwise, for the answers would then be irrelevant, as not going to prove either the guilt or innocence of the accused.

Exceptions and Conditions.

As to the burden of proof in cases of provisoes, or exceptions from the operation of a particular law, Code 717 provides, that when the information negatives any exception, proviso or condition on which the prosecution is founded, it shall not be necessary for the prosecution to prove such negative; but that it lies on the defendant to prove the affirmative thereof. And Code 1125 (c) provides, that a conviction shall not be held invalid because of the omission to negative circumstances, the existence of which would make the act lawful, whether they are stated by way of proviso or exception, in the same or another section of the statute.

If an exception occurs in the description of the offence in the statute, it must be negatived by the prosecution, otherwise the defendant is not within the description of the offence; but if the exception occurs by way of proviso, and does not alter the offence, but merely states what persons are allowed to take advantage of the proviso, then it is for the defendant to prove that he is within the exception: Simpson v. Ready, 12 M. & W. 736; R. v. White, 21 C.P. 354; R v. McNicol, 11 O.R. 659; see R. v. Nunn, 10 P.R. 395, in which it was held that a proviso allowing military bands to play in the public streets, was not an exception requiring to be negatived by the prosecution on a charge of playing musical instruments contrary to a by-law.

But a conviction was held bad, notwithstanding sub-sec. 855 for not negativing the exception in a by-law, under sec. 583 of the Ontario Municipal Act prohibiting hawkers and peddlers trading without license, but excepting from its operation the manufacturer or his agent peddling goods manufactured in Canada: R. v. McFarlane, 33 C.L.J. 119; R. v. Smith, 31 O.R. 224; and see Ex p. Herrell, No. 2, 12 Man. R. 522; 3 Can. Cr. Cas. 15; R. v. Strauss (B.C.), 1 Can. Cr. Cas. 103, 108.

Public Documents.

As to proof of public documents, see Canada Evidence Act, secs. 19-29; Ont. Evid. Act, sec. 21. And as to proof of private documents see 3 Russell, 469.

Municipal by-laws are proved by producing the original by-law, or a printed copy certified by the municipal clerk; Ontario Municipal Act, R.S.O. ch. 223, sec. 334; and they can only be so proved: R. v. Dowsley, 19 O.R. 622; R. v. Banks (N.W.T.), 1 Can. Cr. Cas. 370.

Proclamations or orders of the Governor-General, or Lieut.-Governer in-Council; or rules, regulations or by-laws made by the Governer-in-Council in pursuance of a statute, and published in the *Canada* or *Ontario Gazette,* do not require to be proved, but are judicially noticed: Canada Evidence Act, sec. 22-30; Ontario Evidence Act, sec. 25. But a cutting from the *Official Gazette* is not sfficient evidence: R. v. Lowe, 48 L.T. 768.

Matters of Record.

On a trial for perjury it is necessary to prove the record of the proceedings and evidence, either by production of the original record; or an exemplification, or a certified copy under sec. 23 Can. Ev. Act;; and the *viva voce,* testimony of the clerk of the court and of the stenographer is insufficient: R. v. Drummond, 10 Can. Cr. Cas. 340.

Proof of Age of Young Person.

In proving the age of a young person for the purposes of secs. 211, 215, 242, 243, 245, 294, 301, 302, 315 and 316 of the Cr.

Code, the following is *prima facie* evidence: an entry or record by an incorporated society or its officers, having had control or care of the young person at about the time it was brought to Canada, if such entry was made before the alleged offence was committed; or in the absence, or in corroboration, of the evidence of age, the justice, holding a preliminary enquiry, may infer the age from the young person's appearance: Code 984.

Accomplices.

Generally speaking, one competent witness is sufficient to prove all disputed facts: 3 Russell p. 636; and also see 3 Enc. of the Laws of Eng. 447.

But in some particular cases corroborative evidence is required by statute before a conviction can be made; as in the cases of the offences mentioned in Code 1002, and in some others, although not expressly required by the law, it is unusual to convict without corroborative evidence; for instance, it is unsual to convict on the uncorroborated evidence of an accomplice; R. v. Hargrave, 5 C. & P. 170.

The evidence of an accomplice is receivable on either side, and a conviction upon such evidence, without any corroboration, is valid in law: R. v. Beckwith, 8 U.C.C.P. 274; R. v. Fellowes, 19 U.C.R. 48, followed by R. v. Andrews, 12 O.R. 184; and although it is the rule of practice for the judge at the trial to advice the jury that they ought not to convict on the totally unsupported testimony of an accomplice; still it is not necessary to the validity of the conviction that he should do so: R. v. Andrews, *supra;* Re Menier (1894), 2 Q.B. 415; and the jury may convict, notwithstanding such advice, if they are statisfied of the truth of the accomplice's evidence: R. v. Jones, 2 Camp. 132; R. v. Seddons, 16 C.P. 389; R. v. Stubbs, 7 Cox C.C. 48; R. v. Gallagher, 15 Cox 291; R. v. Beckwith, 8 C.P. 277; Re Menier (1894), 2 Q.B. 415; 3 Russell, 636. So a justice should send a case of an indictable offence for trial on similar evidence.

On a summary trial, however, the justice or magistrate, is in the place of both judge and jury; and the degree of evidence, and the credit due to the witness, is exclusively in the judgment of the justice who tries the case. He should not convict upon the unsupported testimony of an accomplice without some satisfactory evidence going to shew the truth of the accomplice's story. There should be some fact deposed to, independently of the evidence of the accomplice, leading to the inference that the accused is implicated in the offence: R. v. Stubbs, 7 Cox C.C. 48: see notes to 2 Can. Cr. Cas. 261; 10 Can. Cr. Cas. 128. The unconfirmed evidence of several accomplices is of no greater weight than that of one: R. v. Noakes, 5 C. & P. 326. The evidence of the wife of an accomplice was held to be of no greater weight than that of the accomplice himself, in R. v. Neal, 7 C. & P. 168.

"An accomplice is one who knowingly, voluntarily and with common intent with the principal offender unites in the commission of a crime": see 10 Can. Cr. Cas. at p. 127.

Corroboration.

By Code 1002, 1003, no person is to be "convicted" of any of the offences specially mentioned in those sections upon the unsupported testimony of *one* witness, or of a child of too tender age to be sworn. But these sections apply only to the *trial* of the case at which the accused may be *convicted,* and does not apply to a preliminary enquiry before a justice; and the accused may be committed for trial without any corroborative evidence being given before the justice: Re Lee, 5 O.R. p. 597; Re Lazier, 30 O.R. p. 419; 3 Can. Cr. Cas. 167. So also sec. 16 of the Can. Evidence Act provides that no case shall be *decided* upon the evidence of a child which has been taken without oath, unless such evidence is corroborated.

The word "decided" in this section refers to the "final decision" or conviction (see Imp. Dict.; Naas v. Backman, 28 N.S.R. 504), and it does not refer to the preliminary enquiry before the justice upon an indictable offence; the result of the inquiry not being a "final decision," but only that there is a proper case to be sent to a higher court for decision. It is submitted that the word "decided" in sec. 16 of the Can. Evidence Act, is equivalent to the word "convicted" in Code 1003 (2); and if so, the case may be sent for trial on the unsupported and unsworn statement of the child: see Re Lee, 5 O.R. at p. 597; Re Caldwell, 5 P.R. 217; Re Lazier, 30 O.R. 419; R. v. Peacock, R. & R. 278; R. v. Wood, 5 E. & B. 49; Ex p. Vaughan Q.R. 2 Q.B. 114; Mould v. Williams, 5 Q.B. 469.

But on the summary trial of a case before a justice or magistrate, the unsworn statement of a child taken under sec. 16 of the Can. Ev. Act would have to be corroborated before any conviction could be made: R. v. DeWolfe, 9 Can. Cr. Cas. 38 and cases noted at p. 42.

As to what is sufficient corroborative evidence: See A. & Eng. Enc. of Law, 7th ed., p. 866; R. v. Wyse, 1 Can. Cr. Cas. 6; R. v. Conolly, 1 Can. Cr. Cas. 468; R. v. Giles, 6 C.P. 84; R. v. Vahey, 2 Can. Cr. Cas. 258, and notes; R. v. McBride, 26 O.R. 639; R. v. Brindley, 6 Can. Cr. Cas. 196, and notes at p. 200.

Dying Declarations.

The dying declaration of a deceased person, touching the cause of his injuries, and the circumstances of, and as to who was responsible for, the cause of death, may be proved, upon a charge of murder or manslaughter by the production of a written statement taken by a justice or any other person, or even by the oral evidence of a verbal statement by the deceased: R. v. Mahon, 18 O.R. 502. This is an exception to the general rule that only sworn and "first hand" evidence can be received; and it is on the ground of necessity, and that the dying person's consciousness of impending death is of such a solemn character that it is equivalent to the sanctity of an oath, and creates an obligation equal to that which is imposed by a positive oath, and so need not be on oath: R. v. Ashton, 2 Lewin, 147; R. v. Woodcock, 1 Leach, C.C. 500; R. v. Bernardotti, 11 Cox 316; Shurla v. Freccia, 5 App. Cas. 623.

But the statement must have been such as would have been receivable on the oath of the deceased if he had survived: R. v. Sellers, Car. Supp. 233; R. v. Jenkins, L.R. 1 C.C.R. 187.

Before evidence of the dying person's statement can be received, it must be proved that at the time it was made, the deceased believed that his death was impending, and that he had not even the slightest hope of recovery: R. v. Jenkins, *supra*, in which a statement by the dying person that she had "at present" no hope of recovery, was held to invalidate the evidence. There must be a settled, hopeless expectation of death: R. v. McMahon, 18 O.R. 502; R. v. Mitchell, 17 Cox C.C. 503; and that almost immediately: R. v. Osman, 15 Cox C.C. 1; or within an approximately short time: R. v. Laurin, 6

Can. Cr. Cas. 104; See R. v. Davidson, 1 Can. Cr. Cas. 351, in which the statement by deceased that he was shot in the body and was "going fast," was held sufficient. Even if the belief of his immediately impending death was not well founded: R. v. Whitworth, 1 F. & F. 382; but was the result of panic, the evidence is admissible; and the fact that the surgeon thought him likely to recover: R. v. Peel, 2 F. & F. 21; R. v. Whitworth, *supra;* or the fact that he subsequently entertained a hope of recovery, will not exclude his testimony: R. v. Davidson, 1 Can. Cr. Cas. 351; R. v. Hubbard, 14 Cox C.C. 565; R. v. Taylor, 3 Cox C.C. 84.

It is a question as to the state of mind of the deceased, at the time he made the declaration, and what his belief then was, as to his recovery: R. v. Reaney, Dears & B.C.C. 151; R. v. Morgan, 14 Cox C.C. 337; R. v. Cleary, 2 F. & F. 850. So lapse of time between the declaration and the death is immaterial, if it is clearly shewn that he believed himself to be hopelessly dying when he made the statement: R. v. Tinckler, 1 East P.C. 354; R. v. Mosely, 1 Mood. C.C. 97; R. v. Bonner, 5 C. & P. 385.

In R. v. Bernardotti, 11 Cox C.C. 316, the declaration was received, although the deceased lived for three weeks; and in R. v. Reaney, Dears & B.C.C. 151, *supra,* the deceased survived eleven days after making the declaration.

But it is prudent to have the statement made or repeated at as late a period as possible.

The burden of proof of the facts rendering the declaration receivable, is upon the prosecution: R. v. Jenkins, L.R. 1 C. C.R. 187; 20 L.T. 372; or on the accused, if the evidence is offered in his behalf, as it may be: R. v. Scaife, 1 M. & Rob. 551.

See further, R. v. Forrester, 10 Cox C.C. 471; R. v. Goddard, 15 Cox C.C. 7; R. v. McKay, 11 Cox C.C. 148; R. v. Smith, 16 Cox C.C. 170; R. v. Gloster 16 Cox C.C. 471; R. v. Steele, 12 Cox C.C. 170; R. v. Whitmarsh, 62 J.P. 711 and cases cited 3 Russ. 354; Archbold, 22nd ed. 294.

A sense of danger is not sufficient: R. v. Thomas, 1 Cox C.C. 52.

If the belief is not of almost immediate death, *e.g.,* not on the same day, it will be insufficient: R. v. Fagent, 7 C. & P. 238; R. v. Whitworth, 1 F. & F. 382; R. v. Osman, 15 Cox C.C. 1: and see notes of cases at page 111 of 6 Can. Cr. Cas.

It seems that the deceased's belief in impending death will not be presumed from the nature of the wound, and from the fact that he must have known of his condition unless these circumstances are accompanied by some other evidence going to shew such belief: R. v. Morgan, 14 Cox 337; R. v. Cleary, 2 F. & F. 850; R. v. Bedingfield 14 Cox, 341.

The declarant need not have *expressed* his expectation of immediate death, if it can be clearly inferred from the circumstances that he so believed: R. v. Dingler, 1 Leach, 504; R. v. Jenkins, L.R. 1 C.C.R. 187; R. v. Bonner, 6 C. & P. 386.

A dying declaration can only be received in a case of homicide, and in connection with a charge of causing the death of the deceased person, who made the statement, and cannot be received to prove previous transactions however relevant, but only upon the cause and circumstances of death: R. v. Mead, 2 B. & C. 605; R. v. Baker, 2 M. & R. 53; R. v. Lloyd, 4 C. & P. 233; R. v. Hutchison, 2 B. & C. 608; R. v. Newton, 1 F. & F. 641; R. v. Hind, 29 L.J.M.C. 147.

The dying declaration of a very young child, who could have no idea of a future state, is not receivable; and the declaration of a child four years old was rejected: R. v. Pike, 3 C. & P. 598.

But if the child is of sufficient intelligence to understand the solemnity of its circumstances, and expects immediate death, the evidence will be received; the evidence of a child ten years old was received: R. v. Perkins, 9 C. & P. 395.

The statement of a dying person was received although it related to the general conduct of the prisoner towards her generally, and not to any particular act of ill-treatment: R. v. Murton, 3 F. & F. 492.

A dying declaration of an accomplice (*e.g.* to a case of suicide) was received in R. v. Tinckler, I Den. V. 6; R. v. Drummond, 1 East P.C. 353.

The question of the admissibility of the evidence is for the judge: R. v. Woods (B.C.), 2 Can. Cr. Cas. 159; and its weight is for the jury: R. v. Smith, 18 Cox C.C. 470; Arch. 22nd ed. 294; so both are for the justice in a summary trial.

The dying declaration is receivable on behalf of the defence or of the prosecution, and statements therein exculpatory of the accused are admissible: R. v. Scaife, 1 Mo. & Rob. 551.

Form and Manner of Taking Dying Declaration.

The form of declaration is immaterial. It was held that a verbal statement of the deceased might be orally proved, even if a subsequent statement which had been reduced to writing and signed by the deceased, was not produced: R. v. Tranter, Fost. 292. But see *contra* R. v. Gay, 7 C. & P. 230: R. v. Trowter, 1 East, P.C. 356; and see R. v. Wallace (1898), 19 N.S.W. Rep. Laws 155.

As above indicated the declaration need not be on' oath.

It was held that the statement might be made in answer to questions, and even leading questions: R. v. Fagent, 7 C. & P. 238; R. v. Smith, 10 Cox C.C. 82. But in more recent cases it has been decided that if the statement is reduced to writing it must be in the actual words of the deceased; if in answer to questions the actual words used in both the questions and answers must be proved: R. v. Mitchell, 17 Cox C.C. 503; dissenting from R. v. Mann, 49 J.P. 743; see also R. v. Whitmarsh, 62 J.P. 680: R. v. Woodcock, 1 Leach C.C. 502.

The declaration may be oral or written; but if possible should be taken down in writing before a justice or magistrate; and signed by the declarant and justice, being first read over to the declarant.

It need not be made before a justice; but should be so when possible: Roscoe C.E., 10th ed. 38; R. v. Simpson, 62 J.P. 825.

If the declaration is taken in writing, it should be in the dying person's identical words; first taking down his statements as to his settled and hopeless belief that his death is impending almost immediately and that he has no hope of recovery; and then taking down a statement of the cause of his injuries, who inflicted them, and under what circumstances.

If practicable, the declaration should be signed by the person making it, as well as by the justice. The declaration may be taken in the absence of the accused; and even if no charge has been made against any person. But, if practicable, it is only fair to the accused that he should have an opportunity to be present, and if so, it would add to the weight to be given to the testimony: R. v. Woodcock, 1 East P.C. 356.

A statement made in the presence of the accused, but which cannot be received either as a dying declaration or as a deposition, cannot be received as an admission by the accused, unless it is shewn that the accused had the opportunity to answer or deny it, and also that he would have reasonably done so if it were untrue and did not by word or act dissent from it: R. v. Smith, 18 Cox C.C. 470; if so, it is receivable as an admission by the accused: R. v. Steele, 12 Cox C.C. 168.

An examination taken before a justice under the Criminal Code, but which turns out to be inadmissible as evidence, by reason of non-compliance with the requirements of the law, may be admissible as a dying declaration if the proper conditions are fulfilled: R. v. Woodcock, 1 Leach C.C. 502; R. v. Woods (B.C.), 2 Can. Cr. Cas. 159.

If a written declaration is lost secondary evidence of what it contained cannot be given: R. v. Gay, 7 C. & P. 230; but see 3 Russ. 395: but oral evidence may be given of what the deceased said.

If the dying person is a person who cannot speak English, his statement may be taken through an interpreter: R. v. Louie, 7 Can. Cr. Cas. 347.

As to the value to be attached to a dying declaration: see R. v. Spilsbury, 7 C. & P. 187; R. v. Ashton, 2 Lewin C.C. 147; R. v. Reaney, Dears & B. 151.

If the evidence of the dying person can be taken on oath in the usual way under Code 995 in the presence of the accused, it may be so taken.

The opposite party may give evidence to explain, or contradict, or otherwise invalidate the dying declaration: Carver v. U.S., 17 S.C.U.S. 228.

A justice or magistrate, in conducting a preliminary inquiry, should receive the evidence of the dying declaration, if it fairly appears that the conditions above indicated are complied with; and ought not to scrutinize it too closely, or reject the testimony, except on the very plainest grounds; but should leave any arguable questions for the court to decide.

Reference is directed to the copious notes in the following volumes of the Canadian Criminal Cases, upon this subject: 5 Can. Cr. Cas. 328; 6 Can. Cr. Cas. 111; 7 Can. Cr. Cas. 356.

Statements Made by Deceased as Part of Res Gestae.

Evidence of declarations made by a person since deceased immediately after an assault upon him, but not made in the presence of the accused, are receivable, if the circumstances and declarations were so connected with the main fact under consideration as to illustrate its character, to further its object or form in conjunction with it one continuous transaction: Gilbert v. The King, 38 S.C.R. 284.

Statements Made in Performance of Duty.

Another exception to the rule that hearsay evidence is not admissible (R. v. Saunders (1899), 1 Q.B. 490) occurs in the case of evidence of a statement made by a person since deceased, orally or in writing, of a transaction done by or to him, if it is shewn that it was his duty not only to be a party to the doing of the act but also to record it, and that the record was made at the time; and if it is shewn that he had no interest in misrepresenting the facts: Smith v. Blakely, L.R. 2 Q.B. 326; The Henry Coxon, 3 P.D. 156; Massey v. Allen, 13 Ch. D. 558; Chambers v. Bernasconi, 1 C.M. & R. 347; Polini v. Gray, 12 Ch. D. 411, 5 App. Cas. 623.

And another instance is, in the case of evidence of statements made to any one by a deceased person as to his state of health. This evidence is receivable on the investigation of a charge relating to the cause of the death of the deceased person: R. v. Johnston, 2 C. & K. 354; Aveson v. Kinnaird, 6 East 188.

Confessions.

Section 685 of the Criminal Code declares that nothing therein contained shall prevent any prosecutor from giving in evidence any admission or statement made by the person charged, which by law is evidence against him.

Any confession or any statement tending to shew guilt, (even if it does not amount to a confession: R. v. Martin, 9 Can. Cr. Cas. 371.), if it was freely and voluntarily made, is receivable in evidence; and if duly made and satisfactorily proved, is of itself, and without any corroboration, sufficient to warrant a conviction: 3 Russell, 6th ed., 478; Rogers v. Hawken, 33 L.J. 174; R. v. Eldridge, R. & R. 440; R. v. Sutcliffe, 4 Cox C.C. 270.

A statement made by one of two defendants jointly tried may be given in evidence even if it tends to incriminate the other defendant: R. v. Martin, 9 Can. Cr. Cas. 371.

Before evidence of a statement made by the accused *after his arrest* can be received it must be proved that he was warned that any statement made by him may be used against him at his trial: R. v. Kay, 9 Can. Cr. Cas. 403, and notes at p. 406.

Before any evidence of a confession or admission, if made to a *"person in authority,"* either before or after the accused has been charged with or arrested for the alleged offence, can be received, it must be proved affirmatively by the prosecution, that it was made without any inducement or suggestion by way of promise or threat, direct or implied or however slight, of a temporal nature, with regard to the charge: 3 Russell, 6th ed. 478; Enc. of the Laws of Eng., vol. 3, 147, 263.

The test is whether the words import either a threat of evil or a promise of good: R. v. Jarvis, L.R. 1 C.C.R. 96.

The onus is on the prosecution to satisfy the court upon these points, beyond any doubt; and if not satisfied, the court will reject the evidence: R. v. Warringham, 2 Den. C.C. 447 (note); R. v. Thompson (1893), 2 Q.B. 12.

The ground of exclusion is, not that there is any presumption of law that a confession, not given freely, is false; but, that it having been made under a bias, it would not be safe to receive a statement made under any influence or fear, as the truth of it becomes uncertain under such circumstances: R. v. Gardner, 1 Den. C.C. 329; R. v. Thompson (1893), 2 Q.B. 12; R. v. Baldry, 2 Den. C.C. at p. 442.

And in the latter case it was pointed out, that the objection to telling a person charged with an offence that "it would be better for him to speak the truth" is, that these words import that it would be better for him to say *something*, thus holding out a temptation to make a false statement, into which the prisoner might fall, under the influence of the emotions thus aroused, especially in a moment of great distress.

The principles above referred to and laid down in the Warringham and Baldry cases, were affirmed in R. v. Fennell, 7 Q.B.D. 147, in which it was stated, that any sort of threat, or violence, or improper influence, direct or implied excludes the evidence. And these cases were approved and followed by the Court of Crown Cases Reserved in an important and authoritative decision in the case of R. v. Thompson (1893), 2 Q.B. 12; and also in R. v. Romp, 17 O.R. 567.

In R. v. Thompson it was said, "If these principles and the reasons for them are, as it seems impossible to doubt, correct, they afford to magistrates a simple test. Is it proved satisfactorily that the confession was free and voluntary; that is, was it preceded by inducements to make a statement, held out by a person in authority? If so, and the inducement has not clearly been removed before the statement was made, evidence of it is inadmissible."

The inducement or fear, to invalidate a confession, may be by words or conduct, or both: R. v. Gillies, 11 Cox 69, and when the confession is obtained by words or conduct, which naturally must create hope or fear, although not made in express terms, it will be excluded: Bram v. United States, 18 Supreme Court (U.S.) 183; see also R. v. Partridge, 7 C. & P. 551; R. v. Drew, 8 C. & P. 140.

If a confession is obtained by an implied threat, or by means of a false statement of fact; by a person in authority, it is not receivable. As, where a person charged with stealing post letters, was induced to confess, by a false statement made in the presence of the Post Office Inspector, that he had been seen taking the letters: R. v. McDonald, 2 Can. Cr. Cas. 221; 32 C.L.J. 783.

But it is no objection that the confession was made under a mistake in supposition of fact by the prisoner, even if some artifice, not amounting to a falsehood, was used to draw him into that supposition: R. v. Burley, cited in 3 Russell, 6th ed., 485 (m); R. v. Ryan, 9 Can. Cr. Cas. 353.

The inducement or threat need not be held out directly to the person accused; so if a statement, such as "It will be the right thing for him to do to make a confession," is made to a brother of the accused, or to any person likely to communicate it to the latter, the confession so obtained is not receivable. And it is immaterial in such case, whether such statement was or was not, as a matter of fact, communicated by such person: R. v. Thompson (1893), 2 Q.B. 12, at p. 18.

A confession made to a person who did not himself hold out any inducements or threats, is nevertheless invalid, if the circumstances shew such a connection as that it appeared that the confession might really have been induced by a threat or promise by *someone*: R. v. Hope Young, 10 Can. Cr. Cas. 466; R. v. Rae, 13 Cox 209; R. v. Doherty (1), 13 Cox 23; R. v. Doherty (2), 13 Cox 24; see also R. v. Gillis, 11 Cox 96; R. v. Dingley 1 C. & K. 637. A confession must not only be without inducement but must be otherwise voluntarily made: R. v. Boyds, 8 Can. Cr. Cas. 209.

The requirement that it is the duty of the prosecution to prove that the confession has been duly made, was held not to be satisfied by the evidence of an interpreter that he remembered that any statement the prisoner made was voluntary; as it was not shewn that the interpreter knew what was in law a voluntary statement: R. v. Charcoal, 4 Can. Cr. Cas. 93.

The onus is on the prosecution to shew that the confession or statement was made without inducement or threat, and voluntary; and this, not merely by the officer so swearing affirmatively, but he must specifically deny the possible inducements by way of hope or fear, that would have made the statement or confession inadmissible: R. v. Tutty, 9 Can. Cr. Cas. 544; R. v. Boyds, 8 Can. Cr. Cas. 209: and notes of cases at p. 211 of same volume.

If the inducement has clearly been removed before the confession, and it appears that it no longer operates, the evidence is receivable: 3 Russell 495. For instance, the effect of the inducement will be considered to be removed if, after it was held out, but before the confession was made, the prisoner, upon the hearing before the committing justice, has been duly cautioned by the latter in pursuance of Code 684 and in the words there set out; and it is sufficient proof that such caution was given, that it appears on the face of the prisoner's statement returned with the depositions: R. v. Bate, 11 Cox 686 cited, 1 Russell, p. 498 (w); R. v. Lai Ping, 8 Can. Cr. Cas. 467.

But in R. v. Finkle, 15 C.P. 453, a confession having been made under an inducement held out by the prosecutor; and, afterwards, the prisoner, after having been duly warned in the usual way, by the magistrate, made a second confession; the second confession as well as the first was rejected; the judge not being satisfied under the circumstances appearing in evidence, that the promise of favour had not continued to act on the prisoner's mind. The warning in such a case should, besides the usual caution, also include the distinct statement to the prisoner, that the first confession cannot be used against him.

A confession made to a mere stranger to the matter and not a "person in authority" is receivable, no matter what statements the latter may have made, for no hope or fear could properly, or would naturally, arise in the mind of the accused from statements by a person having no authority: R. v. Taylor,

8 C. & P. 733; R. v. Moore, 2 Den. 526; R. v. Todd, 4 Can. Cr.
Cas. 514. But a confession may be invalidated by an inducement held out by a person not in any authority nor connected in
any way with the matter, in the presence of one who is in authority, and who does not dissent from what is said: R. v. Taylor,
supra; R. v. Hewett, C. & Mar. 534; R. v. Garner, 1 Den. 329 ·
R. v. Luckhurst, 23 L.J.M.C. 18; R. v. Pountney, 7 C. & P. 302 ·
R. v. Dunn, 4 C. & P. 543; R. v. Slaughter, *ib.* 544; R. v. Laugh-
ter, 2 C. & K. 225; R. v. Parker, 30 L.J.M.C. 144.

The persons in authority whose inducements will prevent
the reception of confessions, include all who are in any degree
engaged in the apprehension, detention, prosecution or examination of a prisoner, whether public officials or not. These
are more fully designated in 3 Russell on Crimes, 6th ed. 501,
and are stated to include "the prosecutor, his wife, or attorney, or a constable or other officer, or some person assisting
the constable or the prosecutor in the apprehension or detention of the prisoner, or a magistrate acting in the business, or
any other magistrate or magistrate's clerk, or a gaoler, or the
chaplain of a gaol; or any person having authority over the
prisoner, as the captain of a vessel to one of his crew, or a
master or mistress to a servant, or any person in presence of
one in authority, with his assent, whether direct or implied."
The rector of a church is a "person in authority" over the choir
boys: R. v. Boyds, 8 Can. Cr. Cas. 209: and see notes thereto.

An Indian agent under the Indian Act, R.S.C. ch. 81, is
such a "person in authority": R. v. Charcoal (S.C.N.W.T.),
4 Can. Cr. Cas. 93. A private person left in temporary charge
of the accused by the constable is a person in authority: R.
v. Enoch, 5 C. & P. 539; and so are the wife and relations of
the prosecutor, the master of a servant who had stolen his
property: R. v. Warringham, 2 Den. 447; R. v. Simpson, 1
Mood. C.C. 410; R. v. Upchurch, *ib.* 465; but see exception
in R. v. Moore, 2 Den. 522, in which case the above rule was
held not to apply to confession in a case of concealment of birth
by the servant.

If the confession is made after the accused was charged
with the offence, and even before being taken into custody;
or if he has been arrested; it will not be receivable, unless it
is first proved that he was distinctly warned that he was not
obliged to say anything, and that anything he says may be

used against him. As to what inducements or threats will, under the rules above referred to, exclude a confession: see 3 Russell, pages 479-493.

A confession, made under the statement that "it would be better for you to tell the truth," has always been disqualified · see R. v. McDonald, 32 C.L.J. 783; R. v. Fennell, 7 Q.B.D. 147; R. v. Jarvis, L.R. 1 C.C.R. 96; R. v. Jackson (S.C.N.S.), 2 Can. Cr. Cas. 149, and cases cited; or a statement that "it would be worse" for the accused if he did not confess; or "better" for him if he did: R. v. Rose, 67 L.J.Q.B. 289; R. v. Jackson (N.S.) 2 Can. Cr. Cas. 149. But a mere moral exhortation to tell the truth; or any statement not directly or indirectly importing any inducement or threat, is unobjectionable: R. v. Jarvis, L.R. 1 C.C.R. 96; R. v. Sleeman, Dears 249. As where it was said "you had better as good boys, speak the truth": R. v. Reeve, L.R. 1 C.C.R. 362; R. v. Rowe, R. & R. 153; R. v. Gibbons, 1 C. & P. 97; R. v. Tyler, ib. 129; R. v. Clewes, 4 C. & P. 221; but an admonition by the constable that the prisoner "had better not add a lie to the theft," excluded the confession in R. v. Sheppard, 7 C. & P. 579.

The inducement must be some hope of benefit or threat of disadvantage, in relation to the offence charged, or its consequences: R. v. Todd, 4 Can. Cr. Cas. p. 520. For instance, a promise to take off the handcuffs if the prisoner will confess, is not such an inducement: R. v. Green, 6 C. & P. 655; nor a promise to give liquor to the accused: R. v. Sexton, 3 Russ. C. & M. 462; and it is said that even making the accused drunk, will not exclude the confession; but it will be a matter for observation by the judge to the jury: R. v Spillsbury, 7 C. & P. 187. A threat to send for a constable unless the accused confesses will exclude the confession, but a promise to let the accused see his wife if he will confess, is not an inducement which will exclude the confession: R. v. Lloyd, 6 C. & P. 393.

The inducement must be as to some temporal benefit, and not such as is referable only to a future state: R. v. Gilham, 1 Mood. C.C. 186; R. v. Wild, 1 Mood. C.C. 452; R. v. Sleeman, Dears 249. If it plainly appears from a consideration of all the circumstances, that any threat or promise made did not effect the prisoner's mind in making the confession, but that, notwithstanding, it was entirely voluntary, the confession will be received in evidence: R. v. Thompson (1893), 2 Q.B. 12.

The statement made by an informer in expectation of turning King's evidence is not admissible afterwards on his refusing to prosecute: R. v. Gillis, 11 Cox C.C. 69.

Although a confession may be invalidated by an inducement or threat, yet the subsequent acts of the accused, or anything discovered as a result of the confession, may be given in evidence. For instance, where the stolen property was found in the prisoner's apartments in consequence of a confession improperly obtained, the fact of the finding, but not the confession, was received in evidence. And so much of the confession as relates strictly to the fact or thing discovered, and what the prisoner says, at the time of doing any act after the confession are receivable: 3 Russell 521.

A letter referred to in the defendant's confession may be read as part of the subject matter of it: R. v. Attwood, 20 O. R. 574.

Evidence of a statement by the prisoner's counsel at a previous trial, made on behalf of the prisoner, was admitted as evidence against him: R. v. Bedere, 21 O.R. 189.

What a person is overheard to say to another, or even to himself, is evidence against him; but must be accepted with reserve as being very apt to be misconstrued by the person who overheard it: R. v. Simons, 6 C. & P. 540.

A statement made by a third person in the prisoner's presence and not denied by him, is some evidence against him, even if some inducement was held out to the third person; but such evidence is of very little weight: R. v. Janouski, 10 Cox C.C. 365, unless the conduct of the accused, when such statements were made in his presence, clearly indicated his assent to what was so stated. And before such statements can be received, it must be very clearly shewn that the accused had the opportunity to deny them if he chose to do so, and that the circumstances were such that he naturally would have done so if they were untrue, and that, by his conduct, he appeared to acquiesce in them: R. v. Smith, 18 Cox 470; R. v. Steele, 12 Cox C.C. 168; see also R. v. Mallory, 13 Q.B.D. 33; Kelly v. The People, 55 N.Y. 573, noted in 7 Can. Cr. Cas. p. 90.

Upon a preliminary inquiry, evidence of a confession or statement by the accused should be received by the justice, if there is any evidence at all of its having been properly made and not unduly obtained, leaving the question of its sufficiency or validity to the court. But on a summary trial the justice must, of course, adjudicate upon it, as the court would do on a trial.

Sweatbox System.

Subject to the foregoing considerations, statements made to police officers, whether before or after the accused has been arrested or charged, are receivable as evidence, although they were elicited by questions put by the officer. A person suspected of crime may be questioned by an officer before being arrested or charged with the offence, without being cautioned, and what he says is receivable in evidence against him. After being charged or arrested, the statements so obtained are generally considered to be receivable in evidence if the court is fully satisfied that they were not obtained by any undue or improper means: R. v. Day, 20 O.R. 209; and if the accused was expressly warned that anything he said, might be used in evidence against him but not otherwise.

The case of R. v. Day was followed by the Appellate Court of Quebec in R. v. Viau, Q.R. 7 Q.B. 362: see also R. v. Elliott, 31 O.R. 14; 3 Can. Cr. Cas. 95; R. v. Ryan, 9 Can. Cr. Cas. 347.

There has been and is a great divergence of judicial opinion both in England and in Ontario upon the question of the reception of evidence elicited by questions put by an officer of the Crown, some judges refusing to receive such evidence; the practice of so obtaining confessions has been strongly reprobated, and an eminent English judge, while receiving the evidence as valid, threatened to have the officer who had made it a practice, dismissed from office: R. v. Brackenbury, 17 Cox C.C. 628.

There is no positive rule excluding evidence of admissions made by the accused in answer to questions by a police officer, either after arrest or (*a fortiori*) before arrest. Admissions so received were allowed in evidence in R. v. Brackenbury, *supra* and notes to same case. In which case the contrary decision in R. v. Gavin, 16 Cox C.C. 656 was overruled.

The question of the admissibility of evidence so obtained must be determined with reference to all circumstances of each particular case: R. v. Miller, 18 Cox C.C. 54, and as decided in R. v. Day, 20 O.R. 209 , and R. v. Ryan, 9 Can. Cr. Cas. 347, the officer has the right to question the accused, after duly warning him, and what the latter says is receivable in evi-

dence, if it is clearly shewn to the satisfaction of the court
that the admission so made was not obtained by any undue or
improper means: see notes in 1 Can. Cr. Cas. 398; 9 Can. Cr.
Cas. p. 356: R. v. Knight (1905), 21 Times L.R. 310; see also
R. v. Goddard, 16 J.P. 491, *per* Cave, J.; R. v. Coley, 10 Cox
C.C. 536; R. v. Reason, 12 Cox C.C. 228; R. v. Bodkin, 9 Cox
C.C. 403; R. v. Thornton, 1 Moo. C.C. 27; R. v. Kerr, 8 C. & P.
177; R. v. Jones, 12 Cox C.C. 241; R. v. Male, 17 Cox C.C.
689; R. v. Hirst, 18 Cox C.C. 374. Where the prisoner awaiting
trial in prison was questioned by a constable without being
cautioned and the court was of opinion that the questions were
put with the object of unfairly entrapping him, the answers
were held inadmissible: R. v. Histed, 19 Cox C.C. 16.

When it is proposed by the prosecution to give evidence of
a confession, the counsel for the defendant may interpose and
cross-examine the witness as to the circumstances under which
the alleged confession was given, with a view of shewing that
it was not voluntary but under pressure of promise or suggestion of advantage, or threat of disadvantage: R. v. Thompson,
(1893), 2 Q.B. 17; R. v. Lewis, 9 Can. Cr. Cas. 233.

Privileged Communications.

The rule that voluntary statements made by the accused
are admissible as evidence against him is subject to the following exceptions:

1. Communications between a client and his solicitor or
counsel, *bona fide* communicated in professional confidence.
These are considered, as a matter of public policy, sacred and
inviolable; and are not only absolutely privileged, but the solicitor is prohibited from divulging them, not only during the
continuance of the relation of solicitor and client, but for all
time: Cleave v. Jones, 7 Exch. 421; R. v. Cox, 14 Q.B.D. 153;
if they were professional and made in a professional character:
Hamelyn v. White, 6 P.R. 143, *per* Strong, J.; Gardner v. Irvin,
4 Ex. D. 49; O'Shea v. Wood (1891), P. 286; and even if no
legal proceedings were existing, or in contemplation: Minet v.
Morgan, L.R. 8 Ch. App. 361; see also, Hoffman v. Crerar, 17
P.R. 404; McBride v. Hamilton Prov., 29 O.R. 161.

This privilege is limited, however, to communications made
to counsel and solicitors, and it appears that no privilege ap-
pertains to communications made to a priest or clergyman:

Broad v. Pitt, 3 C. & P. 518; R. v. Griffin, 6 Cox C.C. 219; R. v. Hay, 2 F. & F. 4; R. v. Gilham, 1 Mood. C.C. 186. But the court will not compel a clergyman to disclose communications made to him in the confessional, if he refuses to divulge, although the evidence will be received if the clergyman chooses to disclose it: Broad v. Pitt, 3 C. & P. 518; R. v. Griffin, 6 Cox C.C. 219; R. v. Hay, 2 F. & F. 4.

The privilege extends, not only to communications made to the solicitor, but also to an interpreter (re De Barre v. Leverett, 4 T.R. 756) or an agent (Parkins v. Hawkshaw, 2 Stark. 239), between the solicitor and his client; and to the solicitor's clerk; Taylor v. Forestor, 2 C. & P. 195. But the privilege does not extend to a person who is not acting as a solicitor for the person making the communication, although he is one by profession, and may have received the communication in confidence: Rudd v. Frank, 17 O.R. 758; Wilson v. Rastall, 4 T.R. 753; nor does it extend to a conveyancer, 4 Atk. 525. Communications not made to the solicitor alone, or which were not intended to be kept solely to himself are not privileged. So a letter written by a solicitor for his client is not inadmissible on the ground of privilege; R. v. Doroner, 14 Cox C.C. 486. The privilege extends, however, to communications between the town and city solicitors of the party: Reid v. Langlois, 1 MacN. & G. 627. A solicitor who puts his name to a deed as a witness, is bound to disclose all that passed at the time, relating to its execution: Robson v. Kemp, 4 Esp. 233; 5 Esp. 52; Crawcour v. Salter, 18 Ch. D. 30; McGee v. The Queen, 3 Can. Exch. Ct. R. 304; and he may be called to prove his client's handwriting to a bail bond witnessed by the solicitor: Hurd v. Moring, 1 C. & P. 372.

The privilege does not extend to illegal transactions; and a communication made to a legal adviser in furtherance of an illegal purpose, as in the case of a solicitor being consulted previous to an offence being committed, in regard to the best means of committing it, is not privileged: R. v. Cox, 14 Q.B.D. 153; Williams v. Quebrada Rail Co. (1895), 2 Ch. 751; and not only so, but it is the duty of a solicitor to immediately inform the authorities of any intention to commit crime divulged to him by a person consulting him as a solicitor: Annesley v. Anglesea, 17 Howard's State Trials, 1139, cited in 3 Russell, 6th ed. p. 587. The privilege referred to does not extend to communications in regard to matters based on fraud:

Smith v. Hunt, 1 O.L.R. 334; Williams v. Q.R.L. & C. Co., (1895), 2 Ch. 751.

No privilege attaches to telegrams in the possession of a telegraph company. The Dominion Statute does not give any absolute privilege: Re Dwight and Macklan, 15 O.R. 148.

And a bank has no privilege in regard to a customer's account beyond what is provided by the Banking Act, which only prohibits voluntary disclosures as to customer's account: Hannum v. McRae, 18 P.R. 185; following the principle in Re Dwight and Macklan, *supra.*

A communication of a patient to his physician is not privileged: Wilson v. Rastall, 4 T.R. 753.

Admissions in Depositions.

Analagous to evidence of a confession, or voluntary statement above mentioned, is that of a statement made by the accused in his depositions on a prior examination; *e.g.*, before the coroner; or in any previous proceeding, civil or criminal. And the sworn depositions of a prisoner, made by him before a justice in a prosecution against another party, in connection with the same offence, are receivable as evidence against the former; the rule of law excluding the statement of a prisoner under examination before a justice on a preliminary inquiry, if sworn to, and so not taken in the manner provided by secs. 682-684 of the Cr. Code, only applies when the charge is against himself: R. v. Field, 16 C.P. 98.

Prior to the Canada Evidence Act, a witness could not be compelled to answer questions which would tend to incriminate himself if he objected and claimed the privilege or right not to answer on that ground. But, as already mentioned, sec. 5 of the Act referred to, provides that a witness is not to be excused from answering questions on the ground that the answer might tend to incriminate himself, but that the evidence so given can not be used against the witness afterwards, except in a prosecution for perjury in giving it.

The Canada Evidence Act, sec. 5, applies only to cases brought under Dominion laws, and proceedings over which the Parliament of Canada has jurisdiction; and they do not apply to proceedings founded on statutes of the Ontario Legislature, which, as pointed out at page 35, *ante,* has the power to regulate the giving of evidence in cases for infractions of its own laws: R. v. Douglas, 1 Can. Cr. Cas. 221.

The Ontario Legislature, by the Ontario Evidence Act, R. S.O. ch. 73, sec. 5, has retained the common law principle above alluded to, and under its provisions, a witness (except as provided in sec. 9, with reference to the defendant or the wife or husband) can not be compelled to answer any question tending to criminate himself, if he objects or claims privilege on that ground.

In regard to the question of the reception afterwards, of statements in the depositions of a witness as evidence on a criminal prosecution against himself, the rule is this: if the witness did not claim privilege, when he was giving his evidence, but answered voluntarily, then whether the charge against him is under Dominion or Ontario law, the evidence he previously gave in any court or place, in any proceeding, civil or criminal, will, notwithstanding sec. 5 of the Canada Evidence Act, be receivable as a voluntary statement made by him. There is no difference between a voluntary statement made in court, and one made anywhere else: R. v. Garbett, 1 Den. C.C. 236; R. v. Madden L.T. 505; R. v. Coote, L.R. 4 P.C. 599; 9 Moo. P.C. N.S. 463. The same rule will apply although the evidence previously given by the accused was in a civil proceeding under a provincial law, and although it was given compulsorily; unless he claimed privilege, it will be received against him: R. v. Douglas, *supra*.

But if the proceedings in which the witness gave his evidence, shew that he objected or claimed privilege, the depositions will not be receivable as evidence against him, except on a prosecution for perjury in giving such evidence.

A coroner's court is a criminal court within the jurisdiction of the Dominion Parliament, and a witness there is bound to answer incriminating questions; and if he does not claim privilege at the time, his evidence may afterwards be used against him; but if he objects, it cannot be so used. The same rule applies in regard to the reception of statements made in evidence taken in proceedings before the Exchequer Court of Canada: R. v. Connelly, 25 O.R. 151.

And the statements made by a witness before a committee of the House of Commons, may be used on a subsequent charge against himself; but only if the House so orders. The only protection the witness has in that case, is the protection from the use of the evidence without the consent of the House: R.

v. Connelly, 22 O.R. p. 229; and see R. v. Merceron, 2 Stark, N.P. 366.

The original depositions of the witness are the best evidence of what his statements were, and must be produced. But if they have been lost, or have not been so taken as to be used in evidence, the statements may be proved by parol; and the person who took down the notes of the evidence may be such witness, and may refer to the notes of evidence to refresh his memory: R. v. Erdheim (1896), 2 Q.B. 260; R. v. Troop (N.S.), 2 Can. Cr. Cas. 22. So, in cross-examination, a witness's former deposition may be read, to contradict him, if it was duly taken, and is a verbatim record; but not if the document called a deposition contains mere notes of the evidence and not what the witness has said: R. v. Ciarlo, 1 Can. Cr. Cas. 157; R. v. Graham, 1 Can. Cr. Cas. 388; as to the sufficiency of the depositions in this respect see Code 999; Jervis on Coroners, p. 219. Depositions of a witness, speaking in French and taken down in English, are not admissible to contradict him on a subsequent proceeding: R. v. Ciarlo, *supra*.

A grand juryman, or a constable who was in attendance upon the grand jury, may be called, at the instance of the Crown, to prove statements made by a witness before such jury; the privilege of secrecy being, in such a case, a matter which the Crown may waive, if in the public interest: 3 Russell, 595.

Evidence must be given indentifying the accused, as being the person whose depositions are offered in evidence against him; and evidence by the sheriff's officer that he believed him to be the same person, although he couldn't speak positively, is sufficient *prima facie* proof: R. v. Douglas, 1 Can. Cr. Cas. 221. And in a prosecution for a second offence under the Liquor License Act, proof of identity of the defendant must be given apart from the certificate of the former conviction: R. v. Herrell, 1 Can. Cr. Cas. 514.

Section 164 of the Cr. Code provides that wilful disobedience of any Act of any provincial legislature is an offence under the Cr. Code of Canada, and punishable with one year's imprisonment, unless some penalty or other mode of punishment, is expressly provided.

A prosecution under the above sec. 164 of the Cr. Code, for an offence against a Provincial statute, would therefore be "a matter respecting which the Dominion Parliament has jurisdiction to regulate the evidence": Can. Evidence Act, sec. 2.

But if the Provincial law provides a penalty or mode of punishment for its infraction, the proceeding must be in accordance with it, and there would be no authority to proceed under Code 164.

Subject to the provisions of the Canada Evidence Act, and other Dominion statutes, the laws of evidence in force in the various provinces apply to criminal proceedings taken in them: see R. v. Garneau (Q.B. Que.), 4 Can. Cr. Cas. 69, and notes.

In civil actions based on criminal proceedings under Dominion laws, the law of evidence of the provinces will apply, and not the Canada Evidence Act: O'Neil v. Atty.-Gen., 2 Can. Cr. Cas. 303.

CHAPTER VII.

THE JUSTICE OR MAGISTRATE.

Appointment.

The British North America Act, sec. 92, sub-sec. 14, gives the Provincial Legislature power to pass statutes authorizing the appointment of justices of the peace: R. v. Bennett, 1 O.R. 455; R. v. Bush, 15 O.R. 398; and R.S.O. ch. 86, provides for their appointment, which is by Royal Commission under the Great Seal of the province.

Justices in unorganized districts are appointed under the authority of R.S.O. ch. 109, secs. 45, 46.

Ex Officio Justices.

Certain officials are justices by virtue of, and while holding their official positions; thus, a police magistrate for a part of a county is an *ex officio* justice of the peace for the whole county, and has authority of two justices sitting together: R.S.O. ch. 87, secs. 27, 30; the head of every council, mayor of a city or town, reeve of a village or township, warden and members of county council, are *ex officio* justices of the peace: Municipal Act, 1903, ch. 19, sec. 473; aldermen are justices for cities.

Special Justices.

The following officials have authority as justices in connection with matters within their official charge: viz., provincial game wardens: R.S.O. ch. 287, sec. 22; fisheries overseers: R.S.O. ch. 288, sec. 42; crown timber agents and wood and fire rangers: R.S.O. ch. 267, sec. 16; Indian agents: R.S.C. ch. 81, sec. 161; quarantine officers: R.S.O. ch. 74, sec. 7.

Judges of the courts are *ex officio* justices of the peace for every county in the province: R.S.O. ch. 86, sec. 1.

Property Qualification.

A justice (other than one for an unorganized district, who requires no property qualification: R.S.O. ch. 109, sec. 45), must be in the actual possession of real estate (legal or equitable: Crandall v. Nott, 30 C.P. 63), as owner, or tenant for life, or tenant under lease for 21 years or upwards, of at least the value of $1,200, over and above incumbrances: R.S.O. ch. 86, sec. 9.

It is not necessary that his interest in the real estate should in all cases be worth $1,200; thus a life lease, or a lease for twenty-one years in real property of that value, is sufficient; even if the value of such life estate or lease is not worth that amount: Fraser v. McKenzie, 28 U.C.R. 255; Weir v. Smith, 19 A.R. 433; and an estate as tenant by the courtesy in the property of a deceased wife, such property being worth $1,200, is sufficient: Weir v. Smith, 19 A.R. 433. The justice's interest must be *in* the real estate, and not merely a claim *on* it, such as a mortgage on land.

Oaths of Office.

An *ex officio* justice is not required to take any oath of office or of property qualification except the oath of the office in respect of which he is such justice: R.S.O. ch. 54, sec. 13; Ont. Stat. 1903, ch. 19, sec. 475; but he must have taken the latter oath before acting as a justice: R. v. Boyle, 4 P.R. 256.

An appointed justice must, within three months from the date of the commission, take the three oaths of allegiance, office and property qualification; otherwise his appointment becomes absolutely revoked: R.S.O. ch. 86, sec. 12.

Forms of Oaths.

For form of oath of allegiance, see R.S.O., page 288; and forms of oaths of office and qualification at page 966. The clerk of the peace supplies these forms on application.

The oaths can only be taken before a justice of the peace who has previously qualified; or before the clerk of the peace, or a commissioner *per dedimus potestatem* appointed for the purpose by the Lieutenant-Governor in Council: R.S.O. ch. 86, sec. 10; the ordinary commissioners for taking affidavits have no authority to administer justices' oaths of office.

The oath must be filed with the clerk of the peace, who is entitled to a fee of twenty-five cents for filing each oath, and to twenty cents for the certificate, if it is desired: R.S.O. ch. 101; items 51, 58 of tariff.

If the oaths are taken within the three months, and transmitted at once to the clerk of the peace, they will be in time, even if the latter does not receive them until after the period has expired.

A justice who took the oaths under a former commission of the peace, need not do so again under a new commission; unless he has parted with the property on which he formerly qualified; in which case he must take a new oath of qualification, but no other oath is necessary: R.S.O. ch. 86, sec. 15.

A justice who acts without taking the oaths, or having parted with his property has not the necessary property qualification, or does not take a new oath on a change of property qualification, is liable to a penalty for each occasion on which he so acts; same statute, sec 16; and he may be prosecuted by indictment: Margate v. Hannen, 3 B. & Ald. 266.

Game wardens and commissioners are only required to take the oath given in R.S.O. ch. 287, sec. 22 (2-3.), before acting as justices. The refusal of a person who has been appointed is qualified to do so, in an indictable offence: Dickenson's Guide to the Quarter Sessions, 290.

Oaths of Justices for Unorganized Districts.

The forgoing provisions of the statutes relating to oaths of justices under R.S.O. ch. 86, apply also to justices appointed for unorganized districts: R.S.O. ch. 109, sec. 46.

Police, and Stipendiary Magistrates' Oaths.

The forms of oaths of police and stipendiary magistrates in Ontario, are given for the former in R.S.O. ch. 87, sec. 31 · and for the latter in R.S.O. ch. 109, sec. 38. They must also take the oath of allegiance; form in R.S.O. ch. 16, sec. 3.

These oaths may be taken before any of the officials before whom justice's oaths are required to be taken, *ante*; and are to be filed with the clerk of the peace: R.S.O. ch. 87, sec. 32.

There is no provision limiting the time within which this is to be done, or the oaths taken; but magistrates are not to act, not being duly qualified to do so, until the oaths are taken.

Magistrates are not required to be possessed of any property qualification, or take any oath regarding it: R.S.O. ch. 87, sec. 33; R.S.O. ch. 109, sec. 39.

Justices De Facto and De Jure.

The failure of a justice or police magistrate or deputy, to take the required oaths, does not necessarily invalidate his acts, and will not do so, if his authority is not objected to on that ground at the time he acts. This is on the ground that, although not an officer *de jure* unless he has taken the oaths, still he is a *de facto* officer; and unless his right to act is challenged at the time, his action is valid: Ex p. Mainville, 1 Can. Cr. Cas. 528; Ex p. Curry, 1 Can. Cr. Cas. 532; R. v. Hodgens, 12 O.R. 367; O'Neill v. Attorney-General, 1 Can. Cr. Cas. 313; 26 S.C.R. 122; Margate v. Hannen, *supra*: Turtle v. Euphemia, 31 O.R. 404; Attorney-General v. Bertrand, L.R. 1 P.C. 520; R. v. Gibson, 3 Can. Cr. Cas. p. 454.

An officer de jure, is one who has the lawful right and title to the office, and has done everything necessary to make himself a good officer in point of law; while an officer de facto, is one who has the possession and performs, the duties of the office, under colour of right, by appointment, and has the public reputation of being the officer, without being actually qualified by law, by reason of the omission of some precedent act, such as the taking of the oaths, or some defect in his appointment: R. v. Bedford, 6 East 356; Parker v. Kett., 1 Lord Ray. 658, 19 A. & E. Ency. 394; see also Wilcox v. Smith, 5 Wend. (N.Y) 231.

The presumption of law is in favour of the right of the person acting: R. v. Jones, 2 Camp. 131; Gordon's case, I Leach 581; Berryman v. Wise, 4 T.R. 366; until such presumption is rebutted: R. v. Verelst, 3 Camp. 432; R. v. Fearman, 22 O.R. 456; R. v. Excell, 20 O.R. 633; R. v. Fee, 3 O.R. 107; Smith v. Redford, 12 Gr. 316; School Trustees v. Neil, 28 Gr. 408; R. v. Hodge, 23 O.R. 450; cases cited Taylor on Evidence, 8th ed., p. 187.

If, however, his right to act is objected to at the time, the officer who has not qualified, has no jurisdiction, and his acts are void: Re Chapman and London, 19 O.R. 33; and the accused will be released on habeas corpus, if taken into custody under a warrant issued by such officer after objection being taken · Ex p. Curry, 1 Can. Cr. Cas. 532: or the proceedings will be quashed on application to the High Court.

The acts of a mere usurper or intruder who has no colour of title, by election or appointment to the office, are utterly void whether objection is taken or not: cases above cited; Fletchburg v. Grand Junction Ry., 1 Allen (Mass.) 552.

If an officer is one *de facto* and not a mere intruder, (for instance, an officer who continues to exercise his functions after his term has expired; or an officer acting as deputy or delegate to a delegate; or one who has failed to take oath of office; or if his appointment is invalid; or if it turns out that he has not been appointed by the proper and lawful authority), and if he has some colour of right to the office, his acts are valid, unless objected to at the time, as regards all persons other than the holder of the real legal title to the office: O'Neil v. Atty.-Gen., 1 Can. Cr. Cas. 303; Turtle v. Euphemia, *per* Meredith, J., 31 O.R. 404; Speers v. Speers, 28 O.R. 188; Atty.-Gen. v. Bertrand, L.R. 1 P.C. 520; and see R. v. Gibson, 3 Can. Cr. Cas. 454, 465.

The above rules apply to a judicial, and, *a fortiori,* to a ministerial officer: O'Neil v. Atty.-Gen., *supra.*

See also Code 27: McInstry v. Tanner, 9 Johns (N.Y.) 135 McGraw v. Williams, 33 Grattan (Vir.) 510; Woodside v. Wagg, 71 Me. 207; Re Ah. Lee, 6 Sawyer (U.S.C.C.) 410; Re Gagnor v. Greene, 9 Can. Cr. Cas. 240; and the cases there cited as to officers acting *de facto* and *de jure.*

CHAPTER VIII.

JURISDICTION OF THE JUSTICE OR MAGISTRATE.

By What Laws Conferred.

Jurisdiction is the authority which an official has by law, to hear and determine and do justice between the parties in a cause or matter brought before him. It is never presumed; but must appear affirmatively in some authorizing statute, otherwise his proceedings are absolutely void. No power or right to hear and determine a cause can be given otherwise than by some jurisdiction conferred by and emanating from Sovereign authority: R. v. Breckenridge, 7 Can. Cr. Cas. at p. 118; R. v. Carter, 5 O.R. 567; Cullen v. Trimble, L.R. 7 Q.B. 416.

So in the absence of legal authority, jurisdiction cannot be conferred even by the express consent of all the parties concerned, much less by waiver, or by failure to object; and either party may afterwards repudiate the assumed jurisdiction or authority of the tribunal which he himself has selected, if it appears that it had no lawful authority in the matter: Farquharson v. Morgan (1894), 1 Q.B. 552; R. v. Essex, J.J. (1895), 1 Q.B. 38; R. v. Smith, 3 Can. Cr. Cas. 467.

So the justice or magistrate before proceeding in any matter, must look to see if there is statutory authority for it, either express or necessarily implied. If, for instance, a statute relating to an offence says, that a person committing a certain act is liable to a penalty upon summary conviction (not saying by a justice of the peace or magistrate), this would necessarily imply an authority on the part of any justice or magistrate having territorial jurisdiction in the matter.

The laws to which a justice or magistrate must look for his authority, include the Criminal Code and other statutes of Canada; the provincial statutes; and the by-laws and regulations of municipal councils, of police commissioners, under the Municipal Acts, of license commissioners under the Liquor License Acts, of boards of health, under Health Acts, and other bodies authorized by statute to pass by-laws or regulations, and impose penalties for their infraction; all of which come under the authority of justices of the peace.

In addition to these, the criminal law of England is in force in several of the provinces of Canada, except where repealed or altered:

The following are provisions of the Criminal Code in that regard:

In Ontario:

Code 10, 589, provide that the criminal law of England as it existed on the 17th September 1792, unless repealed or amended as there stated, shall be the criminal law of the province: R. v. Cole, 5 Can. Cr. Cas. 330.

In British Columbia:

By Code 11, the criminal law of England as it existed on 19th November 1858, except as it has been repealed or altered in the way there stated, is the criminal law of that province.

In Manitoba:

Code 12, makes similar application to that province of the English criminal law as it existed on 15th July 1870: see R. v. Carlisle, 13 B. & Ald. 161; R. v. Cole, 5 Can. Cr. Cas. 330.

In all the provinces the English criminal law is a part of their constitution.

Nothwithstanding the Criminal Code, the English common law as to crime, is still operative in Canada, even in cases provided for by the Criminal Code or criminal law of Canada, unless there is such repugnance as gives prevalence to the latter law.

No subsequent statute as to crime passed by the British Parliament applies to Canada, unless the Act is by the express terms thereof, or of some other Act, made applicable to Canada or some portion thereof as part of His Majesty's dominions: Code 589.

In the various laws above referred to, are to be found the provisions for the trial and punishment of offenders against the law; and the duty of administering them is imposed upon justices of the peace and the courts of the province, as will be particularly described in the following pages.

JURISDICTION, IN REGARD TO THE PLACE WHERE OFFENCE COMMITTED.

A justice or magistrate has jurisdiction to proceed against persons charged with crime, or offences against the law, in the following circumstances only:—

1. Offences Committed in the Justice's County.

In the case of a person accused of committing an indictable offence (that is, one which the clause of the statute relating to it designates as *"indictable"*), if it was alleged to have been committed within the justice's county or territory, wherever the accused person may be at the time the proceedings are commenced: Code 653 (*b*): see notes and cases cited, in 1 Can. Cr. Cas. 284.   This jurisdiction extends also to the case of a person committing an offence, for which he may be summarily tried and convicted, within the justices or magistrates territoral jurisdiction, under the summary convictions clauses of the Cr. Code: Code 707 (2).   But no authority can be exercised over the person of a defendant in a summary convictions case, while he is out of the province: Ex p. Donovan, 3 Can. Cr. Cas. 286; Ex p. Simpson, 37 C.L.J. 510; Ex p. Fleming, 14 C.L.T. 106; and see cases cited in 1 Can. Cr. Cas. p. 285, on the question of the locality of the offence

2. Offences Committed in Another County.

When the indictable offence, but not one which is the subject of summary conviction: Code 707 (2); was committed in some other than the justice's territory, but the accused is, or has his residence, within that territory or county: Code 653 (*a*), 577; R. v. Burke, 5 Can. Cr. Cas. 29; and cases cited in Tachereau p. 72.

The offence, in order to give the justice jurisdiction, must have been committed (or partly committed) within the Province, *e.g.*, the courts of the province of Ontario have no jurisdiction over an offence committed wholly in another province, even if the offender is in Ontario: Code 653-577-888: see R. v. Blyth, 1 Can. Cr. Cas. 263; R. v. Gillespie, 1 Can. Cr. Cas. 551; 2 Can. Cas. 309; R. v. Ellis (1899), 1 Q.B. 230.

If an offender is brought before a justice under Code 653 (*a*), for an offence committed in another county, the justice may either proceed with the case himself, or send the accused to be dealt with by any justice in the county where the offence was committed: Code 665 (2).   In that event, the first mentioned justice is to issue a warrant (Form 9 in the schedule to the Criminal Code): Code 665 (3); and a constable will then take the prisoner, with the warrant, information and any depositions that may have been taken, to a justice for the county where the offence was committed; and the latter will continue the case, as if it had originally been brought before himself: Code 665 (3), 666, giving a receipt for the prisoner and papers: Form 10. The justice for the county where the prisoner was arrested, has jurisdiction over the case, as well as the justice for the county where the offence was committed; and either may act: R. v. Burke, 5 Can. Cr. Cas. 29. In deciding which course to take, the justice who first has the case will be guided by the considerations of expense and convenience to the parties and witnesses.

A justice has no jurisdiction if the offence was not committed, and the accused is not present or does not reside, in the justice's county; except in unorganized districts, as to which see Code 585, and *post* under "Unorganized Districts"; and even if the accused should be brought before a justice on a summons or warrant, he does not under such circumstances thereby waive the objection, or come under the justice's jurisdiction: Johnston v. Colam, L.R. 10 Q.B. 544.

3. Receiving Stolen Property.

A justice's jurisdiction also extends to cases in which the accused is charged with having, *anywhere,* unlawfully received property which was unlawfully obtained by some other person, in the justice's county, e.g., a charge of receiving stolen property knowing it to have been stolen, even if the receiving was in another county: Code 653 (c).

4. Bringing Stolen Property into the County.

And also to cases in which the accused is charged with having in his possession in the justice's county, any stolen property, wherever it was stolen, either in Canada or a foreign country: Code 653 (d).

5. Offences Committed on the Boundaries of Counties, etc.

A justice has also authority over all offences, (whether indictable or summary convictions cases, and wherever the accused may be at the time), which have been committed in the justice's county; or which have been committed on any bridge, or in any water, whether tidal or otherwise, between the justice's county and an adjoining county; or anywhere in another county within five hundred yards of the boundary of the justice's county. In such cases a justice of either county has jurisdiction: Code

584 (a), (b), 707 (2). The five hundred yards are to be measured "as the crow flies": Mouflet v. Cole, L.R. 8 Exch. 32.

6. Offences Begun in One County and Continued in Another.

If an offence is begun in one county and completed in another, a justice in either county has jurisdiction even if the counties are in different provinces: Code 584 (b); R. v. Hogle, 5 Can. Cr. Cas. 53; R. v. Blythe, 1 Can. Cr. Cas. 284. For instance, in a case where a merchant in Ontario wrote a letter to a party in Quebec and obtained goods on a false statement in such letter of his affairs, a justice in either place may take the proceedings: R. v. Gillespie, 1 Can. Cr. Cas. 551; R. v. Ellis, (1899), 1 Q.B. 230; R. v. Essex, 2 East P.C. 420; 3 Russell, 6th ed. 722 (p).

7. Offences Regarding the Mails or Travellers, etc,

see the Post Office Act, and secs. 3, 209, 364, 365, 366, 510 D. (b) (c) (d), of the Criminal Code; or to a mail carrier, or a letter or anything sent by mail: or a person or any property in or upon any vehicle employed on a journey; or on a vessel employed in a navigable river, canal or other inland navigation. A person charged with any of these offences may be brought before any justice in any county through which the vehicle passed on its journey; or if it passed along a boundary of two counties, a justice of either may act: Code 584 (c). As to what are offences in or upon any vehicle, see R. v. Sharpe, Dears C.C. 415.

8. A Person Aiding or Abetting,

in one county an offence committed in another county, may be brought before a justice for either county: Code 707 (2).

9. Offences Committed in Unorganized Districts.

Or on any lake or river not embraced in any organized county or district, may be taken before a justice of any county in the province, and dealt with as if the offence was committed in the justice's county: Code 585.

10. Offences Committed in the Unorganized Regions North of Ontario and Quebec

May be brought before a justice of any county or district in either province: Code 586.

11. Offences Committed at Sea.

A justice has authority to conduct a preliminary enquiry and commit for trial, any person who is, or is suspected to be within the justice's territorial jurisdiction, and who is suspected of having committed any indictable offence on the high sea, or in any creek, harbour, haven or other place in which the Admiralty of England has jurisdiction: Code 656.

The jurisdiction of the Admiralty of England extends to all British ships on the high sea, in British and foreign ports, and in other places where great ships go, to and from the high sea. A British ship is part of British territory, and has been likened to a British floating island; and a foreigner as well as a British subject committing an offence on board a British ship on the high sea, or in any foreign haven, river or place where great ships go, commits an offence within the jurisdiction of the Admiralty, and is amenable to British laws; and may be tried for the same before any British court within whose territorial jurisdiction he may afterwards happen to be found, or be brought: R. v. Lopez, 27 L.J.M.C. 48; R. v. Anderson, L.R. 1 C.C. 161; R. v. Carr, 10 Q.B.D. 76.

Code 138 specially provides for the arrest and trial of cases for piratical acts committed on the high sea.

All persons of whatever nationality on board any ship, British or foreign, in any Canadian port or place, are on Canadian territory; and amendable to Canadian laws. And by Imp. Statute 41 & 42 Vict. ch. 73, this is extended to the territorial waters of British possessions; that is, within three marine miles of the coast, measured from low water mark.

The above Imp. Statute expressly applies to all British possessions, and is in force in Canada: Code 10, 11, 12; and a justice may proceed in such cases in the same way as if the particular offence was committed within his territorial jurisdiction.

There is no authority for a justice or magistrate to summarily convict the master of a British ship for non-payment of wages, if the ship is of Canadian registration and in Canadian jurisdiction: R. v. Merkle, 7 Can. Cr. Cas. 369.

The leave of the Governor-General must be obtained when the offender is not a British subject, before any prosecution is begun for an offence committed within the Admiralty jurisdiction: Code 591; R. v. Heckman, 5 Can. Cr. Cas. 242.

The Merchant Shipping Act, 1894, Imp. Stat., 57 and 58 Vict. ch. 60, gives extensive jurisdiction to courts in British possessions, including Canada. Sec. 684 provides that every offence against that Act shall, for the purpose of giving jurisdiction, be deemed to have been committed either in the place where it was actually committed, or in any place where the offender may afterwards be found.

So, anyone contravening anywhere, any provisions of that statute, and afterwards being found in Canada, even if brought here as a prisoner by force (R. v. Lopez, 27 L.J.M.C. 48), may be dealt with here as if the offence had been committed in the county or place in Canada where the offender is so found.

. Sec. 685 gives to courts, justices and magistrates, for any district or place abutting on any lake, river or navigable water, jurisdiction over any vessel being in or near such lake, river or navigable water, and over all persons on board or belonging to such vessel, as if the vessel or persons were within the limits of the original jurisdiction of the court, justice or magistrate. This applies to all offences whether triable summarily or indictable; and any offence committed on such vessel, or by any one on or belonging to her, which would, if committed in Canada, be an offence against the laws in force there, may be dealt with (as if it were committed in Canada) by any justice for any district abutting on the lake, river or water on or near which the vessel was when the offence was committed.

Sec. 686 provides, that if a British subject commits an offence on a British ship on the high sea, or in any foreign port or harbour, or on board any foreign ship to which he does not belong; or if any person who is not a British subject commits an offence on board a British ship on the high sea; and such person is afterwards found in any British possession, the courts there have jurisdiction to try the offence as if it had been committed within the limits of their ordinary jurisdiction.

So that a justice for the place where the accused is found, may proceed in such case, as he would in the case of an offence committed in his county.

Sec. 687 further provides, that all offences against property or person committed at any place, afloat or ashore, out of British dominions, by any master, servant or apprentice who is then, or was within three months employed on any British ship (whether such person is a British or foreign subject), shall be deemed to be offences of the same nature, and be liable to the same punishment, and be enquired into and tried in the same manner, and by the same courts, as if the offence was committed within the jurisdiction of the Admiralty of England.

So that an offence by such master, seaman or apprentice, committed out of British dominions, may be dealt with in Canada, just as if the offence had been committed in the justic's county in Canada, if the offender is found there.

Sec. 711 also provides that any offences under the Act shall be punishable in any British possession, by any court or magistrate by whom an offence of the like character is ordinarily punishable, or in such other manner as may be determined by any local Act or law in such British possession. The local courts, and local laws, are applied.

By sec. 689 a British consular officer is empowered to send any master, seaman or apprentice who is, or was within three months, master, seaman or apprentice on a British ship, and who commits an offence, at any place, afloat or ashore, out of His Majesty's dominions, or any master, seaman or apprentice belonging to any British ship, who commits any offence on the high sea, in custody to any British possession, to be proceeded against before any court capable of dealing with the offence.

A justice before whom such offender is brought will proceed as if the offence was committed in his own county.

Section 712 makes all the provisions of the above statute, from sec. 680 to sec. 712, applicable to all British possessions, unless otherwise provided.

Section 745 repeals all previous statutes on the subject except 41-42 Vict. ch. 73, above referred to and 12-13 Vict. ch. 96.

By the provisions of sec. 1 of the latter statute, which is expressly preserved in force by sec. 686 of the above Imperial Act of 1894, any offence committed upon the sea or within the jurisdiction of the Admiralty, shall, in any British colony where the person is charged with the offence or brought there for trial, be dealt with as if it had been committted within the limits of the local jurisdiction of the courts of criminal jurisdiction of such colony; and by sec. 3 of the same statute,

if any person dies in any colony in consequence of having been
feloniously hurt or poisoned upon the sea, or within the limits
of the Admiralty, or at any place out of the colony, the offence
may be dealt with in the colony as if it had been wholly committed there.

12. Offences Committed on the Great Lakes.

The boundaries of the province of Ontario, and of each
county therein, bordering on the great lakes and rivers
extend to the centres of such lakes and rivers; and all offences
committed thereon, and within such boundaries, may be dealt
with by a justice for the county on which the lake or river
fronts: R. v. Mickleham, 10 Can. Cr. Cas. 382.

The great lakes are also within the Admiralty jurisdiction,
being a place where great ships go to and from the high sea;
and anyone committing an offence aboard a British ship, whether
within Canadian or American waters, is amenable to Canadian
law, and may be tried in Canada: R. v. Sharp, 5 P.R. 135; R.
v. Mickleham, 10 Can. Cr. Cas. 382.

Canadian ships are British ships, and the above Imperial
statutes apply to them: R. v. Sharp, *supra*.

Proof that the ship was a British ship need not be by producing the register; but it is sufficient to shew that the ship
belongs to British owners, and carries the British flag: R. v.
Allan, 10 Cox C.C. 405; R. v. Severy, L.R. 1 C.C. 264; R. v.
Jornsen, 10 Cox C.C. 74.

13. Fugitive Offenders.

Persons committing any criminal offence in any part of His
Majesty's dominions, other than Canada, are to be dealt with
as provided by the Fugitive Offender's Act, R.S.C. ch. 154.

14. Justices are Keepers of the Peace.

The English statutes, 18 Edw. III. ch. 3, and 34 Edw. III.
ch. 1, provided for the appointment of justices assigned to be
"Keepers of the Peace": and by the Royal Commission now issued to all justices they are charged expressly with that duty, and
invested with that authority. Their duties in that regard are
prescribed by the various clauses of the Criminal Code, and
will be dealt with more fully in the subsequent pages, under
the title of, "Articles of the Peace."

15. Juvenile Offenders.

Code 800-821 give two or more justices authority to try summarily the class of offences there specified, in which the offender is, or appears to be, under the age of sixteen years; and the proceedings are set out in Chapter XV. *post*

16. Neglected or Dependent Children.

A justice also has authority to deal with children of this class, as defined by the Act respecting the Industrial Refuge for Girls, R.S.O. ch. 310; and the Children's Protection Act of Ontario, R.S.O. ch. 259.

17. Offences Against Ontario Statutes or Municipal or Other By-laws or Regulations,

Are within the jurisdiction of any justice for the county where the offence was committed.

NATURE AND EXTENT OF JURISDICTION OF JUSTICES AND MAGISTRATES.

The authority of a justice of the peace in regard to offences which are alleged to have been committed against any of the laws above referred to, within the territorial jurisdiction above indicated, consists:

(*a*) In conducting a preliminary enquiry in the case of an indictable offence (that is, one which is, by the statute relating to it, termed "indictable"), with the view of ascertaining; whether there is, in the facts adduced in evidence, ground for the accused being committed for trial upon indictment before a higher tribunal.

These will be dealt with in Chapter XII., *post*, on Preliminary Enquiries in Indictable Offences. See also synopsis of indictable offences, *post*.

(b) In the summary trials of those offences in regard to which, it is provided by the particular statutes relating to them that one justice, (or two justices, as the case may be,) has express or implied authority to summarily convict the offender and award punishment.

These will be dealt with in chapter XIII. *post;* see also synopsis of summary convictions cases, *post*.

(c) In making any investigation or order which is specially authorized by statute. *e.g.*, under the statutes relating to neglected or abused children, or under the clauses of the Criminal Code relating to the suppression of riots; as to which see the synopsis of offences, under that heading.

Jurisdiction of two Justices Sitting Together.

Generally one justice is sufficient to deal with any of the foregoing matters, *e.g.*, one justice may hold any preliminary enquiry upon a charge for an indictable offence: Code 653; and except in special instances in which the statute or clause requires two justices to act, one justice has authority to conduct the trial of a summary conviction case: Code 707 (2).

But sometimes the statute or section relating to the offence requires that two justices must act in the trial of it: Code 707.

When this is required, a note to that effect will be found at the end of the form of charge in the synopsis of summary convictions cases. *post*: when not so noted, one justice alone has jurisdiction, although others may be associated with him in the trial, upon his invitation but not otherwise.

But in all cases, it is necessary to examine the particular statute or clause relating to the offence, to see whether one or two justices are required by it.

Special cases.

Two justices sitting together at the request and in the place of a police magistrate are invested with all his authority: R.S. O. ch. 87, sec. 29; but this only applies to cases of offences against Ontario statutes, and not to those under Dominion laws: same section.

Indictable Offences.

Two justices sitting together have also, in cases under the Criminal Code, sec. 771 (a), (iii) (iv) (v) (vi) (vii), special authority conferred upon them in the provinces there mentioned to try summarily a certain class of indictable offences there named. These will be presently discussed: *post*, p. 197 *et seq.*

Juvenile Offenders.

Two justices have also, under Code 800, 821, special author-ity to try charges of certain offences against juvenile offenders as there stated. These will be considered in Chapter XV., *post*.

Justices in Unorganized Districts in Ontario.

Two justices are also given special jurisdiction to try certain indictable offences in unorganized districts, and have the same authority and powers, within their territorial jurisdiction, as justices for counties, as above described: R.S.O. ch. 109, sec. 46.

Police, Stipendiary and District Magistrates.

The authority of these officials includes all the matters which are within the jurisdiction of one or more justices as above mentioned: *e.g.*, to hold preliminary enquiries in all indictable offences; and to summarily convict in all summary convictions cases, as above indicated; and to deal with cases of juvenile offenders and neglected children under the statutes before referred to.

They have in Ontario in these regards, authority and powers co-ordinate with those of justices of the peace; and may also sit alone and convict and do all acts in all cases in which two justices are required: Code 604; R.S.O. ch. 87, sec. 30; R.S.O. ch. 109, secs. 39, 40.

Jurisdiction of Police and Stipendiary Magistrates under Code 777.

But in addition to these functions, special authority and jurisdiction of a very important character, namely in the trial of indictable offences, is conferred upon "magistrates" in the several provinces by various provisions of the law. These will now be mentioned.

By Code 777, all police and stipendiary magistrates in *Ontario;* and also those for *cities* and incorporated *towns* in every *other* part of Canada: Code 777 (2); have authority and jurisdiction to try summarily, with the consent of the accused, all those cases which are within the jurisdiction of the court of general sessions of the peace; and to award the same punishment as that court has authority to impose.

This authority includes power to try by consent, cases of thefts of over ten dollars in value, whether the accused pleads guilty or not guilty; notwithstanding Code 782, 783, which do not interfere with the authority conferred by Code 777, on these officials: R. v. Bowers, 6 Can. Cr. Cas. 264.

The offences which are within the jurisdiction of the general sessions, (and so also within that of the magistrates above mentioned on consent), are set forth in Code 582 and 583.

In the synopsis of indictable offences, *post*, those offences are noted, which are not within the jurisdiction of the above mentioned magistrates to try summarily upon the consent of the accused. The procedure in the latter cases and in other summary trials of indictable offences mentioned below, will be described in Chapter XIV., *post*.

It is to be noted that sec. 777 of the Criminal Code confers the above jurisdiction upon police and stipendiary magistrates only; and a district magistrate has no such authority: R. v. Breckenridge, 7 Can. Cr. Cas. 116: see below under "district magistrates jurisdiction." Nor does Code 777 (2), confer this authority upon county or district stipendiary magistrates in other provinces than Ontario; the jurisdiction being restricted by that sub-section to stipendiary magistrates for cities and towns only. As to the authority of county stipendiary magistrates, see *post,* p. 202.

A county stipendiary magistrate in New Brunswick does not possess jurisdiction under Code 777, even although he may have certain functions, as such stipendiary magistrate, *in* a city forming part of the county; he not being a stipendiary magistrate *for* the city, and so not included in the functionaries mentioned in Code 777: R. v. Benner, 8 Can. Cr. Cas. 398.

The measure of jurisdiction conferred by Code 777, is that of the courts of general sessions of Ontario; and although there are no such courts in the other provinces, the police and stipendiary magistrates for cities and towns there, have nevertheless the same jurisdiction as that which has been created for police and stipendiary magistrates in Ontario, by Code 777: Ex p. Van cini, 8 Can. Cr. Cas. 164; sustained on appeal by the Supreme Court of Canada, reported in 8 Can. Cr. Cas. 228.

A police magistrate, when acting under Code 777, has authority to impose the same punishment as the general sessions could do. notwithstanding the offence may also be triable before him in his capacity of an *ex officio* justice of the peace; and he is not limited to the lesser punishment applicable to the offence on a summary conviction before a justice; *e.g.*, in the case of a common assault, he may if he is acting under Code 777, inflict the punishment as for an indictable offence; although if he acted as an *ex officio* justice in the case he could only inflict the lesser punishment prescribed by the latter part of Code

291: R. v. Hawes, 6 Can. Cr. Cas. 238.   So also he may under Code 777 impose more than six months' imprisonment for an aggravated assault under Code 773 (c), notwithstanding Code 781 limits the punishment to six months; the general sessions having authority to inflict the punishment stated in Code 295: R. v. Archibald, 4 Can. Cr. Cas. 159; and in a case of theft under $10 in value the magistrate may impose the punishment provided by Code 386, notwithstanding the provisions of Code 780: R. v. Conlin, 1 Can. Cr. Cas. 41; and so also in the case of a charge of being the keeper or inmate of a disorderly house: R. v. Spooner, 4 Can. Cr. Cas. 209.   When the magistrate deals under Code 777 with any case in which he has a double juris-diction as above mentioned, he should shew clearly on the face of the proceedings that he was acting under that section of the Criminal Code; otherwise the presumption may be that he acted under his summary jurisdiction as an *ex officio* justice; and if the punishment was greater than he could impose as such justice on a summary conviction, the conviction would be invalid: R. v. Carter, 5 Can. Cr. Cas. 401.

Sub-sec. 3 of 777 was added to the Cr. Code 1892 after the decision in the Conlin case above cited; and made clear the law as stated in that case; viz., that the magistrate may impose the punishment stated in Code 777 notwithstanding the same offence may be included in Code 773, and punishable under Code 780, 781.

All police and stipendiary magistrates in Ontario, and for cities and towns elsewhere have also authority to try with the consent of the accused, any of the offences mentioned in Code 773. If the offence is one of those mentioned in Code 773 (f), no consent is necessary; neither is consent required in any case if the charge is against a seafaring person, who is only transiently in Canada, and who has no permanent domicile therein; and if he is charged within the city of Quebec or Montreal, or in any seaport town or city in Canada; or if the charge is preferred on the information of a seafaring person who is an essential witness: Code 774, 775.   In all other circumstances, a charge mentioned in Code 773 may only be tried summarily upon the consent of the accused to such trial; except, however, that in British Columbia, Prince Edward Island, Saskatchewan, Alberta, the North-West Territories and the Yukon all of these offences may be summarily tried without such consent, before any of the functionaries designated by the name of magistrates in Code 771 (iii), (iv), (v), and (vi) : Code 776; provided however that the cases referred to in Code 782, 783, (viz., thefts, false pretences and receiving stolen goods over ten dollars in value), cannot be so tried without consent unless either the accused or the person making the charge and who is an essential witness is a seafaring person : Code 776.

Trials of Indictable Offences by two Justices of the Peace. ·

In any of the provinces, two justices sitting together, may summarily try, without the consent of the accused, a charge of keeping or being an inmate of a gambling house, betting house, or house of ill-fame or bawdy house : Code 771(vii), 773 (f), 774; R. v. Flynn, 9 Can. Cr. Cas. 550; Ex p. Cooke, 3 Can. Cr. Cas. 72. They may also try summarily without such consent, a case of theft under ten dollars in value, but only when the prosecutor or defendant is a seafaring person as above mentioned, and if the offence occurred in Montreal, Quebec or a seaport town or city : Code 771 (vii), 773 (a).

Two justices in Ontario, Quebec, Manitoba, Nova Scotia and New Brunswick cannot try summarily, even with the consent of the accused, a charge of *attempting* to commit theft under ten dollars in value, (but in the other provinces they have that authority.)   Code 771 (a) (i), (ii), do not include two justices amongst the functionaries designated as "magistrates" in the provinces just named.   The offence of attempted theft comes under Code 771 (b); and is given to two justices in these provinces by Code 771 (vii) over those offences only which come under Code 773 (a) and (f), and these do not include the offence of attempted theft : Code 771 (vii) ; R. v. Morgan No. 2, 5 Can. Cr. Cas. 272.

In cases of theft of anything over ten dollars in value, secs. 782, 783 of the Cr. Code give a limited jurisdiction to the officials therein designated as magistrates and they may convict the accused if he pleads guilty and consents to summary trial; but not if he pleads not guilty.   The term magistrates in these secs. 782, 783 does not refer to or limit the jurisdiction of police and stipendiary magistrates in the province of Ontario, or police and stipendiary magistrates of cities and incorporated towns in other parts of Canada : for we have already noticed that the jurisdiction of these police and stipendiary magistrates under

Code 777, with the consent of the defendant, is co-ordinate with that of the general sessions, which has authority to try every case of theft.

So Code 782, 783 do not interfere with the authority given by Code 777 to police and stipendiary magistrates in Ontario, and in cities and towns elsewhere, to try offences of thefts of over $10, on the defendant's consent, even after a plea of not guilty: R. v. Morgan, 5 Can. Cr. Cas. 272; R. v. Bowers, 6 Can. Cr. Cas. 264.

The jurisdiction under Code 777 of all police and stipendiary magistrates in Ontario, and those cities and towns elsewhere, includes authority to convict of an *attempt* to commit the theft on the trial for a charge of the theft itself, if the evidence fails to prove the completed commission of the offence of theft, but establishes the attempt: R. v. Morgan, 5 Can. Cr. Cas. 272: and the consent of the accused to be tried summarily for theft, is to be taken as a consent to be tried summarily for any offence for which the accused might be found guilty on a trial at the general sessions, were he being there tried on a like charge: *ibid.*

Before any "magistrate" proceeds to try under Code 773 (formerly Code 783), a case of theft under ten dollars value, he must before he asks the question whether the accused consents to a summary trial, satisfy himself, firstly, that the property is alleged to have been stolen; and secondly, that the value does not exceed ten dollars: R. v. Morgan, 5 Can. Cr. Cas. 272.

Jurisdiction of District Magistrates, etc.

The first paragraph of Code 777 only refers to police and stipendiary magistrates in Ontario; and paragraph (2) does not include district magistrates or county stipendiary magistrates but only police and stipendiary magistrates for cities and towns; although in the cases coming under Code 773, 782, 783, district magistrates have the same authority as police magistrates. They, however, have also a conditional and exceptional jurisdiction over cases covered by Code 777, and may try such cases summarily, on consent, if the accused had previously been committed for trial upon the usual preliminary enquiry: Code 604-605; and they have the authority of a justice to hold such preliminary enquiry; and if they find, upon taking that proceeding, that the evidence is sufficient to put the accused on his trial, they may commit him for trial; and may then, but not before, call upon the accused to state whether he consents to be tried summarily; and upon such consent, the district magistrate may proceed to try the case summarily and convict: R. v. Breckenbridge, 7 Can. Cr. Cas. 116.

So also a stipendiary magistrate for a county who is not a stipendiary magistrate for a city or town in British Columbia, has no jurisdiction to proceed with a summary trial under Code 782, 783, until he has first taken preliminary evidence for the prosecution, shewing that there is a sufficient case to put the accused upon his trial. He must first take the evidence for the prosecution; and then if it is sufficient, he may call upon the accused to say whether he consents to a summary trial, and to plead to the charge; and may proceed as indicated in Code 782, 783: R. v. Williams, 10 Can. Cr. Cas. 330.

Magistrates cannot Convict When Holding a Preliminary Enquiry only.

A magistrate who has summary jurisdiction over an indictable offence, but is holding a preliminary enquiry only, cannot at the conclusion of the examination of the witnesses for the prosecution, turn the enquiry into a summary trial and proceed with the evidence for the defence and convict the accused. He must commence *de novo* and hold the summary trial in a regular way: Ex p. Duffy, 8 Can. Cr. Cas. 277.

But a magistrate holding a summary trial by consent for an indictable offence, may convict for a lesser offence, proved by the facts, for which a justice might convict without consent, and which is involved in the greater offence charged: *e.g.*, on a trial for an aggravated assault he may convict for a common assault: Code 949 applying to such trials as well as to trials on indictments: R. v. Coolen, 8 Can. Cr. Cas. 157, and notes, or he may convict for an indecent assault, upon the trial of a charge under the Charlton Act, Code 301: R. v. Cameron, 4 Can. Cr. Cas. 385:

The converse is not true however; and a magistrate cannot enlarge or extend by his adjudication the offence which is tried by consent, so as to convict for any more serious offence: R. v. Walsh, 8 Can. Cr. Cas. 101; R. v. Hogarth, 7 Can. Cr. Cas. at p. 130:

Nor can he try the accused on one charge by consent, and convict the accused of one which is altogether different.

When the accused has consented to a summary trial before a magistrate and has made his defence, it is no longer competent for the magistrate to turn the proceedings into a preliminary enquiry and commit the accused for trial nor to accept the prosecutor's recognizance to prefer an indictment: R. v. Burns, No. 2, 4 Can. Cr. Cas. 330.

Officers of the Royal North-West Mounted Police.

The commissioner and assistant commissioners respectively have within their respective territorial jurisdictions, all the powers of two justices of the peace under all statutes in force in Saskatchewan, Alberta, the North-West Territories and the Yukon: R.S.C. ch. 91, sec. 12; and the superintendents and such other officers as the Governor in Council approves, are *ex officio* justices of the peace: sec. 12 (2)

These powers also extend to the provinces and territories adjacent to the provinces and territories just named: sec. 13. See also secs. 18, 19 as to further powers of the above mentioned force.

The commissioner and each of the assistant commissioners of the force is, by virtue of the above statute sec. 12, "a functionary having the powers of two justices of the peace"; and therefore a "magistrate" under Code 771, (iv.) (v.), with all the authority to try any of the offences mentioned in Code 773; awarding therefor on conviction, the punishments provided by Code 778; if such offence is one within his territorial jurisdiction above mentioned. By Code 776, such authority is absolute in all such cases without the consent of the accused; except in cases coming within the provisions of Code 777, and except in the cases mentioned in Code 782, 783. The procedure is provided by Code 778; but in cases under Code 782, he is to deal with them in the manner described in Code 782, *et seq.*, and if the accused pleads not guilty he is not to try the case, but to proceed to hold a preliminary enquiry and commit for trial: Code 783, 784.

The offence of keeping or being an inmate or habitual frequeuter of a disorderly house, which is one of the offences within the summary jurisdiction of the police commissioner and assistant commissioners: Code 773 (*f*), includes a common gaming house as well as a house of ill-fame or bawdy house: R. v. Flynn, 9 Can. Cr. Cas. 550.

The jurisdiction of the superintendents of police and such other officers as the Governor in Council approves: (R.S.C. ch. 91, sec. 12); includes all the authority of a justice of the peace: *e.g.*, to try all summary convictions cases (see *post* Chapter XIII; and to hold preliminary enquiries in all indictable offences (see Chapter XII.); and the commissioner and assistant commissioners, as *ex officio* justices, have the same authority.

PLACE WHERE JUSTICE OR MAGISTRATE TO PERFORM JUDICIAL AND OTHER FUNCTIONS.

A justice or magistrate can only perform judicial acts within the limits of his territorial jurisdiction; but he may do merely ministerial acts anywhere: Paley on Convictions, 6th ed. 17; R. v. Beemer, 15 O.R. 266; Langwith v. Dawson, 30 C.P. 375.

Judicial and Ministerial Acts.

A judicial act is one in regard to which the functionary may exercise a discretionary or judicial power; but a ministerial act is one which he is obliged to perform as a matter of course: Staverton v. Ashburton, 4 E. & B. 526; Paley, 6th ed., 19 (note m)

The following are examples of judicial acts, viz.:—Admitting to bail: Linford v. Fitzroy, 13 Q.B. 240; issuing a summons or warrant to arrest: R. v. Ettinger, 3 Can. Cr. Cas. 387; taxing costs: R. v. Cambridge Recorder, 8 E. & B. 637; taking evidence, making remands, hearing and adjudicating on the case: R. v. Benn, 6 T.R. 198; see also Harper v. Carr, 7 T.R. 270; Painter v. Liverpool, 3 A. & E. 433; Skingley v. Surridge, 11 M. & W. 503; Paley, 6th ed., 19.

The following are ministerial acts which may be done anywhere, viz.:—Taking an information: Thompson v. Desnoyers, 3 Can. Cr. Cas. 68; issuing a certificate of dismissal: Handock v. Summers, 28 L.J.M.C. 196; Costar v. Hetherington, 28 L.J. M.C. 198; Paley 8th ed. p. 20 (note m); "backing" a warrant: Clark v. Woods, 2 Exch. 395; R. v. Kynaston, 1 East, 117; Dews v. Reilly, 11 C.B. 434; issuing a distress warrant or commitment: R. v. Fleming, 27 O.R. 122.

WHEN CONSENT OF GOVERNMENT OFFICIAL REQUIRED BEFORE PROSECUTION.

No foreigner is to be prosecuted for any offence alleged to have been ·committed within the jurisdiction of the Admiralty of England, except with the leave of the Governor-General; and on his certificate that it is expedient.   Code 591.

Sections 592-598 of the Criminal Code, also provide for the consent on the part of the Government before prosecutions are begun; and particular statutes also contain similar provisions in regard to the offences to which they relate; *e.g.*, the Lord's Day Act, 1906.

These will be noted at the end of the respective forms of charges in regard to which such consent is required, in the synopsis of offences; *post*, when such consent is required before prosecution is commenced.   It must be obtained before the preliminary proceedings before the magistrate are commenced: R. v. Barnett, 17 O.R. 649; except as provided in Code 545, for the offence there mentioned; and except for an offence committed on board ship within the jurisdiction of the Admiralty, in which case it must be obtained before the accused can be *convicted*, Imp. stat. 41 & 42 Vict. ch. 73, sec. 3.

Such consent must in all cases be given by the official named, personally; and his authority cannot be delegated: Abrahams v. The Queen, 6 S.C.R. 10.

CHAPTER IX.

Exceptions to a Justice's or Magistrate's Authority in Certain Cases.

A Justice Cannot Act:—

1. In Cases of Persons Under Disability to Commit Crime.
Infants.

A child under seven years old cannot be convicted of any offence: Code 17. This is declaratory of the common law principle that a child under seven is conclusively presumed not to have sufficient knowledge or discernment of good and evil, to be guilty of crime: R. v. Owen, 4 C. & P. 236; R. v. Smith, 1 Cox C.C. 260; R. v. Boober, 4 Cox C.C. 272; Marsh v. Loader, 14 C.B.N.S. 535. A child over seven and under fourteen years old cannot be convicted, unless it is shewn that he was competent to know the nature and consequences of his conduct, and to appreciate that it was wrong: Code 18.

The presumption is that a child under fourteen years and over seven years old does not know the nature of his conduct; but this may be rebutted by shewing that he did the act with guilty knowledge of wrong-doing; and the nature of the act itself, together with the child's conduct in connection with it, may afford proof that he had guilty knowledge: 2 Russell 115; R. v. Owen, 4 C. & P. 236; R. v. Vanplew, 3 F. & F. 520; R. v. York, Foster 70.

A boy under fourteen is conclusively presumed by the common law to be physically unable to commit any sexual offence whatever; and this cannot be rebutted by proof of the contrary: R. v. Allan, 1 Den. C.C. 364; R. v. Phillips, 8 C. & P. 736; R. v. Hartlen, 2 Can. Cr. Cas. 12. Code 298 expressly provides that a boy under fourteen is incapable of committing rape; but this provision does not supersede or exclude the above common law rule as to other sexual offences: R. v. Hartlen, 2 Can. Cr. Cas. 12; R. v. Cole, 5 Can. Cr. Cas. 330, and note. So a boy under fourteen cannot be convicted of an offence under Code 301, although proved to have arrived at puberty: R. v. Jordon, 9 C. & P. 118; R. v. Waite (1892), 2 Q.B. 600; nor assault with

intent to commit rape: R. v. Phillips, 8 C. & P. 736; R. v. Brim-
ilow, 9 C. & P. 366; nor of sodomy: R. v. Hartlen, 2 Can. Cr.
Cas. 12; but he may be convicted of an indecent assault: R. v.
Williams (1893), 1 Q.B. 320; R. v. Hartlen, *supra;* see Code 293;
or of aiding another to commit any of the above offences: 1
Hale P.C. 630. A person over 14 years old is presumed to have
capacity to commit any crime unless the contrary is proved: R.
v. Owen, *supra;* see also R. v. Wilson, 5 Q.B.D. 28; R. v. Mc-
Donald, 15 Q.B.D. 323; Lovell v. Beachamp (1894), A.C. 607.

Idiots and Insane Persons.

No person can be convicted of an offence who is labouring
under either natural imbecility or disease of the mind, so as to
render him incapable of appreciating the nature and quality of
the offence, and of knowing that it was wrong: Code 19; nor a
person otherwise sane, but having specific delusions, if the delusions caused him to believe in the existence of a state of things
which, if it actually existed, would justify what he did: Code
19 (2).

Everyone is presumed to be sane until the contrary is proved:
Code 19 (3): and see cases above cited.

Drunkenness,

Involuntary drunkenness is in the category of insanity, if
it was of such a degree, that the accused was incapable, even for
a time, of distinguishing right from wrong: 7 Can. Cr. Cas. 277;
but voluntary drunkenness is no excuse: 1 Hale P.C. 32. Acts
committed under delirium tremens, although the result of voluntary drunkenness, are not criminal: *Ib.,* R. v. Davis, 14 Cox C.C.
563. But even voluntary drunkenness is a factor in considering the question of criminal intention or *mens rea,* when that is
an essential ingredient of the offence: Pearson's case, 2 Lewin
144; R v. Doody, 6 Cox C.C. 463; R. v. Scaife, 1 M. & Rob. 551

Ignorance of the law is no excuse for crime: Code 22.

2. A Justice Has no Authority to Intervene,

Or take any part in any case which has arisen within the territorial jurisdiction of a police magistrate, except upon the request, illness or absence of the latter; nor can he take any part
in any case which has been initiated before a magistrate, without the latter's request: R.S.O. ch. 87, secs. 7, 17, 22, 23. But
this does not apply to proceedings against a police magistrate
himself: R. v. Chipman, 1 Can. Cr. Cas. 81. A justice may,

however, sit in a town or place for which there is a police magistrate, when hearing a charge which has arisen outside such town or place: R. S. O. ch. 87, sec. 23; R. v. Clark, 15 O.R. 49; R. v. Lee, 15 O.R. 353. A justice acting in the absence or illness of a police magistrate, at the latter's request, has only the jurisdiction of one justice; but if two justices act together *for* the magistrate, at his request or in his absence, they are invested with all the magistrate's authority: R.S.O. ch. 87, sec. 29: and justices acting "in the place of a police magistrate," should be so designated in the proceedings: R. v. Lyons, 2 Can. Cr. Cas. 218.

A stipendiary magistrate for a county appointed under R. S. Nova Scotia, ch. 33, has jurisdiction over offences arising in an incorporated town in the county, although there is a stipendiary magistrate for such town; unless the jurisdiction of the latter is expressly made exclusive: R. v. Giovanetti, 5 Can. Cr. Cas. 157.

3. A Justice or Magistrate Cannot Intervene,

Or take any part, in a case which is already in the hands of another justice, without the latter's consent.

The justice who issued the summons may hear the case, and convict, even if there should be several other justices present who decide to dismiss the case; unless they took part in the case or acted with the first justice's consent: R. v. McRae, 28 O.R. 569; R. v. Stansbury, 4 T.R. 456. But, at the request of the summoning justice, any others may sit with or for him; and in that event, the majority governs; and when the bench is equally divided there is no decision; but in such event, the case can be re-tried before any justice: Kumis v. Graves, 57 L.T. (Q.B.) 583. All of the justices adjudicating in a case must have heard the whole of the evidence, and if any of the evidence was taken in the absence of any of them, a conviction or commitment by him, or a majority (made up by including him), will be invalid: Re Nunn, 2 Can. Cr. Cas. 429.

If a justice takes an information and proceeds to convict after another justice has taken an information and issued proceedings, the former information and conviction are utterly void; and will constitute no defence to the first complaint: R. v. Bombadier, 11 Can. Cr. Cas. 216.

4. Disqualification of Justice or Magistrate by Interest.

A justice's or magistrate's authority in a case is ousted if he is a party to or, has any *pecuniary* interest whatever in it, direct or indirect, however small; or if he has any *substantial* interest, not pecuniary: R. v. Farrant, 20 Q.B.D. 58; R. v. Sproule, 14 O.R. 381; R. v. Fleming, 27 O.R. 122. And he will be restrained by prohibition if he attempts to act in such a case: Hutton v. Fowke, 1 Rep. 648; and any proceedings taken by him in it may be quashed; and the court will even punish him by attachment for so doing: Hereford's case, 2 Ld. Raymond 766.

By Relationship.

Near relationship, or business or other connection, between the justice and either of the parties, invalidates his authority in it; such as, one of the parties being a daughter of the justice: R. v. Langford, 15 O.R. 52; or his servant: Gallant v. Young, 11 C.L.T. 217; or niece of justice's wife: State v. Wall (Fla.), 19 C.L.T. 21; or when one of the parties was the justice's father: R. v. Steele, 26 O.R. 540; 2 Can. Cr. Cas. 433; or if a civil suit was pending at the suit of the defendant's husband against the justice: Ex p. Gallagher, 4 Can. Cr. Cas. 486; and notes at p. 490 of the same volume; or if the justice is engaged in the same kind of business as a defendant who is being prosecuted as a transient trader: R. v. Leeson, 5 Can. Cr. Cas. 184; or if the justice belongs to a temperance alliance which is prosecuting: Daigneault v. Emerson, 5 Can. Cr. Cas. 534. A justice who is a member of a municipal council, which expressly directed the prosecution, is disqualified: Tessier v. Desnoyers, 12 S.C. (Que.) 35; or who is a member of a local board of health, and who was present when a resolution was passed directing the prosecution: R. v. Lee, 9 Q.B.D. 394; in these cases it was held that where the statute which provided that the fact of the justice being such member, should not disqualify him, did not relieve him, in these particular cases; as he was present, when the prosecution was directed, and.for that reason he was likely to be biased. The authorities on the subject are fully summarized in the case of Leeson v. Medical Council, etc., L.R. 42 Ch. D. 384: see also Code 578.

Bias or Likelihood of Bias.

If a state of things exists, whether arising from relationship, interest or any other cause whatever, which would be *likely* to create a bias, even though it be an unconscious one, and even if there existed no actual bias in the justice in favour of either party, he is nevertheless disqualified; if the party effected was · not aware of that state of things, and so did not object: R. v. Steele, 26 O.R. 540; Wakefield v. West, L.R. 1 Q.B. 84; or if, knowing it at the time, he objected. But if the party affected was aware of it and did not object until the justice had decided the case or expressed an opinion in it, he cannot afterwards object: R. v. Clarke, 20 O.R. 642; R. v. Stone, 23 O.R. 46.

A physician who attended the deceased professionally before his death, was prohibited from holding, as a coroner, an inquest as to the cause of death: Re Harvey & Mead, 34 C.L.J. 330.

If one disqualified justice sits with others who are not so, the whole bench is disqualified, even if the disqualified justice did not actually interfere; the court is improperly constituted by reason of his presence with the others, and its proceedings are invalid; he must entirely withdraw: R. v. Klemp, 10 O.R. 143. See also, R. v. Yarmouth J.J., 8 Q.B.D. 525; R. v· Budden, 60 J.P. 166; Re Southerick, 21 O.R. 670. The court will not enter into an inquiry as to whether the disqualified justice took part in discussing the case with the others; if interested, his presence disqualifies the bench: R. v. Meyer, 1 Q.B.D. 173; R. v. London, 8 T.L.R. 175; R. v. Rand, L.R. 1 Q.B. 230.

It is no answer to the objection that there was a majority of the bench of several justices in favour of the decision, exclusive of the disqualified justice, or that he withdrew before the decision: R. v. Hereford Justices, 6 Q.B. 753.

If one of the convicting justices sits at the sessions on an appeal from his conviction, the proceedings will be void: Ex p. Clarke, L.R. 26 Ir. 1. But his mere presence, during a part of the proceedings during the same sessions, will not do so: R. v. London (Jus.), 18 Q.B. 421; Paley, 8th ed. 413.

The fact that a justice is subpœnaed as a witness by one of the parties does not disqualify him: R. v. Middlesex, 2 W.R. 459; R. v. Tooker, 32 W.R. 753; R. v. Farrant, 20 Q.B.D. 58; and a sitting justice may be called as a witness and examined upon the question whether he has any interest in the subject matter, or upon any other question of fact in the case: R. v. Sproule, 14 O.R. 375; but that decision was disapproved of in R. v. Brown, 16 O.R. 41; which decided that the question whether the justice was interested, was not for the bench of justices,

but a matter for subsequent proceedings to set aside the conviction or dismissal, and the justice may afterwards resume
his place on the bench: 3 Bacon's Abridgement, 7th ed. 206;
R. v. Tooke, *supra;* R. v. Farrant, *supra.*

It is said that if the justice refuses to be sworn or to give
evidence, the conviction may be quashed on the ground that the
accused was not allowed his "full answer and defence" as required by Code 715. The parties have the right to the benefit
of the justice's evidence of facts within his knowledge, bearing
on the case. But the conviction will not be quashed on the
refusal of the justice to be sworn as a witness, unless it is shewn
that the request that he should testify was made *bona fide*, and
that the justice could have given material evidence, and that
the defendant was prejudiced by such refusal: Ex p. Flannagan, 2 Can. Cr. Cas. 513.

In R. v. Petrie, 20 O.R. 317, Armour, C.J., discussing the
question of the propriety of a justice resuming his seat on the
bench after giving evidence, compared the position of a justice
to that of a juror, and said: "If the evidence given by a juror,
called as a witness, is contradicted, is he to join in determining
whether his evidence or that in contradiction is to prevail? If
his credibility is attacked, is he to join in determining the question of his own credibillty?

When the functions of a juror are united with those of a
judge, as in the case of a justice trying a case, he cannot be
both a material witness in the case, and also sit in judgment
upon it.

In R. v. Sproule, 14 O.R. 375, Cameron, C.J., said that the
defendant cannot be deprived of the benefit of the justice's
evidence; but that it would seem he ought not to take his seat
on the bench afterwards; and if he is the sole justice, he should
adjourn the case for some other justice to hear it, if his evidence
is of such a nature that it would be unseemly for him to try
the case.

The justice is bound to testify if called in good faith to
give evidence of material facts which cannot be otherwise proved;
and it would seem that he is not legally prohibited from going
on the bench again: Morth v. Campernoon, 2 Ch. Cas. 79; but
if the case can be proceeded with without the aid of the justice,
it would be proper that he should not further act; and if his
evidence was upon some contested point he ought, by no means,

to sit in judgment upon it, but should have some other justice take the case.

If, however, the evidence given by the justice is upon some uncontested fact or technical or formal matter, it would seem that there could be no objection to his resuming his seat on the bench.

The objection that the justice is interested may be waived: Wakefield v. West, L.R. 1 Q.B. 84; R. v. Clarke, 20 O.R. 642; R. v. Stone, 23 O.R. 46.

If it is desired to call the justice as a witness an affidavit must be produced shewing that the justice's evidence is absolutely necessary to the case and what it is proposed to prove by him, and that the application is made in good faith: Ex p. Herbert, 4 Can. Cr. Cas. 153; R. v. Johnston, 11 Can. Cr. Cas. 6.

5. Proceedings on Sunday.

Judicial proceedings on Sunday are prohibited by the English statute, 29 Car. II. ch. 7, sec. 6, which is still in force in Canada: Re Cooper, 5 P.R. 256; R. v. Murray, 28 O.R. 549; Foster v. Toronto Ry. Co., 31 O.R. 1; R. v. Cavalier, 1 Can. Cr. Cas. 134; and now by the Dominion Lord's Day Act of 1906. Such proceedings are void, even if both parties expressly consent: Taylor v. Philips, 3 East 155.

The prohibition is only as to *judicial*, and not to merely *ministerial* acts. Taking an information on a criminal charge is a merely ministerial act, and so may be done on Sunday. And issuing or executing a warrant to arrest on Sunday is expressly allowed by Code 661 (3). "Backing" a warrant of arrest from another county, is a ministerial act, and so may be done on Sunday: Clarke v. Woods, 2 Exch. 395. Issuing a summons is a judicial act: R. v. Ettinger, 3 Can. Cr. Cas. 387.

Holidays other than Sundays are juridical days and judicial and all proceedings on them are valid: Foster v. Tor. Ry. Co., 31 O.R. 1.

If the time limited for any proceeding expires or falls upon a holiday; it may be done on the next following day which is not a holiday: R.S.C. ch. 1, sec. 31 (*h*); R.S.O. 1897, ch. 1, sec. 8 (17).

6. Expiry of Time Limited for Prosecution.

Proceedings cannot be commenced in a criminal case after the time limited by law has elapsed. The following are the provisions of the law in that respect:—

The various periods of time within which prosecutions must be taken in respect of the offences set out in 1140 of the Criminal Code, are stated in that section.

In cases of offences punishable by a justice on *summary con viction* under the Criminal Code or any Dominion law, the information must be laid within six months from the time the offence was committed, (except in Saskatchewan, Alberta, the N.W.T. and the Yukon, where it is twelve months), unless the particular section or statute relating to the particular offence provides some other limitation: Code 1142. The months are calendar months: R.S.C. ch. 1, sec. 34 (16); R.S.O. ch. 1, sec. 8 (15). This section 1142 does not apply to summary conviction cases before magistrates under their extended jurisdiction conferred by Part XVI. of the Cr. Code.

It only applies to charges brought before justices or magistrates under the summary jurisdiction clauses, Part XV. (the summary conviction clauses) of the Criminal Code; and it does not apply even to a conviction for an offence which might have been summarily tried before a justice, but of which the defeudant was convicted before a magistrate under Part XVI. on the trial of a charge for a higher offence.

For instance, a conviction by a magistrate for common assault on a trial of a charge for an aggravated assault is valid, even if the prosecution was brought after the time within which the defendant could have been prosecuted summarily before a justice, for common assault: Code 1142 has no application to a trial for an indictable offence upon which the accused is convicted for a lesser one, even if the latter might have been the subject of a summary conviction before a justice: R. v. Edwards, 29 O.R. 451; R. v. West (1898), 1 Q.B. 174.

The principle on which the West case was decided is that a prosecution for the larger offence includes the lesser, and the commencement of prosecution for the former relates also to the latter.

In prosecutions under Ontario laws, including municipal by-laws, etc., section 2 of the Ontario Summary Convictions Act, R.S.O. ch. 90, as amended by the Ontario Statutes of 1901, makes the provisions of section 1142 of the Criminal Code apply; and the time limited for beginning the prosecution is six calendar months: R. v. McKinnon, 5 Can. Cr. Cas. 301. In many cases, both under Dominion and Ontario laws, the statute relating to the particular offence limits the time within which prosecutions must be commenced; and in such cases, the time so limited prevails.

The time is computed from, but not including, the day on which the offence was committed, that is, completed: Jacomb v. Dogson, 27 J.P. 68; unless otherwise specially provided by the statute relating to the offence: London v. Worley (1894), 2 Q.B. 826; Allen v. Worthey, L.R. 5 Q.B. 163. But if it was a continuing offence the time runs from the last day on which it was committed: Knight v. Halliwell, L.R. 9 Q.B. 412; Ex p. Burnby (1901), 2 K.B. 458.

The day next following that on which the offence was committed will be the first day counted; and the day on which the information was laid will also be counted as part of the time: Radcliffe v. Bartholomew (1892), 1 Q.B. 161.

If the time expires on any holiday, the information may be laid on the next following day which is not a holiday: R.S.C. ch. 1, sec. 31 (h); R.S.O. 1897, ch. 1, sec. 8 (17). The term "holiday" is defined by R.S.C. ch. 1, sec. 34 (11), and the days there mentioned will be those applicable to cases under Dominion laws; but in cases of offences against Ontario laws, by-laws, etc., the holidays are prescribed by R.S.O. 1897, ch. 1, sec. 8 (16); and see also the Ontario Statutes of 1903, ch. 7, sec. 2, which constitute the following Monday a holiday when any of the holidays prescribed by the Ontario Statutes falls on a Sunday.

In that case the Monday would also be excluded from the computation of time in cases under Ontario laws. There is no provision similar to this in any Dominion law.

If the offence is an indictable one, and is not one of those mentioned in Code 1140, and the particular statute does not provide for it, there is no time limited for beginning the prosecution.

There can be no prosecution for an offence by which one person kills another, unless the death occurs within a year and a day of the cause of death: Code 254; e.g., murder, manslaughter, etc.

Commencement of the Prosecution.

Laying the information is the commencement of the prosecution: R. v. Kerr, 26 C.P. 214; Thorpe v. Priestnell (1897), 1

Q.B. 159; and is sufficient even if the summons or warrant is issued after the time limited has expired: R. v. Lennox, 34 U.C.R. 28; Ex p. Wallace, 33 C.L.J. 506; R. v. Kerr, 26 C.P. at p. 218; R. v. McKenzie, 23 N.S.R. 6; R. v. Carbray, 14 Que. L.R. 223; Turncliffe v. Tidd, 5 C.B, 553. But the prosecution must be followed up without delay; unless it is unavoidable, as in the case the defendant cannot be found: Paley on Convictions, 6th ed. 91; R. v. Casbolt, 11 Cox C.C. 385; Ex p. Wallace, *supra*. Sometimes, however, the particular statute relating to the offence requires the defendant to be "served with the summons" or "apprehended," or "convicted," within a time stated; and if so, merely commencing the proceedings within the time will not suffice: R. v. Mainwaring, El. Bl. & El. 474; R. v. Bellamy, 2 D. & R. 727. In the absence of any special statutory provision applying to the case, and of the case not falling within any of the above provisions, there is no time limited for commencing prosecutions: 7 Enc. of the Laws of England, 471.

In the case of a common assault tried *summarily* under Code 291, before a justice, the time limited for the commencement of the prosecution is six months: Code 291, 1142; but it is provided by the same section that a common assault may be treated as an *indictable* offence; and if the justice for any reason deems it a fit case to be dealt with by a higher tribunal, instead of disposing of it by summary conviction, he will hold a preliminary enquiry and commit the defendant for trial; and in that event Code 1142, limiting the time for prosecution to six months, will not apply and there is no limit to the time for beginning the prosecution.

7. A Previous Conviction or Aquittal.

It is a principal of the common law, as well as being expressly provided by Code 730, 907, that a person shall not be tried twice for the same offence; and a previous conviction or acquittal by a competent tribunal is available as a defence to a person who is put in peril a second time for the same act or offence, whether on a summary trial before a justice, or before a jury, and a justice has no authority to entertain an information for an offence, if the accused has been already *tried* by a tribunal having competent jurisdiction, and either acquitted or convicted for the same offence, or upon any other charge, indictable or otherwise, upon the *same facts*: R. v. Dann, 1 Moo.

C.C. 424; R. v. Walker, 2 M. & R. 446; R. v. Stanton, 5 Cox C.C. 324; Wemyss v. Hopkins, L.R. 10 Q.B. 378; Lockyer v. Ferryman, 2 App. C. 519; and see R. v. London J.J., 25 Q.B.D. 357; R. v. Ashplant, 52 J.P. 474; Ex p. Evans, 63 L.J.M.C. 81; R. v. Monmouthshire, J.J., 4 B. & C. 844. A conviction or acquittal is a bar to a subsequent charge for continuing the offence, if the circumstances remain the same: Kinnis v. Graves, 78 L.T. 502.

The defence that the defendant was previously tried and either convicted or acquitted by a competent tribunal is good, even if the former conviction was in a foreign country: R. v. Hutchinson, cited in 1 Leach, C.C. 134 note (a); R. v. Roche, 1 Leach, C.C. 125; and even if no punishment was awarded on the former conviction: R. v. Miles, 24 Q.B.D. 423.

But in order to constitute it a bar, the former decision must have been *upon the merits;* and a dismissal on a technicality, or for non-attendance of the prosecutor, or on other grounds of non-suit; or if the certificate is otherwise illegally granted; or if there was a withdrawal of the case before decision; it is not a bar to a second prosecution: R. v. Strington, 1 B. & S. 688 · R. v. Green, Dears & B. C.C. 113; R. v. Machen, 14 Q.B. 74; Reed v. Nutt, 24 Q.B.D. 669; R. v. Herrington, 3 N.R. 468.

Even if the form of the second *charge* is altogether differently framed from the first, if it is based upon precisely the *same facts* it will be barred: R. v. Drury, 18 L.J.M.C. 189; R. v. Quinn, 10 Can. Cr. Cas. 412; and even if the second charge is in a more aggravated form: R. v. Elrington, 1 B. & S. 688; and see R. v. Hill, 7 Can. Cr. Cas. 38, and cases cited in notes at p. 43-45 of the same volume: also R. v. King (1897), 1 Q.B. 214; and notes in 2 Can. Cr. Cas. 497. But a second charge based upon the same facts with additional material facts, which have *subsequently arisen,* and which constitute it an offence of a different character from the one previously decided, is not barred. For instance, a conviction on a charge of assault is no bar to a subsequent charge of manslaughter, the person assaulted having died after the conviction for assault, the death making the case a substantially different one: R. v. Friel, 17 Cox C.C. 325; R. v. Morris, L.R. 1 C.C.R. 90.

A former decision does not prevent the court from inquiring into matters which have since arisen: Heath v. Weaverham Overseers (1894), 2 Q.B. 114.

By the same unlawful acts a person may be guilty of two separate offences, for both of which he·may be separately convicted: R. v. Smith, 19 O.R. 714; R. v. Handley, 5 C. & P. 565.

If the defendant may be convicted on the same facts under two statutes or laws, for substantially the same offence, a conviction under one law is a bar to a charge under the other; the offender may be tried under either statute, but cannot be tried twice: Code 15: Wemyss v. Hopkins, L.R. 10 Q.B· 378.

In order to be a bar the issue in the second proceeding must be identical with that in the first one, although the facts may vary, and although the charges formulated may not be the same: R. v. King (1897), 1 Q.B. 214; see notes of cases in 2 Can. Cr. Cas. 497. The test is whether the evidence necessary to support the second charge would have been sufficient to procure a legal conviction upon the first: R. v. Skeen, 2 C. & P. 634; R. v. Bird, 2 Den. 94; R. v. Drury, 3 C. & K. 193.

An acquittal on a charge of committing an offence is a bar to a charge of attempting to commit it: R. v. Ryland, 2 Russell, 55, for he might have been convicted of the attempt on the trial on the charge of committing it: Code 949: and a conviction for an attempt is a bar to a charge of committing the offence: Code 950 (2).

The adjudication on a previous trial by a justice in collusion with the defendant will not be a bar, and will be quashed: R. v. Gilliard, 12 Q.B. 527; and upon the trial of a subsequent proceeding the court will inquire into the circumstances under which a certificate of acquittal or conviction was made, and will recognize its futility, although the conviction has not been quashed: Reed v. Nutt, 24 Q.B.D. 669, (by Esher, M.R., Coleridge, C.J., doubting); Miller v. Lee, 25 A.R., p. 434.

A previous conviction which is void, as being beyond the jurisdiction of the convicting justice, is no defence to a second charge, even if the former has not been quashed: R. v. Lee, 2 Can. Cr. Cas. 233; Keating v. Graham, 26 O.R. 361; Forbes v. Michigan Cen. Ry., 22 O.R. 584.

The following are the special provisions of the Criminal Code, upon the subject ·—

It is a good defence, to an indictment for an offence that the defendant has previously been lawfully acquitted or convicted on the same charge; or on any other charge on which he might have been convicted upon his former trial upon the same facts: Code 907; see also Code 909. But it is no defence if he could not have been so convicted: R. v. Vandercomb, 2 Leach. 708. So an acquittal on a trial for murder is not a bar to a subsequent charge of assault on the same facts: R. v. Smith, 34 U.C.R. 552.

When the charge is substantially the same, but adds a statement of intention or circumstances of aggravation, tending to increase the punishment, the previous acquittal is, notwithstanding, a good defence: Code 909; unless the facts constituting the aggravation occurred subsequently to the conviction or acquittal, making it a new offence. In a case of theft of several articles at the same time, a conviction or acquittal on the charge for the theft of one of the articles is no defence to a subsequent charge upon the other articles: 2 Russell, 6th ed. p. 60.

These defences will be available upon the preliminary inquiry before the justice; for if the conviction or acquittal upon the previous trial is established, there is no proper case to be sent for a trial a second time.

On a summary trial before a magistrate for an indictable offence under sec. 771, etc., of the Criminal Code, the magistrate if he dismisses the case, is required to give the accused a certificate: Code 790; Form 57 to the Criminal Code, may be used: Code 799; and the person obtaining such certificate of dismissal, or who is convicted of the charge, is released from all further or other criminal proceedings for the same cause: Code 792.

A conviction by a magistrate under Part XVI., has the same effect as a conviction upon indictment: Code 791; and so is a bar to any further charge.

A justice who tries a case and dismisses it, is required to give the accused a certificate: Form 38 in the Criminal Code; and such certificate, without proof, is a bar to any subsequent information for the same matter against the same defendant· Code 730.

In the case of juvenile offenders, similar provision is made by Code 813 and 815: Form of certificate 58.

On a charge of assault or battery, preferred under Code 733, by or on behalf of the person aggrieved, if the justice dismisses the charge as not proved, or if he finds the assault to have been so trifling as not to merit any punishment, and so dismisses it, he is forthwith, on request, to make out and deliver to the person charged a certificate of dismissal (Form 38 to the Criminal Code), and upon obtaining such certificate, or if he has been convicted, and undergoes the punishment awarded, he is relieved from all further civil or criminal proceedings for the same cause: Code 734.

A certificate of dismissal of a charge of assault tried before a justice or magistrate, is a bar to a subsequent charge for an aggravated assault on the same facts: Wemyss v. Hopkins, L.R. 10 Q.B. 378; Holden v. King, 35 L.T. 479; Larin v. Boyd, 11 Can. Cr. Cas. 74; or to a charge of unlawfully wounding: R. v. Ellrington, 32 L.J.M.C. 14; R. v. Bibby, 6 Man. R. 472.

Code 733 and 734 apply only when the prosecution has been brought by or on behalf of the "party aggrieved."

If not so brought the certificate will be no bar to civil proceedings; but criminal proceedings will be barred under the general law.

The defendant must take the objection that there was a previous trial and dismissal or conviction, before the justice decides the case on the second trial, or it will be waived: R. v. Bibby, 6 Man. R. 472; R. v. Herrington, 13 W.R. 420.

A collusive conviction and certificate is not a bar: R. v. Bombadier, 11 Can. Cr. Cas. 216.

A conviction under Code 228, for keeping a disorderly house at a specified place from 3rd May to 3rd November is a bar to a charge under Code 773 (f), of keeping a disorderly house at the same place on 3rd November: R. v. Clark, 9 Can. Cr. Cas. 125; and no evidence of identity other than the certificate is necessary, ibid.: Ex p. Flannagan, 5 Can. Cr. Cas. 82; but a charge under the Can. Temp. Act, laid as between certain dates, is not necessarily a bar to another charge for an offence committed during the same period, but not identical with the first one: Ex p. Flannagan, 5 Can. Cr. Cas. 82; R. v. Stevens, 8 Can. Cr. Cas. 76.

A charge of personation at an election, is barred by a previous acquittal on a charge of taking a false oath of identity on the same occasion: R. v. Quinn, 10 Can. Cr. Cas. 412. In this case the subject is fully discussed.

If the offence is one which gives the party injured, an action for damages for the private wrong done by it, and a civil action is pending between the parties, in respect to it, the justice is not estopped from proceeding upon a criminal charge involved. But when it appears that civil proceedings are pending in respect of the same matter, the justice should either dismiss the complaint or impose a nominal penalty, unless there has been an outrage on public order; or unless by statute the civil and criminal proceedings are not to interfere with each other. For instance, when a civil action for damages for an assault is pending, a judgment will not be given on a criminal charge for the assault: R. v. Mahon, 4 A. & E. 575; Paley on Convictions, 8th ed. 172. But if the proceeding before the justice is merely to indemnify the complainant for an alleged wrong, a previous civil decision as to the same matter will be conclusive, e.g., judgment against a servant in an action of the latter for wrongful dismissal, is an answer to an application to a justice to recover wages: Routledge v. Hislop, 29 L.J.M.C. 90; Paley on Convictions, 8th ed. 172.

And criminal proceedings arising out of a civil action should not be proceeded with further than is necessary to apprehend the alleged offender, and hold him to bail, pending the conclusion of the civil proceedings, unless by direction of the civil court.

Even in cases in which the prior trial and adjudication are not a legal bar to a second prosecution; a second prosecution against the same party upon the same facts would be discreditable, to the administration of justice and should be avoided unless there has been a gross miscarriage of justice in the first case: see R. v. Williams, 10 Can. Cr. Cas. p. 332.

A dismissal on a preliminary enquiry before a justice for an indictable offence, does not prevent the charge being brought' up again before the same or any other justice: R. v. Hannay, 11 Can. Cr. Cas. 23

8. Title to Land.

In a case in which the title to land comes in question, on the hearing of a criminal charge, the justice's jurisdiction over the charge is ousted; this is on the ground that such question must be tried by a judge and jury in the civil courts; whereas the justice by convicting would be settling a question of property or other legal rights of the parties conclusively, and without remedy; if his decision happened to be wrong: R. v. Davidson, 45 U.C.R. 91. It is not for the justice to say whether the question of title is well founded or not; if it is honestly raised, and really believed in by the defendant, and there is some *colour of right* or shew of reason for it, the justice must dismiss the case, without at all investigating the legal grounds for the claim of title: Watkins v. Major, L.R. 10 C.P. 662; Scott v. Baring, 18 Cox C.C. 128; R. v. Davidson, 45 U.C.R. 91. The expression "colour of right" means "an honest belief in a state of facts which, if it existed, would be a legal justification or excuse"; because that takes away from the act its criminal character; but to do an. act in ignorance that it is prohibited by law, is not to do it with "colour of right": R. v. Johnston, 8 Can. Cr. Cas. 123; Ex p. Blaine, 11 Can. Cr. Cas. 193.

And when an offence consists of a positive act, the offender cannot escape punishment because he holds an honest and sincere belief which impels him to think that the law he has broken ought not to exist: R. v. Lewis, 7 Can. Cr. Cas. p. 267.

If the justice finds it is a mere pretence, raised for the purpose of avoiding penalties; or if the facts lead to only one possible conclusion on the question, and that is against the defendant, and there is no contradictory evidence on it, then there is no *bonâ fide* question of title raised, and the jurisdiction will not be ousted: Re Moberly v. Collingwood, 25 O.R. 625. The claim set up must be one which (if it were sustained by the facts) would be good in law; and not one that could not exist in law; Watkins v. Major, *supra*: Hargreaves v. Didams, L.R. 10 Q.B. 582; Reece v. Miller, 8 Q.B.D. 626; Pearse v. Scotcher, 9 Q.B·D. 162; Leatt v. Vine, 30 L.J.M.C. 207. The question for the justice to decide is whether the defendant's liability is contingent upon a decision as to the title to land, upon which there is a real dispute; if so, he cannot try it, and has no jurisdiction over the case: South Norfolk v. Warren, 12 C.L.T. 512.

9. Claim of Right.

In a case in which the defendant raises a *bonâ fide* claim of right to do the act complained of and which forms the substance of the charge, the above observations also apply. A *bonâ fide* claim of right ousts the justice's jurisdiction, as the parties are entitled to have it tried in the civil courts.

But in some instances the legislature has qualified this restriction, by enacting in effect, that in order to oust the justice's jurisdiction in the particular case, there must be not only a *bonâ fide* claim of right, but also that the defendant must give evidence to satisfy the justice that he really has fair and reasonable grounds to suppose he had the right to do the act complained of. Thus, in cases under Code 539, 540; and under R.S.O. ch. 120, sec. 1, it is provided that if the accused acted under a fair and reasonable supposition of right, he cannot be convicted. In prosecutions under such provisions, mere honest belief or claim of right to do what is complained of, is not sufficient to protect the accused; he must shew that there really were fair and reasonable grounds for such belief. It is for the justice, in such cases, not to try the question of right, but merely to enquire whether there were *reasonable grounds* for claiming the right; and if there were not, his jurisdiction over the charge is not ousted: White v. Feast, L.R. 7 Q.B. 353; R. v. Pearson, L.R. 5 Q.B. 237; R. v. Davidson, 45 U.C.R. 91.

The defendant in such case, must give evidence of facts upon which he could reasonably found a belief that he had the right to do the act in question: R. v. Malcolm, 2 O.R. 511; R. v. Davy, 27 A.R. 508, 4 Can. Cr. Cas. 28; R. v. Mussett, 26 L.T. 429.

In assault cases, Code 709 provides that the justice is not to try the case if any *bonâ fide* question as to the title to land, or bankruptcy, or the execution of any process of any court arises. In this section of the Code there is no provision requiring proof of reasonable grounds for the defendant's belief in his claim of title; the requirement is, merely that there must be a real question as to title, and that it is honestly raised; if so, the jurisdiction is ousted; no assault case, however clearly established, can be summarily tried by a justice if a *bonâ fide* question of the title to land is raised in it: R. v. Pearson, L.R. 5 Q.B. 237.

But if the assault was independent of the question of title, the fact that there was such a question, is no defence, even if the assault arose out of a dispute between the parties as to the title to land: R. v. Edwards, 4 W.R. 257:

In R. v. Clemens (1898), 1 Q.B. 556, (a wilful damage case), Lord Russell, C.J., held, that though the defendants were acting upon supposed rights, yet if they exceeded what was necessary for the assertion or protection of these rights, and thus committed damage, they were responsible criminally for such excess: Erison v. Marshall, 32 J.P. 691: referred to in R. v. Johnston, 8 Can. Cr. Cas. p. 129. But in R. v. Pearson, L.R.

5 Q.B. 237, it was held, that in assault cases a question of right is a good defence, even if excessive force was used, because the words of the proviso in the statute are large enough to exclude any cases of assault whatever, in which a question of right or title arises.

The question of title, to be a defence in assault cases, must be a question as to land; and not as to personal property: Code 709; White v. Fox, 49 L.J.M.C. 60.

Code 316 (2), makes it a good defence to a charge, under that section, of abduction of a child, that the accused claimed in good faith a right to possession of the child taken away. In that case the mere *bonâ fide* claim of right is a sufficient defence, if there is any colour of right whatever. But in bigamy cases Code 307 (3a) provides that no one commits bigamy by going through a form of marriage, if he or she in good faith, and on reasonable grounds believes his wife or her husband to be dead. In such case proof of such honest belief, and also, that there are reasonable grounds for it must be given by the defendant: R. v. Sellars, 9 Can. Cr. Cas. 153; R. v. Tolson, 23 Q.B.D. 168.

The questions of fact as to whether or not the defendant acted upon a *bona fide* belief that he had the right to do the act complained of; and as to whether he had reasonable grounds for his belief; and as to whether he sets up a question of title *bona fide;* are for the justice to decide, but may be reviewed by the court on motion to quash a conviction if the evidence is clearly the other way: White v. Feast, *supra;* R. v. Davey, *supra.*

When the evidence shewed clearly, that the defendant had acted upon a reasonable supposition of right, and there was no contradicting evidence, the conviction was quashed: R. v. Macdonald, 12 O.R. 383.

Criminal Intent and Mens Rea.

The principle upon which the defendant is allowed to set up an honest claim of right as a defence is similar to that which makes it generally necessary, to a conviction in criminal prosecutions, to shew that the defendant acted with guilty knowledge or intent.

The general rule of law is that a person cannot be convicted in a proceeding of a criminal nature unless it is shewn that there was a blameworthy condition of mind; a *mens rea,* such as neglect, malice, or guilty knowledge: Chisolm v. Doulton, 22 Q.B.D. 736; R. v. Atwood, 20 O.R. p. 576; R. v. Farnborough (1895), 2 Q.B. 484; Dickenson v. Fletcher, L.R. 9 C.P. 1; Aberdare v. Hammitt, L.R. 10 Q.B. 162; R. v. Potter, 20 A.R. 516, 523.

There must be a mischievous intent in order to constitute an act a criminal one; but such intent need not be that of doing the very act prohibited, if it is intended to do something wrong: R. v. Martin, 8 Q.B.D. 54; Beatty v. Gillbanks, 9 Q.B.D. 308; R. v. Pembliton, L.R. 2 C.C. 119; or if the act was in itself unlawful: R. v. Slaughenwhite, 9 Can. Cr. Cas. 53; in which this subject is very fully discussed and the authorities cited: or if the defendant acted in bad faith; or was suspicious, and took his chances: R. v. Mellon, 7 Can. Cr. Cas. 179.

But the principle of *mens rea* is not now of such general application as it formerly was; and there are many cases of offences against statutes to which the above rule does not apply.

So, in a prosecution under the provisions of a liquor license law, prohibiting the supplying of intoxicants to a person who is intoxicated, the fact that the person who obtained the liquor was apparently sober, and that there was no intention to contravene the statute, would be no defence: Cundy v. Lecocq, 13 Q.B.D. 207; Commissioners of Police v. Cartman, (1896) 1 Q.B. 655. And it is no defence to a charge of assaulting a peace officer in the execution of his duty that the defendant did not know he was such officer: R. v. Forbes, 10 Cox C.C. 362. So in offences against the Act prohibiting the adulteration of food, etc.: Fitzpatrick v. Kelly, L.R. 8 Q.B. 337; and against the statutes forbidding the disposal of animals infected with contagious diseases: R. v. Perras, 9 Can. Cr. Cas. 364; and against the Fruit Marks Act: R. v. James, 6 Can. Cr. Cas. 159.

In this class of cases the existence of a *bona fide* mistake, or the entire absence of knowledge of wrong doing, or of any intention of it, is no answer to a charge; and only applies in mitigation of penalty.

It is a question of the intention of the statute relating to the offence, whether in a particular case absence of wrong intent is a good defence or not. "The result of the reported cases is that it is necessary to look at the object of each statute that is under consideration, to see whether, and how far, knowledge is of the essence of the offence created": *per* Stephen, C.J., Cundy v. Lecocq, *supra.*

The legislature may enact, and in some cases has enacted that, "a man may be punished for an offence although there was no blameworthy condition of mind, but this is against the general principle of law; and it lies on those who assert it, to make it out convincingly by the language of the statute: *per* Cave, J., Chisholm v. Doulton, 22 Q.B.D. at p. 74 approved in Somerset v. Wade (1894), 1 Q.B. p. 576; Massie v. Morris (1894), 2 Q.B. 412; Bank of N.S.W. v. Piper (1897), 66 L.J.P.C. p. 76; R. v. Vachon, 3 Can. Cr. Cas. 558.

Generally a blameworthy condition of mind of a servant cannot be imputed to the master: Chisholm v. Doulton, *supra*:

But in some cases a master may even be held responsible criminally for the acts of his servant in the course of his employment, although such acts were done contrary to the master's orders. "The question is, whether upon the true construction of the statute in question, the master was intended to be made criminally responsible for the acts done by his servants in contravention of the Act, when such acts were done within the scope or in the course of their employment": *per* Lord Russell of Killowen, Coppen v. Moore (1898), 2 Q.B. 300, p. 313, in which case the subjects of *mens rea* and the responsibility of the master for the servant's act, were discussed and authorities collected. For instances under particular statutes where it is unnecessary to shew *mens rea*: See R. v. Smith, 3 H. & N. 227; R. v. Prince, L.R. 2 C.C.R. 154; Mullins v. Collins, L.R. 9 Q.B. 292; Somerset v. Hart, 12 Q.B.D. 360; Small v. Waugh, 47 J.P. 20; Benford v. Sims, 14 T.L.R. 424; Core v. James, 7 Q.B.D. 135; Newman v. Jones, 55 L.T. 327; Wilson v. Stewart, 3 B. & S. 913; R. v. Perras, 9 Can. Cr. Cas. 364.

In the leading case of R. v. Tolson, 23 Q.B.D. 168, decided by the Court of Crown Cases Reserved, the principle upon which the question whether, in a particular case, absence of wrong intent is, or is not an excuse, was fully considered. The rule as stated in that case is, that while it is undoubtedly a principle of law that, ordinarily speaking, a crime is not committed if the mind of the person doing the act be innocent, yet it is not an invariable rule, and a statute may be so framed, and use such prohibitory words as to make the act punishable whether there has been an intention to do wrong or not. Such as in the case of statutes or municipal by-laws passed for the special purpose of regulating matters for the general welfare of the community; or to protect particular rights; or to absolutely prohibit certain things from being done or omitted; the breach of them is *ipso facto* an offence; and a man must take care that such regulations are obeyed, and he fails to do so at his peril: see Fowler v. Papst, 7 T.R. 509. But on the other hand, and irrespective of the wording of the statute, and however prohibitory such wording may be, the subject matter of the enactment, the nature of the offence, and of the consequences of penalties, the mischief to be cured, and all the circumstances indicating the intention of the legislature in passing the statute, are to be taken into consideration; and if these indicate that there was no intention to punish an act as a crime, when there was no tainted mind it is a good defence that it was done innocently and with an honest belief on the part of the accused, based upon fair and reasonable grounds, that he had the right to do the act complained of.

In all cases in which there must be a *mens rea*, in order to constitute an offence, an honest claim of right will frustrate a summary conviction; but in cases where the absence of *mens rea* is not necessarily a good defence, the person who sets up a claim of right must shew some reasonable ground for its assertion: R. v. Hibbert, L.R. 1 C.C.R. 184; Watkins v. Major, L.R. 10 C.P. p. 666; Reece v. Miller, 8 Q.B.D. 626; R. v. Bone, 16 Cox C.C. 437; Sherras v. DeRutzen (1895), 1 Q.B. 918; Paley on Convictions, 8th ed. 173.

If the act charged is against the policy and letter of the law, it can only be made innocent by shewing facts which in law justify it; and it is not enough to shew merely that the party had a mistaken belief in the existence of such facts; this only mitigates punishment: State v. Prestnell, 12 Iredale, (N.C.) 103.

Ignorance of law is no defence: Code 22. But ignorance of fact is generally a good defence: R. v. Tolson, *supra*; but it is not so, if the act itself was an improper one; or in cases in which a wrong intent is not a necessary ingredient of the offence: R. v. Prince, L.R. 2 C.C.R. 154. See upon the question of criminal intent: R. v. Slavin, 21 C.L.T. 54; R. v. Preston, 5 Cox C.C. 390; R. v. Glyde, L. R. 1 C.C.R. 139; R. v. Deaves, 11 Cox C.C. 227; R. v. Thurburn, 1 Den. C.C. 387; R. v. Wood, 3 Cox C.C. 453; R. v. York, 3 Cox C.C. 181; R. v. Ollis (1900), 2 Q.B. 158.

Upon the question of fact whether there was a wrong intent, proof of previous similar acts, although not admissible in corroboration of the fact that the act charged was committed, is receivable, after such fact has been duly proved, to shew criminal intent: R. v. Komienski, 7 Can. Cr. Cas. 27. So even voluntary drunkenness is a fact which may be proved upon the question of criminal intent when that is an essential ingredient of the offence: Pearson's case, 2 Lewin C.C. 144; R. v. Doody, 6 Cox C.C. 463; R. v. Scaife, 1 M. & Rob. 551: notes in 7 Can. Cr. Cas. at p. 277.

CHAPTER X.

Authority as to Contempt of Court.

The extent of the authority and powers of magistrates and justices to regulate the proceedings, and enforce order in their courts, and to deal with persons guilty of disorderly or insulting words or conduct or other contempt of court, is fully explained in the case of Young v. Saylor, 23 O.R. 513, affirmed on appeal, 20 A.R. 645; and the authorities on the subject are cited and discussed in the original case.

The general effect of the decision in that case, and of the authorities cited in it, may be stated as follows:

A Justice's Authority.

Any judicial officer (which includes a justice of the peace) when trying a case or performing other judicial acts, but not while doing merely ministerial acts, has authority, without formal proceedings, to order the removal and exclusion from the place where the trial is being held, of all persons who interrupt or obstruct the proceedings by any disorderly conduct, insulting words, or in any other way; such authority being indispensable for the proper exercise of the officer's judicial functions.

But the justice's sitting not being a court of record, and his authority being limited to that expressly given by statute, and no statute having given him the power to summarily punish by fine or imprisonment a contempt, even if it is committed in *facie curae*, it is questionable whether his authority extends beyond the exclusion of the person offending.

But the offender, or any one assisting him, may be prosecuted for a breach of the peace, or for obstructing a "peace officer" (which includes a justice: Code 2 (26) in the exercise of his duty, whether judical or ministerial: Code 169 (*a*).

A justice or magistrate has no authority to deal with any person for insulting words used behind the officer's back, out of court; but only for words or conduct in his presence, and by means of which the proceedings and order are disturbed: R. v. Lefroy, L.R. 8 Q.B. 134; R. v. Weltje, 2 Camp. 142; R. v. Brompton Judge (1893), 2 Q.B. 195.

The justice should be careful that the misconduct justifies the order for exclusion; and that he has not by his own words or conduct been to blame: see Clissold v. Machell, 25 U.C.R. 80; 26 U.C.R. 422.

For a person to say of a justice in court in reference to his judgment, "That is a most unjust remark," is a wilful insult and contempt: R. v. Jordon, 36 W.R. 589, 797; or to reflect in any way on the honesty or impartiality of the justice:. R. v. Skipworth, 12 Cox C.C. 371.

In case a justice orders, as he has the right to do, the exclusion of a person acting in an improper manner, it would be better to issue a written order or a warrant under seal, to a constable, authorizing such exclusion and stating the grounds and the particulars of the contempt or other improper conduct.

Police Magistrate's Authority.

The authority of a police, stipendiary, or district magistrate while holding court, is very much more extensive than that of a justice.

By sec. 607 of the Criminal Code, such magistrate has the same power and authority to preserve order in court, and by like ways and means, as may be exercised and used in like cases, and for the like purposes, by any court in Canada, or by the judges during the holding of the court: see also Code 608.

The power given includes punishment for contempts committed "during the holding" of the court, but there is no power to proceed for contempts committed out of court: Re Scaife, 5 B.C.R. 153; Re Pacquette, 11 P.R. 463; Re Elliot, 41 Solicitor's Journal, 625; R. v. Surrey Judge, 13 Q.B.D. 963, and cases, supra.

A magistrate has power not only to order the expulsion by force, but also to commit to gaol, a person guilty of contempt by insulting him, or otherwise, when acting in his judicial capacity; but not when acting ministerially: 3 Burns' Justice, 30th ed., p. 160; see also Young v. Saylor, 23 O.R. 513. As to what are "judicial" and what "ministerial" acts, see *ante,* p. 205.

A person who obstructs a magistrate or justice in the exercise of his duty, whether judicial or ministerial, may be prosecuted under Code 169 A, 2 (26).

A small room communicating with the court room is not open court: Kenyon v. Eastwood, 57 L.J.Q.B. 454.

It is not clear that a magistrate can punish for contempt committed while he is executing his duty in his own house, and not proceeding in any "court": McKenzie v. Mewburn, 6 O.S. 486; and the same case decides that if a magistrate commits a person for contempt, he must proceed regularly to convict for the offence; that is, he must call upon the party to defend himself, and shew cause why he should not be convicted; and should hear evidence and anything the party or his counsel may have to say and enter an adjudication convicting the party and awarding punishment; and he should issue a formal warrant of commitment under his hand and seal, and setting out the contempt.

The particulars of the insult need not be stated in the commitment: Levy v. Moylan, 10 C.B. 189; but upon committal on a duly issued warrant setting out the facts of the contempt, the High Court, on application for certiorari or habeas corpus (while it has jurisdiction to intervene and prevent any usurpation of jurisdiction, by the magistrate treating as a contempt that which there is no reasonable ground for so treating,) yet it has no jurisdiction to act as a court of appeal from the magistrate's finding upon a matter of fact, nor to review the facts stated in the warrant; but, on the other hand, if there is no formal warrant issued setting out the contempt, the magistrate must establish by evidence such facts as will justify his course, if it is questioned: R. v. Jordan, 36 W.R. 589; Ex p. Porter, 5 B. & S. 299; Ex p. Lees and Judge of Carleton, 24 C.P. 214; Young v. Saylor, 23 O.R. 513, and cases cited. The committal should therefore be by warrant setting out the facts constituting the contempt; and must be made for a definite period: Ex p. Porter, 5 B. & S. 299, and other cases above cited.

There is no power to award hard labour, in such a case.

The exercise of the power of exclusion or punishment for contempt should be done with great forbearance, and not hastily, or under feelings of exasperation, however natural; but with the sole view to the maintenance of proper order and decorum during the prosecution of the officer's judicial proceedings: Heywood v. Wait, 18 W.R. 205; Day v. Carr, 7 Ex. 887.

If the magistrate in the exercise of his jurisdiction, is defiantly disobeyed he may commit the offender instantly for contempt: Watt v. Ligertwood, L.R. 2 H.L. (S.C.) 361.

The contempt may be shewn either by language or manner, and even by language which might not in itself be offensive, if it is uttered offensively: Carus Wilson's case, 7 Q.B. p. 115; Ex p. Lees and County Judge, Carleton, 24 C.P. 214; Re the Judge of the Division Court, Toronto, 23 U.C.R. 6. An order or warrant made while the offender is in court may be enforced notwithstanding he may have gone outside before arrest: Mitchell v. Smith, 2 Ir. R. 351.

A person indemnifying another against the consequences of contempt involves himself in the same: Plating Co. v. Farquharson, L.R. 17 Ch. 49.

The following is a form of commitment:—

WARRANT OF COMMITMENT FOR CONTEMPT.

Canada,
Province of Ontario, }
County of

    To all or any of the constables and other peace officers in the County of   , and to the keeper of the common gaol at   , in the said County of

    Whereas, on the   day of   , A.D. 19 , at the   of   , in the County of   , one, C.D., was brought before me, E.F., then and yet a police (*or* stipendiary) magistrate in and for the   of   , and the said C.D. was then charged before me, upon the information of one, A.B., that he, the said C.D. (*set out the charge*).

    And, whereas G.H., maliciously intending and contriving to scandalize and vilify me, the said E.F., as such police (*or* stipendiary) magistrate aforesaid, and to bring the administration of justice in this province into contempt, afterwards, and during the hearing of the said charge, and whilst I, the said E.F., was examining and taking the depositions of divers witnesses against the said C.D. in that behalf, to wit, on the day and year aforesaid, wickedly and maliciously in the open court and in the presence and hearing of divers subjects of our lord, the King, did publish, utter and pronounce, declare and say with a loud voice to me, the said E.F., and whilst I was so acting as such police (*or* stipendiary) magistrate as aforesaid (*here set out the language used, as for instance* "That is a most unjust remark,") to the scandal and reproach of the administration of justice in this province, and to the great scandal and damage of me, the said E.F., as such police (*or* stipendiary) magistrate, in contempt of our said lord, the King, in open violation of the laws of this province, and to the evil and pernicious example of all others in like case offending.

    And whereas the said G.H. having been then and there duly required and called upon by me, as such police (*or* stipendiary) magistrate (*or* having been duly served with a summons commanding him to be and appear before me on the   day of   , A.D. 19 , at   o'clock in the forenoon), to answer the said contempt, and to be dealt with according to law, after hearing the said G.H. and his counsel (or solicitor): (or if served with a summons and the party fails to appear: and the said G.H. having neglected to be and appear at the time and place appointed, although it has been proved to me upon oath that the said G.H. was duly summoned in that behalf): I did adjudge that the said G.H. was guilty of the said contempt, and I did further order and adjudge the said G.H. should for his said offence forfeit and pay the sum of $, to be paid and applied according to law, and that in default of such payment being made forthwith, the said G.H. should be committed to the common gaol of the said County of   for the term of   days, unless the said fine should be sooner paid.

And whereas the said G.H. did not pay the said fine in obedience to said order: these are therefore to require and command you, the said constables or peace officers, or any one of you, to take the said G.H., and him safely to convey to the common gaol at   , in the County aforesaid, and there to deliver him to the keeper thereof together with this precept; And I command you, the said keeper of the said common gaol, to receive the said G.H. into your custody in the said common gaol, there to imprison him for the term of   days, from the time of his arrest under this warrant, unless the said fine amounting to the sum of $ is sooner paid, and for your so doing this shall be your sufficient warrant.

Given under my hand and Seal this   day of   in the year 19 , at   , in the County of

                                        E.F.   [Seal.]
                                police magistrate.

Exclusion of the Public from the Court.

On a summary trial before a justice or magistrate, the place is an open court, and all persons have the right of access so far as there is room: Code 714-787, subject to removal for improper behaviour; except in cases in which the justice is authorized to exclude the public in the interest of public morals: Code 645 (2), and particularly in the cases specified in Code 645 (1); and cases of juvenile offenders: Code 644.

But on a preliminary inquiry, the place is not an open court, and the magistrate or justice may exclude all persons, other than the parties and their counsel or solicitor, if it appears to him that the ends of justice will be best answered by so doing: Code 679 (d); and he may even exclude the counsel or solicitor for gross contempt or impropriety by which the hearing is obstructed: Colter v. Hicks, 2 B. & Ald. 663; in the latter event it would be necessary to adjourn the case to afford the party an opportunity to obtain other counsel, to which he has the right.

On the Trial of Juvenile Offenders.

In trials of juvenile offenders under 16 years old, Code 644 provides that such trials are to take place without publicity and apart from the trials of other accused persons. See further under heading, Juvenile Offenders, *post*.

Ordering Witnesses out of Court.

A justice or magistrate may order all witnesses out of court, at the commencement or at any time during the course of the proceedings: Southey v. Nash, 7 C. & P. 632; R. v. Murphy, 8 C. & P. 297. The attorney for either party is not within the rule: Pomeroy v. Baddeley, Ry. & M. 430. But there is no jurisdiction to punish a witness for disobedience of the order, or to forcibly exclude him, nor to refuse to receive his evidence, if he does not go out when ordered, or if a witness should afterwards come into court after such order has been made; but that fact, and the fact that he may have heard the evidence of another witness in the case, will be weighed by the court in considering the credit to be given the testimony of the witness who has thus disobeyed the order: Cobbett v. Hudson, 1 E. & B. 11, at p. 14; see also R. v. Colley, M. & M. 329; R. v. Brown, 4 C.P. 588 (*n*) ; Chandler v. Horn, 2 M. & Rob. 423.

CHAPTER XI.

Consent or Waiver.

It is a common understanding, almost amounting to a legal maxim, that in criminal cases, at least those of a more serious character, (such as those formerly known as felonies) a prisoner can admit nothing.

"The object of a trial in a criminal case is the administration of justice in a course as free from doubt or chance of miscarriage as merely human understanding of it can be—not the interests of either party": Attorney-General v. Bertrand, L.R. 1 P.C. at p. 534; see also cases cited in R. v. St. Clair, 27 A.R. 308. But in cases formerly classified as misdemeanors, admissions may be made: R. v. Foster, 7 C. & P. 495, Roscoe, 12th ed., 120.

It has, however, been provided by Code 978 that on the *trial* for an *indictable* offence the accused or his counsel may admit any facts, so as to dispense with proof; and this applies to a trial of indictable offences before magistrates under secs. 771-799 of the Code: R. v. St. Clair, 27 A.R. 308.

In case of Attorney-General v. Bertrand, *supra,* it was held that the consent of the accused to the mode of taking the evidence on a second trial, by reading to the witnesses the notes of their evidence taken on a former trial instead of taking it again in the usual way, did not justify such a course; which was one likely to cause a substantial miscarriage of justice; and that the trial so conducted was invalid, notwithstanding such consent: and see similar decision in R. v. Brooks, 11 Can. Cr. Cas. 188.

Nor is the absence of specific objection a waiver of objection on the part of a person who, happening to be present, is unexpectedly, and without previous notice, called on to answer a charge against himself; such a proceeding being against natural justice and so an excess of jurisdiction: R. v. Vrooman, 3 Man. R. 509.

And even independently of the statutes relating to the Lord's Day, a justice has no jurisdiction to take judicial proceedings on Sunday, even if both parties consent: Taylor v. Phillips, 3 East 155.

Where there is absolutely no jurisdiction over the subject matter, no consent or waiver can give it: Jones v. Owen, 5 D. & L. 669; R. v. Tolley, 3 East 467; Buse v. Roper, 41 L.T. 457; Knowles v. Holden, 24 L.J. Ex. 223; Lee v. Cohen, 71 L.T. 824; Foster v. Underwood, 3 Ex. D. 3; Farquharson v. Morgan (1894), 1 Q.B. 552; R. v. Essex (Jus.), (1895) 1 Q.B. 38; and the accused may object to the tribunal he himself has selected: R. v. Smith, 3 Can. Cr. Cas. 467.

For instance, a justice has no jurisdiction at all over a defendant not found in his county, and who is charged with an offence committed outside his county, even if the defendant appears without objection, or even if he consents: Paley, 7th ed. 109; Johnston v. Colam, L.R. 10 Q.B. 544; R. v. Herbert, 5 Q.R. 5 S.C. 424.

A consent to a trial before a person who has, by law, no jurisdiction, will not give it, and the trial is invalid: Smith v. Brown, 2 M. & W. 851; Lawrence v. Wilcock, 11 A. & E. 941; and in matters essential to jurisdiction there can be no waiver: see cases in Douglass, p. 14. The statutory conditions upon which jurisdiction depends cannot be waived: R. v. Breckenridge, 7 Can. Cr. Cas. 116; Cavanagh v. McImoyle, 6 Can. Cr. Cas. 88; and recent cases noted there at p. 92.

If, however, there is jurisdiction over the subject matter, defects or even contingencies affecting jurisdiction, may be waived by taking a step in the matter without objection: Taylor v. Best, 14 C.B. 487; Forbes v. Smith, 10 Ex. 717; Re Jones v. James, 19 L.J.Q.B. 257; Stamford v. Richmond, 13 W.R. 724; Moore v. Gamgee, 25 Q.B.D. 244; Lee v. Cohen, 71 L.T. 824; Re Guy v. G.T.R., 10 P.R. 372; Re Soules v. Little, 12 P.R. 533; and in order to prevent fruitless litigation and merely technical objections regarding mere matters of procedure being raised after conviction, they must be taken before the justice at the trial: Code 882.

So if defendant appears, he waives any defect in the information and proceedings, and even the total absence of any information or process—unless such was by the particular statute relating to the offence made essential to the justice's jurisdiction: R. v. Hughes, 4 Q.B.D. 614; Dixon v. Wells, 25 Q.B.D. 249; Turner v. Postmaster-General, 41 L.J.M.C. 10; R. v. Berry, 8 Cox C.C. 121; R. v. Shaw, 10 Cox C.C. 66; R. v. Millard, 22 L.J.M.C. 108; Gray v. Commissioners of Customs, 48 J.P. 343;

Douglass on Summary Procedure 11; R. v. Clarke, 20 O.R. 642; Re Merchants Bank v. Van Allen, 10 P.R. 348; Ex p. Sonier (S.C.N.B.) 2 Can. Cr. Cas. 121.

The facts stated in R. v. Vrooman, 3 Man. R. 502 (cited in 2 Can. Cr. Cas. 93) were held, however, not to amount to waiver of process.

The objection that two offences are included in one information, is waived by not being taken before the justice: R. v. Hazen, 20 A.R. 633; Rodgers v. Richards (1892), 1 Q.B. 555.

If an adjournment is made for more than eight days, contrary to Code 661 and 722, it is waived if defendant consented; or if he appears on the adjourned hearing: R. v. Heffernan, 13 O.R. p. 626.

The provision that the justice's adjudication must be announced in open court in the presence of the parties may be waived: Chase v. Sing, 6 B.C.R. 454; and if the trial is conducted in an irregular, but not an improper manner, without objection, the defendant waives it: Re Jones v. Julian, 28 O.R. 601.

The objection that the case is required to be tried by two justices instead of one is waived by non-objection: R. v. Starkey, 7 Man. R. 489; Re Crow, 1 L.J.N.S. 302; Graham v. McArthur, 25 U.C.R. 478; or that the justice's jurisdiction had been ousted: R. v. Salop (Jus.), 2 E. & E. 386; or that the justice is disqualified by interest: Wakefield v. West R. Ry. Co., L.R. 1 Q.B. 84. Waiver must be an intentional act, with knowledge: Darnley v. L. C. & D. Ry., L.R. 2 H.L. 43; Re Marsden, 26 Ch. D. 784.

For instance, the objection that the justice was disqualified is not waived unless the party was aware of the disqualification: Lancaster v. Heaton, 8 El. & B. 952; R. v. Cambridge, 27 L.J.M.C. 166; R. v. Aberdare, 14 Q.B. 852.

A party who objects to the jurisdiction, does not waive it by taking part in the proceedings subject to objection: Re Brazill v. Johns, 24 O.R. 209; Blake v. Beech, 1 Ex D. 320; Emeris v. Woodward, 43 Ch. D. 185; Hamlyn v. Betterley, 6 Q.B.D. 63; R. v. Nutt (S.C.N.S.), 3 Can. Cr. Cas. 184; see Farquharson v. Morgan (1894), 1 Q.B. 552.

For definition of "waiver" of irregularities in proceedings before justices, and the reason for the rule, see Cairncross v. Lorimer, 3 Macq. H.L. 829; Douglass' Summary Procedure, 14.

CHAPTER XII.

Procedure Before the Justice or Magistrate.

The King, as the representative of law and order in the community, is named as the prosecutor in all proceedings for infractions of the criminal law: and by virtue of the authority vested in magistrates and justices of the peace by the Royal Commission, by which they are appointed, and the statutes to which reference has been made in the foregoing pages, they are to deal with all charges of such infractions laid before them, in the manner which will be now described. Such charges are of two classes, viz.:—

1. *Indictable Offences.*

Those which are designated in the particular statutes relating to them, as "indictable" offences; or for which it is stated that the offender may be "prosecuted by indictment." In such cases it is the duty of a justice of the peace or magistrate to hold a "preliminary enquiry," with a view of ascertaining whether there is a proper case to be sent for indictment and trial by a higher court.

An alphabetical list of many indictable offences is given at the end of the present chapter; and the procedure in such enquiry will be considered in this present chapter.

2. *Summary Convictions Cases.*

Those in which one or more justices, as the particular statute requires, have authority to convict and punish the offender Code 706, see, *post*, at the end of Chapter XIII., for an alphabetical list of such offences; and the procedure is given in Chapter XIII.

Trials of Indictable Offences by "Magistrates."

But in addition to the foregoing, an extraordinary jurisdiction is conferred upon certain officials who come under the designation "magistrates," as defined by Code 771, to hold summary trials in certain indictable offences. This jurisdiction is fully discussed, *ante* p. 198 *et seq.*; and the procedure in such cases will be explained in Chapter XIV. *post.*

A justice has no authority to convict and punish a person for an indictable offence, and can only hold a preliminary enquiry with the view of a commitment for trial.

Blank forms of the proceedings in all criminal cases, are supplied to justices and magistrates on application, by the clerk of the peace of the county: R.S.O. ch. 96, sec. 8.

In all cases of serious indictable offences, the justice should at once communicate with the Crown Attorney, and act under his advice; and in all matters, he is entitled to the advice and assistance of the Crown Attorney, upon application to him: R. S.O. ch. 96, sec. 6.

1. Preliminary Enquiries in Indictable Offences.

The proceedings are prescribed by sec. 653, *et seq.*, of the Criminal Code of Canada.

Information.

The first step to be taken by the justice is to receive a written information.

Who May Lay an Information.

Anyone who, upon reasonable or probable grounds, believes that any person has committed an indictable offence, may lay an information, in writing and under oath, before a justice of the peace having territorial jurisdiction (as described *ante* p. 188), in respect to such offence: Code 654: R. v. St. Louis, 1 Can. Cr. Cas. 141.

Form and Essentials of Information.

The information may be in the Form 3, in the schedule to the Criminal Code, or to the like effect: Code 654 (2). The information must, as required by this section, be in writing (which includes signature by the complainant and justice), and under oath: Code 654; or it may be affirmed if the complainant, on the ground of conscientious scruples, objects to taking an oath: Can. Ev. Act, R.S.C. ch. 145, sec. 14.

The form of oath is: "You sware that this information is true: So help you God."

If an affirmation is administered instead of an oath, the form prescribed by the Can. Ev. Act, R.S.C. ch. 145, sec. 15, is as follows :—

"I, A.B. (name) do solemnly affirm" that this information is true.

An information for an indictable offence, must be sworn or affirmed before a summons or warrant of arrest can legally be issued by the justice, who would be liable to an action for damages, if he issues a warrant and the defendant is arrested without a valid information: Friel v. Ferguson, 15 U.C.C.P. 584; McGuiness v. DeFoe, 27 O.R. 117, 23 A.R. 704; R. v. Mc-Donald, 3 Can. Cr. Cas. 287.

The essentials of a valid information are: a statement of the date when the information was laid; the place where laid; the name or names of the justice or justices before whom it is laid; a description of the charge or offence, with date and place when and where committed: signature of the complainant; the jurat, or statement of its being sworn or affirmed; and the signature of the justice to the latter.

Description of the Offence.

The nature and essential particulars of the offence should be set out carefully in the information and process; but Code 723(3), 852, provide that it is sufficient if the offence is stated in the words of the statute relating to it: R. v. France, 1 Can. Cr. Cas. 321; and see examples in Form 64 to the Cr. Code.

In the alphabetical synopsis of offences at the end of this chapter, forms of various charges are given, which may be used in the information and other proceedings. The charge should contain so much detail of the circumstances of the alleged offence as is sufficient to give the accused reasonable information of the matter to be proved against him and to identify the transaction; but the absence of such details will not vitiate the proceedings: Code 853.

The examples or forms of statements of charges given in Code Form 64 are not only sufficient for the particular offences stated: but are examples of the manner in which other offences may be sufficiently stated: R. v. Skelton, 4 Can. Cr. Cas. 467; and the effect of Code 852, 853 is to validate the particular form of statement of the offence, not only in an indictment but also, *a fortiori*, in all prior proceedings: R. v. George. 5 Can. Cr. Cas. 469; R. v. Coolen, 8 Can. Cr. Cas. 157; R. v. Cameron, 2 Can. Cr. Cas. 173.

Code 852, 853, do not make valid, however, a statement which does not contain a description of facts sufficient to constitute a criminal offence: R. v. Goodfellow, 10 Can. Cr. Cas. 427. A charge not in the words of the statute, but otherwise sufficiently describing the offence, is valid: R. v. Weir, 3 Can. Cr. Cas. 102.

A form of charge alleging an act to have been "unlawfully" committed does not sufficiently charge the offence of "wilfully" doing it: Ex p. O'Shaunessy, 8 Can. Cr. Cas. 138; R. v. Tupper, 11 Can. Cr. Cas. 199. The information must state the date of the offence or such reference to the time when it was committed, as will shew that the prosecution was begun within the time limited by law for so doing: R. v. Breen, 8 Can. Cr. Cas. 146; R. v. Boutillier, 8 Can. Cr. Cas. 82.

A charge of wilfully or unlawfully damaging property must state the property damaged, and by what means and in what respect such damage was done: Re Donnelly, 20 U.C.C. P. 165; R. v. Spain, 18 O.R. 385, and whether it was real or personal property, stating what: R. v. Caswell, 20 U.C.C. P. 275; Smith v. Moody (1903), 1 K.B. 56. A charge that a person is a loose, idle person, and a vagrant, (without stating in respect of which of the various things in Code 238, the offence of vagrancy consists), the defendant was guilty, is insufficient: R. v. McCormack, 7 Can. Cr. Cas. 135; R. v. Keeping, 4 Can. Cr. Cas. 494, 498; or a charge of using profane language in a public place, without setting out the language used: R. v. Smith, 2 Can. Cr. Cas. 485.

A charge of attempting to steal from the person of an unknown person, the property of the latter, is good without stating the name of the unknown person or describing the property: R. v. Taylor, 5 Can. Cr. Cas. 89. For other examples see R. v. Beckwith, 7 Can. Cr. Cas. 450; R. v. Morgan, 5 Can. Cr. Cas. 63; R. v. Thompson, 4 Can. Cr. Cas. 265; R. v. Reynolds, 11 Can. Cr. Cas. 312; R. v. Wright, 11 Can. Cr. Cas. 221; R. v. Whiffin, 4 Can. Cr. Cas. 141. It is not necessary to state that the offence was "against the form of the statute; or against the peace of our Sovereign Lord the King," etc.: R. v. Doyle, 2 Can. Cr. Cas. 335; R. v. Weir, 3 Can. Cr. Cas. 499: Taschereau's Cr. Code 675.

But, in case the information does not disclose sufficient facts to enable the defendant to make his defence, he may be entitled to particulars: Code 723 (2); or, if there are good reasons for withholding particulars, in the beginning of the case, reasonable opportunity will be given afterwards to the defendant to meet the case made by the evidence for the prosecution: see *post* p. 257.

Information to Contain one Offence only.

Code 853 (3). See forms, *post*.

To charge that the accused person "procured *or* attempted to procure," etc., is to state two distinct offences in the alternative: R. v. Gibbons, 2 Can. Cr. Cas. 302.

A charge of attempting to compound an offence "with a view of stopping *or* having the charge dismissed," is for two distinct offences: R. v. Mabey, 37 U.C.R. 248; R. v. Haggard, 30 U.C.R. 152.

But a charge of *stealing* "in *or* from" a building, is a charge of one offence committed in alternate ways, and is valid: R. v. White, 4 Can. Cr. Cas. 430.

Against whom Information May be Laid.

Any number of accused persons who have been jointly concerned in committing an offence, whether as principal or as accessories after the offence was committed, or as abettors in it, may be joined in one information: Code 69; but separate information may be laid against each offender: Paley on Convictions, 8th ed. 85.

Corporations.

Cannot be made subjects of a preliminary enquiry before a justice: R. v. T. Eaton Co., 2 Can. Cr. Cas. 252; R. v. Toronto Ry. Co., 10 Can. Cr. Cas. 106; Union Colliery Co. v. The Queen, 31 S.C.R. 81, 4 Can. Cr. Cas. 400; but may be prosecuted before a justice in cases within his summary jurisdiction: see *post*: summary convictions.

Justices Must Receive Informations.

A justice cannot refuse to receive an information from any person who offers to make oath or affirmation to the commission of an indictable offence against the law, over which the justice has territorial jurisdiction. It is a breach of the justice's oath of office for him to so refuse; and if he does, he is liable to be compelled by a mandamus from the High Court of Justice: R. v. Richards, 20 L.J.Q.B. 352; Re Monmouth, L.R. 5 Q.B. 251; and he may even be prosecuted for neglect of duty in office: R. v. Penney, 5 C. & P. 254; R. v. Kennet, 5 C. & P. 282.

Search Warrants, Generally.

When an information has been taken, the next matter for consideration may be, whether a search warrant should be issued. The common law right of search, which only applied to stolen goods, has been greatly extended by section 629 of the Criminal Code; and it is expedient in many classes of cases, to have search warrants issued. This may be done either to recover stolen property; or to secure the implements which have been used in the commission of crime; or to obtain possession of anything which has been the subject of an offence, or which may afford evidence to bring it home to the guilty party: Code 629.

The sections of the Criminal Code relating to search warrants are 629 to 643; and the form of information is Form I. to the Criminal Code. The form of search warrant is No. 2. Forms of material to be filled in these forms are given in the synopsis of indictable offences, *post*, under "Search Warrants."

The particular place where the search is to be made must be definitely stated and described in the information and search warrant: McLeod v. Campbell, 26 N.S.R. 458. Enclosed grounds constitute a "place" within the words of the statute, no matter how extensive they may be, and even if not roofed in: Eastwood v. Miller, L.R. 9 Q.B. 440; R. v. McGarry, 24 O.R. 52; and it must be stated that a criminal offence has been committed, and what it is; and that the things to be searched for relate thereto as above mentioned, and that there are reasonable grounds (stating clearly what such grounds are) for believing the things are in the place stated.

Searching in Another County.

A search warrant cannot be issued authorizing a search in another county; but a warrant may be issued there by a justice for such county where articles liable to be searched for are reasonably suspected to be. Goods seized under search warrant cannot be taken out of the county where they are seized: Hoover v. Craig, 12 A R. 72; but are to be taken to the justice who issued the warrant under which they are seized, and he is to deal with them in the way described in Code 631.

Grounds for Issuing Search Warrant:

The information for a search warrant must not merely state that the informant has reasonable and probable grounds for the issuing of a search warrant but must state clearly what those grounds are, and if no grounds, which would be reasonably sufficient to satisfy the justice, are stated, the search warrant will be quashed on application to a superior court: R. v. Kehr, 11 Can. Cr. Cas. 52. The justice or magistrate, in' granting a search warrant, is exercising a judicial authority and discretion, and must see that the facts alleged and set out in the information are sufficient to justify him in a breach of the inviolability of a man's house by authorizing a constable to enter therein to make a search: R. v. Walker, 13 O.R. at p. 95; R. v. Townsend, 11 Can. Cr. Cas. 115.

It is the "*justice*" who must be "*satisfied*" by information that there is reasonable ground for believing the matters stated in Code 629, before he issues the warrant.

Executing Search Warrant.

A search warrant can only be executed by day; unless the justice by the warrant authorizes its execution by night: Code 630; and that should only be done upon the ground of urgent necessity.

The officer must have the warrant with him when making the search; and must produce it if required: Douglas 309. He may, if necessary, break open outer' or inner doors: Douglas 309. But should only do so in case of extreme necessity, and after demanding admittance, giving notice to those within that he has a legal warrant and is an officer: Foster 137. It is not necessary that the search warrant should specify in detail the exact goods for which search is to be made: Jones v. German, (1897), 1 Q.B. 370. But a description of them, as well as a statement of the offence in respect of which the search is made, is required by Form No. 2 Cr. Code. The officer should take some one with him to indentify the goods or things searched for: and the constable should satisfy himself that they are so: Hamilton v. Calder, 23 N.B.R. 373.

Disqualification of Constables.

A constable who laid the information on which a search warrant, or warrant of arrest, is issued is not disqualified from executing it, in proceedings under the Criminal Code: Gaul v. Township of Ellice, 6 Can. Cr. Cas. 1; R. v. Heffernan, 13 O.R. 616; though it was held in New Brunswick that a constable is disqualified for executing a search warrant, for liquor alleged to be kept contrary to the Canada Temperance Act, which was issued on the constable's own information. If the constable has any personal or pecuniary interest to serve in the matter, and is not acting in a purely official capacity, he is disqualified from acting as constable in executing any warrant in a case in which he has laid the information; but not otherwise: Gaul v. Township of Ellice, 6 Can. Cr. Cas. p. 19 and cases there cited, and at the end of that case.

Search for Weapons or Liquor near Public Works.

As to the authority and procedure to search for weapons or liquors in proclaimed districts near public works and the forfeiture of same, and conviction of offender: see Code 142-154, 610-618.

Search for Gold or Silver ore.

Which has been unlawfully deposited in any place, or held by any person contrary to law, see Code 637.

Search for Timber, Lumber, etc.,

improperly detained: Code 638.

Search for Liquors, near His Majesty's Ships.

Code 639.

Search for Woman or Girl.

Enticed into a house of ill-fame: Code 640.

Search in Gaming House.

Or any place where a lottery is being carried on, or lottery tickets being sold; and seizure of money, etc.; and destruction of devices: Code 641, 642.

Search for Vagrant.

Harboured or concealed in any disorderly house, or tavern or boarding house: Code 643, 238.

Issuing and Executing of Search Warrant on Sunday.

All warrants including search warrants issued *under the Criminal Code*, may be issued and executed on a Sunday or statutory holiday: Code 661 (3).

Search Without a Warrant.

A constable or peace officer has authority to search without a warrant for public stores which have been stolen, if he is deputed to do so by any public department: Code 636; for timber or lumber, etc., improperly detained: Code 638; under the Ontario Liquor License Act: R.S.O. ch. 254, secs. 130-133; under Code 544, 545 respecting the unloading of cattle during a journey for rest and food.

Considering the Information.

Upon receiving an information charging an indictable offence, the next duty of a justice is "to hear and consider the allegations of the complainant"; and to carefully question him, and if necessary any of the witnesses, touching the facts and reasons for suspecting and believing the defendant to have committed the offence complained of. If upon these facts the justice is of opinion that a case is made out for so doing, he may issue either a summons or a warrant of arrest, against the party charged: Code 655. But the mere bald statement in an information, even under oath, by any person, that he believes a criminal offence to have been committed by the accused, without any facts or reasons being given to the justice to warrant such belief, and to *satisfy him* that such facts are sufficient, does not authorize him in issuing process: Ex p. Boyce, 24 N.B.R. 353. A justice who issues a warrant of arrest even upon a sworn information, without enquiring at all into the grounds which the complainant has for making the charge, and whether these are sufficient, so that he may be able to exercise a wise discretion in the matter, thereby sets at naught the requirements of Code 655, which authorizes him to issue the process, only "if on hearing allegations of the complainant he is of opinion that a case for so doing is made out," and the justice who so recklessly issues process by which a man's liberty is taken away, may be liable to an action for damages for so doing, if it turns out that the proceedings were not based upon any reasonable or probable grounds whatever: Murfina v. Sauve, 6 Can. Cr. Cas. 275; Ex

p. Boyce, 24 N.B.R. 333; R. v. Lizotte, 10 Can. Cr. Cas. 316; Ex p. Coffon, 11 Can. Cr. Cas. 48; and cases there cited· R. v. Townsend, No. 2, 11 Can. Cr. Cas. 115. It was held in the latter cases that the information itself should shew the grounds for proceeding; see also Re Dickey, 8 Can. Cr. Cas 321. But if the justice really enquires into the grounds, and hears the facts, and exercises his discretion, and then issues the process, his so doing is a judicial act: R. v. Ettinger, 3 Can. Cr. Cas. 387; and no officer, exercising a judicial act, is responsible for any error of judgment, no matter how erroneous it may be.

Before issuing process a justice should particularly enquire into all the matters referred to in Chapter IX., *ante*.

Sunday.

An information, being a ministerial act, may be taken on Sunday: See *ante* p. 213. And a warrant to arrest may be issued on Sunday: Code 661(3), but a summons cannot be issued on Sunday, it not being a ministerial, but judicial, act and not allowed by Code 661(3).

Whether Summons or Warrant to be Issued.

The question whether a warrant to arrest the offender should be issued in the first instance, or whether a summons will suffice, is a matter for the justice's discretion; and he should include this question when "considering the information" as described, *ante*. He will be guided by the nature of the offence, the general character of the defendant, and whether he is a known resident; keeping in view the consideration that the only object is to secure the presence of the accused to answer the charge. Unless the charge is a serious one, a warrant must not be issued if a summons will suffice: O'Brien v. Brabner, 78 Eng. L.T. 409. But upon a serious charge, a warrant should always be issued no matter who the accused may be. The summons or warrant must be issued by the justice who took the information; no other has authority to do so: Code 654.

The Issuing of the Warrant of Arrest,

Its form, what it is to contain, etc., are set forth in Code 659, 660. The form is given at the end of the Criminal Code—Form 6. All blanks, including the name or description of the defendant, must be filled in, before the justice issues it. "No warrant shall be issued in blank" is the salutary provision of the law in Code 659 (2), preventing the possibility of the recurrence of the gross abuses which at one time prevailed by means of blank warrants.

The warrant must be under the hand and seal of the justice; and may be directed to one (by name), or to all, of the constables of the county, without naming any of them: Code 660.

If the name of the offender is unknown the warrant must so state, and a description of him must be given in it instead of the name.

The warrant never runs out, but is in force for any length of ·time until executed; and it need not be returnable at any particular time: Code 660 (3).

Summons Instead of Warrant.

If a summons is issued, its form and contents are provided by Code 658. The form is given in the schedule of forms in the Criminal Code—Form 5. The time and place where the accused is to appear must be mentioned; and the place should be a convenient one, reasonably near to where the defendant resides or is at the time. He ought not in any case to be unnecessarily brought, either by summons or warrant, a long distance from home. It would be an abuse of the justice's authority to cause such to be done; and a defendant may be unjustly inconvenienced, or even prevented from getting bail when far from his friends. But the jurisdiction of the justice extends to all parts of the county, and prohibition will not lie against his proceedings on this ground: R. v. Chapman, 1 Can. Cr. Cas. 81.

The summons must give a reasonable time for the defendant to appear: Re Smith, L.R. 10 Q.B. 604; R. v. Langford, 15 O.R. at p. 53, in which it was held that a summons requiring the defendant to appear immediately, or on the same day, is irregular. Service on the same day on which the defendant was to appear, or late on the previous evening, is not sufficient, and is an excess of jurisdiction: Ex p. Cowan, 9 Can. Cr. Cas. 457.

Service of Summons.

It must be served by a constable or other peace officer: Code 658 (4). Who are peace officers is described in Code 2 (26). The summons is to be served:—

1. Personally upon the person to whom it'is addressed, by delivering a duplicate, or *copy*: R. v. Chandler, 14 East. 267; Code 658 (4).

2. Or "if he cannot conveniently be met with," it may be left *for him* at his last or most usual place of abode, with some inmate apparently not under 16 years old: Code 658 (4).

It is not necessary to give positive proof that the person with whom it was left was actually an inmate; it is sufficient if the person was apparently an inmate (*e.g.*, a domestic servant there): R. v. Chandler, 14 East 267. But it must be proved that some reasonable effort was made to serve the accused personally; and when the summons was served upon an adult at the defendant's residence, but there was no proof whatever that such person was really an inmate, or that any effort had been made to serve the defendant personally, it was held to be insufficient: Re Barron, 4 Can. Cr. Cas. 465; R. v. Carrigan, 17 C.L.T. 224.

The constable must state to the person served for the accused, what the nature of the summons is, and who it is for: Ex p. Smith, 39 J.P. 614.

Procedure on Default of Appearance on Summons.

If the accused, after due service, does not attend, or'if the constable cannot serve the summons in any of the ways mentioned above, the constable will at the time and place appointed for the hearing be sworn as a witness and his evidence will be taken, in writing and signed by him and the justice in the way evidence is usually taken (see *post*), shewing that the summons was duly served, or that it cannot be served, stating what efforts the constable has made, and why he cannot effect service; or an affidavit of the constable may be drawn up and sworn to to the same effect: Code 658 (5)

An affidavit that the constable served the accused by delivering to and leaving the same with the wife of the accused for him (naming the accused) at his most usual place of abode, naming it and shewing the efforts to effect personal service, was held to be sufficient service and proof: R. v. McAuley, 14 O.R. 643.

The time when service was made must be shewn; and proof that the summons was served the previous day without proving the hour of service and the distance from the place of hearing, is not sufficient proof of service at a reasonable time before the hearing: Re O'Brien, 10 Can. Cr. Cas. 142; and notes at 10 Can. Cr. Cas. p. 135. But it was held in R. v. Craig, 10 Can. Cr. Cas. 249; that even if the service was made late the previous night, the defendant cannot ignore the service, but should apply for an adjournment.

Warrant of Arrest on Default.

Upon due proof of service of the summons, and the accused not appearing, or if the affidavit or evidence of the constable shews that the summons cannot be served, the justice is to issue a warrant to arrest the accused: Code 660 (5)—Form 7.

In case of necessity, (as where it appears that after a summons has been issued or served, the accused is about to abscond, or that there is reasonable ground to apprehend that he may do so), a warrant of arrest, as in the' first instance, may be issued, either before or after the time mentioned in the summons for his appearance: Code 660 (4). Form 6 above mentioned.

The justice cannot proceed with a preliminary enquiry in the case of an indictable offence in the absence of the accused, even if he has been served with a summons, or even if a solicitor appears for him and offers to waive the defendant's personal attendance; he must be brought personally before the justice, and must be personally present at all the proceedings.

Execution of Warrants.

A warrant of arrest may be executed in the same county; or in an adjoining county or territory within seven miles of the boundary, without being "backed" or endorsed in the latter county, in the case of "fresh pursuit": Code 666 (1). "Fresh pursuit" means that if the constable is pursuing the accused and the latter, during such pursuit, escapes beyond the boundary, the constable may follow him and arrest him within seven miles of the boundary. The seven miles are computed in a straight line from the boundary: Mouflet v. Cole, L.R. 8 Exch. 32; see also R. v. Saffron Waldren, 9 Q.B. 77.

A warrant can only be executed by the constable, or one of a class of constables, to whom it is directed: Code 661 (2); as, for instance, where it is directed to any or all of the constables of the county of Huron, it must be executed by one of them: Symonds v. Curtz, 16 Cox 726. A constable after making an arrest is entitled, without any warrant, to place his prisoner in any lockup or gaol until he can take him before a justice: McKellar v. McFarland, 1 U.C.C.P. 457: Code 20 (2) ; R.S.C. ch. 148, sec. 36. As to when a constable is disqualified from executing a warrant issued on his own information, see *ante* p. 244.

Arrest on Sunday.

The warrant may be issued and executed on Sunday, or other holiday: Code 661 (3) ; and by night or day: 4 Russell 110.

Breaking Open Doors.

The constable may break open an outer or inner door, or both, of any place where the accused is suspected to be, for the purpose of making the arrest. But before breaking open by force, he must make a reasonable demand of admittance and explain who he is, and his business there. An outer door should only be broken open in a case of necessity, when an immediate arrest is requisite: 1 Burns' Justice 275; and when there are reasonable grounds to believe that the defendant is secreted in the premises.

Arrest Without a Warrant.

See Code 646, 652, for cases in which arrests may be made without a warrant.

What Amounts to Arrest.

Mere words do not constitute an arrest; the constable must place his hand on the person to be arrested, or otherwise restrain his liberty: 1 Burns' Justice 275. But this may be waived; and if the accused examines the warrant and agrees to go with the constable; or if he so agrees on being told by the constable that he has a warrant for his arrest, it is complete.

It is the constable's duty to have the warrant with him and produce it if required: Code 40. And·when practicable he should give notice of the cause of arrest: Code 40 (2) ; and should serve the accused with a copy of the warrant, which the justice is required to furnish for that purpose: Code 711.

The omission of these details will not invalidate the arrest, however: Ex p. Lutz, 27 N.S.R. 491; but may become a factor in considering the question of the amount of force which was necessary and proper to be used in effecting the arrest, if resisted: Code 40 (3).

"Backing" or Indorsing Warrants.

If the accused cannot be found in the county in which the warrant was issued, the constable may take it before a justice in any other county or district in Canada, where the accused is suspected to be, and have it endorsed as follows; Code 662. The constable is to be sworn by the latter justice in the usual way, and his evidence taken shewing that he was present and saw the warrant signed by the justice who issued it. Upon receiving such evidence an indorsement is to be made upon the warrant or annexed to it in Form 8 to the Criminal Code. The warrant so "backed" may then be executed by the constable who brought it, or by any other constable, either of the county where the summons was issued, or of that where it was so "backed": Code 662 (2). The same process may be repeated in other counties in any part of Canada where the accused is supposed to be: Code 662. An arrest made in another county than that in which it was issued, before being "backed" is unlawful, even if the warrant is afterwards duly "backed": Southwick v. Hare, 24 O.R. 528; and the accused may lawfully resist an arrest under an unbacked warrant: R. v. Crumpton (1880), 5 Q.B.D. 341, cited in R. v. Whitesides, 8 O.L.R. 625.

What Force May be Used in Making Arrest.

An officer lawfully executing any warrant or process, or making any arrest, and everyone lawfully assisting him, is justified, or protected from criminal responsibility, in using such force as may be necessary to overcome any force used in resisting such execution or arrest, unless the process or warrant can be executed or the arrest effected by reasonable means in a less violent manner: Code 39.

Where his authority to arrest is resisted the officer may repel force by force, and will be justified, even if death should be the consequence: yet he will be responsible if he comes to extremities without necessity: 3 Russell, 6th ed. 130; Arch. 22nd ed. 778. And so an officer, or anyone assisting him, is likewise justified, if the person takes to flight to avoid arrest, in using such force as may be necessary to prevent an escape by such flight, unless such escape can be prevented by reasonable means in a less violent manner: Code 41.

Where a person guilty of a serious offence, such as would formerly constitute a felony, flies from justice and is killed by the officer in pursuit, the homicide is justifiable if the offender could not be othérwise overtaken; but not if the offence was one which would have been formerly classified as a misdemeanor: 3 Russ., 130; Arch., 779.

The provisions of Code 39 also apply to cases when the arrest may lawfully be made without a warrant, by a private person; provided that such force is neither intended, nor likely, to cause death or grievous bodily harm: Code 42; and Code 43 also extends the provisions of Code 39, so as to include other persons than peace officers, provided that the necessary force which may be used is neither intended, nor likely, to cause grievous bodily harm..

Everyone who has lawfully arrested a person for any offence for which he may be arrested without a warrant, is protected from criminal responsibility in using such force to prevent his rescue or escape, as the person making the arrest believes, upon reasonable grounds, to be necessary for that purpose: Code 44; and the same provisions are made applicable, by Code 45, to cases of arrest under a warrant for an offence other than that for which the offender may be arrested without a warrant: provided the force used to prevent the rescue or escape is neither intended, nor likely, to cause grievous bodily harm.

Everyone making an arrest, with or without a warrant, must give notice of the process or warrant under which he is making the arrest, or of the cause of the arrest; and if arresting under a warrant, must have it with him and produce it if demanded. But the failure to do so is no justification for resistance by the person being arrested, nor does it invalidate the arrest, but will be a factor in any question which may arise as to whether the arrest might have been made in a less violent manner: Code 40 (3)

Treatment of Prisoner on Arrest.

Upon effecting an arrest for an indictable or other serious charge, the constable should, as a general rule, at once search the person of the prisoner, and take from him any weapons and anything which it might be unsafe to leave with him, and anything which possibly may be in any way connected with the offence charged. But the prisoner's money or any other property (unless it may possibly be connected with the offence) ought not to be unnecessarily taken away from him. It may be very important to him to have the means of carrying on his defence: R. v. O'Donnell, 7 C. & P. 138; R. v. Kinsey, 7 C. & P. 447; R. v. Jones, 6 C. & P. 343; R. v. Burgess, 7 C. & P. 488; Dillon v. O'Brien, L.R. 20 Ir. 300. See also R. v. Boulton, 12 Cox C.C. 95; Agnew v. Jobson, 13 Cox C.C. 625; Gordon v. Denison, 24 O.R. 576, 586, 605; 22 A.R. 315, 325; R. v. Bass, 2 C. & K. 822.

It would be a trespass for a constable to search a person arrested on a trivial charge: Bessell v. Wilson, 17 J.P. 52; and there is no authority to search a witness arrested for non-attendance on a summons: Gordon v. Denison, *supra.*

If a constable improperly deprives a prisoner of his property an application may be made to the justice for its restoration, which on hearing all the parties concerned, he should order, if it appears just. If the property is clearly not the produce or evidence of the crime to be investigated, or of any other crime, and is not such as it is unlawful for the prisoner to have upon his person on the public streets, if he is arrested there; and is not of such a nature that it will be unsafe to allow him to retain it, it ought to be restored: R. v. Barnett, 3 C. & P. 600; R. v. Frost, 9 C. & P. 129.

If the justice refuses to restore to the prisoner, property which ought not to be taken from him, an application may be made to the High Court for an order for such restoration: Ex p. McMichael, 7 Can. Cr. Cas. 549.

Handcuffing.

A prisoner arrested for a trifling offence should not be handcuffed especially a known resident in the community. No one should be handcuffed, unless from the nature of the offence, and the prisoner's supposed character, or for violent resistance to arrest or attempt to escape, or for some other sufficient reason, the constable has reasonable apprehension that the prisoner would otherwise escape, or that there is danger that he might do so. Except on some sufficient grounds, there is no justification for handcuffing a prisoner. There must be some good reason for that degree of violence and restraint: Wright v. Court, 4 B. & C. 596; Griffin v. Coleman, 4 H. & N. 265; Hamilton v. Massie, 18 O.R. 585; Addison on Torts, 660; R. v. Taylor, 59 J.P. 393.

The accused should be treated in a manner consistent with his possible innocence; having careful regard, however, to what is necessary for his safe custody, and the elucidation of the charge against him. Unnecessarily hustling and haling any prisoner, and especially a possibly innocent man, along the public streets, as well as other unnecessarily harsh treatment, is a trespass and an assault. The law bearing upon the subject of the treatment of a prisoner, is fully discussed in the following authorities: Leigh v. Cole, 6 Cox C.C. 329; R. v. O'Donnell, 7 C. & P. 138; R. v. Kinsey, 7 C. & P. 447; Gordon v. Denison, 22 A.R. p. 326; Russell on Crimes, vol. 3 (6th ed.) 329.

Constable's Duty on Making Arrest.

Upon effecting an arrest under a warrant, either in the county of the justice who issued it, or elsewhere, it is the duty of the constable, as soon as practicable, to bring the accused before the justice who issued the warrant, or some other justice of the same county: Code 662 (2); whether in the province where the arrest took place, or "in any part of Canada": Code 662; R. v. Gillespie, 1 Can. Cr. Cas. 551.

But if the prosecutor or some of his witnesses are in the county where the arrest took place, and if the justice who backed the warrant directs that the accused be brought before himself, or some other justice for the same county, and if the arrest and the offence both took place in the same province (but not otherwise) the justice is authorized to make such direction, and it will be the duty of the constable to comply with it; and the justice who backed the warrant, or any other justice for the same county, may then proceed with the case, as if the warrant had originally been issued by himself: Code 663.

Proceedings on Appearance of Accused.

Note that the summons or warrant can only be issued by the justice who took the information; but by his direction or consent (not otherwise) all further proceedings subsequent to issuing the process, may be taken by any other justice having territorial jurisdiction: Code 655, 660, 680.

When the accused appears, whether voluntarily or upon summons or under arrest, or while in custody for the same or *any other* offence, the justice is authorized to proceed to enquire into any matters charged against him: Code 668. The justice must state to the accused what the charge is, and proceed with the enquiry; or he may postpone it to another time if sufficient reasons are given.

Objections to Information or Warrant of Arrest.

A justice or magistrate has no right to issue a warrant to apprehend a person accused of crime without first receiving a sworn information; (*ante*, p. 239.); but when the accused appears or is brought before the justice, any objections to the validity of the information or warrant, cease to be of any importance whatever. The information being required merely to guide and give authority to the justice in issuing the warrant or summons, and the warrant being merely the means of procuring the defendant's appearance, they have no bearing on the case when these objects have been attained. Any irregularity or defect in substance or in form, in the information, summons or warrant, or any variance between the latter and the charge stated in the information, or between them and the evidence adduced, or even the entire absence of any information or process, or if the defendant has been illegally arrested without a warrant; none of these things have then any effect on the proceedings before the justice, who is to proceed (without any necessity to amend any information) to hear any charge whatever for an indictable offence within the justice's jurisdiction, which may then be brought against the accused, whether it be the charge mentioned in the information or any other charge based even on wholly different facts: Code 668, 669; R. v. Hughes, 4 Q.B.D. 614; the word "charged" in Code 668, in no way involves a written information; and it is sufficient that a person charged is brought before the justice somehow or other; all that is necessary to the justice's jurisdiction is that, the person being once before him, the crime with which the accused is charged is within the jurisdiction of the justice: *per* Pollock, B.: Re Maltby, 7 Q.B.D. 18; "when a defendant is actually charged and appears before the justices, and they have jurisdiction; and though the defendant may have been brought before them by illegal process; yet in as much as the justices have jurisdiction, the adjudication cannot be disputed by objecting to the arrest": Grey v. Commissioners of Customs, 48 J.P. 343; R. v. Brown (1895), 1 Q.B. 119; R. v. Clarke, 20 O.R. 642; R. v. Stone, 23 O.R. 46; see also McGuinness v. Dafoe, 3 Can. Cr.

Cas. 139; R. v. McLean, 5 Can. Cr. Cas. 537; R. v. Giberson, 4 Can. Cr. Cas. 537; R. v. Doherty, 3 Can. Cr. Cas. 505; R. v. Mason, 29 U.C.R. 431.

But if the charge taken up differs from that laid in the information the accused must be distinctly informed of its nature; and it ought (though not necessary, but for expediency's sake) to be formulated in writing for that purpose; and if the accused desires further time to prepare to meet it, such time must be granted, the fullest opportunity being allowed him to do so; the accused being remanded to gaol or bailed, according to the nature of the case: Code 670; Re Daisey Hopkins, 56 J.P. 263; R. v. Vrooman, 3 Man. R. 509, referred to in 2 Can. Cr. Cas. page 93; R. v. Bowman, 2 Can. Cr. Cas. 93; R. v. Doherty, 3 Can. Cr. Cas. 505.

It is to be carefully noted, however, that there are some special cases which are exceptions to this general rule; and that it is necessary to refer to the particular clause or statute relating to the offence, to see whether there is any special provision in this regard. If such clause or statute requires, either expressly or by necessary implication, that an information or process is a condition precedent to the justice's jurisdiction, it must be done. For instance, in a case in which a particular statute, relating to a certain offence, provided that a summons against the party charged must be served within a certain period after the offence was alleged to have been committed, it was held that the service was a condition precedent to jurisdiction in the case: Dixon v. Wells, 25 Q.B.D. 249.

Particulars of the Facts on Which the Charge is Founded,

May be ordered to be furnished to the accused, in any case: R. v. Doherty, 3 Can. Cr. Cas. 505. The principle on which the justice should act in ordering particulars is "to give such information as is sufficient to enable the defendant fairly to defend himself; but on the other hand, not to fetter or embarrass the prosecutor in the conduct of his case," or to prematurely disclose the prosecutor's hand, and so enable the accused to make an attempt to make away with evidence which he may have the means of controlling: R. v. Hamilton, 7 C. & P. 448; R. v. Stapylton, 8 Cox C.C. 69; R. v. Rycroft, 6 Cox C.C. 76. If it should appear that giving particulars would in any way unfairly prejudice the prosecution and endanger the elucidation of the truth, particulars should be denied; and instead of giving particulars, further time may afterwards be given the defendant to meet the facts disclosed in the evidence when it has been adduced by the prosecution. On an application by defendant for particulars, he should furnish an affidavit denying knowledge of the accusation: R. v. Stapylton, above quoted.

FORM OF AFFIDAVIT FOR PARTICULARS.

Canada.
Province of Ontario.   }   The King v. C.D.
County of

I, C.D., of the   of   , in the County of   '
(*occupation*) make oath and say:—

1. That I am the above named defendant.

2. That I am not aware what are the nature and particulars of the alleged offence charged against me herein, or any of them, and do not possess sufficient information regarding the charge to enable me to meet the same.

3. That I am advised and believe that it is necessary to enable me to defend myself against the charge brought against me, and to a fair hearing thereof, that further particulars should be furnished me by the prosecutor, in regard to the said charge.

Sworn before me at the   }
of   in the County of   }   (Signed) C.D.
this   day of   , A.D. 190   . }

J.P. (or a commissioner, etc.).

Adjournments and Remands; Bail.

The justice may, at any stage of the hearing, adjourn it from time to time, as the interests of justice may require: Code 679 (c). An ordinary remand is made by a warrant remanding the accused to gaol or lockup, according to Form 17 in the Criminal Code. Or bail may be taken in a bailable case, with or without sureties according to the nature of the matter: Form 18. The following cases are not bailable by justices, viz., offences punishable with death, and treason and all treasonable offences. In all other cases the justice may on adjourning the case take bail as above mentioned. In a case for a trifling offence, and if the defendant is a known resident of the locality, he may be allowed to go at large pending the adjournment, upon his own recognizance to appear, according to the above Form 18. If bail is taken, it should be sufficient to ensure the defendant's appearance, but must not be excessive. To impose excessive bail is practically to refuse bail. If bail is taken, the proposed surety or sureties may be examined on oath as to their property and sufficiency, their evidence being taken down and signed in the same way as other evidence in the case; as to which see subsequent pages.

Respectable householders (not necessarily freeholders) may be accepted as bail, if they possess sufficient property of any kind in the province: Petersdorf on Bail, 506. If a person becoming bail for another should take security from the latter, he will not be accepted as sufficient bail, no matter what property he is possessed of: Con. Ex. & F. Co. v. Musgrove (1900), 1 Ch. 37. Money may be deposited by the accused in place of sureties if the justice sees fit to accept it: Moyser v. Grey, Cro. Car. 446.

The justice should in a large measure be guided by the Crown Attorney in the matter of bail, as he is in a position to have fuller knowledge of the facts of the case.

The remand must not be for more than "eight clear days" at one time, the day following that of the remand being the first day counted: Code 679 (c).

The term "clear days" means that the time is to be reckoned exclusively of the day on which the remand is made and of the day on which the case is to be again taken up: R. v. Aberdare, 14 Q.B. 854; Sams v. Toronto, 9 U.C.R. 181. If a Sunday intervenes it will be counted as one of the eight days: Re Railway Supply Co., 29 Ch. D. 204. A remand on the first day of the month, for eight clear days, would mean until the tenth day of the month.

Any number of such remands may be made (from time to time) if the interests of justice so require: Code 679 (c); but good grounds should be shewn for them: Connors v. Darling, 23 U.C.R. 547.

Short remands, not exceeding three clear days at one time, may be verbally made remanding the accused into the charge of the constable, who then becomes responsible for him, and may place him in a lock-up house, if there is a fit one in the locality: Code 679 (2). A remand for more than three days must be by warrant; and the accused must be personally present when it is made: Re Sarrault, 9 Can. Cr. Cas. 448.

Applications by the Crown Attorney, or person representing the Attorney-General, for remands, should generally be granted upon his stating sufficient reasons for them. But some evidence should be taken in the case within a reasonable time, justifying the prosecution.

The defendant cannot be lawfully remanded in his absence; he is entitled to be present personally throughout; and if a remand is made in his absence; or if a remand is made for longer than 8 clear days at one time, the High Court will order his discharge on habeas corpus as being illegally detained: Re Sarault, 9 Can. Cr. Cas. 448. A remand cannot be made in the magistrate's absence by his clerk; a magistrate or justice must make the remand or adjournment: Paré v. Recorder of Montreal, 10 Can. Cr. Cas. 295.

If it is found expedient, *e.g.*, if a witness is going away and will be absent at the time fixed, or for any other reason, the case ought to proceed earlier; the accused, after being remanded until a day stated, may be brought before the justice and the hearing proceeded with on an earlier day; and the gaoler must produce the prisoner on the justice's order: Code 680.

FORM OF ORDER.

To the Keeper of the Common gaol at   County of
    You are hereby required to have C.D. now in your custody at
in the   of   on the   day of   A.D.
190 , at   o'clock   noon, before me to answer to the charge of
         , upon which he was heretofore remanded by me to your custody. to be dealt with according to law
    Dated, etc.

                                   J.P., County of

Failure of Accused to Attend an Adjourned Hearing When Out on Bail.

In that event a new warrant of arrest must be issued: Form 6 to the Criminal Code; and it may be executed in the same manner as the warrant issued in the first instance. And by Code 1097, the justice is to endorse on the back of the recognizance above mentioned the certificate, Form 73 to the Cr. Code, and transmit it to the clerk of the peace for the county in order that it may be estreated at the next general session of the peace: Code 1097, 1098. The case will then be adjourned until the accused can be again arrested and brought before the justice, when proceedings will be continued as follows. See as to bail and estreating same: Re Barretts bail, 7 Can. Cr. Cas. 1, and numerous cases at the end of that case.

Proceedings to Procure Attendance of Witnesses.

Summons to Witness.

Upon the application of either party, the justice "may" issue a summons for any material witnesses residing anywhere within the province: Code 671; Form 11 to the Code. The word "may" in this section implies a duty, and it is therefore a matter for the exercise of a judical discretion on good reasons, and the summons cannot be refused arbitrarily. It is usual and proper to grant any subponeas applied for unless there is some reason to think that the right, is being abused; and subponeas must not be refused unless in a very clear case for doing so, on the ground that the evidence is not material or necessary.

Production of Documents.

The summons may contain a direction to the witness to produce any documents in his possession; or under his control or in his power even if not in his actual possession: Code 671; and the following form of words may be inserted in the summons: "And that you bring with you and produce at the said time and place all books, papers, writings and documents in your possession or power relating to the said matter, and particularly," (here mention any specific book or paper it is desired to have produced).

Serving Witnesses.

The summons must be served by a constable or peace officer: Code 672. It may be served: (1) Personally; (2) Or if the witness cannot conveniently be met with, it may be left "for him" at his last or most usual place of abode, with an inmate apparently not under sixteen years of age: Code 672. In the latter event, the constable should explain the nature of the summons, and who it is for: R. v. Smith, L.R. 10 Q.B. 609.

The "most usual place of abode" means his present place of abode; and the words "last place of abode" mean the last place of abode he had so far as known: Ex p. Rice Jones, 1 L.M. & P. 357.

Some reasonable effort should be made to serve the witness personally: and before any warrant to arrest a witness for non-attendance is issued, it should appear that the summons has come to his knowledge: Gordon v. Denison, 22 A.R. 315.

Warrant to Arrest Witness.

Code 673. If the witness does not attend, "and no just excuse is offered," the justice is to swear the constable as a witness, and take his evidence proving the service of the summons. The constable's evidence should shew that the summons was served personally, or if not, what efforts the constable made to find the witness, that he could not find him and that an inmate (of at least sixteen years of age) was served at the witness's residence, and also any other facts and circumstances going to shew that the witness is keeping out of the way to avoid service; or that the summons has come to his knowledge. Evidence must also be taken shewing that there is reason to believe that the witness is likely to give material evidence. If the witness fails to attend after being served, it should appear in the evidence that the summons was served a reasonable time before the witness is required to appear: Ex p. Hopwood, 15 Q.B. 121.

The justice may then issue his warrant: Form 12 in the Criminal Code; for the arrest of the witness, who is to be *forthwith brought before the justice*, to give evidence: Code 673. Great care should be used before issuing a warrant to arrest a witness and the reason for his non-attendance should be first enquired into.

Proceedings to arrest a witness should only be resorted to in cases of wilful disobedience or defiance, or if it appears that the ends of justice may otherwise be defeated; and there should be evidence taken to satisfy the justice conclusively on these points. The above provisions do not apply to permit the arrest of a prosecutor in the case of a minor offence which he does not wish to proceed with: Cross v. Wilcox, 39 U.C.R. 187.

The warrant to arrest a witness must be "backed" as described for other warrants, see *ante* p. 252. If the witness is to be arrested in another county; and it may be executed in any part of the province where it is "backed": Code 673 (3).

Witnesses' Travelling Expenses.

There is no provision in the law for payment of the witnesses' travelling expenses; and all witnesses are bound to attend on preliminary enquiry in criminal cases before the justice, without being paid their expenses: R. v. James, 1 C. & P. 322, the Ontario statute relating to payment of witnesses in criminal cases only applying to witnesses before the court and not before the justice. But as a warrant is not to be issued unless "no just excuse is offered" for non-attendance of a witness, it would appear that if the witness would have to come from a distance, and is a person in circumstances in which he would be unable to pay his own expenses, these circumstances would constitute a "just excuse," and a warrant should not be issued against him: Roscoe Cr. Ev. 11th ed. 104. In important cases the Attorney-General may direct the payment of witness' fees in such a case. In such case application may be made through the Crown Attorney.

Execution of Warrant to Arrest Witness.

The warrant when issued may be executed by a constable, anywhere in the county to which it was issued; or if the witness is not in the county, he may execute it in any county in the province, upon getting the warrant "backed" in the same manner as a warrant for the arrest of a person accused for crime under Code 662, 673 (3). It cannot be executed out of the province.

Treatment of Witness When Arrested.

The constable is at once to take a witness when arrested before the justice who is holding the enquiry; and he may order his detention by the constable, or in the common gaol or in a police cell or lockup; or the justice may order his release on his own recognizance, or with sureties, in order to secure his presence at the time and place fixed for the hearing: Code 674: Form 18.

The witness must not be searched, nor placed by the constable in the gaol or police cells without the justice's order. The witness is not to be treated as a criminal; and the justice should not allow any unnecessary harshness or interference with the witness's rights or liberties; the one thing to be kept in view being to secure his attendance to give evidence: Gordon v. Denison, 22 A.R. 315.

The warrant may be issued to arrest a witness either for the prosecution or the accused: Code 671, 673.

Warrant Against a Witness in the First Instance.

Provision is made by Code 675 for the arrest of a witness in the first instance, if it appears upon evidence being taken before the justice upon oath, and in writing, that such witness is within the province, and that, upon the facts and circumstances shewn to the satisfaction of the justice, the witness is likely to give material evidence either for the prosecution or the accused, and will not attend without being compelled to do so by a warrant.

This extreme course should never be resorted to, unless from the facts and circumstances, it clearly appears to be necessary. But, if it appears from the character of the witness, and his not having any permanent residence, or other sufficient reason, that the ends of justice would be otherwise defeated, and particularly if some serious crime has been committed, this necessary means of preventing the loss of important testimony must be taken.

Form of the warrant, 14 in the Criminal Code.

Witness in Canada, but not in Province.

In the case of a witness resident in Canada, but who is not in the province, a justice's summons will be of no effect; and a subpœna from a Superior Court, or a County Court, must be issued. The subpœna will be issued upon an order of a judge of such court, on the application of either party (prosecution or accused) or the Attorney-General. The application must be supported by an affidavit, shewing that the witness is likely to give material evidence, and is a resident in Canada, but out of the province; and the subpœna may require the witness to produce documents: Code 676.

The following forms may be used:—

AFFIDAVIT FOR SUBPŒNA TO WITNESS OUT OF THE PROVINCE.
(CODE 676).

In the High Court of Justice, or
In the County Court of the County of   .

In the matter of an information laid by A.B. against C.D. before E.F., Esquire, a justice of the peace in and for the County of   , for that (state offence as charged).

I, A.B., of, etc., make oath and say:

1. I am the above named informant, A.B.

2. That on the   day of   , A.D. 19 , I duly laid an information before the above named justice of the peace, a true copy of which information is now shewn to me, marked Exhibit "A."

3. That the said justice of the peace thereupon issued his warrant for the apprehension of the said C.D., who has been arrested and is now in custody (or on bail, or as the case may be) upon the said charge, and the said justice has appointed the   day of   , A.D. 19 , for the holding of the preliminary inquiry upon the same, and the prosecution of the said C.D. upon the said charge is now pending before the said justice.

4. That one, G.H., is, as I am informed and believe, likely to give material evidence for the prosecution respecting the said charge, the nature of such evidence being, as I am informed and believe, that (state in general terms the nature of the evidence so as to satisfy the judge or court that the proposed witness is likely to give material evidence).

5. I am informed and believe that the said G.H. has in his possession or control certain documents relating to the matter in question, namely, (state what documents are desired to be produced).

6. That the said G.H. resides at   , in the Province of Quebec, within the Dominion of Canada, and is out of the Province of Ontario, and I desire that a subpœna should issue requiring the said G.H. to appear before the said justice, at the said time and place, to give evidence respecting the said charge, and to bring with him any documents in his possession or control relating thereto, and particularly the documents above mentioned.

Sworn, etc.

ORDER FOR SUBPŒNA TO WITNESS OUT OF THE PROVINCE.
(CODE 676).

In the High Court of Justice. ⎫
    The Honourable   ⎪
        Mr. Justice   ⎬
           In Chambers. ⎪
                  or

In the County Court, etc. ⎫
    His Honour   ⎪   day the
    judge of the said court ⎬ day of
           In Chambers. ⎭ A.D. 19 .

In the matter of, etc. (*as in above affidavit*).

Upon the application of A.B., the informant above named, and it appearing that one, G.H., residing at the   of   , in the Province of Quebec, out of this Province, and not being in this Province, is likely to give material evidence for the prosecution in the above matter now pending before the said justice, and that he is alleged to have in his possession or control certain documents relating to the said charge, and particularly (*state what documents it is desired to have produced*).

It is ordered that a Writ of Subpœna, be issued under the Seal of this court, requiring the said G.H. to appeal before the said justice at   in the   of   , in the County of   , on the   day of   , A.D. 19 , to give evidence respecting the said charge, and to bring with him, and produce at the said time and place, any documents in his possession, or under his control, relating thereto, and particularly the documents hereinbefore specially mentioned.

The subpœna must be served on the witness personally and an affidavit, sworn before any justice of the peace, is sufficient proof of service: Code 676 (2).

AFFIDAVIT OF SERVICE OF SOBPŒNA OUT OF THE PROVINCE.
(CODE 676(2)).

In the High Court of Justice (*or as the case may be*).

In the matter of, etc.

I,   of the   of   , in the County of (*occupation*), make oath and say, as follows:

1. That I did, on the   day of   , A.D. 19 , personally serve   with the subpœna hereto annexed, marked A., by delivering to and leaving with him, the said   , a true copy of the said subpœna, at the   of   aforesaid.

2. That at the time of affecting such service as aforesaid, I produced and shewed to the said   the said original subpœna hereto

annexed, and that the said   so served by me is the person named in the said original subpœna.

    3. That in order to effect such service I necessarily travelled miles.

    4. (*If witness's fees are paid add a clause to that effect.*)

Sworn before me at the
       of
in the County of   (Signature).
this   day of
A.D. 19 .
        C.D.
A justice of the peace in and for
    the County of

If the witness does not attend on the subpœna, and no just excuse is offered for his non-attendance, the justice upon proof on oath of the service, (that is, on the filing of the above affidavit, which by Code 676 (2), is declared to be sufficient proof) may issue a warrant signed by the justice holding the enquiry, for the arrest of the witness anywhere in Canada, and to bring him before such justice, or any other justice, at a time and place to be mentioned in the warrant, to give evidence: Code 677; see warrant, Form 15 to the Criminal Code.

This warrant is not to be directed to a constable of the justice's county, but to any or all constables or peace officers in the county or place where the witness is: Code 677; and it may be executed there without being "backed"; but the warrant may be "backed" in the manner directed by Code 662 (see p. 252) in any other county and be executed there: Code 677 (2).

Witness Fees.

There is no provision made for the payment of the witness's travelling expenses under sec. 676 of the Code; and a witness is bound to attend in criminal cases without being paid his expenses: R. v. James, 1 C. & P. 322.

But as a warrant is only to be issued, if "no just excuse" is offered: Code 667; it appears that the absence of payment of necessary expenses, especially if the witness has to come a considerable distance, and if he is unable to pay his own expenses, would constitute a "just excuse" and a warrant would be refused. The justice has a discretion to refuse in such a case: R. v. Clements, 4 Can. Cr. Cas. 553.

The power under this sec. 676, is to bring a witness even from one end of the Dominion to the other.

In consequence of the difficulty of enforcing in one province, proceedings for contempt against a witness in another province, Code 976 provides, as follows:

The courts of the various provinces, and the judges of the said courts respectively, shall be auxiliary to one another for the purposes of the Criminal Code; and any judgment, decree or order made by the court issuing such subpœna, upon any proceeding against any witness for contempt, or otherwise, may be enforced or acted upon by any court in the province in which such witness resides, in the same manner and as validly and effectually as if such judgment, order or decree had been made by the last mentioned court.

Commission to Examine Witnesses Out of Canada.

The evidence of a witness, on either side, who is out of Canada may be taken under commission, to be issued under order of the judge of the High Court, or County Court: Code 997.

AFFIDAVIT FOR COMMISSION TO TAKE EVIDENCE OUT OF CANADA.
(CODE 997).

(*Heading and style of cause as in next preceding form.*)

I, A.B., etc., make oath and say:
1. I am the above named informant in this matter.
2. On or about the   day of   , A.D. 19   , I duly laid an information against the above named C.D., before E.F., Esquire, a justice of the peace in and for the County of   , for an indictable offence, namely, that (*set out the charge*).
3. The prosecution of the said C.D. for the said offence is now pending before the said justice of the peace.
4. That G.H., a person who resides at   , out of Canada, and is not now in Canada, is, as I am informed and verily believe, able to give material information relating to the said offence, such information being that (*state in a general way the evidence the witness will give, so as to satisfy the court that it is material*).
5. That J.K., of (*residence and occupation*), is, as I am informed and believe, a fit and proper person to be appointed a commissioner to take the evidence of the said G.H.

Sworn, etc.

If it is desired that the evidence should be taken in short-hand by a stenographer, as may be done (Code 683), add a clause stating the facts, shewing the expediency of so doing, and naming a fit person to act as such.

NOTICE OF MOTION FOR COMMISSION TO TAKE EVIDENCE OUT OF CANADA.
(CODE 997)

In the High Court of Justice.
or
In the County Court of the County of Huron.
(Style of cause as in preceding forms.)

Take notice that an application on behalf of the above named A.B. (*or* C.D., *as the case may be*) will be made to the Honourable the presiding judge in Chambers, of the High Court of Justice at Osgoode Hall, Toronto, (*or* to His Honour the judge of the County Court of the County of   , in Chambers at the Court House, in the town of   , in the County of   on   , the   day of   , A.D. 19   , at ten o'clock in the forenoon, or so soon thereafter as the application can be made, for an order appointing a commissioner to take the evidence *viva voce*, upon oath or affirmation, of G.H., a witness who resides out of Canada, and is able to give material information relating to the charge of an indictable offence, for which a prosecution is now pending upon the information of the above named A.B., against the above named C.D., for that (*state the charge*). And take notice that the name and address of the commissioner proposed to be so appointed is L.M., of the of   , in the State of   , one of the United States of *America* (*or as the case may be, adding the person's occupation*). And further take notice that upon such application will be read the affidavit of the said   , this day filed, and the exhibits therein referred to.
Dated at   the   day of   A.D. 19   .
To
The above named (C.D. *or* A.B.), and to
his Solicitor.

Solicitor for the
said (A.B. or C.D.)

ORDER APPOINTING COMMISSIONER TO TAKE EVIDENCE OUT OF CANADA.
(CODE 997).

(Heading and style of cause as in preceding forms.)

Upon the application of the above named A.B., and upon reading the affidavit of   filed, and upon hearing both parties by their solicitors or counsel, and it appearing that G.H., who resides out of Canada, is able to give material information relating to an indictable offence for which a prosecution is now pending in this matter;

1. It is ordered that J.K. of (*residence and occupation*) be and he is hereby appointed a commissioner to take the evidence *viva voce* upon oath or affirmation of the said G.H., at   aforesaid, and that a commission do issue for that purpose under the seal of this court directed to the said commissioner.

2. That   days' previous notice of the mail or other conveyance, by which the said commission is to be sent out, shall be given by the said A.B. to the said C.D., or to his solicitor.

Code 997 (2), expressly provides that the practice and procedure on the appointment of a commissioner to take evidence out of Canada is to be, as nearly as practicable, the same as in like matter in civil causes. As to such practice and procedure in Ontario: see Con. R. 499-515; Holmested and Langton, 677.

If the evidence is to be taken in shorthand by a stenographer insert a clause in the order and commission so providing; and provide for his being sworn: see Con. R. 509-511.

The provisions of Code 997, as to taking evidence of witnesses out of Canada, applies to preliminary proceedings before justices and the commission may issue pending the same, and for use thereon: R. v. Verrall, 16 P.R. 444; 17 P.R. 61. A commission may issue for a witness resident abroad, even though he is temporarily in Canada, but about to return to his own country: R. v. Baskett, 6 Can. Cr. Cas. 61.

The form of commission is furnished by the officer who issues it, and the form of commissioner's oath, oath of witness, and return to the commission are endorsed on it, with directions as to the execution of the commission which must be strictly followed.

If the evidence is taken by a stenographer the latter must first be sworn to truly and faithfully report the evidence: Code 683.

For form of stenographer's oath see *infra.*

Taking the Evidence of a Witness who is in Prison.

If a witness is in any prison (see Code 2 (30)) in Canada the justice holding a preliminary enquiry has no authority to bring such witness before him to give evidence. Code 977 appears to apply only to a witness at the trial before a court of criminal jurisdiction by indictment and not to proceedings before justices.

Such witness can only be brought before the justice under order of the Superior Court for a writ of habeas corpus *ad testificandum*: see Spellman v. Spellman, 10 C.L.T. 20; R. v. Townsend, 3 C.L.J. 184.

Witness Dangerously Ill.

If the evidence of a witness who is dangerously ill and not likely to recover is required, a justice has no power to issue a commission to take it, but a Superior or County Court judge may on the application of either the prosecutor or the accused, issue a commission to take such evidence, and the evidence when taken is, in case the accused has not already been committed for trial, to be sent to the clerk of the peace or the proper officer having charge of the records and proceedings: Code 995.

Affidavit for Commission to Examine Witness who is Dangerously Ill.
(Code 995).

In the High Court of Justice (or In the County Court of the County of   ).

In the matter of an information laid by A.B. against C.D. before E.F., Esquire, a justice of the peace in and for the County of   , for an indictable offence, to wit: for that (*state the charge*).

I, A.B., of the   of   in the County of (*occupation*) make oath and say:

1. I am the informant A.B. above-named.
2. On the   day of   A.D. 19 , I duly laid an information against the above-named C.D. for the indictable offence above-mentioned, and the proceedings thereon are now pending before the said justice.
3. That G.H. of the   of   in the County of   , is a material and necessary witness, and is able to give material information relating to the said offence, and he, the said G.H., is, as he has informed me in an interview which I had with him on the   day of   instant, willing to give such information ,which is (*here state in a general way the evidence which the witness is able to give so as to shew its materiality*).
4. That the said G.H., according to the opinion of J.K., of   , a duly licensed medical practitioner, which is now shewn to me marked exhibit A., to this my affidavit, and which·was given to me by the said J.K. on the day of its date, is dangerously ill and not likely to recover from such illness, and the attendance of the said G.H. to give evidence cannot by reason thereof be procured.
5. That L.M., a justice of the peace residing at   , is a fit and proper person to take the evidence of the said witness.
6. The said C.D. is now in actual custody in the common gaol of the County of   , and has been served with the notice now shewn to me marked "B." (*see Code 996, 998*).

Sworn, etc.,

The opinion of the medical practitioner should, if practicable, be given in an affidavit by him.

Order Appointing a Commissioner to Examine a Witness Dangerously Ill.
(Code 995).

In the High Court of Justice.
The Honourable
Mr. Justice
In Chambers.   Tuesday, the
day of
A.D. 19
or In the County Court of the County of
His Honour
Judge of the said court
In Chambers.

In the matter of, *etc.* (*as in the above affidavit*).

Upon the application of the above-named A.B., upon reading the affidavits of   , and   filed, and it appearing to my satisfaction that one G.H., a person who is dangerously ill, and who, in the opinion of a duly licensed medical practitioner, is not likely to recover from such illness, is able and willing to give material evidence relating to the indictable offence above-mentioned.

1. It is ordered that L.M., of   , a justice of the peace in and for the County of   , (or, *as the case may be*), be and he is hereby appointed a commissioner to take in writing the statement on oath or affirmation of the said G.H., pursuant to section 995 of the Criminal Code of Canada, the examination of the said witness to be *viva voce*.

2. And it is further ordered and directed that the keeper of the common gaol for the County of   , in whose custody the above-named C.D. now is, do convey the said C.D. to the Town Hall, in the Town of   , on the   day of   , A.D. 19 , at   o'clock in the   noon, being the place mentioned in the notice served on the said C.D. of an intention to take the said statement, for the purpose of being present at the taking of the said statement. (*See Code* 996).

The form of commission is supplied by the officer issuing it.

If the accused is in actual custody, the judge who makes the above order will, by an order in writing, direct the officer having the prisoner in custody, to convey him to the place where the evidence is to be taken, under the above sec. 995, so that he may be present; and the expense of so doing is to be paid out of the county funds for prison maintenance: Code 996.

This order may be inserted in the order for commission (see paragraph 2 in the above form.)

A notice of the time and place for taking the evidence must be *"served"* on the opposite party a reasonable time before the evidence is taken: Code 998.

This notice must be in writing, and if a written notice is not served upon the accused, in the case of evidence being taken on behalf of the prosecution, the evidence taken cannot be used, even if the accused, being in custody, was taken to the place where the evidence was given, and was present throughout: R. v. Quigley, 18 L.T. 211; R. v, Shurmer, 17 Q.B.D. 323.

At the time and place fixed, the commissioner will proceed to take the evidence on oath, and the opposite party is entitled to cross-examine: Code 998.

The statement when completed is to be signed by the commissioner, and it should also be signed by the witness, if practicable, although it is not expressly required under this section: Code 995 (2).

The commissioner is to add to the statement, a certificate, shewing who were present when it was taken, and transmit it back to the clerk of the peace for the county where the prosecution is pending: Code 995 (2).

NOTICE OF INTENTION TO TAKE THE EVIDENCE OF A WITNESS WHO IS DANGEROUSLY ILL.
(CODE 998).

To C.D.

Take notice that it is intended on the   day of   A.D.
19 , at (*place where evidence to be taken*) in the Town of   , at
the hour of   o'clock in the   noon, to take the statement
of G.H., of   , on oath or affirmation, under an order of a judge
of the High Court of Justice (or of the County Court of the County of
          , *as the case may be*) appointing L.M., of   , a commis-
sioner to take such statement touching the matter of a charge for an indictable offence now pending against you before E.F., Esquire, a justice of the
peace for the County of   , upon the information of A.B. for that
(*state the charge*).

Dated, etc.

Solicitors for the said A.B.

FORM OF DEPOSITIONS TAKEN ON COMMISSION.

(*To be attached and returned with the commission.*)

Canada   ⎫   The deposition of L.K., of the
Province of   ⎬   of   in the County of
County of   ⎭   (*occupation*),

Taken on oath (or affirmation) before the undersigned E.F., the commissioner named in the commission hereto annexed, at the   of
          , in the County of   , on this   day of   ,
A.D. 19 , under the said commission, in the presence and hearing of
C.D. named in the said commission (*or* after notice to the said C.D.) and
of A.B. (*the prosecutor*) also named therein (*or* after notice to him).

The said deponent, L.K., upon his oath (*or* affirmation), says as follows: —

(*Here insert the witness's statement in the words used by him as nearly
as possible, and at its conclusion have the same signed at the foot by the
witness and also by the commissioner.*)

The depositions of the above-named L.K., written on the several sheets
of paper, to the last of which my signature is subscribed, were taken in
the presence and hearing of the above-named A.B. and C.D., and signed
by the said L.K. in their presence, and I further certify that th' solic't r
or counsel for the said A.B. (*or* C.D., *naming the prosecutor or defendant
as the case may be against whom the evidence is to be used*) had (*or* might
or would have had if he had chosen to be present, *as the case may be*) full
opportunity of cross-examining (*and* did cross-examine *if it be the case*)
the said witness, L.K., upon his said examination before me under the said
commission.

Dated at   this   day of   A.D. 19 .

E.F.

Commissioner.

Code 999 provides that the depositions of any witness taken
under Code 995, by a justice on a preliminary or other investigation of any charge may be read at the trial (not only of the

same charge, but of any other charge against the same defendant: Code 1000), upon proof of facts from which it can reasonably be inferred that the witness is dead, or so ill as not to be able to travel, or is absent from Canada; and that the deposition was taken in the presence of the accused, and that his solicitor or counsel had full opportunity to cross-examine.

For instances of what is an "illness" within the meaning of Code 687: see R. v. Marsella, 17 T.L.R. 164; R. v. Katz, 17 T.L.R. 67; R. v. Jones, 3 F. & F. 285; R. v. Farrell, L.R. 2 C.C.R. 116; R. v. Stephenson, 31 L.J.M.C. 147; R. v. Scaife, 17 Q.B. 238; R. v. Cockburn, Dears, & B. 203; R. v. Wilson, 8 Cox C.C. 453. The illness should be proved by medical testimony: R. v. Welton, 9 Cox C.C. 296; and such evidence must shew the state of health, up to the time of the trial, or such a short time before as to involve the inference that the witness is at the time of the trial unable to attend: R. v. Bull, 12 Cox C.C. 31.

When the witness was taken ill during the cross-examination by the prisoner's counsel, and before it was concluded, it was held that the depositions were not receivable, as the defendant· had not full opportunity to cross-examine as required by Code 686: R. v. Mitchell, 17 Cox C.C. 503.

As to what is sufficient proof of the witness bein̰ out of Canada so as to let in depositions under Code 998-1001: see R. v. Nelson, 1 O.R. 500; R. v. Pescaro, 2 B.C.R. 114.

The evidence of a constable that he could not find the witness and was told the witness was out of Canada, is not sufficient to let in the deposition as evidence on that ground, it being merely hearsay: R. v. Nelson, 1 O.R. 500; R. v. Graham, 2 Can. Cr. Cas. 388; R. v. Wellings, 3 Q.B.D. 426.

A coroner is not a "justice" within the meaning of Code 999-1000, and the depositions taken before him are not evidence at the trial even if the witness is then dead: R. v. Graham, 2 Can. Cr. Cas. 388.

And the unsworn evidence of a child, taken under Code 1003, or the Canada Evidence Act, sec. 16, are not receivable as "depositions" under Code 999: R. v. Pruntey, 16 Cox C.C. 344.

The depositions taken before a justice, in order to be admissible at the trial, under Code 999, must have been taken in exact conformity, in all respects, with the requirements of that section.

Requisites of Depositions.

The three requisites there mentioned are:—(1) That it be proved that the deposition was taken in the presence of the opposite party; (2) that he or his solicitor or counsel had the opportunity to cross-examine the witness; (3) and the deposition must "purport to be signed by the justice before whom it was taken."

The first two requisites may be proved by extrinsic evidence, if they do not appear on the face of the deposition; but the third cannot be so proved, but must appear on the deposition, and cannot be otherwise supplied; for no extrinsic evidence will make the deposition "purport" to be signed otherwise than it is: R. v. Miller, 4 Cox C.C. 166; R. v. Hamilton, 2 Can. Cr. Cas. pp. 399, 403, 409. But evidence contra may be given to shew that the deposition was in fact not so signed: Code 999.

In order to constitute the evidence in any case a regularly taken "deposition," Code 999 evidently presupposes other necessary formalities and requisites, in addition to those expressly mentioned in that section; and it may well be held that *all* the provisions of Code 682 (which regulates the manner in which depositions are to be taken on a preliminary inquiry) are necessary to constitute the writing a regularly taken deposition: see Attorney-General v. Davison, McClel. & Y. 160; R. v. Woodcock, 1 Leach C.C. 500; R. v. Dingler, 1 Leach C.C. 504. For a statement of these formalities, see *post,* p. 277.

The usual presumption in favour of the proceedings of a judicial officer being regular, will be made if, in other respects, the depositions are in proper form: Roscoe's Cr. Ev. 72; and if the prisoner was present the presumption is that he had opportunity to cross-examine; but this may be rebutted: R. v. Peacock, 12 Cox C.C. 21.

Admissibility of Depositions at Common Law.

Even if a deposition does not strictly comply with Code 999, it is probable that it may still be admissable at common law and apart from any statutory provision, if it is a regularly taken deposition before a justice duly holding a preliminary inquiry which is regulated by Code 682.

It was held prior to the English statute, 11 & 12 Vict. ch. 42, sec. 17, from which Code 999 is copied, that the taking of a deposition before a justice on a preliminary hearing was a judicial proceeding, and that, without any statutory provision, it was receivable as evidence at the trial, as a judicial record of the evidence; provided it was a properly taken deposition, and if the witness was then dead: R. v. Scaife, 17 Q.B. 238; R. v. Beeston, Dears. C.C. 405.

The intention of 11 & 12 Vict. ch. 42, sec. 17 (and so of Code 999) was to extend, rather than to restrict, the operation of the common law. So if the depositions are irregularly taken, and therefore cannot be used, parol evidence may be given of what the deceased witness said; and the depositions may be referred to in order to refresh the memory of the person proving it: R. v. Galvin, 10 Cox C.C. 198; 3 Russell, p. 558.

The justice in taking evidence on a preliminary enquiry should be careful to observe all the requirements of both secs. 682 and 999 of the Code, so that if any witness should at the time be dead or ill, or out of Canada, there may be no question as to the depositions so taken being then receivable in evidence.

Proceedings on the Hearing Before the Justice.

When the parties and their witnesses are before the justice, the hearing and subsequent proceedings are regulated by section 678 and subsequent sections of the Criminal Code. Anyone present before the justice may be called and compelled to give evidence, although not subpœnaed: Code 678. It is not necessary that the accused should plead; and the justice will proceed to take the evidence.

Who to Conduct the Hearing.

Either the justice or magistrate who took the information, and issued the process, or any other justice or magistrate for the same territorial jurisdiction, is competent to proceed with the hearing of the case: Code 664. But, as has been mentioned at page 209, another justice cannot intervene without the consent of the justice who took the information and issued the summons or warrant. One justice has authority to conduct a preliminary enquiry: Code 665; but with the consent of the justice having the case before him, any number of justices may join with him in hearing it, or act in his place: Code 665. But in that case, all the justices who join in the commitment, must hear the whole of the evidence taken in the case, and merely hearing the evidence read will not suffice: Re Nunn, 2 Can. Cr. Cas. 429;

R. v. Traynor, 4 Can. Cr. Cas. 410; R. v. Watts,.33 L.J.M.C. 63; Re Guerin, 16 Cox C.C. 596. If the case is heard before two justices, and they disagree, there can be no commitment; there must be a majority in favour of it. If the justices are equally divided, the case may be re-heard, or a fresh information may be laid before another justice. A discharge on a preliminary enquiry does not prevent the accused from being brought up before another justice, upon a fresh information for the same offence: R. v. Morton. 19 C.P. 26; R. v. Watters, 12 Cox C.C. 390.

The justice may, in his discretion, regulate the course of the enquiry, in any way not inconsistent with the general provisions of the law: Code 679 (e); and he may from time to time change the place of hearing: Code 679 (c).

Excluding the Public.

All persons except the prosecutor and the accused, their counsel or solicitors may be excluded from the place where the hearing is taking place, if it appears that the ends of justice would be best served by so doing: Code 679 (d); and under Code 645, the justice should order the exclusion of the public, on the hearing of any of the cases mentioned in that section; or in any case in which he is of opinion that it would be in the interests of public morals: Code 645 (2); or when he deems such exclusion necessary or expedient: Code 645 (3)

Excluding Witnesses.

At the request of either party the justice must exclude the witnesses on both sides: see *ante*, p. 234.

Juvenile Offenders.

The hearing of the cases of juvenile offenders under sixteen years must be private, and their trial must take place without publicity and separately and apart from the trials of other accused persons and at suitable times to be designated for that pur pose: Code 644. See further in Chapter XV, *post*: "Juvenile Offenders."

Waiving Preliminary Examination.

The accused may waive the preliminary examination, and consent to be committed for trial without any evidence being taken: R. v. Gibson, 3 Can. Cr. Cas. 451. But if so committed without any depositions being taken the prisoner cannot elect to be tried before the County Court Judge's Criminal Court: R. v. Gibson, *supra;* R. v. McDougall, 8 Can. Cr. Cas. 234; R. v. Jodrey, 9 Can. Cr. Cas. 477; see also notes at p. 126, 5 Can. Cr. Cas. It is therefore necessary that in all cases some evidence should be taken.

Taking the Evidence.

The evidence of each witness in the case must be taken in writing, in the form of a deposition: Code 682 (3).

The form of caption and ending of the deposition is given in the Criminal Code—Form 19. The caption or heading is to be filled up with the following particulars: 1. The names in full of the witnesses and their residence and occupation; 2. The names of the justice or justices who are hearing the case, and a statement that they are justices for the county where the evidence is being taken; 3. The date and place where the evidence is taken; 4. A statement of the charge under investigation; 5. A statement that the evidence is taken on oath or affirmation and in the presence of the accused: Code 682 (2).

One caption and ending will suffice for the depositions of any number of witnesses, in the same case, taken on the same occasion: R. v. Hamilton, 2 Can. Cr. Cas. 390; but if there is an adjournment to another day, a new caption and ending will be used for the witnesses then examined.

The depositions of several witnesses, taken on the same occasion, may be written on several sheets of paper, afterwards fastened together in any manner. The evidence must be read over to and signed by the witness in the presence of the accused and justice: Code 682 (4). The signature of witnesses must not be taken in the defendant's absence: R. v. Trevane, 6 Can. Cr. Cas. 124. The signature of the justice may be either at the end of each witness's deposition; or at the end of all of the depositions, in such a form as to shew that the signature is intended to authenticate each witness's deposition (*e.g.*, by naming the witnesses referred to): Code 682 (5). This must be done before the accused is called upon for his defence: Code 682 (4). The depositions must be written in a legible hand, and on one side of the paper only: Code 683. All the requirements of Code 683 must be carefully followed, as if that is not done they may not be receivable at the trial.

It is not essential that the justice should write down the evidence with his own hand, anyone may do so at his request, but he must be present when all the evidence is being taken: R. v. Traynor, 4 Can. Cr. Cas. 410; and see notes in 7 Can. Cr. Cas. page 342.

Presence of the Accused.

If any part of the deposition is taken in the justice's absence a commitment on it will be invalid. The accused must also be present during the taking of the whole of the evidence: Code 682 (2); and also when it is signed: R. v. Trevane, 6 Can. Cr. Cas. 125. It will not suffice to read over to him any evidence taken in his absence and have it re-affirmed by the witness; the accused and his counsel have the right, with a view to cross-examination, to hear what the witness says, and observe how his answers are given. Any infringement of this rule will invalidate the commitment, and it cannot be waived; and the commitment for trial on evidence so improperly taken will be set aside: R. v. Watts, 33 L.J.M.C. 63; R. v. Traynor, 4 Can. Cr. Cas. 410; R. v. Lepine, 4 Can. Cr. Cas. 145.

Taking Evidence in Shorthand.

If not taken in shorthand the evidence is to be written in a legible hand, and on one side of the paper only: Code 683.

If it is so desired, the evidence or any part of it may be taken in shorthand by a stenographer: Code 683; and in that event the depositions need not be read over to, nor signed by the witnesses; but the evidence is to be transcribed afterwards, and signed by the justice. An affidavit of the stenographer will be annexed, stating that it is a true report of the evidence: Code 683 (2).

Oath of Stenographer.

The stenographer must be sworn before commencing to take down the evidence: Code 683.

FORM OF STENOGRAPHER'S OATH.

"In the matter of the *King* v. *C.D.;* You swear that you shall truly and faithfully report the evidence to be given in this case; so help you God."

FORM OF AFFIRMATION.

(In case the stenographer objects to take an oath.)

"I, E.F., do solemnly affirm that I will truly and faithfully report the evidence to be given in this case": See Code 683.

Affidavit of the Stenographer.

The transcript of the evidence is afterwards made out under the caption above mentioned: Form 19; and signed by the justice, with the following affidavit annexed: Code 683 (2).

AFFIDAVIT OF STENOGRAPHER.

Province of Ontario.
County of
The *King* v. *C.D.*
I, E.F., of the   of   , County of   (*occupation*), make oath and say (or do solemnly affirm):

1. That I am the stenographer appointed by G.H., one of His Majesty's justices of the peace in and for the County of   , to report the evidence in this case.

2. That the transcript of evidence hereto annexed, signed by the said G.H., as such justice of the peace, is a true report of the evidence taken in this case before the said G.H., and taken down by me as such stenographer as aforesaid.

E.F.

Sworn (*or* affirmed), *etc.*

Evidence to be Taken Down Verbatim.

It should be taken in the witness's words as nearly as possible: R. v. Graham, 2 Can. Cr. Cas. 388. In R. v. Thomas, 7 C. & P. 817, Parke, B., said: "Justices are required to put down *all* of the evidence, not merely what they *deem* material." They should record a full statement of all the witness says upon the matter; and everything of a material nature which may be *said* or *done* by the witness or the accused, in the presence of the justice during the course of the enquiry, should also be taken down: R. v. Grady, 7 C. & P. 650.

Witnesses Must be Sworn

Before giving evidence: Code 682 (2). It is not sufficient to take down a witness's statements first and then swear him to the truth of them: R. v. Kiddy, 4 D. & R. 734. The oath need not be administered by the justice himself, though it is usually so done; his clerk or any person by his direction may administer it; but the justice must be present: 3 Russell 658 (*o*).

Forms of Oaths.

The usual way is as follows:

"In the case of the *King* v. *C.D.*, you swear that the evidence you shall give touching the matter in question shall be the truth, the whole truth, and nothing but the truth: so help you God."

The witness, holding the Bible in his naked right hand while this oath is being read, is then to kiss the Bible.

By the Ontario Statute of 1902, ch. 12, sec. 29, the use of the Bible may be dispensed with and the usual Scotch oath administered as follows:—

"I, A.B., do swear by God himself, as I shall answer to Him at the great day of judgment, that the evidence that I shall give touching the matter in question, is the truth, the whole truth, and nothing but the truth: so help me God."

Witness Affirming Instead of Swearing.

A Moravian or Quaker is sworn as follows:—

"I, A.B., being one of the persons known as the united brethren called Moravians do solemnly, sincerely and truly declare and affirm," etc.

If any witness objects from conscientious scruples, to take an oath, or if he objects for any reason to do so, he may affirm in the following form: Can. Ev. Act, R.S.C. ch. 145, sec. 14:—

"I solemnly affirm that the evidence to be given by me shall be the truth, the whole truth, and nothing but the truth."

Absence of Religious Belief

Does not disqualify a witness, but only affects the value of his testimony.

Such witness cannot be cross-examined as to his absence or otherwise of religious belief if he alleges either that he has, or that he has not, any religious belief: R. v. Serva, 2 C. & K. 53; but the justice should ascertain from the witness what his grounds are on which he objects to his oath; that is, whether it is because he has no religious belief, or because it is contrary to his religious belief: R. v. Moore, 61 L.J.M.C. 80.

Heathen Witnesses

Are to be sworn in the form, and with the ceremony, which they consider most binding on their consciences.

For instance: If the witness is a non-christian Chinaman, "the King's Oath" should be administered in the case of a capital offence, such as murder. If the offence is a minor one, the "paper oath" is sufficient: R. v. Ah Wooey, 8 Can. Cr. Cas. 25.

Forms of these oaths are given in 8 Can. Cr. Cas. 25. See also Roscoe 121.

An Indian Witness,

Or any witness, although non-Christian, if he believes in the future state and a Supreme Being, may be sworn in the same way as a Christian witness: R. v. Pah-Mah-Gay, 20 U.C.R. 195; and one who, although destitute of any knowledge of God, or of any fixed and clear belief in religion, or in the future state of rewards and punishment, may affirm (without oath) to tell the truth, the whole truth and nothing but the truth, in such form as a court approves: R.S.C. ch. 81, sec. 151; but in such case the justice must caution the witness that he will be liable to incur punishment if he does not tell the truth, the whole truth and nothing but the truth: sec. 153.

A Jew

Is sworn on the Pentateuch, with his head covered: Roscoe 148.

A Mahometan

Is sworn on the Koran; placing his left hand on his forehead and his right hand on the book, bringing the top of his forehead down to the book, and touching it with his head.

Deaf Mute Witness.

Such a witness may be sworn and give his evidence by signs or by written questions and answers, or in any way in which he can be communicated with: Can. Ev. Act, R.S.C. ch. 145, sec. 6; and any one able to communicate with him by signs or otherwise may be sworn as an interpreter as mentioned below.

Interpreters.

Witnesses who cannot speak English may be sworn and examined through an interpreter.

The interpreter is first to be sworn, as follows: —

"You shall well and truly interpret the evidence to be given by the witness A.B. (*naming him*), so help you God."

The interpreter will then, under direction of the justice, communicate the usual oath or affirmation to the witness and repeat the question put, and the answers given. A witness who speaks two or more languages may be examined in that which he understands best, but if he can be communicated with in English the communication must be in that language; and the opposing counsel may first question the witness in English to test his competency to speak that language: R. v. Wong On, 2 Can. Cr. Cas. 343; and he may if he chooses cross-examine in English without an interpreter if the witness has any knowledge of that language: same case.

Children as Witnesses.

In the case of a young child offered as a witness, the justice should first question him as to his knowledge of the nature of an oath, and his moral obligation in taking it and to tell the truth. If this does not appear, his evidence may nevertheless be taken, if the justice is of the opinion that the child 'is of sufficient intelligence, and understands the duty of speaking the truth; in that case the child will not be sworn, but his statements will be taken down in the usual way, like any other witness, and the justice will sign the statement noting the circumstances under which it was taken, and that it was without oath: see Can. Ev Act; sec. 16. As to corroboration required in such cases; see Can. Ev. Act, R.S.C. ch. 145, sec. 16 (2), *ante* p. 162.

Examination of Witnesses.

The witnesses for the prosecution are first called, and examined by the private prosecutor or his counsel, or by the Crown Attorney.

Cross-Examination.

The accused or his counsel or solicitor, is entitled to cross-examine all witnesses for the prosecution: Code 682 (2); and the justice should so state to the accused before closing the evidence of each witness. The private prosecutor or his counsel may then re-examine the witness in explanation of anything said in cross-examination; not bringing in any new matter without the justice's permission, which the justice may grant; if there is any new matter permitted the accused must be allowed the opportunity to cross-examine as to it: R. v. Perras, 9 Can. Cr. Cas. 364.

When the witness's cross-examination was interrupted by his illness and no further opportunity was afterwards given the defendant to continue it, the commitment was held to be invalid: R. v. Trevane, 6 Can. Cr. Cas. 124.

Reading the Deposition to a Witness.

When the evidence of a witness is completed, it is to be read over to him (unless the evidence is taken in shorthand), as above explained, *ante* p. 278. On the evidence being read the witness may correct any error the justice may have made in taking down his statements; but if he wishes to change or withdraw anything he has actually said, and which has been taken down, it is not to be erased, but the correction is to be made at the end of the deposition, before he signs it.

If Witness Refuses to be Sworn

Or to answer questions, or to sign his deposition, when ordered to do so by the justice, without just excuse, the justice may adjourn the case for not more than eight clear days, and may issue a warrant—Form 16 in the Criminal Code—committing the witness to gaol: Code 678. To justify a committal of a witness under this section it must appear that the witness not only refuses without just excuse to answer a question, but that the question asked was relevant to the issue; that is, that the matter asked about tended, either directly or indirectly, to prove or disprove a fact in issue, or some relevant fact: Re Ayotte, 9 Can. Cr. Cas. 133; Phipson on Evidence 43.

The justice should note the demand upon, and the refusal of the witness, and state any reason the witness gives; and the questions which the witness refuses to answer should be taken down, with the witness's statement regarding them, if any; and the justice should himself repeat the questions, or make the demand, formally to the witness. All the facts should be noted so as to shew the grounds on which the justice's warrant is issued. The accused will be remanded to gaol, or bailed, meantime.

If the witness "sooner," that is, before the expiry of the remand, signifies to the justice "his consent to do what is required of him," the parties should at once be notified, and brought before the justice, and the matter proceeded with: Code 678. At the time and place to which the case has been remanded (unless the witness has meantime consented to do what is required of him), the parties and witness are to be brought before the justice, who will again demand of the witness, formally, to do what has been required, and upon refusal, may again adjourn the case and re-commit the witness for another period of not more than 8 clear days; and so on from time to time, until the witness obeys:

Code 678 (2). • The justice may, however, proceed to dispose of the case without the evidence of this witness, if he sees fit: Code 678 (3).

Reading Evidence Again at the Conclusion of the Prosecutor's Case.

When the evidence of the witnesses for the prosecution is completed, the prisoner is to be asked if he wishes the whole evidence taken to be read to him again; and it is to be so read, unless he dispenses with it: Code 684. The usual course is for the accused to dispense with the second reading of the evidence.

Warning to Accused.

When the evidence for the prosecution is completed the justice will note that fact on the proceedings and will then proceed in the manner directed by Code 684; and is to read to the accused the question and the warning provided by that section; the form of it will be found there.

Statement by Accused.

What he then says is to be taken down in writing in Form 20: Code 684 (3).

It should be left entirely to the accused whether he will make any statement or not. A prisoner is not to be entrapped into making any statement, nor should he be dissuaded from doing so, because that would be shutting up one of the sources of justice: R. v. Greene, 5 C. & P. 312. If the statement is made in answer to a question by the justice, it is nevertheless receivable in evidence at the subsequent trial; but questions ought to be put only for the purpose of explaining anything the prisoner may have already stated. Questions calculated to lead to answers prejudicial to the prisoner should not be asked; and the power of asking questions should be used with caution and discretion. Anything said by a prisoner in answer to cross-examination by or before the justice, in this connection, will not be allowed to be given in evidence at the trial: 3 Russell 542; R. v. Berriman, 6 Cox C.C. 388.

The statement of the accused should be taken down in the actual words used and should be read to the accused, and he should be got to sign it if he will; but he cannot be compelled to do so, nor is it necessary. He should not be sworn before making this statement. These observations only apply to statements taken under Code 684 (3), and not to the statements made by the accused when subsequently called as a witness.

Evidence for Defence.

The justice will then proceed to ask the accused if he wishes to call any witnesses, and if so all the evidence for the defence must be taken: Code 686; including the evidence of himself as witness if he so desires: Can. Ev. Act; in which case he will, of course, be sworn like any other witness before giving his evidence.

Hearing the Parties.

It is usual and proper, though not obligatory on the justice to hear the prosecutor as well as the defendant, in summing up the case; if such is done, the practice on trials in the highest courts will be followed: R. v. Le Blanck, 6 Can. Cr. Cas. 348.

Disposition of the Case.

There are four ways of disposing: 1. By dismissal; 2. By committing the prisoner for trial; 3. By bailing him for trial; 4. By binding the prosecutor to prosecute an indictment if he so requires. The justice may adjourn the case to consider his decision; but must fix a time and place to dispose of the case. He cannot adjourn *sine die*, and give his decision in the absence of the accused. The latter is entitled to be present in order to protect his interests: R. v. Quinn, 2 Can. Cr. Cas. 153.

1. Dismissal: Code 687.

2. By Committing the Accused for Trial.

Code 690; warrant Form 22 to the Criminal Code.

The question for the justice in deciding the case is, whether or not on considering the whole evidence on both sides, it is sufficient to put the accused upon his trial: Code 690. The justice is not to try the case, nor to decide between conflicting witnesses, any controverted fact. This is for a jury to decide under the judge's direction. If there is a substantial question to be tried, the justice has no right to assume the functions of the judge and jury, but should commit the accused for trial. If, however, the evidence for the defence explains away the facts on which the prosecution is founded there remains nothing for trial;

but if any substantial and apparently credible evidence is given by anyone, which if true would justify conviction, the justice should send the case up for trial. The justice may commit the accused for trial for any indictable offence which the evidence discloses, even if it is different from that laid in the information: See observations *ante* p. 256. But the justice cannot turn a preliminary enquiry for an indictable offence into a summary trial for a lesser offence, and convict the accused of the latter, even if the evidence proves him to be guilty of it. Fresh proceedings would have to be commenced and carried on in the manner described in the subsequent pages for a "summary conviction" case: Re Mines, 1 Can. Cr. Cas. 217; R. v. Lee, 2 Can. Cr. Cas. 233; R. v. Dungey, 5 Can. Cr. Cas. 38; Ex p. Duffy, 8 Can. Cr. Cas. 277. Neither can a person be committed for trial for an offence which is within the justice's summary jurisdiction to convict: R. v. Beauvais, 7 Can. Cr. Cas. 494; R. v. Lalonde, 9 Can. Cr. Cas. 501; in which case a prisoner was in custody under a warrant according to the Form 22 of warrant of commitment for trial, but the offence stated in it was one in which the justices had power to summarily convict, and the prisoner was discharged on habeas corpus.

Warrant of Commitment.

If the justice decides to send the case up for trial he will issue a warrant of commitment: Form 22 to the Criminal Code.

To What Court Accused to be Committed.

The commitment is usually "to the next court of competent jurisdiction"; but by section 697 of the Criminal Code, the accused may be committed for trial at the next sittings of the court of general sessions of the peace for the county (even if the assizes should intervene), in cases in which the general sessions has jurisdiction; as to which: see Code 582, 583. This is to prevent petty cases, triable at the general sessions, from being sent to the assizes. Code 582 gives the general sessions jurisdiction over all indictable offences, except those specified in Code 583, to which refer. All cases which the court of general sessions has authority to try should as a general rule be sent to that court, notwithstanding the assizes may be held at an earlier date. After committal the justice is *functus officio* and cannot take bail and the prisoner must apply to the court if so advised.

3. Bailing the Accused for Trial

Without committal: Code 696. If the justice is of opinion that the evidence is sufficient to put the accused on his trial, but that it does not furnish such a strong presumption of guilt as to justify committing him to gaol, he may admit the accused to bail, with one or more sureties, for his appearance for trial at the next general sessions or assizes as the case may require: Code 696. Form of recognizance, 28 in the Criminal Code. In this event, the justice must call in another justice with him to take the recognizance as it requires two justices if the offence is one for which the maximum punishment prescribed by the statute is more than five years' imprisonment; but if it is punishable with less than five years one justice alone may take the recognizance: Code 696.

If the offence is treason, or any offence punishable with death, or any of the offences mentioned in sections 76 to 86 inclusive of the Criminal Code, section 696 does not apply and the justices have no power to bail the prisoner accused of any such offences.

In taking bail as above mentioned, the proposed surety or sureties may be required to "justify," *e.g.*, to make an affidavit as to his property and other sufficiency as bail: Code 696 (2).

FORM OF AFFIDAVIT OF JUSTIFICATION BY SURETY.

Province of Ontario, ⎫   The *King* v. *A.B.*
County of   ⎬

I, E.F., of the   of   in the County of   ,
(*occupation*) make oath and say:—

1. That I am the surety (or one of the sureties) proposed and named for the above named A.B. in the recognizance in this matter hereto annexed.

2. That I am a freeholder (or householder) residing in the of   , in the County of   •   .

3. That I am worth property to the amount of   dollars over and above what will pay all my debts and liabilities and every other sum for which I am now liable, or for which I am bail or surety in any other matter.

4. That I am not bail nor surety for any person except in this matter and except (*stating in what matter and for how much, if any*).

5. That my said property consists of (*describe what it consists of, e.g., farm stock, land, etc.*), to the value of at least   dollars.

Sworn before me at   ⎫   •
            of   ⎪
in the County of   ,   ⎬   (Signed) E.F.
            on the   ⎪
day of   , A.D. 19   ⎭
      J.P., County of

If there are two sureties, a second affidavit similar to the foregoing will be added.

But if the surety is known to the' justice to be sufficient no affidavit is necessary.

' The question is chiefly as to the property qualification of the proposed sureties, but regard will also be had to their character and standing: R. v. Saunders, 2 Cox 249; R. v. Badger, 4 Q.B. 468. Any householder having sufficient personal property out of which the amount of bail can be recovered, even if he is not a freeholder, may be accepted as bail: Petersdorf on Bail, 506.

Warrant of Commitment in Default of Bail

Under Code 696. If the accused does not give sufficient bail, the justice may commit him to gaol, by warrant: Form 22 to the Criminal Code.

Recognizances of bail need not be signed by the parties, but must be signed and sealed by the justice. It is an obligation taken *viva voce* in court, and the procedure is for the justice to read the recognizance to the parties and at the conclusion ask them "Are you content?" to which they then signify their assent.

4. On Dismissal of Case, Prosecutor May be Bound over to Prosecute.

If the justice dismisses the case the accused is entitled to be discharged: Code 687. But if the prosecutor still expresses his desire to carry the case before the grand jury, he has the right to do so; and in that event, and upon the prosecutor's request, the justice must take his recognizance to prosecute an indictment against the accused before the grand jury at the next court of competent jurisdiction: Code 688; recognizance, Form 21 to the Criminal Code.

The justice cannot refuse this request, but must take the prosecutor's recognizance to prosecute, if so requested by the prosecutor, and if the information or evidence alleges an offence known to the law: R. v. Eyre, L.R. 3 Q.B. 487; R. v. London (Jus.) 16 Cox C.C. 77; but if the information and evidence shew that the charge (even if true) is an impossible one, the justice would rightly decline to bind over the prosecutor: Ex p. Wason, L.R. 4 Q.B. 573.

This recognizance can only be by a person who has preferred the charge before the justice. See 10 Can. Cr. Cas. 216.

Binding Over Prosecutor and Witnesses for the Trial.

Upon committing the accused for trial the prosecutor and witnesses should be required to enter into their own recognizance to appear at the trial and give evidence: Code 692; Forms 23, 24 or 25 to the Criminal Code. If the witness refuses to be bound over the justice may, if he thinks it necessary commit him to gaol: Form 26; until the trial or until he consents to be bound over, when any justice may take the recognizance and order the witness's release: Code 694.

Proceedings to be Sent to the Clerk of the Peace.

This should be done without delay after the accused has been committed for trial: Code 695.

Taking Bail Under Judge's Order: Code 698.

Upon a judge's order for bail being brought before any two justices for the county the accused and sureties are to be also brought before the justices, who will take their recognizance for bail, which may be in a form similar to Form 28 of the Criminal Code.

The justices may, before taking the recognizance, require the proposed sureties to be sworn, and examined on behalf of the prosecutor as to their property and liabilities. No question can be put to them except as to their property and means. The justices are to decide as to the sureties' sufficiency; and if they are not sufficient, others must be obtained, and the accused will meantime remain in custody.

Upon taking the recognizance of bail, the justices are to issue a warrant of deliverance—Form 29; See Code 698 (2), and 702, and the warrant of deliverance, with the judge's order of bail attached—Code 698—are to be delivered to the gaoler, who must forthwith release the accused, unless he is detained for some other offence: Code 702.

Surrender of Accused by Sureties after being Bailed: Code 703.

If, after the accused has been released on bail, there is reason to believe that he is about to abscond, one of the sureties, or some person by his authority, may appear before any justice and lay an information in the following form: —

19—MAG. MAN.

Canada.
Province of   }
County of

      The information of A.B., of the   of   in the County of   (*occupation*), taken this   day of   , A.D. 19 , before the undersigned K.L., one of His Majesty's justices of the peace in and for the County of   , who saith that the said A.B., together with C.D. (*insert names of sureties*), were on the   day of   , A.D. 19 , duly bound by recognizance before E.F., Esquire, a justice of the peace in and for the said County of   , conditioned for the appearance of G.H., at the then next court of competent jurisdiction (*or as the case may be*), and then and there surrender himself into the custody of the keeper of the common gaol at   , in the said County, and plead to such indictment as should be found against him by the grand jury, in respect of a charge upon which he had theretofore been committed for trial, namely: (*state the charge*), and stand his trial thereon and not depart the said court without leave; and that there is reason to believe that the said G.H. is about to abscond for the purpose of evading justice in the premises.
      Sworn, *etc.*   (Sgd.) A.B.

                (Sgd.)   K.L.,
     J.P., County of

On hearing the facts alleged, the justice may issue a warrant for the re-arrest of the accused: Code 703.

Canada.
Province of   }
County of

      To all or any of the constables and peace officers of the said County of

      Whereas A.B. and C.D. were on the   day of   , A.D. 19 , duly bound by recognizance before E.F., Esquire, a justice of the peace in and for the said County of   , conditioned for the appearance of G.H. at the next court of competent jurisdiction (*or as the case may be, following the statements in the above information*), and then and there surrender himself into the custody of the keeper of the common gaol at   , in the said County, and plead to such indictment as should be found against him by the grand jury, in respect of a charge upon which he had theretofore been committed for trial, namely: (*state the charge*), and stand his trial thereon, and not depart the said court without leave. And whereas information has been this day laid before the undersigned K.L., a justice of the peace in and for the County of   , by (*or, on behalf of*) the said A.B. and C.D. (*or, as the case may be*), that there is reason to believe that the said G.H. is about to abscond for the purpose of evading justice in the premises.

*These are therefore to command you, the said constables, or other peace officers, or any of you, in His Majesty's name, forthwith to apprehend the said G.H., and to bring him before me, or some other justice or justices in and for the said County of   , in order that he may be further dealt with according to the law.

Given under my hand and seal at the   of   in the said County of   , this   day of   , A.D. 19
(Sgd.) E.F.,   (Seal.)
J.P., County of

The warrant may be executed in the manner described at p. 250, for the arrest of the accused in the first instance.

Upon the accused (and the prosecutor, who should also be notified) being brought before the justice, evidence will be taken in the usual way; and if the evidence satisfies the justice that the ends of justice would otherwise be defeated, he may commit the accused to prison until his trial, or until the accused produces other sufficient surety or sureties in like manner as before: Code 703.

WARRANT OF COMMITMENT.
Under Code 703.

Proceed as in the next preceding form down to the asterisk*.

And whereas I (*or* the said   , *naming the justice who issued the above warrant to apprehend*)   did thereupon issue my (*or* his) warrant to the constables and all other peace officers for the said county to apprehend the said G.H., and bring him before me (or the said   ), or some other justice or justices in and for the said county, to be dealt with according to law.

And whereas the said G.H. has been apprehended under the said warrant, and is now brought before me, the undersigned, one of His Majesty's justices of the peace in and for the said County of   , and it thereupon appearing to my satisfaction, upon hearing the evidence then adduced in the presence of the said G.H., that the ends of justice would otherwise be defeated;

These are therefore to command you, the said constables or peace officers in His Majesty's name, forthwith to take and safely convey the said G.H. to the said common gaol at   , in the said County of   , and there deliver him to the keeper thereof; and I hereby command you, the said keeper, to receive the said G.H. into your custody in the said common gaol, and him there safely to keep until his trial, or until he produces another sufficient surety or sureties in this behalf.

Given under my hand and seal at the   of   in the County of   , this   day of   , A.D. 19 .
(Sgd.) E.F.,   (Seal.)
J.P., County of

If other sureties are allowed to be given, and are produced, two justices, without any further order, may take a new recognizance in the same manner as before, and issue another warrant of deliverance: See *ante* p. 289.

Costs in Preliminary Enquiries.

Prior to the Ontario Statutes of 1904, ch. 13, secs. 1 and 3, justices were not entitled to any fees in a preliminary enquiry in indictable offences. But by that statute a justice is now entitled to be paid by the county a lump sum of $2 for all services in connection with the case where the time occupied is not more than two hours, with 50c. per hour every additional hour. The account for this fee, in the following form, should be sent to the clerk of the peace to be paid by the county treasurer on the order of the county board of audit of criminal justice accounts. This board sits quarterly early in the months of January, April, July and October for the purpose of examining such accounts.

FORM OF JUSTICE'S ACCOUNT.

Goderich, , 19

The County of Huron.

To E.H., J.P.

190 .

(*Date*)

To all services in the preliminary enquiry in the case of *Rex* v. *G.H.*
for (*name the charge*) hours, $.

An affidavit or declaration is required verifying the account (form of which will be supplied by the clerk of the peace on aplication to him).

As only one justice is required to sit on a preliminary enquiry, though several justices may join, only one fee can be paid, that being all that the statute authorizes. The parties to proseentions for indictable offences are not liable for any costs, whatever the result of the enquiry may be; and it would be illegal for any justice to receive any costs from either party. A penalty of $40 and costs may be imposed upon any justice who illegally receives fees: Ontario Statutes 1904, ch. 13, sec. 2. The costs provided by the tariff contained in Code 770 and in R.S.O. ch. 95, have no application to these proceedings, but only to cases of summary convictions.

The Constable's Costs.

The tariff of these is given in R.S.O., p. 1046. The fees of constables in connection with preliminary enquiries in indictable offences cases are payable by the province, if the accused is committed or bailed for trial; but if the case is dismissed the constables' fees are payable by the county. In either case the account should be made out and sworn to, on a form which will be furnished by the clerk of the peace. These accounts should be sent to the clerk of the peace quarterly, for submission to the Board of Audit.

If assistance is necessary in making an arrest, the party whether a constable or private person, who assists, is entitled to $1.50 besides mileage at 13c. per mile one way, for such assistance. The person assisting must make out and send to the clerk of the peace an account for it in a similar form to a constable's account; with usual affidavit.

In making out these accounts care must be taken to give the date for each item of work done; also the exact place from, and to which (with lot and concession of township) the constable travelled should be shewn in the item for mileage.

If a constable cannot find the accused to make an arrest or serve a summons, at the place to which he goes, he is entitled to his mileage on shewing by his account or affidavit that he used due diligence and the reason for failure.

The mileage covers the conveyance, or railway fares and hotel bills of the constable, but not those for conveying the prisoner to the justice, or to gaol. Necessary meals for the prisoner are also allowed.

Accounts against the province must be in duplicate, but those against the county need not be.

Witness' Fees.

There are no witness' fees allowed in preliminary enquiries; the tariff in Code 770 only applying to summary conviction cases.

ALPHABETICAL

SYNOPSIS OR LIST OF INDICTABLE OFFENCES IN WHICH JUSTICE IS TO HOLD
A PRELIMINARY ENQUIRY.

———

*One Justice Sitting Alone has Authority to Conduct any Preliminary En-
quiry as Described in the Preceding Chapter.*

*Certain Magistrates have Jurisdiction on Consent to Try Any of the Follow-
ing Indictable Offences, Except Those to Which a Note
is Appended to the Contrary.*

*For particulars as to the Officials Included in the "Magistrates" Who Have
This Authority and Explaining This Jurisdiction:
See ante p. 198, et seq.*

———

Abandonment of Child Under Two Years Old.
Code 245.
That A.B., at   , on   , A.D. 19 , did unlawfully abandon
and expose A., a child (*or* a child whose name is unknown) then under
the age of two years, whereby the health of the said child is permanently
injured (or, whereby the life of the said child was endangered).

Abduction.
Of an Heiress: Code 314(a)
A.B., on   , at   , did, for motives of lucre, unlawfully take away (*or* detain), against her will, a woman, named C.D. with
intent to marry (*or* carnally know) the said C.D., *or* with intent to
cause her to be married to (or carnally known by) E.F., she the said C.D.,
then having a legal (*or* equitable) present absolute (*or* future absolute, *or*
future conditional, *or* contingent) interest in real (*or* personal estate; *or*,
she then being a presumptive heiress (*or* co-heiress, *or* presumptive next
of kin) of G.H., who then had a legal (*or* equitable) present absolute (*or*
future absolute, *or* future conditional, *or* contingent) interest in real (*or*
personal) estate.

Of Woman Under 21 Years: Code 314(b).
A.B., on   , at   , with intent to marry (*or* carnally
know) a woman, named C.D., she then being under the age of 21 years,
did fraudulently allure (*or* take away, *or* detain) the said C.D. out of the
possession, and against the will, of her father (*or* mother. *or* of E.F., a
person having the lawful care (*or* charge) of her, the said C.D.

Of a Girl Under Sixteen: Code 315.
A.B., on   , at   , did unlawfully take (*or* cause to be
taken) an unmarried girl named C.D. out of the possession and against
the will of her father (*or* mother, *or* of E.F., a person then having the lawful care or charge of her, the said C.D.) she, the said C.D. then being
under age of 16 years.

Of a Woman of Any Age: Code 313.
A.B., on   , at   , did unlawfully take away (*or* detain) against her will a woman named C.D., with intent to marry her (*or*
carnally know her), or with intent to cause her to be married to (*or* carnally known by) E.F.

Children Under Fourteen: Code 316(a).

A.B., on   , at   , did unlawfully take (*or* entice) away (*or* detain) a child named C.D., then under the age of 14 years, with intent to steal a certain article, namely: (*describe the article*) then being on or about the person of the said child; *or* with intent to deprive E.F., the parent (or the guardian, *or* the person then having lawful charge) of the said child of the possession of such child, (*or if the charge is under Code 316(b) the above form may be changed so as to state the charge, to be that of "receiving or harbouring" the child "knowing it to have been theretofore taken," etc.*).

Abduction.

Code 297. *See* Kidnapping.

Abortion.

Advertising Drug to Procure: Code 207(c).

A.B., at   , on   , did unlawfully, knowingly and without lawful excuse or justification publish an advertisement of (or offer to sell *or* had for sale or disposal) a medicine (or drug, *or any article stating by what name it is called*) intended (*or* represented) as a means of preventing conception (*or* causing of abortion or miscarriage).

Attempt to Procure: Code 303.

A.B., on   , at   , did unlawfully administer to (*or* cause to be taken by) a woman, to wit, C.D., a drug (*or* "a noxious thing") to wit (*state what the drug or noxious thing was*), with intent to procure the miscarriage of the said C.D., or did unlawfully use upon a woman, to wit, C.D., an instrument (or *if other means were taken describe them*), with intent thereby to procure the miscarriage of the said C.D.

Woman Procuring, on Herself: Code 304.

A.B., a woman, did on   , at   , unlawfully administer to herself (*or* permit to be administered to her, the said A.B.) a drug (*or* a noxious thing), namely, (*state what*), with intent thereby to procure her miscarriage, or did unlawfully use upon herself (*or* permit to be used on her) an instrument (or *if other means are used describe them*) with intent, etc., *as in the next preceding form*.

Supplying Drugs to Procure: Code 305.

A.B., on   , at   , did unlawfully supply to C.D. (*or* procure) a drug (*or* a noxious thing, *or* "an instrument," *or if any other thing, name it*), the said A.B. then knowing that the same was intended to be unlawfully used or employed, with intent to procure the miscarriage of a woman, to wit, E.F.

Killing Unborn Child: Code 306.

A.B., at   , on   , A.D. 19 , did unlawfully and wilfully, and with malice aforethought, cause the death of a child of one (C.D.), which was then unborn and which had not then become a human being.

Accessory.

Before the Fact.

Is chargeable as a principal, with the offence: Code 69, 70, 269.

After the Fact.

Or who assists the principal to escape, is chargeable as such: Code 71, 574, 575.

That on   at   some person or persons unknown (*or* A.B.) did unlawfully (*state the offence committed according to the form given for it*) and the said C.D. (*the informant*) has just cause to suspect and does suspect that E.F., well knowing the said person (*or* the said A.B.) to have so committed the said offence, did afterwards unlawfully receive (*or* comfort) the said person (*or* the said A.B.) (*or* assist the said person *or* the said A.B.) in order to enable the said person (*or* the said A.B.) to escape.

The Offence of Being such Accessory is Indictable, if the Principal Offence was so.

Accusing of Crime and Compounding Same.

Code 453, 454. *See* Extortion, etc.

Adulteration of Food.

See Food.

Affray.

Code 100.

A.B. and C.D., on   did commit the act of fighting on the public street (*or* highway) in the said   of   (*or* did commit the act of fighting to the alarm of the public in the bar-room of the hotel known as the   Hotel in the said   of   , being a place to which the public then had access, or *state any other public place*) and did thereby then and there unlawfully take part in an affray.

Apprentice or Servant.

Master Neglecting to Provide Necessaries for: Code 243. *See* 'Neglect.'

Causing Bodily Harm to: Code 249.

A.B. on   , at   , being then and there the master of C.D., an apprentice (*or* a servant) and being legally liable to provide for the said C.D. as such apprentice (*or* servant) unlawfully did bodily harm to the said C.D. (*state the nature of the harm and how inflicted*) whereby the life of the said C.D. was endangered (*or* the health of the said C.D. was likely to be permanently injured).

Arms.

See Weapons.

Arson.

See Fire, Illegal Use of.

Assault.

Causing Bodily Harm: Code 295.

A.B. at   , on   , did unlawfully commit an assault and beat C.D., and did thereby then and there occasion actual bodily harm to him the said C.D.

With Intent to Commit any Indictable Offence: Code 296(a).

On   , at   , A.B. did unlawfully assault C.D. with intent to commit an indictable offence, namely, (*describe the offence intended, following the form of charge for the offence*).

On Constable, etc.: Code 296(b).

On , at , A.B. did unlawfully assault C.D., a public officer (*or a* peace officer), to wit, a constable of the said county of , (*or as the case may be*), then and there engaged in the execution of his duty as such constable, to wit, while (*describe the duty being performed*).

On Constable to Resist Arrest: Code 296(c).

On , at , A.B. did unlawfully assault C.D. with intent to resist (or prevent) the lawful apprehension (or detainer) of him the said A.B. (or one C.) for a certain offence, to wit, (*state the offence according to the forms given*)

On Officer Executing Legal Process: Code 296(d).

On , at , A.B. did unlawfully assault C.D. who was then and there, in his quality of a duly appointed bailiff of (*state the court*), duly engaged in the lawful execution of a certain process duly issued out of the said Court in a case of E.F. and G.H., and directed to said C.D. as such bailiff against (*or* in the making of a lawful seizure of lands *or* goods), *or* with intent to rescue certain goods which had then and there been taken under such process.

During an Election: Code 296(e).

A.B., on , at , being a day upon which a poll for an election of (a member of the Dominion Parliament *or* of the Legislative Assembly for the said county *or* for municipal councillors for the municipality of), was there being held and proceeded with, did, within a distance of two miles from (*state the place*), where a poll in the said election was then being taken and held, unlawfully assault (*or* assault and beat) C.D.

Lying in Wait for Persons Returning From Public Meeting: Code 128.

A.B., at , on , did unlawfully lie in wait for C.D., who was then returning (or expected to return) from a public meeting, with intent then and there to commit an assault, upon the said C.D. (*or* with intent by abusive language, opprobrious epithets or other offensive demeanour directed to the said C.D., to provoke him, or those who accompanied him, to a breach of the peace).

Indecent, on Females: Code 292(a).

On , at , A.B. unlawfully and indecently did assault C.D., a female.

or (*b*).

On , at , A.B. unlawfully did (*state what the act was*) to C.D., a female, by her consent, such consent having been obtained by false and fraudulent representations, that the said A.B. was a medical practitioner, and that such act was necessary in order to the medical treatment of the said C.D. by the said A.B. (or *as the case may be*).

Indecent, on Males: Code 293.

On , at , A.B., a male person, unlawfully and indecently did assault C.D., another male person (or assault C.D. with intent to commit sodomy).

And Wounding. See Wounding.

On Workman. See Workman.

Attempts.
Code. 570-572.
A.B., at   , on   , did unlawfully attempt to (*state the offence attempted in the words of the form given*).

Bawdy House.
See Disorderly House.

Bestiality.
See Buggery.

Betting.
See Gambling.

Bigamy.
Code 307, 308.
A.B., on   , at   , being then a man (or woman) already married, did unlawfully marry, and go through a form of marriage with another woman (or man), to wit, C.D., and did thereby commit bigamy.

Birth, Death, etc.
Defacing, etc., Official Register: Code 480.
A.B., at   , on   , did unlawfully destroy (or deface or injure or insert an entry then well-known by him to be false, *stating what*) in a register of births (or of deaths, or of marriages or baptisms) authorized to be kept by the laws of the Province of Ontario, by the division registrar for the municipality of the   of   in the said county of

Issuing False Certificate of, and Other Offences: Code 481, 482.

Blasphemous Libel.
Code 198. *See* Libel.

Breach of Contract. .
Code 499.
At   , on   , A.B. unlawfully and wilfully did break a certain contract, namely (*describe it and state how broken*) theretofore made by him, he then well knowing (or having reasonable cause to believe) that the probable consequence of his so doing would be to endanger human life (or cause serious bodily injury to others, or expose valuable property to destruction or serious injury).
Other charges for offences under the sub-sections to Code 499 may be framed from the above in regard to contracts for

Supplying Electric Light; or *Water,* or *Carrying the Mails.*

. *Defacing Notices as to*: Code 500. *See* also under "Workmen."

Breaking Prison.
See Escape.

Bribery in Election.
R.S.C. ch. 6, sec. 265.

Bribery of Witness or Juryman.
Code 180.

A.B., at   , on   , did unlawfully dissuade (or attempt to dissuade) one C.D. by threats (describe) or bribe (stating it), or by corrupt means, to wit, (describe) from giving evidence in a civil (or criminal) cause (or matter) then pending in   , between (style of cause);

or (b).

Did influence (or attempt to influence) by (describe the means as in the preceding form), a juryman, to wit, C.D., then summoned as a juryman to serve as such at the court of general sessions of the peace, then to be held at   , in and for the county of   , (or as the case may be), in his conduct as such juryman;

or (c).

Did unlawfully accept a bribe, to wit,   (or any other corrupt consideration stating it), to abstain from giving evidence in a certain matter (or cause) then pending in   , or on account of his conduct as a juryman at   ;

or (d).

Did unlawfully attempt to obstruct (or pervert, or defeat) the course of justice by (stating the corrupt means used).

Bribing Officer of Justice, etc.
Code 157.

A.B. then being a peace officer, to wit, a constable for the county (or district) of   , employed as such for the detection or prosecution of offenders, did unlawfully and corruptly accept (or obtain, or agree to accept, or attempt to obtain) for himself (or for one C.D.) a certain sum of money, to wit, the sum of   (or a certain valuable consideration, or an office or place of employment, stating it) with intent to interfere corruptly with the due administration of justice (or to protect from detection and punishment one E.F. a person who had committed or intended to commit the crime of (stating it).

Bribing Member of Parliament: Code 156.

Gifts, etc., to Officers of the Government: Code 158(a).

Government Officer Accepting Gifts, etc.: Code 158.

Breach of Trust by Public Officer: Code 160.

Corruption in Municipal Affairs: Code 161, 163.

Selling or Buying Office: Code 162.

"Magistrates" Cannot Try Any of the Above.

Bucket Shop.
Keeping: Code 231, 232.

A.B., in his premises at   , on   , did unlawfully make a contract with C.D. purporting to be for the sale of certain stock in (name the company; or of certain goods; or merchandise, to wit, wheat, or state whatever the thing purporting to be dealt in was) in respect of which no delivery was made or received and without the bonâ fide intention to make such delivery and with intent to make gain or profit by the rise or fall of the said stock (or merchandise, etc.), and the said A.B. was thereby then and the e a keeper of a common gaming house.

Frequenting: Code 233.

A.B. on　　　　　, at　　　　　, did unlawfully habitually frequent an office wherein the unlawful making of contracts purporting to be for the sale of (*etc., proceed as in the above form*)..

Buggery.

Code 202, 203.

A.B. at　　　　　, on　　　　　, did unlawfully commit (or attempt to commit) the abominable crime of buggery with a living animal, to wit, a mare (or with C.D.).

Burglary and Housebreaking, etc.

Burglary: Code 457 (a).

A.B., at　　　　　, on　　　　　, A.D. 19　, by night, unlawfully and burglariously did break and enter the dwelling-house of C.D., there situated, with intent unlawfully to commit, in the said dwelling-house, an indictable offence, to wit (state *the offence committed as*) the crime of theft.

or (b).

Did by night, unlawfully break out of the dwelling-house of C.D., there situated, after having committed an indictable offence therein, to wit (state *the offence*), or after having unlawfully entered the said dwelling-house with intent to commit an indictable offence therein, to wit, (*state the offence*). *If the accused had a weapon in his possession add an aver-ment to that effect.*

or 458 (a).

Did unlawfully break and enter by day the dwelling-house of C.D., there situated, and did then and there commit an indictable offence in the said dwelling-house, to wit (state *the offence*).

or (b).

Follow the next preceding form, substituting the words "break out of the dwelling-house of C.D., there situated, after having committed," *etc.*

or Code 459.

Did unlawfully by day break and enter the dwelling-house of C.D., there situated, with intent to commit an indictable offence therein, to wit (*state the offence*).

or Code 460.

Did unlawfully break and enter the shop of C.D. there situated (or *any of the other places named in this section,* or a building within the curtilage of the dwelling-house of the said C.D. there situated)*, and did then and there commit in the said shop (or *other place mentioned*) an indictable offence, to wit, (state *the offence*).

or Code 461.

*With intent to commit therein an indictable offence, to wit (state *the offence*)

or Code 462.

Did unlawfully by night enter (or was by night unlawfully in) the dwelling-house of C.D. therein situated, with intent to commit an indictable offence therein, to wit (*state the offence, e.g.*), unlawfully to steal the goods and chattels of the said C.D.

Being Found Armed with Intent to Break a Dwelling-house: Code 463 (a). .

A.B., at　　　　　, on　　　　　, was found by day unlawfully armed with a dangerous or offensive weapon (or instrument), to wit, (*mention what it was*), with intent to break and enter into the dwelling-house of C.D., there situated, and to commit an indictable offence therein.

or (b).

(*The same form to be used by substituting the words* "by night" *instead of* "by day," *and* "a building" *instead of* "dwelling-house.")

Housebreaking Instruments, Being Disguised or in Possession of: Code 464(a).

Was found by night unlawfully, and without lawful excuse, in possession of an instrument of housebreaking, to wit (*describe it*).

or 464(b).

Was found by day unlawfully having in his possession an instrument of house-breaking, to wit (*describe it*) with intent to commit an indictable offence, to wit (burglary, or *as the case may be*).

or 464(c).

Was found by night unlawfully, and without lawful excuse, with his face masked (or blackened, or disguised by, *stating the manner of the disguise*).

or 464(d).

Was found by day unlawfully having his face masked (or blackened, or disguised by, *stating how*), with intent to commit an indictable offence, to wit (*state the offence intended, such as,* to commit an assault upon C.D.).

Of Place of Worship: Code 455.

A.B., at   , on   , did unlawfully ·break and enter a place of public worship, to wit (*describe the place*), and therein did commit an indictable offence, to wit (*state the offence, for instance,* did steal; *mention the article,* the property of C.D.).

or

Did unlawfully commit an indictable offence, to wit (*state the offence*), in a place of public worship, to wit (*name the place*) and that after committing the said offence, in the said place of public worship, the said A.B. did then and there unlawfully break out of the said place of public worship.

or 456.

Did unlawfully break and enter a place of public worship (*name the place*) with intent then and there unlawfully to (*state the offence*) therein.

Cheating at Play.

Code 442.

A.B., at   , on   , unlawfully, and with intent to defraud C.D., did cheat in playing at a game with cards (or *other game stating it*); *or* in holding the stakes; or in betting on the event of (*state the event bet on*).

Childbirth.

Neglect to Obtain Assistance in: Code 271.

A.B., at   , on   , she being then with child, and about to be delivered thereof, unlawfully did neglect to provide reasonable assistance in her delivery, whereby the child of which she was then delivered was permanently injured (or died just before, or during, *or* shortly after, birth), the intent of such neglect being that the child should not live (or to conceal the fact of the said A.B. having had a child).

Concealing Dead Body of Child: Code 272.

A.B., at   , on   , with intent to conceal the fact that the said A.B. (or one, C.D.) had been delivered of a child did unlawfully dispose of the dead body of the said child, of which the said A.B. (or C.D.) had been so delivered, by (state *the disposition made of the body, e.g.,* by placing it in a water closet).

Choking, etc., to Commit Crime.

See, Garroting.

Clergyman.

Obstructing or *Offering Violence to an Officiating:* Code 199.

A.B., on   , at   , by threats (or force) did unlawfully obstruct (or prevent, or endeavour to obstruct or prevent) C.D., a clergyman or minister, in (or from) celebrating divine service in the church, *or* meeting house, or school house (or *other place for divine worship, naming* or *otherwise describing* it), or in, or from, the performance of his duty in the lawful burial of the dead in the churchyard (or cemetery, or *other burial place, naming or* describing it, *and* describe *the nature of the* obstruction *offered).*

or Code 200.

Did unlawfully strike (*or* offer violence to, or upon a civil process, or under pretence of exciting a civil process, did arrest) C.D., a clergyman, who was then engaged in (or to the knowledge of the said A.B. was then about to engage in *proceed as in previous form).*

Coinage Offences.

Code 546-569.

Counterfeiting Coins: Code 552(a).

A.B. did unlawfully* make (or begin to make) a counterfeit coin resembling (or apparently intended to resemble or pass for) a current gold (or silver) coin known as a five dollar gold (or fifty cent silver) piece.

or (b).

*Gild or silver a coin resembling (*or* apparently intended to resemble or pass for) a current gold (or silver) coin.

or (c).

*Gild (or silver) a piece of silver (or copper, *or* coarse gold, or coarse silver, or a metal or mixture of metals) being of a fit size and figure to be coined with intent that the same shall be coined into counterfeit coin resembling (or apparently intended to resemble or pass for) a current gold (*or* silver) coin known as a five dollar gold (or a twenty-five cent silver) piece.

or (d).

*Gild (or file, or alter, *describing how*) a current silver coin, known as a twenty-five cent silver piece, with intent to make the same resemble (or pass for) a current gold coin, to wit, a five dollar gold piece.

or (e).

*Gild (or silver) a current copper coin (or file or alter, *describing how*) a current copper coin known as a one-cent piece, with intent to make the same resemble (*or* pass for) a current gold coin known as a five dollar gold piece (or a current silver coin known as a twenty-five cent piece).

Clipping Current Coin: Code 558.

A.B., at   , on   , did unlawfully impair (or diminish or lighten) a current gold (or silver) coin called a one dollar gold coin (or a fifty cent or ten cent silver coin), with intent that the said piece so impaired (or diminished *or* lightened) might pass for a current gold (*or* silver) coin.

Defacing Current Coins: Code 559.

A.B., at   , on   , did unlawfully deface one current gold (or silver or copper) coin, to wit (describe *the coin*) by stamping thereon certain names or words, to wit (*describe*), and did afterwards unlawfully tender the same.

Prosecutions for uttering defaced coin must be with consent of Attorney-General: Code 598.

Current Coin, Possessing Clippings of: Code 560.

A.B., at   , on   , unlawfully had in his possession, or custody, certain filings or clippings (or certain gold; *or* silver bullion; *or* certain gold, or silver in dust, or solution, or *otherwise stating how*), which were produced or obtained by impairing (or diminishing, or lightening) gold (or silver) coin, he then knowing the same to have been so produced or obtained.

Counterfeit Coins, Possessing: Code 561(a).

A.B., at   , on   , unlawfully had in his custody or possession, one counterfeit coin resembling, or apparently intended to resemble or pass for a current gold (or silver coin), to wit (describe *it*), with intent to utter the same, he then knowing the same to be counterfeit.

or Code 561(*b*).

Had in his custody or possession, three (or more than three) pieces of counterfeit coin resembling, or apparently intended to resemble, or pass for current copper coins called one cent pieces, with intent to utter the same, he then knowing the same to be counterfeit.

Foreign Coins, Offences Respecting: Code 563(a).

A.B., at   , on   , did unlawfully make, or begin to make, a counterfeit coin resembling, or apparently intended to resemble, or pass for a gold (or silver) coin of a foreign country, to wit, the gold (or silver) coin of (*name the country*) called (*name the coin*).

Uttering Light Coins or Medals: Code 565.

A.B., at   , on   , did unlawfully utter as being current a certain silver coin, to wit, a silver dollar of less than its lawful weight, he, the said A.B., then well knowing the said coin to have been impaired (or diminished, or lightened) otherwise than by lawful wear.

or (b).

Unlawfully, and with intent to defraud, did utter, as being a current silver dollar, a certain silver coin, not being a current silver coin, but resembling in size, figure and colour a current silver dollar, and being of less value than a current silver dollar.

or (b).

Unlawfully, and with intent to defraud, did utter, as being a current silver dollar, a certain medal (*or* piece of metal), resembling, in size, figure and colour, a current silver dollar, and being of less value than a current silver dollar.

or (c).

Did unlawfully utter to C.D.. one piece of counterfeit coin resembling (or apparently intended to resemble and pass for) the current copper coin called one cent. he, the said A.B., then well knowing the same to be counterfeit.

Uncurrent Copper Coins, Uttering: Code 567.

A.B., at   , on   , did unlawfully and with intent to defraud, utter, or offer in payment a copper coin, other than current copper coin, to wit (describe *the coin*).

Counterfeit Money, Advertising, etc.: Code **569**.

A.B., at   , on   , did unlawfully print (or write, or state *any other means of advertising, etc.*, mentioned *in Code* 569(a)), a letter (or writing, or circular, or *other thing mentioned, stating it*) advertising (or offering, or purporting to advertise, or offer) for sale, (*or* loan, *as the case may be, using the words of the* statute), or to furnish, or procure or disturb (or *as the case may be*), any counterfeit token of value, or a (*counterfeit bank note of the bank of*   , or *other thing, naming* it), which purported to be a counterfeit token of value.

Coining, Making Instruments for: Code 556(a).

A.B., at   , on   , did unlawfully and without lawful authority or excuse make (or mend; or begin, or proceed to make or mend or buy or sell; or have in his custody or possession) one puncheon (or *describe the instrument*) in or upon which there was then made and impressed, or which would make and impress, or which was adapted and intended to make and impress the figure, or stamp or apparent resemblance, of one of the sides of a current gold or silver coin, to wit (*describe the coin*).

or (b).

A.B., did (*as above*) make, (*etc., as above*), one edger (or *as the case may be*) adapted and intended for the marking of coin around the edges, with letters (or grainings, or marks or figures) apparently resembling those on the edges of a current gold or silver coin, to wit (*describe the coin*), he then knowing the same to be so adapted and intended.

Counterfeit Coin, Dealing in: Code 562(ii).

A.B., at   , on   , did unlawfully and without lawful authority or excuse buy (or sell, or receive, or pay out, or put off) one piece of counterfeit coin resembling (or apparently intended to resemble or pass for) a current silver fifty cent piece (or gold five dollar piece, or *as the case may be*) of current money at and for a lower rate and value than the same imported (or was apparently intended to import).

Company.

False Prospectus of: Code 414.

A.B., (*etc.*), being then a promoter (or manager, *etc.*) of a public company (or body corporate) then intended to be formed (or then existing) and called (*name of company*) did unlawfully make (or circulate, or publish) a prospectus which he then well knew to be false in the following material particulars (*set out the false* statements) with intent to induce persons to become shareholders in the said company (or with intent to deceive the members or shareholders, or creditors of the said company).

> *False Prospectus of Company under Ontario Law*: Ont. St. 1906, ch. 27, secs. 6, 7. One justice may summarily convict under the Ontario Statute.

Compounding Penal Actions.

Code 181.

A.B., at   , on   , having theretofore brought (or under colour of bringing) an action in (state *what* Court) against C.D., in order to obtain from him a penalty under a penal statute, namely (*state what* statute), did unlawfully compound the said action without the order or consent of the said Court.

Covering Up Offences.
Taking Reward for: Code 182. *See* Rewards.

Concealment of Birth..
See Childbirth.

Conspiracy to Commit an Indictable Offence.
Code 573.
A.B., at   , on   , did unlawfully conspire with C.D.
to commit an indictable offence, to wit, the crime of (describe *the crime,
with particulars in the form given for the alleged* crime).

Counterfeiting *P*ostage or Revenue Stamps.
Code 479.
A.B., at   , on   , did unlawfully and fraudulently
counterfeit (or knowingly sell; or expose for sale; or utter) a stamp used
for the purposes of revenue by the Government of Canada (or of the
Government of the Province of Ontario), to wit, a two-cent postage stamp
of the Dominion of Canada (or *as the case may be*).

Damage.
Wilful. See Wilful *I*njuries.

Dead Human Body.
Neglecting to Bury: Code 237(a).
A.B., at   , on   , did unlawfully and without lawful
excuse neglect to perform a duty imposed upon him by law with reference
to a dead human body, to wit (to bury the dead body of his infant child,
or *as the case may be*).
or
See Code 237(b) as to other misconduct.

Disorderly House.
Keeping: Code 225, 226, 227, 228, 232, 986.
A.B., at   , on   , and on divers other days and times
since that date did unlawfully keep and maintain a disorderly house to
wit, a common bawdy (*or* a common gaming, or betting) house at (*describe
locality, e.g., at a house known as No.* 1 *on*   Street *in the city
of*   ).

Drug.
Administering to Procure Abortion. See Abortion.

Drugging with *I*ntent.
To Commit Indictable Offence: Code 276(b).
A.B., at   , on   , with intent thereby to enable the
said A.B. (or one, C.D.) to (state *the indictable offence committed or attempted*), to one, E.F., did unlawfully apply (or administer, or attempt
to apply or administer) to (or cause to be taken by) the said E.F. chloro-
form (or laudanum or a stupefying or overpowering drug, matter or
thing, stating *what it was*).

*To Endange*r *Life*: Code 277.
A.B., at   , on   '   , A.D. 19 , did unlawfully administer
(or cause to be administered) to (or cause to be taken by) C.D., a poison
(or a destructive or noxious thing), namely (*state what it was*), so as
20—MAG. MAN.

thereby to inflict upon the said C.D. grievous bodily harm (*or* endanger the life of the said C.D.).

With Intent *to* Injure: Code 278.

A.B., at　　　　　　, on　　　　　　, A.D. 19　, did unlawfully administer (*or* cause to be administered to, *or* to be taken by) C.D., a poison (*or* a destructive *or* noxious thing) namely (*state what it was*), with intent thereby to injure (*or* to aggrieve, *or* to annoy) the said C.D.

Duel.

Challenging: Code 101.

A.B., at　　　　　　, on　　　　　　, did unlawfully challenge C.D. to fight a duel (*or* did unlawfully endeavour to provoke C.D. to challenge E.F., to fight a duel; *or* endeavour to provoke E.F. to challenge G.H. to fight a duel).

Election Documents.

Offences Respecting: Code 528.

For Form *see* Wilful Injury to Election Documents.

Election Offences.

R.S.C. ch. 6, secs. 255, 256, 260, 262, 264, 265, 269, 274.

"Magistrates" cannot try these offences.

Escapes and Rescues.

Breaking Prison: Code 187.

A.B., at　　　　　　, on　　　　　　, by force (*or* violence) did unlawfully break a prison, to wit, the common gaol of the county of　　　　　, with intent to set at liberty himself, the said A.B. (*or* one, C.D.), he, the said A.B. (*or* C.D.), then being a person confined in the said prison on a criminal charge, to wit (*state the charge*).

Break Prison, *Attempt to*: Code 188.

A.B., at　　　　　　, on　　　　　　, then being a prisoner confined in the common gaol or prison at　　　　on a criminal charge, did unlawfully attempt to break the said prison (*or* forcibly break out of his cell in the said prison, *or* make a breach in his cell in the said prison) with intent to escape therefrom.

Escape From Custody, Either Before or After Conviction: Code 189, 190.

A.B., at　　　　　　, on　　　　　　, having theretofore, to wit, on the day of　　　　　, A.D. 19　, been lawfully convicted of the offence (*state the offence*), and being on the day and at the place first above mentioned, in lawful custody under such conviction, to wit, in the common gaol in the county of　　　　　(*or* in charge of a peace officer by whom he was then lawfully being conveyed to prison, *or as the case may be*), under a lawful warrant issued upon such conviction, did unlawfully escape from such custody.

Rescue or Assisting: Code 191.

A.B., at　　　　　　, on　　　　　　, did unlawfully rescue C.D. (*or* assist C.D. in escaping, *or* attempting to escape from lawful custody under sentence of (*state the sentence*) upon a criminal charge, to wit (*describe the crime*).

Constable, Voluntarily Allowing Escape: Code 191, 192(b).

A.B., at   , on   , then being a peace officer, and having one C.D. in his lawful custody as such (*or* he then being an officer of a prison, to wit, the keeper *or* guard, *or* turnkey of a prison, to wit, the common gaol of the county of   , in which C.D. was then and there lawfully confined), under sentence of (*state the sentence*) upon a criminal charge of (*state the charge*), he, the said A.B., did then and there unlawfully and voluntarily and intentionally permit the said C.D. to escape.

Peace Officer, Permitting Escape by Neglect of Duty: Code 193.

A.B., at   , on   , being a peace officer, and as such having then and there in his lawful custody one C.D., on a criminal charge, to wit (*state the charge*), did unlawfully, and by failing to perform a legal duty then imposed upon him, the said A.B., in the premises, to wit, by (*state the neglect or failure of duty of the officer*) permit the said C.D. to escape from such custody.

Aiding Escape From Prison: Code 194.

A.B., at   , on   , unlawfully and with intent to facilitate the escape of C.D., a prisoner lawfully imprisoned in the common gaol of the county of   , did convey (*or* cause to be conveyed), a certain (*state the article*) into the said prison.

Convict Being at Large Before Expiration of Sentence: Code 185.

A.B., at   .   , on   , having been theretofore sentenced to imprisonment upon a criminal charge, to wit (*state the charge*), afterwards at the time and place aforesaid, and before the expiration of the term for which he was so sentenced, was at large without a lawful excuse.

Explosives.

Unlawfully Making or Possessing: Code 114.

A.B., at   , on   , did unlawfully make (*or* unlawfully and knowingly have in his possession, *or* under his control), an explosive substance, namely (*describe or name it*), under such circumstances as to give rise to a reasonable suspicion that he was not making (*or* that he had not in his possession *or* under his control) the said explosive substance for a lawful object, which circumstances were as follows: (*state them*).

Explosion.

Causing Dangerous: Code 111.

A.B., at   , on   , by an explosive substance, namely (*name or describe it*), unlawfully and wilfully caused an explosion (*state the locality and particulars*), of a nature likely to endanger life (*or* to cause serious injury to property).

Doing any Act (or Conspiring) to Cause: Code 113(a).

A.B., on   , at   , unlawfully and wilfully conspired with C.D. to cause by an explosive substance, to wit (*name it*), an explosion likely to endanger life (*or* to cause serious injury to property, *describe the locality and give particulars*).

Having Explosive With Intent: Code 113(b).

A.B., at   , on   , unlawfully and wilfully made (*or* had in his possession *or* under his control) an explosive substance, to wit, (*name it*) with intent by means thereof to endanger human life (*or* to cause serious injury to property, *or* to enable C.D., *or* some person unknown by means thereof to endanger human life, *or* to cause serious injury to property).

No further proceedings are to be taken for an offence under Code 113 until the consent of the Attorney-General has been obtained, except such as necessary for the arrest and detention of the offender: Code 594.

Using Explosive With Intent: Code 112.

Did unlawfully place (*or* throw) an explosive substance into (*or* near) a building (*or* ship, *describing the same*) with intent to destroy (*or* damage) certain machinery or working tools therein.

Attempt to Cause Bodily Injury by: Code 279.

A.B., on   , at   , by the explosion of a certain explosive substance, to wit (*name it*), unlawfully did burn (*or* maim, *or* disfigure, *or* disable, *or* do grievous bodily harm to) C.D.

Attempts to Injure, etc., by: Code 280 (a) (i).   •

A.B., on   , at   , unlawfully and with intent thereby to burn (*or* maim *or* disfigure, *or* disable, *or* to do greivous bodliy harm to) C.D. (*or* to certain persons being therein) did cause a certain explosive substance, to wit (*name it*) to explode.

or Code 280 (a) (ii) *substitute the following.*

send or deliver to (*or* cause to be taken by, *or* received by) C.D. an explosive substance (*or* a dangerous or noxious thing), to wit (*name it*).

or Code 280 (a) (iii).

put or lay (*name the place;* as on the sidewalk upon the public street in, *etc.*), *or* did cast *or* throw at (*or* apply to) C.D. a corrosive fluid *or* a dangerous or explosive substance, to wit (*name it*).

or Code 248 (b).

Did unlawfully and with intent to do bodily injury to C.D. (*or* to certain persons then being therein) throw in or upon or against or near a certain building or ship or vessel (*describing it*) an explosive substance, to wit (*name it*).

Extortion.

Demand With Menaces: Code 452.

A.B., on   , at   , did unlawfully with menaces (*state what*) demand from C.D. a sum of money, to wit, the sum of five dollars (*or* one horse, *or as the case may be*) the property of the said C.D. with intent to steal it.

By Accusing of Crime: Code 453, 454.

A.B., at   , on   , did unlawfully accuse (*or* threaten to accuse) C.D. (*or* one E.F.) of the offence of having (*state any of the offences mentioned or referred to in Code* 453, 454) with intent thereby to extort (*or* gain) money (*or anything stating what*) from the said C.D., or whereby the said A.B. compelled (*or* attempted to compel) the said C.D., (*or* one E.F., *or any one*) to (*do any of the things mentioned in the last clause of Code secs.* 453, 454, *stating what*).

By Defamatory Libel: Code 332.

A.B., at   , on   , did unlawfully publish (*or* threaten C.D. to publish, *or* offered to C.D. to abstain from publishing, *or* offered C.D. to prevent the publishing of) a defamatory libel with intent to extort money from the said C.D. (*or* from E.F.), or with intent to induce C.D., (*or* E.F.) to confer upon the said A.B. (*or* upon one G.H.) an office of profit.

By Threatening Letter: Code 451, 453 (c).

At   , on   , A.B. did unlawfully send or deliver to (*or* cause to be received by) C.D. a certain letter (*or* writing) demanding of the said C.D. with menaces, a certain sum of money, to wit (*state what*) the said demand being without reasonable or probable cause, and he, the said A.B., then well knowing the contents of the said letter (*or* writing)

False Return by Official of Penny Savings Bank.

R.S.C. ch. 31, secs. 41, 42.

False Warehouse Receipts.
Code 425, 427 (a).

A.B., on   , at   , being the keeper (*or* a clerk *or* a person in the employ of C.D. the keeper) of a warehouse (*or* a miller, *or* master of a vessel, *or* a wharfinger, *or* a keeper of a yard for storing lumber, *or* any of the places mentioned in Code 425) did unlawfully and knowingly and wilfully give to C.D. a writing purporting to be a receipt for certain goods or property, to wit, 5,000 bushels of grain (*or* 100,000 feet of lumber, *or* as the case may be) as having been received into his said warehouse (*or* place mentioned) before the said goods or property mentioned in the said receipt had been actually received by him as aforesaid with intent to mislead (*or* deceive, *or* defraud) the   of (*or* E.F., *or* some person then unknown).

Fraudulently Alienating Property Covered by Warehouse Receipt.
Code 427 (b).

False Entry in Government Book, etc.
Code 484.

A.B., at   , on   , he then being an official of the Provincial Government of Ontario (*or* a clerk in the bank of   as the case may be) did unlawfully and with intent to defraud make an untrue entry or an alteration in (*or* did wilfully falsify a certain book of account kept by the Government of the Province of Ontario (*or* by the said bank for the Government of the Province of Ontario) in which book were kept the accounts of the owners of certain stock (*or* a certain annuity or public fund, describing it) transferable in such book, by (stating in what the false entry or alteration consisted).

False Ticket, Obtaining Passage by.
Code 412.

A.B., on   , at   , by means of a false ticket purporting to have been issued by the   Railway Co., did fraudulently and unlawfully obtain (*or* attempt to obtain) passage on a   railway train.

(Similar charges in respect to steamboat.)

Falsifying Book, etc., by Official.
Code 413.

A.B., on   , at   , he then being a director (*or* manager) of a body corporate called the   bank (*or* as the case may be) did unlawfully and with intent to defraud, falsify (*or* destroy, *or* alter, *or* mutilate) a certain book (*or* writing, *or* valuable security) belonging to the said bank (*or* make a false entry, *or* concur in making or omitting to enter material particulars in a certain book, set out what the book was, and what the false entries consist of, or what entries were omitted).

False Return by Public Official.
Code 416.

A.B., at   , on   , he then being (state official position. e.g., collector of the said   of   ,) entrusted with the receipt(*or* custody *or* management) of a part of the public revenues (state what) did unlawfully and knowingly furnish to the (Town Treasurer of the said town of   , or as the case may be) a false statement (*or* return) of the money collected by him (*or* entrusted to his care, *or* under his control).

False Pretences, Obtaining Money, etc., By.

Code 404, 405.

A.B., on   , at   , did unlawfully and* with intent to defraud obtain a sum of money, to wit, $ (*or any article or property, stating what*) by false pretences, to wit, by the false pretence that he, the said A.B., was the owner of property to the actual value of $ over and above all claims against it (*or as the case may be, stating the false pretence, which must be of some alleged existing fact*).

or Code 406.

*With intent to defraud (*or to injure*) C.D. thereby did induce the said C.D. to execute (*or make, or endorse, as the case may be*) a promissory note (*or other valuable security, stating it*) by false pretences, to wit, that (*set out the particulars of the false pretences*).

Falsely Pretending to Enclose Money in a Letter.

Code 407.

A.B., on   , at   , did wrongfully and with wilful falsehood, pretend or allege that he, the said A.B., did enclose and send (*or cause to be enclosed and sent*), in a post letter, a sum of money, to wit (*ten dollars, or as the case may be*), or a valuable security, to wit (*state what*), or a chattel, to wit (*state what*), to one C.D., which sum of money (*or as the case may be*) he did not in fact so enclose and send (*or cause to be enclosed and sent*) in the said letter.

False Telegram.

Sending in False Name: Code 475.

A.B., at   , on   , with intent on the part of the said A.B., to defraud one C.D., unlawfully caused or procured a telegram to the effect (*state its purport*), to be sent, or delivered, to the said C.D., as being sent by the authority of one E.F., he, the said A.B., then knowing that the said telegram was not sent by the authority aforesaid with intent on the part of the said A.B. that the said telegram should be acted upon as being sent by the authority of the said E.F.

Telegram or Letter Containing False Matter: Code 476.

A.B., on   , at   , with intent on his part to injure (*or to alarm*) C.D., did unlawfully send (*or cause or procure to be sent*) a telegram (*or a letter or other message, stating by what means*) containing matter which he then knew to be false, to wit (*state the matter of the telegram or letter*).

False News.

Spreading against public interest: Code 136

"Magistrates" cannot try.

Food, Selling Things Unfit for.

Code 224.

A.B., on   , at   , did, unlawfully, knowingly and wilfully expose for sale (*or have in his possession with intent to sell*) for human food a certain article, to wit (*name it*), which he, the said A.B., then knew to be unfit for human food by reason (*state why unfit*)

See, also, The Adulteration Act: R.S.C. ch. 133.

The Inspection and Sales Act: R.S.C. ch. 85.

The Canned Goods Act: R.S.C. ch. 134.

The Animals Contagious Diseases Act: R.S.C. ch. 75, sec. 38.

The Ontario Public Health Act: R.S.O., ch. 248, secs. 108, 109.

Also *Synopsis of Summary Convictions Cases Under "Food," post.*

Forcible Entry.

Code 102(1), 103.

A.B., at   , on   , did unlawfully and forcibly and in a manner likely to cause a breach of the peace, or in a manner likely to cause reasonable apprehension of a breach of the peace, to wit (*set out the force or violence used*), enter on land, to wit (*describe it*), which was then in the actual and peaceable possession of C.D.

Forcible Detainer.

Code 102(2), 103.

A.B., at   , on   , was in actual possession without colour of right of certain land being (*describe it*), did unlawfully detain it in a manner likely to cause a breach of the peace, or reasonable apprehension of the same, from C.D., who was entitled by law to the possession of it, by (*describe the violence used*).

Forgery.

Code 466-470.

A.B., at   , on   , did unlawfully and knowingly commit forgery of a certain document, that is to say (*describe the document as mentioned in sub-sections of Code 468*)

Forged Bank Notes, Possessing.

Code 550.

A.B., at   , on   , did unlawfully and without lawful authority or excuse purchase (*or* receive) from C.D. (*or* have in his possession *or* custody) a forged bank note, to wit (*describe it*), or a forged blank bank note (*describe it*), he the said A.B. then well knowing the same to be forged.

Forged Documents, Uttering.

Code 467.

A.B., at   , on   , then knowing a certain document, to wit (*describe it*), to be forged, did unlawfully use, or deal with, or act upon it (*or* did cause, *or* did attempt to cause, one C.D., to use, *or* deal with, *or* act upon it), as if it were genuine, by (*state how it was used or attempted to be used*).

Forgery of Depositor's Book in Post Office Savings Bank.

R.S.C. ch. 30, sec. 18. See other offences: Code 466-494.

Forgery of Election Documents.

R.S.C. ch. 6, sec. 255.

Fortune Telling.

Code 443.

A.B., at   , on   , did unlawfully * pretend to exercise certain witchcraft (*or* sorcery *or* conjuration, *etc.*).

or

*Undertake to tell fortunes.

or

*Pretend from his skill or knowledge in an occult and crafty science, to wit (*describe*), to discover where, or in what manner certain goods or chattels, to wit (*state what*) supposed to have been stolen from C.D. (*or* lost by C.D.) might be found.

Fraud on Creditors.

Trader Failing to Keep Proper Books: Code 417(c).

A.B., being a trader at　　　　, and then indebted to an amount exceeding in all $1,000 and being on the　　　　day of　　　　, 190 , and still being unable to pay his creditors in full, did not for five years next before such inability and while he continued to be a trader as aforesaid keep such books of account as according to the usual course of the business in which he was engaged were necessary to exhibit and explain his transactions.

Code 417(a)(i).

A.B., at　　　　, on　　　　, with intent to defraud his creditors (*or* C.D., one of his creditors) to whom he was then lawfully indebted in a certain sum of money, did unlawfully, to wit, on the said　　　　day of　　　　19 , make a certain conveyance (*or* assignment, *or* transfer, *or* delivery) of his property, consisting of (*describe it*) to E.F.

or (a)(ii).

Unlawfully remove a part of his property, to wit (*state the articles removed*), from his store in the said　　　　of　　　　(*or* conceal, *or* dispose of a part of his property, to wit, *state the articles, and in what manner they were concealed or disposed of*)

or (b).

A.B., at　　　　, on　　　　, with the intent on the part of the said A.B. that one C.D. should defraud the creditors (*or* one E.F., one of the creditors) of the said A.B., did unlawfully receive from the said A.B., certain property of the said A.B., to wit (*state what*).

Destroying or Falsifying Books; or Making False Entries: Code 418.

A.B., at　　　　, on　　　　, with intent to defraud his creditors did unlawfully destroy (*or deal with in any of the ways mentioned, stating how*), a certain book of account of the said A.B. (*or* a certain writing or security, to wit, *state what, e.g.*, a certain promissory note theretofore made by one E.F. to and then held by the said C.D. and unpaid) *or* made, *or* was privy to the making of a false and fraudulent entry in a book of account kept by the said A.B., whereby it appeared that a certain debt then due by G.H. to the said A.B. had been theretofore paid, whereas in truth and in fact the said debt had not been paid, but was then still owing and due to him, the said A.B.

Fraudulent Concealment of, Incumbrance, etc.

By Mortgagor, or Seller of Land, or Chattel: Code 419.

A.B., at　　　　, on　　　　, then being the seller (*or* mortgagor) of a certain parcel of land (*or* chattel, *describing it*) to one C.D. (*or* then being the solicitor *or* agent of one A.B., the seller (*etc., as above*), and having been served on behalf of the said C.D., as such purchaser or mortgagee, with a written demand of an abstract of title of the said land (*or* chattel) before the completion of the said purchase or mortgage by the said C.D., did unlawfully and with intent to defraud and in order to induce the said C.D. to accept the title offered to him, conceal a deed or incumbrance (*or* other instrument, *naming it*) material to the title (*state what the instrument was and shew its materiality, e.g.*) a vendor's lien on the said chattel in favour of one G.H., under a written instrument signed by the said A.B., whereby the said G.H. had, at the time of the completion of the said purchase (*or* mortgage), and still has, a lien upon the said chattels for the price thereof on the sale of the same by him to the said A.B.

Consent of Attorney-General required before prosecution: Code 597.

Fruit Trees, Diseases of.
San Jose Scale; Importation of Trees Infected With: R.S.C. ch. 127, secs. 2, 3.

Furious Driving, Injury by.
Code 285.

A.B., on   , at   , being in charge of a certain vehicle, to wit, a four-wheeled cab (*or as the case may be*), did then and there by his wanton and furious driving (*or racing*) of and with the said vehicle unlawfully do (*or cause to be done bodily harm to C.D. (give particulars*)

Fire, Illegal Use of.
Arson: Code 511, 541.

At   , on   , A.B., unlawfully, wilfully, without legal justification or excuse, and without colour of right, did set fire to a certain building, to wit, a dwelling-house (*or to a certain stack of vegetable produce, called hay; or mineral fuel called coal; or to a mine known as naming it; or to a well of oil; or to a ship or vessel called name; or to certain timber describing it*) belonging to C.D.

or

At   , on   , A.B. unlawfully, wilfully, without legal justification or excuse, without colour of right, and with intent to defraud, did set fire to a certain building, to wit, a store belonging to him the said A.B.

Threatening to Burn, etc.: Code 516.

A.B., at   , on   , did unlawfully send (*or state as in Code 516*) to C.D. a letter (*or writing*) threatening to burn (*or destroy*) a certain building (*or other thing mentioned, describing it*), (*or certain grain, or hay or straw, or certain agricultural product, stating what it was, in or under a certain building, or in a certain ship, describe the building or ship*).

Attempt to Set Fire to Crops, Forest, etc.: Code 514

A.B., at   , on   , did unlawfully, wilfully and without legal justification or excuse and without colour of right* attempt to set fire to certain (*state what*) to wit (*describe*), the same being the property of C.D.

or

*Set fire to (*state what, e.g., a quantity of wood and brush*) which was then so situated that he, the said A.B. then knew that a certain crop belonging to C.D. then growing on adjacent land (*or any of the things stated in Code 513, stating what*) was likely to catch fire therefrom.

Forest, Reckless Setting Fire to: Code 515.

A.B., at   , on   , did unlawfully by such negligence as shewed him to be reckless or wantonly regardless of consequences (*describing how*) set fire to the forest or to certain manufactured lumber, or to square timber, or logs then being on the Crown domain, or then being on land leased or lawfully held by C.D. for the purpose of cutting timber; or on the private property of C.D. on (*here state one of the places mentioned in the above section*) so that the same was then and thereby injured (*or destroyed*).

Setting Fire to Crop, etc.: Code 513(a), 541.

A.B., at   , on   , unlawfully, wilfully and without legal justification or excuse and without colour of right, did set fire to (*here*

state any of the things mentioned in Code 513(*a*)) the same being the pro
perty of C.D.

or Code 513(b).

A.B., at   , on   , unlawfully and wilfully did set fire to
a tree (*or any of the things mentioned in Code* 513(*b*), *describing the
same*) and did thereby injure (*or* destroy) the said (*describe the thing
injured*).

Gambling.

On Public Conveyances: Code 234.

A.B., on   , at   , in a railway car on the Grand Trunk
Railway (*or in a steamboat called*   ), then being used as a public
conveyance for passengers did unlawfully by means of a game of cards (*or
dice, or by any instrument or device of gambling, describing it*) obtain
from C.D. (*or* attempt to obtain from C.D. by actually engaging the said
C.D. in such game) a sum of money (*or any other valuable security or
property, naming it*).

Poolselling or Betting: Code 235, 987.

A.B., on   , at   , did unlawfully use (*or* knowingly
allow to be used) certain premises under his control being (*describe*) for
the purpose of recording or registering any bet (*or wager or selling pools*
upon the result of a horse race at   ; *or* did unlawfully become
custodian or repository of a sum of money (*or state any valuable thing*)
staked upon the result of a horse race at

Lottery or Raffle: Code 236(a).

A.B. at   , on   , did unlawfully advertise a proposal
or plan for disposing of property, to wit (*describe*) by lots (*or by any mode
of chance, describing it*).

or

Sell a certain lot (*or card, or other device, stating it*) for disposing
of property, to wit (*describe*) by lots (*or describe the mode of chance
adopted*).

or

Conduct a certain scheme (*describing it*) for the purpose of determining the holders of what tickets (*or numbers, etc.*) are the winners of a
certain property (*describing it*) disposed of by lot (*or chance, describing
how*).

Buying Lottery Tickets: Code 236(2).

Gaming in Stocks or Merchandise: Code 231. *See* Bucket Shop.

Frequenting Place Where Above Carried On: Code 233. *See* Bucket
Shop.

Gaming House, Keeping Common: Code 226-228, 985, 986.

Betting House, Keeping Common: Code 227, 228, 985, 986.

A.B. on   , at   , did unlawfully keep a disorderly house,
to wit, a common gaming house (*or* common betting house).
See also Gaming House, in Summary Convictions Cases.

Garrotting or Gagging.

Code 276(a).

At   , on   , A.B., with intent thereby to enable him, the
said A.B. (*or* one C.D.) to rob (*or* commit a rape upon) E.F. unlawfully

did attempt to render the said E.F. insensible (*or* unconscious, *or* incapable of resistance) by gagging (*or* garrotting) or (*mention the means used*) the said E.F. in a manner calculated to choke (*or* suffocate, *or* strangle) the said E.F., or to render the said E.F. insensible, unconscious or incapable of resistance.

Grain and Produce, Receipts, False.
See False Warehouse Receipts.

House Breaking.
See Burglary.

Indecent or Scurrilous Books, Letters, etc.
Posting: Code 209.
A.B., at   , on   , did unlawfully post for transmission, *or* delivery by *or* through the post to one C.D., an obscene *or* immoral book (*or any of the things mentioned*) of an indecent *or* immoral *or* scurrilous character.

or

A letter *or* an envelope addressed to one C.D., upon the outside of which letter *or* envelope (*or* a post card, *or* a post band *or* wrapper upon which) there then were words *or* devices *or* matter of an indecent *or* immoral *or* scurrilous character.

or

A letter *or* a circular concerning a certain scheme devised (*or* intended) by the said A.B. to deceive and defraud the public (*or* for the purpose of obtaining money from the said C.D. under false pretences, to wit, *state what the device or scheme was*).

Incest.
Code 204.
A.B., and one C.D., at   , on or about   , and at divers times since that date, being brother and sister (*or* parent and child; *or* grandparent and grandchild) did unlawfully have sexual intercourse with each other, the said A.B., being then aware of their consanguinity and did thereby commit incest.

Indecency, Gross.
Code 206.
A.B., *etc.*, a male person, did unlawfully commit an act of gross in-decency with C.D., another male person.

Indecent and Obscene Pictures, Selling or Exposing.
Code 207.
A.B., *etc.*, in a certain open and public place did unlawfully, knowingly and without lawful justification or excuse manufacture (*or* sell, *or* expose for sale, *or* expose to public view) an obscene picture (*or* book called   , *or* photograph, *or* model) representing (*describe it*) and having a tendency to corrupt morals.

Inland Revenue Act, Breaches of.
R.S.C. ch. 51.
Distiller, Offences By: Secs. 180, *et seq.*
Compounder, Offences By: Secs. 187, *et seq.*
Brewer, Offences By: Sec. 197.
Maltster, Offences By: Sec. 208, *et seq.*

Bonded Manufacturer, Offences By: Sec. 246, *et seq.*
Tobacco and Cigar Manufacturer, Offences By: Sec. 269, *et seq.*

Jurymen, Attempting to Corrupt.
Code 180. *See* Bribery.

Kidnapping.
Code 297.
A.B., on   , at   , did, without lawful authority, kidnap
C.D., with the intent to cause the said C.D., against his will, to be secretly confined or imprisoned in Canada, *or* to be unlawfully sent (*or* transported)
against his will, out of Canada, *or* to be sold *or* captured as a slave (*or*
held to service against his will); *or* that A.B., on   , at   ,
did, without lawful authority, seize and confine (*or* imprison) C.D. within
Canada.

Landlord and Tenant.
See Tenant.

Landmarks, Removing or Injuring.
Code 531, 532.   Also R.S.C. ch. 55, secs. 222-224.

Larceny: Merged in Theft.
See Theft.

Letter, Unlawfully Dealing with Post Letter.
See Post Office Offences.

Letter, Sending False.
See False Telegram, etc.;   Code 476.

Libel.
Blasphemous: Code 198.
A.B., on   , at   , unlawfully did publish in a certain newspaper (*or* book *or as the case may be*) a certain blasphemous and
profane libel of and concerning the Christian religion in the following
words (*here set out libellous words*).
Libel: Code 334.
A.B., on   , at   , unlawfully did publish of and concerning C.D. a defamatory libel in a certain letter directed to E.F. (*or*
in a newspaper called   , *or state how otherwise published*) in the
words following, that is to say (*set out the words*), thereby imputing that
the said C.D. (*state what was the meaning of the libel*) he, the said A.B.,
then knowing the said libel to be false.
"Magistrates" cannot try the latter.

Lodger or Tenant, Theft by.
Code 360. *See* Theft by Tenant, etc.

Lottery.
See Gambling.

Lying in Waiting Near Public Meeting.
Code 128. *See* Assault.

Mail, Offences Against.
See Post Office Offences.

Manslaughter.
Code 261, 250-260.
A.B., at   , on   , did unlawfully kill and slay C.D.

Maiming.
See Wounding.

Marriage.
Solemnizing Without Authority: Code 311(a).
A.B., at   , on   , without lawful authority, did unlawfully solemnize (*or* pretend to solemnize) a marriage between C.D. and E.F.
or Code 311(b).
A.B., at   , on   , then knowing that C.D. was not lawfully authorized to solemnize a marriage between E.F. and G.H. did unlawfully procure the said C.D. to unlawfully solemnize a marriage between the said E.F. and G.H.
Solemnizing Contrary to Law: Code 312.
A.B., at   , on   , a clergyman of (*state what denomination*), having lawful authority to solemnize marriages, did, then and there, a marriage between C.D., a man, and E.F., a woman, solemnize unlawfully, wilfully and knowingly in violation of the laws of the Province of Ontario in which the said marriage was so solemnized, to wit, by solemnizing the same without due publication of banns and without any license in that behalf (*or, set out particular illegality complained of*) as required by the laws of the said Province of Ontario.
Feigned: Code 309.
A.B., at   , on   , a man, did unlawfully procure a feigned and pretended marriage to be peformed between himself and C.D., a woman.
(*Assisting in same*) unlawfully assist E.F., in procuring a feigned and pretended marriage between the said E.F., a man, and C.D., a woman.

Marine Signals.
Wilful Interfering With: Code 526.
At   , on   , A.B. unlawfully, wilfully, did alter (*or* remove, *or* conceal, *stating particulars*) a certain signal (*or* mark; *or* buoy; *describe it and where situated*) used for the purpose of navigation.
Or Buoy; Fastening Vessel to: Code 526(2).
At   , on   , A.B., unlawfully made fast a vessel or boat to a signal (*or* buoy; *describe where it was situated*) used for the purposes of navigation.

Mines, Frauds in Relation to.
Code 424. *See* also Mines Act, 1906, in list of Summary Convictions Cases.

Mines and Mining Machinery, Injuries to.
Code 520. *See* Wilful Injuries.

Murder.
Code 259, 260; also 250-263.
"Magistrates" cannot try any of the offences under this heading.

A.B. murdered C.D. at   , on

Attempt to: Code 264(a)

At   , on   , A.B. unlawfully did administer (*or* cause to be administered) to C.D. certain poison (*or* a certain destructive thing), to wit (*describe*) with intent, thereby, then and there, to murder the said C.D.

or Code 264(b).

Unlawfully did wound (*or* cause grievous bodily harm to) C.D. with intent, thereby, then and there, to murder the said C.D.

or Code 264(c).

Unlawfully did, with a certain loaded gun (*or* pistol, *or* revolver) shoot (*or* attempt to discharge a loaded arm) at C.D., with intent, thereby, then and there to murder the said C.D.

or Code 264(d).

Unlawfully did attempt to drown *(or* suffocate, *or* strangle) C.D. with intent, thereby, then and there, to murder the said C.D.

or Code 264(e).

Unlawfully did by the explosion of a certain explosive substance, to wit (*describe the explosive*) destroy (*or* damage) a certain building situate and being in (*place*) street, in (*state where*), aforesaid, with intent, thereby, then and there, to murder C.D.

or Code 264(f).

Unlawfully did set fire to a certain ship to wit (*state where*) with intent, thereby, then and there, to murder C.D.

or Code 264(g).

Unlawfully, did cast away (*or* destroy) a certain ship, to wit, with intent, thereby, then and there, to murder C.D.

Attempt to by Any Means: Code 264(h).

By then and there (*describe what the attempt consisted of*) did unlawfully attempt to murder C.D.

Threats to: Code 265.

Unlawfully did send (*or* deliver), to (*or* cause to be received by) C.D. a certain letter (*or* writing) threatening to kill (*or* murder) the said C.D., he, the said A.B., then knowing the contents of the said letter (*or* writing)

or

A.B., on   , at   , unlawfully did utter a certain writing threatening to kill (*or* murder) C.D., he, the said A.B., then knowing the contents of the said writing.

Conspiracy to: Code 266(a).

A.B., on   , at   , and C.D. did, with other parties unknown unlawfully conspire and agree together to murder E.F. (*or* to cause E.F., to be murdered).

Counselling Murder: Code 266(b).

A.B., on   , at   , did unlawfully counsel (*or* attempt to procure) C.D. to murder E.F.

Accessory After the Fact to: Code 267.

That some person or persons, on   , at   , did unlawfully (*state the offence committed by the principal offender*), and that the said A.B. (*the informant*) has just cause to suspect, and does suspect that C.D. did commit the said offence, and that E.F., at   , on   , well knowing the said C.D. to have committed the said offence, did afterwards, at the   of   in the County of   , on the day of   , A.D. 19 , unlawfully receive (*or* comfort) the said C.D. (*or* assist the said C.D.) in order to enable the said C.D. to escape.

Mutiny, Inciting to.

Code 81.

"Magistrates" cannot try.

Necessaries for Children, Parent, etc., Omitting to Supply.

Code 242, 244.

A.B., on   , at   , and on and at divers other days and times before and since that date, he being then the father (or the guardian) of C.D., a child under sixteen years of age, who was then and there a member of the said A.B.'s household, and the said A.B. being as such father (or guardian) under a legal duty and bound by law to provide sufficient food, clothing and lodging and all other necessaries for the said C.D., his said child (or ward), did unlawfully and in disregard of his duty in that behalf refuse and neglect without lawful excuse to provide necessaries, to wit, food (or clothing, etc.) for the said C.D. while a member of the said A.B.'s household aforesaid, by means whereof the life of the said C.D. was endangered (or the health of the said C.D. was likely to be permanently injured; or the death of the said C.D. was caused).

(A similar form may be used in the case of a husband neglecting to provide necessaries for his wife): Code 242(2), or anyone having charge of another who is unable to provide for himself: Code 241: or master neglecting to supply necessaries to apprentice: Code 243.

Negligence Causing Injuries.

Code 284.

A.B., at   , on   , being then and there the agent at the station of the   railway and having as such duly received orders to detain a certain freight train No.   on the said railway at the said station to allow a passenger train then proceeding in an opposite direction to pass at the said station did unlawfully, and negligently, omit to detain the said freight train, in consequence whereof the same proceeded without waiting for the said passenger train to pass as aforesaid, by means and as a result whereof a collision occurred between the said trains and the said A.B. by his said omission of duty did then and there unlawfully cause grievous bodily injury to C.D.

Charges similar to the above may be framed for doing negligently or negligently omitting to do any act which it was a person's duty to do, thereby in any way causing grievous bodily harm to any one.

Negligently Causing Injury by Furious Driving.

Code 285.

A.B., at   , on   , he then and there having the charge of a certain vehicle did unlawfully and by wanton (or furious) driving (or racing, or by wilful misconduct, or wilful neglect, stating in what the neglect or misconduct consisted) did bodily harm (or cause bodily harm to be done) to C.D.

Nuisance, Common.

Code 222.

At   , on   , and on and at divers other days and times before and since that date, A.B., unlawfully and injuriously did and he does yet continue to (set out the particular act or omission complained of) and thereby unlawfully did commit and does continue to commit a common nuisance, which did then and there occasion injury to the person of C.D. (or endangered the lives, or safety, or health of the public).

Oath.
Administering Unauthorized: Code 129.

Administering an Unlawful: Code 130.
A.B., on   , at   , did unlawfully administer or cause
to be administered to C.D. a certain oath and engagement purporting to
bind the said C.D. not to inform or give evidence against any associate
confederate or other person of or belonging to a certain unlawful association and confederacy; and which said oath and engagement was then and
there taken by the said C.D.
Taking Unlawful: Code 130.
Commence as above]—Did unlawfully take a certain oath and engagement purporting (*etc., as in the last form*).
"Magistrates" cannot try these.

Obscenity.
See Indecency.

Offensive Weapons.
See Weapons.

Oil Wells, Injuries to.
Code 250. *See* Wilful Injuries.

Perjury.
Code 170-174.
A.B., at   , on   , did unlawfully commit perjury at
the court of   , on   , on the trial of C.D. for   ,
by swearing to the effect (*state in what the perjury consisted*) contrary
to the truth.
Subornation: Code 170(2)-174.
(*Proceed as in the above form to the end and add*)—And that before
the committing of the said perjury by the said A.B., to wit, on the
day of   , at   , E.F. did unlawfully counsel and procure the
said A.B. to commit the said perjury.
False Statement in Affidavit: Code 172.
False Declaration: Code 176.

Personation at an Examination.
Code 409.
A.B., at   , on   , falsely and with intent to gain an
advantage for himself (*or* for one C.D.) did personate E.F., a candidate
at a competitive (*or* qualifying) examination duly and lawfully held in
connection with the University (*or* college, *or as the case may be*) of
(*naming it*).
This case may also be tried by one justice summarily: *see Summary
Convictions Cases, post*.

Personating an Owner of Stock.
Code 410.
A.B. did unlawfully, falsely and deceitfully personate C.D., who was
then the owner of a certain share or interest in certain stock, to wit (*describe the stock*), then transferable at the   bank (*or*, at the head
office of the   company) and did thereby then and there transfer
(*or* endeavour to transfer) the share and interest of the said C.D. in the
said stock as if he, the said A.B. were the lawful owner thereof.

Pickpockets.
See Theft from the Person.

Prison Breaking.
See Escape.

Promise of Marriage.
See Seduction.

Poisoning.
See Drugging.

Polygamy.
Code 310.
At   , on   , and at divers others days and times before and since that date A.B., a male person, and C.D. and E.F., females unlawfully did practice (or agree and consent to practice) polygamy together.
or
Did unlawfully by mutual consent enter into a form of polygamy together.

Post Office Offences.
Theft of Post Letter Bag, Letter or Mail Matter: Code 364(a).
A.B., at   , on   , did unlawfully steal * one post letter bag, the property of the Postmaster-General of Canada;
or (b).
*A post letter addressed to E.F., from a post letter bag, or from the post office at   ; or from C.D., a mail clerk on the Grand Trunk Railway, then and there employed in the business of distributing and delivering the mail; (or as the case may be);
or (c).
*A post letter the property of the Postmaster-General of Canada, which said letter contained a sum of money, or a valuable security, or chattel (stating what);
or (d).
*Certain money or a certain valuable security, or chattel, (stating what) from or out of a post letter, the property of the Postmaster-General of Canada.
See Code 365, 366, for other offences.
Unlawfully Opening or Detaining Letter: R.S.C. ch. 66, sec. 121.
A.B., at   , on   , did unlawfully open (or did unlawfully and wilfully keep, or secrete, or delay, or detain, or cause to be opened, etc.) a post letter, to wit, a letter transmitted by post (or deposited in the post office of   ; or in a letter box put up at   under the authority of the Postmaster-General of Canada), and addressed to C.D.
Other Post Office Act, Offences Against: R.C.S. ch. 66, secs. 117-137.
Opening Letter Bag, etc.: Sec. 117.
Forging Postage Stamps: Sec. 119.
Forging Post Office Order: Sec. 120.
Enclosing Explosive Substance in Letter, etc.: Sec. 122.
Obstructing the Mail: Sec. 125.
Mail Carrier Drunk on Duty: Sec. 126.
Post Master Issuing Money Order Without First Receiving the Money: Sec. 129.
Postmaster, Other Offences by: Secs. 131-133.
21—MAG. MAN.

Post Office Official Converting Property Mailed: Sec. 133.
Mail, Stopping the: Code 449.
    At   , on   , A.B. unlawfully did stop a certain mail,
to wit (on a railway *or* mail coach, *stating what*), the mail for the conveyance of letters between   and   , with intent to rob (*or*
search) the same.

Raffle.
    See Gambling.

Railway Passengers, Wilfully Endangering.
    Code 282.
    A.B., at   , on   , upon and across a certain railway
there called (*e.g.*, the Grand Trunk Railway), a certain piece of wood (*or*
stone, *or as the case may be*) did unlawfully put (*or* throw) with intent
thereby to injure or endanger the safety of persons travelling or being upon
the said railway.
                                  or
Upon a certain railway there called (*name it*) a certain rail (*or*
switch, *or as the case may be*) there belonging to such railway, did unlawfully take up (*or* remove, *or* displace; *or* injure *or* destroy the track, *or*
bridge, *or* fence, of such railway) with intent thereby to injure or endanger
the safety of persons travelling or being upon the said railway.
                                  or
A certain point (*or other machinery, stating what*) then belonging
to a certain railway called (*name*), did unlawfully turn (*or* move, *or*
divert), with intent thereby to injure or endanger the safety of persons
travelling *or* being upon the said railway.
                                  or
Unlawfully did make (*or* shew, *or* hide, *or* remove), a certain signal
or light upon *or* near to a certain railway called (*name*), with intent
thereby to injure *or* endanger the safety of persons travelling *or* being upon
the said railway.
                                  or
Unlawfully did throw (*or* cause to fall, *or* strike) at, *or* against (*or*
into, *or* upon) an engine (*or* tender, *or* carriage, *or* truck), then being
used and in motion upon a certain railway there called (*name*), a piece of
wood (*or* a stone, *or other matter as the case may be, stating it*) with intent, thereby, to injure or endanger the safety of persons then and there
being upon the said engine (*or* tender, *or* carriage, *or* truck, *or* another
engine, *or* tender, *or* carriage) of the train of which the said first mentioned
engine, tender, carriage or truck then formed part.

Railway, Wilful Neglect of Duty Causing Danger, etc.
    Code 283.
    A.B., on   , at   , he then and there being a switch
tender on the   railway, by wilful omission and neglect of his
duty as such, to wit, by wilfully omitting to replace a switch which it
was his duty to have closed or replaced did thereby unlawfully endanger
the safety of persons being conveyed or being upon the said railway (*or*
set forth any other omission or neglect of duty by any employee of a
railway).
    See also R.S.C. ch. 37, sec. 415.

Rape.
    Code 298-299.
    At   , on   , A.B., a man did unlawfully have carnal
knowledge of C.D., a woman, who was not his wife, without her consent (*or*

with her consent, which was there and then unlawfully extorted by threats, *or* fear of bodily harm, *or* which consent was there and then obtained by the said A.B. personating the husband of the said C.D., *or* by false and fraudulent representations as to the nature and quality of the act, that is to say (*set out the representations*).

Attempt to Commit: Code 300.

At   , on   , A.B., a man, did unlawfully attempt to have carnal knowledge of C.D., a woman, who was not his wife, without her consent (*if with her consent obtained by fraud, add the allegations in the preceding form*).

"Magistrates" cannot try the above offences.

Receiving or Retaining in Possession Stolen Goods.
Code 399, 993, 994.

A.B., at   , on   , did unlawfully receive, *or* retain in his possession (*state the article*), the property of C.D., and which had been theretofore obtained by the said C.D. (*or* one E.F.) by an offence punishable on indictment, to wit, by theft (*or other indictable offence, describing it*), the said A.B. then knowing the said   , to have been obtained by the said E.F. by the said indictable offence.

Rescue.
See Escape, etc.

Robbery.
Code 447.

A.B., at   , on   , did unlawfully steal the moneys (*or* the goods and chattels, to wit, *state what*) of C.D. with violence (*or* threats of violence, *describing the threat*) to the person (*or* property) of the said C.D. such violence (*or* threats) being used to prevent resistance to the same being stolen and did thereby unlawfully commit robbery.

Robbery with Wounding or Violence; or by Two or More Persons; or When Armed: Code 446.

Rob, Assault with Intent to: Code 448.

A.B., at   , on   , did unlawfully assault C.D. with intent the moneys (*or* the goods and chattels, to wit, *describing what*) of him the said C.D. then and there did steal unlawfully and with violence (*or* with threats of violence, *stating what*) to the person (*or* property) of the said C.D. then and there used to prevent resistance to the same being so stolen, and did thereby unlawfully attempt to commit robbery.

Rewards, Corruptly Taking, for Procuring the Return of Property Which has been Stolen, etc.
Code 182.

A.B., at   , on   , did unlawfully and corruptly take from C.D. a sum of money, to wit (*state the amount*), (*or* a certain reward, *stating what*) for, and under the pretence (*or* upon account of the said A.B., helping the said C.D. to recover certain money (*or* a certain chattel, *or* valuable security, *or other property, naming it*) which had theretofore been unlawfully stolen from the said C.D. (*or state the circumstances shewing that the property had been obtained from the owner by an indictable offence*). he the said A.B., not having used all due diligence to cause the offender to be brought to trial for the said offence of stealing (*or as the case may be*) the said money or chattel.

Riotous Destruction or Damage to Buildings.
Code 96.

A.B., (C.D. and E.F.) together with divers other persons, they all being then and there riotously and tumultuously assembled together, to the disturbance of the public peace, did unlawfully and with·force demolish (or pull down, or begin to demolish or pull down, or injure, or damage) a certain building (or a certain erection used in farming land, or in carrying on a certain trade, or manufacture, or in conducting the business of a certain mine, or a certain tender, or wagon way, or track for conveying minerals from a certain mine: describing it).

Inciting Indians to Riotous Acts.
Code 109.

A.B. did unlawfully induce (or incite, or stir up) certain Indians (or half-breeds) belonging to the   reservation at   , to the number of three or more, then and there apparently acting in concert to make a certain request or demand of C.D., an agent or servant of the Government of Canada, in a riotous (or disorderly, or threatening manner, or in a manner calculated to cause a breach of the peace) by demanding (describe the demand and threats).

Search Warrants.
Code 629, 643.

The Forms 1 and 2 are to be filled in as exemplified by the following:—
Information for Search Warrant.

That on or about the   day of   , 19 , one bay horse about   years old, with white nigh hind foot and a white star in the forehead, the same being the personal property of C.D. (or describe *what the property was, so that it can be identified*) was unlawfully stolen by A.B. (or by some person unknown) and the complainant has just and reasonable cause to suspect and does suspect that the same is concealed in the barn (or *describe the place*) on the farm of A.B. (or E.F.) and the causes of such suspicion are as follows (*describe them, as, for instance, that the said A.B. was seen driving a horse of a similar description from the direction of (the place from which the horse was stolen) towards the place where the said A.B. resides and where the said barn is situated.*)

or

That on   , at   , A.B. in his office where he was then carrying on a loan business did unlawfully (obtain from C.D. the sum of $ by false pretences) and there was at that time in the said office certain books of account apparently kept by the said A.B. for recording his loan transactions there, and books of account appearing to be the same books above mentioned are still in the said office of the said A.B., at No.   on   Street, in the said   of   , and the complaint believes that entries in the said books will afford evidence as to the commission of the said offence (*explaining and stating facts to justify that belief*).

(A justice is not authorized to issue a search warrant unless the information sets forth the causes and grounds of suspicion sufficient to satisfy him that there is reasonable ground for the suspicion that there is stolen property in the place indicated and described, or that there is something there which will afford· evidence as to the commission of the offence claimed. R. v. Kehr, 11 Can. Cr. Cas. 52.)

See also, *ante* p. 243, as to Search Warrants.

Seduction.
Inveigling a Woman into a House of Assignation, etc.: Code 216 (b).

A.B. (*etc.*) did unlawfully inveigle or entice C.D., a woman (or a girl), to a house of ill fame (or assignation) for the purpose of illicit intercourse (or prostitution).

or Code 216(*c*).

Did procure (*or* attempt to procure) C.D. a woman (*or* a girl) to become a common prostitute.

or Code 216(*d*)(*e*).

Did procure (*or* attempt to procure) C.D., a woman (*or* a girl), to leave Canada (*or* to come to Canada from abroad) with intent that she should become an inmate of a brothel elsewhere (*describing where*) (*or* in Canada).

or Code 216(*i*).

Did apply to (*or* administer to, or cause to be taken by) C.D., a woman (*or* a girl) a drug (*or* intoxicating liquor) with intent to stupify or overpower the said C.D. so as to enable him, the said A.B. (*or* one E.F.) to have unlawful carnal connection with the said C.D.

For other offences see same section and sections 214, 215, 217, 218, 220.

Carnal Knowledge of Girl Under Fourteen: Code 301, 302.

A.B., at   , on   , did unlawfully and carnally know (*or* attempt to carnally know) C.D., a girl then under the age of fourteen years, she not being his wife.

Of Girl Between Fourteen and Sixteen: Code 211.

At   , on   , A.B. unlawfully did (*or* attempted to) seduce (*or* have illicit connection with) C.D., a girl of previously chaste character, then being of (*or* above) the age of fourteen years and under the age of sixteen years.

Under Promise of Marriage: Code 212.

At   , on   , A.B., being then above the age of twenty-one years did, then and there, unlawfully, and under promise of marriage, seduce and have illicit connection with C.D., she then being an unmarried female of previously chaste character and under the age of twenty-one years.

By Guardian of Ward: Code 213(a).

At   , on   , A.B., then being the guardian of C.D., a female, then and there did unlawfully seduce (*or* have illicit connection with) the said C.D., his ward.

Of Factory Employee: Code 213(b).

A.B., at   , on   , unlawfully did seduce (*or* did have illicit connection with) C.D., a woman of previously chaste character, and then being under the age of twenty-one years, and who was then in the employment of the said A.B. in his factory (*or* mill, *or* workshop, *or* shop, *or* store).

Carnally Knowing Idiot or Imbecile Woman, etc.: Code 219.

A.B., on   , at   , did unlawfully and carnally know (*or* attempt to have carnal knowledge of) C.D., a female idiot (*or* an imbecile, *or* an insane, *or* a deaf and dumb woman *or* girl) the said A.B. then well knowing that the said C.D. was an idiot (*or* imbecile, *or* insane, *or* deaf and dumb).

Ship, Sending Unseaworthy Ship to Sea.

Code 288, 289.

A.B., on   , at   , being the owner (*or* manager, *or* master) of a ship called (*name it*) which by reason of overloading (*or* being insufficiently manned, *or other cause, naming it*) was in such an unseaworthy state that the lives of the seaman (*or* passengers) on board the same were likely to be endangered thereby did unlawfully send (*or* was a party to sending) the said ship on a voyage on the inland waters of Canada.

The consent of the Minister of Marine and Fisheries is necessary before prosecution for this offence: Code 595.

Ship-Wrecked Person, Preventing the Saving of.
Code 286(a).

A.B., on   , at   , unlawfully did prevent and impede (*or* endeavour to prevent and impede) C.D., a shipwrecked person, in his endeavour to save his life.

or Code 286(*b*).

Did without reasonable cause prevent or impede (*or* endeavour to prevent or impede) C.D. in his endeavour to save the life of E.F., a shipwrecked person.

Sodomy.
See Buggery.

Spring-guns or Man-traps, Setting.
Code 281.

A.B., on   , at   , unlawfully did set (*or* place, *or* cause to be set *or* placed) in a certain (*describe where set*) a certain spring-gun (*or* man-trap) which was calculated to destroy human life (*or* inflict grievous bodily harm) with intent that (*or* whereby) the same might destroy (*or* inflict grievous bodily harm upon) any trespasser (*or* person) coming in contact therewith.

Suicide.
Aiding and Abetting: Code 269.

A.B., on   , at   , and on divers other days before that date, unlawfully did counsel and procure C.D. to commit suicide, in consequence of which counselling and procurement by the said A.B. the said C.D. then and there, actually did commit suicide.

Attempt to Commit: Code 270.

A.B., at   , on   , unlawfully did attempt to commit suicide by then and there endeavouring to kill himself.

Surveyor, Obstructing or Molesting while Surveying Dominion Lands.
R.S.C. 55, sec. 221.

Surveyors' Posts or other Landmarks, etc., Removing, etc.
Secs. 222, 223.

Telegram, Sending False.
Code 475, 476. *See* False Telegram.

Tenant.
Wilful Injury to Property by: Code 529. *See* Wilful Injuries.
Theft by: Code 260. *See* Theft.

Theft.
From the Person: Code 379.

A.B., on   , at   , did unlawfully steal a certain chattel *or* valuable security, *or* a certain sum of money (*describing what was stolen*) from the person of C.D.

By Agents, Trustees, etc.: Code 355.

A.B., at   , on   , having theretofore received from C.D., a sum of money (*state amount*), or a certain (*state what, e.g.*, 500 *bushels of wheat*), on terms requiring him, the said A.B., to account for, *or*

pay over, the said money (or the proceeds of the said wheat) to one E.F.
(or to the said C.D.), he, the said A.B., did afterwards, to wit, at the time
and place aforesaid unlawfully and fraudulently convert the said money (or
the proceeds of the said wheat) to his own use, or did unlawfully and
fraudulently omit to account for, or pay over the said money (or the proceeds of the said wheat) to the said E.F. (or to the said C.D.).

By Bank Employee: Code 359(b).

A.B., at   , on   , being there and then employed as
*cashier (or other officer, named in above section of the Cr. Code, stating
what)* of the Bank of (*name*), did unlawfully steal a sum of money, to
wit (*amount*), or a certain bond (*or bill, or note, or as the case may be,
describing one of the things mentioned in the above sections*) of the said
bank; *or a bond (or note, or state what)* belonging to one C.D., which
was there and then deposited or lodged with the said bank of (*name*).

By Clerks and Servants: Code 359(a)(b).

A.B., on   , at   , being then and there employed in the
capacity of a clerk to C.D. did unlawfully steal (*state what*) belonging to
(or then and there in the possession of) the said C.D.

By Tenants or Lodgers: Code 360.

A.B., on   , at   , did unlawfully steal a certain chattel (*or fixture*), to wit (*state what*) which had theretofore been let by
C.D., the owner thereof, to be used by the said A.B. in, or with a house,
or lodging, namely (*describe it*).

By Government Employee: Code 359(c).

At   , on   , A.B. being then and there employed in
the service of His Majesty (or the Government of Canada, or the Government of the Province of Ontario, or the municipality of   ),
and being then and there, by virtue of his said employment in possession
of certain moneys (or certain valuable securities, to wit (*describe*), did
unlawfully steal the said moneys (or the said valuable securities).

By Post Office Employee: R.S.C. ch. 30, secs. 19, 20, 41.

See also Post Office Offences, Thefts, etc., *ante.*

By Partner, in Mining Adventure: Code 353.

A.B. and C.D., being then and there co-partners (or co-adventurers) in
a mining claim (*describe it, or in a share, or interest in a mining claim,
describing it*), the said A.B. on or about   , at   , unlawfully
and secretly kept back and concealed certain gold (or silver) found in or
upon (or taken from) such claim.

By Husband or Wife: Code 354.

A.B., then being the wife of C.D., they then living apart from each
other, did unlawfully steal (*describe the property stolen*) the same being
the personal property of the said C.D.

By Owner: Code 352.

A.B., at   , on   , was the owner of a certain portable
steam engine and had theretofore delivered the same to C.D., a machinist
for repairs, which the said C.D. afterwards made thereto by means whereof
the said C.D. then had a lien upon or a special interest in the said engine
for the cost of such repairs and the said A.B. without the consent of the
said C.D., and while the said engine was still in the actual possession of the
said C.D., who was entitled to the said lien or special property therein did
unlawfully and fraudulently take the said engine out of the possession of the
said C.D. without paying said costs of said repairs, then due and owing to
him by the said A.B., and the said A.B. did thereby commit theft.

Of Stray Cattle: Code 392, 989.

A.B., on   , at   , unlawfully and without the consent of
C.D., the owner of a certain steer which was found astray, did fraudulently

take (*or* hold, *or as the case may be, following the words of the statute*) the said steer; or did fraudulently wholly (*or* partially) obliterate (*or* alter, *or* deface) a brand mark (*or* make a false brand mark) on the said steer; or did unlawfully and without reasonable excuse refuse to deliver up the said steer to the said C.D., *or* to E.F., who was then and there in charge thereof on behalf of the said C.D., *or* who was then and there authorized by the said C.D. to receive the said steer.

Killing any Living Animal with Intent to Steal: Code 350.

A.B., at   , on   , did unlawfully kill one (*state what the animal was*), the property of C.D., with intent to steal the hide (*or* the carcass, *or* a part of the carcass) thereof.

Stealing Anything in a Dwelling, of the Value of $25 or With Menaces: Code 380(a).

A.B., on   , at   , in a certain dwelling-house of C.D., then and there situated, did unlawfully steal certain goods and chattels of C.D., to wit (*describe*),* the said goods then being of the value of $25 at least.

or 380(b).

*And the said A.B., then and there, by menace or threat, to wit, (*state it, e.g.*), by pointing a pistol at, and threatening to shoot one E.F., then lawfully being in the said dwelling-house, did put the said E.F. in bodily fear.

From Ships, Wharves, etc.: Code 382.

A.B., at   , on   , did unlawfully steal certain goods or merchandise, to wit (*state what*), in a vessel called the   , in the harbour or port of   , being the port of entry or discharge of said vessel; *or* from a certain dock or wharf adjacent to the port of (*etc., as above*).

On Railways: Code 384.

A.B., at   , on   , did unlawfully steal in or from the railway station of the   Railway at   (*or* from the engine, *or* tender, *or* passenger car, *or* freight car on the said railway, *or as the case may be*), a certain (*state the article*), the property of C.D., *or* of the Railway Company.

Of Goods Under Seizure: Code 349.

A.B., on   , at   , did unlawfully steal certain personal property, to wit (*describe it*), which was then and there under lawful seizure under an execution duly issued out of (*name the court*) in a certain cause (*name it*).

NOTE.—This does not apply to things seized under landlord's distress warrant or under chattel mortgage.

From a Wreck: Code 383; Code 2(41).

A.B., at   , on   , did unlawfully steal (*describe the article*), which was then and there a portion of the cargo of (*or* belonging to, *or as the case may be*) a certain vessel called (*name the ship*) which had been then and there sunk (*or* stranded) and wrecked.

Of Ore, etc., From a Mine: Code 378, 988.

A.B., at   , on   , unlawfully did steal a *quantity* of ore, the property of C.D., from a certain   mine of the said C.D., situated in   , aforesaid.

(*Similar form for theft of any of the things mentioned in Code 378*).

By Pick Lock: Code 381.

A.B., at   , on   , unlawfully by means of a pick lock (*or* false key) did steal the sum of $ (*or state any other property*), the property of C.D. from a locked and secured receptacle.

Of Goods in Mannufactories: Code 388.

A.B., at   , on   , unlawfully did steal (*describe the property*) belonging to C.D. in a certain   manufactory of the said C.D., then situated whilst the same was placed (*or* exposed) during a certain stage, process or progress of the manufacture thereof in or upon the premises of the said manufactory.

Of Domestic Animal, etc., (*Over* $20 *Value*) : Code 370.

A.B., at   , on   , did unlawfully steal one dog (*or* one goose, *or* three hens, *or as the case may be*), being a beast (*or bird, or other animal*) ordinarily kept for domestic purposes (*or for profit, or* ordinarily kept in confinement) the same being of the value of more than twenty dollars and being the property of C.D.

For same offence when property under $20 in value, *see* Summary Conviction Cases.

Of Drift Timber, etc.; Code 394(a), 990.

A.B., at   , on   , without the consent of the owner thereof did unlawfully and fraudulently take (*or* hold, *etc.*, *using any of the words in the section referred to* appropriate *to the charge*) certain timber (*or* sawlog, *or other* property *mentioned*), which was found adrift in (*or* cast ashore on the beach of Lake   , *or as the case may be*) the same being the property of C.D.

(Similar forms for other offences under Code 394.)

Of Judicial Documents, etc.: Code 363.

A.B., on   , at   , did unlawfully steal a certain record (*or* writ, *or other document, stating it*) belonging to and being in the office of the clerk of (*state what court*) in a certain cause of A. B. v. C.D.

Of Cattle: Code 369.

At   , on   , A.B. unlawfully did steal certain cattle, to wit, one horse (*or* one cow), the property of C.D.

Of Things Fixed to Buildings: Code 372.

A.B., at   , on   , unlawfully did steal a quantity of lead (*or* copper, *or any fixture, describing it*), the property of C.D., then being fixed in a certain dwelling-house (*or* stable, *or* coach-house), belonging to the said C.D. and situated in (*describe where*) aforesaid.

Of Trees Worth $25 *or More*: Code 373.

A.B., at   , on   , unlawfully did steal one ash (*or* maple, *or as the case may be*) tree of the value of at least twenty-five dollars, the property of C.D., then growing in a certain (*describe the* place) belonging to the said C.D., and situated in   , aforesaid.

If of value of less than $25.00, *see* Summary Convictions Offences, under Theft.

Of a Will: Code 361.

A.B., at   , on   , did unlawfully steal a certain testamentary instrument, to wit, the last will and testament (*or* a codicil to the last will and testament) of C.D.

Of a Document of Title: Code 362.

A.B., at   , on   , did unlawfully steal a certain document of title to goods, to wit, one bill of lading (*or* one ware-house keeper's receipt for two thousand bushels of wheat, *or as the case may be*) ; *or* a certain document of title to lands to wit, a deed from C.D. to E.F. of (*describe what land*).

Of Electricity: Code 351.

A.B., at   , on   , did unlawfully and fraudulently (*or* maliciously) abstract (*or* divert, *or* consume, *or* cause to be wasted) electricity then being carried on the wire of the   power company (*or as the case may be*) by (*describe as accurately as possible the method by which the electricity was diverted, etc.*)

Of Tree or Plant, etc., From Orchard or Garden, Over the Value of Five Dollars: Code 373.

If under five dollars in value one justice may convict; *see* Summary Convictions.

Stolen Property; Bringing into Canada: Code 398.

A.B., at , on , unlawfully did bring into (*or* have in) the Province of Ontario in the Dominion of Canada certain personal property (*describing it*), which had theretofore been unlawfully stolen by him, the said A.B. (*or* which the said A.B. then well knew had been unlawfully stolen), in the city of (New York) in the State of (New York), one of the United States of America (*or as the case may be*).

In Cases Not Specially Provided for: Code 386.

A.B., at , on , did unlawfully steal (*state what*) the personal property of C.D.

Trade Mark Offences.
Code 488, 489, 490, 491(a), 992, 335(5).
See also Trade Mark Offences in Summary Convictions Cases.

Trading Stamps.
Supplying to Merchant: Code 505, 335(u) (v) (2).
Merchant Supplying to Customer: Code 506.
Customer Receiving Trading Stamp: *See* Trading Stamps in Summary Convictions Cases.

Trade Combines.
Code 496-498.
"Magistrates" cannot try any offence under this head.

At , on , A.B. did unlawfully conspire (*or* combine, *or* agree, *or* arrange) with C.D. (*or* with the railway *or* steamboat, *or* transportation company known as the *naming it*),

(*a*)

to unduly limit the facilities for transporting (*or* producing, *or* manufacturing, *or* supplying, *or* storing, *or* dealing in) a certain article (*or* commodity) which was the subject of trade *or* commerce, namely (*naming it*).

or (*b*)

to restrain (*or* injure) trade or commerce in relation to certain article (*continue as above*).

or (*c*)

to unduly prevent (*or* lessen) the manufacture or production of a certain article (*continue as above*).

or (*d*)

unduly prevent (*or* lessen) competition in the production (*or* manufacture, *or* purchase, *or* barter, *or* sale, *or* transportation *or* supply) of a certain article (*proceed as above*), or in the price of insurance upon certain property (*describe how*)

Treason.
Code 74.
Accessories to: Code 76.

Treasonable Offences.
Code 77-79.
"Magistrates" cannot try.

Trustee, Criminal Breach of Trust by.
Code 390.
A.B., at , on , he then being a trustee of certain property, namely (*describe it*), for the use and benefit of C.D. (*or as the case*

may be) under (*deed or will or any other written or verbal trust, stating
it*), unlawfully and with intent to defraud, and in violation of his trust,
did convert the said property to a use not authorized by the said trust, to
wit, to his own use (*or as the case may be*).

The consent of the Attorney-General is necessary before prosecution
for this offence: Code 596.

Warehouse Receipt, etc., False.
Code 425.
See False Warehouse Receipt.

Weapon, Bringing Within Two Miles of Meeting.
Code 127.
A.B., at   , on   , he not then being the sheriff or deputy
sheriff or a justice of the peace for the county (*or* district) of   ,
(or the mayor, or a justice of the peace, or other peace opcer for the city (*or*
town of   (*or as the case may be*) in the county (*or* district of   ),
in which a certain public meeting was held on the said day (*or* appointed
to be held) at (*describe it*) or a constable or a special constable employed
by any of the officials aforesaid for the preservation of the public peace
at the said meeting, did unlawfully come within one mile of the place appointed for such meeting as aforesaid, armed with an offensive weapon, to
wit, a pistol (*or describe what the weapon was*).

Weapon is defined by Code 2(24).

Wilful Injuries.
Defined and Explained: Code 509 *See* Explosions, Fire.
*Add to each of the following forms a description of the particular thing
injured and how injury was done.*
*Destroying or Damaging any of the Properties Mentioned in Code
510(A).*
A.B., at   , on   , did unlawfully and wilfully, and without legal justification or excuse, and without colour of right, destroy *or*
damage certain property, to wit: (*** a dwelling-house then and there
situated, and belonging to C.D.; *or* a ship *or* boat called (*naming it*), and
belonging to C.D.; such destruction, *or* damage, being caused by an explosion, and causing actual danger to the life of C.D. (*or* E.F., *etc.*) who was
(*or* were) then in the said dwelling-house, *or* ship, *or* boat;
or
(c) * A certain bridge *or* viaduct, *or* aqueduct (*describing it*) over *or*
under which a highway *or* the   railway *or* the   canal then
and there passed. which said destruction, *or* damage, was so done by the said
A.B., and so as thereby to render the said bridge, *or* viaduct, *or* aqueduct, *or*
the said railway, *or* highway, *or* canal so passing over *or* under the same as
aforesaid (*or* a part, *etc.*), dangerous *or* impassable;
or
* A railway known as the   railway, the said damage *or* destruction being done by the said A.B. as aforesaid with the intent thereby to
render the said railway dangerous *or* impassable.

Code 510(B). (a) (*Proceed as in the above form to the**) a ship called
(*state the name*), the property of C.D., and which was then and there in
distress, *or* wrecked: or certain goods. or merchandise. or articles (*naming
them*), which belonged to a ship called   , which was then and there,
or had theretofore been in distress *or* wrecked;
or
(b)* Certain "cattle" (*see definition in Code* 2(5)), to wit. a cow then
belonging to C.D.; *or* the young of certain cattle, to wit (*a calf*), then be-

longing to C.D., which said damage was so caused as aforesaid by killing, or maiming, or poisoning, or wounding the said cow (or calf).

or

Code 510(C)* (a) A ship called (name it), with intent thereby to destroy or to render useless the said ship.

or

(b)* A mark or signal (describing it) then and there used for purposes of navigation.

or

(c)* A bank or dyke or harbour works, etc.

or

(d)* A navigable river, or canal, etc.

or

(e) * The flood gate or sluice of a private water.

or

(f) * A private fishery or salmon river belonging to C.D. and situated (describe it), which said damage was caused by the said A.B. by putting lime or a noxious material (describing what) into the water of the said private fishery with intent thereby to destroy fish then being in the said fishery, or which were then to be put into the said fishery.

or

(g)* The flood gate of a certain mill pond or reservoir or pool (describing it), the property of C.D., which said damage was caused by the said A.B. by cutting through the said flood gate, or by destroying the said flood gate by (state the means used).

or

(h)* Certain goods, to wit (state what), the property of C.D., which were then and there in process of manufacture in a certain (mill or factory, etc.), such damage being then and there done by the said A.B. with intent thereby to render the said goods useless.

or

(i)* A certain agricultural or manufacturing machine or manufacturing implement (stating what), the property of C.D., the said damage being then and there done by the said A.B. with intent thereby to render the said machine or implement useless.

or

(j)* A hop bind then and there growing in a plantation of hops of C.D., situate (describe where), or a grapevine then growing in a vineyard of C.D., situate, etc.

or

Code 510(D) (a)* A tree, or shrub, or underwood, the property of C.D., and which was then growing in a certain park, or pleasure ground, or garden, or in a certain piece of land adjoining or belonging to the dwelling of the said C.D., situate (describe): the said tree (etc.), being thereby injured to an extent exceeding in value five dollars.

(b)* A post letter bag, or post letter, the property of the Postmaster General of Canada.

or

(c)* A street letter box, or pillar box, or a certain receptable, (e.g., a letter box in the office of   Hotel, in the   of   ), then and there established by the authority of the Postmaster General of Canada for the deposit·of letters or other mailable matter.

or

(d)* A certain parcel sent by parcel post, or a package of patterns, or samples of merchandise, or goods, or of seeds, or cuttings, or bulbs, or roots, or scions, or grafts, or a printed vote or proceeding, or a newspaper, or book, or mailable matter (describing it), sent by mail, and the property of the Postmaster General of Canada.

or

(e)* Certain real or personal property (describing it), belonging to C.D., and which was then and there so damaged by the said A.B., by night, to wit, between the hours of nine o'clock in the afternoon and six o'clock in the ensuing forenoon, and to the value of twenty dollars. ("Property" defined: Code 2(32); "by night": Code 2(23).)

or

Code 510(E)* Certain real, or personal property (describing any other property than those above mentioned), of C.D., and which was then and there so damaged by the said A.B. by day to the value of twenty dollars.

Attempts to Injure or Poison Cattle: Code 536.

That A.B., on   , at   , did unlawfully and wilfully attempt to kill, or maim, or wound, or poison, or injure certain cattle, or the young of certain cattle, to wit (state what), the property of C.D.; or place poison in such a position as to be easily partaken of by certain cattle, etc., (describe where the poison was placed, e.g.) to wit, upon the grass in certain pasture in which the said cattle then were feeding (or in salt placed in a field or lane where the said cattle then were for the purpose of the same being partaken of, etc., describing the locality).

"Cattle" defined: Code 2(5).

Cattle, Threats to Injure: Code 538.

To Buildings by Tenants or Mortgagors: Code 529(a).

A.B., on   , at   , being then and there possessed of a certain dwelling-house (or other building, describing it), or part of a certain dwelling-house, etc., which was then built on land, to wit (describe the land) subject to a mortgage held thereon by C.D. (or which land was then held for a term of six months, or as the case may be, or at will, or held over after the term of a tenancy under a lease thereof to the said A.B. from C.D., the owner thereof), did unlawfully and wilfully, without legal justification or excuse, without colour of right, and to the prejudice of the said C.D.,* pull down or demolish (or begin to, etc.), the said dwelling; (state the nature of injury and how done).

or (a).

*Remove (or begin to remove) the said dwelling-house or building (or a part of, etc.) from the said land and premises on which it was so erected and built. *

or (b).

*Pull down or sever from the freehold of the said land a certain fixture, to wit (state what) then fixed in or to the said dwelling-house or building (or the said part of, etc.).

To Election Documents: Code 528.

At . on   , A.B., unlawfully and wilfully did destroy (or injure, or obliterate, or make, or cause to be made) an erasure (or addition of names or interlineations of names in or upon) a certain writ of election (or return to a writ of election, or pollbook, or voters' list, or ballot, or other document, stating what) to wit (describe), prepare and draw out according to the law in regard to Dominion (or provincial, or municipal) elections.

Rafts, Booms, Dams, etc., Wilfully Injuring: Code 525.

At   , on •   A.B., unlawfully and wilfully, did break (or injure, cut, loosen, remove, or destroy), a certain dam (or pier, or slide, or boom, or raft, or crib of timber, or sawlogs), or block up (or impede) a channel (or passage-way) intended for the transmission of timber, the property of C.D. (describe the acts by which injury or interference was done).

Mines or Oil Wells, Injury to or Interference With: Code 520.

At   , on   , A.B. did unlawfully (*a*) cause water (*or*
earth, *or* rubbish, *or* other substance, *stating it*) to be conveyed into a
certain mine, *or* well of oil;

or

(*b*) Damage the shaft (*or* a passage) of a certain mine (*or* well of
oil);

or

(*c*) Damage with intent to render useless a certain apparatus (*or*
building, *or* erection, *or* bridge, *or* road, *stating what*) belonging to a
certain mine, (*or* well of oil) by (*stating how damage done*);

or

(*d*) Hinder (*stating how*) the workings of a certain apparatus (*stating
what*) belonging to a certain mine, *or* well of oil);

or

(*e*) Damage (*or* unfasten) with intent to render useless, certain rope
(*or* chain, *or* tackle, *stating what*) used in a certain mine (*or* well of oil);
(*or* upon a certain way *or* walk, *stating what*, connected with a certain
mine (*or* well of oil);
Add in each case:
Belonging to C.D., with intent to injure (*or* obstruct the working of),
the said mine (*or* well of oil).

Witchcraft, Fortune Telling, etc., Pretending to Practice.
Code 443.
A.B., at   , on   , did unlawfully * pretend to exercise *or*
use certain witchcraft (*or* sorcery, *or* conjuration, *or* enchantment).

or

*Undertake to tell fortunes.

or

*Pretend from his pretended skill in an occult or crafty science, to wit,
(*describe*); to discover where or in what manner certain goods *or* chattels,
supposed to have been stolen (*or* lost), might be found.

Witness, Corrupting or Attempting to Corrupt.
Code 180. *See Bribery.*

Workman, Assault On.
Code 502.
At   , on   , A.B. and C.D., having before then unlawfully conspired (*or* combined) together with others to raise the rate of
wages in a certain trade (business *or* manufacture), to wit (*state what*) did,
then and there, in pursuance of said conspiracy, unlawfully make an assault
upon (*or* use violence, *or* threats of violence to) E.F. with a view to hinder
him from working (*or* being employed) at such trade (business *or* manufacture).

Wounding.
With Intent: Code 273.
A.B., at   , on   , with intent to maim (*or* to disfigure, *or*
to disable) C.D. (*or* with intent to resist the lawful apprehension of the
said A.B. (*or* of one E.F. by C.D.) under a lawful warrant legally authorizing such apprehension) did * unlawfully wound (*or* cause grievous
bodily harm) to him, the said C.D., by (*stating how wound was inflicted*).
or *Code* 273.

*Unlawfully shoot at the said C.D. (*or* attempt, *describing how*, to
discharge a loaded pistol *or* gun, at the said C.D.).
Unlawfully Wounding: Code 274.

A.B., at   , on   , did unlawfully wound (*or* inflict grievous bodily harm upon) C.D. by (*state how*).

A Public Officer While on Duty: Code 275 (b).

A.B., on   , at   , did unlawfully maim (*or* wound) C.D. who was then and there a public officer, to wit, an Inspector of the Inland Revenue of the Dominion of Canada (*or as the case may be*) he, the said C.D., being then and there engaged in the execution of his duty as such officer, by (*state how wound was inflicted*).

or

Did unlawfully wound E.F., a person acting in aid of a public officer (*beginning and ending as in the preceding form*).

CHAPTER XIII.

Summary Convictions by Justices.

In What Cases.

The jurisdiction of a justice to convict and punish for offences against the law, is limited to those matters in regard to which some statute, either expressly or by necessary implication, gives him that authority: R. v. Craig, 21 U.C.R. 552; R. v. Carter, 5 O.R. 651. For instance, if a statute provides that a person who does something prohibited by law, shall be guilty of an offence, and upon summary conviction before a justice (or two or more justices) of the peace, may be fined or imprisoned; this expressly gives jurisdiction. If, however, the statute says that such person is liable to punishment on summary conviction (not saying by whom) it necessarily means by a justice of the peace, and his jurisdiction is implied: Cullen v. Trimble, L.R. 7 Q.B. 416.

A justice cannot convict a person for an indictable offence; but is merely to hold a preliminary enquiry as described in the last preceding chapter.

In the "Synopsis of Offences, Summary Convictions" at the end of this chapter, many examples are given of those offences for which the justice may summarily convict an offender; while examples of those in regard to which he is to hold a "preliminary enquiry," are stated in Chapter XII. under "Synopsis of Indictable Offences."

See *ante*, p. 196 on the question of jurisdiction in cases under consideration.

Offences Under Dominion Statutes.

A justice has authority to convict for any offences over which the Parliament of Canada has legislative authority (such as offences under the Criminal Code), and for which by the particular statute or clause a person offending is declared to be liable on summary conviction, to punishment: Code 706 (*a*); and also in those matters in which the justice is given power to make an order for the payment of money, or for the performance of some act: Code 706 (*b*).

Offences Under Provincial Statutes.

Justices have authority also under provincial statutes, *e.g.*, under the Ontario Summary Convictions Act, R.S.O. ch. 90, to summarily convict for breaches of provincial statutes and of by-laws or regulations passed under municipal Acts, regulations of boards of health, or of liquor license commissioners, etc., by which penalties are imposed.

Territorial Jurisdiction.

Except in the special cases stated in p. 189, *et seq.*, *ante*, the offence in regard to which the justice assumes to act summarily, must have been committed within the justice's county or territory. He has no authority to convict for an offence committed in another county: for an example of this, see: R. v. Dowling, 17 O.R. 698.

Place Where the Justice is to Act.

He must perform all *judicial* acts within his county or territorial jurisdiction as defined by his commission; but he may perform merely *ministerial* acts anywhere: Paley on Convictions, 8th ed. 19; R. v. Beemer, 15 O.R. 266; Langwith v. Dawson, 30 U.C.C.P. 375.

Taking an information is a ministerial act, and may be done anywhere; but issuing a summons or warrant of arrest and trying a case are judicial acts, and must be done within the justice's county.

A judicial act is one in which the justice is to exercise a judicial discretion to do it or not, according to the rights of the matter; while a merely ministerial act is one which he is to perform as a matter of course. See further as to this, *ante* p. 205.

In What Cases Two Justices are Required.

One justice sitting alone, has complete jurisdiction, unless the statute relating to the particular offence requires that there shall be two or more justices: Code 707; but if two justices are required a conviction by one is invalid: R. v. Plows, 26 O.R. 339. If two or more justices are required by the particular statute, they must all be present and act together during the whole of the hearing and determination of the case: Code 708 (4). Two justices have authority to try without consent of the defendant, an offence under Code 169, of resisting or wilfully obstructing

22—MAG. MAN.

a peace officer in the execution of his duty or any one assisting him; or any person lawfully executing process against lands or goods or making a distress: R. v. Jack, 5 Can. Cr. Cas. 304.

In the "Synopsis of Offences—Summary Convictions," at the end of this chapter, it is noted at the end of the forms, when two justices are required; when not so noted, one justice suffices. But in any case several justices may sit together, with the consent of the justice who is first seized of the case, but not otherwise: see *ante*, p. 209.

If any one of two or more justices, sitting together in any case, should be absent during any part of the taking of the evidence or hearing, he must not act in the determination of the case.

In those cases in which the particular statute requires two justices to *hear* the case, one justice may receive the information and issue the process against the accused, and summon the witnesses and do everything preparatory to the hearing: Code 708; but the hearing must take place before at least two justices.

If, however, the statute relating to the offence requires the *prosecution to be brought* and not merely the *hearing* to take place (before at least two justices) both justices must be present together when the information (which is the *bringing* of the prosecution), is laid; and both justices must be named in the information and stated to be present together; but the information need only be *signed* by one of them: R. v. Ettinger, 3 Can. Cr. Cas. 387; R. v. Brown, 23 N.S.R. 21; Ex p. White, 3 Can. Cr. Cas. 94.

A police, stipendiary or district magistrate is an *ex officio* justice of the peace; and has the authority of two justices sitting together; and so may convict in any case in which one or more justices has the authority: Code 604: See *ante*, p. 198.

Procedure.

By section 711 of the Criminal Code the procedure in summary convictions cases (concerning the compelling of the appearance of the accused before the justice, receiving an information, and respecting the attendance of witnesses, and the taking of evidence), is to be the same as that provided for preliminary enquiries for indictable offences which has been fully described in the next preceding chapter. The Ontario Summary Convictions Act: R.S.O. ch. 90, as amended by Ontario statute, 1 Edw.

VII· ch. 13 sec. 1, provides that the procedure in the trials of offences against Ontario statutes, by-laws, etc., is to be the same as that provided by the Criminal Code. So the procedure described in the foregoing chapter XII., is that to be followed throughout in all cases, except when otherwise specified in following remarks.

Summary convictions cases are of two classes:—

1. Those in which an order may be made for the payment of money merely; or for the performance of some act.

2. Penal offences, in which by some statute it is provided that the justice may summarily convict and punish the offender: Code 710 (2).

The Information.

In the first mentioned class the complaint need not be in writing, unless it is so required by some particular Act upon which the complaint is founded and if only a summons is to be issued: Code 710.

In the second class of cases the information need not be on oath or affirmation unless so required by some particular statute relating to the offence: Code 710 (2) ; but *it must be in writing*. But a warrant of arrest is never to be issued in any case unless the information is under oath, notwithstanding the provisions of Code 710 (2) ; as the recital in the form of warrant—6 to the Criminal Code—states that an information under oath has been laid: R. v. McDonald, 3 Can. Cr. Cas. 287.

And if the particular statute on which the case is founded, specially requires it, the information must be under oath; and in *all cases* it is a proper safeguard to require any person, who charges another with an offence, to pledge his oath to the *bona fides* of the charge.

When an accused is brought before a justice under a statute which requires a sworn information and the justice thereupon amends the information in the presence of both parties, it should be re-sworn; but if that is not done and no objection thereto is taken it is waived: R. v. Lewis, 6 Can. Cr. Cas. at p. 504.

For forms of oaths and affirmations, and the different modes of administering the same, see *ante*, p. 279.

By Whom Information May be Laid.

The complaint may be laid by the informant himself or by his solicitor or by anyone by his authority: Code 710 (4).

As a general rule any person may lay the information; but in cases of private injuries being constituted, by some statute, the subject of a criminal charge, as in cases of wilful injuries to private property (see "Synopsis of Summary Convictions Offences" *post*), the party aggrieved or someone authorized by him must be the complainant. And when an act (such as a trespass to private property under the Petty Trespass Act, R. S.O. ch. 120, see "Synopsis of Offences" *post*) must, in order to be unlawful, have been done against the consent of the person aggrieved, the information must be laid by the owner of the property or person aggrieved, or on his behalf and at his instance: Paley, 8th ed. 81 (*c*); notes 7 Can. Cr. Cas. 218; R. v. Frankforth, 8 Can. Cr. Cas. 57; Robinson v. Currey, L.R. 7 Q.B.D. 465. A complaint against a tenant for fraudulent removal of property, or for wilful injury to the premises, must be laid by the landlord, or by his authority: Paley, 8th ed. 81 (*d*); and in all cases when the particular statute so expressly provides, the information must be laid by the party aggrieved or his agent.

Any person may prosecute summarily for infraction of a municipal by-law (or of the Ontario Health Act) even if the whole penalty goes to the municipality: R. v. Chipman, 1 Can. Cr. Cas. 81.

Against Whom Information to be Laid.

Generally it must be laid against the person who actually commits the act complained of. But in some cases the charge must be laid against the employer and not against the servant who is following his employer's instructions and acting within the scope of his authority; as in the case of locomotives being used on highways, without the precautions required by law; in such case the employer is the person liable, and not the man running it: R. v. Toronto Ry. Co., 30 O.R. 214; Re Chapman & London, 19 O.R. 33; R. v. T. Eaton Co., 29 O.R. 591; Consumer's Gas Co. v. Toronto, 23 A.R. 551; R. v. Verral, 18 O.R. 117.

A master is liable for the act of his servant when the latter is acting within the scope of his authority, even if the particular act was done contrary to the master's orders: R. v. McAuley, 14 O.R. 649; Commissioners v. Cartman (1896), 1 Q.B. 655; R. v. Stephens, L.R. 1 Q.B. 702. But not so in cases in which *mens rea* is an essential ingredient of the offence: Chisholm v. Doulton, 22 Q.B.D. p. 741, see also *ante*, p. 226.

Informations Against Several Defendants.

Any number of defendants may be joined in one information and conviction for an offence in which they are jointly engaged. "Where the offence is in its nature single and cannot be severed, then the penalty shall only be single; because though several persons may join in the commission of it, it still constitutes but one offence. But where the offence is in its nature several, and so every person concerned may be separately guilty of it, then each offender is separately liable to the whole penalty; because the crime of each is distinct from that of the others, and each is punishable for his own crime": Lord Mansfield, C.J., in R. v. Clarke, Cowper, p. 610. So for example, if two or more persons jointly pack for exportation one or more barrels of apples, otherwise than in accordance with the provisions of "The Inspection and Sale Act": R.S.C. ch. 85, sec. 323, they may be jointly prosecuted; but there is only one offence and only one penalty of 25 cents per barrel, (sec. 330) can be imposed, and not a penalty of 25 cents per barrel against each defendant. It is, of course, improper to join two persons in one proceeding if the offence charged against one of them has nothing to do with that charged against the other: R. v. Hagerman, 31 O.R. 637.

An assault by two persons upon the same party may be charged and punished as separate offences, or may be joined in one charge: Re Brighton (Mag.), 9 T.L.R. 522. Whether or not the offence is a joint one, if two or more persons are joined in the one proceeding, each defendant must be made separately liable for his own fine and costs only: Morgan v. Brown, 4 A. & E. 515; R. v. Cridland, 7 E. & B. 853. A conviction is invalid if it awards one fine against different persons: Gault v. Ellice, 6 Can. Cr. Cas. 15; R. v. Sutton, 42 U.C.R. at p. 224; Re Rice, 20 N.S.R. 294; R. v. Ambrose, 16 O.R. 251.

Corporations

Are liable to summary conviction: R. v. Toronto Railway Co., 30 O.R. 214, 2 Can. Cr. Cas. 481; but a justice or magistrate cannot compel a corporation to appear before him in respect of an indictable offence: Re Chapman v. London, 19 O.R. 33; R. v. T. Eaton Co., 2 Can. Cr. Cas. 252 and notes at p. 254, 482. In a summary conviction case service is made by issuing a summons and serving (not the summons but) a notice,

on the mayor or chief officer or secretary of the corporation: R.
v. Toronto Railway Co., *supra;* Newby v. Colt, L.R. 7 Q.B. 293.
The punishment upon conviction of a corporation can only be
by fine, and can only be enforced by distress: R. v. Toronto Railway Co., *supra.* See, also, R. v. Union Colliery Co., 3 Can. Cr.
Cas. 523; s.c., 31 Can. S.C.R. 81, as to the liability of coropora-
tions. A corporation cannot be charged with an offence of which
mens rea is an ingredient: R. v. G. W. Laundry Co., 3 Can. Cr.
Cas. 514.

FORM OF NOTICE.

Canada.
Province of Ontario. }   *The King* v. *The (name the corporation).*
County of Huron.

    To C.D., chief officer (*or* secretary) of the (*name of corporation*).

    Take notice that upon the information of A.B., of   , a sum-
mons was on the   day of   , 19 , duly issued by the
undersigned, a justice of the peace in and for the County of   ,
against the above named (*name of corporation*), requiring the said (*name
of corporation*) to appear before me on the   day of   ,
19 , at   in the   of   in the County of   ,
at the hour of   o'clock   noon, to answer to the charge
that (*here set out the charge as laid in the information*).

    And take notice that unless the said (*name of corporation*) appears
before me at the said time and place and pleads to the said charge I shall
proceed with the summary trial thereof as if the said (*name of corporation*)
had duly appeared.

    Dated at   this   day of   , 19
                                            J.P., County of

Description of the Offence.

The "Synopsis of Offences—Summary Convictions," at the
end of this chapter contains forms of charges to be inserted in
informations.

An information need not allege that the offence was "against
the form of the statute," or mention the statute: R. v. Doyle,
2 Can. Cr. Cas. 335.

It is sufficient if the description of the offence is given in the
words of the statute or by-law relating to the offence, or any
similar words: Code 723 (3). See *ante,* p. 240⁻ as to what is
necessary in this regard.

If the statement of the offence in the proceedings does not
furnish sufficient information to the defendant, the justice may
order fuller particulars in writing to be furnished to him: Code
723 (2).

Only One Offence to be Charged.

Code 710 (3). The information must be for only one distinct and definite offence: R. v. Mabey, 37 U.C.R. 248. If it should happen that more than one offence is charged in the information, and objection is taken on that ground, the justice should call upon the prosecutor to elect which charge he will proceed with, and all but one charge should be struck out, the information being amended accordingly: R. v. Alward, 25 O.R. 519. This must be done before proceeding with the evidence otherwise the conviction for one is void, *ibid.* But otherwise if no objection was made at the time: R. v. Hazen, 20 A.R. 633. In The King v. Austin, 10 Can. Cr. Cas. 34, an objection of this kind was overruled by the justice and he proceeded to take evidence upon the several charges in the information until the conclusion of the prosecutor's case, when all were abandoned except one; the conviction upon that one was quashed by the court on appeal. And where two offences were charged and a conviction made, and one penalty was imposed, but the conviction did not shew for which offence, the conviction was held to be bad, as it could not be pleaded on any subsequent charge for either of the offences: R. v. Young, 5 O.R. 184 (*a*). But in R. v. Hazen, 20 O.R. 633, the Ont. Court of Appeal held that a charge of two offences under the Liquor License Act did not invalidate a conviction for one of the offences.

A conviction for unlawfully distilling spirits and making or fermenting beer without a license is for only one offence, committed in one of several ways, and is good under Code 723, 724: R. v. McDonald, 6 Can. Cr. Cas. 1.

But a conviction for procuring or attempting to procure, etc., is for two offences in the alternative and bad: R. v. Gibson, 2 Can. Cr. Cas. 302. A conviction for carrying on business as a land and insurance agent without a license is for two offences: R. v. Simpson & Lock, 7 Can. Cr. Cas. 294. A charge of stealing "in or from" a building, is one offence: R. v. Patrick White, 4 Can. Cr. Cas. 430.

A charge for a continuing offence, *e.g.*, that the defendant kept a disorderly house on a certain day, "and on other days and times before that day" being for one offence, was regular: R. v. Williams, 37 U.C.R. 540; Olney v. Gee, 30 L.J.M.C. 222. And see Ex p. Hopper, 27 N.B.R. 496; R. v. Whiffin, 4 Can. Cr. Cas. 141. A charge that the defendant was the keeper

or inmate of a disorderly house is bad: R. v. Farrar, 1 Terr. L.R.
308.   But a charge of being a keeper of a disorderly house,
bawdy house, or house of ill-fame or house for the resort of
prostitutes, is not void either for duplicity or uncertainty; and
was valid as following the words of the statute: R. v. LeConte,
11 Can. Cr. Cas. 41.   See also Ex p. Greaves, 26 N.B.R. 437.

A charge of selling or giving liquor to an Indian is for one
offence only: R. v. Monoghan, 34 C.L.J. 55; or for several acts
on the same day in practising as an apothecary without a certificate: Oxford v. Sankey, 5 J.P. 52, 564; Davis v. Leach, 51 J.P.
118; Bartholomew v. Wiseman, 56 J.P. 455.

The justice should be careful that the information is laid
for one distinct offence; and that the conviction if any is for
that offence only: R. v. Farrar, 1 Terr. L.R. 308.   It must appear
on the face of the information that the offence was committed
within the justice's territorial jurisdiction.   The information
should state, the place where it was laid; the name and style of
the justice before whom it was laid; and a sufficient statement
of the offence charged, with date and place and the name and
description of the offender.

No information or warrant is to be deemed insufficient for
any of the defects or objections mentioned in Code 723, 724.

Nor to charge two offences or be uncertain for any of the
causes mentioned in Code 725.

Amendment of Information.

An information if found defective may be amended at any
time during the progress of the case.   The form of information
is to be the same as Form 3 in the Criminal Code.   If amended
the information should be re-sworn, if the statute requires a
sworn information; but not otherwise, and if it is not done and
no objection is taken it is waived: R. v. Lewis, 6 Can. Cr. Cas. p.
504.

Issuing Summons or Warrant of Arrest.

Upon receiving the information the justice will proceed in
the manner described in preliminary enquiries in indictable
offences, *ante* p. 246, He must first enquire into the facts of the
case as stated by the complainant and any other persons present
(taking their statements on oath, unless the sworn information
discloses sufficient facts to justify further proceedings: R. v.

Lizotte, 10 Can. Cr. Cas. 316). This must be done in order to ascertain whether the facts justify proceeding with the case; and in considering the information, etc., he should take into consideration the matters stated in chapter IX.; such as, whether the time for prosecution has expired or not, etc.

If the justice finds that the facts justify his proceeding with the case he will issue a summons or warrant; see *ante* p. 247, as to whether a summons or a warrant is to be issued.

The summons or warrant must be issued by the justice who took the information and cannot be issued by any other justice; but the case may be heard and determined by him, or by any other justice who acts with his consent, not otherwise. Any justice may take the information and issue the summons or warrant and another justice may hear the case and convict: Code 654, 664, 708.

Proceedings on Sundays and Holidays.

As to this see the remarks, *ante*, p. 213.

Execution of Warrants of Arrest.

The observations and information, *ante*, p. 250, *et seq.*, apply to these proceedings; and also to "backing warrants," for execution in another county, *ante*, p. 250, detention of person pending the hearing; serving summonses and procuring the attendance of witnesses; remands, bail and all other proceedings preliminary to the hearing: Code 711.

Attendance of Parties Before the Justice.

Upon a summary trial the prosecutor need not attend personally; nor can the defendant be compelled to attend personally if only a *summons* has been served; it is sufficient if they appear by counsel, attorney or agent: Code 720; Bissell v. Wilson, 1 E. & B. 488. If at the time named in the summons, the justice should be engaged in other official business, the defendant who has been summoned must wait: R. v. Wipper, 5 Can. Cr. Cas. 17. But a justice has no right to adjourn or delay the hearing to suit his personal convenience.

Warrant on Non-appearance of Defendant.

If the accused (after being served with a summons) does not appear either personally or by his counsel or agent, the jus-

tice may either proceed to hear the case, in his absence: Code
718; Denault v. Robida, 8 Can. Cr. Cas. 501; or he may issue
a warrant for his arrest: Code 718, Form 7, Criminal Code;
but before doing so the evidence, orally or by affidavit, of the
constable who served the summons must be taken on oath,
shewing to the satisfaction of the justice that the summons was
duly served: R. v. Levesque, 8 Can. Cr. Cas. 505. Code 711, 712,
provide that the proceedings to compel the appearance of the
accused are to be the same as in preliminary enquiries: as to
which see *ante*, p. 250, *et seq.*, and follow the directions there.

If a summons is issued it must be served a reasonable time
before that appointed for the hearing: Code 718; and what is a
reasonable time depends upon the circumstances of each particular case. In R. v. Eli, 10 O.R. 727, the summons was served very
shortly before the sittings of the court, the justices refused to
adjourn and convicted the defendant; the conviction was quashed by the High Court as being contrary to natural justice.
Where a summons was served on defendant's wife at his residence at 11.30 p.m., returnable the next day at 10 a.m., at a
place 25 miles distant, and the defendant being absent did not
get the summons till the next forenoon, the conviction was
quashed: Re O'Brien, 10 Can. Cr. Cas. 142. In R. v. Smith,
L.R. 10 Q.B. 604, a summons was served on the defendant's wife
on 10th March for trial on 12th March, the defendant being at
the time at sea as a fisherman, and only returned after the justice had convicted him, and it was held that the summons had
not been served a reasonable time. In that case Cockburn, C.J.,
said: "To convict a person unheard is a dangerous exercise of
power, there being the alternative of issuing a warrant to arrest.
Justices ought to be very cautious how they proceed in the defendant's absence, unless they have very strong grounds for believing that the summons reached him, and that he was wilfully
disobeying it." Service in the morning of, or evening before,
the trial is not sufficient in any case: Ex p. Cowan, 9 Can. Cr.
Cas. at p. 457, and cases mentioned therein.

In the absence of the defendant and of the clearest evidence
to satisfy the justice, not only that someone was duly served for
the defendant, but also stating circumstances to shew that the
summons has without doubt reached him, the justice should adjourn the hearing, and either serve another summons or issue a
warrant to arrest: which may be executed as described, *ante*, p.

250. See also notes on this subject in 4 Can. Cr. Cas. 466, and 10 Can. Cr. Cas. 130. But if it is clear that the defendant is aware of the proceedings and is wilfully absenting himself, the justice may proceed and hear the case in his absence. Code 718 gives the justice authority to adopt either of these courses. If he proceeds in the defendant's absence he can only deal with the case as stated in the information and the summons served, and no material amendment or change can be made in them, so as to charge any separate and distinct offence from that for which the summons was issued: Ex p. Doherty, 1 Can. Cr. Cas. 84; R. v. Grant, 34 C.L.J. 171; R. v. Lyons, 10 Can. Cr. Cas. 130, in which it was held that a conviction in the defendant's absence after substitutional service, for unlawfully keeping liquor for sale, when the information and summons were laid in the first place for a charge of illegally selling liquor was bad. The justice must take the evidence and hear the case with the same formality in defendant's absence as if he was present, and cannot convict without sufficient evidence; the defendant does not confess the offence by failing to appear: Paley 114. See also, *ante* p. 249 for further observations applicable also to summary proceedings in regard to the question, what is sufficient service of summons.

As a justice has no jurisdiction over a defendant who is at the time personally out of the country, a summons served substitutionally during that time, is of no effect; and a justice cannot proceed in the defendant's absence even if service of the summons has been made on someone at his residence: Ex p. Donovan, 3 Can. Cr. Cas. 286; Ex p. Fleming, 14 C.L.T. 106; and see cases noted in 4 Can. Cr. Cas. 466.

If the defendant appears personally or by counsel, but the prosecutor, after due notice, does not appear either personally or by his agent, the justice may dismiss the case with or without costs, as he may see fit: Code 719, 722 (2), (3); or he may adjourn the case to some other day upon such terms as he thinks fit; e.g., he may order the complainant to pay the costs of the day, including the expenses of the defendant and his witnesses in attending: Code 719.

FORM OF NOTICE TO PROSECUTOR.

The King, on information of *A.B.* v. *C.D.* for (*state the charge*).
You, the above-mentioned prosecutor, A.B., are required to take notice that the hearing of the case above mentioned before the undersigned will take place at   in the   of   in the County of

, at the hour of   o'clock   noon on the   day of
A.D. 19 . And in default of your appearing either personally or by your
solicitor or agent at the said time and place, the case may be dismissed
with costs against you, or may be proceeded with in your absence.

Dated this   day of   A.D. 19 .
                                        E.F., justice of the peace,
                                        County of

It must be proved that this notice has been given in due time,
manner and form, before proceeding in the complainant's absence under this section: Code 719.

If the Prosecutor Does Not Appear After Due Notice,

The justice instead of dismissing it may proceed to try the
case and dispose of it; but if the prosecutor is a necessary witness the case may be adjourned, and the prosecutor may be summoned as a witness, and compelled to attend, by the same process as an ordinary witness: Ex p. Bryant, 27 J.P. 277; see, *ante*,
p. 216 as to the proceedings to compel the attendance of witnesses.

If Neither of the Parties Appear Personally,

Or by solicitor, the justice may, if he sees fit, proceed as if
they were both present: Code 722 (2); Paley 112; and may hear
the evidence, if any is offered, and may convict the accused
and award punishment, proceeding with the same formality as if
trying the case in the presence of the parties; or he may dismiss
the case with or without costs against the prosecutor: Code
722 (3).

If Both Parties Appear,

Either personally or by their solicitor, the justice will proceed
to try the case in the manner described in the following pages.
The place in which the justice hears the case is an open public
court and the general public must have access to same so far as
the place can conveniently contain them: Code 714. If the
place become so overcrowded as to inconvenience or interfere
with reasonable comfort or convenience in conducting the case,
the justice may exclude all but a reasonable number of spectators.
See, however, the provisions of Code 644, 645.

Rights of Parties to Counsel.

The defendant must be allowed to make his full answer
or defence, and to have the fullest opportunity to cross-examine

witnesses by himself or his counsel or agent: Code 715. The complainant also has the right to conduct the case and to have all witnesses examined and cross-examined by counsel or solicitor on his behalf: Code 715 (2).

The Hearing, Defects and Objections to Proceedings.

As to defects and objections to the information, warrant or other proceedings taken anterior to the hearing, see Code 723, 724, 725.

While a justice has no authority to issue a warrant or summons without an information or complaint having been first properly laid before him, and he will be liable to an action for false imprisonment, if he issues a warrant without such information and the warrant may be set aside and the defendant released on habeas corpus if arrested under such a warrant: McGuiness v. Dafoe, 27 O.R. 121, 23 A.R. 704.

Still a defect in the information, or even the absence of any information, will be waived by the defendant appearing and allowing the proceedings to go on without objection: R. v. Clarke, 20 O.R. 642; R. v. Berry, 8 Cox C.C. 121; R. v. Simmonds, 8 Cox C.C. 190; Eggington v. Pearl, 33 L.T. 428; Paley, 7th ed., 109; R. v. Shaw, 10 Cox C.C. 66; R. v. Fletcher, L.R. 1 C.C. 320; R. v. Cinque Ports (Jus.), 17 Q.B.D. 191; Peck v. De Rutzen, 46 J.P. 313.

"If the defendant be present at the time of the proceeding, and heard all the evidence, and does not ask for further time to bring forward his defence, this has at all times been deemed sufficient": R. v. Stone, 1 East 639, followed in R. v. Bennett, 3 O.R. 45, in which an information for one offence was changed to another in the defendant's presence, and he was held to be rightly convicted of the latter: see also R. v. Smith, L.R. 1 C.C. 110; R. v. Crouch, 35 U.C.R. 433; R. v. Widdup, L.R. 2 C.C. 3; Stoness v. Lake, 40 U.C.R. 320; Dom. Coal Co. v. Kingswall, 30 N.S.R. 397.

Even if the summons or warrant is illegally issued and void, as being issued without any information being laid, or if the defendant appears without any proceedings, whether voluntarily or under arrest without a warrant (and, it is said, even if the defendant appeared by counsel, only for the purpose of objecting to the insufficiency of the service of the summons: R. v. Doherty, (S.C.N.B.) 3 Can. Cr. Cas. 508), the justice has the right to proceed with the case. The leading case of R. v. Hughes, 4 Q.B.D. 614, establishes that, when a person is before a justice who has jurisdiction over the subject matter, it is not essential to a valid trial that he should enquire how the defendant came there, but he may proceed to try the case. The only conditions essential to a valid trial are, (1) the presence of the accused, no matter by what means, and (2) the justice's jurisdiction over the offence. The information or warrant are merely means of bringing the accused before the justice, and have nothing to do with the latter's jurisdiction to try the case, and a conviction will be valid, even if the defendant objects. The case of R. v. Hughes has been followed in Re Maltby, 7 Q.B.D. 18; R. v. Shaw, 10 Cox 66; Gray v. Commissioners of Customs, 48 J.P. 343; R. v. Roe, 16 O.R. 3; R. v. Clarke, 20 O.R. 642; R. v. Stone, 23 O.R. 46; Ex p. Sonier, (S.C.N.B.) 2 Can. Cr. Cas. 121; R. v. Ettinger, 3 Can. Cr. Cas. 387.

But in some cases the particular statute expressly requires an information to be laid as a condition precedent to the justice's jurisdiction: see R. v. Millard, 22 L.J.M.C. 108; and it may be that the proper proceedings to give jurisdiction have not been taken within the time or in the manner required by law; and if, in such case, the defendant distinctly objects on that ground, the justice would have no right to proceed without a properly sworn information and process, and if he does so, the conviction will be quashed: Dixon v. Wells, 25 Q.B.D. 249; R. v. McNutt, 3 Can. Cr. Cas. 184; see also Blake v. Beech, 1 Ex D. 320; and the conviction will be void if there was no summons and the defendant was not informed of the charge and was not given time to defend, if requested: R. v. Hopkins, 56 J.P. 263.

A defendant cannot be charged and tried for one offence, and convicted of another, even if the evidence shews that he was guilty of the latter; and where a defendant was brought up on an information and process for an indictable offence, and the evidence shewed that he was not guilty of it but was guilty of another offence which the justice could try summarily, and he was thereupon convicted of the latter, the conviction was quashed, the evidence not having been directed to the charge, nor the defendant put upon his defence for it: R. v. Mines, 25 O.R. 577, 1 Can. Cr. Cas. 217; R. v. Lee, 2 Can. Cr. Cas. 233; Miller v. Lea, 2 Can. Cr. Cas. 282.

And a justice has no jurisdiction to take up unexpectedly a charge against a person whom he chances to find in his presence: R. v. Vrooman, 3 Man. R. 509; referred to in 2 Can. Cr. Cas. p. 93.

By Code 724, none of the defects there mentioned are valid objections to any information or other proceeding, but if the justice deems it necessary to a fair trial, he is to order further particulars as to the charge, to be furnished to supply such defects. See further, *ante*, p. 257 where the subjects above mentioned are also referred to.

Juvenile Offenders.

If the accused seems to be under the age of 16 years, he must be dealt with differently from an older person, and under the laws relating to "Juvenile Offenders," as to which see, *post* Chapter XV., where the proceedings to be taken are set out, and see Code 779.

The Proceeding on the Hearing.

The justice in the first place is to state to the accused or his counsel or solicitor, the substance of the information (usually by reading it to him), and he is to be asked if he has anything to say why the accused should not be convicted (that is whether he pleads guilty or not guilty to the charge); or why the order asked for by the complainant should not be made: Code 721.

Exclusion of the Public.

The room or place where the trial takes place is an open public court in which the public have the right of access so far as the same can conveniently contain them: Code 714. But the trials of young persons under 16 years of age are to be held without publicity: see "Juvenile Offenders," Chapter XV And the justice may in other cases exclude the public if in the interest of public morals: Code 645.

Plea of Guilty.

If the defendant, either personally or through his agent or solicitor or counsel, admits the truth of the information, and shews no sufficient cause why he should not be convicted, the justice will then proceed to convict him or make the order against him: Code 721 (2).

But if the accused is not personally present the justice should require written authority to enter a plea of guilty offered on the defendant's behalf by any other person, and this extends to his counsel or solicitor appearing for him: Ex p. Gale, 35 C.L.J. 464.

Plea of Not Guilty,

If the accused does not admit the charge, the justice will proceed to take the evidence: Code 721 (3).

Procuring Attendance of Witnesses and Taking of Evidence.— Witnesses in Canada.

The proceedings will be the same as in preliminary enquiries: Code 711, 721 (3). These are described at pp. 264, *et seq., ante,* with this difference that in summary convictions cases the summons to witness may be served on a witness (and a warrant on default may be executed) anywhere in Canada, and by a constable or "any other person" to whom it may be entrusted for service, or to whom the warrant of arrest may be directed: Code 713. A witness in summary convictions cases cannot be arrested unless witness fees have been prepaid or tendered to him, differing in this respect from preliminary enquiries in indictable offences: R. v. Chisholm, 6 Can. Cr. Cas. 493. It should also be shewn that the witness was a material one.

Witnesses Out of Canada.

A commission may be issued by the High Court or County Court to take evidence out of Canada, but only with the leave of the Attorney-General, first obtained: Code 716 (2).

Taking the Evidence.

The evidence for both parties is to be taken on oath or affirmation (and it is to be taken in writing in all cases, otherwise a conviction upon it will be invalid: Denault v. Robida, 8 Can. Cr. Cas. 501; but see, *contra,* Ex p. Doherty, 3 Can. Cr. Cas. 310; Re Stanboro, 1 Mod. R. 325; Ex p. Danaher, 27 N.B.R. 554; R. v. McGregor, 10 Can. Cr. Cas. 313) and it is to be taken in the same manner as in preliminary enquiries, described, *ante,* p. 277: Code 721 (3), 716.

The evidence for the prosecutor is taken first, followed by the evidence for the defence, after which the prosecutor is entitled to offer further evidence in reply if he sees fit; but no evidence in reply can be given on the part of the prosecutor if the only evidence offered for the accused, was as to his general character; if evidence on the merits is given on behalf of the accused, then evidence for the prosecutor may be received in reply: Code 721 (4). No new matter can be so introduced by the prosecutor without the justice's leave, but only such as tends to explain any new matter arising in the evidence for the defence. If, however, new evidence is permitted by the justice, the defendant is entitled to cross-examine and adduce evidence to meet it, if he so desires.

Evidence Negativing Exceptions or Conditions in the Statute.
See Code 717.

Cross-Examination of Witnesses.
Each party has the right to fully cross-examine the opposing witnesses: Code 715. If called as a witness the prosecutor is not bound to disclose on cross-examination the source of the information on which he laid the charge; for his answers to such questions would not tend either to prove or disprove the charge, and are irrelevant; unless it clearly appears to be necessary in the interests of the elucidation of the truth of the charge or defence: R. v. Sproule, 14 O.R. 375.

As to the scope of the cross-examination of the prosecutor who gives evidence, and also of the defendant, if called as a witness on his own behalf, see the above case of R. v. Sproule, and R. v. D'Aoust, 5 Can. Cr. Cas. 407, 413, where the subject is fully treated: R. v. Grinder, 10 Can. Cr. Cas. 333.

Witnesses for the Defence.
All witnesses for the defence as well as for the prosecution must be allowed to give evidence: Code 715.

As to evidence generally, see *ante,* Chapter VI.

Taking Evidence in Shorthand.
The same proceedings will be taken in that event as are provided for preliminary enquiries and as described *ante* p. 278.

Adjournments and Remands
Are provided for by Code 722; and see also observations *ante* at p. 258 as to these, and as to the taking of recognizances

23—MAG. MAN.

for defendant's appearance or his remand to jail; estreating such recognizances on defendant's failing to appear, and issuing warrant for his arrest.

An adjournment on a summary trial cannot be for longer than "eight days" at any one time, differing in this respect from adjournments on preliminary enquiries, which may be for eight *clear* days: see p. 259. There will be one day less maximum time of adjournment in a summary trial case. If the defendant expressly consents to allow a longer adjournment than eight days he cannot afterwards object: R. v. Heffernan, 13 O.R. 616; R. v. Hazen, 20 A.R. 633. In computing the eight days the day of the adjournment is excluded and the day of the adjourned hearing is included: R. v. Collins, 14 O.R. 613. There may be several adjournments from time to time as the interests of justice may require: Code 722; Messinger v. Parker, 18 N.S.R. 257; but they must be for good and sufficient reasons. A justice has no right to adjourn and remand the accused to custody merely to suit his own personal convenience; and he would be liable in trespass for so doing. He must either go on with the case himself or direct that the accused be taken before another justice for trial: Gray v. Customs Commissioners, 48 J.P. 343.

One justice may adjourn the case, although the statute requires two justices to hear it: R. v. Manary, 19 O.R. 691. The time and place to which the adjournment is made must be stated in the presence and hearing of both parties or their counsel then ' present. And the adjournment must be made by the justice, and not in his absence by his clerk: Paré v. Recorder of Montreal, 10 Can. Cr. Cas. 295. After an adjournment if the defendant does not appear at the time and place to which the case was adjourned the justice may proceed in his absence: Denault v. Robida, 8 Can. Cr. Cas. 501; but only on the charge for which the defendant was summoned for or charged with when he appeared before the justice.

Hearing of Argument.

At the conclusion of the evidence for both parties, the justice must hear what each party or his counsel or solicitor has to say: Code 715, 726.

Adjudication.

After considering the whole matter the justice is to proceed to determine the case, and either dismiss it, or convict, or make the order against the defendant: Code 726; or he may allow the case to be withdrawn, in a proper case; Ex p. Wiseman, 5 Can. Cr. Cas. 58. The justice may adjourn the matter to consider his judgment, but must in the presence and hearing of both parties, fix a time and place to announce his adjudication. He cannot adjourn *sine die*, and then give judgment in the absence of either of the parties, without previous notice to them; a conviction so made will be invalid: Therrien v. McEchren, 4 Rev. de Jur. 87. The parties have the right to be present when the decision is given, in order to protect their interests; and any order made in the party's absence, and not at the time and place fixed for delivering judgment is invalid: R. v. Morningstar, 11 Can. Cr. Cas. p. 16. But if at the time fixed or after notice to them they do not attend, he may adjudicate in their absence: R. v. Quinn, 28 O.R. 224; R. v. Doherty, 3 Can. Cr. Cas. 505; R. v. Kennedy, 17 O.R. 159; R. v. Maybee, 17 O.R. 194.

The justice in deciding the case must act upon the evidence only; and if he views the *locus in quo*, the conviction will be bad, even if the accused was present at such view: R. v. Petrie, 20 O.R. 317; Re Sing Kee, 5 Can. Cr. Cas. 86.

If the defendant does not attend at the time appointed to give judgment the justice can only adjudicate upon the charge for which accused was tried: Ex p. Doherty, 1 Can. Cr. Cas. 84. He cannot, after adjourning a case for the purpose of considering his judgment, amend the information in the defendant's absence; and a conviction on such amended information will be quashed: R. v. Gough, 22 N.S.R. 516; R. v. Grant, 30 N.S.R. 368.

If the justice tries two separate charges against the same defendant at the same sitting he should adjudicate and dispose of one before proceeding to try the second case: Hamilton v. Walker (1892), 2 Q.B. 25; 7 Can. Cr. Cas. 299; R. v. Burke, 8 Can. Cr. Cas. 14. But if the evidence in the one case is altogether different to that in the first case and is such as would not be at all likely to affect the mind of the justice in the consideration of the other this rule does not apply: R. v. Butler, 32 C.L.J. 594; 7 Can. Cr. Cas. 299; R. v. Fry, 19 Cox 135; 7 Can. Cr. Cas. 300; R. v. Bullock, 6 O.L.R. 663; R. v. Bigelow, 8 Can. Cr. Cas. 132; R. v. Burke, 8 Can. Cr. Cas. 14; R. v. Sing, 6 Can. Cr. Cas. 156. But in all cases it is more expedient to decide the case first tried before taking the evidence in the second case. This is especially so if both informations relate to the same occasion; as the defendant should not be deprived in the second case, of the right to set up the defence that he had been either convicted or acquitted on the same facts in the previous case: Hamilton v. Walker (1892), 2 Q.B. 25, 7 Can. Cr. Cas. 299.

Memorandum of Adjudication: Code 727.

Immediately after announcing his decision the justice should make a full note of it at the foot of the proceedings. This is called the "minute of adjudication," and should be done carefully, and before the justice leaves the bench; and it should be read, or the purport of it announced to both parties. It is the basis of all the future proceedings; the formal conviction afterwards made out is only the entering in proper form of the proceedings which have already taken place: R. v. Mancion, 8 Can. Cr. Cas. 220. A copy of the minute is to be served on defendant: Code 731.

The minute or memorandum should contain a full minute of the *conviction*, the *penalty* by fine or inprisonment, *amount of costs, when* the money is to be paid and *what* the proceedings are to be to enforce payment in case of default. The formal conviction may be made out at any time afterwards and it must be in conformity to the memorandum of adjudication. Where the formal conviction provided for hard labour which was not mentioned in the minute of adjudication, the conviction was held to be bad and the defendant was discharged on habeas corpus: Ex p. Carmichael, 8 Can. Cr. Cas. 19; R. v. Beagan, 6 Can. Cr. Cas. 56, and notes at page 59 and 8 Can. Cr. Cas. p. 20, on the subject of non-conformity. If there has been any omission in the minute of adjudication, however, the defendant may be brought back and the minute corrected in his presence: R. v. Brady, 12 O.R. 358-363; R. v. Hartley, 20 O.R. 481-485; 8 Can. Cr. Cas. p. 20. If the justice prefers to make out the formal conviction or order before leaving the bench he may do so and the minute of adjudication will then of course be unnecessary and may be omitted: Ex p. Flannigan, 2 Can. Cr. Cas. 513. Forms of convictions 31, 32, 33, in the Criminal Code; the form of order of dismissal is Form 37.

The decision of a majority of several justices who have tried the case governs; if the bench is equally divided, there is no decision, and another information may be laid and the case tried again: Kumis v. Graves, 57 L.J.Q.B. 583; or the case may be adjourned before another justice or justices and the trial taken *de novo* including the taking of evidence: Douglas, p. 87.

Punishment on Conviction.

In all cases except those referred to in section 729 of the Criminal Code (to which refer), the justice may if he thinks fit discharge the offender without punishment, if it is a first offence, and upon the offender making such satisfaction to the party aggrieved·as the justice ascertains to be proper: Code 729. If punishment is awarded it must be strictly in accord with the provisions of the statute governing the offence; and must not exceed the maximum, nor be less than the minimum punishment if the minimum is fixed by the statute. If an offence is punishable by three months in jail, a conviction awarding ninety days is bad; as that period may exceed three months: R. v. Gavin, 1 Can. Cr. Cas. 59. Upon a conviction under the liquor license laws the justice cannot suspend sentence or impose less than the minimum penalty provided by law: R. v. Verdon, 8 Can. Cr. Cas. 352: or when a definite penalty for the offence is fixed by statute: R. v. Hostyn, 9 Can. Cr. Cas. 138. A magistrate upon making a conviction for an indictable offence, may suspend sentence: Code 1081. This section does not apply to summary convictions by justices, whose only authority in this regard is that provided by Code 729-733.

Subject to the limitations provided by law, the quantum of punishment is entirely in the discretion of the convicting justice: Code 1028-1029. When the statute provides for a fine *and* imprisonment, both or either may be awarded. The justice is not compelled to inflict both: R. v. Robidoux, 2 Can. Cr. Cas. 19; unless the statute relating to the offence expressly provides that both are to be imposed: Ex p. Kent, 7 Can. Cr. Cas. 447.

If the particular statute does not limit or state the punishment to be awarded for the offence, section 1052 (2) of the Criminal Code applies, and provides that it shall be by a fine not exceeding $50, or by imprisonment for not more than six months, with or without hard labour; or both fine and imprisonment, as the justice thinks the nature of the case requires: Code 1052 (2).

If the defendant is convicted of two or more offences under two or more charges at the same sitting the sentences of imprisonment may run concurrently, or may take effect one after the other, as the justice directs: Code 1055. It is usual to make them concurrent. Imprisonment may be with or without hard labour: Code 1057.

When Fine to be Paid.

The fine and costs may be ordered to be paid forthwith, or time may be given. If no time is stated, it is payable forthwith: R. v. Caister, 30 U.C.R. 247.

Costs.

Code 735, 736, provide that the justice may in his "discretion" award and order that costs shall be paid. The award of costs against the prosecutor on dismissal is provided for by Code 736; and against the defendant on conviction by Code 735, in cases under Dominion laws; and by R.S.O. ch. 90, sec. 4, in cases of breaches of Ontario laws. The amounts must be specified in the conviction or in the order of dismissal: Code 737; and the payment of them may be enforced in the same manner as a penalty or fine may be enforced as mentioned below: Code 737; or if there is no penalty they are to be recoverable by distress, and in default of no sufficient distress by imprisonment as stated by Code 738.

What Costs to Include.

They may include the justice's, the constable's and also witness fees if the justice in his discretion awards them.

Tariff of Costs.

The tariff for justice's, constable's and witness fees in cases under the Criminal Code and in other Dominion laws, is contained in Code 770: See *post*, pp. 375-379, for the tariffs of costs under the Cr. Code, and under the Ontario statute.

The tariff in cases for breaches of Ontario law, by-laws, etc., is given in R.S.O. ch. 95, secs. 1 and 4, as to justice's fees and witness fees; and in R.S.O. ch. 101, p. 1046, as to constable's fees. These tariffs differ from each other in some respects; and care must be taken to apply the right tariff. The Dominion tariff does not apply to cases for breaches of Ontario laws, by-laws, etc.; and *vice versa*: R. v. Excell, 20 O.R. 633. No costs except those provided by the above tariffs can be charged; and if any costs should be included which are not so provided the conviction will be invalid and may be set aside: Ex p. Lon Kai Long, 1 Can. Cr. Cas. 120. A conviction which included in the costs awarded, a charge for the use of the hall where the trial took place, was quashed: R. v. Elliott, 12 O.R. 524. If the justice fixes an excessive *amount* of costs, it will not invalidate the conviction; taxing costs being a ministerial act merely: R. v. Brown, 16 O.R. 41; Ex p. Howard, 32 N.B.R. 237; Ex p. Rayworth, 2 Can. Cr. Cas. 230. But an order for payment of costs which the justice has no authority to award will do so: Ex p. Lon Kai Long, 1 Can. Cr. Cas. 120.

If a justice takes excessive costs by mistake, he may be compelled to refund: McGillivary v. Muir, 7 Can. Cr. Cas. 360; and if he does so wilfully, he may be prosecuted criminally: Code 1134; Ex p. Howard, 32 N.B.R. 237; McGillivray v. Muir, 7 Can. Cr. Cas. 360; and is liable to a penalty: Code 1134; Ontario Statutes, 1904, ch. 13, sec. 2.

To Whom the Costs are Payable.

The costs awarded on conviction or dismissal must be ordered to be paid to the prosecutor or defendant as the case may be, and not to the justice: Code 735, 736; R. v. Binney, 1 E. & B. 810; R. v. Roache, 32 O. R. 20; R. v. Law Bow, 7 Can. Cr. Cas. 468.

The constable's costs (but not those of the justice or witnesses) are paid by the county in cases of summary convictions if they cannot be realized from the parties to the case or if the justice has not ordered payment of them. For instance, in vagrancy cases in which the accused is committed to prison and other similar cases, the county pays the constable's fees. The account for same is to be sent to the clerk of the peace for submission to the board of audit quarterly. Such account need not be in duplicate, but in other respects the directions at page 293' *ante*, apply.

The Ontario Statute, 1904, ch. 13, sec. 1, respecting justice's fees, applies only to cases of preliminary enquiries in indictable offences and not summary convictions; so that in vagrancy and other cases of summary convictions in which no costs can be collected from the parties the justice is not entitled to recover any fees from the county under that statute.

Security for Defendant's Good Behaviour.

By section 748 of the Criminal Code, the justice may in addition to or in lieu of any punishment, order that the defendant give sureties for his future good behaviour for any time *not exceeding twelve months* (Re Smith's Bail, 6 Can. Cr. Cas. 416), if the offence is one directly against the peace, such, for instance, as riot, assault, fighting or gross disorderly conduct in a public place, etc., and if the offence was committed under circumstances which render it probable that the defendant will again be guilty of the same, or some other offence, against the peace, unless he is bound over to good behaviour; as for instance, if he had been previously guilty of similar conduct. In such case, the justice will add to the usual form of conviction the following clause:—

And I do further order and adjudge that in addition to the said sentence hereinbefore imposed by me upon the said   as aforesaid, the said   be and is hereby required forthwith to enter into his own recognizance and give security in two sufficient sureties in the sum of   , to keep the peace and be of good behaviour for a period of (*state time, not exceeding twelve months*).

Recognizance for Good Behaviour.

Form 49 in the Criminal Code.

Commitment for Default of Sureties.

If the defendant does not give security for good behaviour as ordered, he may be committed to jail: Form 50. For further observations on this subject see "Articles of the Peace" in the "Synopsis of Offences—Summary Convictions."

Formal Record of Conviction.

Forms of Convictions 31, 32 and 33 are to be used according to the circumstances. The formal conviction may be made out at once at the trial or it may be made out afterwards: Code 727. It must be signed and *sealed* by the justice, or by all the justices if more than one tried the case; or by a majority of them if some dissent. The majority may convict. The conviction must shew on its face all things requisite to the justice's jurisdiction: as to which see notes at page 48 of 8 Can. Cr. Cas.

How Penalty is to be Ordered to be Enforced.

In awarding, by the minute of adjudication and conviction, the measures to be taken to enforce payment, the justice may either apply those which are provided by the particular statute or clause relating to the offence, or he may (whether the same does or does not provide such measures), adopt those contained in Code 738, 739, 740.

These latter provisions of the Criminal Code are made applicable also to convictions for offences against Ontario laws, by R.S.O. ch. 90, sec. 2 (3). The following are the proceedings authorized by the above sections of the Criminal Code.

Distress Warrant.

Form 39. The first proceeding to be awarded by the conviction for enforcing payment, is a warrant of distress; but distress should not be ordered if the justice finds that it will be ruinous to the defendant or his family; or if the defendant acknowledges, or it otherwise appears, that he has not sufficient seizable goods to make the money: Code 744. In either of these events, the distress should be omitted, the reason for so doing being stated in the memorandum of adjudication and formal conviction; and in that case the justice will award commitment alone, in default of payment and not order distress. It was held, however, in Ex p. Casson, 2 Can. Cr. Cas. 483, that the conviction was good when the distress was omitted, without expressly stating the reason for it, in the conviction. But if the reason is so stated the truth of it cannot be controverted: Mechian v. Horne, 20 O.R. 267.

The defendant is entitled to be heard on the question of dispensing with the distress, before that is done: Re Clew, 8 Q.B.D. 511; R. v. Rawding, 7 Can. Cr. Cas. 436, 441, 442; notes 9 Can. Cr. Cas. 562. So before dispensing with distress, the justice must state to the defendant that he proposes to do so, for either of the reasons above mentioned, and ask him if he has anything to say upon the subject; and anything he may say should be taken down and inquired into, before ordering that distress be dispensed with. The defendant may prefer to have the penalty recovered by distress, instead of being committed to gaol; but even so, that course will not be allowed if it really appears that there are not sufficient goods to meet the amount; or that it would be ruinous to the defendant or to his family, to levy a distress. In deciding whether or not to omit distress the justice is exercising a judicial function, and should do so only in the presence of the parties and on hearing what they have to state; see cases cited in 9 Can. Cr. Cas. 564.

Warrant of Commitment.

If distress is dispensed with as above mentioned, the minute of adjudication should award that, on default of payment of the fine and costs, the defendant be committed to gaol; and the formal conviction, afterwards made out, will be Form 32 in the Criminal Code.

If, however, distress is ordered, the minute of adjudication will state that, if payment is not made, a distress warrant is to be issued; and that if sufficient goods to realize the money cannot be found, the defendant is to be committed to gaol; and in that case, the formal conviction will be Form 31, in the Criminal Code.

The period of imprisonment to be awarded, in default of payment, is usually stated in the statute or clause relating to the offence; and if so, it must not exceed what is so stated; but if the statute or clause does not so provide, section 739 of the Criminal Code applies; and by that section the imprisonment may be for any period not exceeding three (calendar) months.

Such imprisonment may be with or without hard labour, in the discretion of the justice; if any imprisonment *for the offence* may be ordered to be with hard labour, then imprisonment *in default of payment* of the fine may also be with hard labour: Code 739(2).

The period of imprisonment provided by the statute in default of payment of the fine, is to be distinguished from that provided as punishment for the offence itself.

In his award of imprisonment, whether as a punishment for the offence, or in default of payment of a fine, .the justice may in the conviction make the following directions:—

1. If the offender is already in goal undergoing punishment for another offence, the justice may order that the imprisonment for the subsequent offence shall begin at the expiration of the imprisonment then being undergone: Code 746.

2. If the defendant is convicted by the same justice at the same sitting of more than one offence, he may award either that the sentences may run concurrently, or that they shall take effect one after the other.

3. Or the justice may award (in cases where a fine and imprisonment are both awarded) that the imprisonment imposed for default in payment of the fine shall begin after the expiry of the term of imprisonment imposed as punishment for the offence: Code 740.

All the above matters are to be considered and dealt with by the justice before he leaves the bench, and while the parties are before him; and are to be inserted in the minute of adjudication.

The minute of adjudication should contain the following: that the justice has found the accused to be guilty and that he has convicted him of the charge; that the defendant is adjudged to forfeit and pay a fine, stating the amount, and costs, fixing the amount, and when they are to be paid; that if not so paid a distress warrant is to be issued; and that if no sufficient distress is found the defendant is to be imprisoned (stating in what goal) for the time adjudged, unless the fine and costs are sooner paid.

If distress is dispensed with, or if the punishment awarded for the offence is to be by imprisonment only, or by both fine and imprisonment, the minute of adjudication will include suitable provisions. The formal conviction may be drawn up at any time afterwards.

Issuing and Executing Process to Enforce Punishment.

Issuing Distress Warrant.

If the fine and costs are not paid as provided in the conviction (and distress has not been omitted as stated *ante* page 361), a distress warrant will be issued: Code 741 in the Forms 39 or 40, as the case requires.

Who to Issue Warrants.

The warrant of distress (and also the warrant of commitment mentioned below) may be issued either by the convicting justice; or by any other justice for the same county or district: Code 708(3); and one justice may issue the warrant (of distress or commitment) even if the statute relating to the offence requires two justices to try the case and convict: Code 708(2).

What Constable to Execute Warrant.

It may be directed to any constable of the county by name, or "to all or any of the constables" of the county, according to the form given in the Criminal Code.

The constable who laid the information and so is the private prosecutor, is not disqualified from executing a warrant issued in a prosecution under the Criminal Code: *Gaul* v. *Town-*

ship of Ellice, 6 Can. Cr. Cas. 15; *R.* v. *Heffernan,* 13 O.R. 616; but if the constable has any personal or pecuniary interest to serve in the matter, and is not acting in a purely official capacity, he is disqualified from acting as constable in executing warrants in a case in which he has laid the information: *Gaul* v. *Township of Ellice,* 6 Can. Cr. Cas. p. 19, and cases there cited and in the notes at end of the case.

Remand During Execution of Distress Warrant.

On a distress warrant being issued, the defendant may either be allowed to go at large on his own recognizance, or with sufficient sureties, pending its enforcement (see Recognizance on Remand *ante* p. 258; or he may, by verbal or written order, be kept in safe custody until the constable can make his return to the distress warrant: Code 745.

Where Goods Out of County.

If the constable cannot find sufficient goods of the defendant in the county, but there is reason to believe the defendant has sufficient goods elsewhere, the warrant may be "backed" or endorsed (Form 47) in any other county. The warrant may then be executed by a constable of either the county in which it was issued or by a constable of the county in which it was so "backed": Code 743.

Which Goods are Exempt From Seizure.

The Ontario exemption law only applies to exempt goods from seizure under civil process from Ontario Courts, and there is no law providing for exemptions from seizure under a distress warrant in a criminal case; but, as has been seen, the justice is not to issue a distress warrant if it appears that it would be ruinous to the defendant's family: Code 744. If the only goods seizable are the defendant's household effects necessary for his family's use, and his implements of trade which are necessary to earn a living, they should not be taken. So that goods named in the Ontario Exemptions Act, R.S.O. ch. 77, sec. 2, should not be seized under distress.

There is no provision made by any Dominion or Ontario statute as to the proceedings to sell the goods seized; but in analogy to sales under distress warrant for rent, etc., notices of the sale should be put up for eight days, and a notice of it should be given to the defendant; a list and appraisement of the goods seized should also be made by at least one competent and disinterested person.

The tariff provides a fee for *advertising* and *appraising* the goods (see Tariff in Code 770), indicating that the goods must be *appraised* and *advertised* for sale.

The following forms of the constable's proceedings are submitted:—

CONSTABLE'S INVENTORY OF GOODS SEIZED UNDER WARRANT OF DISTRESS.

An inventory of goods and chattels of C.D. by me this day seized and distrained in the   of   in the County of   , by virtue of a distress warrant issued by E.F., Esquire, a justice of the peace in and for the County of   , dated the   day of   , A.D. 19 , under a conviction (or order) made by the said E.F., as such justice on the   day of   , A.D. 19 ; that is to say, (*specify the articles seized*).

Dated this   day of   , A.D. 19 .
          A constable of the said county.

APPRAISEMENT.

We,. G.H. and I.K., having at the request of L.M., a constable of the County of   , examined the goods and chattels mentioned in the annexed inventory, do appraise the same at the sum of $.
Witness our hands this   day of   , A.D. 19 .
          G.H.
          I.K.

NOTICE OF SALE OF GOODS DISTRAINED.

To C.D.
By virtue of a distress warrant issued by E.F., Esquire, a justice of the peace in and for the County of   , under a conviction (or order) made by the said justice against C.D., I have distrained of the goods and chattels of the said C.D. to wit: (*describe property*). All of which goods and chattels will be sold by public auction at   on the   day of   , A.D. 19 , at the hour of   o'clock in the   noon; unless the moneys to be levied under the said distress warrant, with the costs of executing the same, amounting in all to $ are sooner paid.

Dated the   day of   , A.D. 19
          L.M., Constable.

A copy of this notice should be served on the party whose goods have been seized.

The distress warrant must fix the time within which after seizure the defendant is to pay the fine, etc., in order to avoid the goods being sold: See Forms 39 and 40 to the Criminal Code;

and the constable must wait for the time mentioned in the warrant before he sells the goods seized.

The constable should on seizure remove the goods from the defendant's premises immediately. He will be liable for trespass if he remains on the defendant's premises an unnecessarily long time: Paley, 8th ed. 339.

The constable may break open an outer door to execute a distress warrant for a penalty, the whole or any part of which goes to the Crown; but not on a warrant for a mere order for payment of money such as wages, or damage to private property, nor for penalties which are payable wholly to the complainant: Paley 339.

Before breaking open an outer door the constable should verbally notify those within, who he is, and his business there, and demand admittance.

Constable's Fees for Executing Distress Warrant.

For the costs of distress in cases of convictions for offences against the Cr. Code or other Dominion laws, see Tariff under Code 770. The items will be as follows: Tariff, item 9, executing warrant of distress, and returning same, $1; item 10, advertising under warrant, $1; item 11, mileage to seize goods, per mile (one way only) 10c.; item 12, appraisement, 2 cents on the dollar on the value of the goods; item 13, commission on sale, 5 per cent. on the net produce of the goods. Item 13 will not be included in the above mentioned notice, as it would not be payable if the money is paid before sale of the goods.

The constable's costs of distress in cases of convictions for offences against Ontario laws and by-laws are provided by R.S.O. ch. 101, page 1046, as follows: Executing and returning warrant, $1.50; advertising, $1; mileage, per mile, one way, 13c.; appraisement, 2 per cent. on the value of the goods; commission on sale, 5 per cent. on net produce.

By R.S.O. ch. 75, sec. 2(d), $1 a day is allowed for keeping possession of the goods; and by sub-section (e), a commission of 3 per cent. may be charged if the money is paid before the sale. But this only applies to cases under Ontario laws; no commission is provided for by the Criminal Code before sale, in cases of convictions under Dominion laws.

Release on Payment.

Under Code 747 the defendant may at any time pay or tender to the constable the amount payable under the warrant, with the expenses of the distress, up to that time; and the officer must then cease to execute the warrant.

The constable, upon such payment, or upon sale of the goods, must return the warrant and money to the justice who issued it.

When There is not Sufficient Goods.

The constable should not make a seizure or execute a warrant of distress unless he finds sufficient goods to yield, on sale, the *full amount* to be realized under the warrant; for if part only is realized the defendant cannot afterwards be committed for the balance. If the goods are not sufficient, they ought not to be taken; and the warrant should be so returned: Paley, 8th ed. 341; *Sinden* v. *Brown*, 17 A.R. 173; *Trigerson* v. *Cobourg* (Police), 6 O.S. 405; *R.* v. *Wyat*, 2 Ld. Raymond 1189; 1 Burns' Justice, 30th ed., 867; see also 10 Can. Cr. Cas. 68.

Issuing Warrant to Commit.

Upon receiving the constable's return, Form 43, of no sufficient goods to answer the distress (or in case distress was omitted as explained *ante* p. 361, any justice of the peace for the county or district may issue the warrant to commit, as ordered by the conviction: Form 44, Code 741(2). The want of sufficient distress to justify commitment in default, can only be proved by the constable's return of no sufficient goods to the distress warrant, or by hearing the defendant upon the subject: *R.* v. *Rawding*, 7 Can. Cr. Cas. 436.

The constable must make a real effort to find sufficient goods before making a return of no-goods. In *Re Authers*, 22 Q.B.D. 345, cited in 7 Can. Cr. Cas. 442; a form was gone through of issuing and making a return of *nulla bonâ* to a distress warrant, but the only effort to find goods was to ask the defendant if he had any, his reply being in the negative which turned out to be incorrect; and the courses pursued was held to be improper and might even make the commitment illegal.

Even when the constable has made a return of no-goods, the justice should, before issuing a warrant of commitment, satisfy himself by inquiries on the subject that the constable actually made reasonable efforts to find goods upon which to distrain: *R. v. Skinner,* 9 Can. Cr. Cas. 558 and notes.

The cost of commiting and conveying the defendant to gaol must be fixed and inserted in the warrant of commitment: In re Bright, 1 C.L.J. 240; R. v. McDonald, 2 Can. Cr. Cas. 504; R. v. Beagan, 6 Can. Cr. Cas. 56. If the justice dispensed with distress as mentioned *ante* · P. 361; the justice must so state in the warrant of commitment. A warrant of commitment must shew on its face either a return of no sufficient distress, or that the distress was dispensed with under Code 744: *R. v. Skinner,* 9 Can. Cr. Cas. 558.

The costs of commitment, etc., will be, 25c. to the justice for the warrant, and mileage one way at 10c. to constable for conveying the defendant to gaol (also $1.50 for arresting the defendant if he is at large, but not if he is already in custody; and 13c. per mile one way, to make such arrest) ; and the actual expenses of conveying prisoner to the gaol.

If the particular statute only authorizes costs of conveying (and not of "committing") defendant to gaol, then the justice's fee for warrant of commitment must be omitted or the warrant will be bad.

Execution of Warrant of Commitment.

The warrant is to be addressed to any or all of the constables of the county or district, and may be executed anywhere in Canada; but if executed out of the justice's county it must be first "backed" as described *ante* p. 250.

Part Payment.

If part of the money has been realized by distress or paid by defendant, it must be returned to him before a warrant to commit can be issued, as he cannot be committed for part only of the money: *Ex p. Gilbert,* 36 N.B.R. 492; *Ex p. Bertin,* 10 Can. Cr. Cas. p. 66, and notes p. 68; *Sinden v. Brown,* 17 A.R. 173. But in some special cases the particular statute relating to an offence expressly provides, contrary to the general rule, that a warrant of commitment may be issued notwithstanding part payment; such as the provision in the Indian Act, R.S.C. ch. 81, sec. 127(4).

Acquittal; **and Dismissal of Case.**

If the justice finds the charge not proved he will dismiss the case: Code 726, 730. Form of Order 37; and he must, if required, give the defendant a certificate of the dismissal—Form 38: Code 733; and such a certificate releases him from all further proceedings for the same cause: Code 734. But a certificate of dismissal is only to be given when a case has been heard on its merits, and not where it is withdrawn, or dismissed on a technicality: *Reid* v. *Nutt*, L.R. 24 Q.B.D. 669.

The justice on dismissing the case may order the prosecutor to pay the costs, including the witness fees: Code 736; and may direct that they are to be recoverable in the same manner and by the same warrants, as penalties are recoverable under a conviction, described above. Code 737, 738, 742.

If such costs are given against the prosecutor on dismissal, the order will include an adjudication stating their amount and when they are to be paid; and also that in default of payment it is to be enforced by distress, or if that is omitted for similar reasons to those stated *ante* p. 361; or if there are not sufficient goods of the prosecutor to realize the costs, then that the prosecutor be committed to gaol for not more than one month (Code 742(2)), with or without hard labour, as the justice sees fit, unless the costs, together with costs of conveying him to gaol, are sooner paid.

The directions in the foregoing pages in regard to issuing the processes for enforcing payment of a fine under a conviction will apply to process for enforcing payment of costs by the prosecutor on dismissal—and warrants of distress (if awarded), and of commitment, will be issued and executed as above described: Code 742. The forms are given in the schedule to the Criminal Code, Form 45, for warrant of distress, and 46 for warrant of commitment.

Place of Imprisonment on Committal.

The imprisonment, if for less than two years is to be in the common gaol of the county or district where the sentence is pronounced; or if there is no gaol there, then in the nearest one Code 1056.

In the cases of offenders under sixteen years old, the justice may commit to a reformatory for an indefinite time, instead of other punishment, for serious offences or in the cases of incor-

rigible youthful offenders, or those who by reason of the neglect
or vice of parents are within the scope of the law respecting
juvenile offenders or neglected children: R.S.O. ch. 304; R.S.O.
ch. 310; R.S.O. ch. 259.

Payment of Fine, etc., to Gaoler.

The person imprisoned for non-payment of fine or costs may
at any time pay the money to the gaoler, who is to receive it and
discharge the defendant, if not in custody on any other matter,
and the money is to be paid to the justice who issued the commitment: Code 747(2).

Prosecutions Under the Ontario Municipal Act.

The Ontario Statute, 1903, ch. 19, secs. 704-709, provides the
proceedings in prosecutions for offences against municipal by-
laws; and the Criminal Code does not apply to these prosecutions.
In such prosecutions there is no authority to omit recovery of
fines by distress, as there is in cases under the Criminal Code;
and the conviction must direct that in default of payment of
the fine a distress warrant is to be issued and imprisonment in
default of sufficient distress only.

Sections 711, 712, of the same Act make provisions for compelling the attendance of witnesses and taking of evidence in
such cases.

In prosecutions under by-laws care must be taken to prove
the by-laws; sec. 710(2). This may be done by the production
of the original by-law—section 333—or a copy, written or
printed, without erasure or interlineation, and under the seal of
the corporation and certified by the clerk, or a member of the
council, to be a true copy: Section 334.

Prosecutions Under Ontario Statutes Other Than the Municipal Act.

In such prosecutions the Ontario Summary Convictions Act,
R.S.O. ch. 90, provides that the proceedings are to be the same
as in cases under the Criminal Code, as before described; subject,
however, to any special variation contained in the Ontario statute
last mentioned. The proceedings generally will be the same as in
cases under the Criminal Code.

Appeals from Convictions.

An appeal from the justice's conviction under the Criminal Code is to be taken in Ontario to the court of general sessions of the peace, if the punishment is imprisonment only; and in all other cases, *i.e.*, when a fine is imposed, an appeal lies to the Division Court of the division in which the cause of compaint arose: Code 749 (*a*).

In the district of Nipissing the appeal is to the general sessions for Renfrew County if the punishment ordered was imprisonment only; and in all other cases to the Division Court of Renfrew nearest to the place where the cause of complaint arose; Code 749(2).

See chapter on appeal, *ante*, p. 99.

Appeals from Convictions Under Ontario Laws.

The above provisions do not apply. Appeals from such convictions lie to the general session in Ontario unless the particular statute under which the conviction is made otherwise provides: R.S.O. ch. 90, sec. 7; and the convictions, depositions and papers are to be transmitted to the clerk of the peace: Section 6.

Particular statutes, however, sometimes provide for an appeal to another court than the general sessions. Thus an appeal under the Ontario Liquor License Act, is to the judge of the County Court, and the depositions and conviction must be transmitted to the clerk of the latter court and not to the clerk of the peace.

So also, appeals under the Master and Servants Act are to be made to the Division Court in which the cause of complaint arose, or in which the parties complained against, or one of them resides at the time when the complaint is made, or where the parties complained against or one of them carried on business R.S.O. ch. 157, sec. 18.

In these and other cases where the appeal is to some other court than the general sessions, the conviction and depositions must be transmitted to the clerk of such other court.

The conviction in all cases is to be transmitted to the clerk of the court to which an appeal lies: Code 757; and the information and depositions are to accompany it: *R.* v. *Rondeau*, 9 Can. Cr. Cas. 523.

See chapter on this subject, *ante*, p. 143.

Cases Stated under Dominion Laws.

In cases under Dominion laws: Code 761-769. Upon the application of either party the justice may state a case for the opinion of the proper court to which an appeal lies as above indicated, upon a point of law arising in the case, and which is claimed to have been erroneously decided by the justice; or upon the ground of excess of jurisdiction.

The proceedings in that event are laid down in the above sections of the Code: and are described, *ante*, p. 122.

The justice should not refuse to sign a "case stated" unless he is of opinion that the application is frivolous; nor can he refuse if the application is made on behalf of the Attorney-General: Code 763. If the justice refuses to sign a "case stated" an application for an order may be made to the court: Code 764.

Case stated in cases under Ontario law: See R.S.O. ch. 91.

Quarterly Returns of Convictions.

Justices are required, quarterly on or before the second Tuesday in March, June, September and December, to transmit to the clerk of the peace a return in the form which will be provided by him on application—Form 75 in the Criminal Code—of all convictions made by him up to the end of the previous month and of all moneys received by him and not included in some previous return: Code 1133, 1134.

In Nipissing, the return is to be to the clerk of the peace of Renfrew: Code 1133(6).

Similar provision is made for return of convictions under Ontario laws by R.S.O. ch. 93.

These returns are to include all moneys for fines payable under convictions made during any previous quarter, but not received till a later date.

If two or more justices join in a conviction they must make a joint return: Code 1133(3)

Penalty for Neglect or False Return.

Code 1134 and R.S.O. ch. 93, sec. 3, provide for a penalty of $80 for neglect to make proper return or wilfully making a false, partial or incorrect return; or wilfully exacting or receiving improper fees: See also Ont. St., 1904, ch. 13, sec. 2.

To Whom Fines to be Paid Over.

Fines and penalties received by justices are to be paid over by them in accordance with the special direction (if any) contained in the statute under which the conviction was made.

Fines Levied Under Ontario Municipal Act.

All fines levied under the Municipal Act or by-laws are (unless otherwise specially directed by the particular clause of the statute relating to the offence) to be paid, one moiety to the informer or prosecutor and one moiety to the municipal treasurer; that is, to the county treasurer under county by-laws, or to the treasurer of the minor municipality when the offence was against the by-laws of that municipality. But if the prosecution is brought by a member of the police force or an employee of the corporation or local board of health the whole of the penalty is payable to the treasurer of the county or minor municipality whose employee the prosecutor is.

Fines Under Other Ontario Laws,

Are to be paid in the manner provided for by the particular statutes under which they are imposed, or if there is no such provision, to the Provincial treasurer: R.S.O. ch. 107, sec. 2, amended by the statutes of 1901, ch. 12, sec. 12.

Certain fines under Imperial statutes in force in Ontario are payable to the treasurer of the county (or of any city or town separated from the county) in which the conviction took place: R.S.O. ch. 107, sec. 1.

Fines for Breaches of Canadian Revenue Laws,

or for malfeasance in office by a Dominion official, or in cases in which the prosecution is taken at the instance of the Dominion Government (if the latter bears the costs of prosecution), are to be paid to the Receiver-General of Canada.

Fines Imposed Under The Criminal Code.

Fines imposed for any offence under the Criminal Code or other Dominion statute, except as above mentioned, are payable to the Provincial treasurer: Code 1036.

Fines to be Remitted to the Crown Attorney.

All fines payable to the Provincial treasurer of Ontario are required, by order of the Lieutenant-Governor in Council, to be paid by justices and sheriffs to the Crown Attorney for the county for transmission by him to the Provincial treasurer.

Fines for Cruelty to Animals.

Code 542, 543.   Fines levied for this offence may be ordered by the justice to be paid, one-half to the county, town, village or township treasurer where the offence was committed, and the other half with the costs of prosecution to such other person as to the justice seems proper (*e.g.,* to any society or persons enforcing the law) : Code 1043.

Lockup Houses.

The Ontario Municipal Act, 1903, ch. 19, secs. 518-523, provides for the erection and maintenance of lockup houses.   And by the statute of the late Province of Canada, 1866, ch. 51, sec. 409 (which is not repealed), a justice of the peace is authorized by warrant under his hand and seal to direct the confinement in any lockup house within his county, for any period not longer than two days, of any person charged with crime, whom it may be necessary to detain pending the hearing of the case and until he may be conveyed to jail; also for the confinement for not more than twenty-four hours of any person found in a public street or highway in a state of intoxication, or of a person convicted of desecrating the Sabbath; and generally justices may commit to the lockup any person summarily convicted by them of any offence cognizable by them and liable to imprisonment therefor under any Ontario statute or by-law. Notwithstanding these provisions the present condition of most lockup houses is such that they ought not to be used for any but the most transient purposes.   .

Compounding or Settling Offences.

This offence consists in any person receiving anything from another upon an agreement, expressed or implied, not to prosecute the offender for a criminal act: *R.* v. *Burgess,* 16 Q.B.D. 141.

It is a serious offence against the law, to make a bargain to drop, or not to bring, a criminal prosecution for a criminal offence.   Such a bargain or arrangement between parties, even though not actually expressed, will be implied, if the nature of the transaction indicates that no prosecution will be brought; or, if brought, will not be proceeded with.

While reparation is a duty which the offender owes to the person he has injured, quite independently of his fear of prosecution or otherwise; and the law is not anxious to discourage reparation; yet there must be no bargain or understanding in regard to what is the clear duty of the person who has been wronged, to himself and to others, not to cover up a criminal offence.

The law must taken its course; and the fact of reparation being made is one for the court in awarding or suspending punishment, after conviction: *Jones* v. *Merionethshire* (1892), 1 Ch. 173; *Legatt* v. *Brown,* 30 O.R. 225.

By Code 729 the justice is authorized, in the cases therein referred to, to discharge the offender from the conviction, if it is the first conviction, upon reparation being made. And in other cases of mainly a private nature, such as wilful destruction of property, petty trespass, etc., there can be no objection to the charge being dropped upon compensation being made. But if the offence is of a public character or one against which the public should be protected, an indictment will lie against parties settling it: 1 Can. Cr. Cas. 316; Archibald, 22nd ed., 1035; *Baker* v. *Townshend,* 7 Taunt. 422. No settlement between parties ousts the jurisdiction of justices to proceed with a criminal case; and if a justice finds or suspects that the parties are likely to stifle a criminal prosecution, he should immediately inform the Crown Attorney, so that the public interest may be protected.

TARIFF OF COSTS.

In cases under the Criminal Code or other Dominion laws: Code 770.

(Justices' Fees.)

1. Information or complaint and warrant or summons..$0.50
2. Warrant where summons issued in the first instance... 0.10
3. Each necessary copy of summons or warrant.   0.10
4. Each summons or warrant for witness (only one sum
    mons on each side to be charged for in each case, which
    may contain any number of names).......   0.10

5. Information for warrant to arrest witness and warrant.$0.50
6. Each necessary copy of summons or warrant for witness 0.10
7. For every recognizance 0.25
8. For hearing and determining case 0.50
9. If case lasts over two hours 1.00
10. Where two justices are required to hear the case the associate justice is also entitled to a similar fee, but if one justice can lawfully hear the case there is only one fee even if other justices assist.
11. For each warrant of distress or commitment.......... 0.25
12. For making up Record of Conviction, in those cases where it is ordered to be returned to the session or on certiorari 1.00

But in all cases which admit of a summary proceeding before a single justice and wherein no higher penalty than $20 can be imposed, the fee for making out the conviction is 0.50
13· For copy of any paper connected with any case, per folio of 100 words 0.05
14. For every bill of costs when demanded to be made out in detail 0.10

(Items 13 and 14 to be charged only when there has been an adjudication.)

(Constables' Fees.)

In cases under Dominion laws.

1. Arrest of each individual upon a warrant $1.50
2. Serving summons 0.25
3. Mileage to serve summons or warrant per mile (one way) necessarily travelled 0.10
4. Same mileage when service cannot be affected, but only upon proof of due diligence.
5. Mileage taking prisoner to gaol, exclusive of disbursements necessarily expended in the prisoner's conveyance (the constable's expenses not included as the mileage covers same) 0.10
6. Attending justices on the trial for each day necessarily employed in one or more cases, when engaged less than 4 hours. 1.00

7. If the case or cases lasted more than 4 hours..........$1.50
8. Mileage travelled to attend trial before justices (when public conveyance can be taken only reasonable disbursements to be allowed) one way per mile 0.10
9. Serving warrant of distress and returning same 1.00
10. Advertising under distress warrant..........   1.00
11. Travelling to make distress, or search for goods to make distress when no goods found (one way) per mile... 0.10
12. Appraisements, whether made by one appraiser or, more, 2c. on the dollar on the value of goods.
13. Commission on sale and delivery of goods, 5c. on the dollar of net proceeds.

(Witnesses' Fees.)

In cases under Dominion laws.
1. Each day attending trial $0.75
2. Mileage travelled to attend trial (one way) per mile.. 0.10

TARIFF OF COSTS.

In cases under any Ontario statute or law.

(Justices' Fees: R.S.O. ch. 95.)

1. For information and warrant for apprehension, or for information and summons $0.50
2. For each copy of summons to be served on defendant or defendants............................... 0.10
3. For every subpœna, only one subpœna on each side to be charged for.............................. 0.10
4. For every recognizance (only one to be charged in each case) 0.25
5. For information and warrant for surety for the peace or for good behaviour (to be paid by the complainant) 0.50
6. For warrant of commitment for default of surety to keep the peace or for good behaviour (to be paid by complainant) 0.50
7. For hearing and determining the case 0.50
8. Where one justice alone cannot lawfully try the case an additional fee for the hearing to be allowed the associate justice................................ 0.50

9. For warrant to levy distress $0.25

1U. For making up record of conviction when the same is ordered to be returned to the sessions or on certiorari. 1.00

11. But in all cases of summary proceeding before one justice and wherein no higher penalty than $20 can be imposed, the fee for the conviction is 0.50

12. For copy of any paper connected with any trial per folio of 100 words 0.10

13. For every bill of costs (when demanded to be made out in detail) 0.10

(Items 12 and 13 to be only chargeable when there is a conviction.)

(Constable's Fees under Ontario laws: R.S.O. ch. 101.)

1. Arrest of each individual upon a warrant $1.50

2. Serving summons or subpœna 0.25

3. Mileage to serve summons, subpœna or warrant, per mile (one way) 0.13

4. Mileage when service cannot be effected, upon proof of due diligence 0.13

5. Mileage taking prisoner to gaol, exclusive of disbursements necessarily expended in the prisoner's conveyance only 0.10

6. Returning with prisoner after arrest—conveyance or railway fare for prisoner only.
Only reasonable disbursements to be allowed and public conveyance to be used when available.

7. Attending justices on trials, etc., for each day necessarily employed in one or more cases. 1.50

16. Serving distress warrant and returning same   1.50

17. Advertising under distress warrant 1.00

18. Travelling to make distress or to search for goods to make distress if no goods found per mile (one way).. 0.13

19. Appraisement of goods distrained, whether by one appraiser or more, 2c. on the $ of the value of the goods.

20. Catalogue, sale and commission and delivery of goods. 5c. on the $ of the net proceeds.

21. Executing search warrant 1.50

(Witnesses' Fees, in cases under Ontario laws.)
R.S.O. ch. 95, sec. 4.

Each day's attendance before the justice to give evidence,
   where the distance travelled does not exceed ten miles.$0.50
Mileage, over ten miles travelled 0.10

NOTE.

The above tariffs apply only to cases of Summary Convictions under Part XV. (secs 705 *et. seq.*,) of the Cr. Code, for
breaches of Ontario laws, and not to cases of indictable offences.

ALPHABETICAL

SYNOPSIS OR LIST OF OFFENCES WHICH ARE THE SUBJECT OF SUMMARY
CONVICTIONS BY JUSTICES OF THE PEACE.

*One Justice has Authority to Convict for any of the Following Offences,
Except Those Where a Note is Made at the End of the Statement of the Offence That Two Justices are Required.*

A magistrate has the authority of two justices.

Abandoned Mine.
Neglect to Guard. See Neglect.

Advertisements or Circulars Like Bank Notes, Using.
Code 551.
Two justices required.

Automobiles.
See Motor Vehicles.

Agricultural Society Exhibitions.
Ont. St. 1906, ch. 16, secs. 26, 29.
Appointment of constables by a justice of the peace on the request of
the Society; and the powers of such constables and of Provincial constables
at exhibitions are provided for in this statute.
Offences Against this Statute.
Obstructing Officers: Sec. 27.
A.B., at   , on   did unlawfully and wilfully hinder
(or obstruct) C.D., an officer of the   Agricultural Society in the
execution of his duty as such (or gain admission to the ground of the
said society contrary to the rules of the said society).
Entering Horse *in Wrong Class or by False Name:* R.S.O. ch. 254.
A.B., at   , on   , did on the   day of   ,
at   , unlawfully enter for competition for a purse offered by the
     Agricultural Society at its exhibition where the contest was to
be decided by speed a horse in a class different to that to which the said
horse properly belonged by the rule of the said society in reference to the
said contest.
Gambling Devices, etc., at: Sec. 28; Ont. Stat. 1898, ch. 31.

Algonquin Park Act, Offences Under.
R.S.O. ch. 46.
Using Firearms in Park: Secs. 8-16, 22.
Fishing in Without a License: Sec. 9(2)-16, 22.
Or with Net, Trap, Spear or Night Line.
Cutting Wood or Timber on: Sec. 13.
Sale of Liquor In: Sec. 15.

Anatomy Act, Offences Under.
R.S.O. ch. 177; Ont. Stat. 1899, ch. 11, sec. 37.

Animal, Selling Diseased.
R.S.C. ch. 75, sec. 38.
A.B., on   , at   , did unlawfully sell (or dispose of)
to C.D. (or offer, or expose for sale, or attempt to dispose of) * * * *
an animal, to wit, a heifer (or as the case may be) infected with or

labouring under a certain infectious (*or* contagious) disease, to wit, *name the disease*: (*or* * * * * the meat, *or* skin, *or* hide, *or* horns, *or* hoofs, *or other parts, stating what*, of an animal, to wit, a heifer infected with or labouring under a certain infectious disease, *stating what*, at the time of its death).

See also secs. 35-46 as to other offences.

Also see R.S.C. ch. 75, secs. 36-40, 48.

Two justices of the peace required.

See also offence of selling things unfit for food, under "Food."

Animals, Diseased.

R.S.O. ch. 273.

The following are the proceedings to be taken in the order here given.

Notice by Anyone to Justice: Sec. 2(1).

I hereby notify you that it appears to me that a horse (*or other animal, describing it*) now in the possession of C.D., of the   of   , and now being at (*describe locality where animal is*) is diseased, that is to say, is affected with glanders or farcy.

Dated at   this   190

To G.H., Esq., J.P.   A.B.

(*Address*)   of

Notice by Justice to Veterinary: Sec. 2(1).

Having been notified in writing by A.B., of   , that a horse (*or other animal, describing it*) now in the possession of C.D. of the   , of   , and which is now at (*state where the animal is*) is diseased:

I hereby direct you to inspect the said animal as required by the statute in that behalf.

To E.F., Veterinary Surgeon.

(*Address.*)

          G.H., Justice of the Peace County

Report to Justice by V. S.: Sec. 3.

I beg to notify and report to you that having this day inspected, pursuant to your directions a horse (*or other animal, describing it*) in the possession or charge of C.D. of the   , of   , I find that the said animal is diseased, that is to say, is affected by glanders or farcy.

Dated at   this   190

To G.H., Esq., J.P.   E.F., Veterinary Surgeon.

(*Address.*)   (*Address.*)

Notice by Veterinary to Person in Charge of Animal: Sec. 3.

Take notice that having this day inspected by order of G.H., Esq., a justice of the peace for the county of   , a horse (*or other animal, describing it*) in your possession or charge I find that the same is diseased, that is to say, affected with glanders or farcy.

Dated at   this   190 .

To C.D., of (*residence*)   Signed E.F., Veterinary

          Surgeon (*Address*).

Justice's Order Thereon.

To I.J., a constable of the county of

Whereas I was on the   day of   , 190 , duly notified under the statute in that behalf that a horse (*or other animal, stating what*) was diseased and affected with glanders or farcy; and I did thereupon notify E.F., a veterinarian, to inspect the said animal, and the said E.F., having this day reported to me that he has found the said animal to be diseased as aforesaid:

You are thereby ordered to seize and detain the said animal and to cause the same to be kept in some place where it will not be brought into contract with or be in danger of transmitting the said disease to other animals until the case has been determined by the court.

Dated at   this   190

G.H., a justice of the peace in
and for the county of

Summons to Person in Charge of Animal: Sec. 6.

Canada.   ⎫
Province of Ontario. ⎬   To C.D. of
County of   . ⎭

Whereas it appears by the report this day made to me a justice of the peace in and for the county of   , by   , a veterinarian, that a horse (*or state what animal*) now in your possession *or* charge is diseased, that is to say, is affected with glanders or farcy.

These are therefore to command you in His Majesty's name to be and appear before G.H. and L.M., two of His Majesty's justices of the peace in and for the county of   , or such other justices as shall then be there at the   in the   of   in the county of   , on the   day of   , A.D. 190   , at   o'clock in the   noon to shew cause why the said animal should not be destroyed. Herein fail not.

Given under my hand and seal this   day of   , A.D. 190   , at   , in the county aforesaid.

G.H.   (Seal)
Justice of the peace in and for
the county of   .

The case will then proceed before two justices as in summary conviction cases as described *ante* p. 348; and upon "the evidence of one or more competent veterinarians" (sec. 8) that the animal is diseased as above mentioned and other evidence taken in the usual way the following order is to be made:—

ORDER FOR DESTRUCTION OF ANIMAL.

Canada.
Province of Ontario.
County of   .

Be it remembered that on the   day of   a notice was given by A.B. to G.H., a justice of the peace for the county of   , that a horse (*or state what animal*) then in the possession of C.D., of   , at   , the said   of   was diseased and affected with glanders or farcy; and thereupon the said G.H. did duly direct E.F., a veterinarian to inspect said animal, and afterwards on the   day of   , 190   , the said E.F. duly reported to the said G.H. in writing that said animal was so diseased; whereupon the said G.H. duly issued a summons to the said C.D. as required by the statute in that behalf:

And now on this day, to wit, on the   day of   , 190   , at   , the parties aforesaid appear before the undersigned, two of His Majesty's justices of the peace in and for such county of   , and having heard the matter of such complaint and it appearing by the evidence of   , a competent veterinarian (*or veterinarians if more than one*), that the said animal so in the possession of C.D. as aforesaid is diseased and affected with glanders or farcy.

We do order and adjudge that within twenty-four hours from this time, to wit, from the hour of   o'clock   noon of this present day, the said C.D. shall kill and bury (*or burn*) *or* cause to be killed and buried (*or burned*) the said animal.

And we do further order and adjudge that the said C.D. do pay to the said A.B. the sum of   for his costs in this behalf. And in default

of the said C.D. killing and burying (*or* burning) the said animal or causing the same to be so killed and buried (*or* burned) within the time aforesaid we do further order and adjudge that the said C.D. for his said default
shall forfeit and pay the sum of   , to be paid and applied
according to law.   And if the said several sums of money or either of them
is not paid on or before the   day of   , we do order and adjudge
that the same be levied by distress (*then* proceed *as in Form* 31 *in the
Criminal Code*).

G.H.   (Seal)
L.M.   (Seal)
Justices of the peace in and for
the said county of   .

No means are provided in the Act under consideration for enforcing
the payment of the penalty; but it is provided by R.S.O. ch. 90, sec. 2(3),
that the means for enforcement of payment of penalties under the Criminal
Code shall be adopted.   These are provided by section 739 of the Criminal
Code.

The order in regard to costs is also authorized by R.S.O. ch. 90, sec.
4(1)(3).

If the animal is not killed and buried as ordered a warrant of distress for
the fine will be issued and if not sufficient distress is found it will be followed
by a warrant of commitment for the period ordered unless the animal is
sooner disposed of as directed.

The forms of distress and commitment, *Forms* 40 and 44 in the Criminal Code may be used, making necessary changes.

If a fine is levied it goes to the municipality: Sec. 8(1).

The justices may give the veterinary or veterinaries acting in the
matter an order on the treasurer of the municipality for witness fees and
remuneration not exceeding four dollars for each day the veterinary was
engaged in making inspection and report and in attendance at court:
Sec. 11.

FORM OF ORDER ON TREASURER.

To the treasurer of the town (*or as the case may be*) of   .   **Pay**
to E.F. the sum of   dollars for his witness fees and other remuneration for his services in inspecting, reporting and attending court to give
evidence in the case of A.B. against C.D. for having in his possession an
animal affected with glanders or farcy.

Dated   , 19   .

G.H.   (Seal)
L.M.   (Seal)
Justices of the peace for
the county of   .

Add to the veterinarian's fees the cost of horse hire or other travelling
expenses if such was necessary in travelling to inspect the animal and in
attending court.

See also Dom. Stat. R.S.C. ch. 75.

Animals.
   Cruelty to or Abusing: Code 542.   *See* Cruelty to Animals.
   Two justices required.
   In Transit on Railways, etc., not Unloading for Rest, Food, etc: Code
   544.

Animal, Neglect to Bury Dead Animal.
   See Public Health Act, also Municipal By-law.

Apprentices and Minors, Offences by or Against.
   R.S.O. ch. 161.

Architect, Practising Without Authority.

R.S.O. ch. 181.
(Similar form to that under "Medicine.")

Articles of the Peace.

Code 748(2)(3).

Any person being threatened with personal violence to himself or his wife or child, or with injury to his property, may lay an information before a justice in the Form 49 to the Criminal Code, and the justice may summon or issue a warrant to arrest the defendant to answer to the complaint.

The proceedings are to be the same as in the case of any other charge laid against an offender; witnesses may be summoned and examined and the parties heard and the matter dealt with in the manner prescribed in Chapter XIII.; and if the justice is satisfied that the complainant has reasonable grounds for his fears, he may make an order that the defendant enter into a bond with one or more sureties to be of good behaviour and keep the peace. See the form of recognizance, 49 in the Criminal Code.

If the defendant does not furnish security as ordered the justice may issue a warrant committing the defendant to gaol: Form 50 in the Criminal Code.

Under the first clause of Code 748, a justice before whom a person is convicted of the class of offences there mentioned, may without any information or complaint of threats, and in addition to or in lieu of punishment for the offence of which he has been convicted, make an order that the defendant furnish securities to keep the peace and enter into the recognizance above mentioned, and in default may commit him to gaol as above stated.

See also *ante* p. 360.

Assault.

Common: Code 290, 291.

.A.B.. at   , on   , did unlawfully assault (*or in the case of assault and battery*, assault and beat) C.D.

Unreasonable Chastisement of Minor: Code 63. 290, 291.

A.B., at   , on   , did unlawfully assault, beat and ill-use C.D.

Assault on Workmen.

Code 501. *See* Workmen.
Two justices required.

Assembly, Unlawful.

See Riotous Acts.

Bank Note, Printing Circulars, etc., to Imitate.

Code 551.

A.B., at   . on   , did unlawfully engrave (*or* print *or* make, *or* execute. *or* circulate, *or* use, *stating how*) a certain business card (*or* notice, *or* placard, *or* circular, *or* hand bill, *or* advertisement) in the likeness or similitude of a bank note of the   bank (*or* of a share, *or* debenture of the   bank, *or* a debenture of the government of

Two justices required.

Bawdy House, Frequenting.

See Disorderly House.

Barberry Shrub, Planting, etc.

Ont. St. 1900, ch. 48; 1902, ch. 38, sec. 1.

A.B., at   , on   , did unlawfully plant (*or* sell, *or* does unlawfully cultivate) the shrub known as the barberry shrub.

Bees.

Selling Bees with Foul Brood: R.S.O. ch. 283, sec. 5.

Omitting to Give Notice of Foul Brood: R.S.O. ch. 783, sec. 10.

Begging.

Code 238(d). *See* Vagrancy.

Betting.

See Gambling in List of Indictable Offences. Also Gaming House.

Billiard Rooms.

Unlicensed. See R.S.O. ch. 247.

Minors, Admitting to: R.S.O. ch. 247.

A.B., at   , on   , being there and then the keeper of a licensed billiard, *or* pool, *or* bagatelle room, for hire or gain, did unlawfully admit C.D., a minor, who was then under the age of sixteen years, to the said billiard room, (*or* did unlawfully allow C.D. (*etc., as above*) to remain in the said billiard room), without the consent of the parent, *or* guardian of the said C.D., he, the said C.D., then not being a member of the family, *or* the servant of the said A.B., and then going to the said billiard room for the purpose of loitering, *or* to play billiards therein, and the said A.B., not then having reasonable cause to believe that such consent had been given by the parent *or* guardian of the said C.D., *or* that the said C.D. was not under the age of sixteen years.

Birds, Insectivorous, Protection of.

R.S.O. ch. 289.

Killing or catching any kind of wild birds whatever is unlawful, except hawks, crows, blackbirds and English sparrows; and also the birds specially mentioned in the Ontario Game and Bird Protection Act, during the close season: Secs. 2, 3. And the destruction or having in possession their eggs is also unlawful: Sec. 4.

But robins may be destroyed by a person to protect the fruit on his own premises: Sec. 2(2).

A permit may however be issued by the chief game warden to certain persons mentioned in section 6.

Fines imposed under this Act are to be paid to the prosecutor unless collusion between him and the offender is suspected: Sec. 8(2).

Births, Deaths, etc., Failing to Register Such.

R.S.O. ch. 44, secs. 15, 29.

A.B., being the father of a child born at the   of   on or about the   day of   , did unlawfully neglect to report such birth within thirty days from the date of the said birth.

(Similar forms for neglect to report death before interment: Sec. 25; or marriage within thirty days: Sec. 20; or making false statements in report: Sec. 28; or other offences: Sec. 30).

Breach of the Peace.

See Articles of the Peace; Riotous Acts, etc.

Butter and Cheese, Frauds in Sale of.

R.S.O. ch. 251.

25—MAG. MAN.

By-laws, Municipal, Breaches of.

Con. Municipal Act, 1903, ch. 19.

One justice has jurisdiction to convict for all breaches of this Act and of municipal by-laws passed under it; except that where there is a police magistrate for the municipality a justice has no authority without the magistrate's request: Secs. 476, 705.

All penalties are enforced by distress, or if no sufficient distress, by imprisonment: Secs. 705, 706.

Form of conviction is given in section 707.

Fines are to be disposed of in the way provided by section 708.

Canned Goods Act, Offences Against.

R.S.C. ch. 134.

Cattle in Transit, Not Unloading for Rest, Feed and Water.

Code 544, 545.

Cheese and Butter.

Fraud in Manufacture of: R.S.O. ch. 251.

Interfering with Testing of the Milk: Secs. 4, 5.

Supplying Cheese or Butter Factory With Milk from Which Cream has been Taken, Without Notice: Sec. 6.

or

Keeping Back Part of the Milk, Without Notice: Sec. 7.

or

Supplying Tainted Milk to Factories: Sec. 8.

FORM OF CHARGE UNDER SECTIONS 6, 7, OR 8.

A.B., at   , on   , did unlawfully supply deteriorated milk (see section 9(41)) to the   cheese (*or* butter) factory without notifying in writing the owner or manager of the said   factory thereof as required by the Act to Prevent Frauds in the Manufacture of Cheese and Butter.

Penalty is to go one half to complainant and one half to the factory: Sec. 10.

Two justices required.

Children.

Employing in Factories. *See* Factories Act.

Employing in Shops. *See* Shops Regulations.

Neglecting: R.S.O. ch. 259.

Child Immigration: R.S.O. ch. 262. *See* also under Minors.

See "Juvenile Offenders" *post*.

Coin.

Uttering Defaced: Code 566.

A.B., at   , on   , did unlawfully utter a certain coin which had theretofore been unlawfully defaced by having stamped thereon certain names or words, to wit (*state the words*).

Two justices required.

The consent of the Attorney-General is necessary before prosecution: Code 598.

Uttering Uncurrent: Code 567.

Making or Importing Uncurrent Copper Coin: Code 554.

Cock-pit, Keeping.

Code 543.

At   , on   , A.B. did unlawfully keep (*or* allowed to be kept) a cockpit on premises belonging to (*or* occupied by) him (*describe where*).

Two justices required.

Cock or Dog Fighting, etc.

Code 542(c).

At   .   , on   , A.B. did unlawfully encourage (or aid, or assist, describing in what manner) at the fighting (or baiting) of certain dogs (or cocks, or bulls, or bears, or badgers, or other animals, describing it or them, or a dog and a bear, or as the case may be).

Two justices required.

Cruelty to Animals.

Code 542(a).

At   , on   . , A.B. did unlawfully, wantonly, cruelly, and unnecessarily beat (or bind, or ill-treat, or abuse, or over-drive, or torture) a certain animal, to wit, a horse (or steer, or dog, or any domestic animal, describing it).

or 542(b).

While driving a horse (or steer, or heifer, or other animal, describing it) by negligence (or ill-usage) in the driving thereof was unlawfully the means whereby damage (or injury) was done to the said (animal, describing it, and describing the negligence or ill-usage).

Two justices required

Constable, Obstructing, etc.

Code 169.

A.B., at   , on   ·   , did unlawfully resist (or wilfully obstruct) C.D., who was then and there a peace officer, to wit, a constable of the county of   in the execution of his duty as such, to wit, in executing a lawful warrant of arrest against E.F.

or

Did unlawfully (or wilfully obstruct) one E.F., who was then and there lawfully aiding C.D., a peace officer (proceed as in the preceding form to the end).

This offence is either indictable or may be tried by two justices.

Contagious Diseases.

Of Animals. See Animals.

Public Health Act: R.S.O. ch. 248.

Cullers of Sawlogs.

See Sawlog Cullers.

Damage to Property.

See Wilful Injuries.

Dentist, Practising Without License.

R.S.O. ch. 178, secs. 26, 27. *See* Form under "Medicine."

Desertion of Wife.

R.S.O. ch. 167. *See* Husband and Wife.

Desertion, Persuading Soldier or Seaman to; Code 82.

A.B., at   , on   , he not then being himself an enlisted soldier in His Majesty's service (or a seaman in His Majesty's naval service) did unlawfully persuade (or procure, or endeavour to procure) C.D. then and there being a soldier in His Majesty's service (or a seaman in His Majesty's naval service) to desert from and leave such service by (describe the means used).

This offence is either indictable or triable summarily before two justices.

Disorderly Conduct or Vagrancy.
See Vagrancy.

Disorderly House.
Frequenter of Gaming House: Code 229.
A.B., at   , on   , did unlawfully play (*or* look on while another person was playing) in a common gaming house at (*describe locality*).
Two justices required.
See Disorderly House, Keeper of, in List of Indictable Offences.
Obstructing Police From Entering: Code 230(a)(b).
A.B., at   , on   , did unlawfully prevent C.D. (*or* obstruct, *or* delay C.D. in) entering a disorderly house (*or* a room constituting a part of a disorderly house) at (*describe locality*), he the said C.D., being then and there a constable of the said county of   (*or* a police officer of the said city of   ), and being then and there duly authorized to enter the same.
or Code 230(*c*).
By a bolt (*or* chain, *or other contrivance, stating it*) did unlawfully secure an external (*or* an internal) door of a common gaming house situate (*describing where*) for the purpose of preventing C.D. from (*or* obstructing, or delaying C.D. in) entering the said common gaming house (*or* room being a part of the said house), he, the said C.D., being then and there a constable of the said county of   (*or* a police officer of the said city of   , and duly authorized to enter the said house (*or* room).
Two justices are required to try the above cases.

Disturbing Public Meeting or any Assemblage of Persons Met for any Moral, Social, or Benevolent Purpose.
Code 201.
That A.B., at   , on   , did unlawfully disturb, *or* interrupt, *or* disquiet, an assemblage of persons then met together at (*name and describe the church, hall, or house where the meeting was*) for religious worship, *or* for a moral, *or* social *or* benevolent purpose, by profane discourse, *or* by rude *or* indecent behaviour, *or* by making a noise, (*describe the conduct*) within the said place of such meeting, (*or* so near the said place of such meeting as to disturb the order *or* the solemnity of the said meeting), then and there being so held.

Dogs, Recovering Damages from Owner of Dog Which has Worried Sheep.
R.S.O. ch. 271, sec. 15.
A.B., on   , at   , was the owner of a certain sheep *or* lamb, which was then and there unlawfully killed by a dog of which C.D. was then and there the owner (*or* keeper) the said sheep or lamb being of the value of   dollars, and the said A.B. claims to recover from the said C.D. the value of the said sheep (*or* lamb).
In case there are two or more dogs owned by different persons the justice may apportion the damage: Secs. 5, 15(2).
An appeal lies to the Division Court, where the sheep was killed or where the owner of the dog resides: Sec. 15(6).
The convictions and proceedings will be sent to the clerk of that court.
There can be no claim for sheep killed on the highway: Sec. 20.
Neglect of Owner to Destroy Dog After Notice of Injury: Sec. 16.
Keeping or Harbouring a Dog Which Has Worried Sheep: Secs. 11-13.

Making False Statement to Assessor by Owner of Dog: Sec. 4.
Justices are to make returns of convictions to the clerk of the municipality besides the usual return to the clerk of the peace.

Driving Furiously.
See under Indictable Offences: There is generally a municipal by-law against this, under which a summary conviction can be made.

Druggist, Practising as Without Diploma.
See Pharmacy.

Drunk and Disorderly.
Code 238(f). Also see Municipal By-law.

Engineer, Operating Stationary Engine Without Certificate.
Ont. St. 1906, ch. 26, 27.

Factories Act, Ontario.
Offences Against: R.S.O. ch. 256; Ont. Stat. 1901, ch. 35; 1902, ch. 36.
Employing Children in Factories: Secs. 3, 5.
A.B., at   , on   , being then and there the employer in charge of a factory within the meaning of the Ontario Factories Act, did unlawfully employ C.D., a child, being a boy (*or* girl) under the age of fourteen years of age in the said factory.
For other offences see the various sections of the above Act and use similar forms.
Two justices required: Sec. 46.
For provisions as to description of offence see section 47(2-5).
The information must be laid within two months: Sec. 47.
Fine is to be paid to the factories inspector.

Fire Escape.
Hotelkeeper, Not Providing: R.S.O. ch. 264.
A.B., at   , on   , he being then and there the owner (*or* lessee, *or* proprietor) of an hotel known as   , which exceeded two storeys in height did not erect *or* cause to be erected and maintained at least one permanent outside stairway or ladder from the several landings or floors above the first storey thereof of the kind and description required by section 2 of the Act for the Prevention of Accidents by Fire in Hotels and Other Like Buildings.
Keeping a proper rope in each bedroom is sufficient: Sec. 3(2); or the fire escape known as "The Natural Drop Fire Escape," described in Ont. St. 1900, ch. 44.
Factory Owner, Not Providing: Ont. Stat. 1902, ch. 36.

Fire.
Negligently Setting Out, Within Districts Proclaimed by the Lieutenant-Governor: R.S.O. ch. 267.
Setting Out Fire Between April 1st and November 1st Without Taking Reasonable Precautions: Secs. 5, 6.
Dropping Burning Match, Lighted Cigar, Pipe Ashes, etc., Within Fire District: Sec. 7.
Engine Driver on Railway not Seeing that Engine Provided With Proper Appliances to Protect from Fire while Passing Through Fire District: Sec. 10.
Prosecutions must be within three months: Sec. 12.

Fire Arms, Discharging so as to Disturb.
Code 238(g).
A.B., at　　　　, on　　　　, did unlawfully by discharging firearms in a street (or highway) wantonly disturb the peace and quiet of the
inmates of the dwelling-house of C.D., situated near the said street (or
highway).
See also municipal by-laws against discharging fire-arms on the public
streets.

Fisheries Act.
Ont. St. 1900, ch. 50.
Trespassing on Land Covered by a Fishing Lease: Sec. 25.
A.B., at　　　　, on　　　　, did unlawfully enter upon or pass
over the land described in, and the subject of a fishing lease in favour of
C.D. being (*describe the locality trespassed on*) without the permission of
the said C.D. or his representative.
Fishing Within the Fishing Limits of Another Person: Sec. 26.
*Obstructing or Interfering With by Violence or Threats, or Giving
False Information to Fishery Overseer, When in Discharge of His
Duty*: Sec. 30.
*Neglecting to Move Nets as Directed by Fishing Overseer After Forty-
eight Hours' Notice*: Sec. 34, amended by Act of 1901, ch. 37,
sec. 9.
*Shipping or Transporting Out of Province Salmon Trout, Lake Trout
or White Fish, Weighing Less Than Two Pounds*: Sec. 39.
*Transporting Out of Province Fish Caught in Provincial Waters Out of
Season*: Sec. 40.
Catching Sturgeon Without License: Ont. St. 1901, sec. 14.
*Catching More than Twelve Bass or Twenty Pickerel or Four Maski-
nonge in One Day by Angling*: Ont. St. 1900, ch. 50, sec. 46.
*Catching More than Fifty Speckled Trout or More than Fifteen Pounds
in All*: Sec. 47.
Catching Speckled Trout Between Sept. 1st and May 1st, Inclusive:
Sec. 47.
*Not Returning to the Water Bass Less Than Ten Inches or Speckled
Trout Less Than Six Inches, or Maskinonge Less Than Eighteen
Inches in Length*: Sec. 48.
*Non-resident Tourist or Summer Visitor Catching More Than Ten Lake
Trout*: Sec. 49.
*Catching Lake Trout or Whitefish Under Two Pounds Undressed or
One and Three-quarters Pounds Dressed, or Sturgeons Less Than
Ten Pounds Dressed*: Sec. 50.
*Fishing In Lake Nepigon, River Nepigon or Tributaries Without Per-
mit*: Sec. 51.
Penalties under above Act: Sec. 53. In default of immediate pay-
ment imprisonment, not distress.
Information must be laid within three months: Sec. 59(1). Fines are
to be paid one-half to the prosecutor and one-half to the fisheries com-
missioner: Secs. 64, 66.
The following are offences under R.S.C. ch. 45:—
Catching Brook Trout Between Sept. 15th and Jan. 1st: Sec. 24(d).
Catching Salmon Trout Between Oct. 1st and Dec. 1st.: Sec. 24(c).
*Catching or Having Whitefish Between the First and Tenth Nov. In-
clusive*: Sec. 31(a).
Not Providing Fish-ways: Sec. 46.
For other offences under this Act see sections 71-95. The fine under
the above Dominion Statute is to be paid one-half to the prosecutor and
one-half to the Crown: Sec. 104.

Food.

See Canned Goods Act.

Offering for Sale Things Unfit for: Public Health Act, R.S.O. ch. 248,
secs. 108, 109; sec. 11 of by-law at the end of above statute.

A.B., at   , on   , did unlawfully offer for sale as food a
diseased animal (*or certain meat, or fish, or any of the articles mentioned
in the above statute or by-law*) which by reason of disease (*or adulteration,
or impurity, or any other cause, stating what*) was then unfit for use.

The above by-law is by section 122 of the statute declared to be in force
in every municipality.

Two justices are required to try this case.

See, also Health Laws, *post*; also Animal, Selling Diseased, *ante*.

Forest, Wilful Injury to Dominion Forest Reserve or Park.

R.S.C. ch. 55, sec. 225.

Two justices required.

Fruit, Marking and Fraud in Sale of.

R.S.C. ch. 85; R.S.O. ch. 253.

Game Protection Laws.

Offences Against: Ont. Stat. 1900, ch. 49; amended by Stats. 1902, ch.
39; 1904, ch. 28; 1905, ch. 33.

Non-resident of Ontario, Hunting Without a License: Ont. Stat. 1900,
secs. 3, 29(1).

A.B., at   , on   , he not then being a resident of and
domiciled in Ontario, did unlawfully hunt certain game, birds (*or animals*),
to wit, wild ducks (*or deer, or as the case may be*) without having first
obtained the license therefor required by the Ontario Game Protection Act.

Deer Hunting Between 15th Nov. and 1st Nov. Following: Secs. 4(1)
29(1).

A.B., at   , on   , did unlawfully hunt deer during the
time prohibited in that behalf by the Ontario Game Protection Act.

Deer, Moose, Reindeer, or Caribou Hunting Without a License:
Sec. 8(1).

Hunting Cow Moose, or Young Moose or Caribou Under One Year Old:
Sec. 8(2).

*Killing More Than Two Deer, or One Bull Moose, or One Bull Caribou,
in a Season*: Sec. 8(3).

*Killing Deer in Water or Immediately After Coming Therefrom (in
Indian Peninsula, County of Bruce only)*: Sec. 8(4).

Hunting by Crusting or Yarding: Sec. 8(5).

*Hunting Deer With Dogs or Allowing Hunting Dog Loose in Close
Season*: Sec. 8(6).

*Hunting Ducks From Sailboat, or From Yacht or Launch Propelled by
Power; or With Swivel Gun*: Sec. 9.

Using Poison: Sec. 10.

*Trapping Game; or Setting Nets or Barbed Lines, Except for Beaver,
Otter or Muskrats*: Sec. 10(2).

*Shooting Game Bird Between Half an Hour After Sunset and Half an
Hour Before Sunrise*: Sec. 11.

Hired Hunters: Sec. 12.

Destroying or Having Game Birds' Eggs: Sec. 13.

*Carrying Gun, etc., and Being Masked or Disguised Near Game
Preserve*: Sec. 14.

Trespass While Hunting: Sec. 20.

Failure to Produce License on Demand by any Person: Sec. 25(2).

Hunting Wild Geese or Swans Between 1st May and 15th Sept.: Sec. 4(4c).

Hunting Ducks or Water Fowl Between 15th Dec. and 1st Sept. Following: Sec. 4(4d).

Penalties and Application of Same: Sec. 29.

Penalties are Enforceable by Imprisonment (not Distress): Sec. 31(6).

Prosecutions Must be Within 3 Months: Sec. 31.

Parties Charged not to be Taken Before a Justice More Than 10 Miles Distant, Except as Stated: Sec. 31(2).

The Form of Charge to be Drawn up in the Words of the Section Violated: Sec. 31(3); *Giving Name or Description of Offender With Time, Place and Circumstance of Offence.*

One justice or game warden has jurisdiction in all above cases.

Hunting Snipe, Rail, Plover, or Waders Between 15th Dec. and 15th Sept. following: Sec. 4(4e).

Hunting Muskrats Between 1st May and 1st Jany. Following: Sec. 5(2).

Shooting Muskrat, or Breaking Muskrat House During April: Sec. 5(3).

As to exceptions see above section.

Hunting on Sunday: Sec. 6.

Being Possessed of Game in Close Season, Except as Stated: Sec. 15(1).

Selling or Buying Game Without a License, Except as Stated: Sec. 15(2).

Hotel or Restaurant Supplying Game at Meals for Pay During Close Season: Sec. 15(3).

Exporting Game in Close Season, Except as Provided in this Section: Sec. 16.

Hunting Beaver or Otter Before 1st Nov., 1910: Sec. 5(1); as amended in 1905.

Hunting in Rondeau Park: Sec. 17.

Hunting Grouse, Partridge, Woodcock, Black or Grey Squirrels, or Hares Between 15th Dec. and 15th Sept. Following: Sec. 4(4a).

Hunting Quail or Wild Turkies Between 1st Dec. and 1st Nov. of Following Year: Stat. of 1902, ch. 39, sec. 2(b).

or

Hunting Moose, Caribou, South of Main Line of C.P.R., Between Mattawa and Manitoba, Between 15th Nov. and 1st Nov. Following; or North of Above Limit Between 15th Nov. and 16th Oct. Following: Stat. of 1904, ch. 28, sec. 1(2).

Hunting Capercalzie Prior to 15th Sept., 1909; Sec. 2.

Carrying Gun in Tamagamie Forest Reserve in Close Season: Stat. of 1905, ch. 33, sec. 4.

Common Carriers Having or Transporting Game Without Coupon and Affidavit Attached, After Close Season: Stat. of 1900, amended in 1905, ch. 33, sec. 5(1)

Gaming House, Looking on or Playing in.

Code 229.

A.B., at   , on   , did unlawfully play (*or* look on while certain persons unknown were playing) in a certain common gaming house at (*describing where*).

Two justices required.

Garden, Destroying.

See Wilful Damage.

Health Act, Offences Against.
See Public Health Act: R.S.O. ch. 248.

Horses, Glandered.
R.S.O. ch. 273; R.S.C. ch. 75. *See* Animals Diseased. *See*, also, Dom. St. 1899 as to regulations for preservation of health on public works.

Highway.
Disobeying Regulations for Use of: R.S.O. ch. 236; Ont. St. 1900, ch. 40.
Persons Driving and Not Turning Out to the Right to Enable Person Meeting Him to Pass: Sec. 1(1).
Or to Allow Person on Bicycle to Pass: Sec. 1(2).
Or to Allow Another to Pass When Overtaken: Sec. 2(1).
Not Turning Out to the Left When Overtaking and Passing Another Vehicle: Sec. 2(2).
Bicyclists or Person Driving and Overtaking Another Not Giving Audible Warning Before Attempting to Pass: Sec. 2(4).
Person With Heavy Load, Not Turning Out or Stopping and Assisting Another to Pass: Sec. 3.
Driver of Vehicle Being Too Drunk to do so With Safety: Sec. 4.
Racing and Furious Driving or Shouting or Using Blasphemous or Indecent Language: Sec. 5.
Driving Sleigh Without Bells: Sec. 6.
Driving Over Bridge More than Thirty Feet Long Faster Than a Walk if Legible Notice is Conspicuously Placed Thereon: Secs. 8, 10.
Driving of Traction or Portable Engine Meeting Horse Vehicle and Disobeying Regulations: Ont. St. 1900, ch. 40, sec. 2.

Husband and Wife, Desertion by Husband, Order for Maintenance.
R.S.O. ch. 167.
A.B. is a married woman deserted by her husband C.D., who being able to maintain his said wife A.B., has unlawfully refused and neglected so to do and has deserted her at the   of   in the county of   , on or about the   day of   ; and the said A.B. applies for an order that the said C.D. shall pay to her a weekly sum for her support and that of her family.
Two justices required.
The proceedings to enforce payment of amount ordered are described in section 3, and must be closely followed.
The order can only be enforced by distress and not by commitment.
See, also, Neglect to Supply Necessaries.

Ice, Leaving Unguarded Holes in.
Code 287. *See* Neglect.

Indecent Theatrical Performances.
Code 208.
A.B., at   , on   , he being then and there the lessee (*or* manager, *or* person in charge) of a theatre known as the   opera house situated in the said   of   , did unlawfully give (*or* allow to be presented, *or* allow to be given) therein an immoral (*or* indecent, *or* obscene) play, *or* concert, *or* performance, *or* representation.
NOTE.—This offence may be treated either as indictable; or it may be tried summarily by one justice.

Indecent Act.
Code 205(a).
A.B., at   , on   , unlawfully and wilfully in the presence of one or more persons did an indecent act (*describing it*)* at

the same being a place to which the public have (*or* are permitted to have) access.

or 205(*b*).

* Intending thereby to insult or offend C.D.

Two justices required.

Indian Act.
Offences Under: R.S.C. ch. 81.
Trespass by Outsider, Cutting Trees or Sapling on Indian Reserve: Sec. 127.
• *Indian of Band, Trespassing on Another's Land and Cutting Trees or Removing Stone, Soil, etc.*: Sec. 128.
Buying or Acquiring a Present Given to Indian: Sec. 133.
Supplying Liquor to Indian, etc.: Secs. 135, 136, 140, 141.
Indian Making or Having Liquor in His Possession: Secs. 136, 137.
Two justices or Indian Agent have jurisdiction in the above offences.
Trespass by Outsider on Indian Reserve, etc.: Secs. 33-37, 124-126.
Drunken Indian, etc.: Secs. 139, 144.
Indian Refusing to Give Information from Whom Liquor Obtained: Sec. 146.
Celebrating Certain Indian Festivals: Sec. 149.
One justice or Indian Agent has jurisdiction in these cases.

Inland Revenue Act, Breaches of.
R.S.C. ch. 51.
Brewer, distiller or tobacco or cigar manufacturer not keeping license posted up: Sec. 99.
Two justices: Sec. 132(b).

Insane and Dangerous Person.
Ont. St. 1906, ch. 60.
A.B., at   , on   , is insane and dangerous to be at large.
NOTE.—*The proceedings to be taken are described and the forms will be found in the above statute; blank forms will be furnished by the clerk of the peace.*

Insurance Company.
On Mutual or Assessment System, Using Policy, etc., Not Marked "Assessment System": R.S.O. ch. 24, secs. 61, 62.
Carrying on Business Without a License: Secs. 66-68.
Limit of time for prosecution, one year.
Two justices required.

Inspection and Sale of Staple Commodities.
R.S.C. ch. 85.
Offences under sections 36, 39, 40, 41, 102, 104, 105, 108, 304, 305, 306, 307 and 308 must be tried by two justices.
Offences under sec. 103 may be tried by one justice.
Offences under sections 106, 107, 235 are indictable, and justices can only hold preliminary enquiries.

Junk or Marine Stores.
Dealer Buying from Person Under 16 Years Old; or From Any Person Between Sunset and Sunrise: Code 431.

Juvenile Offenders, 16 Years Old or Under.
Code 800-821, 644; R.S.O. ch. 259 and 304.
Theft by Juvenile Under 16: Code 802.

The proceedings are fully set out in sections 800-821 of the Criminal Code.

Two justices have jurisdiction to try such case summarily and convict, on proof of guilt, unless the offender or his parent or guardian objects as provided by section 807. If such objection is made the justice may hold a preliminary enquiry and commit for trial.

Justices have no jurisdiction to try summarily any case of theft except those against juvenile offenders under these sections of the Code, and except those mentioned *ante* p. 196.

As to liability of juveniles to punishment for crimes, see *post* ch. XV.

On a youthful offender being brought before a justice the parent or guardian should be notified and also the executive officer of the Children's Aid Society if one has been organized in the county, so that the child's rights may be protected: Code 779.

Trials of juveniles must be held without publicity and separately and apart from other accused persons, and at suitable times to be appointed for that purpose: Code 644.

Young offenders under fourteen years old should never be placed in the police cells or in gaol with any other prisoner; nor those over 14 years old, if it is possible to arrange for their safe keeping elsewhere or if they can furnish sufficient bail.

In dealing with the cases of juveniles, reference should be had particularly to the provisions of the above sections of the Criminal Code; and also to the above mentioned Ontario statutes, in which provision is made in regard to juvenile offenders against Ontario laws, and also for the cases of children who are being abused or neglected.

Lake Shore of Lakes Erie, Ontario or Huron, Taking Sand or Stones From Without Leave.

R.S.O. ch. 270, secs. 3-10.

Two justices required: Secs. 7, 12.

Appeal is to the County Court and the conviction and papers must be transmitted to the clerk of that court.

Land Surveyor, Practising as Without License.

R.S.O. ch. 180. (Similar form under "Medicine.")

Liquor License Act, Offences Under.

Neglecting to Keep License Exposed: R.S.O. ch. 245, sec. 47.

A.B. having a license by wholesale (*or* shop, *or* a tavern, *or* a vessel license) on   , at   , unlawfully and wilfully (*or* negligently) omitted to expose the said license in his ware-house (*or* shop, *or* in the bar-room of his tavern, *or* in the bar-saloon, *or* bar-cabin of his vessel, *as the case may be*).

Neglecting to Exhibit Notice of License: Same statute. sec. 48.

A.B., being the keeper of a tavern (*or* inn, *or* house of public entertainment) in respect of which a tavern license has duly issued and is in force, on   , at   , unlawfully did not exhibit over the door of such tavern (*or* inn, etc.) in large letters the words "licensed to sell, wine, beer, and other spirituous or fermented liquors," as required by the Liquor License Act.

Sale Without License: Same statute, sec. 72.

A.B., on the   day of   , A.D. 190 , at   . in the county of   , unlawfully did sell liquor without the license therefor by law required.

Two justices required unless offence committed in township or incorporated or police village, where one justice may try: Secs. 72, 97, 118.

Keeping Liquor Without License: Same statute, sec. 50.

A.B., on   , at   , unlawfully did keep liquor for the purpose of sale, barter and traffic therein, without the license therefor by law required.

Two justices required: Secs. 97, 118.

Selling Without License, Second Offence: Same statute, sec. 72.

If the prosecution is for a second offence, insert one of the charges stated above, and add the following:—

And further that the said A.B. was previously, to wit, on the day of   , 19   , at the   of   , before C.D. and E.F., justices of the peace for the   of   ,in the county of   , duly convicted of having on the   day of   , 19 , at the town (or village, *etc.*) of   ,in the county of   , unlawfully sold liquor without the license therefor required by law (or *as the case may be, setting out the previous conviction*).

If the charge is for a third offence, add to the above the second conviction in the same form.

Two justices required, except in cases where the offence was committed in township, incorporated or police village or territorial district: Sec. 97. 118.

Sale Under Wholesale License in Less Than Wholesale Quantities: R.S.O. ch. 245, secs. 2(4) and 51(2).

A.B., having a license to sell by wholesale on   , at   , unlawfully did sell liquor in less quantity than five gallons (or than one dozen bottles of three-half pints each, *or* than two dozen bottles of three-fourths of a pint each).

Two justices required unless offence occurred in a township, or incorporated or police village, or territorial district: Secs. 97. 118.

Allowing Liquor to be Consumed in Shop: R.S.O. ch. 245, sec. 62.

A.B., having a shop license on   , at   , unlawfully did allow liquor sold by him (or in his possession), and for the sale of which a license is required, to be consumed within his shop (or within the building of which his shop forms part, *or* within a building which communicates by an entrance with his shop) by a purchaser of such liquor (or, by a person not usually resident within the building of which such shop forms a part).

One justice may try the case if the offence was committed in a township, or incorporated, or police village. Otherwise two justices required.

Allowing Liquor to be Consumed on Premises Under Wholesale License: R.S.O. ch. 245, sec. 63.

A.B., having a license by wholesale, on   , at   , unlawfully did allow liquor sold by him (or in his possession for sale) and for the sale of which such license is required, to be consumed within his warehouse (*or* shop, *or* within a building which forms part of or is appurtenant to *or* which communicates by an entrance with a warehouse *or* shop, or premises) wherein an article to be sold (*or* disposed of) under such license, is sold by retail (or wherein there is kept a broken package of an article for sale under such license).

Two justices required unless offence was committed in a township, or village, or territorial district.

Allowing Liquor to be Drunk in Wholesale Shop: Same statute, sec. 80.

A.B., on   , at   , being then and there the purchaser of liquor from C.D., who was not licensed to sell the same to be drunk on the premises, did unlawfully drink (or cause E.F. to drink) such liquor on the premises of the said C.D., where the same was sold by him to the said A.B., and such drinking was unlawfully with the privity and consent of the said C.D.

Illegal Sale of Liquor by Druggist: R.S.O. ch. 245, sec. 52.

A.B., then being a druggist on   , at   , did unlawfully sell liquor for other than strictly medicinal purposes (or sell liquor in packages of more than six ounces at one time; or sell liquor without the prescription of such liquor signed by a duly qualified medical practitioner required by law, *or* sell liquor without recording the same) as required by the Liquor License Act.

Keeping a Disorderly Tavern: Sec. 81.

A.B., being the duly licensed keeper of a tavern (*or* ale-house, *or* beer-house, *or* house of public entertainment), situate in the city (or town, or village, *or* township), of   , in the county of   , on   , in his said tavern (or house) unlawfully did sanction (*or* allow) gambling (or riotous, *or* disorderly conduct) in his said tavern (or house).

Two justices required, or one justice and the mayor or reeve of municipality.

Harbouring Police Constable on Duty: Sec. 82.

A.B., being licensed to sell liquor at   , on   , unlawfully and knowingly did harbour (or entertain, or suffer to abide and remain on his premises) C.D., a constable belonging to a police force, during a part of the time appointed for his being on duty, and not for the purpose of quelling a disturbance or restoring order, or executing his duty.

Compromising or Compounding a Prosecution: Sec. 83.

A.B., having violated a provision of the Liquor License Act on   , at   , unlawfully did compromise (or compound, or settle, or offer, or attempt to compromise, compound or settle) the offence with C.D., with the view of preventing any complaint being made in respect thereof (or with the view of getting rid of or stopping, *or* of having the complaint made in respect thereof dismissed, or *as the case may be*).

Being Concerned in Compromising a Prosecution: Sec. 83.

A.B., on   , at   , unlawfully was concerned in (or a party to) a compromise (or a composition, or a settlement) of an offence committed by C.D. against a provision of the Liquor License Act

Tampering With a Witness: Sec. 85.

A.B., on a certain prosecution under the Liquor License Act, on   , at   , unlawfully did tamper with C.D., a witness in such prosecution before (or after) he was summoned (*or* appeared) as such witness on a trial (or proceeding) under the said Act (or unlawfully did induce, or attempt to induce C.D., a witness in such prosecution, to absent himself, or to swear falsely).

Refusing to Admit Policeman: Sec. 130.

A.B., on the   , at   , being in (or having charge of) the premises of C.D., being a place where liquor is sold (or reputed to be sold), unlawfully did refuse (or fail) to admit (or did obstruct, or attempt to obstruct E.F., an officer demanding to enter in the execution of his duty or did obstruct, or attempt to obstruct E.F., an officer making searches in said premises, and in the premises connected with such place).

Officer Refusing to Prosecute: Secs. 129, 130.

A.B., being a police officer (or constable, or inspector of licenses) in and for the   of   , in the county of   knowing that C.D. had on   , at   , committed an offence against a provision of the Liquor License Act. unlawfully and wilfully did and still does neglect to prosecute the said C.D. for his said offence.

Two justices required.

Order for Destruction of Liquor Seized: R.S.O. ch. 245, sec. 132.

We, E.F. and G.H., two of His Majesty's justices of the peace for the county of   (or C.D., police magistrate of city of   ), having on the   day of   , 19   , at the township of   in said county, duly convicted J.K. of having unlawfully kept liquor for sale without license, do hereby declare the said liquor and vessels in which the same is kept, to wit, (*describe the same*), to be forfeited to His Majesty, and we (or I) do hereby order and direct that A.B., License Inspector of the of the said county, do forthwith destroy the said liquor and vessels.

Given under our (*or* my) hands and seals, this   **day of** A.D. 19 , at the   of   , in the said county.

E.F. [L.S.]
or G.H. [L.S.]
C.D. [L.S.]

Inebriate, Notice Prohibiting Sale to: Ontario Stat. 1906, ch. 47, sec. 33.

NOTICE.—Given under section 125 of the Liquor License Act.

To E.F. (and G.H., *several names may be included in one notice*) of the   of   , in the county of   , a person (*or* persons) licensed to sell intoxicating liquor under the Ontario Liquor License Act.

I, A.B., of (*residence and occupation*), the wife (or husband, or parent, son, daughter, brother, sister, master, guardian or employer, *as the case may be*) of the person hereinafter named, hereby notify you not to deliver liquor to C.D., of the   of   , in the county of   , being a person who has the habit of drinking intoxicating liquor to excess.

Take notice that in the contravention of this prohibition, or in case you suffer or permit the said C.D. to linger or loiter in the bar-room or other place upon your premises in which liquor is disposed you will incur the penalties provided by section 125 of the Liquor License Act.

Dated at   this   day of   , A.D. 190 .

(*Signature.*)

This notice may be given by the license inspector: Same statute, sec. 33(3).

Inebriate, Notice to: Same statute, sec. 33(3).

NOTICE.—Given under section 125 of the Liquor License Act.

To C.D. (*name of the inebriate*).

I, A.B., (*name of person giving notice, adding occupation*) of the of   , in the county of   , hereby notify you that I have this day given notice to the license holders of the   license district of   (or to E.F., or to E.F. and G.H., *etc., name of persons notified*), not to deliver liquor to you, you having the habit of drinking liquor to excess.

Take notice that should you directly or indirectly purchase *or* procure, or attempt to purchase *or* procure upon the premises of any of the said license holders (or upon the premises of the said E.F., *etc., naming the particular license holders notified*) *or* be found lingering or loitering in or about the bar-room or other place in which liquor is disposed upon such premises you will incur the penalties provided by section 125 of the Liquor License Act.

(*Signature.*)

NOTE.—*These notices may be given by mailing in registered letters*: Same sec. (4).

Inebriate, Furnishing Liquor to, After Such Notice: Same statute, sec. 33(5).

That on the   day of   , 190 , A.B., the wife (or parent, *etc.*) of C.D., a person who then had the habit of drinking intoxicating liquor to excess, duly gave notice in writing signed by her (or him) to E.F., a person then licensed to sell intoxicating liquor, not to deliver intoxicating liquor to the said C.D.; and within twelve months next after the service of such notice,* the said E.H. unlawfully did deliver (*or* suffer to be delivered) in or from the place then and there occupied by the said E.F. being a place where intoxicating liquor was authorized to be sold, intoxicating liquor to the said C.D., otherwise than in terms of special requisition for medicinal purposes signed by a duly qualified medical practitioner. (See sec. 25(1) as to what the medical requisition must contain).

Inebriate, License Holder Permitting Loitering by: Same statute, sec. 33(6).

*Proceed as in the next preceding form to the * and add the following*:—

And E.F., being then and there the keeper of a licensed tavern after service upon him of the said notice did unlawfully suffer (*or* permit) the said C.D. to loiter or linger in and about the bar-room of the said licensed tavern in which liquor was dispensed upon the said licensed premises.

Inebriate, Third Person Providing or Purchasing Liquor for: Same statute, sec. 33(8).

*Proceed in the form given above to the * and add*:—

And on the   day of   , 190 , the said A.B., (*name*) did also duly give notice in writing to the said C.D. in the form and manner required by the statute of the Province of Ontario, 6 Edw. VII. ch. 47, sec. 33, sub-sec. 3, * *, and thereafter on   , at   , G.H. with a knowledge of the said notices having been so given, did unlawfully give (*or* sell), or purchase for and on behalf of C.D., (*or* for the use of C.D.) intoxicating liquor.

Inebriate, Himself Procuring Liquor: Same statute, sec. 33(7).

*Proceed as in the above forms to the second * *, and add*:—

And the said C.D. within twelve months after service of the said notices as aforesaid did unlawfully purchase (or procure, *or* attempt to purchase or procure) intoxicating liquor (*or* was found unlawfully lingering *or* loitering) in and about the bar-room of the licensed tavern of E.F. being a place in which liquor was dispensed.

Intoxicated Person, Supplying Liquor to: R.S.O. ch. 245, sec. 76.

E.F., at   , on   , he being a duly licensed person under the Ontario Liquor License Act, did unlawfully deliver intoxicating liquor to C.D., a drunken person; (*or* unlawfully permit and suffer C.D., a drunken person to consume liquor upon his premises).

Minors, Supplying Liquor to: Same statute, sec. 78.

E.F., at   , on   , he being then and there a licensed person under the Ontario Liquor License Act, did unlawfully allow liquor to be supplied on his premises to C.D., a person apparently (*or* to the knowledge of E.F.) under the age of twenty-one years, (Stat. of 1905, ch. 30, sec. 1)

Minor, Allowing to Loiter in Bar-room: Same statute, sec. 78(4).

E.F., at   , on   , he being then and there a licensed person under the Ontario Liquor License Act did unlawfully and without proper cause suffer (or permit) C.D., a person apparently (*or* to the knowledge of the said E.F.) under the age of twenty-one years and not accompanied by his parent (or guardian) and not being a resident or a *bonâ fide* lodger or boarder on the premises of the said E.F. to linger (or loiter) without good and sufficient reason in and about the bar-room on the said premises in which liquor was dispensed.

Minor, Loitering in Bar-room: Same statute, sec. 78(4).

Form may be adapted from the foregoing.

Drunkenness, Permitting on Licensed Premises: Same statute, sec. 76.

E.F., on   , at   , he being then and there a licensed person under the Ontario Liquor License Act, did unlawfully permit drunkenness (*or* violent, or quarrelsome, *or* riotous, *or* disorderly conduct, *stating what*) to take place on his premises.

Gambling, Permitting on Licensed Premises: Sec. 76.

E.F., at   , on   , he being then and there a duly licensed person under the Ontario Liquor License Act, did unlawfully suffer gambling (or *any unlawful game*) to be carried on on his premises (*state what the gambling* or *the game was*).

Prohibited Hours, Disposing of Liquor During: Statute of 1906, sec. 13.

E.F., at   , in his premises (or on, *or* out of, or from his premises) known as (*state the place*), being a place where liquor was then and there authorized to be sold, unlawfully did sell (or dispose of) intoxicating liquor during the time prohibited by the Liquor License Act (or by by-law of the municipal council of   , or of the license commissioners for the district of   , *as the case may be*) for the sale of the same, to wit, after the hour of seven of the clock in the afternoon of Saturday the   day of   , A.D. 190 , and before the hour of six of the clock on Monday morning next thereafter without any requisition for medical purposes as required by the said Act being produced by the vendee or his agent. (See section 25(1) as to what medical requisition must contain.) Two justices required, unless offence was committed in a township, or village, or territorial district in which case one justice has authority.

Prohibited Hours, Allowing Liquor to be Drunk on Premises During: Same statute, sec. 13.

E.F., at   , in his premises known as the   , being a place where intoxicating liquor was authorized to be sold, unlawfully did allow and permit * the sale of such liquor upon the said premises during the time prohibited by the Liquor License Act for the sale of the same, to wit, after the hour of seven of the clock in the afternoon of Saturday the   day of   , A.D. 190 , and before the hour of six of the clock on Monday morning next thereafter * *, without the requisition for medical purposes required by the said Act being produced by the vendee or his agent.

or

*Allow and permit such liquor to be drunk upon the said premises being the same (*etc., proceed as in above form to the * *).

Two justices required unless offence was committed in a township, village or territorial district.

Prohibited Times, Sale at Other: Same statute, sec. 13.

The above forms may be adapted to such charges.

Two justices, except as above mentioned.

Shop License, Sale of Less Than Three Half Pints Under: R.S.O. ch. 245, sec. 2(3).

E.F. having a shop license under the Ontario Liquor License Act on   , at   unlawfully did sell liquor in less than three half pints.

Two justices, except as above mentioned.

Keeping Two Bars: Same statute, sec. 65.

E.F., on   , at   , in his house or premises duly licensed under the Ontario Liquor License Act and known as the   hotel, did unlawfully keep in the said house or premises more than one bar.

Two justices, except as above mentioned.

Prohibited Hours, not Keeping Bar-room Closed During: Same statute, sec. 66.

A.B., at   , on   , being then and there the keeper of a licensed tavern in the said city (or town) of   , unlawfully did* not keep the bar-room (or room in which liquor was trafficked in) in the said tavern, closed against all persons other than those permitted to enter the same during the hours in (or day on) which the sale of liquor was prohibited by law.

Or, same section.

*Did allow certain persons to be present in the bar-room in the said tavern during the hours in (or day on) which the sale of liquor was prohibited by law.

NOTE.—Informations must be laid in writing within thirty days after the commission of the offence: R.S.O. ch. 245, sec. 95.

The next day after the offence was committed will be the first day to be counted.

The information may be laid by any person (sec. 95); and need not be sworn (sec. 95).

Only one offence to be included in one information.

The costs are the same as in summary conviction cases (Ontario tariff; see *ante* p. 377), except the license inspector is entitled to the fees mentioned in section 117 of R.S.O. ch. 245, which will be added.

Justices have no power to remit or reduce penalty or suspend punishment: Sec. 88.

License Holder Taking Articles for Liquor or in Pawn: Same statute, sec. 67.

E.F., at   , on   , being then and there a person holding a liquor license under the Ontario Liquor License Act did unlawfully * purchase from C.D. certain wearing apparel (or *any of the articles mentioned in the above section, stating what*) the consideration for which was (or was in part) intoxicating liquor (or the price of intoxicating liquor).

or

*Did unlawfully receive from C.D. certain goods, to wit, (*stating what in pawn*).

Two justices are required to try this charge.

Bar-tender, Unlicensed: Statute of 1906, sec. 6.

E.F., the keeper of a licensed tavern in the city (or town) of   , in the Province of Ontario, did on   , at   , employ A.B. as bar-tender (or permit A.B. to act as bar-tender) in the licensed premises of the said E.F., the said A.B. not being then the holder of a bar-tender's license.

Medical Practitioner, Giving Requisition Without Stating Particulars: Same statute, sec. 25(2).

or

Giving False Requisition: R.S.O. ch. 245, sec. 74.

License Holder Supplying Liquor on Improper Requisition: Statute of 1906, sec. 25(1)(3).

Drugging Liquor: Same statute. sec. 26(3)(4).

For other offences see the several clauses of the above statutes.

Forms of information and of convictions and warrants of commitment are given at the end of the R.S.O., 245; see sec. 103, and should be carefully followed.

Bottled Liquor, Mixing or Re-filling Bottle: Ont. St. 1906, sec. 26(1)(4).

A.B., at   , on   , being then and there the keeper of a licensed tavern did procure certain bottled liquor (*describing it*) for the purpose of supplying the same to his customers or guests did while the said liquor was on the said licensed premises unlawfully omit to keep such liquor in the bottle in which the same was delivered to him and removed and kept the same in another vessel (*or put or allow, or suffer to be put into such bottle other liquor, or any substance of liquor, stating what*); or re-fill. or partially re-fill. the said bottle for the purpose of supplying liquor therefrom to his customers or guests after the said bottle had been emptied, or partially emptied, of the said bottled liquor contained in the said bottle when so procured by him as aforesaid.

Bottle, Tavern or *Shop Keeper Using False Label On, etc.*: Same statute sec. 26(2)(4).

Fines and penalties received are to be paid over as stated in R.S.O. ch. 245, sec. 90.

As to appeals, see sec. 218, *et seq.*

Refer to and follow the special forms of informations, convictions, warrants of commitments, etc., given in the schedule to R.S.O. ch. 245.

As to search warrants for liquor, see secs. 131, 132.

Supplying Liquor *to Railway Employee in Uniform*: Ont. St. 1906, ch. 30, sec. 244.

A.B., at 　　　, on 　　　, did unlawfully sell (or give) spirituous or intoxicating liquor to C.D., who was then and there a servant or employee of (*here name the railway company*), and while he, the said C.D. was actually employed in the course of his duty on a train or car (or while he the said C.D. was in uniform as such employee, as the said A.B. then well knew).

Supplying Liquor *to Railway Employee on Duty*: R.S.C. ch. 37, sec. 414.

Railway Employee Being Intoxicated on Duty: Same statute, sec. 245; R.S.C. ch. 37, sec. 413.

A.B., at 　　　, on 　　　, was unlawfully intoxicated while in charge of a locomotive engine (*or* an electric motor of 　　　 railway company, or while acting as the conductor of a car or train of cars) of the railway company.

Liquor, Sale of Within Three Miles of *Public Works*: R.S.O. ch. 39, secs. 1, 2.

A.B., on 　　　, did unlawfully sell (or barter, or exchange, *or* dispose of) to C.D. (*or* expose, *or* have in his possession for sale, *etc.*), intoxicating liquor at the 　　　 of 　　　, such place not being within the limits of a city, town or incorporated village, and being within three miles of a railway then and there in process of construction, the said liquor not being so sold by wholesale, by a licensed distiller or brewer.

Search warrants for such liquor. See secs. 6, 7, 8.

Liquors, Sale of, Near Public Works: Code 150-154.

A.B., at 　　　 on, 　　　, upon (or after) the day named in a certain proclamation putting in force in the said place an Act respecting the *Preservation* of the *Peace* in the *Vicinity of Public Works*, and while the said proclamation remained in force, did unlawfully at the said 　　　 of 　　　, which was within the limits specified in the said proclamation, sell (*or* barter, or exchange, *state* for *what, or* supply, or dispose of) intoxicating liquor (*or* expose, or keep on hand in his possession intoxicating liquor intended to be sold or bartered, *etc.*).

See, also, Ont. Stat. 1906, ch. 30, sec. 244.

Liquor, Offences Under Indian Act in Regard to: R.S.O. ch. 81, secs. 135-146. *See* Indian Act.

Supplying Liquor *to Indian*: R.S.C. ch. 81, sec. 135.

A.B., at 　　　, on 　　　, did unlawfully supply an intoxicant (*naming what*) to C.D., an Indian and known by the said A.B. to be such.

Two justices required.

Lord's Day Act, Breaches of.

Dom. St. 1906, ch. 27; Con. St. U.C. 1859, ch. 104.

A.B., at 　　　, on 　　　, did unlawfully engage on the Lord's Day in a public game or contest, to wit, the game of hockey (or *as the case may be*) for gain (*or* for a prize, or reward)

or

Was unlawfully present at a public game (*etc., as in the above form*)

or

Did unlawfully provide (or was present at, or engaged in) a certain performance (*describing it*).

or

At a public meeting elsewhere than at a church, namely (*describe where*) at which a fee was charged for admission.

Excursion On: Sec. 6.

Shooting On: Sec. 8.

Selling Foreign Newspaper On: Sec. 91.

Selling or Purchasing Merchandise On, etc.: Sec. 2.

Carrying On Ordinary Calling On:

The various Acts of the Ontario Legislature as to the Lord's Day have been declared by the *Privy* Council to be *ultra vires* and inoperative: Atty.-Gen. v. Ham. St. Ry. L.R. (1903) A.O. 524, 7 Can. Cr. Cas. 326; but the Court also decided that the Act of the late *Province* of Canada, Con. Stat. U.C. 1859, ch. 104, relating to the observance of the Lord's Day is still in force in Ontario.

Since then the Dominion *Parliament* has passed the Lord's Day Act, 1906, ch. 27; but by section 14 that statute does not repeal or affect any provisions of Con. Stat. U.C. 1859, ch. 104. Both these statutes are therefore in force in Ontario, and a violation in Ontario of any of the provisions of either statute is punishable in the way stated in the same. Prosecutions for offences against the Dominion Statute, 1906, cannot be commenced without the leave of the Attorney-General. In proceedings under the above Consolidated Statutes a summons must be issued in the first instance and not a warrant of arrest, unless the defendant fails to appear on the summons: Sec. 9.

Prosecutions under Con. Stat. must be begun within one month; and under the Act of 1906 within sixty days. Under section 18 of the Con. Stat. any fine under that Act is to be paid one-half to the prosecutor and one-half to the county or city treasurer. Fines under the Act of 1906 will be paid to the Crown Attorney to be transmitted to the provincial treasurer.

One justice may try all cases under either statute, except charges against corporations, under section 12 of the Act of 1906, in which two justices are required.

The Ontario Legislature has authority to legislate so as to prevent electric railways which are subject to the jurisdiction of the province, from running on Sunday; and by Ont. Stat. 1904, sec. 79, it has so legislated by prohibiting cars to be run on Sundays, with certain exceptions there mentioned; and the conductor in charge of a car of an electric railway running on Sunday, is liable to summary convictions for doing so.

Lunatic, Dangerous.

See Insane and Dangerous *Person*.

Machinery, Not Having Couplings, etc,. Protected.

R.S.O. ch. 265. *See* also, Threshing Machines, Factories Act.

Master and Servant Act, Offences Under.

R.S.O. ch. 157; Ont. Stat. 1901. ch. 12.

Wages, Non-payment of: Secs. 9-12, 17.

A.B., on   , at   , was engaged by C.D. to work for him the said C.D. as a labourer (or a domestic servant, or *as the case may be*) at the wages of (*state the rate of wages and how payable*) and the said A.B. from thence until the   day of   190 , continued to work for the said C.D. at the said employment. and on the   day of 190 , the said A.B. became entitled to be paid by the said C.D. under said hiring and service the sum of   , being the amount of wages then due and payable to him by the said C.D., which said overdue wages the said C.D. neglects (or refuses) to pay to the said A.B., although payment has been duly demanded.

The information in wages cases must be on oath or affirmation; and the claim must not exceed forty dollars: Sec. 11.

The order for payment can only be enforced by distress.

Information must be laid within one month after the time the employment ceased or after the last installment of wages fell due: Sec. 12.

See, also, Apprentice.

Marine Stores, Junk, etc.
Dealer *in Buying From a Person Under Sixteen Years Old*: Code 431.
or
From Any Person Between the Times of Sunset and Sunrise: Code 431(2).

Milk, Frauds in Sale of.
R.S.O. ch. 252.

Mines Act.
Ontario, 1906, ch. 11.
Removing Boundary Marks: Sec. 209.
A.B., at   , on   , did unlawfully and without being authorized by, and contrary to the provisions of the Mining Act, 1906, wilfully deface (or alter, or remove, or disturb) a certain stake or post (or boundary line, *describing it*) placed or made (or a figure or writing by law permitted to be made on a stake or post planted or made, *etc.*) under the provisions of the said Act, marking the boundary of a certain mining camp of C.D.,' (*describing where situated*).
Contravening an Order of the Mining Commission: Sec. 17.
A.B., at   , on   , did unlawfully and wilfully refuse to obey a lawful order of the mining commissioner appointed under the Mines Act, 1906, that is to say (*set out the order and in what respect it was disobeyed*).
Prospecting Without a License: Secs. 84, 103.
A.B., on   , at   , and at and on divers days and times since that date did unlawfully explore (or attempt to explore, or occupy, *or* work) certain Crown lands for minerals otherwise than in accordance with the provisions of the Mines Act, 1906, that is to say (*describe what was unlawfully done*).
Employing Boys Under Fifteen in Mine: Sec. 192, 196.
A.B., at   , on   , did unlawfully employ a boy named C.D., who was then under the age of fifteen years (*or* did allow a boy named C.D., who was then under the age of fifteen years to be for the purposes of employment) in a mine, to which the Mines Act of 1906 applied, below ground.
Employing Woman or Girl in Mine: Secs. 192, 196.
Employing Boy Under Seventeen in Mine on Sunday (or *for More than Forty-eight Hours in any One Week, or for More than Eight Hours in One Day*: Secs. 193, 196.
Neglect to Keep Register of Boys Employed in Mine: Secs. 194, 196.
Paying Wages to Employee in Mine at or in a Public House, etc.: Sec. 200.
Neglect to Fence Abandoned Mine: Sec. 203(1).
See form of charge under Neglect to Fence Hole in Ice, etc.
Keeping Magazine Within Four Hundred Feet of Mine: Sec. 203(2)—(6).

Not Providing Places of Refuge and Manholes for Miners: Sec.
    203(13)(14).
Workmen Being Lowered or Hoisted in Mine Contrary to sec.
    203(22)(23).
Staking Claim Without License: Sec. 209(6).
  See sections 209, 214 as to penalties, etc. Two justices required to try
offences under the Act: Secs. 17, 215. Complaint must be laid within
three months: Sec. 216.
  Fines to be enforced in the manner described: Sec. 225.
  See also Mines, Offences Regarding in List of Indictable Offences.

Medicine, Practising Without Registration.
  R.S.O. ch. 176, sec. 49.
  A.B., on   , at   , being an unregistered person within the
meaning of the Ontario Medical Act, did unlawfully practise medicine for
hire or reward contrary to the said Act by attending professionally and
prescribing medicine for one C.D. and also for one E.F.

Milk, Adulteration of.
  R.S.O. ch. 252.
  Two justices required.

Minors.
  Under Eighteen, Supplying Tobacco or Cigarettes, etc., to: R.S.O. ch.
    261. *See* form under Tobacco.
  Supplying Liquor to or Allowing Minor Under Eighteen to Loiter in
    Bar-room. See Liquor Laws.
  Admitting Minor to Billiard Room. See Billiard Room. *See* also
    under Apprentices; Master and Servant; Juvenile Offenders;
    Neglected Children.
  As to extent of authority of parents, teachers and masters to discipline
child, pupil or apprentice, see Code 63, 64.

Mortgagors, Fraudulent Injury to Property by.
  Code 529.

Motor Vehicles.
  Ont. Stat. 1906, ch. 46.
  Driving on Highway Without License: Sec. 2.
  A.B., at   , on   , was the owner of a motor vehicle known
as an automobile which was then and there driven on the highway without
* the said A.B. having paid the registration fee and obtained a permit re-
quired by section 2 of the Statutes of Ontario, 6 Edw. VII. ch. 46.
or
*Without the said automobile having attached thereto and exposed
on the front and back thereof a number of the kind and description required
by section 3 of the statute (*proceed as in the above form*).
  Not Sounding Alarm at Crossing: Sec. 5.
  Not Carrying Lighted Lamp with Number on it After Dark: Sec. 5.
  Using a Searchlight: Sec. 5(3).
  Speeding at More than Ten Miles an Hour in or Near Cities, Towns or
    Incorporated Villages: Sec. 6.
  Reckless or Negligent Driving: Sec. 7.
  Intoxicated Chauffeur: Sec. 9.
  Breach of Provisions as to Passing and Meeting Vehicles: Sec. 10.
  Leaving Motor Unlocked on Highway When Not Used: Sec. 14.
  Penalties: Secs. 19, 20.
  Constable may arrest offenders without warrant: Sec. 21.

Municipal By-laws.
See By-laws, *ante.*

Neglect to Guard Holes Made in the Ice.
Code 287 (a).

A.B., at , on , did cut or make (or cause to be cut or made) a hole (or opening, *or* place) of sufficient size to endanger human life through the ice on certain water then open and frequented by the public, to wit, the harbour (or the bay, *or* lake, or river, *designating the place*) and did unlawfully leave such hole or opening while so in a state dangerous to human life unenclosed by bushes or trees and unguarded by a guard or fence of sufficient height and strength to prevent anyone from accidentally driving or walking *or* skating *or* falling therein.

Neglect to Guard Abandoned Mines.
Code 287.

Obscenity.
See Indecency.

Pawn Brokers Act, Ontario, Offences Under.
R.S.O. ch. 188.

Neglect to Put up Sign: Secs. 7, 8.

Taking Goods in Pawn From Journeymen: Sec. 18.

Search Warrant for a *Certain Form of Goods*: Sec. 19.

Selling Pawned Goods Without Exposing a Catalogue: Secs. 26, 27.

In the above cases two justices are required. In all other offences under this Act one justice may act: Sec. 41.

Prosecutions must be commenced in twelve months: Sec. 40.

Penalties are to be paid to the municipal treasurer.

See also Pawnbrokers' Act of Canada: R.S.C. ch. 121.

Peace Officer, Obstructing, etc.
See Constable.

Personation at Examination.
Code 409.

See same heading under list of indictable offences.

This offence is either indictable or may be tried summarily by one justice.

Patent Medicines.
Ont. St. 1898, ch. 30.

Pharmacy Act, Offences Under.
R.S.O. ch. 179, amended in 1905. ch. 16, and 1906, ch. 25.

Practising Pharmacy Without Certificate: Sec. 26.

See form for practising medicine *ante.*

Poison.

Selling Poisons Mentioned in the Statute Without Certificate as Chemist: Sec. 26; Schedule A. to Act.

Chemist Selling Poisons Mentioned in Schedule A, in Bottle or Package Not Marked Poison, and With the Seller's Name and Address: Sec. 28.

Chemist Selling Poisons Mentioned in Part I. of Schedule A, Without Making an Entry in a Book in the Form C to the Act, with the Purchaser's Signature to the Entry: Sec. 28.

or

Selling any of the Drugs or Medicines *Mentioned in Ont. St. 1905, ch. 16, sec. 9, Without a Certificate as Chemist.*

Pigeon or House Dove, Killing, Wounding or Taking.
Code 393.
At   , on   , A.B. did unlawfully and wilfully kill (or wound, *or* take) a pigeon or house-dove, the property of C.D.

Poisons.
See Pharmacy Act Offences.

Public Buildings, Churches, etc., Doors not Hinged to Open Outwards.
R.S.O. ch. 216.
A.B. (*or a* company, *or as the case may be, giving the name*) on   ,
at   , was the owner (*or* possessor) of a public hall (or theatre, or church, or *other building, naming and describing it*) then and there used for holding public meetings or being a place of public resort, in which building the doors were not so hinged that they might open freely outwards.
Two justices required.
Half the fine goes to informant and half to the minor municipality: Sec. 3.

Public Health Laws, Offences Against.
The laws are to be found in the R.S.O. and amendments thereunder noted; and in the Municipal Act, 1903, secs. 550-554; and in the by-laws and regulations passed by the Boards of Health and the municipal councils under these statutes.
The statutes are: R.S.O. ch. 248; and Ont. Stats. for 1901, ch. 12, secs. 28, 29, 35, and ch. 34; also for 1902, ch. 34; 1903, ch. 29; and 1905, ch. 32.
The statement of the offence in the proceedings must say that the act objected to was done unlawfully; and should follow the words of the statute or by-law or regulation which has been broken, giving time, place and particulars of the act which constituted the offence.
Two justices are required to try a charge under the Health Act.
See also the following headings in the lists of offences:—
Food, Selling Things Unfit for: In list of Indictable Offences.
Animal, Selling Diseased: In list of Indictable Offences.
Food, Selling Things Unfit for: In Summary Convictions list.

Post Office Offences.
R.S.C. ch. 66.
Selling Postage Stamps Without License: Sec. 134.
Using Stamps Previously Used: Sec. 135.
Unauthorized Person Delivering Letters: Sec. 136.
Enclosed Letter in Parcel, etc.: Sec. 123.

Prize Fight.
Code 108.

Engaging in as Principal: Code 105.
A.B., at   , on   , did unlawfully engage as a principal in a prize fight.
Attending or *Promoting:* Code 106.
A.B., at   , on   , was unlawfully present as an aid (or second, or surgeon, *or* umpire, *or* backer, or as assistant, or reporter, *or* did advise, *or* encourage. *or* promote by. *state in what manner*) a prize fight between E.F. and G.H. (or *between two persons unknown*).

Leaving Canada to Engage in: Code 107.
Challenging: Code 104.

Pound Keepers.
Neglecting to Supply Food and Water to Animals Impounded: R.S.O.
ch. 272, sec. 23.
or
*Neglecting to Make a Return to the Clerk of the Municipality at the
Beginning of Each Year as to the Animals Impounded*: Secs. 27-29.

Poultry or Geese, Trespassing After Notice.
R.S.O. ch. 272, sec. 3.
Notice must first be given.

FORM OF NOTICE.

Take notice that you are hereby required to prevent poultry (or geese)
owned by you from trespassing upon my premises. This notice is given
pursuant to section 3 of the Revised Statutes of Ontario entitled an Act
Respecting Pounds.
Dated at   this   19
To A.B., of   ,   C.D.

FORM OF CHARGE.

A.B., at   , on   , did unlawfully refuse (*or* neglect) to
prevent certain poultry (or geese) then and there owned by him from
trespassing upon the neighboring premises of C.D. after notice in writing
had been duly served upon him, the said A.B., of their trespass as required
by the statute on that behalf.

Prostitutes.
See Disorderly House; Keeping or Frequenting; also Vagrancy.

Public Meeting, Disturbing.
See Disturbing Public Meeting.

Public Parks Act, Offences Against.
R.S.O. ch. 233, sec. 18.

Railway Track, Trespassing on.
Ont. Stat. 1906, ch. 30, sec. 240(1).
A.B., at   , on   , being a person not connected with the
          railway or employed by the   railway, did unlawfully
walk along the track thereof.

Railway.
Entering Train Without Paying Fare: Same statute: Sec. 240(2).
A.B., at   , on   , did unlawfully enter upon a railway
train of the   railway company with intent fraudulently to be carried
upon said railway without paying fare thereon.
or
Did unlawfully and wilfully trespass by entering the railway station
(or car, or building, *stating what*) of the said   railway company
in order to occupy the same for his own purposes.
Obstructing Railway Employee.
Did unlawfully and wilfully obstruct or impede (*stating how*) C.D.,
an officer of the   railway company in the execution of the duties

by the said C.D. as such officer or agent upon a train of the said company (or upon the premises of the said company).

Railway Employee, Wilfully Allowing Engine or Car to Stand on Highway for More than Five Minutes at One Time.
R.S.O. ch. 37, secs. 394, 431.

Railway Company.
Not Having Blackboard at Station Giving Information as to Trains: Secs. 395, 431.

Any One Leaving Gate Open at Farm Crossing, or *Taking Down Railway Fence or Taking an Animal on the Railway* Track: Secs. 407, 431.

Trespassing or Walking on Railway Track: Secs. 408, 431.

Railway Regulations, etc.
Any Person Negligently Violating: Secs. 246, 247.

Damage to Electric Railway: Sec. 248(c).

Selling or *Giving* Liquor *to Railiway Employee on Duty* or *in Uniform:* Sec. 244.

Riotous Acts.
Unlawfully Assembly: Code 87-89.

A.B., C.D., E.F., with other persons (or A.B., with other persons to the number of three or more), with intent to carry out the common purpose of assaulting one G.H. (*or of preventing* G.H. from proceeding to his work along the streets of the said   of   ; or, of causing a breach of the peace; or a disturbance on the public street of   ; or of preventing the Toronto Railway Co. from running their cars; *or, stating what the common purpose was, it being immaterial whether such purpose was in itself lawful or unlawful*) did unlawfully assemble themselves together in such a manner (*or,* did assemble together and then and there while so assembled did unlawfully conduct themselves in such a manner) as to cause persons in the neighbourhood of such assembly to fear on reasonable grounds that the said A.B. (C.D. and E.F.) with the said other persons so assembled would disturb the peace tumultuously (*or,* would by such assembly needlessly and without any reasonable occasion provoke other persons to disturb the peace tumultuously).

Riot.
Code 88.

(*Proceed as in the next preceding form to the end and then add the following*): and being so assembled together did then and there actually begin and continue for a long time unlawfully to disturb the peace tumultuously.

Hindering the Reading of Riot Act: Code 91, 92(a).

At   , on   , there were divers persons to the number of at least twelve unlawfully, riotously and tumultuously assembled together to the disturbance of the public peace, whereupon H.J., Esquire, who was then a justice of the peace for the said county of   , pursuant to his duty prescribed by the statute in that behalf, duly resorted to the said place where the said unlawful, riotous and tumultuous assembly then was, and as near to the said rioters as he could then safely come, then and there began (*or* was about) to make the proclamation in the words and manner required by the said statute, and A.B. (and C.D. with others) did unlawfully and with force and arms then and there wilfully oppose (or hinder or hurt) the said H.J., who had then and there begun (or was about) to make the said proclamation whereby, and by means whereof, the said proclamation was not made.

Refusing to Disperse After Reading of Riot Act: Code 92(b).

A.B. (and C.D), with divers other persons to the number of twelve or more, unlawfully, riotously and tumultuously assembled together to the disturbance of the public peace, whereupon, and while the said A.B. and C.D. and said other persons were so unlawfully, riotously and tumultuously assembled together as aforesaid, H.J., Esquire, then a justice of the peace for the said county of   , within whose territorial jurisdiction the said assembly then was, duly resorted to the said place where the said unlawful, riotous and tumultuous assembly then was, and among the said rioters, or as near to them as he could safely come * with a loud voice did duly proclaim and command silence and thereupon did then and there with a loud voice make (*or* cause to be made) the proclamation in the words and in the manner provided by the statute in that behalf, in these words, that is to say (*here insert the proclamation of which the form is given in Code* 91), and the said A.B. (and C.D.) with said other persons so unlawfully, riotously and tumultuously assembled together as aforesaid, to the number of twelve or more, then and there, notwithstanding the proclamation so made as aforesaid, did unlawfully continue together for the space of thirty minutes after the said proclamation had been made as aforesaid. (*Or insert instead of the above words after the * the following:* then and there began (or was about) to make the proclamation in the words and manner required by the statute in that behalf, when certain persons unknown did unlawfully and with force and arms then and there wilfully oppose (*or* hinder, or hurt) the said H.J., who had so begun (*or* was about) to make the said proclamation as aforesaid, whereby and by means whereof the said proclamation was not made, the said A.B. (and C.D.), with other persons to the number of twelve or more so unlawfully, riotously and tumultuously assembled together, as aforesaid, then well knowing that the making of the said proclamation was hindered as aforesaid did then and there unlawfully continue together for the space of thirty minutes after such hindrance).

NOTE.—The foregoing riotous acts are indictable only: Justice will hold preliminary enquiry and commit for trial.

Proceedings to Suppress Riot—are described in Code 91, 93, 94; and in R.S.C. ch. 41, sec. 39; and are as follows:—

Reading the Riot Act: Code 91.

When a justice becomes aware that there are twelve or more persons within his jurisdiction unlawfully, riotously and tumultuously come together to the disturbance of the public peace. it is his duty (of his own motion and without waiting to be called upon to do so: R. v. Penney, 5 C. & P. 254; R. v. Kennet, 5 C. & P. 282), to proceed at once to the place, and either amongst the rioters or as near to them as he can safely come, with a loud voice to command. "silence"; and then with a loud voice make the following proclamation, either reading it himself or causing the sheriff or constable or other person to do it in his presence:—

"Our Sovereign Lord the King charges and commands all persons being assembled, immediately to disperse and peaceably to depart to their habi-. tations or to their lawful business, upon pain of being guilty of an offence, on conviction of which they may be sentenced to-imprisonment for life: God Save the King."

Without these latter words the proclamation will not be valid: R. v. Childs, 4 C. & P. 442.

In proceeding to make this proclamation, it is proper that the justice should be accompanied and protected by such police or constables as may be available, while he is performing his duty.

Hindering the Reading of the Riot Act, etc.

If any persons forcibly oppose, hinder or hurt the justice who is about to make the proclamation or while he is making it, it is his duty to direct the police or constable to forthwith arrest such persons; and it is the duty of the police and constables (and all persons called upon to aid them: Code 95) to apprehend such persons and carry them before a justice of the peace for trial upon the charge, the form of which is above given: Code 93; proceeding in the manner prescribed for indictable offences, Chap. XII., *ante.*

No warrant of arrest is necessary. Form of charge to be drawn up is given above.

The justice is also to direct the arrest of all persons who continue together to the number of twelve, for thirty minutes after reading of the above proclamation, or after they know that it was hindered as above mentioned: Code 93(b).

Form of charge for same is given above,

The police and constables are justified in using reasonable force in carrying out these directions and to disperse the mob; using their batons if necessary.

Before proceeding to use force to disperse the mob, there must be a delay of thirty minutes after reading the proclamation and before employing force for that purpose; but if those assembled together continue their riotous conduct, the justice should proceed to direct their arrest and to quell the disturbance, notwithstanding the thirty minutes have not expired: R. v. *K*ennet, 5 C. & P. 282. All persons who remain together to the number of at least twelve, for more than thirty minutes after the proclamation has been read, do so at their peril; and must take the consequences, even if they are not of the rioters but merely onlookers. It is the duty of peaceable citizens either to come forward and offer their service in aiding to suppress the riot, or to go away.

The reading of the proclamation, or "Riot Act," applies to all gatherings, whether at the place where the riot is going on, or elsewhere; and if twelve or more persons are gathered together in any part of the municipality, they may be dispersed by force if necessary. The reading of the "Riot Act" may be, and if necessary should be, repeated, if the justice thinks expedient.

Special Constables: R.S.O. ch. 99, sec. 23-31.

Authorizes two or more justices to appoint and swear in special constables to suppress a tumult or riot; and this should be done, if the ordinary police force and constables are not sufficient for that purpose.

Before calling upon the citizens as special constables, the justices must first take an information, or evidence on oath, of some credible witness, that a tumult or riot has taken place, or is continuing, or may be reasonably apprehended. at some place within the limits of the justices' jurisdiction: R.S.O. ch. 23, sec. 23.

EXAMPLE OF SUCH INFORMATION.

Canada.

Province of Ontario.

County of

The information and complaint of A.B., of the   of   , in the county of   (*occupation*) taken this   day of   , A.D. 19 , before the undersigned, two of His Majesty's justices of the peace in and for the said county of   who saith that a riot has taken place and is now continuing at (*describe the locality*), disorderly persons to the number of twelve or more having been and being now unlawfully assembled together at the said place and having begun to disturb and are now disturbing the peace tumultuously.

Sworn before me at the said ⎫
  of   the day ⎬   **A.B.**
and year first above mentioned. ⎭

              C.D., J.P.
              E.F., J.P.

If upon receiving the above information, the justices are of opinion that the ordinary police force and constables are not sufficient for the preservation of the peace and the protection of the inhabitants and the security of property, they may call out and appoint in writing so many as they think fit, of the householders or other persons (not legally exempt from serving as constables), resident in the territorial division or its neighbourhood, to act as special constables, for such time and in such manner as the justices may deem necessary: R.S.O. ch. 99, sec. 23.

FORM OF APPOINTMENT.

To J.K., of the   of   , in the county of   (*occupation*).

You are hereby appointed a special constable in and for the ˙ of , for the term of   days, pursuant to the Revised Statutes of Ontario, chapter 99.

Dated, etc.

              C.D., J.P.
              E.F., J.P.

The special constables are to be sworn: Sec. 24.

FORM OF OATH.

I, A.B., do swear that I will well and truly serve our Sovereign Lord the King in the office of special constable in the   of   , without favour or affection, malice or ill will; and that to the best of my power, I will cause the peace to be kept and preserved and will prevent all offences against the persons and properties of His Majesty's subjects; and that while I continue to hold the said office, I will to the best of my skill and knowledge discharge all the duties thereof faithfully according to law; so help me God.

Those exempt from service as special constables are clergymen, aged and decrepid persons, and persons under fifteen years old: 5 Burns' Justice 22.

The justices appointing special constables must at once send notice by letter to the Hon. the *Provincial Secretary*, Parliament Buildings, Toronto, stating that they have appointed special constables under this Act, giving a list of those appointed, and stating fully the facts shewing that it was necessary to take that step: Sec. 25.

Section 26 provides for the justices making orders and regulations, for the more efficient performance of their duties by the special constables so appointed.

Special constables so appointed have the powers and duties of ordinary constables: Sec. 27.

What Force May be Used in Suppressing a Riot.

By Code 48 the justices and constables are justified in using, and in ordering those assisting them to use, such force as reasonably appears necessary to suppress a riot, and as is not disproportioned to the danger reasonably apprehended from continuance of it.

The police (and those assisting them, if so ordered by the justices) may resort to the use of batons or clubs to disperse the rioters; but every reasonable effort to get the crowd to disperse should first be exhausted. The police and citizens must not be armed with or use firearms.

Payment of Special Constables.

The justices are authorized to make an order on the municipal treasurer for the municipality in which the special constables have been required to serve, for the payment of a sum not exceeding $1 per diem in favour of of each of the special constables: R.S.O. ch. 99, secs. 30, 31.

FORM OF ORDER FOR PAYMENT.

To   , Esq,
          Treasurer of the   of   .
     Pay to   special constable appointed by us under the Revised Statutes of Ontario, chapter 99, the sum of $, being for
days, during which he served as such special constable for the   of

Dated, etc.

C.D., J.P.
E.F., J.P.

Calling Out the Militia.

If a riot appears likely to assume such serious proportion, as to be beyond the powers of the civil authorities to suppress, three justices of the peace (one of them being the mayor, or head of the municipality) may by writing require the senior officer of the active militia of the locality (*e.g.,* the Colonel of the city battalion), to call out, with their arms and ammunition, such portion of the active militia as such officer thinks necessary.

The officer of the militia force on its arrival is bound to order the use of such force and means to suppress the riot, as shall be directed by the three justices mentioned; and the militia are protected and justified in obeying, in good faith, the justices' orders, if the same are not manifestly unlawful: Code 49.

As to what force is justifiable, the circumstances of each case will govern; but great care is to be used. At first the mere parading of the military at different strategic points, or where the rioters are gathered, may be sufficient to deter them from further riotous doings. If not, such force as, under the circumstances, appears reasonably necessary and commensurate with the danger to be apprehended, must be used; going even to such extreme measures as firing upon the mob, if ordered by the justices, if it appears to be absolutely necessary for the protection of life or preventing extensive and immediate destruction of property. This, of course, should be a last resort, in order to prevent danger which is apparent and imminent; and is one not likely to be necessary to be resorted to in Ontario.

In all the proceedings above referred to the three justices mentioned are the sole directory authority; and are responsible for what is to be done, and for the orders issued; and although they should confer with the military officers and other authorities, their doing so would be no defence or excuse if the action taken should be wrong. On the justices, and not on the military officers, rests the authority and responsibility for the degree of force to be used; and the military are required by the law to obey the justices' orders.

If, upon a riot taking place, a justice neither reads the Riot Act nor restrains nor apprehends the rioters, it is *primâ facie* evidence of criminal neglect of duty, for which he may be indicted: Code 94.

The duties and responsibility of justices under the circumstances, are fully discussed in R. v. *Penney,* 5 C. & P. 254, and R. v. *Kennet,* 5 C. & P. 282.

Riots, etc., Near Public Works.
     R.S.O. ch. 38.
     Two justices required: Sec. 11.

Rivers and Streams, Obstructing.
     R.S.O. ch. 142, secs. 4-8.

A.B., at   , on   , did unlawfully throw (or he being then an owner, or occupier of a mill on the stream hereinafter mentioned, did unlawfully suffer or permit to be thrown) into the river (*naming it*), *or* into a rivulet, *or* watercourse, *describing it*) slabs (or waste stuff, or refuse, *stating what, or* stumps, or shrubs, *or* tan bark, or waste wood, or leached ashes).

or

Did unlawfully in or across a river (*etc., as above*) fell timber or standing trees and allow the same to remain across the said river (or stream, *etc.*).

The proceedings to be followed are mentioned in section 8, and warrant of distress cannot be dispensed with.

Penalties goes one-third to the informer and two-thirds to the municipal treasurer: Sec. 9.

Rivers, Streams and Lakes, Obstructing by Driving Sawlogs.

R.S.O. ch. 143, sec. 3.
See example in preceding form.

Rondeau Park.

R.S.O. ch. 47.
Breach of Government Regulations: Sec. 5.
Regulations Published in Ontario Gazette.
Hunting in Park: Sec. 9(1).
Shooting or *Killing Birds Within Two Miles of Park*: Sec. 9(2).

Sawlog Cullers Act, Offences Under.

R.S.O. ch. 186.
Culler Making False Measurement: Sec. 16.
A.B., at   , on   , he being then and there a culler duly licensed under the Ontario Cullers' Act (*or* being then and there the holder of a special permit issued by the Commissioner of Crown Lands for the Province of Ontario to act as a culler under the Ontario Cullers Act) and employed as such to measure sawlogs cut upon Crown lands in the Province of Ontario by one C.D. for the purposes of a return to the Crown Lands Department of Ontario, did wilfully and unlawfully undermeasure (*or* mismeasure, *or* improperly cull and reject) certain sawlogs (*describing what logs they were, where measured and in what respect they were improperly measured*), which sawlogs were cut upon Crown lands in the Province of Ontario by the said C.D. and which it was the duty of the said A.B. as such culler to measure fairly and correctly for the purposes of said return.

Culler Making False Return: Sec. 14.
Two justices required in above cases.
See also the offence of obstructing a culler under the Act (Dominion), R.S.C. ch. 84, sec. 84, in which case one justice may convict.

Sawing Machine, Not Having Couplings Protected.

R.S.O. ch. 265.

Sheep Killed by Dogs.

R.S.O. ch. 271. *See* Dogs and Sheep.

Shops Regulation Act, Offences Under.

R.S.O. ch. 257; Ont. St. 1900. ch. 43; Ont. St. 1901, ch. 36.
Employing Children Under Ten Years of Age: Sec. 6.

A.B., at   , on   , being the employer in charge of a shop within the meaning of the Ontario Shop Regulation Act, did unlawfully employ therein C.D., a person then under the age of ten years.

Employing Child Under Fourteen Before Seven A.M. or After Six P.M., Except Saturday, etc.: Sec. 7(1).

or

On Saturday Before Seven A.M. or After Ten P.M.: Sec. 7(2).

or

Not Providing Seats for Female Employees: Sec. 11.

or

Not Providing Eating Room: Sec. 12; or *Separate Water Closets*: Sec. 13(2); or *Fire Escapes*: Sec. 15.

Two justices required: Sec. 28.

Prosecution must be begun within two months: Code 32(1).

Fines are to be paid to the inspector: Sec. 31.

Street Walker.

See Vagrancy.

Sureties to Keep the Peace.

See Articles of the Peace.

Tame Pigeons, Taking or Killing.

See Pigeons.

Tenant.

Wilful Injuries to Buildings by: Code 529.

Fraudulent Removal of Goods by: 11 Geo. II. ch. 19, sec. 1.   (Imperial statutes still in force here).

Thefts by Juveniles.

Code 800-821. *See* Juvenile Offenders, *ante.*

Theft.

Of Tree or Shrub, etc., from Orchard, etc., Under the Value of Five Dollars: Code 375.

Of Anything Under Ten Dollars: Code 771(a. vii.), 773(a) with the consent of accused and if he pleads guilty, but not otherwise: Code 778.

Two justices have jurisdiction.

By Juvenile Offender: Code 802.

Two justices have jurisdiction.

Of Domestic Animals Under Twenty Dollars in Value: Code 370.

Of Trees, Sapling or Shrub: Code 374.

A.B., at   , on   , did unlawfully steal one maple tree (or *as the case may be*) of the value of at least twenty-five cents, the same being the property of C.D.

Of Fruit Growing in a Garden: Code 375.

A.B., on   . at ·   , did unlawfully steal a quantity of grapes (*or otherwise describe the fruit or vegetable stolen*) the property of C.D., which was then and there growing in a certain garden (or orchard) of the said C.D. situated in (*describe the place*).

Of Domestic Animals, etc.: (Under $20 Value): Code 370.

A.B., at   , on   , did unlawfully steal one dog (or one goose, or three hens, *or as the case may be*) being a beast (*or* bird, *or* animal) ordinarily kept for domestic purposes (or for profit, or advantage, or ordinarily kept in confinement) the same not exceeding in value the sum of $20 and being the personal property of C.D.

(Indictable if over $20 in value).

Threshing Machines.

Or *Wood Sawing Machines, not Protecting Couplings of Shafting*:
R.S.O. ch. 265.

A.B., on   , at   , who was then and there running a threshing machine (*or* wood sawing, *or other machine, describing it*) which was connected to a horse (or steam) power by means of a line of shafting, did unlawfully neglect to cause each of the couplings or joints of the said line of shafting to be safely boxed or secured while running with wood, leather or metal covering in such manner as to prevent injuries to persons passing over the same.

Prosecution must be brought within thirty days: Sec. 5.

Fines to be paid, one-half to informant and one-half to the treasurer of the school section where the offence was committed.

Not Providing Spark Arrester On: R.S.O. ch. 278.

Timber Slide Companies Act.

R.S.O. ch. 194.

Impeding Transmission of Timber, etc.: Sec. 50.

A.B., at   , on   , did unlawfully resist (or impede, *or* molest) C.D., a servant of (*name the company*) a company duly empowered by letters patent under the Timber Slide Companies Act for the purposes therein mentioned in the transmission of certain timber through the timber slide owned by the said company at   (*describe where*) by (*describe the manner in which the offence was committed*).

Prosecution must be begun within six months: Sec. 55.

Fines are to be paid to the treasurer of the timber slide company affected: Sec. 54.

Timber or Logs.

Manufacturer of, Not Registering His Mark, or Not Marking Timber With Same: R.S.C. ch. 725, sec. 11.

Using Registered Mark of Another Person: Sec. 12.

Two justices have jurisdiction.

Complaint must be laid on behalf of proprietor of mark misused: Sec. 12(2).

Tobacco, Supplying to Minors Under Eighteen Years.

R.S.O. ch. 261.

A.B., at   , on   , did unlawfully sell (or give, or furnish) to C.D., who was then a minor under the age of eighteen years, tobacco (*or* cigars, or cigarettes), the said tobacco (*etc.*) not being sold to the said minor for his parent or guardian under a written request or order of his said parent or guardian.

Traction Engines on Highways, Breach of Regulations as to Speed, Width of Tires, etc.

R.S.O. ch. 242.

Sections 8 and 9 of this statute do not apply to threshing machines engines, or traction engines used in constructing roadways: Ont. St. 1903, ch. 7, sec. 43.

Trade Mark.

Importing Goods Having False: Code 493.

Other Offences: Code 491(6).

Falsely Claiming to Have Royal or *Government Warrant*: Code 492.
Trading Stamps, Customer Receiving From Tradesman: Code 508, 335(2), 342.
Selling Bottles Having Trade *Mark on Them*: Code 490.

A.B., at , on , did unlawfully sell (*or* offer, *or* expose for sale, *or* traffic in, *stating how*), certain bottles marked with a trade mark blown (or stamped, or having permanently fixed) thereto, to wit (*describe the trade mark*) of which trade mark C.D. was then the proprietor without the consent of the said C.D.

Trade Offences, Other.

Code 486, 487.

Offences referred to in the last two paragraphs may be treated either as indictable or tried summarily by one justice: Code 491. See also trade mark offences in list of indictable offences.

Trespass.

R.S.O. ch. 120.

A.B., at , on , did unlawfully enter into (*or* come upon, or *pass through*) certain lands then being the property of C.D., being (*describe the property*) * and being then wholly enclosed (*or* being a garden or lawn: see Ont. St. 1902, ch. 12, sec. 17) by walking upon (*or* driving a horse, or cattle over the same, *or state in what the trespass consisted*).

*Or (see Ont. St. 1903, ch. 19, sec. 545(7)) and after the municipal council of the township of aforesaid had duly declared by by-law that the (*state what*) boundary line of said land which passed through a marsh or swamp should as regards the said boundary be deemed wholly enclosed within the meaning of section 1 of the Act Respecting Petty Trespasses, and on which posts were then duly put up and maintained along the said boundary line at distances which permitted of each of the said posts being clearly visible from the adjoining post.

Trespass by Walking on Railway Track.

R.S.C. ch. 37, sec. 408.

Vaccination of Children, Compulsory.

R.S.O. ch. 249, secs. 7, 12.
Two justices required.

Vagrancy.

Code 238, 239.

(*a*) A.B., at , on , not having any visible means of subsistence, was found unlawfully wandering abroad (or was found lodging in a barn, or outhouse, *or in a* deserted *or* unoccupied building, or in a cart or wagon, or *as otherwise stated in Code* 238(*a*)).

or

(*b*) Being able to work and thereby (or *by other means, stating them*) to maintain himself and family, wilfully and unlawfully refused or neglected to do so.

or

(*c*) Unlawfully did openly expose, or exhibit in a street (*or* road, *or* highway, or public place, to wit, *state the place*), an indecent exhibition (*see post, "Indecent Exhibition," stating its nature in general terms*).

or

(d) Was unlawfully wandering about and begging (or did unlawfully go from door to door, or place himself in a street, or highway, or passage, or public place, to wit, *name it*, to beg *or* to receive alms), without a certificate signed within six months, by a priest, or clergyman, or minister of the gospel, or two justices of the peace, as by law required.

or

(e) Did unlawfully loiter on a public street (or road, *or* highway, or public place, to wit *describe where*), and obstruct passengers by standing across the footpath (or by using insulting language), to wit (*state the language used*, or *state any other way by which any passenger on the way was obstructed*).

or

(f) Did unlawfully cause a disturbance in (or near) a street (or road, or highway, or public place, *describing it*), by screaming (or swearing, or singing, or by being drunk, *or* by impeding *or* incommoding peaceful passengers. (*Note.*—The gravamen of this charge is *causing a disturbance by any of the means stated*).

or

(g) by discharging firearms (or by riotous, or disorderly conduct) to wit, by *describe it*, in a street, or highway, in the said   of   , wantonly and unlawfully disturbed the peace and quiet of the inmates of the dwelling-house of C.D., situate near the said street or highway.

or

(h) Did unlawfully tear down *or* deface a sign (or break a window, *or* a door *or* a door plate, or the wall of a house, or of a road, or of a garden, or destroyed a fence, *describing the same*).

or

(i) Being a common prostitute (or night-walker), wandered in the fields adjacent to the   of   , (or in the public streets, or highways (or lanes, *or* places of public meetings, or gathering of people, *stating where*), and upon demand being thereupon made of her by C.D., a peace officer of the said   of   , she unlawfully did not give a satisfactory account of herself.

or

(j) Was unlawfully a keeper (or inmate) of a disorderly house, to wit, a common bawdy-house, (or house of ill-fame, or house for the resort of prostitutes, *see* D*isorderly House*).

or

(k) Was unlawfully in the habit of frequenting disorderly houses, or bawdy-houses (or houses of ill-fame, or houses for the resort of prostitutes) and upon being required by C.D., a peace officer, did not give satisfactory account of herself.

or

(l) Having no peaceable profession or calling to maintain himself by, for the most part supports himself by gaming (or by crime, or by the avails of prostitution).

Prosecutions must be begun within six months: Code 1141.

Veterinary Surgeon, Practising Without Authority.
R.S.O. ch. 184.

Wages, Non-payment of.
R.S.O. ch. 157, sec. 11. *See* Master and Servant.

Weapons.
Carrying, Two or More Persons: Code 116.

A.B. and C.D.,   at   , on   , being together did both of them
then and there openly carry offensive weapons, to wit (*state what*) in a
public place, to wit (*state where*), in such a manner and under such circumstances as were calculated to create terror and alarm (*state the manner and
circumstances*).

Two justices required.

"Weapon" is defined by Code 2(24).

Carrying Pistol or Air Gun: Code 118.

A.B., on   , at   , did unlawfully have upon his person a
pistol (or air gun) elsewhere than in his own dwelling-house, shop, warehouse or counting house, to wit (*state where*): the said A.B. not then being
a justice, or a public officer, or a soldier, sailor or volunteer in His Majesty's
service, then and there on duty, or a constable or other peace officer; and
the said A.B. not then and there having a certificate of exemption as required by the statute in that behalf issued by a justice of the peace, and
not having at the said time reasonable cause to fear an assault or other
injury to his person, family or property.

Selling a Pistol, etc., to a Minor: Code 119.

A.B., on   , at   , did unlawfully sell (*or give*) a pistol
(or air gun, or certain ammunition for a pistol, or air gun) to a minor
under the age of 16 years, to wit, to (*name the minor*).

Selling a Pistol or Air Gun Without Keeping a Record: Code 119(2).

A.B., on   , at   , did unlawfully sell a pistol (*or an air
gun*) to C.D. without keeping a record of such sale, and the date thereof,
and the name of the said purchaser thereof, and of the name of the maker
of the said pistol (*or air gun*) or of some other mark by which the said
pistol (*or air gun*) might be identified.

Having Weapon on the Person When Arrested: Code 120.

A.B., on   , at   , having been then and there arrested on
a warrant issued against him by C.D., Esquire, a justice of the peace in and
for the   of   , for an offence, to wit (*state the offence*); (or
having been then and there duly arrested while committing an offence, to
wit, *state the offence*), did then and there unlawfully have upon his person
when so arrested, a pistol (or an air gun)

Two justices required.

Pointing Firearm (Loaded or Not) at any Person: Code 122.

A.B., at   , on   , did without lawful excuse, unlawfully
point at C.D., a firearm (or an air gun).

Two justices required.

Carrying, or Having, or Selling Sheath Knife, etc.: Code 123.

A.B., at   , on   , did unlawfully carry about his person a
bowie-knife (or dagger, or dirk, *or* metal knuckles, or skull cracker, or
slung shot, *or other offensive weapon of that character. stating what*):
(did unlawfully and secretly carry about his person an instrument loaded at
the end; or did sell, or expose for sale., a bowie-knife, *or any of the weapons
above enumerated, naming it*); or that A.B., on   , at   , being
then and there masked (*or* disguised), did unlawfully, and while so masked
(or disguised) carry (*or* have in his possession), a firearm (or air gun).

Two justices required.

Carrying Sheath Knife: Code 124.

A.B., at   , on   , was found in the town (or city) of
        carrying about his person a sheath knife, he, the said A.B. not
being thereto required by his lawful trade or calling.

Two justices required.

Refusing to Deliver Weapon to a Justice: Code 126.

A.B., at   , on   , being then and there attending (or on his way to attend) a certain public meeting at (describe it) did unlawfully decline and refuse to deliver up peaceably and quietly to C.D., a justice of the peace for the said   of   ·   , within whose jurisdiction the said public meeting was then appointed to be held, upon demand then and there duly and lawfully made by the said justice of the peace, a certain offensive weapon, to wit, a pistol (or describe the weapon) with which he, the said A.B., was then armed (or which he, the said A.B., then had in his possession).

The justice may on the spot record the refusal and fine the offender $8, or he may commit him for trial: Code 126(2).

If fine imposed it may be enforced as described, ante p. 360.

Having Weapon Near Public Works: R.S.O. ch. 38, sec. 3(1).

That on   , being upon (or after) the day fixed by proclamation of the Lieutenant-Governor of the Province of Ontario in Council declaring the several places within the limits whereof a railway, the work on which was then being carried on by an incorporated company, to wit (name the company), was then in process of construction, wherein the said Lieutenant-Governor deemed it necessary that the R.S.O. ch. 8, should be in force, A.B. at   , being a place within the said limits in which the said statute was then in force did unlawfully have in his possession or under his control a gun (or any other weapon mentioned in the above statute, describing it), he, the said A.B., not being a justice of the peace or a public officer or a soldier, sailor or volunteer in His Majesty's service on duty, or a constable or a peace officer, and the said A.B. not then having a certificate of exemption from the operation of section 3 of the said Act as provided thereby, and not having at the said time reasonable cause to fear an assault or other injury to his person, family or property

Two justices required: Sec. 11.

The weapon is to be seized by any justice of the peace or constable and forfeited to His Majesty's use: Secs. 6, 10.

As to search warrants see section 8.

·   Similar charge in regard to Dominion Public Works: Code 142-149.

Possessing Weapons Near Public Works: Code 142, 145, 146.

A.B., who was at the time hereinafter mentioned, employed upon or about a certain public work within the   of   . being a place where the statute called an Act respecting the Preservation of the Peace in the Vicinity of Public Works was then lawfully in force by proclamation, did upon (or after) the day named in the proclamation by which the said Act was brought into force at the said   of   , unlawfully keep or have in his possession (or under his care or control) within the said   of   , a certain weapon, to wit, a dirk (or describe the weapon).

Concealing Arms Near Public Works: Code 147.

A.B., within the   of   , being a place where the statute known as an Act respecting the Preservation of the Peace in the Vicinity of Public Works was then lawfully in force, did unlawfully and for the purpose of defeating the lawful enforcement of Part III. of the Criminal Code of Canada, receive (or conceal, or aid in receiving, or concealing, or procure to be received or concealed) within the said place a certain weapon, to wit, a dirk (or describe the weapon) then belonging to (or in the custody of) C.D., a person then and there employed on or about a certain public work (describing it) then being prosecuted at the said   of

Weeds, Neglecting to Cut and Other Offences.

R.S.O. ch. 279, sec. 9(1); Ont. Stats. 1902, 1904.

Weights and Measures Act, Offences Under.
R.S.O. ch. 52.

Wife Desertion, Order for Maintenance.
R.S.O. ch. 167. *See* Husband and Wife.

Wilful Injuries.
To Property: Code 509, 540, 541.
Injuring Goods on Railway, Ship or in Warehouse, etc.: Code 519.
A.B., at   , on   , did unlawfully and wilfully and without legal justification or excuse and without colour of right (*see Code* 541) * destroy (*or* damage, *stating how*) a certain box (*or* package, *or* barrel, *or* crate, *describing it*) containing certain goods, to wit (*state what*) which was then in or about the railway station (*or in a ship called, naming it, or in a warehouse of C.D.*) at the said   of   with intent unlawfully to obtain (*or injure*), the contents thereof
or
* Drink (*or* wilfully spill, *or* allow to run to waste) certain liquor, to wit (*state what*), which was then in or about the railway station (*or in a ship, naming it, or in a warehouse of C.D.*) at the said   of   .
Telegraph, Telephone, Fire Alarm, or Other Electric Wire, Attempting to Injure: Code 521(2).
A.B., at   , on   , did unlawfully and wilfully and without legal justification or excuse and without colour of right, attempt to (*describe any of the offences mentioned in Code* 521(*a*) *or* (*b*).
Harbour Bar, by Removing Earth or Stone, etc.: Code 527.
Fences, Boundary Posts, etc.: Code 530.
A.B., at   , on   , did unlawfully and wilfully and without legal justification or excuse and without colour of right, destroy (*or damage, stating how*) a certain fence (*or a wall, or gate, or a post, or stake then planted or set up*) on a certain land (*or marsh, or swamp, or land covered by water, or as the boundary line of certain land, or in lieu of a fence to said land, etc.*), which land was then the property of C.D., and situated (*describe it*).
Trees, etc.: Code 533.
Vegetable Productions in Gardens, etc.: Code 534.
A.B., at   , on   , did unlawfully and wilfully and without legal justification or excuse and without colour of right, destroy (*or damage with intent thereby to destroy, stating what damage was done*) a certain vegetable production, to wit (*state what*) the property of C.D., and which was then growing in a certain garden (*or orchard, or nursery grounds, or house, or hothouse, or greenhouse, or conservatory*) of the said C.D. situate (*describe the place and also how injury done, as, for instance, by uprooting it*).
Vegetable Productions Elsewhere than in Garden: Code 535.
Dog, Bird or Animal Other than Cattle: Code 537.
A.B., at   , on   , did unlawfully and wilfully and without legal justification or excuse and without colour of right, kill (*or. maim, or wound, or poison, or injure*) a dog (*or any animal not being cattle, describing it*).
Wilfully Impeding the Saving of Wreck: Code 524(2).
Two justices of the peace required to try the last mentioned offence.
By tenants, mortgagors, *or* to Railways, *or* Mines, *or* Oil Wells, *or* by Explosions are indictable offences. *See* list of indictable offences under these headings.
Not Otherwise Provided for: Code 539.

A.B., at   , on   , did unlawfully and wilfully and without legal justification or excuse and without colour of right, commit damage (*or injury. or spoil*) to certain real (*or personal*) property, to wit, belonging to C.D. (*stating what property and how the damage or injury was done*).

Wood-sawing Machine, etc., Couplings Unprotected.
R.S.O. ch. 265. *See* Threshing Machines.

Workmen, and Others, Intimidation with Respect to.
Code 501(a).

A.B., at   , on   , wrongfully and without lawful authority, with a view to compel C.D. to abstain from employing E.F., as a workman, whom he, the said A.B., had a lawful right to so employ (*or to compel C.D. to employ G.H., as a workman, whom he, the said A.B., had the lawful right to abstain from so employing; or to compel the said C.D. to increase or abstain from diminishing the rate of wages of his workmen; or to compel J.K. to abstain from working for C.D.*); did unlawfully * use violence to the said C.D. (*or the said J.K.*), or to the wife, *or* children of the said C.D. (*or J.K.*), or did unlawfully injure the property of the said C.D. or J.K. (*set out the acts of violence, or the injury done*).

or (b).
* Intimidate the said C.D. (*or J.K.*) by threats to (*proceed as in the preceding form*).

or (c).
* Persistently follow the said C.D. (*or J.K.*) from place to place.

or (d)
* Hide certain tools then owned or used by the said C.D. (*or J.K.*) or deprive the said C.D. (*or J.K., or hinder the said C.D., or J.K.*) in the use of certain tools (*etc.*)

or (e).
* With one (*or more*) other persons follow the said C.D. (*or J.K.*) in a disorderly manner in a street in   of

or (f. Picketting).
* Beset or watch the house in which the said C.D. (*or J.K.*) resided (*or the mill or factory, or other place, where the said C.D., or J.K.*) then worked or carried on business (*or happened to be*).

Similar Offences: Code 503.

Two justices required in any of these cases.

Workmen Leaving Employment Without Repaying Advances.
Ont. St. 1901, ch. 12, sec. 14.

A.B., at   , on   , entered into an agreement with C.D. under which the said A.B. did then and there receive from the said C.D. (*or from E.F., the agent of the said C.D.*) as an advance of wages the sum of   (*or a railway ticket from   to   , to enable him, the said A.B,.* to reach the place at which he then and there engaged to perform labour (*or other services, stating what*) for the said C.D. and thereafter, to wit, on the   day of   , at the   of   *etc.*, the said A.B. without the consent of his employer. the said C.D., did unlawfully leave the said employment before the said money (*or the cost of the said transportation*) so advanced as aforesaid had been re-paid.

Wreck.
Includes the cargo. stores. or tackling and all parts of a vessel which has been wrecked and also the property of a shipwrecked person: Code 2(41).

For a statement of the various offences in connection with a wreck, which may be tried by two justices of the peace, see Code 431.

CHAPTER XIV.

SUMMARY TRIALS OF INDICTABLE OFFENCES BY MAGISTRATES.

The summary jurisdiction of police magistrates, and the other functionaries mentioned in Code 771, and therein defined under the designation of "magistrates," in relation to their authority to try indictable offences, has been considered in page 197 *et seq.* There remains to be considered the procedure by which such jurisdiction is to be exercised.

It may be convenient to understand that when the term "magistrate" is used, it is intended to refer to the various officials in the different provinces, who are declared by Code 771 to be included in that term, unless it is otherwise stated.

Consent.

The jurisdiction conferred upon magistrates by Code 773, is sometimes exercisable summarily and absolutely, without any consent of the accused; and sometimes can only be exercised with such consent.

A magistrate has absolute authority, without consent, in the case of a person charged with keeping, or being an inmate, or habitual frequenter, of a disorderly house, house of ill-fame or bawdy house: Code 773 (*f*); and such authority does not depend upon consent, nor is consent to be asked: Code 774.

The term a disorderly house in this section includes a gaming house: Ex p. Cooke, 3 Can. Cr. Cas. 72; R. v. Flynn, 9 Can. Cr. Cas. 550; but see *contra*: R. v. France, 1 Can. Cr. Cas. 321.

The magistrate's jurisdiction is also absolute, without consent in regard to any of the offences mentioned in Code 773, in the case of a seafaring person only transiently in Canada, and having no permanent domicile here, and who is charged either within the city of Quebec (as limited for the purpose of the police ordinance), or within the city of Montreal as so limited, or in any other seaport town or city in Canada where there is a magistrate; and also in the case of any other person charged with any of the offences mentioned, upon the complaint of any such seafaring person whose testimony is essential to the proof of the offence: Code 775.

Such jurisdiction does not depend on consent, nor is consent to be asked: Code 775 (2).

In British Columbia, Prince Edward Island, Saskatchewan, Alberta, the North-West Territories and the Yukon, a magistrate's jurisdiction is also absolute, without consent, except a case coming under Code 777; and also except cases under Code 782 and 783 (thefts, false pretences and receiving stolen goods, over $10, in value), unless the person charged is a seafaring person, such as is above mentioned: Code 776.

In all other cases, the magistrate has jurisdiction to try the offences mentioned in Code 773, only in the event of the accused consenting to be so tried. The procedure thereupon is laid down in Code 778-781.

In cases of theft, false pretences and receiving stolen property of over $10 value, (which are not included in Code 773), a magistrate has jurisdiction to proceed summarily on consent; and the procedure is that prescribed by Code 782, 783.

But he can only convict and award punishment in the last mentioned cases, when the accused not only consents to be tried summarily, but also pleads guilty; and if he pleads not guilty, the magistrate is to hold a preliminary examination only; and may commit the accused for trial: Code 783.

By Code 777, a very extensive jurisdiction is conferred upon the magistrates there mentioned: viz., all police magistrates in Ontario; and all stipendiary magistrates for any county, district or provisional county in Ontario; and also police and stipendiary magistrates in cities and towns in all the other provinces (not including district magistrates, however, elsewhere than in Ontario), and also recorders, exercising judicial functions anywhere in Canada.

Such magistrates have authority, with the consent of the accused, to try summarily, and convict and punish, any offender for any offence for which he might be tried at the general sessions of the peace: Code 777.

Such offences are stated in Code 582, to be all *indictable offences*, except those mentioned in Code 583.

The procedure before the magistrates mentioned, in these cases, is provided by Code 778.

Juvenile Offenders.

In any case coming within the jurisdiction of any magistrate, under any of the provisions above referred to, if the accused appears to be of or about, or under the age of sixteen years, the magistrate is not to ask whether he consents to a summary trial, nor is he to proceed to deal with the case, without first asking the accused what his age is; and if it is stated to be sixteen years or less, and he is not represented by counsel present at the time, the magistrate is first to *give the notice* and take the proceedings mentioned in Code 779.

Offenders Generally.

In any case, if the consent of the accused is requisite, and he does not consent to be tried summarily, a preliminary enquiry only will be held; and in case the accused is committed for trial, the warrant is to state that the defendant elected to be tried by a jury: Code 785.

And even in cases in which consent is given, if it appears to the magistrate that the offence is one which, owing to a previous conviction, or from other circumstances, ought to be made the subject of a prosecution by indictment rather than to be disposed of summarily, the magistrate before the accused has made his defence, may decide not to adjudicate summarily but may hold a preliminary enquiry: Code 784; Re McRae, 4 B.C.R. 18. But he cannot take that course after the accused has entered upon his defence: for to proceed with the summary trial of a case, and at its conclusion commit the accused for trial, would practically be submitting him to be tried twice for the same offence; which is repugnant to the law: Ex p. Cook, 3 Can. Cr. Cas. 73.

By Code 796, if a person is charged before a justice or justices with any offence mentioned in Code 773; and it appears to be a proper case to be tried summarily by a "magistrate," the justice or justices may remand the accused to be tried before the nearest "magistrate" in the same province, in like manner as a justice is authorized to commit a person for trial, and the accused may be so tried.

A district magistrate in Quebec, may, under certain conditions, try any of the cases referred to in Code 777; although he is not one of the *magistrates* given jurisdiction by that section.

He is one of the functionaries to whom is given authority, by Code 823, *et seq.*, (the clauses relating to speedy trials of Indictable Offences), to try cases in which the accused has been

committed for trial by a justice. He also has the authority of
a justice; and may himself hold such preliminary enquiry, as
such justice; and he may afterwards, as such district magistrate, hold a trial by consent of the accused, under Code 823:
R. v. Breckenridge, 7 Can. Cr. Cas. 124.

A "magistrate" who is not a police or stipendiary magistrate
having authority to try cases under Code 777, can only try
cases mentioned in Code 782, (theft, false pretences and receiving stolen goods of over $10 value), after the conditions
mentioned in that section have been complied with; viz., after
he has taken evidence for the prosecution, and has reached the
opinion that such evidence is sufficient to put the accused on
his trial. He may then, but not before, ask the accused whether
he consents to be summarily tried: R. v. Williams, 10 Can. Cr.
Cas. 330.

In all cases the jurisdiction of a magistrate is limited to
those which have arisen within his territorial division as a magistrate.

Consent of Accused to Summary Trial.

In all cases in which a magistrate has authority and assumes
to try an accused person, by consent, for an indictable offence,
it is important, as pointed out in R. v. London, JJ., 17 Cox
C.C. 526, that he should be careful to carry out the provisions
contained in Code 778; and to see that the accused fully understands the effect of his consent: and if the magistrate does not
inform him of his right to be tried by a jury, the conviction
will be quashed for want of jurisdiction. The accused person
must be expressly informed of his right to be tried by a jury:
R. v. Cockshott (1898), 1 Q.B. 582; R. v. Hogarth, 24 O.R. 60;
R. v. Conway, 7 Can. Cr. Cas. 129; R. v. Shepherd, 6 Can. Cr.
Cas. 463.

He must also be informed of the *court* at which the case
can probably be soonest tried by a jury: R. v. Walsh, 8 Can. Cr.
Cas. 101; and he must be informed of the *date* of the sitting
of the court at which the jury trial will likely take place: R. v.
Williams, 10 Can. Cr. Cas. 330.

The omission of any of these particulars goes to jurisdiction,
and will be fatal to the conviction; and it is immaterial whether
the defendant knew of his right to a jury, and other particulars. The omission to do what the statute provides shall be done,

for the protection of accused persons, cannot be waived: R. v. Cockshott (1898), 1 Q.B. 582; R. v. Walsh, 8 Can. Cr. Cas. 101.

It is not sufficient to merely ask the defendant, "How do you wish to be tried: by me or by a jury": R. v. Walsh, 8 Can. Cr. Cas. 101; the words to be used are expressly provided by Code 778 (2), and must be used; viz., "Do you consent that the charge against you shall be tried by me; or do you desire that it shall be sent for trial by a jury at the (*naming the court at which it can probably be soonest tried*)," and stating the date of the sittings of that court.

The question may be put by the magistrate's clerk, speaking for the magistrate in his presence: R. v. Ridehaugh, 7 Can. Cr. Cas. 340.

Before asking the accused person whether he consents to be tried by the magistrate, the nature of the charge is to be stated to him and when he has elected to be tried by the magistrate, the charge is to be reduced to writing and read to the accused, and he is to be asked whether he is guilty of it or not: Code 778 (3).

The charge need not be "reduced to writing" a second time, after the consent, if it was previously done; and the charge as stated in the information laid in the beginning of the proceedings is sufficient: R. v. Shephard, 6 Can. Cr. Cas. 463.

When the accused person has once elected to be tried by the magistrate he cannot afterwards withdraw it: R. v. Keefer, 2 O.L.R. 572.

If the defendant pleads guilty, the magistrate will make a minute of adjudication similar to that described, *ante,* p. 356 or he may make out the usual formal conviction, which, however, can be made out afterwards.

Extent of Authority Conferred by Consent.

The consent to summary trial for the offence stated to the accused is to be taken as a consent to a summary trial for whatever offence the accused might be found guilty of at the court of general sessions in Ontario, if he were tried there on a like charge: *e.g.,* on a trial by consent for committing an offence, he may be convicted, without further consent, of an attempt to commit it; or on a trial for an offence he may be convicted of a lesser offence involved in it; for instance, on a charge of committing an aggravated assault, he may be convicted of an

428 SUMMARY TRIALS BY MAGISTRATES.

assault of a lesser degree than that charged: R. v. Morgan, 5
Can. Cr. Cas. 63; R. v. Morgan No. 2, 5 Can. Cr. Cas. 272; R.
v. Coolen, 8 Can. Cr. Cas. 157. But the charge cannot be en-
larged or extended or made of a different nature by amendment, without the accused being given the right to elect again:
R. v. Walsh, 8 Can. Cr. Cas. 101.

In all cases he must be allowed, if he pleads not guilty, to
make his full answer and defence and to have all witnesses
examined and cross-examined by counsel or solicitor: Code 786;
and every court held by a magistrate, is to be an open, public
court: Code 787. But see the provisions of Code 644, 645 in
particular cases: *ante*, p. 233.

The forms of procedure for compelling the attendance of
witnesses: Code 788 and 789; and other proceedings generally
by information, summons, warrant to arrest, taking evidence,
etc., are similar to those to be taken by justices of the peace as
described in the preceding chapters. If the accused person is
duly under arrest without a warrant, and is brought before a
magistrate and charged with any indictable offence, the written
charge though not under oath, then drawn up and read to him,
is to be read to him, and if he then consents to a summary trial,
the magistrate may proceed with it although no information,
under oath or otherwise, has been laid: R. v. McLean, 5 Can. Cr.
Cas. 67.

Code 799 provides that forms of conviction, etc., Nos. 55,
56 and 57, in the Cr. Code, may be used, making requisite altera-
tions.

Punishment.

The punishment for offences tried under Code 773 (*a*) (*f*) ·
viz., theft, false pretences and receiving stolen goods, not exceeding $10 in value, is that prescribed by Code 780; and in
other cases, under Code 773, (except when they are tried under
Code 777, by a police or stipendiary magistrate), are provided
by Code 780, 781.

But in all cases tried under Code 777, (whether or not they
are included in Code 773, a police or stipendiary magistrate
mentioned in Code 777, may award such punishment as the
court of general sessions of the peace in Ontario could award:
R. v. Archibald, 4 Can. Cr. Cas. 159; R. v. Boucher, 8 P.R. 20,
4 A.R. 191; R. v. Conlin, 29 O.R. 28; R. v. Ridehaugh, 7 Can.

Cr. Cas. 340; R. v. Hawes, 6 Can. Cr. Cas. 238; and see notes in 9 Can. Cr. Cas. p. 370.

The punishment imposed is to be in the manner, if any, prescribed by the statute relating to the offence: Code 1051.

The sections relating to punishment, costs, restitution, etc., (Part XX., secs. 1027-1057 of the Cr. Code), apply to proceedings for indictable offences tried under Code 777, by police and stipendiary magistrates having jurisdiction under that section: Ex p. Kent, 7 Can. Cr. Cas. 447.

When both fine and imprisonment are provided by the statute for the offence, the magistrate may impose òne or both of them ''in his discretion'': Code 1028; R. v. Robideaux, 2 Can. Cr. Cas. 19; Ex p. Kent, 7 Can. Cr. Cas. 447. When the same offence is triable and punishable differently under the same or different sections, and the magistrate has authority to try the case in either manner, his jurisdiction as to punishment, then depends upon which section he is assuming to act under: R. v. Spooner, 4 Can. Cr. Cas. 209; R. v. Carter, 5 Can. Cr. Cas. 401; R. v. Ames, 10 Can. Cr. Cas. 52. And in any of such cases, if he tries the case as a magistrate holding a trial as for an indictable offence, he may inflict punishment as such, and award the punishment applicable to the offence by the section under which he is acting, and is not limited to the punishment fixed by the alternative section. Thus on the trial under Code 777, of a charge of aggravated assault, occasioning grievous bodily harm (Code 274), the magistrate is not limited to the punishment provided for the offence by Code 773 (c), viz., 6 months in gaol (Code 781); but may impose the punishment provided by Code 274: R. v. Archibald, 4 Can. Cr. Cas. 159; so also on a charge of keeping a disorderly house, the magistrate trying the case under Code 777, as an offence under Code 228, is not limited to the punishment provided for the same offence triable under Code 773 (f), viz., six months in gaol (Code 781), but may inflict the punishment which it is competent for the general sessions to inflict under Code 228: R. v. Ames, 10 Can. Cr. Cas. 52.

When the statute provides that an offence is either indictable or may be tried summarily before a justice: e.g., a case under Code 144, of obstructing a peace officer; the justice or magistrate may, if he thinks that course adequate, try the case as a ''summary convictions'' case, without consent, imposing the punishment applicable to it as such, and need not treat it as an indictable offence unless it appears that the interests of justice so require: R. v. Nelson, 4 Can. Cr. Cas. 461.

Suspended Sentence.

A magistrate may suspend sentence in cases tried before him in his capacity of a magistrate and not as an *ex officio* justice: Code 1026, 1081-1083. When sitting for the trial of an indictable offence, the magistrate's court is a "court" within the meaning of Code 1026, 1081 and 1082; and he has the powers given to a court by those sections: R. v. McLellan, 10 Can. Cr. Cas. 5.

The circumstances under which a person convicted of crime may be released on suspended sentence, or probation of good conduct, are stated in the above sections; and the proper time to make enquiry and take evidence under them as to any previous convictions against the accused in order to exclude a suspended sentence, is after the defendant has been convicted; and the magistrate may make the enquiry, even if the Crown counsel does not do so: R. v. Bonnevie, 10 Can. Cr. Cas. 377. Affidavits on both sides may be received and certified copies of any previous convictions may be used; and the Crown officer as well as the defendant's counsel are entitled to be heard in any court on the question of the punishment to be awarded; and if the defendant pleaded guilty the Crown officer is heard first, and the defendant's counsel follows: R. v. Dignan, 7 A. & E. 593; R. v. Bunts, 2 T.R. 683; R. v. Sutton, 7 A. & E. 594; cited in 10 Can. Cr. Cas. 381.

A person released on suspended sentence can only be brought up again under Code 1083, for sentence, on motion of the Crown and not of the private prosecutor: R. v. Young, 4 Can. Cr. Cas. 580; R. v. Siteman, 6 Can. Cr. Cas. 224.

Sureties for Good Behaviour.

The magistrate may, in addition to any sentence imposed, require the person convicted to give security to keep the peace and be of good behaviour for any term not exceeding two years; and may order that in default the defendant shall be imprisoned for not more than one year after the expiry of any imprisonment under his sentence, or until sureties are furnished: Code 1058, 1060.

In drawing up the recognizance and other papers care must be taken that they shew, upon their face, jurisdiction in the magistrate exercising "summary trial" powers: Re Smith's Bail, 6 Can. Cr. Cas. 416; and cases cited there at p. 419.

Restoration of Stolen Property.

See Code 1050.

Property stolen, or obtained unlawfully, may be ordered to be restored to the owner; and compensation for the loss of property may also be ordered: Code 1049. And if it appears by the evidence that the defendant has sold it, or any part of it, any money taken from the prisoner on arrest may be applied in making restitution, if such money belongs to the defendant: Code 1049.

Enforcement of Fine or Costs.

The conviction by a magistrate has the same effect as a conviction upon indictment for the same offence: Code 791; and so the punishment under it may be enforced in like manner. There is no provision for levying the fine or costs by distress, but only by imprisonment: Code 1035.

In issuing warrants of commitment, the magistrate is acting ministerially merely and not judicially and is in no sense "adjudicating" in the matter, and has no authority to so adjudicate. The adjudication was by the magistrate who made the conviction and must be made by him when he did so. So care must be taken by the latter, to fix a term of imprisonment upon default of payment of any fine, which will extend beyond the day appointed for payment, otherwise such term (being "reckoned from the day of adjudication"), may have then elapsed, and there would remain no means of enforcing payment of the fine.

Costs.

The provisions of the law as to costs in these cases are contained in Code 1040, 1044-1047. The tariff of fees, in Code 771, (ante, p. 375, is, in its terms, not applicable to cases of indictable offences, tried before magistrates; and there is no tariff of fees provided for such cases.

The costs, if ordered, are to be taxed according to the lowest scale of fees allowed in the superior courts of the province: Code 1047 (2); and may include a moderate allowance to the prosecutor for loss fo time in and about the prosecution, as may be considered reasonable: Code 1044. Such costs in cases tried under Code 777, can only be recovered by the same process as in a civil action; viz., in the manner described in R.S.O. ch. 76; and the payment cannot be enforced by distress or imprisonment.

But in cases tried under Code 773 (c), (d), (e) and (f), the fine and ·costs (which are both not to exceed $100), may be levied by warrant of distress or by imprisonment, in addition to any inflicted for the offence, for a further term not exceeding six months: Code 781 (2).

Other Provisions.

After a summary trial of an indictable offence before a magistrate by consent the prosecutor is not entitled to be bound over to prosecute by indictment under Code 688; as the matter is *res adjudicata,* and the provisions of the above section have no application: Code 798; Re R. v. Burns, 1 O.L.R. 341.

Restoration of Property.

Stolen property may be restored to the owner or his representative by order of the magistrate: Code 1050; and provision is made for enforcing same by sub-sec. 2. This may be done although the person charged is not convicted, if it is proved to the satisfaction of the magistrate that the property belongs to the prosecutor, or to any witness for the prosecution: Code 1050 (3), and see sub-secs. (4) and (5), for further provisions.

Transmitting Conviction.

A magistrate trying an indictable offence is to send the conviction, (or a duplicate of the certificate of dismissal, as the case may be), and all papers to the clerk of the peace, or other proper officer of the court, to be kept amongst the records of the court of general sessions or other court discharging like functions: Code 793.

Application of Fines.

Fines received by magistrates are to be paid to the Provincial Treasurer, except as mentioned: Code 1036.

By an Ontario Order in Council, such fines are to be paid over to the County Crown Attorney, and are to be transmitted by him to the provincial treasurer: see *ante,* p. 373.

Magistrates' Returns.

By R.S.O. ch. 94, sec. 8, magistrates in Ontario are to forward to the clerk of the peace and to the Inspector of Legal Offices, Osgoode Hall, Toronto, on or before the 2nd Tuesday in March, June, September and December, a copy of the book required by sec. 1 of R.S.O. ch. 94, to be kept by magistrates, shewing the convictions made by them during the quarter ending with the next previous month, including any transactions which may have taken place during the period covered by the return with reference to any previous conviction. The penalty for not keeping this book or making this return in $80: R.S.O. ch. 94, sec. 5; R.S.O. ch. 93, sec. 4. This provision does not apply to the police magistrate for Toronto.

Magistrates' and Constables' Fees.

The provisions for fees and tariffs in summary convictions cases, are not applicable to "magistrates" dealing with indictable offences. But if the magistrate is entitled to receive from the county the fee provided by Ont. Stat. 1904 ch. 13, sec. 2 see *ante,* p. 292, and the constable will also be entitled to be paid by the county, his fees according to the tariff in R.S.O. ch. 101.

The witness fees are also payable by the county, by order of the magistrate, under R.S.O. ch. 105.

Appeal.

As to appeals in magistrates cases, *ante,* p. 138.

CHAPTER XV. .

JUVENILE OFFENDERS.

Against Dominion Laws.

In dealing with young persons charged with offences against the law the usual procedure before described, will be varied, as follows:—

By R.S.C. ch. 148, different provisions are made for the several provinces; but the following apply to all the provinces.

Juvenile Offenders to be Kept Separate From Other Criminals.

By section 28: young persons apparently under the age of sixteen years, who are arrested, or committed to custody, whether for indictable offences, or for cases punishable on summary convictions under any Canadian law, and whether before or after the trial, but before imprisonment under sentence, are to be kept separate from older persons charged with crime; and all persons undergoing sentence; and are not to be confined in lockups or police stations with older persons charged with crime, or with ordinary criminals.

Trials to be Without Publicity.

By Code 644, the trials of such young persons are to take place without publicity, and separately and apart from the trials of other accused persons; and at suitable times to be designated and appointed for that purpose.

Procedure on Trials Before Magistrates for Indictable Offences.

Code 779 applies to juvenile offenders appearing to be of or under 16 years of age, who are charged, before a "magistrate" acting under Part XVI. of the Criminal Code, with an indictable offence which the "magistrate" purposes to try summarily: see *ante*, p 424.

In such a case the "magistrate" is first to ask the accused what his age is: and if it is stated to be sixteen years or less, the "magistrate" must defer further proceedings, and at once cause notice, (Form, *post* p. 437) to be given to the parent, if any, living in the province; or if the parents are dead or unknown, to the guardian or the householder, if any, with whom the child ordinarily resides.

The "magistrate" must allow reasonable time and opportunity for the parent, or other person, to be present and advise the accused, before he is called upon to elect summary trial by the "magistrate."

The notice may be given by registered letter, if the person to be notified does not reside in the municipality where the proceedings are being taken: Code 779. The subsequent proceedings will be similar to those described in Chapter XIV. *ante*, except as varied by the following provisions of the law, which apply to all cases of juvenile offenders against the law of Canada.

Procedure in Cases Generally.

The Statute R.S.C. ch. 148, provides for different modes of procedure in the several provinces in dealing with all cases of juvenile offenders against the laws of Canada; and the following sections of that Act apply to such cases in Ontario only:

By R.S.C. ch. 148, sec. 68, whenever an information is laid against a boy under twelve, or a girl under thirteen years of age, for any offence against the law of Canada; whether indictable or punishable on summary conviction; a justice or magistrate before whom the charge has been laid must give notice in writing to the executive of the Children's Aid Society, if there be one in the county; and allow him to investigate the charge made; and the parent of the child should also be notified, or some other person interested in the child's welfare, if the parents are dead or unknown.

The justice or magistrate is then to advise with the said officer, and with the parents or such other person, and may consider any report made by the officer: sec. 68 (2).

If, after such consultation or advice, and upon consideration of any report so made, the justice or magistrate is of opinion that the public interests and the welfare of the child will be best served thereby, instead of committing the child for trial, or sentencing the child as the case may be, he may

(a) authorize the officer of the Children's Aid Society to take the child and under the provisions of the law of Ontario (*i.e.*, the Act respecting Apprentices and Minors: R.S.O. ch.

161), bind the child out to some suitable person, until the child
is twenty-one years old, or any less age; or

(b) place the child in some foster home; or

(c) impose a fine not exceeding ten dollars: (which may be
enforced with costs in the manner described in Code 739; or

(d) suspend the sentence either for a definite or indefinite
period; or

(e) if the child has been found guilty of the offence charged,
or is shewn to be wilfully wayward and unmanageable, he may
commit the child to a certified industrial school, or to the refuge
for girls: and in such case the report of the officer of the Children's Aid Society is to be attached to the warrant of commitment: sec. 68 (3).

By sec. 69, when such an order has been made, the child may
thereafter be dealt with under the law of Ontario, as if the order
had been made in respect of a proceeding instituted under the
authority of an Ontario Statute: i.e., in any of the ways provided for by the Children's Protection Act of Ontario, or the Industrial Schools Act, or the Act to establish an Industrial Refuge
for Girls.

By sec. 52 R.S.C., ch. 148, further provision is made by
which a police or stipendiary magistrate by whom a boy, not
exceeding the age of 13 years, is convicted of any offence against
the law of Canada, may sentence him to imprisonment in any
certified industrial school for not more than five years and not
less than two years; but not beyond the time when he will be 17
years old.

Similar provisions for the commitment to an industrial
school or refuge for girls under 14 years are made by sec. 62.

Section 67 provides, that if any child apparently under the
age of 14 years is convicted of any offence against the law of
Canada whether indictable or upon summary conviction the
magistrate or justice, instead of sentencing the child, may order
that the child be committed to the charge of any Children's Aid
Society approved by the Lt.-Govenor of Ontario in Council,
or to any industrial school.

Section 70, of the same statute provides that except in the
cases of children cared for in a shelter or temporary home
established under the Children's Protection Act of Ontario, in
a municipality in which there is but one Children's Aid Society,
no Protestant child is to be committed to the care of any Roman

Catholic Children's Aid Society, or to be placed in any Roman Catholic family as its foster home; nor is any Roman Catholic child to be committed to the care of any Protestant Children's Aid Society or to be placed in any Protestant family as its foster home.

By R.S.O. ch. 259, sec. 38 and R.S.O. ch. 304, sec. 17, the committal of any Protestant child to a Roman Catholic industrial school, Children's Aid Society, or institution or foster home; or any Roman Catholic child to a Protestant industrial school, Children's Aid Society or institution or foster home, is likewise prohibited.

Form of Notice to Parent and to the Children's Aid Society. (*R.S.C. ch. 148, sec. 68: Code 779*).

Canada.
Province of
County of .
    To A.B., Esquire, Secretary (or President) of the Children's Aid Society for the County of , and to C.D., parent of boy (or girl), hereinafter named.
    You are hereby notified that, on the day of A.D. 19 , an information was duly laid by E.F. of against G.H., a boy apparently under age of 12 years (or a girl, apparently under the age of 13 years) a son (or a daughter) of you, the said C.D., as it is alleged, for that (*set out the charge with particulars*), and the said C.D. has been arrested upon a warrant thereon (or has been summoned to answer the said charge), and the day of A.D. 19 , at , in the of , in the County of , at the hour of , has been appointed for the hearing of the said charge before the undersigned police magistrate (or two of His Majesty's justices of the peace) in and for the of , against the said G.H.
    Dated at , in the County of , this day of A.D. 19

                          K.L., Police Magistrate;
                  or
                      M.N.,
                      O.R.,
                      J.P.s., County of

The usual affidavit of service will be annexed to the above notice.

Form of Order for Delivery of a Child Charged with a Criminal Offence, to a Children's Aid Society or Industrial School.

Canada.
Province of Ontario,
County of
    Whereas on the day of · , A.D. 19 , an information was duly laid, on oath (or affirmation) before the undersigned, one of His Majesty's justices of the peace in and for the County of (*or*

police magistrate in and for the   of   in the County of   ),
by A.B. against C.D. of   , for that (set out the charge).

And whereas the said C.D., having been brought before me to answer the said charge, and it appearing to me that the said‾C.D. is a boy under the age of 12 years (or a girl under the age of 13 years), I did on the   day of   , A.D. 19 , cause notice in writing to be duly given to the Executive Officer of the Children's Aid Society for the said County of   (or if there is no such society state that fact), and to E.D., the father (or mother) of the said C.D.

And having advised and counselled with the said officer and with the said E.D., (or as the case may be), and having considered the report made by the said officer upon the said charge, and having duly heard the matter of the said information, I am of opinion that the public interest and the welfare of the said C.D. will be best served hereby.

I do order that G.H., Esquire, the said executive officer of the said Children's Aid Society, be and he is hereby authorized to take the said C.D., and under the provisions of the law of the Province of Ontario, to place the said C.D. out in some approved foster-home (or bind the said C.D. out to some suitable person) until the said C.D. shall have attained the age of 21 years (or any less age may be here stated).

(Or, instead of the preceding paragraph beginning "I do order," insert the following) :—

And whereas I did on this   day of   , A.D. 19 , upon the trial of the said C.D. upon the said charge (if it is one within the justice's or magistrate's summary jurisdiction) in the presence and hearing of the said C.D., and of the said officer of the Children's Aid Society, and of the said E.D., the parent of the said child, duly convict the said C.D., and find him guilty of the said offence.

Or (if the child is not tried, insert the following in place of the above recital of conviction) it having been shewn that the said C.D. is wilfully wayward and unmanageable:—

I do order that the said C.D. be and he is hereby committed to the Victoria Industrial School at Mimico (if the child is a Protestant; or if a Roman Catholic, substitute the St. John's Industrial School, East Toronto, in the County of York. If the child is a girl, she is to be committed to the Alexandra Industrial School for Girls, East Toronto, if a Protestant; or to the St. Mary's Industrial School at Toronto, if the girl is a Roman Catholic, for the term of (not more than 5 or less than 2) years: Sec. 52.

And I further order, pursuant to the statutes in that behalf, that, until the said C.D. shall reach the age of   years, or be otherwise provided for, the treasurer of the municipality of the   of   , which I specify to be the municipality responsible for the maintenance of the said C.D. in that behalf, shall pay to the said Children's Aid Society (or to the Industrial School to which the child has been committed, naming it, as the case may be) the sum of $ per week, towards the maintenance of the said C.D.

Given under my hand and seal this   day of   , A.D. 19 , at   in the County of

(Signed)   [Seal]
J.P., County of

A copy of the above order and the depositions in the case with the following certificate of the justice or magistrate, is to be sent to the clerk of the municipality chargeable with maintenance, as to which see *post*, p. 450.

CERTIFICATE OF JUSTICE OR MAGISTRATE.

Province of Ontario,
County of   ; or
City of   .

I do hereby certify that the papers hereto annexed are true copies of the depositions and order made by me in the case of C.D. therein named.

Dated at   , this   day of   A.D. 19

(Signed)
J.P.,
County of
or
Police Magistrate.

The report of the officer of the Children's Aid Society upon the case, is to be attached to the order of commitment.

The following notice must also be attached and sent to the clerk of the municipality :—

NOTICE TO COUNTY (OR CITY, OR SEPARATED TOWN) LIABLE FOR THE CHILD'S MAINTENANCE.

To   .

The clerk of the municipality of the   of   .

Take notice that the foregoing is a true copy of an order made by me, and annexed hereto are copies of the depositions upon which the child therein named has been committed.

You are required to take notice that unless the municipality of the   of   moves before me to set aside or vary the above order within one calendar month from the time of your receiving said order from me, the municipality will be deemed to have consented to the order, and will be estopped from denying liability thereunder.

Dated at the   of   , this   day of A.D. 19

G.H.,
J.P.,
or
Police magistrate, in and for
the   of

The order, with a copy of the depositions and the following medical certificate, is to be furnished to the authorities of the Industrial School or to the officer of the Children's Aid Society.

MEDICAL CERTIFICATE.

I,   , of the   , of   , in the County of   , being a duly qualified medical practitioner in Ontario (*or as the case may be*) do certify that I have this day examined C.D., a boy (*or as the case may be*), committed to St. John's Industrial School at East Toronto, and I do certify that the said C.D. is free from any contagious disease, as well as any mental or physical defect or weakness that might interfere with his industrial training, and that he (*or she*) may be safely admitted as an inmate of St. John's Industrial School (*or as the case may be*), without injury to the health or well-being of the other boys (*or girls*) there.

Dated at   , this   day of   , A.D. 19   .

(Sgd.)   I.K., M.D.

If the parent, or person interested in the child, claims that the disposition made by the above order is illegal, habeas corpus will lie: see chapter on "Habeas Corpus," *ante.*

After being committed to the charge of a Children's Aid Society or to an Industrial School, the child is to be dealt with under Ontario laws as if committed under an Ontario Statute: R.S.C. ch. 148, sec. 69. The Ontario Statutes on the subject are The Industrial Schools Act, R.S.C. ch. 304, amended by Ontario Statute 3 Edw. VII. ch. 37; and The Children's Protection Act of Ontario R.S.O. ch. 259, amended by 3 Edw. VII. ch. 30; and The Act to establish an Industrial Refuge for Girls.: R.S.O. ch. 310.

The Industrial Schools Act, R.S.O. ch. 304, sec. 16 (1), as amended by Ontario Statute: 3 Edw. VII. ch. 37-55, authorizes the authorities of an industrial school to receive and detain boys under 16, who are convicted of an offence against any Dominion law.

Juvenile Offenders Charged With Theft, etc.

Criminal Code.

The Criminal Code, secs. 800, 821, Part XVII., deals with the special cases of juveniles charged with *theft, or attempted theft* or any offence punishable as such; and who appear to be under 16 years old at the time the offence is alleged to have been committed or attempted: Code 802.

Who May Try.

The functionaries in the different provinces, who are authorized to try such cases summarily and to award punishment are those mentioned in Code 800. In British Columbia and Prince Edward Island, these sections of the Cr. Code apply only to cases in which the punishment provided for the offence is less than two years' imprisonment: Code 801.

No special consent by the accused is necessary; but upon reading the charge and before calling upon him to plead to it, the justices are required to say to the accused:—

"We shall have to hear what you wish to say in answer to the charge against you; but if you wish to be tried by a jury you must *now* object to our deciding upon it at once: Code 807.

If the accused, or his parent or guardian, *then* objects (he•
cannot object afterwards), the justices cannot deal with the
case *summarily* under these provisions; but they may proceed
with a preliminary inquiry, in accordance with the sections of
the Criminal Code relating to cases of indictable offences, and
described, *ante,* pp. 255 *et. seq.*: Code 807 (2).

Notice to Parent.

The parent and Children's Aid Society must be notified in
accordance with R.S.C. ch. 148, sec. 68, see *ante,* p. 434 and
Form p. 437.

In proceeding under Code 800 *et seq.*, the justices are not
to try the case if the charge appears from any circumstances to
be a fit subject for indictment, even if the accused does not object to be tried summarily; and in that event, they are to hold a
preliminary enquiry only, proceeding as described in Chapter
XII., *ante,*: Code 808.

If the accused or his parent or guardian objects and elects
trial by a jury, a preliminary enquiry will be held and the war
rant of commitment, if any, committing him for trial will state
that the accused so elected: Code 808 (2). ·

Procedure.

The proceedings for the trial of juvenile offenders under the
above sections 800 *et seq.*, are initiated by a sworn information
by a "credible witness": Code 805.

The usual forms of information, Form 3 in the Criminal
Code; and of summons, Form 5.; and warrant to apprehend,
Form 4, may be adapted to the above proceedings.

The information may be taken and the summons or warrant
may be issued by one justice, although the statute requires
these cases to be tried before two justices; and the form of
summons will be changed so as to require the accused to appear
before two justices or a magistrate: Code 805.

The usual powers of remand or adjournment, and for taking
the recognizance for the appearance of the accused thereon, are
given to one justice by Code 806; see Forms 17 and 18 in the
Criminal Code.

Witnesses may be summoned, and if necessary bound over to
attend: Code 809, 810; and they may be arrested on a warrant
for neglecting or refusing to attend, upon proof of service of

summons; or of the witness being bound over to appear: Code 811.

Summonses for witnesses are served in the manner provided by Code 812; and may be issued and recognizances taken by any one justice: Code 809, 810; Form 11 to the Criminal Code.

One of the justices before whom the witness is required to attend, may receive proof of service, and issue the warrant for the arrest of the witness for non-attendance; Form 15 to the Criminal Code.

The Hearing.

The proceedings on the hearing of the case are the same as ordinary summary trials by justices: see *ante* p. 348; or preliminary enquiries: see *ante*, p..255, except that the provisions of Code 644, and of R.S.C. ch. 148, above referred to at p. 434 *ante*, will apply also to these proceedings in regard to the trial taking place without publicity and apart from the trials of other 'ajccused persons; and that the offender must be kept separate and apart from other accused persons; and that notice of the proceedings must be given to the parent and the Children's Aid Society; and the other requirements of the law, as above stated, in reference to the trials of juveniles, apply and must be followed in the cases under consideration.

Release Without Punishment in Certain Cases.

If the justices or magistrate upon the hearing of the charge of theft under the above sections of the Criminal Code, deem the case not proved; or, if proved, that it is not expedient to inflict any punishment, they are to dismiss the accused; but must first require him, in the latter event, to find sureties for his future good behaviour: Code 813. The grounds stated in Code 1081, would be fit grounds for deeming it not expedient to inflict any punishment: viz., the youth, character and antecedents of the offender; or the trivial nature of the offence; or any extenuating circumstances under which the offence was committed.

Form of Recognizance for Good Behaviour.

See *ante*, p. 360 for form of the recognizance; but instead of the *condition* there given, insert the following:—

The condition of the above written recognizance is such that if the above bounden C.D. shall be of good behaviour for the term of twelve months now next ensuing, then this recognizance to be void, otherwise to stand in full force and virtue.

On finding the case not proved (or, if proved, on sureties being given for future good conduct), no conviction is recorded, but the accused is to be dismissed; and a certificate of dismissal is to be made out and delivered to him, in the Form 58 in the Criminal Code: Code 813; and the accused, upon obtaining such certificate, or if he is convicted, is released from any other criminal charge for the same cause: Code 815.

Conviction.

If the case is tried summarily, and the accused is convicted upon his own confession, or upon proof: Code 810, the form of conviction may be drawn up in the Form 59 to the Criminal Code: Code 814. The conviction must be signed and sealed by both justices, or the magistrate, as the case may be.

Punishment.

The punishment on conviction, is prescribed by Code 802, viz., imprisonment, *with or without hard labour*, for not more than three months, in the common gaol, "or other place of confinement, within the jurisdiction of the justices." This includes an industrial school.

The form of warrant to commit, 41 given in the Criminal Code, may be adapted by making the necessary changes; or the above order for commitment to an industrial school may be made.

Instead of imprisonment as above provided, the justices may "adjudge" that the offender "forfeit and pay" a fine not exceeding $20: Code 802.

The mode of enforcing payment is provided by Code 818. If the fine is not at once paid, the justices may, if they deem it expedient, appoint a future day for such payment, and order the offender to be detained "in safe custody" until such day; unless security is given by recognizance "or otherwise" (meaning, probably, by the deposit of property), for his appearance on the day appointed: Code 818.

If the fine is not then paid, a warrant under the hands and seals of the same or any other justices may be issued (Form 41 above mentioned changed to suit the facts), committing the offender to gaol, or other place of confinement within the justices' jurisdiction, for not more than three months, "reckon-ed from the day of such adjudication": Code 818 (2).

The justice issuing a warrant to commit are merely acting ministerially, and are in no sense "adjudicating." The inten-tion of secs. 802, 818 of the Criminal Code probably is that where the justices have made an adjudication under Code 802 directing the fine to be paid forthwith, but the accused is unable to pay the money then, time may be given, the justices fixing a day for payment, and adjourning the case until that day, naming the hour and place; and if the money is not paid as so ordered, the justices may, at the adjourned hearing, add a clause to the minute of adjudication fixing the term of imprisonment, which is to be "reckoned from the day of such adjudication"; and not from the time the accused may be lodged in gaol, as is provided by the forms of commitment in the Criminal Code. The justices and the gaoler must be careful to observe this dif-ference.

It is very doubtful whether any other justices than those who convicted the accused could award the imprisonment, notwithstanding Code 818.

No provision is made in the statute, for release after com-mitment if the fine is paid before the term of imprisonment expires. Code 747 is only applicable to proceedings under Part XV. of the Criminal Code. Probably Code 1079 may reach the case.

Restitution.

Besides the above punishment the justices have authority to order restitution of the stolen property : Code 817; and if it is not forthcoming, they may enquire and ascertain its value, and order payment of it; and the money so ordered to be paid may be recovered by suit against the offender, as for a debt : Code 817 (2), (3).

Costs.

Code 819 enables the justices, at the request of the prosecutor, or a witness for the prosecution, to order payment of reasonable and sufficient sums to reimburse them respectively for their expenses in attending before the justices, or otherwise, in carry-ing on the prosecution, and for their trouble and loss of time; and they may also order payment of the constable's fees for ·the apprehension and detention of the offender. By Code 819 (2) such payment may be ordered, although no conviction takes place, if the justices are of opinion that the persons claiming such payments acted in good faith. Code 819 does not expressly say that the payment of these costs is to be ordered to be made by the accused, even if he is convicted or found guilty; and probably this section is to be read in connection with sec. 820, 821, which provides for the payment of costs out of the county funds. But the latter sections are practically abrogated, being only applicable prior to the repeal of former Code 827, and the substitution, by the Criminal Code Amendment Act, 1900, ch, 46, of the present sec. 1036, by which the fines levied under these sections are no longer payable to the county treasurer, but to the provincial treasurer, and consequently there will no longer be any county fund provided thereby, out of which alone such costs can be paid as directed by Code 819-821.

Returns.

Convictions and recognizances under the above sections of the Criminal Code are to be forthwith transmitted by the justices to the clerk of the peace, to be kept among the records of the general sessions: Code 816. And the clerk of the peace is required to transmit to the Minister of Agriculture, Ottawa, a quarterly return of such convictions: Code 1139.

Objections to Form of Order or Commitment.

A conviction under the above provisions of the Cr. Code is not invalid if it omits to state the age of the child, or the opinion of the justices on that subject, as it is presumed that they acted rightly; and as the questions of age and of religious belief could not properly and need not be enquired into at the trial of the offence, they would properly form a subject of enquiry on the part of the justices *after* conviction and before sentence, and it would, therefore, be unnecessary to refer to them in the conviction: R. v. Brine, 33 N.S.R. 43: and see R. v. Yates, 9 Can. Cr. Cas. 359; R. v. Quinn, 36 C.L.J. 644.

The foregoing Canadian Statutes only apply to prosecutions for offences against Dominion laws.

Juvenile Offenders Against Ontario Laws.

The Act for the Protection and Reformation of Neglected Children.

By R.S.O. ch. 259, similar provisions to those above mentioned are made for proceedings on the prosecution of juvenile offenders against Ontario laws.

By sec. 29 sec.-secs 1, 2 and 3, it is the duty of cities and towns of more than 10,000 inhabitants to make separate provision for the custody of children under the age of 16 years; and they are not to be put in the ordinary cells or lockups, nor to be tried in the ordinary police court rooms, if practicable; or an interval of two hours must elapse after the other trials for the day.

Hearing to be Private.

By sec. 29 (4), the judge (which term includes a magistrate, or two justices acting together: see sec. 2 (d)) is directed, in all cases in which a child under 16 is being tried or examined, to exclude from the place all persons other than the counsel and witnesses, officers of the law and of the Children's Aid Society, and the immediate friends or relations of the child. And, by sec. 32, no such child is to be placed in the same cell or room with adult prisoners, but is to be kept apart as far as possible. By sec. 31 of the same Act, a magistrate, before whom a child under 14 is convicted of any offence against Ontario law, may, instead of committing the child to prison, order that it be handed over to the charge of any home for destitute or neglected children, or an industrial school, or a Children's Aid Society, who may permit its adoption by a suitable person, or may apprentice it to any suitable trade or service.

By Ont. Stat. 3 Edw. VII. ch. 30, sec. 2, the following sections have been added to the above revised statute:—

Custody of Child Pending or After Conviction.

8a (1) Where a child apparently under the age of sixteen years is brought before a judge charged with any offence against the laws of this province the said judge may, without making a conviction, order the child to be placed under the care of a probation officer and may by such order require a report to be submitted to him by the officer from time to time concerning the progress and welfare of the child.

(2) Any member of a Children's Committee or any officer of a Children's Aid Society duly approved of, may act as a probation officer, but shall not be so appointed without his own consent.

(3) It shall be the duty of the probation officer to take a personal interest in the child placed under his care so as to secure its reformation and enable it to lead a respectable life.

8*b* (1) No child under the age of fourteen years charged with an offence against the laws of this province shall be committed to any gaol or police station or lockup pending trial, nor if so committed shall any sheriff, gaoler or police official receive any child apparently under the age of fourteen years for confinement in any lockup or gaol commonly used for the detention of adults.

(2) Any child under fourteen years of age who has been arrested shall as far as possible be admitted to bail and be placed in the custody of some relative, friend or benevolent person willing to be responsible for his or her appearance.

(3) Where a child cannot be admitted to bail the sheriff or officer having the direction of such matters shall have authority to contract for the temporary care and maintenance of such child with any association or individual possessing facilities for the safe-keeping and proper care of children until the case is disposed of and any expenses thus incurred shall be a charge upon the municipality in which the child has last resided for one year.

Notice to Parents and Children's Aid Society.

By sec. 30, when a boy under 12, or a girl under 13, is charged with an offence against Ontario law, before any court or magistrate of competent jurisdiction, notice in writing is to be given to the executive officer of the Children's Aid Society, if any, and the child's parents should also be notified, and the proceedings and dealings with the case are to be similar to those above described at p. 298, under sec. 4 of the Dominion statute, 57 & 58 Vict., ch. 58.

See Form of notice, *ante* p. 437.

The Industrial Schools Act.

By the Industrial Schools Act, R.S.O. ch. 304 sec. 14, amended by the Ont. Stat. 3 Edw. VII. ch. 37, sec. 3 any one apparently under 16, who has been convicted before a judge or magistrate, or one or more justices, for an offence against Ontario law, may be committed to an industrial school for an indefinite period, and may be obtained there until he is 21 years old.

Section 11 of the same Act, amended by Ont. Stat., 3 Edw. VII. ch. 37, also provides for the committal to an industrial school of a child, apparently under 16 years old, who has been found guilty of petty crime.

R.S.O. ch. 312, sec. 8, prohibits the committal of a child to any institution for adult paupers.

Certified Industrial Schools in Ontario.

The certified industrial schools in Ontario, to which children may be committed or sent under the above laws, are:—

The Victoria Industrial School for Boys, at Mimico (Protestant).

The St. John's Industrial School for Boys, at East Toronto (Roman Catholic).

The Alexandra Industrial School for Girls, at Toronto (Protestant).

The St. Mary's Industrial School at Toronto (Roman Catholic)

Child's Maintenance.

A child who, either under the above Dominion or Ontario laws, has been committed to an industrial school, must be supported by the municipality to which it belongs: R.S.O. ch. 304, secs. 16, 30 (1); as amended by Ont. Stat.: 3 Edw. VII. ch. 37, secs. 5, 7, 8, and 9; or if placed in charge of the Children's Aid Society or in any foster home, it is to be so supported, until the child reaches the age of 12 years if a girl, or 14 if a boy; R.S.O. ch. 259, sec. 6. In the former case the amount is to be not less than $1.25 weekly, and in the latter not less than $1.00 weekly.

The following are the statutory provisions in that regard:—

A judge, magistrate, or two justices, on application of a Children's Aid Society to whose care a child is committed, may order the payment by the county, city or separated town to which the child belongs, of a reasonable sum, not less than $1.00 a week, towards the expense of supporting a boy until he is 14, or a girl until she is 12 years old: R.S.C. ch. 259, sec. 6 (1). The child is deemed to belong to the municipality in which he has last resided for one year, and, in the absence of evidence to the contrary, the presumption is that he belongs to the municipality in which he was taken into custody: sec. 6 (2).

But the latter municipality may recover the amount paid by it from another municipality which may be really responsible: sec. 6 (3) ; or from the child's parent: sec. 6, sub-sec. 4.

The order for committal is to include the order for payment, and may also direct repayment by the parent to the municipality: sec. 5.

If, however, a child is committed to an industrial school, or refuge, for boys or girls, or other institution subject to government inspection, or any other society authorized by law, provision is made by R.S.O. ch. 259, sec. 36, for the child's maintenance so long as it remains there, without reference to its age.

By that section, the judge, magistrate or justices committing a child to any of these institutions, is to specify, by the order of committal, the municipality chargeable with such maintenance. Section 30 of R.S.O. ch. 304, makes provision for ascertaining what municipality is liable for maintenance in such case, as follows:—

If the child is not a resident of the city or separated town where the industrial school is situated, or if it has not resided there for one year, but has resided for that period in some other county, city, or town separated from the county, the latter county, city or town is liable for such maintenance. And sub-sec. 2 provides that even if the child was at one time resident for one year or more in the municipality in which the industrial school is situated, but subsequently resided for at least one year in some other municipality, the latter is liable for the charge of maintenance; the liability is fixed upon the municipality in which the child was last resident for at least one year: sec. 30 (2).

If the child last resided for one year in the municipality in which the industrial school is situated, the later municipality must pay the weekly allowance for its maintenance: sec. 30 (3).

If the child is committed to the care of a Children's Aid Society, the municipality where the child has last resided for the period of one year, may be ordered to pay the weekly allowance.

In dealing with the case of a child under the above laws, evidence should be taken in the usual way upon the question of responsibility for maintenance. It is not necessary to first notify the municipality.

29—MAG. MAN.

Upon an order being made for maintenance against a municipality, a copy of the order and of the depositions is to be sent
to the clerk of the municipality, by registered letter; and the
municipality may give notice and may move against the order
before the judge, magistrate or justice who made it. And in
that event evidence may be taken, all parties interested being
previously notified; and the order may be confirmed, reversed
or amended. But if the municipality does not give notice and
move against the order in this manner, within one month from
the time the clerk received the copy, the municipality will be
estopped from denying liability: R.S.O. ch. 259, sec. 36.

The order may be enforced in the manner provided by R.S.
O. ch. 76.

The liability for maintenance is not affected by the child
being afterwards placed by the industrial school authorities
in a foster home, except that, when the cost of maintenance
is thereby reduced, the municipality is only liable for what the
industrial school actually pays for such maintenance: R.S.O.
ch. 304, sec. 20.

The above provisions apply to cases where child offenders
are committed under Dominion laws, as well as under Ontario
laws: R.S.O. ch. 304, sec. 16 (2) ; and the order for chargeability
for maintenance of an offender against Dominion law, and
transferred from prison to an industrial school, or committed
to such school, may be made by the judge or magistrate before
whom the offender was committed, at any time, as in the case
of an offender against Provincial law: sec. 16 (3).

When a child is committed to a reformatory, industrial
school or refuge, the magistrate or justices are to deliver to the
superintendent a certified copy of the depositions in the case:
R.S.O. ch. 304, sec. 23; R.S.O. ch. 310, sec. 18.

Escape.

It is a criminal offence for a child, who has been committed
to, or ordered to be detained in, an industrial school or other
institution above-mentioned, to escape; and the child may be
arrested without a warrant and brought before a magistrate,
who, upon proof of the the child's identity, may either remand
him back to such institution, or in case of an incorrigible child,
may commit him or her to any reformatory prison for the re-
mainder of the original term, or if such term has expired at

the time of such arrest, for a further time not exceeding one year: R.S.C. ch. 148, secs. 22, 23, 24.

And the police, or stipendiary magistrate may, in any case in which the officers of an industrial school bring a child, who is under detention there, before him (which they may do without a warrant), order that the child be transferred to any reformatory prison: Same statute, sec. 2.

Incorrigibles.

If the child committed to an industrial school is incorrigible or vicious and beyond the control of the officer in charge, he or she may be dealt with as described in R.S.C. ch. 148, secs. 25-27: R.S.O. ch. 304, sec. 15.

Act Respecting Apprentices and Minors.

The provisions of the above statutes for dealing with youthful offenders in Ontario apply to prosecutions under the Act respecting apprentices and minors: R.S.O. ch. 161.

Sections 2 and 3 of that Act empower a parent, or a guardian or person having the charge of a minor, or any authorized charitable institution (such as an authorized Children's Aid Society), with the child's consent, if a boy of 14, or a girl of 12, and without such consent, if under that age, to enter into articles appointing any trustworthy person to be the child's guardian. And, in case of a boy of 14, or a girl of 12, may with the child's consent, bind him or her as an apprentice: sec. 6. And if the father has abandoned the child and left it with the mother, she may, with the consent of two justices, bind the child as an apprentice: sec. 7. The mayor of a town, or a county judge, or police magistrate may, with the consent of the minor, if a girl of 12, or a boy of 14 or upwards, and without such consent if under that age, bind as an apprentice, any child who is a orphan, or who has been deserted by its parents, or whose parents have been committed to gaol or house of correction, or any child who is dependent upon charity: sec. 8.

A judge, or police magistrate, may hear complaints by the apprentice or master: sec. 14; and he may, in his discretion, cancel the articles of apprenticeship: secs. 14-17.

If an apprentice absents himself from his master's service, he may be arrested anywhere in Ontario and brought before a justice or police magistrate; and may be ordered to make satisfaction as directed by the justice or magistrate: secs. 18-19; and in default, the apprentice may be committed to gaol for not more than three months: sec. 19 (2). No such proceeding can be taken after three years next after the expiration of the time served, or from the apprentice's return to Ontario, if he has been absent from the province: sec. 20; and sec. 24 empowers the judge, magistrate or justice to award costs in any proceeding under the Act.

All fines collected under the above Act are to be paid to the treasurer of the local municipality where the offence was committed: sec. 25.

An appeal lies to the general sessions from a decision by a justice or magistrate under the above Act: sec. 26.

And an appeal may be made to a judge of the high court in chambers from the order of the general sessions cancelling or varying articles of apprenticeship, or cancelling guardianship: sec. 27; and the practice upon such appeal is provided by that section.

Juvenile Offenders in Other Provinces Than Ontario.

See R.S.C. ch. 148.

INDEX.

Amendment of Information (see Information), 344

Appeal
what deemed to be "appealing," 38
when certiorari taken away by (see Certiorari), 38, 101
from judgment, on application for certiorari, 45
to Privy Council in criminal matters, none, 73
from an order granting or refusing prohibition, 79
    mandamus, 95
no bar to order for prohibition, 79
from order on application for habeas corpus, 71
right to dependent on statute, 96
provisions of Criminal Code as to, 96
and case stated under Dominion laws, 96
from summary convictions under Part XV. of Code, 96, 99
    by whom, 101
    to what court, 99
    in Ontario to the Sessions, or the Division Court, 99
    in other provinces, 99
    notice of, and form, 101
        requisites of, 102, 103
        service of, 103
        when to be served and filed, 103, 104
        service of second notice giving grounds, 105
    waiver of right to, 106
    to what sittings, 104
    recognizance of, 106-109, and form,
    recognizance, and form of, 106-109
    money deposits instead abolished, 110
    transmission of conviction to appellate court, 110
    entering appeal, 110
    hearing of, 110, 112
        procedure on, 110
        how to be decided, 76, 77, 78
        examination of witness, 112
        no jury, 111
    affidavit to let in depositions on hearing, 74
    powers of appellate court, 112, 115
    objections for defects in substance or form, 114
    adjournment of court, 111
    subpœna to witness, 111, 112
    respondent must produce evidence to sustain his charge, 111
    what orders court may make, 112, 115
    enforcement of order on appeal, 115
    costs, court may make order as to, 112, 116
        what included in, 118
        when appeal abandoned, 116
        how to be determined, 118
        order for, how made, 118
        payment of, now enforced, 119
        when appeal dismissed on preliminary objection, 117
        costs of failure of appellant to prosecute, 117
    abandonment of appeal, 116
        notice of, 116
    default of appearance at hearing, 117

Arrest—*Continued.*
  on Sunday, 251
  duty of constable on making, 252
  breaking into houses or enclosures to effect, 251
  what necessary to constitute arrest, 251
  in county other than that in which warrant issued (see Backing Warrant), 195
  warrant of, not to be issued in blank, 248
  duty of constable after making, 253-255
  use of force in making, 252
  treatment of prisoner after, 253
    searching prisoner, 253-254
    disposition of property found on prisoner, 253
    handcuffing prisoner, when justifiable, 254
  of witness—on failure to attend on summons, 261
    in first instance, 263

Articles of the Peace
  may be ordered in addition to any penalty, 360, 430, 442
  recognizance to keep the peace, ibid.
  warrant of commitment in default of, ibid.
  grounds for awarding, 360
  information and proceedings to obtain Articles of the Peace, 384

Attorney-General or Governor-General or Officer of Government
  consent of, to prosecution, when necessary, 205

Authority (see Jurisdiction)
  of justices and magistrates, how conferred and limited, 187, 238, 336, 423, 434
    while holding court, to prevent disorder, etc., 229

Backing Warrants
  when warrant to be executed outside of county, 250, 252
  duty of justice on endorsing the warrant, 252
  form of endorsement, 252
  procedure after endorsement, 252
  on proceedings for summary conviction by justices, 345

Bail
  on remand, 258, 353
    form of recognizance, 258
    procedure on failure of accused to appear, 260
    in lieu of commitment for trial, 287
    in cases punishable by more than five years' imprisonment, 287
    recognizance in such case, 287
    in cases punishable by less than five years' imprisonment, 287
    committal of accused in default of, 288
      warrant of commitment, 288
        after committal by judge, 289
    procedure after judge's order for, 289
    form of recognizance to be used, 289
    warrant of deliverance thereon, 289
    discharge of accused, 289
  surrender of accused by bail, form of information, 290
    warrant of arrest on, 290
    how warrant executed, 291

Cross-Examination—*Continued.*
contradicting witness on, by depositions in previous examinations, 158
prosecutors not bound to disclose source of information, 159
right of, 274, 278, 353, 282
on examination of witness on commission, 271
necessary to validity of depositions, 274

Crown-Attorney
fines to be remitted to, quarterly, 373
Custody (see Imprisonment)
provisions as to juvenile offenders (see Juvenile Offenders), 434

Deaf Mutes
competent to give evidence, (see Evidence), 152
manner of taking evidence of, 281

Death
does not abate proceedings, 27

Decision (see Adjudication, Conviction),

De Facto Justices (see Justices of the Peace)

Defects
in information or warrant, 241, 256, 343
in conviction cured by statute, 349
in substance or form not allowed without objection, ib.
in information and process, waiver of, ib.

Deferred Sentence
when defendant may be bound over to appear for, 357, 430, 442

Delirium Tremens
acts committed under, not criminal, 208

Depositions (see Evidence),
statement of accused in evidence in previous case, 178
admissibility of, as evidence in appeal from summary conviction, 112, 113
affidavit required in, to let in depositions, 113, 145
on commission for examination of witness (see Witnesses),
taking down on preliminary enquiries, 277

Deposit (see Security),
with justice, in lieu of recognizance, on appeal under Criminal Code, abolished, 110
on appeal to county judge under Ontario statutes, 146
disposition of, after hearing of appeal, 148

Description of Offence (see Conviction),
what requisite in, 240
when exceptions or provisions must be negatived, 159
need not be in words of statute, but if so described will be sufficient, 240
(see particular titles in Synopsis of Offences for forms of charges of indictable offences, 240; and of summary convictions cases, 380)
particulars of may be ordered, 356, 342, 351

31—MAG. MAN.

Lightning Source UK Ltd.
Milton Keynes UK
UKOW06f1924200815

257278UK00017B/396/P